PUBLIC ADMINISTRATION

FIFTH EDITION

Marshall E. Dimock received his PhD from Johns Hopkins University in 1928. Dr. Dimock's professional experience has been almost equally divided between university teacher and governmental practitioner. While he was at the University of Chicago in the 1930s, Dr. Dimock devoted his attention to business, the economy, bureaucracy in large corporations, and public policy. Dr. Dimock has been a member of Vermont State Legislature and a United Nations Resident Representative. He has held executive posts in Washington in the following capacities: U.S. Assistant Secretary of Labor, executive reorganizer and head of the Immigration and Naturalization Service, and head of recruiting and manning in the War Shipping Administration during World War II.

Currently Dr. Dimock is active in the National Academy of Public Administration, specializing in federal personnel policy and administration, and is also consultant to large corporations on organization, policy, and bureaucracy.

Dr. Dimock is author of many books, among which are those on government administration, business, and law and administration.

Gladys Ogden Dimock graduated in 1936 with the first entering class at Bennington College. In 1935 Mrs. Dimock won the Baldwin Prize for an essay on town meeting government sponsored by the National Municipal League. In the 1960s she served as Bennington alumnae president and college trustee.

Mrs. Dimock began her career in public administration during the pioneering period of Louis Brownlow in the 1930s, having worked first with Luther Gulick at the National Institute of Public Administation in New York City, and then in Washington with Arthur Macmahon on a comprehensive study of the federal relief program sponsored by the Committee on Public Administration of the Social Sciences Research Council.

After her marriage to Marshall Dimock, Mrs. Dimock became joint author with her husband of several books on American government and public administration.

Mrs. Dimock is active in civic affairs and is currently on the board of directors of several governmental programs in the areas of education, libraries, health planning, and the handicapped.

After attending Yale University, Douglas M. Fox received his PhD from Columbia University in 1968. Dr. Fox is director of a college master's degree program in public administration. He is also vice-president of the Connecticut Chapter of the American Society for Public Administration (ASPA) and consultant to government and nonprofit organizations; he has also served on numerous public management study groups.

In addition to the present book, which he has coauthored with Marshall and Gladys Dimock, Dr. Fox is author or editor of five other books.

PUBLIC ADMINISTRATION

FIFTH EDITION

45 3873

Marshall E. Dimock
Gladys Ogden Dimock
Douglas M. Fox

350
D 597

Holt, Rinehart and Winston
New York • Chicago • San Francisco • Philadelphia • Montreal • Toronto • London • Sydney • Tokyo
Mexico City • Rio De Janeiro • Madrid

Library of Congress Cataloging in Publication Data

Dimock, Marshall Edward, 1903–
    Public administration.

    Includes bibliographical references and index.
    1. Public administration.   I. Dimock, Gladys
Gouverneur Ogden.   II. Fox, Douglas M.   III. Title.
JF1351.D5 1983   350   81-6847
ISBN 0-03-056212-0   AACR2

CBS COLLEGE PUBLISHING
Holt, Rinehart and Winston
The Dryden Press
Saunders College Publishing

PREFACE

Although this Fifth Edition of *Public Administration* continues to emphasize the practice of public management as its guiding theme, it differs from its predecessors in the following ways:

1. It gives as much attention to state and local governments as it does to the federal government.[1]
2. It integrates short case studies into the text itself, instead of presenting them in a companion casebook.
3. It includes much more visual material: tables, figures, memos, photographs, and cartoons.
4. It contains more real-life examples to illustrate generalizations, including:
   a. changes in budget and grants-in-aid policy under the Reagan administration
   b. numerous vignettes of department heads, program managers, and local chief executives at work
   c. several interviews with government managers about their work, so that the reader can get the feel and flavor of these managerial tasks.

This book has been completely rewritten, just as previous revisions were. It is not a cosmetic revision; it is a different volume from its predecessors. Like its predecessors, however, this editing is organized around the subject of public managerial performance. *Public Administration* asks what you and I need to know in order to make administrative performance more effective, and how to raise our level of living in a time when some resources seem to be declining.

The focus of this book is on the question of relevancy. We are not inclined to choose sides; we do not take this side or that. Nor, at the other extreme, do we believe that a procedure currently being followed is necessarily the best one. In short, we do not believe in playing intellectual games, nor do we think that our students are interested in such games. If we focus on what is relevant and what will serve well in the future, we are bound to include any doctrines or fads that have relevancy now and in the future.

Public administration has a long history. We need to know something about its leaders and landmarks, because only by such means do people acquire perspective and wisdom. Public administration was not born yesterday. Those who believe that it was do a disservice to the broad understanding needed if the nation is not to repeat past mistakes. The best way to gain insight into the central core of administrative performance is to consult the insights of administrators themselves—experience is the greatest teacher. We must, however, constantly add to this pool of knowledge the innovations that serve to bring about better human relations, more humane goals, and an improved culture for everyone in modern society. The appeal of public service is not that it provides more jobs than any other segment of the economy. The real appeal is a challenge to service and to individual growth.

---

[1] Coauthor Douglas M. Fox is responsible for this balance (M.E.D. and G.O.D.).

In writing this book, we have sometimes used the pronouns "he" and "him" to refer to persons of both sexes. The three of us (one female and two males) feel that awkwardness is thus avoided. Our text and its examples presented indicate our belief that women must play an increased role in managing American government.

M.E.D.
G.O.D.
D.M.F.

ACKNOWLEDGMENTS

In addition to those mentioned in previous editions, we wish to acknowledge the valuable assistance of the following persons in the preparation of this Fifth Edition: Mark Keane, Bess Payne, and Mary O'Neal, International City Management Association; Susan Walter, Council of State Planning Agencies, Washington, D.C.; George Esser, George Maharry, John Campion, Richard Chapman, and Fay Kennedy, of the staff of the National Academy of Public Administration, Washington, D.C.; Luther Gulick, Chairman of the Board of the Institute of Public Administration, New York City; Harvey Sherman, Mary Layton, Nancy Greenberg, and Diane Wilson, of The Port Authority of New York and New Jersey; Jacquel-Anne Couinard, Commissioner of Personnel, State of Vermont; Murray Comarow, Adjunct Professor of Public Administration and Administrative Law, American University, Washington, D.C.; the reference librarians of Baker Library, Dartmouth College; Western Connecticut State College librarians Robert Blaisdell, Lorraine Furtick, Barbara Hirsh, Mary Kohn, Marion Pfender, Doris Rourke, and Alesia Szabo; Victoria Weber, Librarian, Vermont Law School; Ernest Griffith, Washington, D.C.; David Stanley and James Sundquist, of the Brookings Institution; Nesta Gallas, of John Jay College, City University of New York; Dwight Waldo, formerly of Syracuse University; former U.S. Senator George D. Aiken; U.S. Congressman James Jeffords; Emmette Redford, University of Texas; William Reynolds, Comptroller, Greenwich, Connecticut; Leo V. Donohue, Connecticut State Auditor; Denny A. Fuller, Connecticut State Comptroller's Office; George Hale, Assistant for Intergovernmental Relations to the Governor of Delaware; Richard Hedman, who drew the cartoons; Robert Whelan, University of North Florida; John Boyle, University of Maryland; Jeffrey Straussman, Maxwell School, Syracuse University; David Schnall, CUNY; and Jeremy F. Plant, George Mason University, who reviewed the entire manuscript; Holt editors Frank Graham, Patrick Powers, Marie Schappert, Donna DiBenedictis, and Sara Boyajian; and Diane Brownell, Cynthia Ardolino, and Nancy Kennedy for editorial and typing services.

CONTENTS

PUBLIC
ADMINISTRATION

PART 1

THE CHALLENGES OF PUBLIC ADMINISTRATION

Elmer Staats, a distinguished career official in federal government, capped his career as comptroller general, head of the General Accounting Office, from 1966 to 1981. (Photo courtesy of the International City Management Association)

1

The Accomplishing Side of Government

Man is a tool-using animal ... without tools, he is nothing; with tools, he is all.

Thomas Carlyle

In this chapter, we define public administration, distinguish between public policy and managerial technique, and seek to give the reader a sense of the nature of the work of the public manager today.

The first thing to be noted about practical public administration is that even when, as in the administration of President Ronald Reagan, concerted attempts are made to curtail the scope of governmental activity (sometimes called interference), there is scarcely a situation in modern life that does not involve governmental action or surveillance at some place or some time.

A second observation is that administrative action is always more evident in times of emergency or of rapid social change than it is at other times. For example, in May 1979, California drivers began to run out of gas. A drop in gasoline supplies produced lines so long that some families camped overnight at gas stations, setting up breakfast tables while they waited. In response to this problem at the pumps, the state government took several steps. First, motorists with license plates ending in an odd number were allowed to buy gas only on odd-numbered days of the month; motorists with even-numbered plates were likewise restricted to buying on even-numbered days. Second, motorists had to pay for a minimum purchase whether they bought gas in that amount or not. Third, in some areas of the state, motorists had to have less than half a tankful of gas before they were allowed to buy more. These emergency measures were enforced by state transportation and motor vehicle department employees and by state, county, and municipal police. Offenders were subject to arrest and fines.

The job done by these California government employees and other public officials is *public administration,* or *the accomplishment of politically determined objectives.* To administer or to manage—increasingly, the terms are used interchangeably, especially in the public sector—is to know how to set goals, to organize, and to gain cooperation, so as to achieve purposes that are established in advance. Sometimes this work is done by empowering legislation, in which case it is called public administration. At other times it is done by businesses on the basis of cost and profit calculations. Whether public or private, service or profit, management has this common ability; it knows how to go from here to there, how to put everything together to accomplish cooperative purposes.

A third observation is that irrespective of whether the function is "housekeeping" and conventional or innovative and halting, something is always going on in public management. The tax collector is taken to court by the millionaire seeking to maintain his tax shelter while at the other end of the spectrum environmentalists charter a vessel to sail for the Arctic, where they hope to stop whaling activities.

The methods of the manager naturally differ depending upon the nature of the business. Steel production is different from care of the mentally retarded. Or, to turn to the public sector, government promotes and subsidizes (scientific research, for example); it legislates about almost everything and regulates a wide range of activities (entry into a profession, for example); and it tries to stabilize or moderate the inflation of the economy and performs certain so-called business services itself (banks, municipal power, for example). The government promotes trade and commerce, abroad as well as at home; it sets labor standards and deals with labor disputes; it provides a gigantic medical service for veterans, the poor, and the aged. Its most rapidly expanding area is that of human services, which are the responsibility of a federal Department of Health and Human Services. The government also carries on diplomatic relations and provides the defenses for the country. No two of these services, or controls, are alike. Hence it stands to reason that too much uniformity, no matter what guise it assumes, is bad for administrative effectiveness.

The government accomplishes its tasks through the executive branch, in which more than 95 percent of government employees work. To be sure, there are important administrative positions within the legislative branch, not only in the United States Congress, but also within state legislatures and the larger city and county legislatures. Moreover, in the judicial branch, federal and state courts have many employees, and some judges manage more employees than do some executive-branch managers. Indeed, some employees shuttle between the executive and one or more of the other branches of government. And there is no question that the laws passed by the legislature and the interpretations of these laws by the judiciary have an enormous impact on the work of the executive branch. Yet it is the executive branch that carries out almost all government programs. Legislative and judicial mandates must be carried out by the executive agencies. This fact was noted by President Andrew Jackson in the 19th century when he commented that the Supreme Court had ordered the executive to carry out a policy but that the president would leave it up to the court to do so. For this reason, the executive branch is the accomplishing side of government. Although in this book we consider at some length the importance of the legislative and judicial branches, the chief object of our attention throughout is the executive branch and its administrative agencies—federal, state, and local.

WHAT IS PUBLIC ADMINISTRATION?

Public administration is the production of goods and services designed to serve the needs of citizen-consumers. As such, it deals with as broad a range of subjects as does economics or physics. Like business management, which it resembles in many respects, public administration deals in a systematic and dynamic manner with the substance of the goods and services that are its concern and with the method, or process, by which they are made or provided. "Substance" means, for example, what the successful city manager must know about highway building and maintenance, water supply and engineering, public buildings and architecture, and revenue collection and public finance. "Process" means obtaining cooperation from law-making bodies, the public, government employees, and special-interest groups in order to supply authorized services as efficiently and as economically as possible and with due regard for public satisfaction, the values of society, and the political philosophy favored by a particular political community at any given time.

The characteristic that makes administrative leadership perhaps even more challenging than a political career, the practice of law, lobbying before a legislature, or other government work is that the administrator is a synthesizer, a doer, an achiever. In one executive's words, the administrator is a member of the "get-it-all-together" profession.[1] In his personality and total makeup he develops a way of looking at things and of coordinating diverse factors so as to produce a rounded and artistic result that is concrete, measurable, and immediately available. A person with these qualities is sometimes said to have an administrative mind; in other words, some people can synthesize and lead, whereas others with different personality traits and motivations are less able to do so.

This managerial skill is observable so widely in everyday life as to justify the claim that it is universal, that it is found in every field where production is involved. The would-be farmer studies agriculture, but only a few farmers are good managers and they are the ones who succeed. The same comment applies to household management; some manage with grace and with a strong sense of priorities and orderliness, which makes the effort pleasurable and artistic. Some carpenters seem to have a fifth sense, which makes every move count; they seem to know what to do almost instinctively and therefore need little or no coaching. In music and painting the same intuitive blending of skills is present among those who become outstanding artists.

These homely illustrations go far to dispel the false assumption that managerial excellence is simply a technique, a matter of following the same rules and habits endlessly so that they become almost automatic. To be sure, technique is required. A physician uses technique when he inserts a needle in a vein; but his skill is really tested when, because of his training, inherent insight, and wide experience, he considers his patient as a whole person in the context of her environment in everything he prescribes. So it is with administrators. Certain common traits and skills make managers successful. Some of these skills are seemingly inborn, though most are learned; and a knowledge of how to put everything together can be achieved and communicated to others. Indeed, countries such as the United States have been following this practice for a long time. Hence public administration, like private administration, has a solid core of material, which can be analyzed, dissected, and logically explained. It is also true, however, that there is considerable variation and social and human complexity in the tasks governments undertake. As a result, public management sometimes seems so diverse and multifaceted that a definition of it is difficult if not risky. The following interview with a public manager should help to increase the reader's understanding of what public administration is.

An Insider's View

In 14 years, the person being interviewed has held four positions as program manager.

Q. What do you like about being a bureau chief? It's not very glamorous, is it?

A. No, most people would say not. But I like it because it challenges me and gives me a feeling of tangible accomplishment.

Q. What is challenging about it?

A. I can see a problem pretty clearly. The spokespersons for the interest groups help me define the problem in terms of what ought to be done, say, in the next 5 to 10 years. Then after talking with my own organization, we develop a plan for the fiscal year and fold this plan into the longer one. Next I talk with my legislative committee and find out whether their ideas and mine happen to jibe. Finally I talk with my boss and after telling him what I've done, I get his approval and his promise to let me handle it my way.

Q. What do you mean by that?

A. I try to put myself in a position where I have agreement all around in advance. Once I have that, I feel like a free man and go ahead full steam, using my initiative and

resourcefulness to make all my moves count.

Q. Doesn't this depend upon whether you are under civil service or have an appointive position?

A. Yes, to some extent. But not so much as you might think. In either case there are a number of bases you want to touch. And all are necessary and important. One advantage of having a political appointment is that you can go all the way to the top—even to the chief executive. Once you have his ideas and blessing, it's surprising how little interference you get from those who are also his appointees. You also want to be sure that the bureau of the budget officials, or whatever they are called, understand your objectives and strategy, because when they do there is none of the nit-picking and polite bullying that you might otherwise encounter.

Q. You sound as if you wanted to have the feeling of owning your own business.

A. Yes, in a sense that is true. The career employees at all levels soon come to have that feeling of proprietorship; and if you want to be one of the team, you try to have that feeling of belonging, too. You know instinctively that you can accomplish only so much as the organization as a whole is inspired to accomplish.

Q. I judge then that being a progressive administrator is not a matter of taking people by surprise but of having them share a goal?

A. Something like that. You want to have a clear mandate from the start so as to be free to exercise your ingenuity to do a superior job. Freedom for the administrator is not license but knowing that he will have support when he exercises imagination and a sound discretion.

Q. Then in a sense you are trying to be political?

A. Yes, if by that you mean knowing what is possible so as to be free to involve others in things they as well as you want to do.

Q. How do you lead? By issuing orders or by giving your lieutenants the same kind of freedom you desire for yourself?

A. Mostly the latter. You talk things out, judge the strengths and weaknesses of the person to whom authority is being delegated. Then when you have such an agreement, in most cases it is not necessary to give orders at all. It is almost accurate to say that the fewer orders you are compelled to give, the better you know you are doing.

Q. This is because people feel challenged when they are trusted and consulted and feel the opposite when these things are withheld?

A. Precisely.

Q. How do you avoid trying to surround yourself with persons just like yourself?

A. Because you realize that opposites make a better team than persons who are temperamentally and in every other respect the same. Everyone has strengths and weaknesses. The skill of the manager lies in matching up these opposing strengths and weaknesses so as to produce a rounded whole. One person is a good thinker, another a good, open-field runner. In a good organization you want to have someone to whom you can throw the ball when a certain move is indicated.

Q. You try to get over the notion that you can do everything yourself?

A. Yes, there is no place for arrogance and conceit in administration. Not only do you admit that others are better than you in certain respects, but when they score successes you tell them they are successful and why you think that is so. The next time they will do even better.

Q. Do you believe that the more employees you have and the more money you have to spend, the more you can accomplish?

A. Far from it. The reverse is true. The fewer you can along with and the more mileage you get out of your colleagues, the better the results are likely to be. Big things are accomplished by small organizations.

Q. Do the labor unions buy this idea?

A. Not always. But when they don't, the bureau chief has an educational job to do. You must talk it out with them just as with everyone else.

Q. Do you believe that the more hours you put in, the better you are? Do you pride yourself on being a night worker?

A. In both cases, no. If you and the organization are on top of the job, you work effectively while you work. When you are physically and emotionally tired, you make mistakes and are out of sorts, and cooperation begins to go out the window.

Q. Why stick to an operating job so long? If you are a proven executive, why not aim at being a top official? Or why don't you run for office? You say some of the qualifications are the same.

A. There are a number of explanations. Maybe you wouldn't be able to assess your accomplishments as readily. Some call that pride of workmanship. Or maybe you don't care particularly about being in the limelight. Or often it's as simple as being loyal to your organization and its program, just as you are to your family and its reputation. Or possibly being a line official is what you do best, and since there are never nearly enough of such persons to accomplish what needs doing, you stick to your post.

Q. You mean you have your own standards of success and don't care what the conventional view is?

A. Something like that.

For this administrator, then, public administration is getting a job done well, and the satisfaction from so doing is immense.

Common Elements of Public Administration

What are the elements common to the job of manager in such fields as farming, teaching, health care, transportation, and public safety?

The first element is people: the consumers, the political leaders and legislators, the pressure groups, and the reformers. They are the employees of the action agency; their motivations, skills, and cooperation are essential to winning. The human element, more than any other element, determines outcomes.

The second element is organization. Organization is central to everything the administrator does: assignment of duties, delegation of tasks, coordination of effort on which efficiency and production mainly depend, the opportunities for challenge and growth.

The third element is money. Public finance is at the center of everything the government does. A knowledge of public finance helps to stabilize and motivate the economy and may be used to achieve the distribution of fair shares in the form of incentives and rewards.

The fourth element is planning. Planning, large or small, is found in everything the government sets out to do. However, paper plans become mere fantasy unless they are translated into action and accomplishment.

The fifth element is public policy. Public policy is defining the problem and determining a solution: passing legislation, issuing policy statements and administrative orders, choosing among alternatives, finding new and better ways of coping with new or persistent problems. In this area the administrator resembles the legislator, with whom he needs to form a close partnership.

The sixth element is administrative performance. Every decision, large or small, requires values. In a discussion about human rights, which human rights are meant? Do they apply to some groups or to everyone? At every level the self-conscious and effective administrator is a continuing student of political and social philosophy, of economics, and of every body of knowledge, such as literature and art, that makes people more human, enriched, and fulfilled.

The seventh element is coordination. But before there can be coordination there must be a definition of tasks, an agreed-upon division of responsibility. There is the real test of successful leadership. What the lone individual can do is strictly limited. What can be done if the person knows how to win cooperation surmounts the stubbornest of social problems.

The eighth element is feedback and evaluation. Progress cannot be taken for granted. It must be tested, measured, analyzed, and improved, if performance is to be improved. Closely related to this element is public relations, defined as informing and educating the public about everything that concerns it and in return obtaining its understanding and support.

The ninth element is the coordination of levels. Things that can be done better at a lower level should be undertaken at that level. There big gains in efficiency and economy are possible. But before responsibilities can be assigned, local and state levels must be able to collect more substantial revenues.

The final, or tenth, element is institutional and human renewal. The stultifying tendency of bureaucracy is a constant problem because habit is a very strong force in human nature. Public administration must adapt to changing circumstances; otherwise it will become more of a burden than an asset. A good administrator knows how to reinvigorate dull procedures without resorting to the costly expedient of starting a parallel division to do the work the original division is not doing satisfactorily.

An Acquired Skill

A famous scientist was asked at the peak of his career to become the chief executive officer of the government research agency in which he worked. He hesitated to accept, saying, "I know I can succeed in science and invention. But management? What is that? Goals, targets, planning, policies, organization, finance, personnel, leadership, delegation, coordination, control, feedback, evaluation, constant adjustment to world and internal economic forces, and human tastes and desires? How can I make any order out of these?"

What did he do? He devoted several months to

the study of management from books and talks with respected executives, after which he accepted the offer. In a year or two, judged by indexes such as productivity, client and employee satisfaction, public opinion, and high departmental morale, he had established a reputation as an able executive. He had become a successful executive because he had demonstrated the same innovative traits he had demonstrated in the laboratory.

Management is not a matter of moving chessmen on a board or of feeding data into a computer. Management is human relations: knowing how to obtain cooperation, what do do, and whom to ask to do it. The following case study illustrates this point.

CASE STUDY: THE UNRECORDED DEED

Bethel is a small township (six miles square) in central Vermont, on the east side of the Green Mountains. It is fairly typical of many small Vermont towns. In addition to the usual retail businesses, including two independent grocery stores, a hardware store, drugstore, lunch counter, and dry goods store, the town has two banks, two printing establishments, a car dealership, a law office, two realtors and a wire cable brokerage. It also has a grain dealer, a lumber and building materials business, a plastics plant, and a container plant, as well as a large plant that changes hands frequently as one after another enterprise tries to use it and fails. There is a brick church, a white wooden church, two other churches, a Rotary Club, a Junior Chamber of Commerce, and the usual clubs and fraternal orders.

In 1970 the town had two schools, an elementary school built in 1903 and a much newer high school built in the 1950s. One night in 1970, however, the elementary school caught fire, and the top story was consumed. All the elementary grades were immediately farmed out to the high school gym, the four churches, and two mobile units brought in by the school board. After some deliberation, the school board proposed to build a new elementary school as a wing on the high school. The voters agreed, and construction began. While it was going on, the old building, minus its top floor, was patched up and the grades were temporarily reassembled there.

When the new wing was finished, the school board was faced with the problem of what to do with the old building, which was still a solid structure with a satisfactory furnace. The board set a price of $20,000 on it; but various proposals to use it as a professional building, medical center, or factory for church organs did not work out.

By 1974 the problem of disposing of the old school house had become acute. A member of the school board called a meeting of interested citizens to discuss the matter. Three committees were appointed to explore three proposals: (1) that the building become a community center, (2) that it become professional offices, and (3) that it be torn down and the land restored to its original use as Bethel Common. The first two proposals soon lost steam, and the committee on the third decided that the citizens would never stand for the destruction of a perfectly solid building with a nostalgic past and a useful future. The third committee investigated the idea that the space should be given to town offices, with the rest going to a senior-citizen center, the Boy Scouts, or other community programs.

By the winter of 1975, matters were at a standstill. At that point a member of the school board remarked to a member of the third committee that perhaps a new citizens' committee should be created to study the problem further. A meeting was called and the eight people who appeared automatically became the committee. They considered such new proposals as razing the building to make a parking lot to supplement the limited parking on Bethel's narrow main street. At the same time, the school board continued to look for solutions.

The school district owned the building and thought it also owned the land on which the structure stood. In fact, however, the school district did not own the land because the original Bethel Common had not been town property but had belonged to the brick church across the street. The congregation of the brick church had merged with that of the white church, facing the school across its playground, in 1927 to form the United Church of Bethel. When articles of confederation were finally signed in 1954, the United Church gave the land on which the school stood, with its playground, to the school district. When the school board tried to find the deed of gift, it discovered that records in the town office contained a blank page marked "save for recording of school deed," but there was no written document, and the church had no copy. Unwilling to accept any plan to turn property in a residential area close to the church into a shopping center or parking lot, the church refused the school board's request for a duplicate deed with the excuse that the church did not know the exact wording of the original. Yet it had become clear that if town offices were not to occupy the building, the alternative was to tear it down and restore the common.

When the experienced town manager, Burt Moffat, who had been away earning an MA degree, returned, he found himself in the midst of a three-cornered conflict among the church, the school board, and the three selectmen who governed the town. He negotiated separately and informally with a member of the citizens' committee, who unofficially spoke for the church, and with the selectmen and the school board. He did not attend further meetings of the citizens' committee in order to avoid controversial situations where he might be forced to state an opinion contrary to that of a selectman or some impassioned citizen. But behind the scenes he was a firm guiding hand, defusing arguments, thwarting proposals he disapproved, and promoting ideas he considered beneficial to the town. When it was finally

obvious that restoration of the common was the only possible solution, he openly and wholeheartedly encouraged it.

Moffat, supported finally by the selectmen, and the committee, with the support of the church, came to a meeting of minds. Moffat also persuaded the school board to agree to receive $10,000 for its interest in the building. Further, he exerted his finely honed talents to obtain funds for the restoration from other sources, such as the federal government and the state.

The first step in the restoration was to hire a firm of landscape architects, who agreed to work for costs only. Their plans, beyond anything the committee had imagined, included razing the building but retaining the foundations as enclosure for a sunken garden with benches, flowers, lawn, flagged walks, and a fountain. There would also be a small parking lot, owned by the church. Existing shade trees would be preserved and new ones added.

The next step was to call a special town meeting to approve the project. Articles and letters in the local paper and the interest of citizens of a small town in its affairs meant that almost everyone was informed about the situation. The meeting, held in the school cafeteria, was well publicized and well attended. Moffat stayed on the sidelines while the plan was presented and discussed, but he was there to head off snags with explanations. The citizens approved the restoration by nearly unanimous vote.

Thereafter Moffat went to work. He used his town crew to do much of the labor at minimum cost. Citizens and groups, including local greenhouse owners, donated funds and even labor. When the church could not find the money to pay half the cost of paving the parking lot, Moffat paid the whole amount and said nothing about repayment.

A few years later Moffat resigned his position to accept another one in the northern part of the state. In his farewell message he said that the restoration of Bethel Common had been the highlight of his career in the service of the citizens of Bethel.

Today Bethel Common is the site of summer

weddings and receptions, church bazaars, concerts, festivals, and the planting of and caring for flowers. It is also a place where people may rest and enjoy a pleasant view of the valley. Bethel has an able town manager to thank for his role in making the common a place of enjoyment and thereby enhancing the quality of life in Bethel.

Keeping Bureaucracy Under Control

Bureaucracy refers to those aspects of organizations concerned with rules and regulations. It is systematic and logical, and as such it stresses correct procedures and uniform policies. Without bureaucracy, large modern organizations could not function; with too much bureaucracy, problems arise.

One problem is a focus on activities instead of results. Another problem is a seeming concern for self-preservation, regardless of whether the agency has done its job or not. Box 1.1 is an example of an agency that has preserved itself.

Certain unmistakable signs betray the fact that a given program is becoming excessively bureaucratic. Instead of being outgoing and consumer oriented, it grows introverted, oblivious to any but its own narrow concerns. The multiplicity of rules reduces opportunity for discretion and creates a degree of inflexibility that makes it hard for the program to adapt to change. Discretion, which is at the heart of change, is the sine qua non of a developing managerial strategy, without which an operating executive is hindered. To the bureaucrat, change itself becomes a threat; only business as usual provides a sense of cocoonlike security. Excuses are found for not acting, and when action does not occur, the pace is slow. Employees behave as though doing business is a favor to the customer, and if something goes wrong, they throw the book at him. They do only what their job descriptions require, are no longer obliging, and become insolent to the point of sadism. One Connecticut resident who received this kind of treatment wrote to his local paper:

On November 6, I went [to the state Motor Vehicle Department office in Waterbury] to change my license plates. During the course of my inquiry I can describe the behavior of the three public officials with which [*sic*] I dealt as rude, surly, arbitrary, and even hostile. "If you don't like it, tell your legislator," was their final remark.[2]

Passing the buck has become a game played by everyone. Those at the service level pass it upwards to top management until at length top management is overwhelmed with a mass of petty decisions that are time-consuming and distracting. Quality is sacrificed to quantity. Things are measured instead of ultimately assessed for their human and social import. Individuals "behave" rather than think. Minimum norms of employee performance are imposed but mean nothing in terms of service to the customer and the public. Rationality is defined as "what do I get out of it?", instead of "what does it do for the effectiveness of the program?" There is little pride in work; esprit de corps vanishes as jealous cliques take over. And a weary management fails to renew itself.

These manifestations of excessive bureaucracy can be traced to four common weaknesses. First is the tendency toward insulation, or grooving, or cloistering, as people try to protect themselves from system and impersonality, seeking a place to hide from the rigidities and frustrations surrounding them. They resist cooperation outside their own small group, wishing only to be left alone.

Second is a dislike for responsibility. People find themselves in an environment where little is expected of them. They cannot develop their personalities or experience daily challenges. "Play it safe" is the attitude; "avoid risk so you cannot be blamed." Motivation is reduced to drawing a weekly check and retiring early so they can begin to live.

Together with these two weaknesses at the service level is the third, seemingly contradictory

Box 1.1

THE 21ST ANNUAL REPORT OF THIS COMMISSION

Legislative Document (1979)

1978 ANNUAL REPORT

OF THE

TEMPORARY COMMISSION OF

INVESTIGATION

OF THE STATE OF NEW YORK

TO

THE GOVERNOR AND THE LEGISLATURE

OF THE

STATE OF NEW YORK

APRIL 1979

weakness of empire building, or encroaching upon others' areas. It most often occurs at the supervisory level. Empire building is intensified when compensations and promotions are gauged primarily by the number of those supervised instead of by the qualitative standards of difficulty of performance and social contribution. Jurisdictional infighting naturally becomes common under these circumstances as each fief strives to profit at the expense of another.

An example of this behavior occurred when the United States and the Soviet Union were vying to be the first to put a satellite in orbit

around the earth. All three U.S. military services—the army, the air force, and the navy—had space and missile programs. In October 1957, the Soviets won the race, orbiting their Sputnik satellite. At one army installation, an excited officer rushed into the general's quarters, saying, "The enemy has put a satellite into orbit!" The general exclaimed, "You mean the air force has beaten us?"

Managers have frequently resorted to reorganization in the hope that combining existing agencies will miraculously infuse new vitality into them. Universal experience, however, demonstrates that vitality must be generated from within. An agency must solve smaller problems before they become larger ones. Instead of doing their jobs better, therefore, in this third manifestation of bureaucratic weakness, competing units wind up doing a number of disparate, similar, or sometimes unrelated tasks less well. This is the basic situation from which the need for higher policymaking and direction arises.

Finally, the fourth bureaucratic weakness is loss of personality and humanness, thus creating a deadening uniformity throughout a program. Employees are afraid to be different lest they be judged disloyal to worker and management norms. Instead of showing independence and enterprise, they feel safer conforming to the system. The system itself develops a life of its own, which continues from one generation of employees to the next, all of them resisting change in the hope of staying comfortable. But consumers often rate individuality and responsiveness higher than machinelike efficiency, rendering the effort self-defeating. A vitalized organization is a living thing and as such it develops personality.

The trouble with bureaucracy is that it is only too rational, nothing else. As such, it appeals to the logician, the engineer, and the pedant whose stock-in-trade is categories and nothing else. It is anathema, however, to those who are productively oriented. If one starts with the assumption that each individual should be a specialist in his field, that what is being administered is a paper plan, that no one should be expected to do more than the position requires, and that the position is more important than the person who fills it—then one has the perfect prescription for bureaucratic excess. The operations man is interested in the opposite of such things; he seeks teams and flexibility, strategy instead of logic, voluntarism instead of fear, and freedom from domination. He is looking for people who can think and innovate, and he does not trust those who use rule making only to enhance their own power and authority. If everything is reduced to rules the life of any operating organization is sapped. The manager is holistic; the bureaucrat, schizoid.

In an attempt to counter some of this bureaucratic behavior, the newly elected California Governor Jerry Brown decreed a ban on state-issued briefcases for state employees. Brown said that paperwork had expanded to fill the briefcases, thus causing problems instead of solving them.[3]

PUBLIC ADMINISTRATION: POLICY AND TECHNIQUE

Although public administration has always interested those who like a subject that combines theory with action, at this stage of American development it is interesting for a number of other reasons.

First, much experience with developing countries has shown Americans that without administrative skills, little progress in economic development is possible; administration is crucial. In underdeveloped countries, the African nation of Zaire, for example, these skills are rarely found.

Zaire, rich in minerals and natural resources, could be a very wealthy country, yet in 1980 it faced ruin. Roads between the provincial capitals were undrivable, half the railroad locomotives were out of order, and Air Zaire canceled more flights than it ran. Corruption was so pervasive that effective management was impossible. The president himself pocketed 10 percent of all international business deals; a former minister of culture sold treasure from the national museum; and the postmaster-general stole money orders from the mail. Under these conditions, it is no surprise that the country is deeply in debt and that the standard of living dropped to an all-time low. When it becomes impossible to manage effectively, no country can prosper.[4]

By extension, it is also now apparent that once a nation reaches a high level of economic and political power, as the United States has done, sound administrative judgment must guide public policy decisions or no amount of effort can offset the consequences of going in the wrong direction. Accordingly, those who have been deeply concerned with the development of public administration during the preceding decade or so have concluded that policy in administration, involving economic principle as much as behavioral science, is infinitely more crucial than mere managerial technique. Once this relative valuation was recognized, the theory of public administration had to be rebuilt and placed on broader and more realistic intellectual foundations.

The record shows that those who argue that the principal problem of government is management technique are mistaken. For example, each new U.S. president sets up a reorganization study team, which argues that increased coordination, achieved through formal restructuring of government agencies, will solve many of the country's problems. President Jimmy Carter said, for example, that the new federal Department of Energy, created in 1977 and combining agencies formerly part of the Department of the Interior, the Atomic Energy Commission, and other agencies, would result in a better energy policy. Although marginal improvements in some areas probably resulted from this change, when Carter left office in 1981 it was obvious that the United States did not have an effective energy policy. The nation continued to import huge amounts of energy, and it had failed to adopt either effective conservation programs or significant new energy sources. Tinkering with the administrative machinery, then, was no substitute for the policy steps that had to be taken to change the nation's disastrous course.

Public policy is deciding what to do. It is the way an administrator goes about deciding on a program. This program is substantive, that is, it involves other fields of knowledge such as construction, medicine, growing crops, or predicting the weather. Should a town road be paved or patched? Should farmers be paid to restrict their acreage in wheat, or should they be encouraged to produce more wheat? Should inflation be tackled by limiting the money supply or by instituting wage and price controls? Sometimes a policy is determined by deciding among alternative approaches; at other times it seems to work better when the government applies several methods in combination with responsibility distributed among several programs or agencies instead of concentrated in one.

Some policy programs embrace the economy as a whole, whereas others deal with a segment of the economy; in either situation the economy as a whole is ultimately affected. The economists refer to the first situation as macro (large) and to the second as micro (small). Either way the alert administrator is constantly aware of the interplay of forces and programs so as to secure the maximum results for the economy as a whole.

Public policy is an integral part of the political process, involving voters, pressure groups, political parties, legislatures, the legal system, and every agency of government so as to produce the desired results. (This matter is discussed in more detail in Part 2.) Public administration is part of a larger team effort. Program management is an integral part of what political scientists call the government's responsibility to distribute values and benefits in a way that is compatible with the freedom, life-style, and objectives of any given society.

Public policy, meaning what should be done, is not the whole of public administration. If public policy were merely a blueprint or a dream, it would never produce goods and services. The decision to do something useful is followed by decisions about how to organize, to provide the funds and personnel, to delegate responsibilities, to control developments, to assess results, to secure efficiency and economy, and to produce the necessary teamwork within action programs.

Viewed from the standpoint of public administration, the program manager needs to be aware of five elements: scope, analysis, pressures, decision, and persuasion. These elements lie at the heart of political philosophy. In dealing with the first element, scope, the relevant questions are as follows. Is the proposed program a proper function? Where does it stand, for example, in terms of a priority list? Is the proposed program indicated at this time? The answers depend upon whether the allocation of resources is likely to produce results that are so limited that the resources would be better diverted to a more deserving purpose. The country may not be ready for the program, or the public, whose support is essential, may not consider the remedy worth the cost. An additional test is also involved. Is the proposed program philosophically and legally justified in terms of its effect on the legal system, the values of society, and the welfare and security of the nation? These decisions cannot be avoided; not only does the public administrator recommend legislation, he also makes law in his action program pursuant to the legislation, thus making him a key figure in the political process as a whole.

The second element, public policy analysis, is a skill needed by the effective administrator. He has research staffs, who help collect facts, organize them, sift alternatives, calculate their cost, and assess their worth. He has a planning function dealing with longer-range, intermediate, and immediate steps to be taken. But in the final analysis, so far as his contribution to legislation is concerned and especially so far as his expertise as a manager is involved, the synthesis must ultimately be made in his own mind and must be accompanied by a feasible scheme of action pursuant to decisions made. (Policy analysis is examined in more detail in Chapter 10.)

The third element, pressure from interest groups on legislatures and the public, results in the enactment of legislation. Once the action stage of administrative execution is reached, this pressure continues. In his role as executor, the administrator acts as both judge and negotiator; in this capacity he needs strongly political skills as well as a knowledge of economics and of relevant substantive fields.

The fourth element, decision making, is a subject that has been carefully examined in recent years by public administration experts. Decision takes many forms. The first decision is whether to act as pressures indicate, whether an alternative solution is desirable, or whether no action at all is indicated. Then, in all day-to-day matters, the administrator is involved in a plethora of decisions, never losing sight of the main social objec-

tive and the strategies needed for achieving tangible and beneficial results.

The fifth element, the test of leadership, may turn on the administrator's persuasiveness. Leadership is needed in dealing with pressure groups, higher officials, legislative committees, and, most of all, the manager's own organization and staff. Clarity, straight thinking, and listening to others and gaining their confidence are hallmarks of the successful executive.

AN ACTION PROFESSION

A United Nations official in New Delhi organizes a conference on economic development. A bureau chief in Washington signs an order for a public housing project in Cleveland. A town manager in Vermont agrees to install a new culvert for a farmer whose brook crosses a road. These instances all represent public administration, and much of what government officials do is no more complicated. In the top ranks of government, where policy is studied and formulated, however, complexity may be very complex indeed. Consider, for example, this aspect of the jet age. In 1977, commercial airlines in the United States carried 245 million passengers; this figure is expected to double by 1990. An immediate result of these developments will be to make the air terminals so overcrowded that new ones will have to be built between large cities as well as around them. Noise is already a major problem. The cost of land in such areas is constantly rising. Government has subsidized commercial aviation from the outset, as it did the railroads. Must it now subsidize private aviation through the purchase, construction, and maintenance of tens of thousands of small airfields for smaller towns and cities, in addition to the larger ones that also will be required? With the air filled with large and small craft alike, how will this traffic be controlled?

Moreover, who is to be allowed in the air? Experience shows that almost anyone can learn to fly, from a 16-year-old to a 70-year-old, the main difference being judgment; some people have good judgment in the cockpit and some do not. Ten years from now, those with poor judgment cannot be allowed to use the air space, because it will be too crowded to allow for more than a very narrow margin of error. Government is responsible for granting pilot licenses, and if the quality of judgment is increasingly to be assessed, the once fairly simple task of testing pilots becomes still more complicated.

The range of policy issues with which public administrators deal today is enormous. Examples include the following:

- establishing programs (recreation, youth centers, community athletic contests, for example) designed to give teenagers something to do with their time and energy
- attempting to lower the level of state air and water pollution while trying to attract new industry at the same time
- mediating conflicts in collective bargaining between private companies and labor unions
- expanding preventive health programs, such as prenatal care and inoculation for communicable diseases
- resolving problems of foreign policy, energy and defense

Operating within the context of these issues of public policy, the public administrator with policy responsibilities is inescapably concerned with problem solving, in the course of which he must understand enough about the economy, the forces that shape history, and the aspirations of society to provide wise counsel to those who translate policy into legislation. His practical skills, his experience, and his intimate knowledge of the machinery of government give vitality to the programs for which he is responsible. Indeed, if anything is to be done about issues such as these, the administrator will do it; otherwise it will not be done.

Examples of active administrators may be found in any part of the country. A U.S. Department of Agriculture official realized that soil is an irreplaceable resource; he launched a demonstration project that proved the utility of enriching and conserving soil; from this humble beginning

the U.S. Soil Conservation Service was born. A fish-and-game club in northern New England became distressed because raw sewage was being discharged from local firms and towns into an otherwise uncontaminated river. The club had enough influence to have a government salmon hatchery established on the river on condition that the river be cleaned up—it was. Veterans of the Korean War flocked in large numbers to the farmlands of the country, seeking the good life; but they had little capital, and everything they needed to start in farming was costly. In one progressive state the legislature exempted this group of young farmers from taxes for 10 years, arguing that because new industries had been exempted, so should the aspiring farmers. In all these illustrations it was the public administrator who was either the prime mover or the strongest ally of the citizens' group. He was neutral about partisan politics, dedicated and resourceful about his profession, willing to take chances, and able to win support for a policy.

CONTEMPORARY CHALLENGE TO PUBLIC ADMINISTRATION

Government and its employees are under a more severe attack today than they have been. The public's opinion of the performance of U.S. government is at an all-time low. Four successive presidential campaigns by the winning candidate made the bureaucracy the major point of attack. President Reagan, beginning in 1981, made deep cuts in many programs and discontinued others, while increasing military expenditures. Many factors have contributed to this trend—the Vietnam War, the Watergate scandal, the inability of government to deal with many of the social problems it has chosen to tackle, and the rising taxes necessary to pay for the increased activities of government. The passage of Proposition 13, which set a lid on California property taxes, and similar measures in other states indicate discontent with government. Government officials at any level can say that the proportion of activist or watchdog groups who want to participate in government decision making has increased greatly and has made their jobs harder. Yet all is not bleak.

One of the few thoroughly scientific studies of the attitudes of citizens toward government agencies found that people who used government services were relatively satisfied with them. They did *not* think the agencies were "inefficient, unfair, and error-ridden . . . nor did they find the personnel in these offices elusive, irresponsible, or authoritarian. Overall, approximately three out of five persons questioned stated that their problem had been resolved."[5] The difference between these findings and generalized discontent with government can be explained by the fact that "people's specific experiences are more positive than their general attitudes. . . . The general low rating of characteristics of governmental services may be a function of stereotypes of public bureaucracy held by Americans."[6] Much of the dissatisfaction with government, then, seems to be due *not* to the work of government agencies, but to a feeling that all is not right with the United States. Working in this environment should challenge rather than discourage administrators. If they can do a good job, the people will be satisfied with the work of their agency. The rest of this book is designed to help public administrators do a good job.

ing than his techniques. The managerial mind not only knows what to do (analysis) but also how to do it (implementation). Unlike the mere logician, or the dreamer, the manager combines the two steps in his action program. He avoids the horns of the logician or dreamer dilemma. This is a useful mind set for individuals in any and all fields, the musician, for example, or the scientist in his laboratory. In short, management-mindedness has a universal appeal and utility.

With this mind set, public administration becomes a challenging subject. It challenges whole countries, whole governments, at all levels, but most of all the individual who wants to become a manager or to understand it.

Accordingly, in Parts 1 and 2 we shall continue to deal with the larger of these challenges: the universal factors, how public and private management differ and are the same, why good management is good politics, how to secure intergovernmental cooperation, why law is so integral a part of everything the manager does and yet tends toward excessive and debilitating bureaucracy, why ethics is necessary to survival but difficult to enforce in practice, and what the satisfactions and problems are of the chief executive at the top. Against this larger backdrop we shall then be enabled in Part 3 to get to the nubbin of what makes a successful manager.

SUMMARY

We have defined public administration, provided living examples of its nature and complexity, and shown how closely management is related to the formulation and execution of public policy. To keep things in balance, we have also warned against the excesses of bureaucracy and have analyzed why they occur and what constructively can be done about the weaknesses that underlie them.

Properly considered, public administration and management are colorful, intriguing subjects, not technical, dull ones. Let us explain this rationale in a concluding paragraph.

The mind set of the manager is more interest-

NOTES

1. Harlan Cleveland, "The Get-It-All-Together Profession," *Public Administration Review* 39 (July–August 1979): 306–309.

2. Letter to the editor, Danbury *News-Times,* 14 January 1981.

3. "Gov. Brown Finds He Is Losing Battle on Bureaucracy," *New York Times,* 12 July 1977, p. 17. See also Herbert Kaufman, *Red Tape* (Washington: Brookings Institution, 1977).

4. John Darnton, "Zaire Could Be Very Rich, But Now It Faces Ruin," *New York Times,* 1 February 1979, p. E 3.

5. Daniel Katz et al., *Bureaucratic Encounters* (New York: Institute for Social Research, 1975), p. 184.

6. Katz, p. 186.

2

The Government Executive Views His Job

We must take a man as we find him; and if we expect him to serve the public, we must interest his passions in doing so.
Alexander Hamilton

In this chapter, we interview the head of a government agency. The reader is able to gain a sense of the actual workings of public administration by listening to this government executive.

THE BUREAU CHIEF

When we talked with the bureau chief whom we quote here, the questions (**Q**) and answers (**A**) developed something like this:

Q. What do you really think of your job?

A. My job is pretty much what I make it. I've been in the service [the Immigration and Naturalization Service] for nearly 30 years and every commissioner I've worked under has had a different view, or style, so to speak. For my part, I like to work through others so I become friends with them. Some of my predecessors were drivers. One was a martinet and got the service into a lot of trouble because he cracked down on aliens and aroused a lot of ill will, which we've been a long time overcoming.

Q. But surely you do more than make friends of your associates, or congressmen, or the people in your interest group?

A. Oh, of course. As a main check on our work, I keep asking myself how the service is doing its job for the country, and this depends somewhat on what kind of difficulty the country is in. If there's a war on, people are suspicious of aliens and the hot-headed ones want to get tough. If there's a depression, the unemployed become hostile and prejudiced toward aliens. Our job is to keep the service's prestige high so that what we do in fairness to aliens will be accepted. Maybe this sounds like saying that what's good for business is good for the country, but we find it works. Ours is an old agency in the government, and most of our higher officials are trained in law. On questions of policy we are concerned with aliens who are poor and unfortunate, and we try to be as soft as the law will allow. But we can also be tough with aliens who are dangerous to the country.

Q. You have explained your service philosophy, but what exactly do *you* do?

A. Well, for one thing, I handle legislation for the service, go up on the Hill a lot, and talk with congressmen and senators. I enjoy that. Then there are 50 or more groups interested in immigration in some way, and I deal with them, too. Also, my boss, the attorney general, calls me quite often and I go over and talk with him.

Then we run a training program for immigration inspectors, border patrolmen, and naturalization examiners. I organized it and I keep close tabs on it. I also have a lot to do with appointments, promotions, and duty transfers in the service; this is one of my most important responsibilities.

I try to work through my key men as much as I can, but there's a lot I must do myself. And I've found that if I don't work hard myself, not many others will. This is no cushy, armchair job. I have to try to know just about everything that's going on, but I have to give the men I trust as much authority as they need, and if they can't be trusted, then I have to fire or reassign them.

Q. You have a large field organization—in fact, some of your employees are stationed abroad. How can you keep track of operations that are so large and far-flung?

A. We have the whole country divided into major regions, and there's a regional commissioner in charge of each one. He's responsible for everything that happens there, and as long as we have good regional commissioners, we don't have too much trouble. If a commissioner turns out to be weak or the wrong man for the job, we move him out of there as soon as we can.

Q. Is there politics, that is, partisan politics, in appointments and promotions?

A. There used to be. But not today.

Q. Why did you join the service, and would you do it again?

A. I started working here in Washington as a clerk while I was attending law school at night. I liked the service and after I got my degree, I never thought seriously of taking another job. I like the work, too. It's interesting and varied. Also I like dealing with people, and in Immigration you meet all kinds.

The service has grown and I've enjoyed being a part of it. Like me, most of those in top positions started at the bottom and went ahead pretty fast as the service expanded. At the top here now, there are four of us (the number varies), and we put our heads together often when something important comes up. So *I* don't run the service, really—*we* run it. I don't always trust my judgment, but when the four of us agree on something—and the test is always the question, "What does this do to the reputation of the service?"—then I can sleep nights.

Yes, sure, I'd do it again. I can't think of any job I'd like better. I even get to travel abroad quite a bit. Today, for example, I'm just back from Ottawa, where I conferred with Canadian immigration officials on a problem of illegal entry we're having with refugees from Europe.

Q. Do you get a kick out of belonging to an elite corps, the supergrades [the top grades, 16–18] in the civil service, or do you never think of that?

A. I never used to think much about it, but now I do. Government service is much more of a career and a respected profession than it was only a few years ago. Yes, I'm proud of being in the supergrades. We even have supergrade meetings sometimes when someone is in town we'd like to hear.

Q. Would you like a chance at a different job in the government? say, in the State Department or something else in the foreign field?

A. You haven't chosen a very practical illustration. State has the Foreign Service and I couldn't crack that. No, I don't know that I *would* like to transfer. I'm in my early 50s now. Ten years ago I might have, but I don't think so, because I find immigration the most interesting work in the world.

THE EXECUTIVE DAY

On a subsequent visit to the bureau chief, we asked him:

Q. What is a typical day like for you in this work?

A. The work varies, naturally, but there are some things I try to do regularly because otherwise it would be upsetting to others, my secretary, for example. I always try to keep on the good side of her.

She comes in early and opens the mail and sorts it so I'll see the urgent things first. Then I try to dictate letters and memoranda before I become too busy with appointments. Also, this gives her a chance to get letters out the same day.

There are some other things I do regularly, too, such as hold a weekly staff meeting at 10 o'clock every Monday morning. Our committee on legislation meets regularly once a month, more often if necessary. But actually, there aren't many things that can be kept on a strict schedule. The work may seem pretty routine to the outsider, but it isn't.

Q. By the time you reach the office in the morning, do you have in mind a work plan for the day?

A. Yes, I do. If you don't keep thinking up new strategies and tactics, you don't get much done in a job like this. I sometimes think the top administrator is one who knows how to use his time to best advantage.

You have to be flexible, of course, because there are certain people in government to whom you must respond on a moment's notice. The attorney general, for example, and the assistant attorney general, who is in charge of administration for the Justice Department. Also people in the State Department—I suppose we have more dealings with them than with anyone else. Then when the chairman of a committee on the Hill asks for something, he has to have instant response. Sometimes one of my own men has to see me right away because, remember, a bureau chief is also father confessor in some ways and must be an amateur psychiatrist as well as friend and counsellor.

Q. What are your plans for today? That is, if we don't stay too long now?

A. I've already taken care of my correspondence, and I've talked with three or four people, one of whom had an appointment. Later I'm going to review the draft of an amendment to the immigration law that was prepared in our office. I'm also going to talk with the head of the Border Patrol about possibly using more helicopters along the Mexican border.

I'll have lunch with one of the attorneys in the Criminal Division—we have a little problem he can help us with. After that I have an appointment in the Visa Division of the State Department about passport procedures. And then sometime before the day is over I must have a conference with my administrative assistant on the figures for next year's budget.

Q. What is your overall strategy? How do you know what to do next, when there are so many things needing your attention?

A. You develop a sort of sixth sense about these things. If you have a general idea of what you want to accomplish, the various parts of your work have a way of falling into place. But first you have to have this fairly definite idea of what is desirable and feasible in terms of your long-range objectives. You look ahead and try to foresee what's coming up.

There are always three things to be considered. The first is emergencies, things you didn't count on. You try to keep them to a minimum but it's not entirely up to you. Someone writes a crank letter to the attorney general. One of our field men gets some

bad publicity. Someone else dies or beats his wife. Little things like these sometimes are blown up out of all proportion, and it takes time to deal with them. A more serious emergency would be excluding an important visitor to this country when we should have let him in, and the press catches us out of line.

Second, there are the routine things that must be done and watched. This takes more time than anything else, as a matter of fact. If you don't supervise even the best men, things have a way of not happening and you don't discover it until you need them most. Then third, if you keep emergencies and routine things under control, you have time to think ahead, to build for the future, to improve the organization, and make the service better.

If I neglect any one of these three things, then I'm no longer on top of my job. My job controls me. And the man who lets that happen for very long loses his self-confidence and his ability to do anything constructive.

RELATING UPWARD TO POLICY EXECUTIVES

A recurrent problem concerns working relations between the civil service executive and the appointed policy executive, because most large government programs have both. This relationship has been brilliantly analyzed by Hugh Heclo in his analysis of the federal government.[1]

From the standpoint of the career executive the problem is to learn to respect and value his political boss without seeking to dominate him, which would not be hard because the career man has a fund of knowledge and experience that the policy man lacks. On his side, the policy executive wants to be able to make changes without losing the support of the careerists in his agency. Thus, the career executive and the policy executive make an odd couple, and developing a working relationship between the two takes time. This relationship must work out if our government is to be both responsive and efficient.

This dual arrangement existed in the organization of the Immigration Service, so we asked some questions of the civil service head of the bureau:

Q. How does it work out, having a political boss?

A. Let's face it. I suppose every normal, human, civil service executive would rather be his own boss. By the time he gets to be head of his service, he's gone through a long process of developing experience. Moreover, he's been continually appraised by his peers, most of whom are also his rivals for each job at the next higher level, so he's also developed quite a bit of savvy and self-confidence. But my observation is that his personal self-confidence is really a sort of group self-confidence. He knows at least as much about the strengths and weaknesses of those who run the service with him as they know about him and as he knows about himself.

Q. How does the policy boss come into this picture? Do you mean he's resented by the service or just tolerated?

A. No, that's not what I mean. As an intellectual proposition, I think the average career person understands why we need a system of dual executives in our form of government. It's only emotionally that he may feel otherwise.

The way we resolve this issue is really quite simple, maybe too simple. When a new policy executive is appointed, everyone in the service has only one question in mind: "What kind of fellow is he? Can we respect him, or can't we?" We'd *like* to respect him, but that isn't always in the cards. If we can, then it's easy enough to work with him. If we cannot, then we simply ignore him as much as possible. You know yourself, there are ways of not doing the things that are

harmful to the program, even when the top man has ordered them.

Q. Does this matter of respect depend on whether the policy man was appointed because he had pull of some kind?

A. No, not really. Some political appointees turn out quite well, and sometimes better than those who got the job merely because of being expert in something. And I'll tell you why. The man who's appointed for political reasons has to act political, and that means he's likely to cultivate others and their points of view. Whereas the specialist is apt to think he knows it all. His attitudes are rigid and he doesn't have much use for anyone who's not as expert as he is. At his worst, he doesn't seem to think much of anyone but himself. He's arrogant, incapable of understanding the other fellow's point of view, even a prig.

Q. What do you do with people like that?

A. My own policy is to try to make friends with them, until our relationship is close enough so that I feel I can be frank with them. Then I say, "I suppose you took this job planning to make extensive changes?" Usually they admit they did. The political type, of course, would deny it even if he *did* have changes in mind. He'd bide his time instead of showing his hand even before he got his seat warm.

Q. So when the expert says he does plan to make changes, what do you say?

A. I ask him to explain, and usually he's only too willing to tell me what's wrong with the service. Later I report on this to others in the service and we discuss it. Maybe some of what he plans won't do the service any harm. Anyhow, we try to be open-minded, and in case we're not sure, we try to give him the benefit of the doubt, after explaining to him the difficulties in doing what he contemplates, naturally.

Q. Suppose he decides to go ahead anyway?

A. Well—intellectually, we're loyal, but emotionally, we never are. In this case, as I said, there are ways of never quite coming to grips with what we have been told to do, of never quite putting harmful reforms into effect.

Q. In effect, then, this means that the man with the new broom must win you over to his way of thinking before he can sweep clean.

A. Yes, I guess that's what it means. But then, you know, everything I do, or anyone else in executive work in the civil service does, involves winning over others to a common plan of action and strategy. Why should there be one rule for the political official and another rule for the career man?

Q. The political official has a higher authority, and democratic theory requires that you do what he says.

A. Not if what he says will do lasting harm to the reputation of the service. We have to take the position that our values and sense of what is good for the service are based on experience and hence are more reliable than those of a newcomer.

Q. In effect, then, this might mean that very little change in policy or organization or anything else can take place in the Immigration Service.

A. Not at all. If you'll study our history you'll see that we're constantly experimenting and changing. One reason is that we have a good research program, and the man who heads it is constantly in touch with academic people and others who have new ideas. We introduce these new ideas through our training program to new employees so that they will be receptive to change.

Q. Can you give me an example of an appointive policy official who had rigid and uncompromising views?

A. I could give you several, but let's take the one I think of first. This man was a lawyer. Of course I'm a lawyer, too, but there are lawyers and lawyers.

This one thought the only important thing in life was the *Morgan* case.[2] You re-

member that had to do with the requirements of administrative due process. If we had allowed him to have his way, administrative procedure would have been the only thing we'd have paid any attention to while he was in office. When we told him that if we were to put his plans into practice it would mean doubling the number of immigration inspectors, do you know what he said? "Why not?" We pointed out that Congress would never agree to such an increased expense, but he waved this aside. If it was right to do it, he said, we should do it, no matter what the expense.

Q. Maybe there was some justice on his side. Maybe you *did* need better safeguards in your administrative procedures.

A. Yes, we did, and we told him so. And over a period of maybe three or four years, as we explained the situation to our congressional committees and told them what we proposed to do with the money, we did get more. So among other things we remodeled our review procedures and extended the right of aliens to be represented by counsel. These were big improvements, but they took time, and also they were compromises between his extreme views and our conservative ones.

Q. So perhaps in the end, this policy official did do some good? He stirred you up, didn't he, and got you to do what you might not have done without his prodding?

A. Yes, you're right, of course. Even the experts who are sort of crazy do some good sometimes. But it's a good thing we know how to handle them.

SATISFACTIONS AND DISAPPOINTMENTS

In a final session with our friend we asked him:

Q. If you were going to change the civil service to make it more interesting for executives like yourself, what would you do?

A. Get more executives like me, of course!

Q. But not everyone has your sense of humor.

A. No, seriously, there's a lot about the civil service that I like. At least for myself. I'm pretty much my own boss. If those of us at the top of the service stick together, we can get pretty much anything we want, including support from Congress. The chairmen of the committees on the Hill whom I deal with are my friends. We're back and forth in each others' homes. They're almost as much career men as I am.

So under the circumstances, I think I have more freedom and independence here than if I worked in a large corporation. Of course, if I owned my own business, that might be different. But if you're going to work for a large organization—and if you're a career man as I am—then I think you have things your own way in government more than you do in business.

Q. Is this necessarily a good thing?

A. That depends on whose view you're considering. I am looking at it from my own standpoint, as you asked me to.

Q. Touché! You're quite right. Well, what don't you like about civil service?

A. The rigid pigeonholes. Setting up a lot of positions and then having to go out and fill them as you would orders from a customer. I'd rather hire some good people and then divide up the work on the basis of their experience. Of course, that's what we *try* to do, really. But all the time we have to fight the system, which is based on pigeonholes.

Q. Do you think you're paid enough?

A. Who ever does? In fact, I think we are paid almost enough. At least it's a lot more than it was a while ago. And for people like me, salary isn't everything. Otherwise we wouldn't work for the government.

Q. In other words, you like your work and you feel you're free enough to be able to act like an executive. Is that it?

A. I guess that's it.

SUMMARY

What has one executive had to say about public administration? First, the effective executive must be an astute administrative politician to do his job. He must know how to get along with legislators and with appointed executives who are his bosses. Second, the executive must know how to delegate authority to subordinates, or he will not be able to accomplish his job. Third, for the same reason, he must learn how to manage his scarcest resource—time. Even though he starts his day with an overall plan, he must remain flexible so that he can cope with emergencies and with requests from the boss. Fourth, he indicates that he has a loyalty to his agency *as an institution,* which is necessarily the same as allegiance to his boss, the political executive. (We return to this last theme in Chapter 8.)

NOTES

1. Hugh Heclo, *A Government of Strangers* (Washington: Brookings Institution, 1977).

2. For a commentary, see Kenneth C. Davis, *Administrative Law* (St. Paul, Minn.: West Publishing, 1951), ch. 8.

3

Administration: Public and Private

Business and government administration are alike in all unimportant respects.

Wallace S. Sayre

In this chapter we compare administration in the public sector with administration in the private sector, examine the historical evolution of management theory and practice, scrutinize trends in management in the United States in the 20th century, and look at the public administration profession today. We turn to the private-public nexus in management to gain some perspective, chiefly analytical but also historical, because both are needed.

Michael Blumenthal was secretary of the treasury in the administration of Jimmy Carter. Before taking that position he had been chief executive officer of the Bendix Corporation, one of *Fortune* magazine's 500 largest corporations. Earlier, he had served in Washington in the administrations of John F. Kennedy and Lyndon B. Johnson. Wanting to record his impressions of the differences and similarities in private and governmental management, in 1978 he volunteered to be interviewed aboard an air force flight to Moscow. During this flight a 150,000-word-long tape was recorded, from which he derived an article that appeared in *Fortune*. The article made some interesting points. Many officials in Washington, Blumenthal thought, are dedicated and work as hard as their counterparts in private business. He said that other, lower-level officials are equally dedicated. "There's nothing inherent in a bureaucrat that makes him less efficient," stated Blumenthal. "It's the way the system is structured." If you want the thrill of serving your country in a really tough job, he told his business colleagues, "don't pass it up." For all the differences between the corporate world and Washington, Blumenthal found, some of the basic principles of good management are valid in both. He stressed four points: be a good picker, delegate, know your facts, and be scrupulously honest.[1]

Secretary Blumenthal suggested one reason for studying the link between the private and the public sectors—the search for valid principles. Other reasons are perhaps obvious: to see how private management and public management differ, to observe principles that may be gainfully applied to the improvement of both sectors, and to appreciate the difficulties of government's dealing with a multitude of diverse functions. Additional reasons are to gain the feel of administration at top and lower levels of operating a huge conglomeration of governmental activities, from grantsmanship to housekeeping, and to lay the foundation for dealing in successive chapters of this book with the distinctiveness of the "system," which Secretary Blumenthal mentioned.

BUSINESS MANAGEMENT AND PUBLIC ADMINISTRATION

Among the first writers on management to take the private-public comparison approach were James Mooney and Alan Reilly. First they coauthored a book dealing with the subject; later, Mooney expanded and centralized their thesis.[2] Believing that the characteristics of organization and management are universal, these authors traced common threads in church, the military, government, business, and other forms of large-scale management, not only setting forth parallels and convergencies but also trying to develop a body of common principles.

Both government and large corporations operate in the same social environment; hence it is inevitable that social forces should affect both. There is the effect of technology on size and on human problems, the growing number of layers in the hierarchy that contribute to remoteness and impersonality, the need to plan goals to accommodate growth and change, the necessity of professionalized staffs for policy and planning purposes, and the realization that the larger the organization, the greater the demands upon leadership.

Many of the similarities between private and public administration, states Donald Rumsfeld, an official in the administrations of Richard M. Nixon and Gerald Ford, are related to size. Rumsfeld, who later went from government into business,[3] noted that business planning can be more rational than government planning, because in the former there are fewer pressures and crosscurrents from the outside. In the White House and the Defense Department, where Rumsfeld served, there was such a flood of information that it was like "drinking water from a fire hose"; this is not true in business. Again, in government, the news hawks are more alert and problems emerge in the press earlier than they do in business. Hence the greater necessity to reach down and know how things are really going. The smartest government executives learn to distinguish between the facade and the reality behind it, that is, how much is really being accomplished.

Points of Comparison

Perhaps the best way to understand how corporate life and governmental life resemble each other and how they differ is to make a checklist.

1. *Profit motive.* In business, said Secretary Blumenthal, "you can dress up profits only so long," because there is a bottom line.[4] In government, profit can sometimes be measured; usually it cannot. Where it cannot, as we see in later chapters, increasing effort is being made to measure productivity as a substitute.

2. *The corporate fiction.* Because corporations are legal entities apart from their individual members and therefore have greater autonomy and managerial freedom and discretion than do government agencies, corporations have greater opportunity to be efficient and innovative.

3. *Holding companies.* The United States government is like a holding company; so are virtually all of the *Fortune* 500. Each has a variety of businesses under the same umbrella. This obviously complicates managerial problems for both.

4. *Pressure groups.* We have already observed that as a rule, pressure-group activity is ordinarily much more intense in government than in the corporate world.

5. *Specialization.* Historically there has been more specialization in business than in government. In the larger corporations product specialization is slowly disappearing. In the days of Adam Smith in the 18th century it was thought that specialization was one of the bases of efficiency and profits.

6. *Power.* It was once thought that the political state had a monopoly of legal power, within its borders, at least. As corporations have become conglomerate and transnational, they have become more and more powerful.

7. *Politics.* Some corporations are very political, oil companies operating abroad, for example. Office politics is also obvious in competition for positions in large corporations. Further, it is acknowledged that political skill—making shrewd

moves and getting things done—is one of the main criteria in rating corporate executives.

8. *Regulation.* Many businesses complain of being overregulated by government. Overregulation of business was a dominant theme of the Nixon, Ford, and Carter administrations and has become one under Ronald Reagan. Even though it is not so clearly recognized, however, there is even more regulation of the government administrator. Such regulation takes various forms: administrative procedure acts, legislative vetoes, legislative surveillance, and various forms of investigations by the General Accounting Office (GAO), personnel departments, inspectors general, and others.[5]

9. *Board of Directors.* In business, most of the initiative is with the paid management; the board of directors merely reviews and approves or disapproves. The reverse is true, historically, of the United States federal government, because Congress is considered the board. Nevertheless, executive initiative has increased sharply in recent years. A similar situation exists at the state level. In city government, the manager usually acts much as the chief executive officer does in industry.

10. *Final authority.* A sign on President Harry S. Truman's desk read "The buck stops here." In general, however, the corporate executive has more final authority than the political one. His sanctions are greater and he is subjected to less "political" interference. But the pattern is changing. The management of the largest corporations frequently operates as executive committees: Each executive has his area of responsibility; the entire group meets to plan and decide; and during the implementing stage each member is boss in his own area.

11. *Organization.* Corporations have more flexibility to change their organization than do the larger governments. But the main difference is that the corporation coordinates better because the staff function, as distinct from the line operating function, is distributed to the operative vice-presidential level instead of being centered in the president, as it is in Washington, for example. This practice not only assures better coordination, but also creates more flexibility, initiative, drive, and executive direction. The motto in in-

dustry is "Everything should be planned together, but administered separately." The fewer the levels of decision, the better it is for vitality. Corporations, unlike government, also do not customarily give independent authority to organization and management (O&M) units. Decisions about organization and personnel are invariably made by operating officials, sometimes acting as ad hoc teams.

12. *Finance.* Finance officials have more power in corporations than they do in government. Part of the reason is that in the corporation there is only one finance department and one department head. In government the finance function is widely distributed among the agency, department, secretary of the treasury, Office of Management and Budget (OMB), GAO, and the ways and means and appropriations committees of Congress.

13. *Purchasing.* In corporations, responsibility is usually centralized, but execution is more widely dispersed than in government.

14. *Contracts.* The larger the corporation, the more it contracts for parts and services. This is done partly to avoid an overload of directive management. The federal government has been moving in this direction, too, since the time of Secretary of Defense Robert McNamara.

15. *Civil service.* In some respects, during the past 40 years the personnel systems of large corporations have come to resemble government's civil service system. Corporations, however, have far more freedom to recruit, to raise salary ceilings, and to fire.

16. *Unions.* Unionism has grown so fast in government that there are now few differences between the private and public sectors. Some corporations awakened to the problem earlier than did most governments. This area is going to be one of the major problems of the 1980s.

17. *Field offices.* Corporations have as much trouble with headquarters-field relationships as does the government. They experiment with regionalism only to discontinue it. They fluctuate between headquarters-field command posts and reporting directly to the functional units at headquarters. There is no easy solution to this matter; there is room for some pioneering work.

18. *Accountability.* Traditionally, it has been said that greater accountability is one of the ways

government differs from business. Both sectors experiment with the same techniques, traveling auditors, for example. And both eventually learn the same thing—too tight a rein stifles initiative, too lax a rein is bound to result in occasional abuses. As a result, real accountability is sometimes promoted more by a good training program than by giving auditors more power to influence management decisions.

The main difference between business and government, it will be seen, is that the business corporation enjoys a far greater *autonomy* than a government agency ordinarily does because the latter is part of, and is controlled by, the larger governmental machinery. Consequently, a government agency is expected to observe set rules enforcing conformity and consistency. Autonomy means separateness, insulation, and self-sufficiency, and it permits various kinds of managerial freedom. If these inherent freedoms are not limited by some outside source, therefore, business executives enjoy a greater degree of discretion and opportunity to experiment and innovate than the government official does.

Insofar as bureaucracy connotes *conformity*—it means many other things as well, of course—public administration is stamped with a higher degree of this characteristic than business management is. Some writers, including the German economist Max Weber, see conformity and uniformity as among the most desirable characteristics of administration because they produce impersonality; every individual and every situation is treated with machinelike efficiency and hence with complete impartiality. Critics, however—and the British historian Arnold Toynbee is one of them—regard excessive uniformity as a major cause of institutional deterioration and eventual decay.

This matter of conformity is a major issue of administration theory today. Herbert Simon, for example, argues that a central responsibility of administrative leadership is to secure cooperation by promoting support for and conformity to the goals determined by the group.[6] One of the present authors, on the other hand, sees an emphasis on conformity—when bureaucracy becomes excessive—as the main obstacle to the promotion of initiative and energy renewal.[7] No doubt there is a point at which both positions may be reconciled.

The Public Service Appeal

Probably the main difference between business and public administration is in *outlook*. Thus, concerned with service and seldom with financial profit, government operates programs that a private business could never undertake and remain in business.

This thumbnail sketch would be remiss if we did not mention the influence of personality—especially that of leaders, the kind that inspires confidence. An example of leadership was found during the Carter administration when, as later, the country was particularly concerned with inflation. In 1977 President Carter was looking for someone to succeed Arthur Burns, who headed the Federal Reserve Board during Republican presidencies. The search finally centered on Paul Volcker, who, like Burns, was known as a two-fisted, tight-money executive. Volcker took the job, although it meant a salary cut of $57,500 from the $116,000 he earned annually as president of the New York Federal Reserve system. Never in years had there been such universal praise of any Washington appointment; businessmen, Congress and the media, gave this lanky, six-foot-seven Wall Street businessman rave notices. Was it mystique or reality? Most people thought it was his record and his approach to things.[8]

EVOLUTION OF PRIVATE-PUBLIC MANAGEMENT

From earliest times, private and public managements have interacted with each other. Volumes have been written on this subject.[9]

Many early civilizations, including the Chi-nese, Egyptian, and Babylonian, not only developed a high level of organizational and managerial effectiveness but in some cases wrote tracts on the subject. These tracts sound quite modern in their discussion of securing cooperation at a distance, preventing graft and dishonesty, and recruiting and training competent officials. During the Middle Ages, European rulers began to develop mining and overseas colonies in order to increase the nation's wealth and territory, and this trend required additional managerial sophistication. The king's principal lieutenants eventually became the heads of departments of government—the treasury, the legal system, the king's business enterprises, and all the rest. Both in the Roman legal system, which has prevailed on the continent of Europe, and in Anglo-Saxon law, dominant in England, the judicial establishment evolved out of administration as a specialization of function. Not until the early 19th century in England did general incorporation laws provide the basis on which larger businesses, as contrasted with crafts and guilds, could be created without express franchise from the king. Earlier, however, around the turn of the 18th century and as a consequence of the Industrial Revolution, modern management began to assume the importance it has since attained. On the Continent public administration and business administration both developed from the law schools, whereas in England the fields adhered to the philosophical tradition and the teaching of history.

The last step in this unfolding story occurred at the turn of the 20th century with the rise of the scientific management movement under Frederick W. Taylor, an American engineer. Taylor's idea of analyzing a process to achieve maximum efficiency of each step and of the process as a whole was soon adopted by business as the basis of mass production and has now become universal; even the Soviet Union has adopted the idea. U.S. public administration built upon its foundations soon after the introduction of Taylor's theory, but like modern business administration, public administration has considerably broadened and deepened its explorations.

STUDY OF PUBLIC ADMINISTRATION IN THE CURRICULUM

Public administration as an academic field is now 100 years old. Many countries look upon the study of public administration primarily as an American innovation, largely because of the influence of Taylor's scientific management movement. Taylorism is a body of knowledge that cuts across several levels of government. It seeks cross-referencing with other fields of management and searches for common principles applicable to all forms of government activity from the smallest to the largest, from the local to the national, and even the international.

In recent times, other countries have been attracted to the United States' approach. If public administration is removed from law and philosophy (as formerly these three subjects were combined in the British Commonwealth), administration can be made more practical and hence can lead to greater efficiency and effectiveness.

There are still interesting differences. In the Soviet Union, for example, where the success of the system plainly depends largely upon good management (because of centralization and state planning), administration is taught for the most part not in separate schools but as an integral part of substantive fields such as engineering, medicine, education, and all the forms of production and distribution. In a Soviet school of engineering, for example, the training of managers, or executives, may be considered the apex of the academic structure. Managers are first trained in engineering, and a few of them are then trained as top executives.

Something analogous, of course, occurs in the United States, where, in schools of engineering, education, and other disciplines, management is usually part of the curriculum. There are also separate schools of business in the United States, more numerous than those that teach public administration.

Both systems have their characteristic advantages and disadvantages. Clearly, there is an advantage in thoroughly understanding engineering, for example, before studying management. One

disadvantage is that engineers may not be attracted to management. When management is taught within a broader scope, including comparative insights and a strong social science orientation, prospective managers are likely to become adept at public policy analysis and the psychological insights of group activity.

A few examples may underscore the point of difference. A bridge contractor was so completely absorbed in the lore of bridge building that he was blind to human nature and human relations. After passage of the Wagner Act of 1935, when company employees sought to form unions of separate company divisions, he doggedly resisted this action in his firm; he refused even to discuss the matter. Eventually, he was forced out of business. The chief reason was his insensitivity to employee needs and problems.

In another example, one of the country's largest corporations discovered that there was almost no employee loyalty to the company. The result was careless work, minor sabotage, and eventually serious crippling strikes. So naive was the management of this engineering enterprise that in desperation it resorted to showing company-made movies of its work. Top executives also put on overalls and labored alongside the blue collar employees. The results were to be expected. The employees laughed at such clumsy tactics and wound up refusing to attend movies on company time. Nor was loyalty improved.

In a third instance, a trained social worker was put in charge of the state police as chief executive. Being insecure in his knowledge of police science and although he was on the job for less than a month, he tried to rule with an iron hand, even telling the state police how they must operate their short-wave radio sets. He did not last very long.

Successive Emphases in the Approach to Public Administration

The study of administration reflects the changes in emphasis that have marked the development of public administration in the United States. Each change was supposed to be the final answer to the problems of effective performance. Although no one emphasis wholly excluded the one immediately preceding it, few real attempts have been made even to this day to create a complete synthesis.

Public administration became a conscious concern of the citizenry in 1882 when Woodrow Wilson wrote his now classic essay, "The Study of Administration,"[10] in which he pleaded for a more businesslike efficiency in government. The country was ready for civil service reform and in 1883 Congress passed the Pendleton Act, which created the federal civil service system aimed especially at frustrating political appointments.

Frederick Taylor's influence began to be felt about 1906, and the theme of efficiency, stressed by Wilson, gained support. Citizen reform groups and bureaus of municipal and governmental research sought to break the power of political bosses and machines in the cities. It was the era of muckraking, a term employed by the newspaper reporter Lincoln Steffens in his articles on municipal corruption and misrule.

Then the group that later became university professors of public administration suggested the idea of budget reform as the best means to achieve efficient government. In line with this approach, in 1911 President William Howard Taft created the federal Commission on Efficiency and Economy. By 1921 the efforts of this group and its supporters had secured the passage by Congress of the Government Budget and Accounting Act.

The first college textbooks on public administration appeared in 1926 and 1927. The first, by Leonard White, developed the efficiency theme and also stressed personnel administration, an area in which White was later to gain eminence as chairman of the U.S. Civil Service Commission.[11] The second textbook, by W. F. Willoughby,[12] also stressed the need for efficiency and, like the first text, relied on the analogy to business management: in the federal government, Congress is the board of directors; civil servants, the professional managers. Willoughby's main interest, however, was in budgetary reform.

Meanwhile, the theme of personnel adminis-

tration was exhaustively studied by the privately supported Commission of Inquiry on Public Service Personnel under the direction of Luther Gulick, director of the Institute of Public Administration in New York. The commission's report[13] and a series of supporting monographs appeared in 1935. Find good people in the first place, the report argued, then treat them right, and they will do an efficient job. This report had a strong influence from the start and set in motion ideas that have since greatly improved the civil service field.

The next distinct emphasis, centered on administrative organization and reorganization, gained ground during the 1930s as a result of the proliferation of agencies and programs under the New Deal. It culminated in the work of the Brownlow Committee and the Hoover Commission, discussed in Chapter 8. Many state, and several of the larger city, governments appointed so-called little Hoover commissions of their own, which eventually resulted in more or less useful administrative reorganizations at those levels. There is a limit, however, to how much efficiency can be achieved through administrative reorganization. Moreover, much of this rearranging upsets orderly procedure and employee morale.

Meanwhile, interest in improved personnel administration continued, having been carried forward through the Brownlow and the Hoover studies. Eventually interest turned to human relations and group dynamics. As early as 1933, the Hawthorne experiments, conducted by Elton Mayo and F. J. Roethlisberger at the Western Electric Company,[14] demonstrated that people respond to attention, negative as well as positive—seemingly a fairly self-evident conclusion. Business management and public administration were beginning to find they had much in common; at the very least, both were conducted by people and had similar problems based on human nature. The influence of psychology and sociology spread into administration, until limitations began to appear here, too: this human relations thing, said the critics, is too soft.

Attention then turned to cybernetics (discussed in more detail in Chapter 17), in which the key word is systems. As applied to administration, success was said to depend upon laying out systems consisting of *everything* in a given undertaking, including its relation to the environment. The effect was immediate and positive. Administrators suddenly became aware of the need for more planning, more careful and rational decision making, a clearer definition of goals, and a more detailed scheduling and timing of the work. To administer by objectives became a slogan as procedures were rationalized and adapted to defined goals, instead of being cherished for their own sake, as is often true in a bureaucratic structure. When automation developed to the point of supplying administration with computers, the new machines strengthened the use of systems. The computer revolution in administration is now in full swing.

When the influence of machine technology became established, it joined with the already existing influence of psychology and sociology to create a new amalgam under the guidance of the behavioral movement. The behaviorists favor what may be called a hard empiricism, which emphasizes a careful, precise methodology based on exact measurements and using mathematical tools wherever possible, to produce a growing body of tested and reliable causal theory.[15] Commonly agreeing that behavior must be understood by observation and verification rather than surmised, some leaders of the behavioral movement were disposed to brush aside all preceding administrative theory and start anew.

Thus, old approaches were labeled unscientific; the new scientific methodology would put everything right. Traditional assumptions were classified as "proverbs," in contrast to rigorously tested and verified fact. Most public administrators were interested, or at least tolerant, until results could be more widely demonstrated. Even some traditionalists usually agreed that systems analysis, which the behaviorists carried over from the cybernetic approach and which stresses all aspects of the administrative process and its environment, might be made to work. This approach merely confirms that administration moves forward smoothly when it combines all elements and limps when something is missing from the compound.

The New Public Administration

Partly because of the reaction to the depersonalization of public administration embodied in some of the foregoing emphases, the next stage, which in its turn was reflected in the teaching of administration, was the emergence of the new public administration.[16] Basically it was a strong revival of the emphasis on the human side of public administration, with stress on values such as fellow feeling and employee aspiration. This stage stressed the ethical element and a return to the idea of public administration in a democracy. Although called new, the change of direction showed a stronger understanding of and sympathy for the historical roots of the subject than had prevailed under the immediately preceding assumptions. Under the influence of Dwight Waldo and others of the Maxwell School of Citizenship and Public Affairs, notably Paul Appleby and Roscoe Martin, this new emphasis sought to revive the connection between the perennial concerns of political philosophy and moral philosophy and the methods employed by modern administration. Organization was deemphasized; so also was hierarchy. In their place appeared a strong emphasis on small-group theory and human relations. This development was a notable contribution to the synthesis of elements that many had been seeking for almost 100 years. The emphasis is still vigorously growing.

Concurrently with this development and influenced (as we see later) by the whiz kids in the Pentagon, led by Robert McNamara, another emphasis was on productivity, a subject much stressed today, as we see in the sections of this book on personnel and finance.[17] The business analogy and the methodology of the professional economist here showed their influence. Public administration at all levels must be made cost conscious and hence efficient by measuring productivity of goods and services at whatever level they originate. Only by this macro means, in which the country is again made fully competitive, it was argued, can the United States hold its position of leadership in the world. Waste must be eliminated and service improved, and the most promising way to achieve both is through computations of cost and benefit and input and output. Since this emphasis markedly resembled Taylorism and budgeting, the cycle was complete.

THE PUBLIC ADMINISTRATION PROFESSION

Paralleling academic development in public administration is professional development, which is achieving great intellectual vigor. Professional associations of public administration began to be formed shortly before the turn of the 20th century, and membership and influence greatly increased as a result of the demands on government during the Great Depression of the 1930s and World War II. In 1939 the American Society for Public Administration (ASPA) was founded and today has a membership of over 20,000. The ASPA's quarterly, *Public Administration Review,* combines the interests of practitioners and academic people in this field. More than 100 chapters are located in major governmental and educational centers throughout the country.

An outgrowth of the ASPA is the National Academy of Public Administration (NAPA), founded in 1967. Both groups have their headquarters in Washington. The NAPA is modeled after the National Academy of Science; members are elected to it on the basis of professional achievement. Total membership is limited to 300 and has not yet reached that figure. It is more than a prestige organization; it maintains a number of panels offering consultation on government programs, has a training and publication program, and is actively concerned with developing the priorities of public administration.

In addition to the ASPA, there are many individual professional associations of practitioners; these are listed, with commentary, in Appendix A of this book. The list is a useful reference to the key groups in the field.

PUBLIC ADMINISTRATION PRIORITIES

In the complexity of public administration practiced in the United States, intensified by increasing technology and the size and variety of programs expanding all over the world as well as at home, what problems are most pressing? The National Academy of Public Administration, through questionnaires and in interviews beginning in 1968, asked top executives of major federal agencies in Washington to list their toughest administrative problems, to arrange them in rank order, and to indicate the priorities as they saw them. Of the 60 issues mentioned in the replies, 27 were repeated most often, and of these, problems relating to personnel administration were raised more than any other. The second major concern was with program fragmentation, an area in which planning and coordination are of primary importance. Some agency heads thought that operating administration at the field level was neglected, that the organization and management of the headquarters-field relationship should be strengthened, with the focus more on the field than on Washington. Communications were also criticized as weak, notably in the headquarters-field network. Overseas administration posed other problems. In yet another area of concern, issues relating to local governments were numerous. Finally, problems of regulatory administration, a distinctive feature of American government, were being neglected.

Implicit in many of the replies from these federal administrators was the question: How can professionally trained specialists—scientists, engineers, doctors, and others—be transformed into effective administrators, since so many of them are destined eventually to join those ranks?

What does the NAPA consider the pressing priorities today? The focus has been broadened and is now called the capacity to govern. This overall interest is centered on the relationship between Congress and the executive establishment. The organization surrounding the president of the United States is receiving intensive study, and a comprehensive report was completed in 1980.[18] Allied to this interest is a concern for better organization in Congress and more effective cooperation between the law-making and law-executing departments. Another task force on the evaluation of the Civil Service Reform Act of 1978 has been empowered to make a final report in 1983–1984 and to submit periodic reports during the interim period. There is far more concern for the future of the economy and government's role in stabilizing it and improving planning and decision making. The perennial problem of government levels continues to receive the attention it deserves. All of this is included under an overriding interest in how to make government more effective and less costly while strengthening democratic values and the contribution of citizens.

SUMMARY

At the very least, corporate and public management can learn much from each other, profiting from each other's mistakes as well as accomplishments. Second, in line with sociological theory, trends in one field are likely to occur at much the same time as in the other. Examples of this parallelism are the productivity emphasis of recent years, the so-called communications revolution, and still more recently the emphasis on quality control and labor-management collaboration at the work level. Third, the private analogy is more likely to be stressed during periods of conservative rule as contrasted with liberal rule, which in the 20th century means during Republican periods rather than Democratic. During the early days and months of Ronald Reagan's administration, for example, even the language of executive Washington was almost identical to that of *Fortune*'s 500, the main reason being that so high a percentage of executives—higher than at any

previous time in history—came directly from corporate management.

Of the points of difference and correspondence mentioned earlier in comparing private and public management, three sensitive areas stand out. All involve the calculus between flexibility and precision. The first of the three is *rules*. Business used to pride itself on being relatively free of them; but with increasing size, corporations have become more and more dependent on rules. Government has expanded rules to the point where they are a main cause of bureaucratic feebleness. Perhaps with the Reagan reforms of bureaucracy and governmental interference, business leadership will recapture some of its flexibility and resiliency. The second area is *accountability*. Accountability has been so much emphasized in Washington administration since World War II that economy and efficiency and especially initiatives from the executive branch have come off a distant second. In business, internal controls have changed little in 50 years. The third area is *motivation*. With the development of departments of government, public affairs, and external relations (the name varies), the largest U.S. corporations have been responding to the demand for an enlightened social conscience. At the same time, government has been tending toward income-output analysis, cost control, and financial incentives. It will be interesting to see whether the tendency to reduce the degree of difference in this vital area will continue.

NOTES

1. Michael Blumenthal, "Candid Reflections of a Businessman in Washington," *Fortune,* 29 January 1979, pp. 36–49.

2. James D. Mooney and Alan C. Reilly, *Onward Industry* (New York: Harper & Row, 1931); and James D. Mooney, *Principles of Organization* (New York: Harper & Row, 1947).

3. Donald Rumsfeld, "A Politician Turned Executive Surveys Both Worlds," *Fortune,* 10 September 1979, pp. 88–94.

4. Blumenthal, "Candid Reflections," p. 36.

5. Marshall E. Dimock, *Law and Dynamic Administration* (New York: Praeger, 1980).

6. Herbert A. Simon, *Administrative Behavior,* 2d ed. (New York: Macmillan, 1957), *passim.*

7. Marshall E. Dimock, *Administrative Vitality: The Conflict with Bureaucracy* (New York: Harper & Row, 1959), *passim.*

8. "A Real Inflation Fighter Takes Charge at the Fed," *Fortune,* 10 September 1979, pp. 62–64.

9. Albert Lepawsky, *Administration: The Art and Science of Organization and Management* (New York: Knopf, 1949); Claude S. George, Jr., *The History of Management Thought* (Englewood Cliffs, N.J.: Prentice-Hall, 1972).

10. Woodrow Wilson, "The Study of Administration," *Political Science Quarterly* 2 (June 1887); reprinted in 56 (December 1941): 481–506.

11. Leonard D. White, *Introduction to the Study of Public Administration* (New York: Macmillan, 1926).

12. W. F. Willoughby, *Principles of Public Administration* (Washington: Brookings Institution, 1927).

13. Commission of Inquiry on Public Service Personnel, *Better Government Personnel* (New York: McGraw-Hill, 1935).

14. Reported in F. J. Roethlisberger and William J. Dickson, *Management and the Worker* (Cambridge: Harvard University Press, 1939).

15. Herbert A. Simon, *Administrative Behavior,* 2d ed., *passim.*

16. Frank Marini, ed., *Toward a New Public Administration: The Minnowbrook Perspective* (Scranton, Pa.: Chandler, 1972).

17. "Symposium on Productivity in Government," *Public Administration Review* 38 (January-February 1978): 1–50.

18. *A Presidency for the 1980's* (Washington: National Academy of Public Administration, November 1980).

PART 2

POLITICS AND PUBLIC POLICY

Patricia Roberts Harris, former secretary of Health, Education, and Welfare, and prior to that secretary of Housing and Urban Development, under the Carter administration, meets with leaders of the International City Management Association. (Photo courtesy of the International City Management Association)

4

The Politics of Public Administration

Politics is the science of how who gets what, when, and why.
Sidney Hillman

In this chapter we position administration in the political process as a whole, judicial as well as legislative. We explain the program manager's role in public policy, his constituency of interests, the way he uses them and is used by them, and the way he walks a tightrope between autonomy and complete absorption in the political process.

Politics and government are inseparable. This relation is sometimes subtle; other times, as in the case of New Jersey's Hudson County, it is blatantly obvious. For example, when Barney Doyle, who was appointed county superintendent of weights and measures in the early 1900s, was asked by a reporter how many ounces there were in a pound, he replied, "How do I know? I just got the job." The author Harold Seidman has summed up the difference between business and government administration in this way: In business, the bottom line is profit or loss; in government, it is votes. Barney Doyle got his job because he was successful in meeting the bottom line of the Hudson County government.

POLITICS AND PUBLIC POLICY

A term that is much used in theoretical discussions of public administration today is *public policy.* Public policy is deciding at any time or place what objectives and substantive measures should be chosen in order to deal with a particular problem, issue, or innovation. It also includes the reasons they should be chosen, as for example, to reduce inflation or to prevent farmlands from being decimated. The term public policy may be, and sometimes is, used in such a way as to be synonymous with the older term *politics.* This confusion is unfortunate because politics has long been equated with government and hence deals with human needs and wants and pressures, as well as with the organization and operation of the entire government. Politics, as the term has come to be used, is virtually synonymous with the word *government,* and includes the organization of the government, its constitution, electorate, and other aspects.

Public policy is thus a subdivision of politics, just as administration may be another. As such, public policy deals with objectives, decisions, and implementation *in specific areas such as* land, water, cities, economics, foreign affairs, defense, poverty, housing, transportation, education, and all the rest—in short, anything in which the government has an interest either as direct provider of the service or as legislator of the service that others administer.

Having distinguished between politics and public policy, readers may now turn their attention to the larger political setting in which the work of practical administrators is done. Administrators are seen to be necessarily political, both in terms of their position in the overall political process and in terms of defining the area of public policy in which they find themselves fashioning objectives, organization, and procedures and making use of public relations while achieving results.

POLITICS VERSUS ADMINISTRATION

In the early 1900s, the efforts of some scholars to distinguish between politics (policy) and administration led to a misunderstanding of what they were trying to say. The scholars were suspected of attempting to create a marked dichotomy, or division, between politics and administration. Critics alleged that the scholars defined policymaking as the job of the elected official and administration of policy as the job of the administrator. Critics further stated that the scholars believed that government would not work well if administrators become involved in policymaking and elected officials become involved in administration of policy. This viewpoint was referred to as the policy-administration dichotomy.[1]

Today, few if any would argue in support of the policy-administration dichotomy. Elected officials *expect* their career administrators to recommend policies to them. In many city-manager governments, for example, the professional manager who does not recommend policies to the mayor and council would be fired for incompetence. Today's public administration professional is inevitably involved in policymaking. The administrator knows that all the political officials discussed in the rest of this chapter may attempt to become involved in and influence policy implementation. If these individuals and groups work hard to institute a policy, they will work hard to make sure it is administered to their satisfaction.

On the practical side, a close kinship that transcends partisanship exists between the public administrator and the political leader. Both are necessarily strategists and tacticians in a drive to get things done. Both must contribute to the solution of society's toughest problems. Both must know how to organize and win support. Both may be equally intelligent, imaginative, and capable, thus creating confidence in their judgment and motives. Because of these common characteristics, the politician wins votes and reelection, and the public administrator wins legislative appropriations and organizational support from all interested parties.

In short, the most able political and administrative leaders are partners, not rivals; they work together to accomplish a task and each knows how to go about it. Enduring political reputations are not likely to be the result of demagoguery, of repeated election from a safe district, or of charisma. Nor, as studies of administration increasingly show, is administrative success due wholly, or even largely, to the position and degree of authority of administrators. In both situations, reputation and influence depend much more on their attitude toward their job, on their political or managerial skills, and on the methods they employ. A conversation with a state government executive tells much about the relation between policy and administration.

Q. How and when did you enter state service?
A. I took the state civil service exam during the depression of the 1930s and was appointed clerk in the state labor department. I had no sponsor or special pull to get me the job.
Q. That entry-level position is a long way from where you ended up.
A. Yes. I served as head of three state departments under four different governors, both Republican and Democratic. Of course, in those positions I was no longer a civil service appointee but a gubernatorial appointee who could be removed at any time.

Q. So you have watched the relation between career and political administrators from both sides of the fence. What advice do you have for young careerists who want to get along with their political bosses?
A. Above all, do your job well. Do your homework so that you always know what is going on in your area of responsibility. I remember when I was promoted to special assistant to the labor commissioner because I knew more about collective bargaining than anyone else in the department. No one is indispensable, but I had become extremely valuable to the commissioner because of my knowledge.
Q. But didn't you have to maneuver against competitors for the job and curry favor with the commissioner to be promoted?
A. Of course, that's true in some departments. It wasn't true in mine. Naturally, you must have some sense of how to get along with your fellow workers and bosses. I never gave my boss unsolicited "political" advice— that is, how to deal with the legislature, governor, political parties, media, and interest groups. But when he realized I know a lot of these people, he began to ask me for such advice. You have to be very careful here, because if your boss sees you as primarily a kind of legislative or interest-group liaison, that is what you will end up doing. Then you'll be cut out of *policy* matters, which is what I came into government to handle.
Q. Tell us about your work after you had had a fair amount of experience.
A. In the 1940s I transferred over to the newly established Department of Economic Development as assistant commissioner, a position covered by civil service. The first commissioner was a businessman without any political experience. Like many newcomers to government, he wanted to "reinvent the wheel"—to do things that had been tried and had failed years previously. I considered it my job to fill him in on those facts,

but his level of arrogance was so high he wouldn't listen. He had contempt for career civil servants and thought he had all the answers. I finally decided that he was going to have to learn the hard way. He put together a plan for development that was shot down quickly in the legislature. This lowered the governor's estimate of the commissioner, and some said his days were numbered. But he showed he was able to learn. He began listening to me and other experienced subordinates. He didn't necessarily accept our ideas—far from it—but he was able to avoid policy catastrophes in the future. We developed a mutual respect and worked well together. And I think we did a damn good job of attracting industry and creating jobs in the state.

Q. Where did you go after that?

A. Governor Brown, elected in 1952, asked me if I would serve as his commissioner of public finance, in charge of budgeting and planning. While I knew this post would mean I would lose my civil service coverage, I felt the challenge was worth it. The work I had done in labor and in economic development had given me a working knowledge of the state's finances, and I knew the top people in most state departments.

Q. What was the difference between that job and your previous ones?

A. Basically that the buck stopped with me. I had the final responsibility for all decisions. This is a sobering responsibility, but I was ready for it because I realized no one could be right all the time. I was entitled to a few mistakes, so long as they weren't disastrous.

Q. What were your relations with career civil servants?

A. Cordial, because they knew I had come up through civil service myself. But there were times I had to get tough with some of them. The fellows in revenue forecasting, for example, were behind the times. They were not using some of the latest econometric methods, so their estimates were off. I told them they were going to have to change. I

didn't care how they did it, but the estimates were going to have to improve. When they failed to respond, I had to replace the chief of the section with a qualified outsider. The others then realized I wasn't kidding, and they got to work. Some of them may have thought I would be soft, because we were all alumni of the same civil service system, but they discovered that wasn't so.

Q. How did you get on with the governors you served under?

A. I had no great problems because I never took on a job I felt I couldn't handle. Governor Brown's successor, Governor Jones, wanted me to be commissioner of education—"to whip that department into line," in his words. I refused because I had no background in the field and knew I would not be accepted by state and local educators, nor by legislators, for that reason. I recommended an excellent woman with the right background whom I knew would sympathize with the governor. He picked her and she did a great job.

Q. Where did you work for Governor Jones?

A. I was made commissioner of the newly created Personnel Department. Because I had come up through civil service, I was accepted by civil servants, the department's clientele. Legislators knew and trusted me because I had always been sure to keep my word to them. We reorganized the civil service system and improved it greatly, in my opinion.

Q. What did you do next?

A. A new governor, David Smith, from the opposition party, was elected in 1962. I was prepared to dust off my résumé and look for a new job when he called me in. He wanted to create a new Department of Transportation, made up of the former Highway Department and the agencies concerned with railroads, airplanes, maritime affairs, and ferryboats. Smith wanted someone who knew state government well and could put together such a department. He was satisfied that even though I had served under the other party, I was a professional, policy-oriented person.

Q. Wasn't serving under both parties unusual?

A. Well, it had been done before in areas such as health and education, which are highly professionalized. That is, most commissioners are MDs or professional educators. So while it had not been done in other departments, there was a precedent.

Q. What was it like creating the new department?

A. My subordinates and I had to show the heads of the different sections that the move made sense for them. None of them was too happy not to be head of an agency anymore. After a while, most of them could see the advantages in coordinating services because it made each of the operations run better. I only had real problems from the man in charge of air transportation. After several talks with him, I told him it was obvious he could not be a willing member of our team and would have to step down.

Q. Wasn't he under civil service? You couldn't fire him, could you?

A. I offered him the chance to transfer to an equivalent civil service position in economic development, where I thought he could do a good job. He took it, and it worked out well for all concerned.

Q. What do you do now?

A. In 1972, I left state service, but I have since been called in to serve as a consultant to several governors. I have worked on a variety of projects ranging from economic development to consolidation of state hospitals.

Q. What are your thoughts and advice about the working relation between career officials and political appointees?

A. They need one another. Government could not work without career people, and we would not be a democracy if elected officials did not have the authority to appoint top executives. When both sides understand the different background of the other and respect each other, they can work well together. If they don't—and I have seen this numerous times in my career—the department is in trouble. Relatively few people have served on both sides of the fence, as I have, which is too bad. It gives you an appreciation for both the careerist and the political appointee.

POLICY ROLES OF THE PUBLIC ADMINISTRATOR

If administrators are to reach the higher levels of their profession, to the point where they may be primarily involved in policy determinations, they must develop the acumen and skill in the use of strategy that distinguish the successful politician or businessperson. Consequently, they must acquire an understanding of all the facets of program administration, including the political.

The Importance of Being Political

In every aspect of public administration, the successful executive is political. Thus, a city manager may be an expert civil engineer, but if he cannot get along with the city council or the pressure groups with which he must deal, highway contractors or unions, for example, or with the voters, he soon finds himself looking for another post. The head of a state government department may be a tax expert, but if he cannot sell his program to the legislature, the governors, and interest groups, he may not accomplish anything memorable. Similarly, the bureau chief, head of one division within a department and a program administrator par excellence, must earn the support of his superiors, colleagues, and subordinates, supporting pressure groups, and the legislature, or his program will falter.

The major work of government is accomplished through programs organized in the major areas of the economy because of their problems: public housing, urban renewal, energy, agricultural productivity, regulation of utilities, social security, medical care, environmental protection, and many more. These programs are served by the career executive under the direction of a politically appointed policy official and the support of his civil service colleagues. At this program level expertise is developed that, combined with dedication and effort, solves problems that have become serious or prevents them from becoming worse.

Few Americans realize how successful these career executives really are and how much political acumen they have acquired. They are the connecting link between partisan and career leadership, and the importance of their role has been clearly illustrated in a number of studies. Indeed, these studies revealed that federal officials engaged in political policy regard top-level career officials as *more skilled in policy and political relations with Congress* and the other centers of political power than they are themselves.[2] (One reason is that appointive policy officials hold office for relatively short periods, changing with each new administration, compared with the lifetime employment of most career officials.) Unlike Britain, the United States has not yet succeeded in making politics a lifelong career.

These men and women deal with policy and politics as a daily concern from the time they reach federal civil service Grade 13. It is they who accompany the top policy person to the Hill when he or she testifies before a congressional committee. The career person may even go alone to these sessions because the person at the top trusts the careerist and believes he or she may do a better job than he can do himself. To the career person, dealing with competing pressure groups becomes second nature. In this connection it may be noted that when bribery or other scandals occur in Washington, the career person is less likely to be involved, because in such matters as in others, he knows the score.

Career employees may have even more influence in state and local government. Fully one fifth of state department heads are covered by civil service, whereas over half the department heads have de facto semipermanent tenure. This is true for some because they have strong interest-group

support and for others because they are highly skilled professionals whose expertise is difficult to replace. In the states, then, many policy executives are long-term office holders and civil servants at once.[3]

In thousands of local governments, department heads and subordinates may be replaced if their party loses the election. But in other thousands of jurisdictions under civil service, department heads are tenured, meaning that they can be removed only for cause. Since cause is usually defined as flagrant insubordination, near-total incapacity to work at the job, or conviction for a felony, many local policy executives are civil servants. And city and county managers, discussed in Chapter 8, are the top policy executives in thousands of local governments. Although they are not tenured, they are professional chief executives.

It is the career executive also who analyzes complicated policy problems and recommends solutions for decision at the higher policy level, dealing with matters in which policy officials have little experience or competence. As complex problems have developed in the nation, so have the career men and women, who today are far more able and more sophisticated than they were even 20 years ago.

The appointed policy executive has rather limited influence compared with that of either the career official or a member of Congress partly because the policy executive does not usually have the long experience in government that the other two have acquired. Nevertheless, the work has many satisfactions as one policy official illustrated by this comment:

The privilege of executive experience in the federal government is strongly affirmative. The daily involvement in critical programs involving large numbers of people offers a stimulation that cannot be equaled in other types of executive positions. . . . The association with other Americans from all segments of the community in a common program contributes significantly to the personal development and understanding.[4]

Even a limited success, continued this official, is satisfactory, because of the process through which it was achieved and the broad impact of its consequences. "It was the most interesting and satisfactory working experience I have had," said an associated official.

Ways to Be Political and Nonpolitical at the Same Time

"It is not political skill that is looked down upon here [in Washington] as much as political commitment is feared,"[5] commented one Washington veteran; the commitment he referred to involved preference or bias. Rufus Miles, who had 30 years of rich administrative experience in the federal government and went on to teach at Princeton, has suggested the practical guidelines by which the public administrator may be political in the sense of being policy oriented, without becoming involved in a partisan political commitment:[6]

1. In a conflict of loyalties between his own program and a policy determined by a higher authority, the program chief should always state his viewpoint openly and, in return, should expect to be consulted before a final decision is made.
2. Although it is true that too many decisions are made at a higher level when they might better be made at the program level, once a decision has been determined, complete loyalty to its promulgator is essential. Furthermore, administrative loyalty should be rewarded and disregard of it punished. Administrators who cannot be loyal should resign.
3. There is no excuse for noncooperation, whether it is illustrated by covert disloyalty or by merely halfhearted efforts at compliance. Cooperation is primarily a matter of attitude, disposition, and discipline. The cohesiveness of society requires disciplined administrative organization. All public administrators moving into supergrade positions should receive a combined orientation and indoctrination course to help them understand what their superiors at specific levels of government expect of them.
4. Interest groups and lobbies, a ubiquitous aspect of

politics, have multiplied like mushrooms since World War II, and public administrators must learn how to deal with them fairly and openly; otherwise, public programs will suffer from fragmentation and ineffectual management.

Miles expresses an understandable concern in these matters. The weakening of respect for the principle of administrative loyalty is no doubt explained in part by the wide questioning of authority that has appeared in American society in recent years. In government, says Miles, the remedy lies with the administrator. In the specific agency, the in-group composed of program experts understands the evolution of program policies and experience, and it is they who must explain the rationale of the policies that are adopted. The members of this group must be open minded in welcoming new ideas on a give-and-take basis and sufficiently imaginative to adapt useful suggestions to the policies at hand. Their responsibility is to create the basis of trust on which all program success finally depends.

THE PROGRAM MANAGER'S CLIENTELE

The strategic role of the program manager is best appreciated if he is visualized as occupying the center of an eight-way relation as illustrated in Figure 4.1. This contrasts with the usual method of showing the manager in a hierarchical framework with one or more layers of organization above or below him. But such an arrangement conveys a false impression, because in fact the higher civil servant resembles no one so much as he does the business entrepreneur, the city manager, or the field commander in time of war. He is the action person with the most direct relation to all parties of interest. A major responsibility, therefore, is to fuse these interests with his overall duties as program manager.

Paul Appleby, a former federal official who later became a professor, probably understood these relations and responsibilities as well as any-

Figure 4.1 The Program Manager's Strategic Position

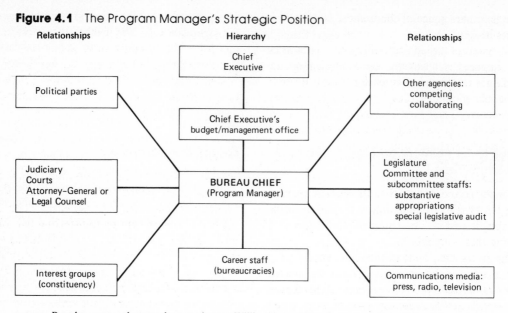

SOURCE: Based on notes taken at a lecture given at Williamsburg, Virginia, by Professor Wallace Sayre during an executive development conference sponsored by the Brookings Institution in 1963.

one. Appleby noted that top-level administrators are "more political" than those at the lower levels. The reason is that the top people relate to more citizens, more competing interests, and more political processes. It is here that the greatest number of clients and factors need to be brought into harmony, here that mighty social forces contend. Consequently, top-level administrators must be generalists. It is more important that they be synthesizers than specialized experts.[7]

The politician, continued Appleby, is also often a generalist, and ideally these two sets of generalists should be able to work side by side, the administrator recommending policy and then executing policy on the basis of the politician's decisions. In the United States, however, political parties have succeeded in only two respects: providing the machinery for developing electoral majorities and elevating candidates having political promise. Consequently, most of the job of government falls on the professional manager.

In the rest of this section, we discuss each member of the program manager's clientele.

Interest Groups

Any kind of nongovernmental association of a voluntary nature can be considered an interest. Once it becomes politically active and lobbies, it is also a pressure group. The National Rifle Association, the Grange, the Teamsters Union, the Chamber of Commerce, the American Association of University Professors, and the Roman Catholic Church are all interest groups when they attempt to influence the policymaking process in areas of concern to them.

Public administrators live constantly with these groups and even help to organize them and to strengthen them. Indeed, if the group supporting a particular program shows signs of weakening, the administrator may even have to step in and share in its management until the crisis is past.

In so close a relation and in a compound in which thousands of pressure groups are the active ingredients, where to draw the line between proper and improper activity on the program manager's part is one of the hardest political decisions he must make.

An interest group, for example, frequently asks the head of a government action agency in which it is interested to *draft legislation* favored by the group on the ground that that person has the necessary know-how and experience. It may also ask *help in securing legislative approval* of the measure on the ground that the head has connections with the chairman of the house of the legislature dealing with the particular program and with others in both houses dealing respectively with budgets and appropriations. The head, says the interest group, is more adept at this sort of thing than they are.

The group may then ask the program manager to *intercede for them with higher administrative authority*. Perhaps the Office of Management and Budget is blocking a certain expenditure, or for political reasons, the White House is about to appoint the "wrong" person to a post in which the group has an interest. The program manager is asked to use influence to secure favorable action.

And finally, the interest group may ask the program manager to *develop a joint public relations program* to push a particular product, service, or solution to a given problem, such as encouraging foreign visitors to the United States, persuading Eskimos to buy more oranges, inducing Arabs to grant more contracts for oil exploration, or prevailing on the Soviet Union to grant reciprocal aviation rights to American carriers.

Faced with such requests from a group whose support he needs, what does the administrator do? Resign himself, and never say no? Or does he go to the opposite extreme and say no to everything? Most successful program managers, of course, wind up somewhere between these two choices. But gradually, over a period of time, administrators tend to do more and more for their interest groups, sometimes until, without even noticing the increase, they are doing a great deal. This is one reason, as Rufus Miles has noted, that an experienced pressure group is able to impose its will on the program it supports and to create internal conflicts between public programs to sup-

plement and reinforce external conflicts between the same interests. The result can only be harassment for the administrator, sometimes to the point where he is no longer a free agent. As Stuart Chase has remarked, interest groups, although lawful and necessary, are sometimes "the despair of patriots."[8]

Legislative Relations

The close relation between program administrators and their interest-group clientele has profoundly influenced some of the basic practices of American government by transferring part of the initiative in the legislative process from the legislature to the executive branch. Thus, most large public agencies working in any major segment of society have created their own committees on legislation to draft administration proposals. In the federal government and in most state governments it is customary to refer to "administration measures," meaning those offered by the executive branch to the legislature and for which priority is demanded. As noted earlier, civil servants instead of the politically appointed chiefs of agencies now frequently appear as official spokespersons before legislative committees. The reason is partly that the relation between the career people and the legislators is customarily of longer duration, is more intimate, and is based on a greater degree of mutual confidence than can be achieved by an appointed official, whose tenure is usually brief and whose political affiliations may be unwelcome. Box 4.1 indicates the importance of good relations with the legislature.

The influence of the professional civil servant begins in the agency he serves on a permanent basis. No departmental head or assistant head, no matter what his prestige, can automatically count on ready cooperation and discipline from his program managers and the bureaucracy *until he earns it*. The attitudes of appointed policy officials, the way they take hold of things the first few days in office, and especially their readiness to consult with career officials instead of springing new policies on them unannounced—such

Box 4.1

DO's AND DON'Ts AT CONGRESSIONAL APPROPRIATIONS HEARINGS

The DO's and DON'Ts listed on the following pages will help you avoid some of the common mistakes made when preparing for and testifying at congressional appropriations hearings. We welcome any suggestions that will improve this list, since we intend to distribute a revised edition at this time next year. Furthermore, your constructive suggestions will be very helpful when we conduct our annual revision to the *Budget Presentation and Justification* student manual. Any recommendations for improvement should be forwarded to: John Edward Murphy, Director of Financial Management Training, Office of Personnel Management, Management Sciences Training Center—WED, P.O. Box 7230, Washington, D.C. 20044.

DO's	DON'Ts
PUNCTUALITY	
Determine the place, time, and scope of the hearing. Recheck on the day before the hearing.	Don't "guess" on these facts. Don't assume that the places and time remain unchanged from the original schedule.
Arrange to have all witnesses present promptly at the time required.	Avoid the need to delay or reschedule the hearing because witnesses are not available.
WITNESSES	
Keep the number of witnesses and back-up personnel to the minimum needed for an effective presentation.	Don't try to impress the subcommittee with numbers.
Before the hearing, submit a list of witnesses to the subcommittee indicating names, titles, and telephone numbers.	Don't depend on identification of witnesses during the course of the hearing.
Obtain prior approval of the subcommittee staff or the chairman if more than the number previously identified are to appear.	Don't "spring" additional witnesses on the chairman.
Have witnesses that are well informed in their program.	Don't have unqualified personnel or unprepared substitutes as witnesses.
Witnesses should be briefed on the subcommittee's composition, desires, interests, and attitudes.	Don't throw witnesses into the hearings "cold."
Ascertain in advance if special witnesses are desired, including any from other agencies. Arrange for alternatives, if considered necessary. Provide biographical data for each new witness for the record.	Don't wait till the hearing is being held to indicate that special witnesses would be helpful to make the presentation more clear.

PRESENTATION

DO's	DON'Ts

Be sure that prepared statements are supplied to the subcommittee in advance, in the number of copies required.

> Do not read a prepared statement that has not been submitted to the subcommittee in advance.

Speak distinctly and to the point in the direction of the chairman and the reporter.

> Do not make a speech directed to no one in particular.

Be sensitive to women members' preference for gender designation (e.g., Mrs., Miss, or Ms.). At the present time there are no women chairpersons on either the House or Senate Appropriations Committees and Subcommittees. Should this change, make sure you know the incumbent's preference. Julia Butler Hansen, who formerly chaired the Interior Subcommittee of the House Appropriations Committee, preferred to be addressed as "Madam Chairman." A future woman chairperson may prefer something different.

> Don't risk annoying a member by falling into the "masculine by preference trap."

Address each incumbent chairman as "Mr. Chairman." Should a woman accede to the chair, determine her preference and address her accordingly (see above). Make sure you know a woman representative's or senator's surname and address her accordingly. If you are sure of a representative's surname address him or her as "Mr. _____," or "Mrs., Miss, or Ms. _____," or in the Senate as "Senator _____." If you are unsure of a male representative's name, address him as "Congressman," or in the Senate as "Senator."

> Do not rely on name plates in front of members, since they sometimes change seats.

When acting as a supporting witness, preface your answer by giving your name and title for the benefit of the chairman and the reporter.

> Do not repeat your name and title upon subsequent questioning unless you feel the chairman and/or reporter do not recognize you.

All remarks should be germane to the hearing and should be made for the benefit of the chairman and the reporter.

> Do not carry on side conversations in the hearing room; they distract.

Focus the presentation on program goals, objectives, plans and financing. Early in the presentation, clearly identify significant changes.

> Don't "fuzz up" the presentation by unnecessary shifting from one subject to another. Don't ramble. Do not wait until late in the hearing to point out a change in policy or program emphasis.

Make sure the opening statement of the initial witness is a crisply written summary of significant matters to be covered in succeeding presentations, and that the interrelationships are clear.

> Don't underestimate the value and impact of this highly important segment of the presentation.

PRESENTATION (*cont.*)

DO's	DON'Ts
Consider the need for a "test run" of the presentation, to identify and strengthen weaknesses.	Don't run the risk of the subcommittee "picking on" an obvious weak spot, thus disrupting an orderly presentation.
Insure that the presentation and supporting material respond to all questions, suggestions, or proposals made by the subcommittee at last year's hearing.	Do not try to avoid embarrassing questions or problems previously posed by the subcommittee.
Be equipped with "back-up" material to respond to questions that might be expected or problems that might be raised.	Don't come to the hearing unprepared to respond quickly to subcommittee questions.
Give direct answers to any questions. Be brief but responsive.	Don't go into long-winded explanations. Don't introduce a new problem in your answer.
Offer to supply for the record any requested information not readily available at the hearing.	Don't take up the subcommittee's time by searching for information. Don't try to bluff the answer. Don't underestimate the member questioning you.
Confine your remarks to your particular field.	Do not attempt to answer questions outside your field.
Keep your language free of technical jargon and alphabetical abbreviations.	Don't use terminology or abbreviations not obviously known to the subcommittee.
Make your presentation in a way that fully supports the President's budget.	Do not volunteer the initial budget request level nor the "cut" by any of the succeeding review levels, e.g., the agency head, OMB, the President.
In response to questions such as "who made that decision," refer to titles and organizations rather than to individuals.	Do not refer to names of individuals in OMB as makers of decisions. Do not criticize a review level for its decisions.
Treat matters about which you have strong opinions factually to avoid misrepresentation by the subcommittee.	Do not volunteer personal opinions unless requested, and if such opinions are inconsistent with the President's recommendations, the witness should make it clear that his opinions do not constitute a request for change or for additional funds.
Use prior year's experience as a guide in organizing your presentation. Introduce variety to bring out new or changing emphasis.	Don't be stereotyped and repeatedly use previous years' formats and style, unless the subcommittee indicates that they want it that way.
Use visual aids, charts, handouts, exhibits, with discretion. Ascertain the desire and attitudes of the subcommittee.	Don't overdo the use of presentation aids. Don't use gimmicks. Don't tell jokes.

Reprinted From the Training Manual, *Budget Presentation and Justification.*

characteristics go far to determine the limits of what the policy official is able to do. His position in the hierarchy and possibly his personal prestige may be of some use to him, but in the long run it is his personality, attitudes, judgment, and willingness to cooperate that determine whether he can accomplish much or only a little.

In practice, therefore, the professional civil servant has a considerable impact on legislation and appropriations, often greater than that of his political superior. Where certain agencies are concerned—those already noted as the favorites of the legislature—the professional career person's influence on legislation may be greater even than that of the chief executive. This tendency of the program manager to become the kingpin in interest-group, legislative, and executive-level politics is a fact of American political life. The triple alliance among policy head, career manager, and legislators, sometimes called the policy triangle, remains an essential fact of American public administration at all levels of government, especially the federal.

Political Parties

When a party wins an election, party leaders need to reward campaign workers. To do so, they must have control over or influence with executive branch agencies, and the chances are that the executive branch will be responsive to their demands. What they desire most, concessions or exceptions for their supporters, often makes their relations with the agencies uneasy and awkward, adding to the difficulties in the day-to-day job of the career administrator.

For example, one category of favors is government jobs. A party worker may want such a job even if he does not have the requisite skills. If he is incompetent, career bureaucrats will be unhappy to accept him as a new employee of the agency.

A second category of favors is government contracts. Enormous sums of money are involved in contracts awarded by urban and state governments, and party leaders want to be sure that the party faithful share in these contracts, regardless of how the agency heads may feel. Finally, a third category, which is quite important to the party leaders, is exceptions for constituents such as fixing a traffic ticket, procuring welfare for an applicant who might be technically ineligible but nonetheless in need, and obtaining a scholarship for a college student. Party leaders desire all these favors to cement the relation between them and their followers. Career employees, on the other hand, resist infringements of the rules.

In regard to the first category, how does a person go about applying for a job in agencies not under the merit system? A 25-year-old Vietnam veteran who wanted to work for the Indiana state highway department was told that the only qualification which he met was Republican registration. In addition to the usual questions in the application were these two: "How long have you been a member of the Republican party?" and "Would you be willing to contribute regularly to the Indiana Republican State Central Committee?" The completed form, along with endorsement from party organization leaders in his area, was forwarded to Republican state headquarters for further processing. The "voluntary" party contribution expected of a patronage employee is 2 percent of his salary, and retaining his job is contingent upon donation to the party. The Indiana arrangement is unique only in the candor with which it is acknowledged; kickback schemes are common. In Illinois and Ohio, for example, they are termed "flower funds," a name derived from the politicians' custom of sending flowers to funerals and wakes. Patronage employees can also expect to participate in such fund-raising devices as testimonial dinners.[9]

Concerning the second category of favors, many state and local department heads are responsible for deciding which banks receive millions of dollars in state highway fund deposits. It is no surprise to find that those banks that have helped them and their political allies are awarded accounts.

While leaders of political parties are much less influential at the federal level than they are at the state and local levels, the experience of the administration under Richard M. Nixon indicates they are not to be discounted. Most federal jobs are covered by the merit system, but under Nixon people who controlled patronage proved ingenious at subverting that system. Many jobholders who had been appointed in the preceding administration were asked to resign. Some were promised excellent recommendations for future jobs. Others were threatened with transfers to another part of the country, to which they did not want to go. Still others were given little or no meaningful work to do. All these techniques were designed to encourage resignations so that jobs could be given to the party faithful. These faithful were then hired in ways equally subversive to the merit system.[10]

Party leaders are influential in the process of implementing policy. They are often able to receive the different kinds of favors and exceptions that they desire from administrators. They are usually not so effective in the process of developing policy, however, except in election law. And they are often apathetic about other decisions in policy development. Thus, party leaders have an uneven impact on policymaking; they are more active in policy implementation than in policy development.

Further, the nature of party leaders' demands places fundamental restrictions on the scope of their involvement in policy implementation. Their focus is quite narrow: favors and exceptions from the bureaucracy, rather than substantive policy preferences. As a result, party leaders are unlikely to have the same impact on policymaking as do chief executives, career bureaucrats, the legislature, and interest groups, even when all their demands are satisfied, which they rarely are. This situation is due to the very nature of the needs of the organizations run by party leaders.

Communications Media

Any treatment of the communications media must distinguish among the kinds of media. The focus here is primarily on mass media, which reach very large numbers of people, instead of on elite media, which appeal to much smaller numbers of leaders. The mass media can be divided into two broad categories: printed (newspapers and magazines) and electronic (television and radio).

Reporters pursue a story only if it conforms to their definition of news. Several studies have found that reporters believe readers prefer certain kinds of stories to others, which is why they concentrate on material dealing with conflict, change, the unique, and names. Reporters pay attention to all kinds of controversy, violent or not. It is inconceivable that the media would regularly play up harmony in Congress, city halls, and state capitols. Any kind of obvious change or departure, such as a new drug rehabilitation program, is reported. Unique events of human interest—for example, a bureau head's volunteering to spend time in jail to appreciate better what prisoners experience—are given prominence. Names are news because reporters believe readers respond to a "star system," as do fans of rock music or opera. For example, one study quotes a reporter as saying that when the chief executive called a press conference or asked to see newsmen, he "would never snub the governor, regardless of how important events occurring elsewhere were."[11]

These focuses have profound implications for the way news is covered. Rarely is consideration given to the background of a story, or is an attempt made to probe deeply into its meaning. As likely as not, the reporter will be concentrating on another subject the next day, so that his approach is descriptive rather than analytical. Moreover, because he is under pressure to meet deadlines and has no time to reflect and write in depth, his efforts often result in superficiality, nonuniformity, and discontinuity of coverage.[12] These statements do not imply in any way that reporters are shallow or do inferior reporting; they simply point out the constraints placed on reporters by the nature of their work.

Recently, however, a new and deeper approach to news reporting, investigatory journalism, has emerged. This approach is graphically illustrated in the spectacular exposés by two *Washington Post* reporters, Bob Woodward and Scott Armstrong, who first uncovered the Watergate story during the Nixon administration and later wrote their best-selling book dealing with the inner workings of the Supreme Court of the United States, a hallowed institution that previously had been immune to such intimate treatment.[13]

Representatives of the news media may often enter into conflict with government officials, who are greatly concerned with media coverage and who attempt to have themselves depicted in the best possible light. Today, government agencies of any size have public relations offices that, whatever their designation, crank out reams of releases and information for the media. The Pentagon, for example, employs hundreds of people in its press offices. In some situations imaginative use of public relations techniques can result in great dividends for the agency. A study of the New Haven antipoverty program describes such efforts, which made the program a national showcase.[14]

In spite of even the most brilliant public relations, the relation between government officials and reporters is often one of conflict, because the goals of each group differ when it comes to the dissemination of information. Reporters want to know as much as possible about government and wish to emphasize disagreement, change, and uniqueness. The more stories they produce that highlight controversy and change, the more likely they are to be featured on the front page of the evening news, to become widely known, and to be promoted.

Government officials, on the other hand, strive to keep private as many matters within their purview as possible in order to enhance their ability to influence the decision-making process. If a proposal for policy development under consideration becomes public knowledge, it will give the opportunity for potential opponents of the project to mobilize. Furthermore, officials may often be trying to cover up practices, legal or illegal, that may prove embarrassing to them. Thus, they attempt to hide many potential news items that reporters tend to exaggerate.

A totally different pattern from the one just described may often exist, and it is difficult to say which pattern is more prevalent. Reporters and government officials may often develop a symbiotic relation, in which the reporter does not dig too deeply so as not to embarrass the government official and in return is given enough material to keep his employer happy. One journalist claims that this relation is perhaps the major problem faced by reporters.[15]

Reportorial norms guarantee that the day-to-day functioning of the executive branch at any level of government will not be covered. Although state capital newspapers publish reams of copy about the deliberations of the state legislature when it is in session, readers will search in vain for comparable coverage of agency programs. The same situation is even more characteristic at the urban level. The daily work of administrators may be of great importance, but it is unlikely to be characterized by spectacular conflict, change, uniqueness, or names. Moreover, the work is becoming increasingly complex, so that the reporter's task of explanation becomes correspondingly more difficult. Further, because agencies are specialized, only a small segment of the readership is greatly concerned with the functioning of any particular bureau.[16] Persons without a relative or friend in a city hospital, for example, are unlikely to be greatly concerned about such institutions.

Career administrators are less likely than other political figures to be influenced by the press. First, administrators are not so prone to develop close ties with reporters as are elected officials, because the reporter's news story is focused on the elected official. Second, administrators may often enjoy a good deal of autonomy in carrying out a program and may therefore not need press support. When such is not the situation, they may seek to cultivate the press.

The Courts

The courts are another important influence on the bureaucracy. Judges are powerful officials, a fact reflected by the way audiences rise to their feet when the judge enters the courtroom. Examples of court influence over administration include ordering desegregation and busing in local school systems, withholding federal grants-in-aid to localities, and the takeover of jails, hospitals, and railroads.

A 1976 survey of the budgetary process in eight states found that one third of 322 agency officials had been ordered by federal courts to alter existing programs or initiate new ones.[17] The prospects are that judicial intervention will increase in the future, given the trends discussed in Chapter 6, which deals with administrative law.

The Chief Executive and Other Agency Officials

Because Chapter 8 is devoted to chief executives and their attempts to coordinate government, we reserve this important discussion for that chapter.

The Career Administrative Corps

Part 4 of this book is devoted to the topic of personnel.

POLITICS AND ADMINISTRATION AS PROCESS

It is now possible to state some conclusions regarding the respective roles of politics and public administration in the conduct of government.

First, there is no sharp dividing line between the making of law and the execution of law because the professional bureaucracy is necessarily involved at all stages of the political process except the partisan stage.

Second, the relation of the professional bureaucracy to pressure groups and legislatures is now the most significant focus of influence in the United States government. The bureaucracy has the *influence,* but not the *legal authority,* to decide issues of public policy. This influence is partly the result of the vacuum created by the relative insufficiency of leadership in the legislature and in the higher reaches of the executive branch compared with the greater continuity of leadership among civil servants and their greater technical competence in most areas of policy decision. Yet another point, discussed in Chapter 8, is certain weaknesses in overall structural coordination at all government levels.

Third, unless people are prepared to be more formalistic than realistic, they must conclude that the *political process and the administrative process overlap at so many points that only by understanding both can either be understood.*

Clearly, in the face of complexities continually generated in technologically highly developed societies, the influence and even the power of trained administrators who understand some of these problems has become very great indeed, and it is becoming even greater as science assumes new influence. The point was underscored by Sir Henry Bunbury, one of the most respected members of the British administrative class, who was not only a practitioner but also a scholar of public administration. He observed:

The technicians and technologists claim a much bigger share in running the shows in which they are engaged—they want, in fact, not to be confined to the laboratories and workshops, but to sit in the boardrooms and decide policy. This is the challenge to the old British tradition of entrusting policy and administration to "gifted amateurs"—politicians and civil servants who, the technical people say, don't know what they're talking about.

I go a good way with them. When I was in the Post Office I urged that it should be possible for a top Engineer to become head of the Post Office Administration, if he were the right kind of chap. I was delighted when this actually happened, after I retired.

But the problem isn't quite as simple as the technician makes out, in my opinion. Public psychology, the economic and financial considerations have to be taken into the reckoning and technicians are apt to be a bit weak in these aspects. And I feel that a society organized and run purely by scientists would be rather a hell to live in.[18]

Although the combination of two kinds of competence, technical and political, adds a new dimension to politics, this mix is badly needed in the administrative systems of most technologically advanced countries.

The needed adjustment might take one of three directions: (1) improve the policymaking and administrative skills and understandings of politicians, (2) improve the policymaking and economic skills of permanent career officials, or (3) improve the skills of both groups and let them work closely together, with the elected political official having the final word. A country must be assured not only that wrong policies are being stopped, but also that right ones are being initiated at the right time. Under existing conditions in the United States, most of the defense against misconceived policies, if it occurs at all, falls on the shoulders of the permanent career official. Strong as many of these people are, they cannot do the whole job alone.

SUMMARY

Perhaps this last observation provides the meat of what needs to be said. The administrator is on the cutting edge of social change. His success depends upon his political skill in the best sense. He provides a continuity no one else can supply. As an expert he knows more about substance than anyone else; his negotiating and mediating skills are vital because of his "permanence." The administrator's impact on public policy can be great or small; but if he commands respect, he can do more than any other person to pull every aspect of the program together and make it work.

NOTES

1. Frank J. Goodnow, in his *Politics and Administration* (New York: Macmillan, 1914), did not try to create a di-chotomy; neither did Woodrow Wilson when he stressed the need for more "businesslike" administration in government—he was, after all, the justly celebrated author of a study of *Congressional Government* (Boston: Houghton Mifflin, 1885). Nor did Luther Gulick as coeditor of *Papers on the Science of Administration* (New York: Institute of Public Administration, 1937). Nor did Marshall E. Dimock (one of the present authors) in his *Modern Politics and Administration* (New York: American Book, 1937) ever regard politics and administration as separate worlds. In all these studies, the two processes were differentiated, not to set up polarities but to find a better basis for studying the administrative process, to repair the earlier neglect of the subject, and to show that the civil service career official is professionally obligated to eschew certain types of partisan political activity.

2. Three excellent studies are Marver H. Bernstein, *The Job of the Federal Executive* (Washington: Brookings Institution, 1958); Hugh Heclo, *A Government of Strangers* (Washington: Brookings Institution, 1977); and Harold Seidman, *Politics, Position, and Power,* 3d ed. (New York: Oxford University Press, 1980).

3. Douglas M. Fox, *The Politics of City and State Bureaucracy* (Santa Monica, Calif.: Goodyear Publishers, 1974), p. 16.

4. Bernstein, *The Job of the Federal Executive,* pp. 216–217.

5. Bernstein, *The Job of the Federal Executive,* p. 195; see also pp. 45, 55–56, 59, 62, and 112.

6. Rufus E. Miles, Jr., "Administrative Adaptability to Political Change," *Public Administration Review* 35 (December 1965): p. 221.

7. Paul H. Appleby, *Policy and Administration* (Tuscaloosa: University of Alabama Press, 1949), pp. 49–50, 170.

8. Stuart Chase, *Democracy Under Pressure* (New York: Twentieth Century Fund, 1945).

9. John Kifner, "Kickbacks Still Thrive in Indiana," *New York Times,* 11 July 1971, p. 21.

10. U.S., Congress, House, Committee on Post Office and Civil Service, Subcommittee on Manpower and Civil Service, *Final Report on Violations and Abuses of Merit Principles in Federal Employment,* 94th Cong., 2d session, 30 December 1976.

11. See Delmar D. Dunn, *Public Officials and the Press* (Reading, Mass.: Addison-Wesley, 1969), p. 55. This is a study of reporters covering Wisconsin state government. Three studies that make similar points about Washington reporters are Douglass Cater, *The Fourth Branch of Government* (Boston: Houghton Mifflin, 1959); Bernard C. Cohen, *The Press and Foreign Policy* (Princeton, N.J.: Princeton

University Press, 1963); and Edward Jay Epstein, *News From Nowhere: Television and the News* (New York: Random House, 1973).

12. Dunn, *Public Officials and the Press.*

13. Bob Woodward and Scott Armstrong, *The Brethren: Inside the Supreme Court* (New York: Simon & Schuster, 1980).

14. Russell Murphy, *Political Entrepreneurs and Urban Poverty* (Lexington, Mass.: Heath, 1971), p. 72. See also Morris Janowitz et al., *Public Administration and the Public: Perspectives Toward Government in a Metropolitan Community* (Ann Arbor: University of Michigan, Bureau of Government, 1958), p. 97.

15. William Rivers, *The Adversaries: Politics and the Press,* (Boston: Beacon Press, 1970). See also Dunn, *Public Officials and the Press,* pp. 95–96.

16. Compare Dunn, *Public Officials and the Press,* p. 57.

17. George E. Hale, "Federal Courts and the State Budgetary Process," *Administration and Society,* November 1979, pp. 357–368.

18. Bunbury to Professor Charles Ascher, formerly of Brooklyn College, New York City, and circulated at a meeting of the National Academy of Public Administration. Sir Henry was born in 1876, entered the British War Office in 1900, became National Health Insurance commissioner in 1913, and was comptroller of the Post Office from 1920 to 1937. Among his publications is *Governmental Planning Machinery* (Chicago: Public Administration Clearing House, 1937). Sir Henry was among the founders of the British study group called Political and Economic Planning (PEP) and of what is now the Royal Institute of Public Administration.

5

Intergovernmental Relations

With a federal system we have diversity; without diversity, there is no choice; without choice, there is no freedom. . . . the great glory of the federal system is that some damn fool at the top can't ruin it.
Frank Bane, Former Chairman, Advisory Commission on
Intergovernmental Relations

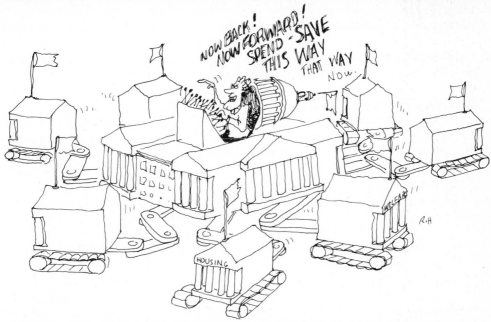

In this chapter, we examine the federal system of the United States and the relations among the federal, state, and local governments. We scrutinize grants-in-aid from one government to another, look at political intergovernment relations, and offer some advice on how to apply for grants. We assume that cost and effectiveness depend largely on the number and kind of governments that need to cooperate and where the lead role is found. In the administration of Ronald Reagan, no issue, perhaps, has been more emphasized than this one. The extremes are the tight federal centralization advocated by the American statesman Alexander Hamilton after 1789, versus the village autonomy advocated by the 20th century Indian leader Mahatma Gandhi. It is a complex problem, fraught with danger and promise, but it is soluble. First the problems and possibilities must be made clear.

Whenever a college course in intergovernmental relations (IGR in this chapter) is offered, some students will likely be puzzled the first day. These students may think they signed up for a course in inter*national* relations, and they may quickly drop out when they discover otherwise. Yet if they stayed, they would find many parallels between the complex diplomatic relations, alliances, and bargaining characteristic of international relations and the behavior of groups and individuals in IGR. An example, unusual only in that it involved a foreign nation as well as other participants in IGR, is that of Vulcan, West Virginia. This hamlet's only access to the outside world was a bridge, which rotted away in 1975. After waiting in vain for a year for state officials to repair the bridge, Vulcan resident John Robinette asked the Soviet Union for a foreign aid grant to accomplish the job. A Soviet reporter came to look around, and just a few hours after his departure, state officials announced they would build a new bridge.[1]

We define IGR as the interaction of government officials and employees of two or more units of government.[2] IGR may occur *vertically*, as in federal-state-local government relations. The governmental system of the United States is a federal one. A federal system, whether governmental or corporate, is one in which power is divided between a central unit at the top and others that are geographically separated, as distinguished from a unitary government, where a single unit at the top operates through subordinate administrative units at the base. A federal system, like a unitary system, has the problem of defining roles and securing cooperation among the various units working on a given program. The scope, however, is wider than in unitary governments, and the problems are correspondingly greater. IGR may also occur *horizontally*, as in interstate or interlocal government action.

CONSTITUTIONAL AND HISTORICAL BACKGROUND

Relations among the different governments in the United States cannot be adequately understood without a brief examination of the historical background. The original 13 states existed as independent colonies before the existence of a national government. The adoption of a constitution uniting the 13 colonies into one nation in 1789 was a lengthy and arduous process. Only after numerous guarantees of state prerogatives and privileges were made was the Constitution ratified.

In the century following the formation of the union, the *limited national government* created by the Constitution showed no evidence of disturbing the balance of powers between the states and the nation. In case of doubt, Congress and the Supreme Court usually decided in favor of allowing the states and local governments to do what the national government might have done. As Emmette Redford has shown,[3] the equilibrium between Washington and the states for the first 100 years of American federal experience was a judicious mixture of centralization, when that was needed to foster and promote development, and decentralization to allow state and local governments to exercise their initiative wherever possible. Under these conditions, there was little splintering or fragmentation of programs—which, of course, were not on a large scale anyway.

By the time the railroads had spanned the continent and business and commerce were nationwide, shortly after the Civil War, the tide turned in favor of national authority and against authority of the states. With the onset of what has been called the second industrial revolution, the Interstate Commerce Commission Act was passed in 1887, and the Sherman Anti-Trust Act in 1890. At the same time, Congress began making wider use of its commerce and taxing powers, and the federal administrative bureaucracy began to expand until it reached a high point in the 1930s, when New Deal programs multiplied to cope with the Great Depression.

With the proliferation of these federal regulatory, agricultural, labor, and welfare programs, federal power vis-à-vis that of the states became fully dominant. Under what may be called the New Deal revolution, federal programs began to invade the hitherto reserved functions of state and local governments, largely through the federal-aid device. Under this arrangement, the national government raises the money and, in effect, contracts with state governments to do or assist in work they are constitutionally entitled to undertake on their own responsibility. Although some notable Supreme Court decisions were unfavorable to this extension of national authority over the states, the total powers of government were in fact redistributed in such a way that the national government came eventually to be concerned in almost every area of state and local activity.

SOME ANALOGIES DESCRIBING IGR IN THE UNITED STATES

The traditional 19th-century view of the U.S. federal system, dual federalism, has been likened to a layer cake. That is, the states carried out their own activities separately from the federal government and vice versa. The two levels did not intersect or interact but were as distinct as two layers of cake.

Students of IGR later came to argue that the layer cake analogy probably was never accurate and certainly did not describe the realities of 20th-century IGR. The late Morton Grodzins, one of the most penetrating analysts of IGR in the 1950s, baked a marble cake to describe the system. The marble cake is "characterized by an inseparable mingling of differently colored ingredients, the colors appearing in vertical and diagonal strands and unexpected swirls. As colors are mixed in a marble cake, so functions are mixed in the American federal system."[4] An example is the public welfare system, in which all three levels of government administer public assistance programs and child welfare services. Sharing of program responsibility and implementation, rather than exclusive control of policy areas by one level of government, characterizes U.S. IGR.

Former North Carolina Governor Terry Sanford has used the term *picket fence federalism* to describe the realities of IGR. The picket fence is diagramed in Figure 5.1. Each picket represents a specific policy area, for example, welfare, highways, education. The significance of the picket fence is that the pickets, not the horizontal bar

joining them, are the most important part of the fence. Specialists in each policy area are the most important participants in the policymaking process.

These specialists, organized into professional associations called intergovernmental guilds by the author Harold Seidman, are key figures in IGR. David Walker, assistant director of the Advisory Commission on Intergovernmental Relations (ACIR, an agency discussed later in this chapter), thought that IGR changed enough in the 1970s to warrant substituting a bamboo fence for the picket fence. Writing in the fall of 1977, Walker cited ACIR surveys indicating that attitudes of administrators of federal-grant programs had changed in some important ways. The administrators in the 1970s were more flexible than those in the 1960s had been. The administrators did not reject out-of-hand any attempts to increase coordination in the system, recognizing that this was an important concern. Walker stated, "A fence would still appear to be the proper metaphor, but not the sturdy, solid wood variety. Instead, one of bamboo would be more apt—given somewhat softer materials, its elaborate horizontal wiring system, and its greater capacity to bend to the prevailing winds."[5] With these cakes and fences in mind, readers may now look at the U.S. system of IGR in more detail.

THE ANATOMY OF IGR

The anatomy of intergovernmental relations is analogous to the anatomy of the human body but on a huge scale. The possibilities for malfunction are equally great.

Interstate Relations

Congress must approve any formal agreement, or compact, between states. (So far some 170 agreements have been signed in the nation's history.) An example is the compact signed by all 50 states agreeing to return to their home states criminals on probation or parole who break the law. The Constitution also requires states to give "full faith and credit" to the laws of other states. Interstate

Figure 5.1 Picket Fence Federalism: A Schematic Representation

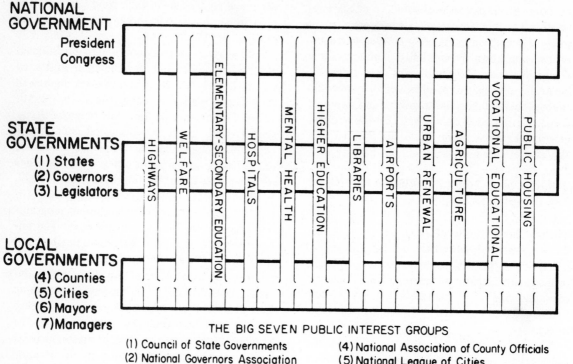

THE BIG SEVEN PUBLIC INTEREST GROUPS

(1) Council of State Governments
(2) National Governors Association
(3) National Conference of State Legislatures

(4) National Association of County Officials
(5) National League of Cities
(6) U.S. Conference of Mayors
(7) International City Management Association

Deil S. Wright
Copyright 1/17/77

conflict occurs as frequently as cooperation. For example, New Hampshire and Maine fought a "lobster war" in the 1970s, each state claiming jurisdiction in contested waters and taking police measures against fishermen from the other state. Numerous interstate and regional commissions, such as the Upper Great Lakes Regional Commission, were founded in the 1970s and will probably play a slowly increasing part in the IGR system.

Interlocal Relations

Local interrelations boggle the mind. Readers may consider first the aggregate figures. The

United States contains 3,000 counties, 16,000 school districts, 24,000 special districts, 17,000 townships, and 18,000 municipalities. As Congressman Henry Reuss put it, "Nowhere but in America have so few ever been governed by so many."[6] On the average, there is one local government for every 2,750 residents of the nation. The average can be misleading because the majority of local governments are found in rural areas, where only 30 percent of the population lives. Even so, there is still a vast proliferation of governments in urban areas. The Philadelphia metropolitan area, for example, has more than 900 governments. (A metropolitan area is defined by the U.S. Census Bureau as a city of 50,000 or more with surrounding suburbs that are economically integrated with the city.)

Whitehall, Pennsylvania, is admittedly an extreme example but indicative of what the U.S. system can produce. In 1972, Whitehall, with a population of 16,000, housed all or parts of 14 local governments within its boundaries: the borough of Whitehall, Baldwin-Whitehall School District, Baldwin-Whitehall Schools Authority, Pleasant Hills Sanitary Authority, South Hills Regional Planning Commission, South Hills Area Council of Governments, City of Pittsburgh, Allegheny County Sanitary Authority, Allegheny County Port Authority, Allegheny County, Western Pennsylvania Water Company, and Southwestern Pennsylvania Regional Planning Commission. Because many of these governments levy taxes, an individual resident of Whitehall pays taxes or user charges to several different governments at once.[7]

Types of Local Government

Local governments can be divided into two broad types: *general governments,* which carry out a number of different functions, such as health, welfare, highways, police, fire, and other functions; and *single-purpose* governments, which carry out only one (or perhaps two) closely related functions such as water and sewerage, education, or public safety. No matter what the formal name of a local government may be, it is necessary to look at what it actually does before concluding whether it is a general or specialized government. Two localities that are called townships, for example, may actually differ greatly in government work load.

Municipalities. The term municipality derives from the Latin word *municipium,* a label given to Roman cities allowed special privileges. The 18,000 U.S. municipalities, which are usually called cities, towns, or villages, were originally established as providers of local services, such as police and fire protection and public works. A municipality is a legally public corporation, granted

a charter from its state legislature that spells out what it can and cannot do.

Townships. The township furnishes far fewer functions for its residents than municipalities do for theirs. It does not have the degree of discretional authority the municipality has. The township is usually responsible for roads, which may be its only function. (In such a situation, it amounts to a de facto, single-purpose government.) In remote rural areas, townships may become rudimentary forms of local government, which provide more services to residents than does any other local government.

The 17,000 townships in the United States are found principally in the north-central states of the Midwest and in the mid-Atlantic states. This land was originally part of the national domain, and townships often evolved from federal surveyors' maps, which explains why many of them have neat, geometrical boundaries.

Special Districts and School Districts. Special districts usually supply only one specific service of government, such as mosquito control or soil conservation, although some special districts provide closely related services, such as water supply and sewerage. We have combined the discussion of special districts with that of school districts because both are *single-purpose governments,* usually providing only one service instead of the range of services a municipality offers. In 1976, there were a total of nearly 24,000 single-purpose governments, outnumbering municipalities and townships.

The growth rates of these two single-purpose agencies are very different. The number of school districts has been drastically reduced from 108,000 in 1942 to 16,000 in 1980. This decrease has not been caused by a reduction in the number of schoolchildren but by the combination of many of the smaller districts into larger ones. Special districts, on the other hand, are the fastest growing type of local government, more than doubling in number from 1952 to 1972. In 1976 there were more than 24,000 special districts, making them the most numerous form of local government in the United States. Eight of the 14 governments of Whitehall, Pennsylvania, listed in a preceding section, are special districts.

Special districts collectively provide almost every type of local government service. In 1972, according to the ACIR, the most common type of special district is the fire protection district; there are almost 4,000 of these. Other common districts are those for soil conservation, housing and urban renewal, water supply, drainage, cemeteries, and sewers, as well as special districts for electric and gas supply, libraries, transit, and health. Less than 4 percent of the districts performed more than one function, and two thirds of these were in the related areas of sewerage and water supply.[8]

Special districts are surging so spectacularly that they pose even more problems for coordination of services than do school districts. Paradoxically, although special districts were created partly to overcome problems in delivering service caused in the first place by governmental fragmentation, they have increased fragmentation. Thus in the post–World War II period, many rural towns quickly became suburbs when city residents moved out to the country. These towns eventually found it necessary to install municipal water supply systems, because there were too many houses for each to have its own well. Yet how was a small town to develop its own reservoir system? A typical solution to the problem was the creation of a special district, which would provide water to several towns, sharing the cost of a reservoir system among them. Thus the problems caused by the fragmentation of local government into small units were overcome in this one policy area. At the same time, however, fragmentation was increased by the creation of yet another local government, the independent water district, which generated its own revenues through the sale of water to users in the district. Although the immediate problem was solved for the time being, future attempts to coordinate policy with related areas such as sewerage disposal and flood control were inevitably complicated by the existence of additional units that would have to be coordinated. For this reason, many specialists in public

administration look askance at the spread of special districts.

An example of the problems that can be created by the spread of special districts is a situation that occurred in Bridgeton Terrace, Missouri, in October 1963. The telephone operator who reported a residential fire to the Community Fire Protection District was advised that the fire was not in the district's jurisdiction. The operator then called the Pattonville-Bridgeton Volunteer District, which went to the fire. These volunteers could not enter the burning house immediately because their masks did not work. Once in the house, they operated their inhalators incorrectly. As a result of the delay and incompetence, two girls died of smoke inhalation. In the wake of the furor over this incident, upset citizens and officials made a serious attempt to merge the county's 52 fire districts into one unit. But the jurisdictional jungle remained intact in the face of opposition from many individual fire districts.[9]

Counties. Counties, a form of general government, are, in area, easily the largest local governments, which explains why there are far fewer (3,000) of them than any other type of local government. King County, Texas, for example, is larger than the state of Rhode Island. It is not uncommon for a county to be comprised of a hundred or more municipalities, townships, school districts, and special districts. In addition, there may be unincorporated areas over which the county does not share its jurisdiction with any other local governments.

Counties are significant units of government in all parts of the country except the six New England states. Early in the history of the New England states, the town existed before the county and assumed a vigorous role. Thus the New England counties had little to do but elect a sheriff and operate a jail. Some no longer even run jails. One source rates counties as very important in 6 states, important in 3, and moderately important in 33.[10]

The county has changed more than other forms of local government. Historically limited in the scope of their powers and responsibilities, many counties have greatly expanded their regulatory activity and delivery of services. In 1976, fully two fifths of the states had granted increased home rule or decision-making authority to the counties, allowing them greater discretion in determining both the form of county government and the scope of activity of county agencies. The National Association of Counties reports that counties offer 58 different services, ranging from fire protection through rehabilitation of crippled children to operation of museums, airports, and zoos. By any measure, counties are spending a larger relative share of each local taxpayer's income each year, and they already account for more than one fifth of the money spent by all local governments. Nassau County, New York, has a vigorous consumer-protection program consisting of both educational and publicity efforts and investigation of complaints.

The four services on which counties spend two thirds of their total budgets are welfare, education, highways, and hospitals. Highways, a traditional county function, have not kept up with the other three functions or with a host of other services in rate of growth, thus indicating that counties are expanding and diversifying their services.[11] It is difficult to deny that the 80,000 local governments of the country need to be combined and consolidated. According to 1977 figures, 20,891 municipalities, townships, and special districts did not have even one full-time employee. Another 3,815 had only one full-time employee, and 5,134 had only two to five. The number would probably be larger if counties and school districts were included, but numbers are not available for these governments. The researchers who gathered the data refer to these jurisdictions as "toy" governments, and urge combining them.[12] How can that be done?

COORDINATING LOCAL GOVERNMENT

The focus of this section is the consolidation of services and regulatory activities offered by several localities into a new and necessarily larger unit of general government. This approach, of which there are several variations, is different from another one that has enlisted growing support in a number of areas: unifunctional regionalization, or consolidation of services, by creating a new special district. There are, for example, some regional police and fire governments. In such unifunctional consolidation, as we have already noted, one kind of fragmentation is exchanged for another. When regionalization of one service occurs under a new government, however, fragmentation is reduced. The focus here is on the attempt to create and enlarge the responsibilities of general governments that are geographically larger than the local governments they take over. Roscoe Martin lists a total of 16 approaches, including unifunctional regionalization.[13] Some of these alternative approaches follow.

City and County Government

A good deal of informal cooperation (for example, mutual aid in fire fighting or sharing of police teletype information) occurs among local governments. Of course, the effectiveness and the very existence of such cooperation depend upon the desire of governmental units to cooperate.

A number of cities and counties buy and sell local services through a *service contract*. Los Angeles County, for example, through what is called the Lakewood Plan, offers to municipalities within the county a range of services, including police protection and water supply. A 1971 survey of 2,000 cities found that 62 percent of them contracted with their counties for services.

Annexation of unincorporated areas into cities and counties has slowed down in recent years, because most areas surrounding large cities are now incorporated. This gives them a legal life of their own, so they cannot be absorbed by cities. Some cities have used their practical monopoly on vital services to force annexation. In the 1960s, Mayor George Sensenbrenner of Columbus, Ohio, informed those suburbs that bought water from Columbus that their days of independent existence were over. Unless they allowed annexation, the water supply would be shut off. Annexation began at once. But increasing suburban power has prevented other cities from using this approach. Milwaukee's attempt to emulate Columbus failed when the suburban-dominated state legislature forced the city to supply the suburbs with water at low cost.

Functional consolidation of city and county services has occurred in a number of areas. For example, the city of Rochester, New York, has combined its welfare, airport, civil defense, health, mental health, and park programs with those of Monroe County.

Councils of government (COG) can be defined as voluntary regional associations of local governments, which are concerned with a broad range of government services and problems. Each member government is represented in the COG by elected officials, who meet to exchange information, discuss problems, and develop policy on matters of common interest. The COGs usually also formulate a comprehensive plan for the area, review applications from members for federal grants to see if these applications are consistent with the plan, and serve as liaison groups with federal bureaus.

The COGs' limitations lie in their lack of authority. A confederal body, they do not have governmental powers and operating responsibilities. They cannot compel participation, attendance, or acquiescence in their decisions. President Harry S. Truman once said about his job that all he had was the power to persuade, to convince others that what he wanted was in their best interest as well. Such is quite literally true about the power of the COG.

Although the COGs are growing in number and importance, they remain, as the ACIR has said, "essentially a device for incremental adaptation to changing needs."[14] No major or sweeping changes are likely to come from an institution that can make decisions only by consensus. The COGs find it relatively easy to agree on a common approach to purchasing whereby all governments will benefit from lower prices resulting from larger orders. But more controversial matters, such as busing central-city schoolchildren to the suburbs or deciding where to place low-in-come housing, are not going to be resolved by the COGs. The very different perspectives of the central city, the county, and the suburbs preclude such decision making.

At the same time, the probable prospect for the future is an increased role for the COGs. The COGs are more active and robust now than 10 years ago. The reasons for their establishment—service coherence and coordination—will probably cause them to become increasingly important in the years ahead.

Metro Government

Metropolitan area-wide government takes two forms. One is consolidation of a central city's government with that of the surrounding county. The other is the two-tier form, which strengthens an areawide government while retaining all or most existing municipalities. Although neither has been very popular in recent years, both have been used more frequently.

Examples of city-county consolidation in the 19th century include New Orleans, Philadelphia, New York, and Boston. Since 1945, there have been consolidations in Baton Rouge, Louisiana; Nashville, Tennessee; Jacksonville, Florida; and Indianapolis, Indiana, among others. For each of these successful efforts, there have been scores of failures.

City-county consolidations usually involve one major city in a rapidly urbanizing county in a moderate-sized metropolitan area. No postwar consolidations occurred in any city of more than 500,000. Seven consolidations occurring between 1969 and 1973 were limited to cities of less than 200,000. Through a referendum, the smaller municipalities are free to join or stay out. The new government is divided into different tax districts, depending on the level of services provided in each area. The consolidated government has an elected chief executive, who usually confronts a fairly large legislature.

The two-tier approach has been carried out in Miami and Minneapolis–St. Paul. Such an approach may or may not require a reallocation of functions, in whole or in part, from one level of government to another. Perhaps the most ambitious two-tier metro government is Portland, Oregon's, three-county government, achieved in 1979.

The future will probably see an increase in both types of metro government, but the United States has a long way to go to achieve coordinated local government.

VERTICAL IGR AND THE ACIR

One way of conceptualizing vertical IGR in the United States is to look at the three levels of government as a division of labor. The federal government gives money to and issues regulations for state and local government. Few federal employees directly carry out programs of state, city, and other local governments. State governments directly administer some important programs such as public higher education, mental health care, and highway construction and maintenance. In other areas, such as primary and secondary public education, welfare, and city and town roads, the states play a role similar to that of the federal government. That is, they issue regulations and provide funds to pay for some of the cost of these functions. Local governments do the work related to programs in their area. From the recordings of birth certificates and death certificates, they accompany citizens every day of their lives. Local zoning and building regulations determine the structures people live in; local police and fire departments protect public safety; local schools, road departments, nursing agencies, libraries, and a host of other divisions provide services. For these reasons, local governments employ more workers than the federal and state governments *combined*. This is the labor-intensive part of the system of IGR, or the place where "street-level" bureaucrats work.[15]

State and local governments have become increasingly dependent on federal aid, as Table 5.1 shows. Correspondingly, local governments have become more financially dependent on state government. (Chapter 21 traces these trends in more detail.) Cuts in the 1982 budget proposed by President Reagan and accepted by Congress could work to reverse these trends, but it is too early to tell.

Even cities such as oil-rich Tulsa, Oklahoma, which has built a 75-foot statue called the Golden Driller, a symbol of its commitment to business and independence, receive large amounts of federal aid. A recent study found that 27 percent of the budgets of Tulsa's departments providing protection of property, health, transportation, and general administration was funded by Washington.[16] Even though Mayor James M. Inhofe stated in 1979 that the city could get along without federal grants, the study indicates that this bastion of free enterprise is deeply dependent on federal aid.

In 1959 Congress created a permanent Advisory Commission on Intergovernmental Relations, which optimists regarded as a move to find solutions to the problems of administrative federalism. With the normal reluctance of Congress to create permanent commissions, a bipartisan advisory body of this nature is something of a rarity. Moreover, the initiative came not from the executive branch but from Congress itself. Although the commission does not "occupy a position of high significance or access to the President," nevertheless almost from the beginning it has had an "extremely productive Staff," and its influence on the national and state scene has grown.[17]

Support for the creation of the ACIR came largely from a small group of congressmen headed by Representative L. H. Fountain (D) of North Carolina, who at the time was chairman of the Subcommittee on Intergovernmental Relations of the House Committee on Government Operations. Able assistance came from organizations representing state and local governing officials: the Council of State Governments, the National League of Cities (formerly known as the American Municipal Association), the National Association of Counties, and the United States Conference of Mayors.

TABLE 5.1   Federal Grants-in-Aid in Relation to State-Local Receipts from Own Sources, Total Federal Outlays, and Gross National Products (1955–1981 est.)

	FEDERAL GRANTS-IN-AID				
	In billions of current dollars		**As a percentage of**		
Fiscal year	**Amount**	**Percent increase**	**State-local receipts from own sources**	**Total federal outlays**	**Gross national product**
1955	$3.2	4.9%	11.8%	4.7%	0.8%
1956	3.7	15.6	12.3	5.3	0.9
1957	4.0	8.1	12.1	5.3	0.9
1958	4.9	22.5	14.0	6.0	1.1
1959	6.5	32.7	17.2	7.0	1.4
1960	7.0	7.7	16.8	7.6	1.4
1961	7.1	1.4	15.8	7.3	1.4
1962	7.9	11.3	16.2	7.4	1.4
1963	8.6	8.9	16.5	7.8	1.5
1964	10.1	17.4	17.9	8.6	1.6
1965	10.9	7.9	17.7	9.2	1.7
1966	13.0	19.3	19.3	9.6	1.8
1967	15.2	16.9	20.6	9.6	2.0
1968	18.6	22.4	22.4	10.4	2.2
1969	20.3	9.1	21.6	11.0	2.2
1970	24.0	18.2	22.9	12.2	2.5
1971	28.1	17.1	24.1	13.3	2.8
1972	34.4	22.4	26.1	14.8	3.1
1973	41.8	21.5	28.5	16.9	3.4
1974	43.4	3.8	27.3	16.1	3.2
1975	49.8	14.7	29.1	15.3	3.4
1976	59.1	18.7	31.1	16.1	3.6
1977	68.4	15.7	31.0	17.0	3.7
1978	77.9	13.9	31.7	17.3	3.8
1979	82.9	6.4	30.9	16.8	3.6
1980 (est)	89.8	8.3	30.5	15.8	3.5
1981 (est)	91.1	1.4	28.3	14.9	3.2

SOURCE: ACIR staff computations based on U.S. Office of Management and Budget, *Budget of the United States Government,* annual, Washington: U.S. Government Printing Office. *Fiscal Year 1981 Budget Revisions,* Washington: U.S. Government Printing Office and unpublished data. Bureau of Economic Analysis, *The National Income and Product Accounts of the United States, 1929–74,* Washington: U.S. Department of Commerce Survey of Current Business, Washington, D.C. U.S. Department of Commerce, various issues, and ACIR staff estimates.

The ACIR is a 26-member body consisting of 9 officials from the federal government, 14 from state and local governments, and 3 representing the public. Six of the 9 federal officials are members of Congress: 3 senators and 3 congressmen are appointed by the vice-president and the speaker of the House, respectively. The other members are appointed by the president, but he does not have any broad discretion in the choice of the 3 officials from the executive branch and the 3 members from the public. He also appoints the commission's chairman and its vice-chairman.

The ACIR (1) is committed firmly and uniformly to increasing the effectiveness of the federal system and (2) recognizes that most problems are not susceptible to analysis and solution by a single level of government but require instead the joint and cooperative action of governments at two or more levels, a kind of "cooperative federalism." The commission (3) rejects "grand alternatives," such as complete centralization or complete decentralization and (4) tries to make its recommendations as practical as possible in order to win acceptance and to increase the chances of making some significant impact. It (5) favors decentralized decision making, spread as widely as possible at the lower levels, and hence strongly objects to the splintering effects of vertical functional autocracies, composed of functional specialists at two or more governmental levels. The commission (6) would abolish many single-purpose special districts and authorities, which splinter the work of government and weaken the autonomy that once characterized the decentralized system of American state and local governmental responsibility. It (7) believes it is the duty of the national government to foster the viability of state and local units and to broaden the range of their discretion, and finally it (8) believes the federal government should develop an administrative system allocating to state and local units the greatest possible discretion consistent with national needs.

The commission has adopted what might be called a progressive or positive approach, whereas at the same time its outlook and temper are middle-of-the-road. Moreover, it takes a sympathetic attitude toward positive government; hence states' righters, whose primary disposition is to oppose federal action of all kinds, are not happy with it. At the same time, the ACIR would make it possible for state and local governments to act more effectively and responsibly in meeting the modern challenges to public administration. One by-product of the ACIR has been the establishment of 18 state ACIRs.

In the 1970s, the ACIR published a large number of first-rate research reports on the functioning of the federal system.[18] But its efforts to improve administrative federalism met with frustration, as we note later in this chapter.

GRANTS-IN-AID

In a unitary system, such as those of France and Britain, the national government rather than local bodies directly provides many services for its citizens. For example, the British police are national government employees.

As described in detail in Chapter 21, the federal government has financial resources superior to state and local governments. It can more easily raise and spend money than can subnational government. Since 1932 it has increasingly provided funds to assist state and local governments. These funds, called grants-in-aid, are an alternative to direct national assumption of subnational governmental functions. They have evolved into a huge and complex system, some highlights of which we discuss in this section.

The precursor of modern grants was the 1862 Morrill Act, under which proceeds from the sale of federal land went to support state colleges. In return, the states had to provide military instruction. By 1980 the number of grants had increased to more than 450, worth more than $80 billion, or almost 16 percent of the total federal budget. This sum constituted 20 percent of the federal budget for domestic expenditures and more than 23 percent of the total budgets of subnational governments. Grants-in-aid, then, are fundamental to the functioning of the federal system.

In January 1982, Ronald Reagan presented a "new federalism initiative" in his State of the Union message. He proposed that the federal government take over the full cost of the Medicaid program—medical aid for the indigent—by 1984; in turn, the states would assume full responsibility for the food stamp and welfare programs, plus over 40 education, transportation, community development and social service programs. The proposition included the establishment of a trust fund by the federal government to equalize gains and losses among the states and to help the states pay for programs they wished to continue during the transitional period. The trust fund, which would be a temporary fund, would get its moneys from excise taxes on tobacco and alcohol, plus federal levies on telephones, gas, and windfall oil profits. At the end of four years, the federal government would reduce the gasoline tax and end the liquor, tobacco, and phone taxes, which the states would be free to reinstitute in addition to whatever excise taxes they might already have. Debate raged over the proposal, whose passage would mean both a shift in federal programs and revenues to the states.

Types of Grants

There are three principal types of federal grants: categorical grants, block grants, and general revenue sharing. There are also state grants.

Categorical Grants. The most numerous and complex type of federal grant is a categorical grant. In 1980 categorical grants accounted for 78 percent of the total federal grant money. The ACIR identified four varieties of categoricals.

One is the *formula* grant, where funds are given to recipients according to criteria listed in statutes and regulations. For example, numerous Office of Education formula grants are allotted on the basis of the number of school-age children in a school district. Others, designed to help the poor, allocate funds on the basis of the number of families below the poverty level. This means that if Highhog Heights has few children per family and all families are affluent, it will not receive nearly so much per capita from a formula grant designed for low-income families as will Ragsville, a low-income area.

A second kind, *project* grants, works quite differently. Applicants submit specific requests, which may or may not be funded by the granting agency. Both Mudville and Solar City may apply for demonstration solar heating projects, for example, but there is no guarantee either will receive them.

A third variety, *formula-project* grants, combines features of both previous types.

Open-end reimbursement grants, a fourth kind, are commitments by the federal government to pay a specific proportion of state and local program costs.

Formula grants and project grants make up the vast majority of categoricals. In 1975, 296 of 442 categoricals were project grants, and 106 were formula grants. (There were 36 project-formula grants and 4 open-end reimbursement grants.) But whereas project grants outnumbered formula grants almost three to one, formula-grant funds totaled twice as much as project-grant funds. Most categorical money, then, is distributed by formula. Note that project grants maximize the discretion of the granting agency. If a granting agency does not like a proposal regardless of merit, it may be able to refuse the application. But if a person applies in correct form for a formula grant, he or she will automatically receive it. This is why Congress allots more money by formula, because formulas remove discretion from administrators and make Congress itself the key decision maker.

Block Grants. The chief characteristic of block grants is that they allow more discretion to the grantee than do categoricals. Within a single-policy area, the grantee has more latitude than under a categorical. The first block grant was the Partner for Health Act, passed in 1967. Since then, block grants in law enforcement (1968), job training (1973), community development and housing (CDBG) (1974), and social services (1974) have been enacted. The last two were created by terminating scores of categorical grants and assigning those grant funds to the block grants. In CDBG, for example, funds previously earmarked specifically for urban renewal can now be spent for a variety of community development projects.

Block grants and funds are assigned on a formula basis, and localities submit applications for these grants. In 1980, block grants came to around 12 percent of total federal grant funds.

General Revenue Sharing. The fewest strings of any type of grant are attached to general revenue sharing (GRS), enacted in 1972. If the residents of Dry Gulch, for example, want to spend their revenue-sharing allotments on gold-plated bird-baths or elephant racetracks, they may. Funds are allotted on the basis of a complex formula, with one third of the total going to state governments and two thirds to general-purpose local governments. Revenue-sharing funds are allotted automatically; applications do not have to be filed. Indeed, when the program was first enacted, congressional district offices were flooded with calls from local officials asking why they had received checks from the United States Treasury. One town, Lazy Lakes, Florida, had to work hard to return its $1,198 grant in 1976, stating that it did not need the money.[19] In 1980, revenue sharing equalled 7.5 percent of all federal grants. In that year, Congress renewed GRS for three years but eliminated the one-third state share for the first two years. For reasons explained later, GRS had lost much of its popularity in Congress.

State Grants. In addition to federal grants are state grants to localities, which totaled $52 billion in 1975. They are disbursed in a manner different from most federal grants. More than 97 percent of these grants are similar to federal block grants. For example, educational grants to school systems have relatively few restrictions.[20]

Administration of Grants

By providing for billions in grants-in-aid, the federal government has recognized the needs of subnational government. Unfortunately, the modes and mechanisms governing grants amount at present to an administrative nightmare. The current system works against coordination and program effectiveness and will be increasingly costly if major changes are not made soon.

Although one is told not to look a gift horse in the mouth, it does not make sense to apply this warning to grants-in-aid. The purpose of such grants is to forge a partnership among the different levels of government in the country. To accomplish such teamwork, the partners must respect one another and must be able to work closely together. Imagine a baseball team in which three of the nine players own the gloves, three the bats, and three the shoes. If they refuse to share what they own—and share in a timely and effective manner—the team would be gravely handicapped. Suppose that the players who own the bats let the other players use them only after the game is over. Unfortunately, analogous practices can be found in American IGR.

Grantees lodge various complaints against the system. One common objection is that reporting requirements are too detailed, diverse, and burdensome.[21] For example, one of the authors of this book once secured a small grant to pay student interns. After his college grants office and business office filled out the lengthy and almost bizarre report required by the granting agency, he was informed that the college had spent more in fulfilling the reporting requirement than it had received in grant aid.

Another frequent frustration is delay in processing grant applications. Many granting agencies do not or cannot make a decision expeditiously. One study found that it is not uncommon for the agency to delay a decision for six months to a year. "Several local officials expressed the view that they would rather be promptly turned down than have to spend months in futilely pursuing project applications."[22]

Another complaint is that there is no timely information about what grants are available and how to apply for them. For example, a year after Medicaid was enacted, states were still waiting for information to guide them in preparing grant applications. As a result, they could not make any specific plans in this crucial area of public health.[23]

Delay in the reimbursement of costs is a fourth problem. For example, construction of the University of Kentucky Medical Center was completed before the university received any of the federal grant funds that were to defray part of construction expenses.[24]

Another burden is borne by those grantees receiving funds from more than one federal agency, a common occurrence in a large city or a state. They may be asked to use a different method of record keeping or accounting for each grant and then be subject to several time-consuming audits by each grantor agency.

Inflexible regulations are a sixth obstacle. Delaware asked for $6 million to rebuild a bridge but was told that applications for less than $10 million could not be considered.[25] Congress later changed the law so Delaware could apply, but only after pressure from the state's Congressional delegation was applied.

Various attempts to combat these problems have been made since 1960. They include the Intergovernmental Cooperation Act of 1968, designed to provide information about grants to the states; various attempts to decentralize, standardize, and simplify administrative procedures; an Interagency Audit Standards Work Group; Federal Regional Councils (FRCs) and grant clearinghouses designed to increase coordination among agencies; and a host of other efforts. A definitive study, however, concludes that not much has changed as a result of these measures.[26] Critics say the process still works as Figure 5.2 diagrams it. In the words of Robert Greenblatt, a New York state official:

The Regional Clearinghouse [is] an attempt to better coordinate the use of federal money, so that you don't

Figure 5.2 Stages of the Approval Process for a Grant-in-Aid Project

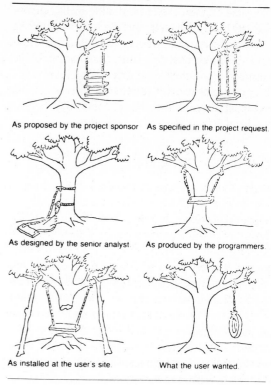

As proposed by the project sponsor   As specified in the project request.

As designed by the senior analyst.   As produced by the programmers.

As installed at the user's site.   What the user wanted.

SOURCE: Adapted from *Front Lines,* a publication of the U.S. Agency for International Development.

have two groups applying to build two sewers on parallel streets in the same town or so that the federal government itself doesn't decide to expand an airport right across a new highway that the state is building. Believe me, it doesn't always work because people still go ahead and do what they please.[27]

During the Carter administration, the entire issue seemed to take a back seat. President Reagan set up study groups and promised to reform the situation, but by fall 1981 it was too early to judge what effect his efforts would have. Before grant administration can be greatly improved, however, the design of the grant system will have to change. And this change will not be easy, as the following section indicates.

GUILDS AND CONGRESSMEN

The present grant system is demonstrably unpopular with elected state and local officials. The U.S. Conference of Mayors, the National Governors' Conference, the National Association of Counties, and other state and local groups have issued statement after statement denouncing the present system. As Box 5.1 indicates, the frustration level is high indeed.

Reasons for the System

Why, then, does this system persist? The answer is support from Congress and associations of specialist officials. Although congressmen work closely with and for officials from their states and districts, their interests do not coincide in grant policy. A congressman likes to be able to announce that a certain program in his district has received a $3-million water system grant. By implication, it is the congressman who obtained it for the town, although his office may have had little or nothing to do with the grant. But woe unto the federal granting agency if it, not the congressman, makes this announcement. For the same reason, congressmen favor categorical grants allocated from Washington. The more centralized the grant-making process, the more influence congressmen will have over grants and the more dependent local officials will have to be on their congressman to receive grants. If grant authority were turned over completely to federal regional or district offices, congressmen would no longer be such central figures in the grant process. Mayors and governors would enjoy easier access to the granting source, and the congressmen would be cut out of the action. It is for this reason that Congress has long resisted both further grant decentralization and the consolidation of more categoricals into block grants. A congressman on one congressional subcommittee may be able to design and control a particular categorical. If that categorical was removed and consolidated with others into a block grant, several congressmen would lose control of their pet projects.

The other groups supporting categoricals are the associations of specialist officials. Many of these groups control an individual's entry into a profession. These groups, examples of which include the National Education Association (NEA), the American Association of State Highway Officials (AASHO), and the American Vocational Association (AVA), cut across levels of government. A number of directors of the U.S. Bureau of Roads were former state highway directors. Many staffers at the U.S. Office of Education are or have been members of the NEA in state and local educational agencies. These groups, which the author Harold Seidman calls guilds because of their control over jobs in their areas, are truly intergovernmental. These specialists are interested in control over their own policy areas and view as a threat any attempts by governors, mayors, and state and local legislatures to assert more control or to coordinate their program areas with others.

For this reason, the guilds join many congressmen in resisting grant consolidation or decentralization. In 1976, for example, groups such as the Child Welfare League of America and the American School Food Service Association opposed grant consolidation in welfare and education.[28]

The Single-State-Agency Requirement

One product of the congressional-guild alliance has been the single-state-agency requirement (SSA). When Congress stepped up aid to subnational governments in the early part of the 20th century, it found that state governments were often a poorly organized hodgepodge of agencies. Congress therefore insisted that many of these grants be administered by one designated agency—the "single state agency." What once made good administrative sense, however, now works to frustrate chief executives striving for better coordination. On many occasions, the reaction of federal agencies to reorganization of state agencies designed to promote better coordination has been a threat to withhold grant funds until the formerly designated SSA is restored.

Box 5.1

THE MAYOR STRIKES BACK

In 1974, Mayor Ernest Angelo, Jr., of Midland, Texas, applied for a grant from the U.S. Department of Housing and Urban Development (HUD). The application process lasted almost a year, and consumed an enormous amount of time. Later, when the mayor received a request from the Dallas regional office of HUD for a reserved parking space at Midland's municipal airport, he replied as follows:

1. You must obtain from the U.S. Government Printing Office, or the National Archives, or the Library of Congress, or someplace, a supply of application form COM-1975. You must submit three executed and fourteen conformed copies of this application . . .

2. With the application submit the make and model of the proposed vehicle together with certified assurances that everyone connected with the manufacturer, servicing, and operation of same (was) paid according to a wage scale that complies with the requirements of the Davis-Bacon Act.

3. Submit a genealogical table for everyone who will operate said vehicle so that we can ascertain that there will be a precisely exact equal percentage of whites, blacks, and other minorities, as well as women and the elderly.

4. Submit certified assurances that this plan has been discussed at length with the EEOC and submit that commission's certification that requirement 3 above has been fully complied with.

5. Submit certified assurances that all operators of said vehicle and any filling station personnel that service same will be equipped with steel-toed boots, safety goggles, and crash helmets and that the vehicle will be equipped with at least safety belts and an air bag to show compliance with the Occupational Safety and Health Act.

6. Submit an Environmental Impact Statement . . . The statement should show the number of times the vehicle will be operated, times of day, the name of the operator of the vehicle, the number of other vehicles that might be coming into or leaving the parking lot at the same time, as well as the number and type of aircraft that might be landing or taking off at the airport at the same time and an exact conclusion as to the effect this will have on the atmosphere in West Texas.

7. In order to obtain approval of a negative Environmental Impact Statement, you will not be able to:

   (a) operate the car on gasoline produced from domestic oil because that would require that someone discover it, process it, and deliver it, and it is possible that some private person, firm, or corporation might realize a profit as a result of such activities . . .

   (b) operate the car from energy produced by coal because this might require digging a hole in the ground . . .

8. Submit a certificate from the Attorney General of the United States that all of the certifiers of the above assurances are duly and legally authorized by Congress to make such certificates . . . and that the United States of America is a duly organized and legally existing independent nation with the full right, power, and authority to operate automobiles in the first place.

   Upon receipt of the foregoing, rest assured that the application will be promptly referred to someone for approval. We cannot state at this time who that someone will be because whatever department he or she is in will be undergoing . . . reorganization . . .

This issue came to a head in the late 1970s, when Florida carried out a comprehensive reorganization of human services agencies. The Department of Health, Education, and Welfare then withheld vocational rehabilitation grant funds from Florida, stating that the reorganization meant that vocational rehabilitation functions were no longer under the control of a single agency; that rather, different bureaus in the Florida department were carrying out different activities relating to vocational rehabilitation. The Tampa *Tribune* stated in an editorial: "We think [Governor] Graham argues correctly that delivery of services to 1.5 million Floridians should not be altered to accommodate the Federal notion of how vocational rehabilitation should be administered to 49,000 persons." Even Robert Humphreys, administrator of the federal Commission of Rehabilitation Services, which administers the law, noted that "the system which works the best to serve disabled people probably should be allowed."[29] (Humphreys noted he had to enforce the law as written by Congress.)

Florida took the case to the United States Supreme Court and lost. In 1979, rather than go back to the old organizational structure to keep its grant money, the state moved to set up a nonprofit organization to administer the vocational rehabilitation program. (This option was allowed by a 1978 federal law.) In expressing frustration with this and other aspects of the categorical system discussed earlier, the National Governors' Conference stated in 1979 that Congress should change the system to "shift power not so much from the federal government to states, counties, and cities, but from the unelected bureaucracy to elected officials at all levels."[30]

Conflict over Categoricals

This, then, is the nature of the conflict over categoricals: guilds and Congress versus *elected* state and local officials. The state and local officials feel that Congress has created an insulated system impervious to the control of local elected officials. Bureaucrats at all three levels carry out programs regardless of the desires of subnational elected officials. This fact explains a paradox, which stupefies those who look at IGR as a question of *the* federal government, *the* state level, and *the* local level. The conflict between elected officials and bureaucrats at any one level may exceed conflict among levels. Certainly it is difficult otherwise to explain a phenomenon noted by V. O. Key, Jr., in 1937. Key related how members of the AASHO came to Washington to insist that federal controls over state highways be tightened. Were they asking to be controlled by another level of government? No, they were asking that their own standards become the legally governing ones. In the words of an ACIR survey, "Many administrators may agree to national performance standards because they view them as a means of exerting leverage on local government units, clientele groups, and/or other state officials. Strict standards may be perceived positively from a programmatic or professional standpoint rather than as a constraint upon their own performance."[31]

This is *not* to say that local administrators relish *all* federal controls. In policy areas without a strong guild structure, such as law enforcement, officials may resent all controls. And in no area will an administrator agree with all standards. But the point is that the federal system in its functioning is far more complex than the layer cake analogy implies.

Congressmen and guilds argue that categorical controls are needed. Representative John Brademas of Indiana, a staunch supporter of the SSA requirement, typifies the congressional stance. He argues that Congress puts up the money and therefore has the responsibility to make sure it is spent effectively by attaching needed conditions. One congressional opponent of block grants was the late Senator Philip A. Hart, of Michigan, who argued that the consolidation of categoricals into the Partnership for Health Act caused a measles epidemic in several states. Governors gave low priority to measles inoculation, and so the disease spread. State and local officials who want money should be willing to accept these conditions, according to these congressmen. Should we forget about requiring the state of Mississippi not to discriminate against minorities, they ask?

The need is to balance local flexibility with national purpose. It is not a question of ending measles inoculation or of protecting minority rights; it is one of increasing efficiency in the system. The SSA secures an outmoded requirement, for example, and many of the delays and much of the red tape are far from inevitable. But so long as the congressional-guild alliance remains in force, citizens cannot expect fundamental change in the system. The alliance demonstrated its power in the summer of 1981, when some of President Reagan's proposals to convert categorical grants into block grants were defeated in Congress at the same time that the president was winning a stunning victory in cutting spending and taxes.

OBTAINING GRANTS

Since grants have become so important to state and local government (and to nonprofit corporations such as hospitals, arts centers, private schools, and so forth), the seeking of grants has become a good-sized business. Consultants who train grant applicants are found all over the country.[32] Not all of them offer the same advice; some common suggestions on grantsmanship are presented here.

First, the grant seeker should pursue a marketing instead of a selling strategy when approaching the grant giver. The marketing approach means that the seeker finds out what objective the giver wishes to achieve. This differs from the selling approach of telling the grant giver what assistance the seeker can provide, regardless of the giver's purpose.[33]

To pursue a marketing approach, the applicant needs to find out all he can about the granting agency. Key written sources include the mammoth *Catalog of Federal Domestic Assistance,* published by the U.S. Government Printing Office, as well as newsletters and other publications of groups such as the International City Manage-

ment Association, the National League of Cities, and the Municipal Finance Officers Association.[34]

When a relevant grant is located, the seeker should read the state or federal legislation that set it up. Then he should write or call the office that administers the grant. Most state and federal officials are happy to talk with potential applicants and to provide guidance. Some even require a preapplication form and strongly encourage such talks. As a recent brochure from the National Endowment for the Humanities Education Division states, "Those applicants who send in their applications close to the deadline date, without first having consulted the staff, are often at a competitive disadvantage...."[35]

One writer recommends that the applicant do so much homework that he "know[s] more about the program than the agencies that fund them. Then [he] can show them what pigeonhole [he] belong[s] in." This grantsman, David Ornstein, obtained $30,000 for the city of Peekskill, New York, to study how to dispose of hot water used to cool a nuclear power plant. Ornstein's coup was in getting this money *not* from the Environmental Protection Agency or the Nuclear Regulatory Agency, but from the National Endowment for the Arts. Ornstein found a grant program designed "to improve the looks and livability of our communities," researched it thoroughly, and received the grant.[36]

When it is time to prepare and submit the grant application, the seeker should *follow instructions carefully*. If the grantor wants a detailed inventory of the seeker's beer can collection, the seeker should provide it. The seeker should be sure to make deadlines. These may seem obvious, but many applications do not contain everything the granting agency requests. A study revealed that several hundred grant applications were rejected because they were carelessly prepared.[37] One program director mentioned that some applicants used out-of-date instructions and forms and submitted proposals just under the deadline. When he advised them to wait and resubmit before the next deadline, the applicants became angry. "What can you do? It's like watching a sinking ship—all you can do is stand there and salute.''[38] In short, when preparing the application, the seeker should *give the granting agency what it requires.*

Grant applicants should be ready to respond if their applications are rejected. Instead of giving up, they should call or write the agency to learn *why* an application was rejected and what could be done to get a grant in the next competition. Initial failure does not mean that eventual success is impossible. Grantor agency officials are usually just as happy to give advice in such instances as they were when the applications were first submitted.

Moreover, applicants should be prepared to accept changes in grant regulations and shifts in program priorities. In such instances the grant may have to be quickly rewritten, or it may be more leisurely rewritten and submitted at a later date. The point is that if the grant is not rewritten, the application is seriously handicapped.[39]

One warning: The applicant should *never* publicly denounce the grantor for refusing a request. After all, the applicant may wish to go back later and try again. And there is not much point in trying to appeal a rejection unless the applicant is sure that a factual or procedural error has been made by the agency. Grantor-grantee relations, like relations among neighbors, should not be permanently shattered because of one disagreement.[40]

Some grantors recommend using political allies, such as legislators or party leaders, to help in obtaining grants. This move is said to be particularly useful after a grant has been turned down. It may work in some instances, but it is a two-edged sword. As our discussion of the guilds indicates, money-granting agencies have substantial autonomy and power and may be able to resist legislative pressure. Or if they give in one time, it may cost the applying agency dearly in the future. One successful city manager's rule is to use "political" help only if he is sure an error has been made and to disassociate himself from the politicians working on his behalf. In this way, he hopes to maintain good working relations with the grantor agency in the future.[41] Note that this approach is used only in rare instances. Many federal agencies

have a kind of gentlemen's agreement with . . . congressmen. If they are asked by a constituent to intercede on behalf of a proposal, they write [the agency]. . . . We reply, saying . . . that the subject proposal will receive our most careful attention. The congressman sends a copy of our letter to the constituent, and he is off the hook. We place the proposal in the same pile as all the others and that is the end of it.[42]

In most situations, political pull will not substitute for the steps outlined above.

IGR TRENDS AND FORECASTS

Several commentators have pointed to trends in IGR about which they are concerned. One trend is *the growing federal role.* We have noted that federal financing has increased relative to subnational governments. (The same trends characterize state-local relations, as Chapter 21 on public finance explains in more detail.) But we have also noted that the existence of powerful guilds makes it more difficult to argue that federal dollars automatically equal more federal control.

David B. Walker, assistant director of the ACIR, goes beyond the financial facts to argue that IGR in the United States has recently become dominated by the federal government. Ironically, in Walker's view, Jimmy Carter's presidency was characterized by steps that omitted subnational government from IGR policymaking. Where the administrations of Richard M. Nixon and Gerald Ford stressed decentralization in IGR, the trend in the Carter administration went in the opposite direction.[43] President Reagan's administration represents a return to decentralization. The centralization-decentralization pendulum is likely to swing back and forth in the future from one president's administration to another.

Another trend of IGR is *the failure, to date, of efforts to improve coordination.* The disjointed, out-of-sync functioning of the system is going to be an expensive luxury indeed as the country moves into a period of slowed economic growth. Innovative solutions attempted during the Nixon and Ford administrations were not emphasized during the Carter administration. Much more needs to be done to end chaos in IGR.

A final and fundamental concern is *equity in IGR.* Formulas for aid established in the earlier part of the 20th century favored the West, then a developing area, and the South, then an economic backwater. Times have changed. Today it is the old industrial Middle West and Northeast that are hurting economically, while the Sunbelt is booming. The "snowbelt" states have organized into a coalition to reshape these formulas in Congress; however, the Sunbelt states understandably resist such a move.[44] The resolution of this problem, as well as the other two problems discussed in this section, will determine the shape of IGR in the rest of this century and the first part of the following century.

SUMMARY

In dealing with intergovernmental administration historically and analytically, we have noted a number of remedies, such as metro government and block grants, that are being tried. We have also suggested some of the more sweeping, long-range remedies, such as amending the Constitution to make state and local government the banker instead of Uncle Sam and possibly relying upon regional government more than is done now. Short of a truly revolutionary change that cannot presently be envisaged, it seems likely that people's strong attachment to states and localities (including counties), will continue to preserve the main outlines of a six-tier system (federal, regional, state, county, local, and special districts for limited purposes). But there is no question that restructuring of governmental hierarchies could provide substantial dollar savings. Short of structural change, the only alternative is closer cooperation by program managers and citizens.

NOTES

1. Bryna Brennan, "Russians Win Praise for Town's Bridge," *Danbury* (Conn.) *News-Times,* 1 July 1980, p. 14.

2. Parris Glendening and Mavis Mann Reeves, *Pragmatic Federalism* (Pacific Palisades, Calif.: Palisades Publishing, 1978), p. 9.

3. Emmette Redford, *Centralized and Decentralized Political Impacts on a Developing Economy: Interpretations of American Experience* (Bloomington: Indiana University, Comparative Administration Group, 1967).

4. Mortin Grodzins, "The Federal System," ch. 12, in President's Commission on National Goals, *Goals for Americans* (Englewood Cliffs, N.J.: Prentice-Hall, 1965), p. 265.

5. David B. Walker, "Federal Aid Administrators and the Federal System," *Intergovernmental Perspective,* Fall 1977, p. 17.

6. Henry S. Reuss, *Revenue-Sharing* (New York: Praeger, 1970), p. 41.

7. Advisory Commission on Intergovernmental Relations (ACIR), *Regional Decision-Making: New Strategies for Substate Districts,* A-43 (Washington: U.S. Government Printing Office, October 1973), pp. 3–4.

8. ACIR, *Regional Decision-Making,* pp. 19–47.

9. Reuss, *Revenue-Sharing,* p. 77.

10. G. Ross Stephens and Gerald W. Olson, *Pass-Through Federal Aid,* Report to the National Science Foundation, 1979, p. 80.

11. Susan Walker Torrence, *Grass Roots Government: The County in American Politics* (Washington: Robert B. Luce, 1974), pp. 21–44.

12. Stephens and Olson, *Pass-Through Federal Aid,* pp. 78–80.

13. Roscoe C. Martin, *Metropolis in Transition* (Washington: Housing and Home Finance Agency, 1963).

14. Advisory Commission on Intergovernmental Relations, *Regional Decision-Making,* ch. 3.

15. Michael Lipsky, "Street-Level Bureaucracy and the Analysis of Urban Reform," in *Blacks and Bureaucracy,* eds. Virginia B. Ermer and John H. Strange (New York: Crowell, 1972), pp. 171–184.

16. John Herbers, "U.S. Aid Contradicts Tulsa's Image of Independence," *New York Times,* 2 February 1979, p. 19.

17. Deil S. Wright, "The Advisory Commission on Intergovernmental Relations: Unique Features and Policy Orienta-

tion," *Public Administration Review* 25 (September 1965): 193–202.

18. For an analysis of these studies, see Douglas M. Fox, "Analyzing the Intergovernmental Grants-in-Aid System," *Center for Study of Federalism Notebook,* Summer 1979, pp. 3–10.

19. "Town Can't Show Federal Money," *Danbury* (Conn.) *News-Times,* 25 July 1976, p. 7.

20. ACIR, *The States and Intergovernmental Aids,* A-59 (Washington: U.S. Government Printing Office, February 1977).

21. ACIR, *Improving Federal Grants Management,* A-53 (Washington: U.S. Government Printing Office, February 1977), p. 95.

22. ACIR, *Improving Federal Grants,* p. 96.

23. ACIR, *Improving Federal Grants,* p. 96.

24. ACIR, *Improving Federal Grants,* p. 97.

25. John Herbers, "Carter to Study Options on Reform of $80 Billion Domestic Aid Plans," *New York Times,* 16 January 1979, p. 1.

26. ACIR, *Improving Federal Grants, passim.*

27. Robert Greenblatt, "A Comment on Federal-State Relations," in James D. Carroll and Richard W. Campbell, eds., *Intergovernmental Administration* (Syracuse, N.Y.: Syracuse University, Maxwell School, 1976), p. 148.

28. Joel Havemann, "State, Local Officials Help Write Consolidation Plans," *National Journal,* 21 February 1976, p. 231.

29. John Herbers, "Governors and Congress Battling over Centralizing Aid Programs," *New York Times,* 5 March 1979, p. 1; and *Intergovernmental Perspective,* Spring 1979, p. 5.

30. Julian M. Carroll, "Balance Budget Through Aid Reform," *National Journal,* 24 February 1979.

31. ACIR, *The Intergovernmental Grant System as Seen by Local, State, and Federal Officials,* A-54 (Washington: U.S. Government Printing Office, March 1977), p. 125.

32. Perhaps the best known such group is the Grantsmanship Center, 1031 S. Grand Ave., Los Angeles, Calif. 90015.

33. Daniel Lynn Conrad, *The Grants Planner* (San Francisco: Institute for Fund Raising), pp. 2–3, 21.

34. Charles A. Morrison, "Identifying Alternative Resources for Local Government," in *Managing Fiscal Stress,* ed. Charles H. Levine (Chatham, N.J.: Chatham Home Publishers, 1980), pp. 235–256.

35. Virginia White, *Grants* (New York: Plenum, 1975), p. 220.

36. Morrison, "Identifying Alternative Resources," pp. 242–243.

37. White, *Grants,* p. 226.

38. White, *Grants,* pp. 227–228.

39. Deil S. Wright, "Intergovernmental Games," *Southern Review of Public Administration,* March 1980, pp. 396–397.

40. David J. Ferguson, Manager, Township of Pequannock, N.J., to intergovernmental relations seminar, William Paterson College, October 4, 1978. Ferguson's main concern was getting grants from or through state government.

41. Ferguson.

42. White, *Grants,* p. 290.

43. David B. Walker, "A New Intergovernmental System in 1977," *Publius,* Winter 1978, pp. 101–116; and "A Tilt Toward Washington," *Intergovernmental Perspective,* Winter 1978, pp. 4–14.

44. A great deal has been written on this subject. Perhaps the best place to start is Joel Havemann et al., "Federal Spending: The Northeast's Loss Is the Sunbelt's Gain," *National Journal,* 26 June 1976, pp. 878–891.

6

Law and the Public Business

Ah, happy world, where all things live, creatures of one great law. . . .

Harriet Prescott Spofford

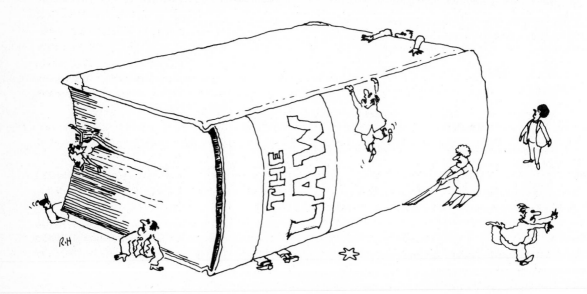

In this chapter we deal with law as the central vehicle of public policy. We are especially concerned with statutory and administrative law, procedure legislation, the legislative veto, judicial review, and administrative due process. The chapter also discusses attempts to protect civil liberties and ensure accountability, attempts that sometimes have the unfortunate side effect of exacerbating some of the weaknesses of bureaucracy. Here pressure-group politics can be seen at work. The lesson is clear: the administrator masters the rudiments of law or becomes its captive.

THE LAW IN ACTION: POLITICAL DYNAMICS

Many of the hardest-fought political battles of the 1980s have arisen within the boundaries of law and administration. In the confrontation between conservatives and liberals, the main issue is the deregulation of the economy by the government through the independent regulatory commissions.[1]

Then there is a major onslaught aimed at limiting the number of bureaucrats and reducing their alleged influence in the government. The usual method recommended is either to abolish their functions or to surround them still further with legal restraints.[2]

A third struggle, which began in earnest shortly after World War II, has been a drive to "judicialize" administration, either by turning over to the courts functions now performed by administrative agencies or by putting judges inside the administrative organization, where they can act independently of the policy officials.[3]

The argument advanced by the conservatives is that free enterprise needs to be made more competitive; 100 years of accumulated regulation interfere with business efficiency and competition. Inflation, it is said, is caused primarily by the increasing cost of government; therefore, if the size of government is reduced and regulation is eliminated or reformed, the country will be able to overcome its inefficiency and compare favorably with the private sector. Before long-range policy can be improved, citizens need to understand why and how the present confluence of concerns came into existence.

PUBLIC ADMINISTRATION AND ADMINISTRATIVE LAW

The first step in the reforms discussed is to realize the close relation among politics, administration, and law. Politics is concerned with setting policies and determining values in the private and the public sectors in an attempt to serve the highest interests of the citizenry. Administration is translating the policies into tangible results. Law is the creation by official means of principles, doctrines, and rules for establishing policies, rights, and duties as guides to human conduct.

In such a three-way relation it is inevitable that conflicts of role and expectation should arise between the administrative and the legal professions. As is the wont of all bureaucratic groups that tend to become doctrinaire and self-centered, lawyers have their view of doctrine and role and administrators have theirs; at some point it would be surprising if the two doctrines and ideas of appropriate method professed by each group did not come into conflict.

Administrative law is concerned with giving concrete effect to the law and policies adopted by the national government and its subdivisions. Both it and public administration are sometimes referred to as the law in action. Administrative law is closely related to constitutional law, which deals with the powers and functioning of the government as a whole and the protection of citizen and private rights under the Constitution.

In two important respects American administrative law differs from administrative law as it has developed under the civil, or Roman, law of Europe. First, in the United States administrative law is not clearly differentiated from constitutional law; nor is it largely administered by a separate court system, as it is in Europe. Second, since the 1930s American administrative law has come to have a much narrower focus than its counterpart in Europe because it now deals almost entirely with the area of government regulation and the protection of individual and business rights. In countries that have civil law the scope of administrative law is virtually the same as that of public administration in the United States.

This narrowing of the focus of American administrative law is explained in part by the fact that government intervention in business and the economy expanded rapidly during the Great Depression of the 1930s and that lawyers, like some businessmen, became concerned with the possibility of socialism and communism. A second fact was that administrative law, as it was first developed by Frank J. Goodnow and other American political scientists between 1880 and 1930, was thought too vast a subject to be taught in a single law school course. Alarmed by the growth of the administrative state, the legal profession turned instinctively to strengthening private rights as the main thrust of administrative law. In so doing the legal profession parted company with the public administration profession, whose concern throughout has been with both governmental powers and the protection of individual rights.[4]

As a result of this shift in emphasis, administrative lawyers have had a limited and often prejudiced view of the nature of public administration. Bernard Schwartz, one of the prolific writers on administrative law, refers throughout his most recent text to the innate colorlessness and political incompetence of public administration as found in Washington and in other national governments.[5] Even Kenneth Davis, whose writings are fair minded and liberal, has sometimes fallen into the error of considering public administration in action as "politically colorless" and having a "chameleonic quality."[6] The underlying assumption is that public administration is dull and nondiscretionary, that it has been reduced to the work of clerks. Many who teach administrative law in the law schools assume that administration is merely a "process" and therefore all that needs to be taught is procedure. In other words, they draw a sharp line between substantive law, which is the concern of others, and procedural law, which they consider all-important. Experienced public administrators, however, have learned that the appropriate procedure arises from substance, such as knowledge of engineering. If substance is not given at least equal attention, public administration's delivery system must perforce break down. The excuse administrative lawyers use for limiting their study to procedure is that, first, procedure is important in ensuring fairness, which everyone will admit, and second, that to go into policy and objectives leads them too far afield. This arbitrary limitation of scope would not per-

haps be socially objectionable, except that on the basis of their limited definition, these people proceed to reduce public administration to overly simplified assumptions which, if accepted, would make dynamic administration virtually impossible. Their simplistic reasoning is that if every step in administration is reduced to uniformity and a rule, the business will run itself automatically. They cannot see that there is a logic in administrative performance, which begins with objectives, moves on to policies, and then deals with organization and leadership. During this progression, strategies are developed relevant to situation, time, place, public opinion, and values. All these steps are necessary before social problems can be solved and the public satisfied.

By oversimplification lawyers distort and mangle. In so doing they create the conditions of an inflexible bureaucracy, which conservatives are the first to criticize. This oversimplification courts national disaster. There *are* imperative objectives of government policy and administration such as security and economic stability; and if the appropriate means are not found to achieve them, the country, whether realizing it or not, is like a machine without controls. In disparaging administrators, narrowly focused administrative lawyers unwittingly weaken the political system and expose it to sluggishness and possible decay.[7]

The practical approach to the resolution of this unfortunate pedagogical conflict is to realize (1) that in dealing with important issues, at least 10 times as many decisions are made by administrative agencies in the course of their work as are made in a year's time by the courts; (2) that a single agency such as the Interstate Commerce Commission (ICC) has as many employees as the whole of the judicial establishment; and (3) that the making of policies (rules) and the formulation of decisions in the course of an agency's work are *integral to* its overall mission and cannot be extracted and turned over to others without producing a condition verging on disaster. A good administrator does away with rules and red tape; lawyers think that proliferating them is their main function.

Then the public must be considered. The average person, says Davis, is much more frequently and intimately affected by public administration than by the judicial process, which theoretically is limited to review and should interfere only when necessary. Most people go through life without experiencing the judicial process, whereas every citizen comes face to face almost daily with the services provided by public servants.[8] There are 16 million of these servants—3 million in the federal government alone (not to mention the military and the postal service). If these servants do not do an effective job, the lawyers and the judiciary can do little to improve national life.

Some of the wiser heads among conservatives have recognized the necessity of supporting efficient administration instead of castigating all bureaucrats as antibusiness. Herbert Brownell, who served as attorney general in the administration of Dwight D. Eisenhower, said in 1955:

Administrative agencies have become an established part of our constitutional governmental authority. . . . They were created as a necessary means for protecting public interests which could not be suitably protected by the courts or other means. . . . Administrative agencies must be enabled and permitted to function efficiently and effectively if the public interest, which is their primary concern, is to be preserved.[9]

His views relative to the effect of the Administrative Procedure Act of 1946, by which administrative procedures, especially in the regulatory commissions, were determined, were prophetic: "These changes would substantially 'judicialize' the administrative structure, with disastrous results to efficiency and effective government." The procedures under this legislation, he suggests, were unsound, unworkable, and too costly, and they should be rejected. Far from achieving economy, efficiency, and improved service in the transaction of public business, they would do exactly the opposite.[10]

Even more insightful are the comments of Federal Judge Charles Wyzanski. The administra-

tor's discretion is an indispensable ingredient of the law. With experience gained by living with a subject, the administrator acquires insight and understanding. He comes to have an appreciation of the history and grammar of his specific subject; he alone understands the probable evolution of the subject; and he alone grasps the values that inhere in the process of growth.[11]

We now need to discuss three offshoots of the judicialization program we have been considering historically and analytically: court review, the role of administrative judges, and the legislative veto.

Judicial Review

The record of the courts in dealing with practical public administration is considerably better than the prejudiced views sometimes found among law school faculty. Of course, there has always been judicial review of administrative action if for no reason other than that the United States is the celebrated home of judicial review. Edouard Lambert, a distinguished law professor at the University of Lyon, called the United States *le gouvernement des juges* ("the government of judges").

Most celebrated of all judicial-governmental relationships, of course, is the power of the highest courts to declare acts of legislatures unconstitutional, a practice that the Supreme Court of the United States enunciated in 1803 in the case of *Marbury* v. *Madison.* This, in a way, was a case in public administration because it concerned the power of a higher official to hand a certificate of appointment to a lower official.

If, unlike courts of other countries, U.S. courts have the power to declare unconstitutional the acts of the people's "courts," the legislature, it stands to reason that executive and administrative acts are fair game. At the very minimum, the courts reserve the right to question the law, that is, its conformity with the law of the Constitution, in all cases, unless, of course, the issue is "political," meaning that it is a privileged matter of another branch of government, such as seating a member of the legislature, and the court thinks it inappropriate to interfere.

Another principle of judicial-governmental relations is that the courts will look into substance as well as procedure. Most of the New Deal cases, which caused such political controversy at the time, were cases of substance. Congress claimed the power to delegate the fixing of prices, for example, regulating the price of petroleum and chickens. Since the New Deal era, however, the rule against delegation has been relaxed. Kenneth Davis states bluntly, for example, "Congress may and does lawfully delegate power to administrative agencies." In 1940, the Supreme Court ruled: "Delegation by Congress has long been recognized as necessary in order that the exercise of legislative power does not become a futility."[12]

The extent to which the Supreme Court has been willing to recognize the expertise of public administrators has varied by periods. It was most restricted during the period of the New Deal, which triggered the Administrative Procedure Act of 1946. Since the end of that period, the Supreme Court has been much more understanding and conciliatory. Most of the gyration of court policy has revolved around the following four central issues.

1. *The fairness doctrine.* Has the administrative decision been objective and impartial? (We shall say something about this later in this chapter under the heading "Administrative Due Process of Law.") The principle is that if administration provides the equivalent of judicial fairness, the courts are less likely to interfere.
2. *Administrative standards.* Is there a norm, a yardstick, which is made manifest in advance and which administration follows without fear or favor? The basic requirement in most recent Supreme Court cases is this: "Congress cannot delegate any part of its legislative power except under the limitation of a prescribed standard."[13] But this command usually means merely "just and reasonable," "public interest," "public convenience and necessity," and the like.
3. *Law and fact.* The principle here is that administration may judge facts because of its expertise,

but the court has a constitutional duty to have the final word on law. But what if the two are so interrelated as to be almost inseparable? In the public utility cases that arose during the New Deal, for example, the question often was "Is a return on the investment of X percent confiscatory or is it reasonable?" The decision often turned on whether the return should be 8 percent, 12 percent, or even higher. Since about 1936, with the decisions in the *B&O* and *St. Joseph Stockyards* cases,[14] the Supreme Court has usually been disposed to recognize the expertise of regulatory tribunals and hence to show moderation with regard to both fact and application of the law.[15]

4. *Substantial evidence.* How much evidence is required to support an administrative decision? The decisions of the higher courts have varied from one class of case to another and from one time to another. The general tendency, however, has been to support the substantial evidence rule and not require as complete proof as it sometimes demanded in ordinary court proceedings. On the whole, therefore, professional public administration has fared better at the hands of the courts than at the hands of the law schools since the subject became so truncated.

Administrative Law Judges

Administrative law judges, who are assigned to hear and decide cases arising in ordinary administration as well as in major regulatory administration, are perhaps the main feature of the Administrative Procedure Act of 1946. They are a breed apart. They come from a central pool, are assigned, and have no direct link with the program they serve; they are not supervised by the action head of the agency in question and hence fracture the unity required by effective administration if it is to be efficient, cogent, and timely. The judges may take as much time as they need. During the course of his service on the Civil Service Reform Panel of the National Academy of Public Administration, one of the present authors heard of a request for 200 more administrative law judges over a two-year period to reduce a backlog of cases, because most judges decided an average of only 20 cases a year. In 1978 the General Accounting Office reported that at the time the request was made 1,000 administrative law judges were working in 28 federal agencies. The budgeted cost to the taxpayer was $3 billion, and the cost to the private sector ranged from $16 billion to $130 billion.[16]

This is a prime illustration of the creeping bureaucracy about which conservatives complain. The administrative law judges used to be called hearing officers, and they heard cases only in those agencies that have a lot of appeals work, such as public utility regulation and social security, for example. Other agencies, such as the Immigration and Naturalization Service, which decides scores of cases a day, were exempt. As so often occurs when red tape makers are on the loose, however, those who administered the act eventually decided that what was good for independent regulatory commissions should be equally beneficial to virtually every agency that makes decisions. It was a boondoggle for the lawyers and a headache for the administrators.

The contention was, to be sure, that the administrative lawyers did not have the final say, that the head of the agency did. If within 30 days the agency did not reverse or change the recommended decision, it would stand. What occurred can be imagined. Most heads found themselves too busy even to read the opinions. Others feared to overturn decisions because of the mystique that surrounds people called judges. Judges are drawn from a civil service roster. Judges may be removed for "good cause" but only by the civil service people, not the operating head of an agency. To make matters worse, judges are tied in with the Administrative Conference of the United States, a government agency created at the same time as the administrative law judge system. It is dominated by legal thinking.

The next step in this creeping paralysis, as might be expected, is a proposal to make the administrative law judges completely independent, just as federal court judges are.[17]

Legislative Veto

One additional topic will round out this phase of the subject. The legislative veto, which is found at the state government level as well as at the federal level, has become a major weight on the administrator's already overloaded back. Like the Administrative Procedure Act and other incursions on executive autonomy, the legislative veto is justified by the legislators as a means of gaining ground lost in recent years by the legislature vis-à-vis the executive branch. Furthermore, it reflects the fact that lawyers and legal thinking dominate legislative assemblies. Many legislators have been prosecutors or district attorneys, and they act as if no one can be trusted. Finally, the same interests that push other forms of control derive satisfaction from slowing down the wheels of administration and causing innumerable delays and stallings.

The legislative veto, which came into prominence during the administration of Lyndon B. Johnson, takes several forms. Under the Administrative Procedure Act two areas are much emphasized: rule making and adjudication.

Rule making has been termed spelling out the law. For example, the legislature specifies that a certain number of people may be hired. The administrative agency issues a policy statement, or rule, to the effect that these people shall receive equal pay for equal work. Or, because the subject is now covered by general legislation, perhaps the agency decides that all employees must live within a certain number of miles from their place of work. Thus rule making is used for many purposes, and much of it has the force of law as if it were part and parcel of the original statute. Rules are sometimes called sublegislation, which usually deals with policy but can also deal with procedure.

There are several forms of the legislative veto. (1) Before issuing its proposed rules, the agency must submit them to the legislature for approval.[18] Under the Administrative Procedure Act, such rules, which are found in many state governments as well as in the federal government, will already have been delayed a long time because extensive hearings are required, often with lawyers taking an active part. (2) The legislature may require that the rules lie before it for a certain number of days (usually 30 to 60); then if there is no adverse action, the rules may go into effect. Otherwise a proposed rule may have to be changed, and the administrator must start all over again. (3) In some cases a member of the legislature or a committee, usually goaded by a pressure group, may prevail on the legislature to interfere with rules already in operation. In other words, if the pressure group loses its battle with the agency, it attacks through the legislature. (4) Still another version of the legislative veto calls for a periodic review. The legislature creates a standing committee on administrative rules, which goes over questions and requires changes in rule making from all agencies. This is by far the most burdensome method of the four. The whole idea seems to be to keep anything from happening in government.

The usual defense of this kind of behavior is that since the legislature makes the law, it wants to be sure that rules having the force of law are consistent with the law. This effort for consistency is sometimes called codirection by Congress and by the administrative agency. As stated earlier, the legislature wants more of a hand in administration because it has lost the face-to-face relation that used to exist between its members and administrators in the executive branch, a situation that is the fault of the legislature itself. Even though it is a natural desire, it is poison to effective administration. This codirection is contrary to the whole history of delegation of power. It is often dominated by pressure-group needling behind the scenes.

Two other kinds of legislative veto have been prominent but need not be of concern here. The first is trying to decide for the president what his choice of options should be under statutory authority, whether to act or not to act, which project to give priority to. President Johnson, the darling of Congress, claimed that its demands were an in-

fringement of the separation of powers. In December 1980, a federal appeals court upheld this argument in a case that may have wide application. As a result of the ruling, President Jimmy Carter issued an executive order instructing federal agencies to ignore all legislative vetoes. But citizens can be sure this is not the last chapter in this story.

THE DEREGULATION ISSUE

The deregulation campaign, which was intense in the early 1980s and reached its climax during the administration of Ronald Reagan, was directed primarily at the independent regulatory commissions dealing with major areas of the economy such as transportation, the stock market, electric power and public utilities, and attempts to control monopoly. When, during the second administration of Richard M. Nixon, the so-called Ash Council wrote the monograph *A New Regulatory Framework*,[19] the conservative president decided that the only matter to be studied was the organization and functioning of eight independent commissions in the areas of the economy mentioned above. At that time, however, leading economists stoutly insisted that the focus should be on abolishing the commissions or limiting their powers because regulation constituted a shield for noncompetitive practices on the part of regulated industries.[20] The advice went unheeded.

Soon thereafter, however, a campaign was started to deregulate not only the areas of the economy controlled by the independent commissions but also others, for example, food and drugs, labor relations, and occupational health and standards. This across-the-board campaign became headed by powerful allies, such as the American Enterprise Institute, chambers of commerce, trade associations, and conservative politicians.[21] Their victory reached its climax with the election of the Reagan administration in 1980. Two main assumptions were stressed: (1) government costs too much and is the cause of inflation and competitive inefficiency and (2) regulation of all kinds, leading to an excess of rules and regulations, causes inefficiency in both industry and government. While removing the protection to airlines, natural gas suppliers, and trucking lines might cause prices to the consumers to rise, it was thought these prices would later come down again because of increased competition and greater autonomy of corporate management.

There was surprisingly little opposition to this campaign, partly because Congress had been deeply concerned for some time with the alleged inefficiencies of some older regulatory agencies, such as the Interstate Commerce Commission. Another reason for so little opposition was that with the rapid growth of mergers, oligopolies, and transnational corporations, the historic backers of the Federal Trade Commission and the Anti-Trust Division of the Department of Justice had become dispirited. Liberals found it questionable politics to seem to oppose the taxpayer revolt against high taxes or to fail to do something constructive against the evil of too much bureaucracy. Besides, at that time they could offer no substitute program that had any chance of success. The media were against the liberals and everyone was clamoring for reform.

Seen in historical perspective, this collapse of liberal opinion and support was truly remarkable. Beginning with the Progressive Party's advocacy of regulation in the 1880-1914 period as a substitute for socialism, and continuing with Woodrow Wilson's advocacy of regulation as a desirable middle ground, conservative presidents such as Herbert Hoover had lavishly praised major regulation by independent commissions as expressing Americans' innate preference for compromise and the middle ground. Hoover believed firmly that so long as regulation was made to work, the American telephone system, for example, would remain under private management despite the fact that practically all other countries, large and small, had opted for government ownership and operation of their national telephone systems.

Regulation was greatly expanded during the period of Franklin Delano Roosevelt. Harry S. Truman, Eisenhower, John Kennedy, Johnson,

Nixon, and Carter were all apparently satisfied that Hoover had made the correct analysis. If extensive deregulation occurs and franchise monopolies mushroom, how will the public react? It is clearly a gamble. Another time something else may be tried.

The main problems of major regulation have been known for years. In all the reorganization studies, starting with the Committee on Administrative Management in 1937, through the Hoover commissions of 1949 and 1955, to the study commissions of the Johnson and Kennedy periods, much the same things were found to be wrong.[22]

1. The many-headed commissions were said to be inefficient.
2. Commissions spent too much time deciding cases instead of planning and making policy.
3. It was hard to sustain a good caliber of personnel.
4. The interests regulated sometimes had too much inside control, and when the regulators left they often joined the industries being regulated.
5. Major public utility cases were in litigation for as long as 10 years. The work was slow and extremely costly. The consumers had to pay the bill. Legislatures did not support the commissions financially as well as they should have. The ICC was blamed for making the railroads bureaucratic and unprogressive. Too many restrictions were placed on truckers and airlines.
6. Rate bases were inflated, and consumers had to foot the bill. Earnings for protected industries were said to be too high. The protection provided for monopoly in public utilities that had exclusive franchises was seen as a temptation to other industries to seek legal protection from competition.

From the standpoint of the effects of regulation by commission on the operation of the government as a whole, the following criticisms emerged:

1. The president or governor had no control over the policies and objectives of the independent commissions.
2. Budget people and personnel agencies did not like the independent regulatory agencies (IRA) being

outside their province. The General Accounting Office also objected to the IRA's independence.

3. Regulation by commission complicated the committee system of Congress and the state legislatures. Legislators complained that their access to the commissions was more difficult than that to the regular departments of government.

4. IRAs had been used for almost 100 years, the first one, the Interstate Commerce Commission, having been established during the Progressive era in 1887. Perhaps it was time for a change.[23]

Of course the battle is not over. It is one thing to advocate change, another to bring it about. Many powerful segments of the legal profession are in favor of the present system in which hearing and deciding powers are combined in the same commission. It would be surprising, therefore, if many real changes in organization will have occurred by the time this book goes to press.

WHAT THE ADMINISTRATOR NEEDS TO KNOW ABOUT LAW

Tied up as they are in rules and regulations, administrators must understand law and lawyers or they have little chance of running their own show. Every large operating program has its own solicitor, or company lawyer. Lawyers can be indispensable in enabling administrators to achieve their goals, or, conversely, they can be martinets. Lawyers by training and inclination are both admirable facilitators and adept at causing a program to slow down or fail. Administrators and lawyers are both politicians in the best sense of the word. Their expertise consists in accomplishing things desired by clients, private or public.[24]

Good administrators constantly fight for enough autonomy to enable their program to be unified and effective. They are like the business entrepreneur in this respect. They prefer principle to rigid rules. When rules are necessary, they want to be able to make them and to reduce their number as teamwork and initiative develop within their organization. In the best example of program success at any level of government, this sense of autonomy will invariably be discovered as the secret of accomplishment. In this effort lawyers become the administrators' indispensable ally.

Discretion is the freedom of executives, public or private, to choose among alternative means of accomplishing objectives. Reduce that discretion and they become merely the clerks some lawyers accuse them of being. Ensure that discretion and if they have the credentials, the executives become powerhouses in serving the public welfare as expressed in legislative intent. When, as Kenneth Davis has admirably pointed out, administrators have sufficient discretion, things begin to move; when the reverse is true, bureaucracy becomes all the stodgy things it is accused of being.[25]

Discretion is not an insulated entity; it is part of a larger strategy or plan. Suppose, for example, an administrator's mandate is to prevent subversion by aliens during wartime. There is a sit-down strike in New York harbor by Chinese crewmen who object to double standards of treatment. The administrator can either crack down on the strikers and throw them in jail, or he can try to find out why they are striking and attempt to bring about equal treatment.[26]

Or suppose a city manager is caught in the middle of a controversy over building an outlying shopping center. He has a choice of favoring the downtown merchants or siding with the would-be developer. If he is a conciliator, he will adduce the facts about long-range municipal growth, adequacy of water, sewers, schools, transportation routes, and the like—all of which are part of the environmental picture—and allow public opinion to form around the two alternatives.

Or suppose a city school superintendent finds that the school population has fallen off because the "baby boom" is over. He may either recommend that some schools be sold and add to the facilities of the remaining ones, or he may fight to maintain the status quo. He is paid to know how to marshal the facts, present the alternatives to the school board and the public, and display a degree of statesmanship.

Decision making and the exercise of discretion are closely related. To the legal mind, decision is a discrete event. In the administrative mind it is vastly more than that. Any decision is an integral part of the complex of factors involved in providing dynamic administration. Decision is a daily, universal need of administration. It occurs at all levels, and all levels are related. These decisions are of varying degrees of importance. Detach them from their context, and the administrator's overall strategy of accomplishment may suffer.[27]

The upshot of this discussion has been well stated by Davis. Discretion, as a tool, is our principal source of creativeness in government and in law. "Rules, alone, untempered by discretion, cannot cope with the complexities of modern government and of modern justice."[28]

ADMINISTRATIVE DUE PROCESS OF LAW

The best way to avoid the debilitating effect of administrative procedure laws and legislative vetoes (and these areas should be radically reformed) is for every would-be administrator to familiarize himself with the area of law called administrative due process. The meaning of the term is derived from several sources, as most law is—the Constitution, statutory law, decided court cases (precedents), and treatises. The main principles underlying administrative due process are these:

1. *Requirement of notice.* The citizen has a right to be notified when his interests are being dealt with by administrative action. This is especially true when proceedings are being brought against him. How much notice is required varies with the subject matter. Sometimes publication in a newspaper with general circulation is sufficient notice.

2. In most kinds of administrative action, but not in all, the citizen has a right to a *hearing.* As with due notice, however, no one rule applies to all kinds of hearings; and differences are permitted according to the subject matter. In some instances, for example, the courts decide that a hearing is not mandatory; in others that an oral hearing is sufficient; and in still others that a writ-

ten record is enough; in some instances both an oral hearing and a written record are required.

3. In some cases, the individual affected has a right to *appear in his own behalf.* This right is called the right of confrontation. Again, the rule does not apply in all classes of administrative action. When it does, allegations can be disputed and any factor that has been overlooked can be brought out by the interested parties.

4. Increasingly, the citizen has the right to be *represented by attorney.*

5. There is a growing requirement that administrative agencies creating sublegislation (through the enunciation of standards) and engaging in administrative adjudication (the settlement of rights among contestants) *state their reasons.* This requirement gives citizens and their attorneys a chance to defend themselves more intelligently and to appeal unfavorable administrative decisions.

6. Administrative officials may be disqualified if they are *prejudiced* in advance, thus supporting the tradition of fairness in the law. Under due process of law, all persons are regarded as having equal rights and privileges, and prejudice precludes the enforcement of fairness.

7. Every citizen or interest affected by an administrative decision in the lower ranks of an agency is generally entitled to an appeal of some kind. The purpose of this procedure is to avoid unfairness and incompetence and, again, to safeguard the symmetry of the law. But this rule also varies. The two kinds of appeal are administrative (that is, appeal to a higher administrative echelon) and judicial; in a growing number of areas the administrative appeal is final. An almost universal rule, moreover, is that administrative appeals must be exhausted before an appeal to a court of law will be entertained. Moreover, the courts deal only with cases and controversies, nothing else, and if there is no case or controversy, the court has no jurisdiction.

8. A court will almost invariably take a case on appeal if the question at issue is whether the deciding administrative level has *jurisdiction.* This rule applies in all judicial business; if jurisdiction is absent, there has been no proper hearing or determination of the case. This rule is to prevent an excessive use of power or a high-handed usurpation of authority.

9. Finally, the courts will not take action where no *remedy* exists under the law. The remedies available are numerous and often complicated, including habeas corpus mandamus, injunctions, quo warranto (less often used today than formerly), trespass, and torts (damages).[29] In a growing number of cases, and usually by express legislative provision, the government and/or the responsible official may be sued, but such cases are by no means universal. Government was originally held to be sovereign and hence immune to suit; but with the growth of democratic assumptions, this immunity has gradually been eroded.[30]

Because a discussion of legal due process is highly technical, the following case is offered to show its application in a concrete situation.

CASE STUDY: THE DEPORTABLE ALIENS

Timothy O'Shaughnessy was a troubled man. He had been a career officer in the Immigration and Naturalization service for 40 years and was now the deputy commissioner, the highest career job. In two hours he had an appointment with Senator James Smith. Smith had introduced a bill providing that all aliens who had been barred from entry into the United States and who had subsequently entered illegally, or who had been found deportable on criminal, subversive, or moral grounds, should either be deported to any country that might accept them (assuming their country of birth would not) or should be held in protective custody until such time as they could be removed from the United States by some other means.

There was a reason for O'Shaughnessy's acute distress. He and the senator had become friends and had met socially; the political officers of the Department of Justice opposed Senator Smith's bill and expected O'Shaughnessy's department to oppose it, too. O'Shaughnessy did not want to offend the senator, nor did he wish to be disloyal to his boss. The appointment proceeded as follows:

SENATOR: Well, Tim, what do you think of my bill?
O'SHAUGHNESSY: As you know, the attorney general is against it on civil rights grounds, and I personally think it ought to have some due process provisions put into it.
SENATOR: I don't see why. The Supreme Court has already upheld secrecy provisions when the alien is, or is thought to be, a subversive.*
O'SHAUGHNESSY: Yes, but this is a liberal regime. Besides, our department is now taking steps to live up to the dicta in the *Morgan* case.†
SENATOR: If I were to agree to put a lot of provisions in my bill about lengthy hearings, appeals, and so on, we'd never get rid of the subversives.
O'SHAUGHNESSY (smiling): I thought you had more confidence in us than that.
SENATOR: Well, maybe with your exemption from the Procedure Act that might not be so bad.
O'SHAUGHNESSY: Our procedure has improved a lot in the past few years, but I don't think it's excessive.
SENATOR: But how about the substantive provision of my bill? You favor getting them out of the country, surely.
O'SHAUGHNESSY (cautiously): Well, since you're adding no new provisions to the grounds for deportation that already exist, I suppose I do agree we ought to deport them if we can.

*The reference here is to the leading case of *O'Shaughnessy* v. *United States ex rel. Mezei,* 345 U.S. 206 (1953), discussed in Davis, *Administrative Law and Government,* p. 170.

†*Morgan* v. *United States,* 298 U.S. 468 (1936), discussed in Davis, p. 217.

SENATOR: But that's just the point. If their home country won't take them, I want them sent somewhere else.

O'SHAUGHNESSY: Our State Department is not too keen about that. No country wants to be regarded as a dumping ground for undesirables.

SENATOR: Are they fighting my bill, too?

O'SHAUGHNESSY: They naturally follow the lead of the president, and he's against it unless you modify it a good deal.

SENATOR: I won't do that.

O'SHAUGHNESSY: You won't even let our departmental committee on new legislation take a crack at it?

SENATOR: No. I know what you'd do to it.

O'SHAUGHNESSY: Then it looks as if the Justice Department and the administration will have to oppose your bill. And that's too bad, both being of the same political party.

SENATOR: I'll talk to the speaker [speaker of the House of Representatives] and see if he can change the president's mind. If he can't, I guess we have a fight on our hands.

O'SHAUGHNESSY: Yes, and one I'll be glad to stay out of.

SOME SUGGESTED AREAS OF CONCENTRATION

If the issues dealt with here are to be agreeably resolved, a number of constructive steps should be taken to strengthen the country's representative government.

It would be an excellent idea, as Kenneth Davis suggests in his introduction to *Administrative Law and Government,* to have the elements of law taught as a liberal arts subject in American universities.[31]

Administrative law, as broadly dealt with in this chapter, should be required of everyone preparing for service in government and public administration. Equally, the law schools should teach courses in administrative law, in which students would learn the rudiments of management and in which substantive and procedural aspects of the subject would be combined. Professors should be required to gain actual administrative experience before teaching the subject.[32]

The issue of government regulation should be dealt with by legislatures, bar associations, and others on a case-by-case basis instead of launching a frontal attack on the whole of regulation, which is now the fashion. Just as there are some essential functions of government, so, equally, there are some areas of government regulation that should be continued and improved in the process.

Administrative procedure acts, which have been imposed on the whole of administration, should be modified to deal with those areas where rule making and decision making are more prominent than they are in others. As the economists suggest, this scrutiny should be undertaken on a segment-of-the-economy basis, permitting a more precise and realistic evaluation of the effects of rules and regulations on business, governmental, and social vitality.[33]

Teams of lawyers and public administrators, drawn from agencies such as the American Bar Association and the National Academy of Public Administration, should combine forces to strengthen the law-making and surveillance functions of Congress and state legislatures. Bill drafting is an area requiring immediate and careful consideration. Too many laws are long, detailed, and insufficiently evaluated with respect to enforcement and the unfolding of practical administration. If the laws are made clear, the need for administrative procedure laws and legislative vetoes would shrink correspondingly.[34]

The administration of Congress and state legislatures should be reorganized in order that members may have more time for law making and for face-to-face consultations with administrators around the committee table. Only by this means will confidence in program administration be reestablished. Equally, the committee structure of legislative assemblies should be adjusted so that it is not so illogical and time-consuming as it now is. Too many committees and subcommittees deal with the same areas and problems. If there were fewer committees and if they were lined up with the corresponding organization in the executive branch of the same government, half the energy would be required and the results would be at least twice as good.

SUMMARY

Administrative law has been defined as the law in action. If it is truly to become that, and if it is to contribute to the solution of America's problems, lawyers once again need to be reoriented to the public service ethic, and public administrators need a better appreciation of law as a civilizing agent. Popular opinion to the contrary, the reading of legal materials (especially cases) is not difficult, and often it is intriguing. An introduction to law belongs in liberal arts curricula; courses on public law (municipal, constitutional, and administrative) are an essential part of the administrator's preparation.

NOTES

1. Emmette S. Redford, "Regulation Revisited," *Administrative Law Review* 28 (Summer 1976): 543–568.

2. American Bar Association, Commission on Law and the Economy, *Federal Regulation: Roads to Reform* (Exposure draft, 5 August 1978).

3. One of those who started this shift of emphasis was Ernst Freund in *Administrative Powers over Persons and Property* (Chicago: University of Chicago Press, 1928). For a fuller discussion, see Marshall E. Dimock, *Law and Dynamic Administration* (New York: Praeger, 1980).

4. The father of administrative law in the United States was Frank J. Goodnow, who was trained in Europe and taught at Columbia. See his *Comparative Administrative Law*, 2 vols. (New York: Putnam, 1893) and *The Principles of the Ad-*

ministrative Law of the United States (New York: Putnam, 1905).

5. Bernard Schwartz, *Administrative Law* (Boston: Little, Brown, 1976), pp. 3–4.

6. Kenneth C. Davis, *Administrative Law and Government* (St. Paul, Minn.: West Publishing, 1960), p. 17.

7. Dimock, *Law and Dynamic Administration*, chs. 1–3, 12.

8. Davis, *Administrative Law and Government*, p. 13.

9. Herbert Brownell, *Interstate Commerce Commission* (ICC) *Practical Journal* 23 (1955): 9.

10. Herbert Brownell, *I.C.C. Prac. Journal* 23 (1955): 195–201.

11. Charles Wyzanski, "The Trend of Law and Its Impact on Legal Education," *Harvard Law Review* 57 (1944): 558.

12. *Sunshine Anthracite Coal Co.* v. *Adkins*, 310 U.S. 381; 60 S. Ct. 914; 84 L. Ed. 1263 (1940). For a discussion of the entire issue of separation of powers and delegation, see Davis, *Administrative Law and Government*, ch. 2.

13. Davis, *Administrative Law and Government*, p. 57.

14. *B&O R. Co.* v. *United States*, 298 U.S. 349 (1936); *St. Joseph Stock Yards Co.* v. *United States*, 298 U.S. 38 (1936).

15. Schwartz, *Administrative Law*, p. 621.

16. "Administrative Law Process: Better Management Is Needed," *Report of the Comptroller-General of the United States*, 15 May 1978.

17. Felix A. and Lloyd G. Nigro, *Modern Public Administration*, 5th ed. (New York: Harper & Row, 1980), p. 104.

18. Allen Schick, "Congress and the 'Details' of Administration," *Public Administration Review* 36 (September-October, 1976); John A. Worthley, "Public Administration and Legislatures: Past Neglect, Present Probes," in "A Symposium: Public Administration and Legislatures," ed. James Heaphey, *Public Administration Review* 35 (September-October 1975): 480–490.

19. President's Advisory Council on Executive Organization, *A New Regulatory Framework* (Washington: U.S. Government Printing Office, 1971).

20. Roger C. Noll, *Reforming Regulation* (Washington: Brookings Institution, 1971).

21. American Bar Association, Commission on Law and the Economy, *Federal Regulation: Roads to Reform* (Exposure draft, 5 August 1978, Washington, D.C.).

22. Emmette S. Redford, *The President and the Regulators* (Washington: President's Advisory Committee on Government Organization, 17 November 1960); Marver Bernstein,

Regulating Business by Independent Commissions (Princeton, N.J.: Princeton University Press, 1955).

23. U.S., Congress, House, Committee on Oversight and Investigations, *Federal Regulation and Regulatory Reform,* 94th Cong., 2d sess., 1976; U.S., Congress, Senate, Committee on Commerce, *Appointments to the Regulatory Agencies, the Federal Trade Commission and the Federal Communications Commission (1949–1974),* 94th Cong., 2d sess., 1976.

24. This analysis is developed at length by Marshall E. Dimock in *Law and Dynamic Administration,* especially in chs. 2–4.

25. Kenneth C. Davis, *Discretionary Justice: A Preliminary Inquiry* (Baton Rouge: Louisiana State University Press, 1969).

26. Marshall E. Dimock, *The Executive in Action* (New York: Harper & Row, 1945), p. 20.

27. Dimock, *Law and Dynamic Administration,* pp. 59–60.

28. Davis, *Discretionary Justice,* p. 25.

29. James Hart, *An Introduction to Administrative Law,* 2d ed. (New York: Appleton-Century-Crofts, 1950), pp. 37–62.

30. Hart, *Administrative Law,* pt. 1, ch. 4; pt. 3. See also Davis, *Administrative Law and Government,* chs. 25–27.

31. Davis, *Administrative Law and Government,* pp. 3–6.

32. Dimock, *Law and Dynamic Administration,* ch. 12.

33. Both the Brookings Institution and the American Enterprise Institute undertook and completed studies so focused in the period beginning in the 1960s and continuing to date. Another organization, the Center for Public Resources, in New York City, has taken this approach beginning in the 1970s.

34. Dimock, *Law and Dynamic Administration,* ch. 8.

7

Ethics in Government

There is a wider diffusion of virtue, morality has become democratic, more men and women are controlled by right principles, but better men and even women than there were 2,000 years ago are not easy to find.

Charles Eliot Norton

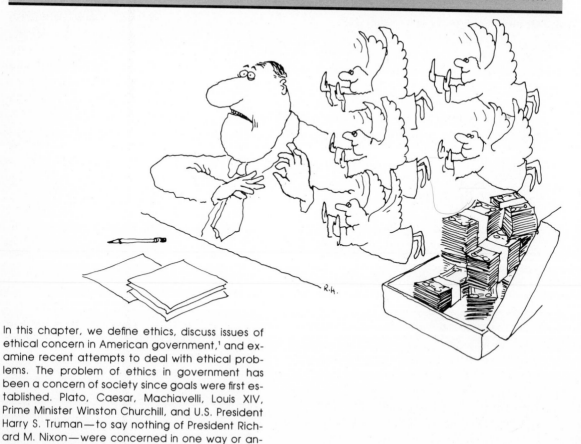

In this chapter, we define ethics, discuss issues of ethical concern in American government,[1] and examine recent attempts to deal with ethical problems. The problem of ethics in government has been a concern of society since goals were first established. Plato, Caesar, Machiavelli, Louis XIV, Prime Minister Winston Churchill, and U.S. President Harry S. Truman—to say nothing of President Richard M. Nixon—were concerned in one way or another with the problem of ethics.

V. O. Key, who was to achieve scholarly distinction in the field of politics and political parties, wrote his doctoral dissertation at the University of Chicago on municipal graft and corruption in Chicago. Chicago, like other large American cities in the 1930s, was ruled by political bosses and their machines; graft was hard to uncover, even more difficult to prosecute. There is far less machine rule in large cities today. But graft and dishonesty constantly take on new forms and crop up where least expected at the local level. If a town clerk pilfers money, for example, he or she is brought to trial, the judge sometimes orders the money returned with interest over a specified period, and the citizens are satisfied.

A PERENNIAL PROBLEM OF DEMOCRACY

All instances of violation of duty involve ethics. Ethics is concerned with establishing and practicing what is right and proper. A code of ethics is based upon moral values, which usually, though not always, derive from religious convictions. According to ethics in the Judeo-Christian tradition, it is wrong to kill, to steal, to covet another's wife or property, and to fail to live up to one's oath as a public official or civil servant. The civil service reform act of 1883 (the Pendleton Act) was largely an offshoot of the public's attempt to clean up the seamy side of American politics, the graft and corruption associated with venality both inside and outside the government.

What this act has to do with the administration side of government is perhaps not entirely clear without further explanation. The first point to note is that in proportion to the number of people involved, the civil service throughout American history has been relatively free of graft and corruption.[2] In other words, the lower ranges of public employment have remained predominantly ethical whereas the celebrated breaches of faith have occurred at higher levels among elected and appointed officials at the top and in legislatures, for example, a city boss, cabinet officer, or member of Congress. Not so many judges are involved, because, professionally, they are more like civil servants.

If most of the trouble is found outside the civil service, why should citizens be concerned with it? The greatest loss deriving from low ethical standards is a loss of confidence in democratic government. There are two possible results: Either the people fail to support their government and the level of economy and efficiency is reduced; or, in a more extreme situation, the prevailing political system is replaced by another system that veers toward the extreme right or left.[3]

A second point is that effective work usually cannot be done under unfavorable conditions. In an attempt to rout out unethical conduct a spy system may be introduced that would have a shattering effect on individual and group initiative and morale. Such a measure would be another cause of excessive, or pathological, bureaucracy, which, as we shall see in later chapters, is already a major problem in many governments, including that of the United States.

A third point to consider is what the legal profession refers to as the principal-agent relationship.[4] The principal, who typically represents a pressure group, is outside the government; his agent is inside, where for a consideration he can do the principal's bidding. This connection has become the main cause of misconduct in American politics and it is hard to reach and correct. Special-interest groups put up candidates, elect them, and sometimes control them afterwards, creating a situation that at times leads to scandal. Though both individual and group pressure are unethical, this kind of situation differs from one in which a town clerk "borrows" money because a relative is sick or the clerk sees a chance to make a killing on race horses or in the stock market, fully intending to return the money later. Both cases are illegal, but in the town clerk's case it was his or her idea, not that of another person. It is not surprising, therefore, that a principle of unethical behavior is this: the larger the government and the larger the financial stakes handled, the greater become the risks of unethical conduct.

The existence of pressure groups gives rise to an unresolved dilemma in American politics. On the one hand, Americans accept pressure groups because their vigor is regarded as a measure of political freedom. On the other hand, Americans are threatened by the excessive influence of pressure groups, which, if it became obnoxious enough, could not only undermine representative government but destroy capitalism itself.

A fourth point in the discussion of governmental ethics, therefore, is that as the size of corporations and other economic interests tends to increase, and as these interests employ full-time lobbyists to promote their interests and secure valuable contracts and exemptions fairly or unfairly, the difficulties of detection, prosecution, and enforcement proceed apace. Most legislation and rules are aimed at government servants, not the interests or individuals on the outside who attempt to corrupt them.[5] In 1978 the U.S. General Accounting Office reported that a possible $250 billion of the federal budget was susceptible to fraud, which, according to a Department of Justice estimate, actually affected from 1 percent to 10 percent of that figure.[6]

To this may be added a fifth point, that the standard of ethical conduct expected of the government by the public is considerably higher than that demanded of the private economic sector. This difference explains why in every recent session of Congress new safeguards have been included in the law and in internal rules and regulations, and proposals for others are currently being entertained. This difference is generally conceded and understood.

In the entire course of political history this dual standard of morality has not always prevailed, quite the contrary. But in the United States from the time of the first English colonizations in the early 17th century it has been true. Ethics, in part, is based upon ideals, and even when reality does not accord with high ideals, people continue to hold them. Those who work for government are supposed to put the public interest above their own; they are subject to a strict interpretation of the law and are not above it;

theirs is a public trust. Businessmen may cut corners, but the public servant must operate according to "moral sentiments," as Adam Smith said in the 18th century in his book of that title. The stability of society demands it. Arnold Heidenheimer capsulizes this thesis in the late 20th century, saying that public servants are trustees of the public good.[7]

A sixth and final point is that people seem to be more uncertain today about which values underlie ethics than they were in most previous periods. Either they are uncertain, or they are reexamining the relative weight assigned to various values. There are not so many Puritans as there were in the 17th century. More people subscribe to the notion that everyone is out to get what he can for himself short of running seriously afoul of the law. And law and ethics are by no means identical.[8] There seems to be no way of avoiding the Aristotelian-Platonic insight that true ethics is based upon virtue and standards that are internalized and durable.

The results to date of legislative enforcement of ethical standards, especially as concerns the executive branch, have been far from reassuring. There are a number of reasons. Offenses are hard to define; the General Accounting Office has consistently reported that not enough money or personnel are committed to enforcement; and the courts have thrown out cases where the gravamen (offense) is too vaguely defined. It is perhaps naive to think that administrative enforcement can succeed when the main actors (large government and corporations) are so conglomerate and hence amorphous. The result is that new offenses are constantly added while the older machinery works a treadmill to keep pace with the old guidelines.[9]

OFFENSES AND THE RECORD TO DATE

In the following discussion we shall deal only in passing with the enforcement of ethical standards in the judicial system. The American Bar Association and state and local bar associations have in many instances adopted codes of ethics for their members. Some of them, notably the New York and District of Columbia bar associations, have intensively studied this problem. Also bar associations throughout the country and administrators of the court system have been increasingly vigilant about the ethical conduct of judges.[10] Because of this vigilance, the ethics of the judicial branch, especially the conduct of judges, is of a higher quality than that of the legislative and executive branches.

Congress' responsibilities for ethical conduct are of two kinds: to ensure the ethical conduct of its own members, and, what is of more immediate interest to readers, to legislate concerning the ethical conduct of the executive branch and the judiciary.

Congress' obligations toward its own members are specifically provided in the Constitution. Each house is the judge of its own elections in contested cases, and each house has the power to discipline or remove its members for misconduct. There has been much of the latter kind of activity since the 1960s. At that time each house of Congress created its own committee on ethics, and both houses adopted codes of ethical conduct for their own members and staff.[11]

Congressional reform as well as the plethora of legislation affecting the executive branch was influenced markedly by the congressional investigations during the last thirty years dealing, among other things, with gambling and crime (the Kefauver Committee), the Internal Revenue Service, the Reconstruction Finance Corporation, campaign expenses, the armed services, the U.S. Maritime Commission, and, during the second Nixon administration, the Watergate scandal. Since the onset of the second Nixon administration in 1968, a vice-president has resigned under pressure for offenses such as tax evasion, bribery, and accepting illegal gratuities. More than 20 congressmen, former senators, and members of Congress have been indicted on criminal charges; more than a dozen have been convicted, and half a dozen have spent time in jail.[12] The most recent cases arose from the so-called Abscam scandals

during the latter part of the administration of Jimmy Carter.

A former professor of economics at the University of Chicago, former U.S. Senator Paul Douglas, has dealt interestingly with these developments in his Godkin Lectures at Harvard University in 1951. Douglas was the prime mover in promoting congressional ethics. His book *Ethics in Government* not only deals with many of the investigations here referred to but deals also with congressional and executive reforms and future steps which he thinks should be taken. It is somewhat paradoxical, says this professor turned politician, that public indignation should concentrate on guilty public officials and leave relatively unscathed equally guilty private corrupters. This contradiction is probably caused by conflicting moral standards on the part of the public.[13]

THE OFFICE OF GOVERNMENT ETHICS

We turn now to the problem of ethics in the executive branch. The main landmark with which we are concerned is the Office of Government Ethics, which was created by the Civil Service Reform Act of 1978. (This legislation is more fully discussed in chapter 19 on personnel administration.)

Why was this office created? There are several possible explanations. First, its creation occurred shortly after the Watergate scandal. Second, Congress had created a modest unit of this kind (committees in both houses) to deal with ethics. Third, Congress was concerned that replacing a civil service commission unit on ethics with the Office of Personnel Management under a single executive head might lead to more danger of partisan or unethical behavior. This concern is evidenced by the fact that Congress hesitated a great deal about placing the ethics office in the new agency for fear it might not be independent enough.[14] The most important factor in Congress' decision, however, may have been its growing worry that it was losing its direct control over the departments and agencies. Congress' face-to-face contacts with government agencies had declined, and it wanted to strengthen its surveillance responsibilities. Beginning with the passage of the Administrative Procedures Act of 1946, Congress has prescribed in growing detail the rules of operation that executives were formerly free to determine themselves.[15]

A further evidence of Congress' seeming determination completely to control the executive branch is that under the 1978 legislation creating the Office of Government Ethics as a central unit, Congress provided for ethics officials in each department and agency, who have authority to issue rules and regulations of their own.

As will soon be seen, the two biggest problems of ethics legislation are conflict of interest and the accompanying difficulty of disclosure of an official's income and its sources. The third problem is postemployment restrictions. Even these problems are quite different from the age-old evils of bribery and graft in their simple form. But readers should consider now what Congress did in its zeal to reduce everything to rote in the 1978 legislation. It provided six prohibitions, or admonitions, applicable to every employee, against any action that might *create the appearance of* or actually result in the following: using public office for private gain, giving preferential treatment to any person, impeding government economy or efficiency, losing complete independence or impartiality, making a government decision outside official channels, or affecting adversely the confidence of the public in the integrity of the government.[16] Such hortatory statements might sound appropriate in the preamble to a piece of legislation, but as a substantive provision of law? It only leads to making more rules and regulations and further weakens dynamic administration.

Another feature found in much congressional legislation since enactment of the Administrative Procedures Act of 1946 is that Congress has a fatal weakness for passing governmentwide regulations. Such action is unrealistic because no two programs are exactly alike and hence executives should be given some latitude for effective oper-

ation. Consider six areas that are covered in the 1978 legislation: gifts, outside employment, misuse of government property, adverse financial interests, wrongful use of official information, indebtedness, and gambling and betting. What do these phrases mean? Are they precise enough to be enforced effectively? Is it not conceivable that some of them are an infringement of the individual's right to privacy?[17] One of the worst features of this kind of legislation, of course, is that every phrase, however innocent it may appear, is a constant invitation, or temptation, to resourceful agency officials to spell out still further the meaning of words. The best way to obtain results in government, as in any endeavor, is to give executives trust and opportunity for freedom. If necessary, the superior official can check up on abuses afterwards in problem areas but without attempting to spell out in advance every move subordinates may or may not make.

Exercises in Government Ethics

The Ethics in Government Act of 1978, as we have noted, deals with certain large categories of behavior designed to keep government ethics more "pure" than private ethics. Before telling the reader what these strictures are, it would be interesting to discover how he or she would decide the following issues guided only by "general principle."

Consultancy Case. Albert Smith is employed as an economist in the Treasury Department in Washington. His former service included that of economist for the Tariff Commission (now called the International Trade Commission). In this position he dealt, among other things, with the importation of television sets from Japan. As part of its jurisdiction against dumping, the Tariff Commission has just decided that in a pending case the importation of television sets from Japan "at less than their fair value" does substantial "injury" to American manufacturers. A Washington law firm asks Smith to assist the firm's attorneys to assemble, collate, and analyze certain factual material involved in the pending case. This situation raises the following issues. Is the taking of this "outside" engagement proper? Would it make a difference whether or not Smith received a fee for his services?

Postemployment Case. Mary Jones, who retired in 1979 from federal service, in the U.S. Department of Agriculture, has taken employment with the University of Maryland. Under the terms of her federal retirement, Jones receives her retirement pay, participates in life insurance coverage, and has official personnel files maintained by the federal government. As a senior employee of the agriculture department, Jones formerly held a paid job with the Maryland Agricultural Extension Service. Her request in 1980 is to continue this connection but without compensation. The issue is Would there be a conflict between her former combination of federal and state employment and her requested combination of private and state employment, although she was paid in the former situation and would not be in the latter situation?

Conflict-of-Interest Case. John Brown is president of a large corporation doing business with the Defense Department. Since 1972 he has served without compensation on three major government committees on defense—the Defense Science Board, Joint Strategic Target Planning, and the Scientific Advisory Group. In 1979 these activities took 42 days of his time. One of Brown's colleagues on the Defense Science Board raises the question of whether there is a conflict of interest between Brown's private and public roles.

Now that the reader has decided these three cases on the basis of his or her perceptions of innate justice, we shall enumerate the main categories of the Ethics in Government Act of 1978 (Public Law 95-52): Title I, Legislative personnel disclosure requirements; Title II, Executive personnel financial disclosure requirements; Title III, Judicial personnel financial disclosure requirements; Title IV, Office of Government Ethics; Title V, Postemployment conflict of interest; Title

VI, Special Prosecutor; and Title VII, Senate legal counsel. Title V prohibits any officer, employee, or special government employee from intentionally trying to influence government agencies for two years following retirement from federal service. Appearances at the behest of the federal government on strictly government business are permissible. Participation in previous actions is broadly defined and includes decision, approval, disapproval, recommendation, rendering of service, investigation, "or otherwise" while so employed.

Conflict of Interest

Several of the provisions cited obviously relate to conflict of interest, which is unquestionably the most difficult area of ethics legislation and enforcement. Its importance is that if the idea is carried to extreme lengths it might, and doubtless already has, discourage some able and experienced people from accepting public employment or from staying in government.[18] It also creates uncertainty and fear. Moreover, conflict of interest is difficult to define. In general it means that public servants are prohibited from taking action or hiding interests which might, or do, result in favoritism and hence lack of thorough dedication to their duty to follow strictly the law and its intent. Even the Association of the Bar of the City of New York, which has worked on this problem as much as any group, has suggested that in the U.S. government it is impossible for government employees to isolate themselves from private interests. The bar's reasoning runs as follows. (1) The growth of government, its involvement in private interests, and its regulation of substantial portions of society mean that the line between private and public has virtually disappeared. (2) Because of changes in U.S. society, which are apparently irreversible, it may be necessary to define conflict of interest, but correspondingly it becomes increasingly difficult to do so without losses in efficiency and morale that are difficult to measure but nonetheless real.[19]

We can therefore take a few examples of how

difficult it is to define and prosecute offenses. One of the grounds constituting conflict of interest is called self-dealing. Not only is self-dealing prohibited when considering candidates for confirmation while working for the government, but there is also a one-year limitation on self-dealing after leaving office. It is also provided that self-dealing covers not only oneself but also members of one's family and associates who might be used indirectly. Once such relationships begin to fan out, it becomes a matter of debate where the circle ends. The situation is similar with speculating on inside government information for purposes of direct or indirect enrichment. True, the regulations attempt to define the implications of this prohibition; but, as so often happens, the more detailed the regulations are, the more confusing the issue becomes in unusual cases.

It is not surprising that lawyers and financiers run into disclosure difficulties, but it is surprising how many others do too. For example, a man was being considered for administrator of the Small Business Administration (SBA). He owned substantial interest in two banks, one of which did substantial business with the SBA. In another instance, a man incurred a campaign debt, decided to throw a party to pay it off, and refrained from inviting those who were associated with industries that could conceivably be affected by his actions as a legislator. In a third instance a person was being considered for a position in the General Services Administration (GSA). A corporation he headed received about a million dollars a year in rent from a building the GSA occupied. This was only a small portion of the income of the corporation, however.[20] Should these people be confirmed?

The Office of Government Ethics operates under a director with broad powers. Some of these relate to issuance and review of rules and regulations concerning ethics, consultation with agencies and with the attorney-general, evaluating the operation of the law and suggesting methods of improving it, and ordering corrective action on the part of agencies and individuals. In short as the director's duties are set forth in Title IV of the 1978 act, the Office of Ethics promulgates,

evaluates, decides, and fashions future policy and direction. As evidence of the sensitive and special character of the office, let it be noted that when the administration of Ronald Reagan succeeded the Carter administration, the incumbent, a graduate of Yale Law School and a highly principled individual, J. Jackson Walter, was continued in office instead of being replaced by a patronage appointment. His was one of a few positions so exempted.

Postgovernment Employment

The criminal provisions of the act, as set forth in Paragraph 207, rely upon stiff penalties: a fine of not more than $10,000 and imprisonment for not more than two years.

Among the main provisions of this section of the act are the following:

- There is a lifelong prohibition against any former employee knowingly acting as agent or attorney for any other person in matters where the employee participated personally and substantially as a government employee.
- The act places a two-year prohibition on the postemployment activities of federal employees regarding matters within their official responsibility; there is a shorter prohibition where the employee's involvement was less extensive.
- Covered by these provisions are not only high-ranking officials such as departmental secretaries, heads of agencies, and their deputies (so-called executive schedule officers) but also military officers and others later designated by the director.
- In order to prevent influence peddling, the act prohibits for one year any higher-level official from knowingly acting as agent or attorney concerning any formal or informal appearance where the former employee was previously employed and where there is a direct and substantial interest involved. Exceptions may be made where the Office of Government Ethics gives its consent or where the matter is personal or individual in character.

Unquestionably many or perhaps all of these objectives of public policy are desirable and necessary. It takes no great knowledge of the law, however, to appreciate that many of these words and phrases are ambiguous. Hence one sees why, as said earlier, courts in some cases have been loath to apply criminal penalties when the terms are so imprecise.

STATE AND LOCAL GOVERNMENT

State and local governments in the United States are beset by the same kinds of problems that affect the federal government. Nor are they doing less, relative to their size and complexity, than the federal government has done to date. In succeeding chapters in this book we shall deal with concrete demonstrations of this interest and intent. In our chapters on personnel administration, for example, we shall show that there are alternatives and in some respects possibly more constructive approaches to the problem of ensuring ethical behavior.

One of these methods, exemplified by the City Management Association, is to develop codes of ethics similar to, or even superior to, those of the American Bar Association and the medical profession. We shall also deal with the importance of training programs and decision making as tools for inculcating ethical standards. Another method is use of the ombudsman. Still others are auditing and accounting controls and the use of evaluation techniques to ensure desirable performance standards.

It should also be realized that, as so often happens, the federal example leads to state government experimentation along the same lines. The problem is more acute, as might be expected in the larger states such as New York, California, Pennsylvania, Ohio, and Michigan, where many of the same devices dealt with in this chapter are being used, sometimes with greater success. This same interest is also manifest in much smaller states and in cities throughout the country. These are the insulated laboratories, to use Justice Louis Brandeis's phrase, where experimentation may be expected and where more constructive approaches than those outlined in this chapter may conceivably originate.

CONCLUDING OBSERVATIONS

For reasons already suggested, the subject of ethics in government deserves continuous and careful consideration by all citizens and especially by those who may some time later find themselves employed in the public sector. It is fortunately, and deservedly, one of the main interests and concerns of those who espouse the "New Public Administration."

One of the spiritual leaders of that group, Dwight Waldo, has remarked, for example, that the organization man has more responsibilities to deal with ethical complexity than almost anyone else has. Further, moral complexity increases as responsibilities in an administrative hierarchy increase. The social-civic costs of failing to accord values and ethics their due outweigh the purely economic considerations.[21] He cites with approval Chester Barnard's statement to the effect that "moral creativeness" is an essential executive function.[22]

The old idea that career employees are politically and morally neutral cannot work any more. Career officials as well as appointive ones do not live in a cloistered compound where their only duties are to give unthinking obedience without careful scrutiny of long-range consequences and their effect upon the country's life-style. If they succumb to the excesses of pressure-group greed and immorality, they fail in their duty. If they allow themselves to be bound up in rules and red tape that undermine their effectiveness, they fail in their trust. Ethics involve positive obligations as well as well-conceived restraints. Hortatory admonitions to be loyal and to provide a full day's work have their place. But the essence of ethics is in means—methods that work and improve a situation—not in high-sounding words. A leading authority on this subject has suggested that the structural essence of ethics is the employee's relation to the public. It is one in which "A public employee acts on behalf of others who are not in a position to control or to monitor effectively the employee's actions."[23] In short, a public employee's duties and obligations run to the government, his superiors, and the "service" of which he is a part; but the employee's primary ethical obligation is always to the public.

SUMMARY

We have seen that enforcement of ethical conduct is an old and growing problem at all three levels of government. All three branches have set up ethics units to cope with problems such as conflict of interest, the taking of bribes, postelective employment prohibited by law, and a growing number of standards and prohibitions. The prosecutory-judicial method is plainly needed, but experience here as elsewhere seems to suggest that it needs to be supplemented by other measures such as education, training, codes of ethics, and inspectors-general. Principally the quality of those elected to office or serving in the government career service must be improved. Sources of potential corruption, such as business, law, and the professions, are often actively involved in setting standards of their own, enforcing them, and thus reducing unethical approaches to government. An excess of control might discourage some able people from entering public service; a neglect of gross abuse might in time undermine people's confidence in free government.

NOTES

1. The best brief analysis of ethics in government, to date, is J. Jackson Walter, "The Ethics in Government Act, Conflict of Interest and Presidential Recruiting," *Public Administration Review* 41 (Nov.–Dec. 1981).

2. Paul P. Van Riper, *History of the United States Civil Service* (New York: Harper & Row, 1958).

3. Aristotle, *Nichomachean Ethics,* bk. 1. See also W. A. R. Leys, *Ethics and Social Policy* (New York: Prentice-Hall, 1941); and George A. Graham, *Morality in American Politics* (New York: Random House, 1952).

4. Robert G. Vaughn, *Conflict of Interest Regulation in the Federal Executive Branch* (Lexington, Mass.: Lexington Books, 1979), ch. 1.

5. Gerald E. Caiden, "Public Administration and Bureaucratic Corruption: A Comparative Perspective" (Paper delivered at Conference on Fraud, Waste and Abuse in Government, University of Pittsburgh, 5–7 October 1980).

6. William Proxmire, *The Fleecing of Government* (Boston: Houghton Mifflin, 1980), p. 51.

7. Arnold Heidenheimer, *Political Corruption* (New York: Holt, Rinehart & Winston, 1970).

8. Vaughn, *Conflict of Interest,* chs. 5–8.

9. Vaughn, *Conflict of Interest,* pp. 6–8, 27–28.

10. *American Bar Association Code of Professional Responsibility and Code of Judicial Conduct* (1976); Association of the Bar of the City of New York, *Conflict of Interest and Federal Service* (Cambridge: Harvard University Press, 1960); Council of State Governments, *Ethics-State Conflict of Interest, Financial Disclosure Legislation, 1972–75* (1975).

11. U.S., Congress, Senate, Special Committee on Official Conduct, *Code of Conduct* (Washington: Government Printing Office, 1977); David A. Frier, *Conflict of Interest in the Eisenhower Administration* (Ames: Iowa State University Press, 1969).

12. Anthony Marro, "Congressional Ethics and the Need for Basic Reform," *New York Times,* 30 January 1977.

13. Paul H. Douglas, *Ethics in Government* (Cambridge: Harvard University Press, 1952), p. 24.

14. Vaughn, *Conflict of Interest,* p. 71.

15. Vaughn, *Conflict of Interest,* ch. 3, and Marshall E. Dimock, *Law and Dynamic Administration* (New York: Praeger, 1980), pt. 2.

16. Civil Service Reform Act of 1978, sec. 735.201(a), in Vaughn, *Conflict of Interest,* appendix.

17. For brief definitions and discussion, see Vaughn, *Conflict of Interest,* pp. 35–40.

18. "A Law That Kept Some Reagan Men Out of Office," *U.S. News and World Report,* 26 January 1981, p. 43.

19. Bar of the City of New York, *Conflict of Interest and the Federal Service* (1960), p. 36.

20. Vaughn, *Conflict of Interest,* pp. 106–107 for information on all three cases.

21. Dwight Waldo, *The Enterprise of Public Administration* (Novato, Calif.: Chandler & Sharp, 1980), pp. 184, 114, 130.

22. Chester Barnard, *The Functions of the Executive* (Cambridge: Harvard Business School, 1947), ch. 17, "The Nature of Executive Responsibility."

23. Vaughn, *Conflict of Interest,* p. 133.

8

The Chief Executive

I look upon my profession as city manager in exactly the same way that a minister of the gospel looks upon his mission, and believe that as a city manager endeavoring to make the city for whose administrative affairs I am responsible better in every way for every man and woman, boy and girl in it, I am doing on earth the work of the Master.

Louis Brownlow

In this chapter, we examine chief executives of the United States and their role in coordinating the fragmented governmental structures. The chief executive is the official who heads an entire government. At the federal level, the chief executive is the president. At the state level, it is the governor. It should be noted that both are elected officials who serve a fixed term of no more than four years before reelection. At the local level, things are more complicated. The elected chief executive is usually called a mayor, though the title of supervisor, warden, selectman, executive, or burgess or some other title is found in some jurisdictions. Yet there is also an appointed chief executive, the professional manager, who shall be scrutinized later.

L. P. Cookingham, one of the most distinguished city managers in American history, was once meeting with two of his Kansas City department heads. These two officials could not work well together and began to argue vehemently. Finally, one lunged at the other and began to chase him around the manager's desk. After Cookingham recovered from a fit of laughter, he got up and put the chase to an end.[1] Such are the tribulations of those who work for coordination at the upper levels.

OVERALL COORDINATION: A POLITICAL PROBLEM

How to secure overall coordination at the top is a major problem of American government today, as it has been for a long time. The difficulty lies partly in the structure of the American governmental system, divided as its powers are among the legislative, executive, and judicial branches. But the difficulty is compounded by the great size to which government in the United States has grown in response to citizen demands translated into law through interest groups and legislatures. (Chapter 21 details that growth.)

The result is a multiplicity of fragmented programs following courses seemingly of their own choosing, because it is now impossible for a single individual at the top of the executive branch to discharge the ordinary responsibilities of a general manager on so vast a scale. For example, the federal government subsidizes the growing of tobacco, while at the same time it warns Americans not to smoke cigarettes.

Coordination means keeping the various parts of an overall undertaking in proper relationship to one another. It is synchronization of action. These parts may be as great as the three branches of government or as small as the details of a specialized program, such as digging drainage ditches in a soil-conservation district.

Coordination is sought through more or less formal structural arrangement. In addition, where chief executives of large jurisdictions can-

not deal personally with more than a few legislators and department heads and can never know everything that is happening at the many lower levels of administration, coordination is also a matter of cooperation willingly offered. As such, coordination is more a matter of motivation and psychology than it is of formal structure or internal administrative organization.

Where cooperation is found in executive-legislative relations and in administrative relations with the top executive, major problems of national importance, such as inflation and deflation, are more easily solved, and the nation moves with more assurance in foreign affairs. To the degree that such cooperation is lacking, the country may find itself embarrassed both at home and abroad. The inability of presidents and Congress to achieve a coherent energy policy in the 1970s was disastrous to the nation.

The administrator looks at this problem a little differently than do some other interested parties. He places a good deal of importance on structural framework as one of the means of securing program results. When, despite the structure that exists for coordination between the legislature and the chief executive, the administrator notes more feuding than cooperation between them, he is likely to regard it as wasteful and possibly even irrational. To him the test of governmental effectiveness is the cooperative relations that can be achieved to solve major problems before they weaken the confidence of the people in themselves and in their institutions.[2]

Thus the administrator is inclined to judge these structural relations by his own standards and outlooks, and his perennial query is Does it work? Even in matters lying outside of his main concern, he cannot help thinking as an administrator. The passage of legislation affecting his agency becomes a personal and programmatic concern; it is "his" law or "his" service's law. Every triumph or failure of coordination is therefore viewed through eyes prejudiced by the needs of a particular undertaking: What does it mean to *my* program? The degree to which any success or failure outside his own group is likely to help or harm his own program becomes the focus of his primary concern.

THE PRESIDENTIAL AND CABINET SYSTEMS

The two principal frameworks of democratic government are the parliamentary, or cabinet, system, as found in Great Britain, and the presidential system, which has reached its highest development in the United States. We use the term presidential to refer to all the state governments and local governments with legislatures and chief executives, which are separate bodies, such as the mayor-council form, as well as to the federal government.

Characteristics

The cabinet and presidential systems each have characteristic strengths and weaknesses.[3] Supporters of one system are not likely to give up its advantages in order to adopt the other, for, as the late British political scientist Harold Laski once observed, "A system of government is like a pair of shoes; it grows to the use of the feet to which it is fitted." But he continued in a manner that strikes a responsive chord on both sides of the Atlantic today: "It is essential for both our countries to realize that we face, in the coming years, problems of a scale and intensity far greater than any we have known at least in our lifetime."[4]

Although it is not necessary here to debate the possible superiority of one governmental system over the other, some of the issues involved may be noted, because Americans are now more widely disposed to correct the coordinative gaps in the presidential system than they were a few years ago. The rapidly growing pressures of policy and other problems created by the United States' involvement in the affairs of other nations leave no choice in the matter.

Laski's principal criticism of the American presidential system was its failure to guarantee cooperation between the legislative and executive branches, whereas under the cabinet system, this relationship is never in doubt. Unlike Congress, Parliament does not make law; it simply debates and approves—or disapproves—what the executive, created out of its own majority party membership, submits to it. Parliament also has an educational function, among its own members and the nation, in its debate of broad principles or problems of national import, thus helping to clarify policy as a basis for legislation. Finally, when a proposal offered by the party in power is disapproved in a no-confidence vote in the House of Commons, Parliament has a selective function as the source from which the new government will be chosen.

In response to Laski, the American scholar Don K. Price, for his part, criticized the British system as weakening the role of the legislature, whereas the American system strengthens it. He also argued that the president, who is elected by the people and whose constitutional powers are clear, is a stronger executive, especially in time of crisis, than the cabinet system—aside from the leadership of strong personalities—is capable of providing. He argued, finally, that to divide powers according to checks and balances is the ideal method of giving vitality to an independent judiciary, an independent Congress, and an independent chief executive. Price concluded that if the British system has worked well, it is largely because of the high caliber of the British civil service. The service provides Britain not only with experience and ability but in addition with wisdom and an indispensable continuity in daily operations, irrespective of the changes that occur in political control at the top. In recent times, the United States has been trying to develop the same useful resource.

From the debate on the merits of these two systems, which has a long history,[5] two issues stand out as of special concern to Americans: (1) whether stronger measures are needed to secure cooperation between the legislative and executive branches than the Constitution seems to provide, and (2) whether the president is as strong an executive, especially in his managerial functions, as has generally been assumed.

There have been many attempts in recent years to strengthen the cooperative relationship between Congress and the president. As the result of two studies made in 1945, Congress was reorganized by the Legislative Reorganization Act of 1946, and the process has been continued, by bits and pieces, to this day. As one result, legislators have had much more staff assistance than previously, in the hope that their own access to research and information would reduce their dependence on the executive establishment.

In more recent times, except for minor reform in 1970, Congress has been trying unsuccessfully to extend the internal reform that began in 1941-1946. Just as it appeared that the legislative reforms were about to succeed, the vested congressional interests, largely those of powerful committee chairmen who considered their positions threatened, defeated the necessary improvements. The only exception is the 1974 budget procedure revision, discussed in Chapter 22.

Other suggestions that have not been acted on are (1) that members of the cabinet appear regularly—on the British example—before Congress to answer questions and improve cooperation by more frequent communication and (2) that a constitutional amendment make it mandatory to hold a new election in the event of an impasse between an implacable Congress and an implacable president in time of serious foreign or domestic crisis.

What is the likelihood that some significant remedies will be enacted by Congress? Short of a crisis of dimensions hitherto not experienced in the national history, the possibility of constitutional change does not appear likely, for Congress has never been disposed to weaken its own powers. And after the Watergate crisis of the 1970s, Congress looks with new suspicion on the presidency.

Bureaucracy's Role

The friction that seems naturally to exist between the legislative and executive branches is due in part to each institution's trying to increase its own power and prestige at the expense of the other. The effect of these struggles on the on-going work of the bureaucracy has yielded interesting results.

The first is that the main action programs of American governments have secured a degree of administrative independence and entrepreneurial opportunity that would not be possible in a tighter system, such as Britain's. Britain has had no such figure as J. Edgar Hoover, who ran the Federal Bureau of Investigation (FBI) for almost 50 years, often ignoring what presidents wanted.

The second result is that since both legislative and executive branches claim certain administrative prerogatives in running the departments and agencies, program chiefs are in a position to play one off against the other and to profit from both. Moreover, any inclination in this direction is reinforced by the natural tendencies of interest groups to muddy the waters for their own benefit.

The ambiguity of the position of administration in the structure of government has increased the influence of career officials on appropriations and other legislation. At the federal level, for example, agency heads are expected to clear with the Office of Management and Budget, which is the president's own agent. In practice, however, the relations of career officials with key members of Congress are so intimate as to constitute a backstairs access to the center of legislative power. Close relations with key congressmen, for example, were the source of J. Edgar Hoover's power. Similar examples can be found at the state and local level.

In short, *the growth and influence of the American bureaucracy is in part a compensation for, and an offset to, the gaps that are inherent in the presidential system.* The only way the situation could be changed—if, indeed, change is desirable—would be to substitute the cabinet for the presidential system of government.

Yet another result of unclear relations in the presidential system is that they increase the difficulty of securing joint policy determination, planning, and execution for programs that belong together. Such coordination is a requirement if large, complex problems are to be tackled in their entirety, in a rational and unified way. Thus, dealing with juvenile delinquency involves, at a minimum, education, recreation, child welfare, the police, the correctional system, mental health programs, and the regulation of child labor. Similarly, solving the problem of technological unemployment involves at least the employment service, unemployment insurance, public welfare, education, science and technology, commerce, and labor.

One example of confusion produced by the presidential system is the Department of Health and Human Services (HHS), labeled a "bureaucratic labyrinth" by its former secretary Elliot Richardson. In the 1970s, HHS's predecessor agency, the Department of Health, Education, and Welfare (HEW), had 300 programs, 54 of which overlapped and 36 of which overlapped with programs of other departments.[6]

In all such instances, how well these public agencies work together is more significant than how well each works within its own limited area. It is true that at the action level, much cross-referencing occurs among all of the agencies of interest; but it is at the higher levels, where goals are identified, policy is determined, and relationships are activated, that coordination is notably lacking. It is at these higher levels that fragmentation becomes a major administrative problem and that Americans become increasingly concerned about structural cooperation.

THE PRESIDENT AS GENERAL MANAGER

In the American system, the coordination of action programs, theoretically at least, is the responsibility of the chief executive. All public chief executives are not identical, of course. As the most powerful chief executive in any constitutional government in the world, the president of the United States has many constitutional duties, of which management coordination is only one. He is also the symbol of national unity (king and prime minister rolled into one), head of the ma-

jority political party, chief proposer of legislation to Congress, commander in chief of the armed forces, chief architect of foreign policy (with the cooperation of the Senate and the secretary of state), and chief catalyst of public opinion in the nation.

While the president's managerial duties are important, they are only one area of responsibility among half a dozen, all of which are either expressly provided for or implied in the Constitution. Consequently, what a man makes of the presidency depends in some degree on his style and his predispositions, and he is likely to concentrate on areas with which he is familiar or which give him the greatest satisfaction. Thus, if he has previously been a manager, he will doubtless continue to take an interest in management; but if not, there immediately opens an area of uncertainty.[7] And no American presidents between Franklin D. Roosevelt (1933–1945) and Jimmy Carter (1977–1981) had had substantial civilian executive experience, although both Carter and Ronald Reagan had previously been state governors.

Since we have spoken mostly about presidents to this point, it is now time to look at the other chief executives in American government.

GOVERNORS

Constitutional provisions relating to control of the administrative branch of state government divide power between the chief executive and the legislature. For this reason, no matter what other ideal conditions may exist in his favor, the governor is going to find himself frustrated at times in his attempt to oversee, coordinate, and manage the administrative apparatus of which he is nominally the chief. While marked variations in the power of policy implementation exist, all governors are often crossed in the attempt to impose their wills on their administrative subordinates. Often these restrictions are imbedded in the state constitution, which is much more difficult to amend than it is to change laws passed by the legislature. Five types of limitations seem particularly relevant to the governor's ability to coordinate.

First, the governor must usually share power with independently elected executive officials. For example, in 1980, 43 states had elected attorneys general; 38, treasurers; 37, secretaries of state; and 18, superintendents of education. When the electorate splits a ticket between candidates of both major parties, the governor has a very difficult time influencing officeholders of the opposition party. A Republican treasurer in Wisconsin, for example, refused to honor the salary voucher of a state commission member appointed by the Democratic governor. Even in situations where the other elected officials may be of the same party as the governor, he may have problems controlling them or influencing them, especially if they are ambitious politicians who covet his job and who owe him nothing for their election. If a governor is a strong party leader whose party sweeps all the top state offices, however, he may be able to overcome the problem of the unresponsive elected executive. He can do so by making sure that the party nominates individuals responsive to him. And, of course, there are variations in the numbers of elected executives per state, so that some governors find this problem negligible or less irksome than others.

Second, the governor's power to appoint persons to and remove them from administrative positions is often restricted. Legislatures seem to enjoy creating boards, commissions, and other executive agencies to which the governor cannot name members. In some instances, appointees serve a fixed term, and only when a term expires can the governor nominate successors. In other instances he has no authority whatsoever to appoint members; it lies with the legislature or other boards or commissions. Even when the governor can name persons to office, he usually has to gain legislative approval for them. One researcher has calculated that the governors in only 13 states name as many as half the appointees to the key departments. In fact, the highest rating of any governor in his evaluation was that for the governor of Tennessee, who has the authority to name 73 percent of the heads of 16 key governmental agencies.[8]

Besides the problem of limited authority, the governor may also often find it difficult to attract persons whom he desires to serve in state government, largely because salaries, set by the legislators, are not so high as comparable positions in industry. An example is that of Governor Thomas Meskill of Connecticut, elected in 1970. Meskill made it known that his prime criterion for appointment to key executive positions was personal loyalty to himself. However, he retained fully one fifth of the political executives, commissioners, and deputy commissioners who had served under his Democratic predecessor. This group of executives, who had spent careers as either professionals or bureaucrats, was presumably kept on because Meskill could not have easily attracted other persons with the necessary expertise.

Third, the governor's authority to manage through budgetary controls may be restricted. The monies appropriated do not automatically go to the bureaus but must be allotted to them by the central budget office, a topic we return to in Chapter 22. Most governors enjoy substantial authority in this area, but a large minority are handicapped. Such controls can be of great importance in influencing bureau behavior; if a governor lacks them, he lacks an important resource for policy implementation.

Fourth, the authority of the governor and his key political executives to control agency personnel is circumscribed. Civil service systems limit the chief executive by establishing criteria for entry, promotion, job classification, and removal. Where a civil service system does not exist, as it does not in many areas of state government, the governor and his key subordinates have wide discretion over matters of personnel. (Chapter 19 has more to say on this aspect of personnel management.)

Finally, most governors have limited powers of reorganization. The president has the authority to submit a plan for reorganization of executive departments to Congress. If neither house of Congress moves within 60 days to veto his proposal, it becomes law. Only 10 of 50 governors, however, enjoy even this limited authority to reorganize their own administrations. Instead, most of them have to go hat in hand to the legislature to ask for such a grant because they have no legal basis to take the initiative in reorganization. Reorganization can be a crucial management tool, as may be seen in Chapter 11.

The most important recent study of the governor argues that he has become much more of an administrative coordinating force in state government in the post-World War II period.[9] A number of changes have concentrated more effective means of management in the governor's hands. Many states had established departments concerned with administration by 1980. Within these departments are management analysts whose task is to devise bureau organization to make program delivery both more effective and more responsive to the governor. State budget offices increasingly stress new types of budgetary systems designed to promote the same goals. Central planning has received greater emphasis and, like the management and budget tools, is coming more and more under the authority of the governor.

For example, in Georgia an Office of Planning and Budget was set up in 1971 under Governor Jimmy Carter. Typically, such state agencies were supposed to coordinate activities, evaluate programs, and troubleshoot problem areas for the chief executive. Many of the states also created central "housekeeping" departments. Again in Georgia, a Department of Administrative Services was established. It coordinated functions such as printing, data processing, purchasing, and property management.[10] In some states, the personnel office, telephone service, travel arrangements, and other service functions have also been included in a Department of Administrative Services. (The General Services Administration has provided these services, except for personnel, for the federal government since 1950.)

Gubernatorial actions to coordinate have seemingly met with some success. A 1965 survey of state administrators found that a majority of them felt that the legislature had more influence over them than the governor had. An identical survey taken in 1978 found the opposite: administrators felt that the governor had more influence over them than had the legislature.[11]

MAYORS AND COUNTY EXECUTIVES

The mayoralty is the foremost form of chief executive in cities of more than 500,000. Over 80 percent of these cities have mayors, while 40 percent of cities of 10,000 to 500,000 have them. While only 50 of the 3,000 American counties have an elected executive, analogous to the mayor, this form of chief executive is rapidly growing in popularity.

Compared to the president and governors, mayors lack formal authority and are thus handicapped in policy coordination. Half of all mayors lack veto power of any kind; half are elected to two-year terms of office; and almost half of all cities elect other executive officials.[12] A survey of cities of more than 50,000 found that only 39 of 151 mayor-council governments had a so-called strong-mayor form.[13] As in the case of the governor, formal authority is a key determinant in making a mayor strong or weak.

Although these formal restrictions make the job of mayor arduous, a skilled political operative and party leader can use limited resources to coordinate policy. The record of Richard Lee, of New Haven, Connecticut, exemplifies this point. Mayor from 1953 to 1969, Lee was able to launch and implement the most comprehensive urban renewal program in any American city. He did so principally through the resources available to him as chief of his party and by his skill at persuasion and negotiation with the federal government and community groups.

Likewise, Jeffrey Pressman's study of mayoral leadership in Oakland, California, a manager-council community, indicates that the extent to which the mayor is able to exercise power in policy development depends largely on his personality and willingness to exploit his meager resources. Pressman points out that a great deal of the mayor's influence is based on his prestige and legitimacy, which he can use to prevail upon different groups to go along with him on certain issues. Further, the mayor is the presiding officer at city council meetings and appoints council committees, which gives him an opportunity to affect discussions and outcomes. The mayor of Oakland cultivated one councilman whose chief interest lay in an airport golf course by creating a golf course committee and making the councilman its chairman and only member. Informal cultivation of councilmen at social occasions may also pay good dividends. Another resource that even a weak mayor may enjoy is the authority to name members to many city commissions; this power can be valuable if he is in office long enough to make a number of appointments.[14] Thus, it is possible for a mayor to exert leadership even in extremely difficult circumstances.

The local chief executive, whether he is mayor or manager, confronts the same kinds of frustrations as the president or governor in trying to manage a bureaucracy. If the mayor is strong in formal authority, he can be a formidable figure in policy coordination because he has substantial power to create or abolish positions, to make temporary transfers, to administer a contingency fund, to appoint and remove officials, and to administer budget funds. If a mayor is a strong party leader, he may be able to circumvent fragmented authority by skillfully using his party role, as did the late Mayor Richard Daley of Chicago and former Mayor Richard Lee of New Haven. For example, Lee gained effective control of the New Haven boards of aldermen, zoning appeals, and finance through his control of the nominating machinery and use of patronage. Nineteen of 33 aldermen were economically vulnerable to mayoral attack (11 were city employees, 3 had close relatives who worked for the city, and 5 did business with the city). Several Board of Finance members did business with the city and could thus be influenced by the mayor.

The mayor's role as chief administrator, however, is still characterized by frequent bargaining with opponents and would-be allies rather than by the imposition of ukases from above. Further, no mayor can be a leader in every or even most areas of his city government. A study of New Haven notes that although Lee was nationally recognized as an exceptionally strong mayor, "in the more traditional areas of city administration [education, police, health], Lee's status never matched his status in urban renewal."[15] (For "more traditional" readers may substitute "more professionalized and more structurally autonomous" in order to have a better idea why these agencies remained more powerful than others.) Another force that has risen to bedevil the mayor is the new militancy of public unions. By demanding a voice in both work conditions and departmental policy, unions have lessened the impact of city chief executives on policy implementation, a topic we return to in Chapter 20.

While the chief executive may have more control over the bureaucracy than any other figure, most mayors, like presidents and governors, come to the job without experience in management. They are thus at a disadvantage vis-à-vis administration.

THE CITY MANAGER AND THE COUNTY MANAGER

More popular than the mayoralty in localities of 10,000 to 500,000 is the executive in the form of a city manager or a town manager. Only one-fifth of cities of more than 500,000 are run by managers. Half the population of the United States lives under government by a city or town manager. Three hundred fifty counties have adopted a county manager system. These counties number about 12 percent of the total but contain 28 percent of the population of the nation.

Characteristics

The city manager is a full-time professional employee appointed by the local legislature to be the chief executive officer of its government. The legislature can remove the manager at any time, by majority vote. The manager usually has full legal authority over administrative matters such as personnel, purchasing, or budgeting but has no formal voting or veto powers.

The successful manager is as likely to be a key policymaker as is the successful mayor. In other words, the split between policy and administration is more apparent than real, a fact acknowledged by the International City Management Association (ICMA) in 1952 when it revised its code of ethics to read: "The city manager as a community leader submits policy proposals to the council and provides the council with facts and advice on matters of policy to give the council a basis for making decisions on community goals."

What resources does the manager possess that explain his key place? First, his functional task in government is to provide and evaluate policy alternatives for the council. He is usually prepared, and often expected, to make a policy recommendation. Second, the manager's resources explain why "there is a strong tendency . . . for administration to devour politics."[16] Pressman notes that in Oakland in 1970 the mayor was paid $7,500 and councilmen $4,600, sums that make it financially difficult for them to work full time, while the manager's $40,000 salary enables him to do so. In addition, the manager usually has far greater staff resources, including not only personal assistants but, potentially, all city employees. Thus, he has much more information about government than others.

City managers constantly walk a tightrope between policy and administration. If they are not tactful or if they are overly aggressive, they find themselves at odds with the council or powerful interests, in which case they are sometimes replaced and must look elsewhere for new posts. To a greater extent than under federal or state civil service, managers can influence policy by direct participation in the policymaking process. In small towns it is not unknown for them actually to preside over council meetings; they know the most about agenda.

Most managers enjoy an edge over other chief executives in policy coordination. The typical city charter grants the manager authority in administrative matters that is equal or superior to that of the strong mayor. Equally important is the manager's training and experience in administration. This administrative primacy may have far-reaching consequences. As Pressman comments in his Oakland study:

> The city manager defines "policy" and "administration" in such ways that "administration" turns out to be very large and "policy" is very small. When Mayor Reading complained in July 1968 that the police chief's stringent restrictions on policemen's use of guns . . . constituted a dangerous policy decision which should be overturned by the council, the city manager disagreed. The manager's reasoning was clear: "A policy decision would be that policemen in Oakland should carry guns. Administrative decisions should be when they should carry guns, where they should carry guns, and how they should use those guns."[17]

There are, however, some manager-council governments where the manager is greatly restricted in authority and has no substantial previous experience in administration. And, of course, managers, like other chief executives, vary in personal skill.

Development of the Concept

The manager movement began around the turn of the century, making it almost three generations old. It has grown because cities and towns need business management. Managers are professionals. Business firms rank good community service as number one in choosing locations. Managers are practical and save money. They do not intrude themselves unnecessarily into politics. They have wide mobility, moving to more desirable positions as they gain experience. Most of them have political savvy. The universities and colleges are equipped to train them.

One may take a town of 1,500 people, for example, which submits a plan for main street improvement and housing for the elderly and low-income families. The initial application is for $186,000 and the manager winds up obtaining $350,000. Small wonder, therefore, that when other towns try to "steal" the manager, the town where he has been so successful makes a concerted drive to retain his services.

Historically, when so much of the community's business was streets and public works (such as water and sewerage), it is not surprising that most town managers were engineers. However, as communities have expanded their range of functions and people have broader concerns, different skills are required, and general managers who know how to carry on public relations are surging rapidly to the fore. The typical younger manager today has an MPA degree from a college program in public administration.

Increasingly, the manager is one who not only knows business and organizational practice but is also able to identify with power groups and minorities when crises arise. This knowledge is illustrated by an experience of Keith Mulrooney, city manager of Claremont, California, site of several colleges. Two months after the burning of the Isla Vista branch of the Bank of America, another bank in Claremont was threatened. Mulrooney describes the scene.

I stood feet planted in the open doorway of the Yale Avenue Branch of the Bank of America . . . and watched while 1,000 singing college protest marchers with picket signs hoisted aloft, red headbands, and Viet Cong flags rounded the corner of Harrison Avenue, about 15 abreast, proceeded forward down Yale, arms linked, and closed up their ranks about 20 feet away while their leader began an anti-Cambodia, anti-Bank of America speech. I could see our police chief, in plain clothes, gauging the mood of the crowd from across the street. I knew our mayor was somewhere in the tight mass of emotion-charged young people, trying to reduce tensions. About 25 SDS [Students for a Democratic Society] types stood immediately in front of me, urging the marchers to enter the bank. Would the protesters maintain order, or would they enter the bank?

Then, in the manner of the author of a case study, which presents the facts and leaves the proposed solution to the reader, Mulrooney, at the end of his 10-page article, appends this postscript: "The protesters didn't enter the bank or burn it down either."[18]

Professional Standards

Professionalization is written into city manager charters and also into the constitution and by-laws of the ICMA. The typical charter reads: "As chief administrative officer, the city manager provides professional counsel to the city council. . . . His work is performed with professional independence. . . ." Similarly, the introduction to the ICMA's Code of Ethics for managers states that its main objective is "to strengthen the quality of urban government through professional management." This code of ethics was adopted in 1924 and has been amended five times since. Before a person may join the ICMA he must sign the "Agreement to abide by the City Management Code of Ethics and service in a professional position . . . recognized by ICMA as providing for overall management responsibilities." This is enforced by the ICMA Committee on Professional Conduct.

By the late 1970s, 20 to 25 ethics cases were handled annually. Some of the ethical grounds were these: conflict of interest, job-hopping (short service), felony convictions, and partisan political activity. The ICMA also produces high morale and an ethical tone by stressing future planning and a positive outlook on government. It is this positive outlook, as contrasted with the suspicious, policeman's attitude, that is often so sharply different from that in federal and state government. The ICMA is positive.

THE PUBLIC ADMINISTRATION VIEW OF THE PRESIDENCY

Presidents of the United States have had many different interests and abilities regarding the administration of the federal government. There have been weak and strong presidents, those deeply interested in administrative policy and execution, and those who were not much concerned about such matters.

Beginning with the creation of the Brownlow Committee in 1936,[19] however—at the height of the Roosevelt administration—the public administration profession, which was to organize the American Society for Public Administration (ASPA) three years later, began energetically to seek ways of making the president a more effective manager.

One of the profession's main interests was to find some solution to the problem of the headless administrative fourth branch and to check the growing tendency toward program fragmentation. Remedies were sought in a greater degree of central direction, more party responsibility, and better coordinated effort at the top. Taken together, these added up to the equivalent of one of the best features of the cabinet system of government, responsibility.

To this end, the Brownlow Committee proposed to institutionalize the presidency. Since the president could not do everything himself, he needed the help of staff services. Consequently, it proposed to strengthen the Bureau of the Budget as the president's planning, financial, efficiency, and coordinating tool. In addition, he was to have as many key assistants (with a "passion for anonymity," said the Brownlow Report) and staff units as might be needed to achieve managerial effectiveness. Here the analogy to business failed, in some respects, because the corporation president is free of such immediate concerns. The point was answered by stating the obvious, that government differs from business in important respects.

Supporting the Brownlow Committee's recommendations, prominent political scientists[20] have argued the constitutional necessity and propriety of thus institutionalizing the presidency. The executive power, says the Constitution, is vested in the president, not in Congress or anywhere else. The president is the only official in the nation elected by all the voters. Consequently, he is the only one one who can speak for them on all matters, and he has a personal obligation, as head of his party and chief legislator, to see that Congress follows his lead. Having secured what is needed from Congress, the president must then have the staff services that will secure coordination among the action programs and prevent them from working at cross purposes.

This view of the presidency expounded by the Brownlow Committee was faithfully followed by the first Hoover Commission, which reported in 1949,[21] and the organization of the Executive Office of the President, created in 1939, has followed this pattern. Consequently, the institutionalized view of the presidential office has been dominant in public administration theory and federal practice for more than 45 years.

In 1970, the federal Bureau of the Budget was renamed the Office of Management and Budget (OMB) to stress this central coordinating role. However, neither it nor the Domestic Council, created the same year, has been able consistently to coordinate policy. Some critics think that the only change in OMB has been its new name.

A Divergent View

Throughout these changes and reorganizations, however, some observers have continued to question the assumptions on which the presidency has been progressively institutionalized. Their arguments and motives differ.

Congress. Political response in Congress, for example, has been mixed from the outset. On the one hand, the members of Congress have not questioned the president's right to strengthen his office and more often than not have understood the need for more coordination and responsibility. On the other hand, however, there has been a good deal of evidence in Congress, on both sides of the aisle, of a feeling that every increase in presidential power serves to diminish the power and prestige of Congress. The unwillingness of

Congress to reorganize its own structure and procedures and to provide for more staff assistance to its own members is partly explained in these terms.

Congress has shown institutional jealousy in several ways. In 1943, for example, against the president's strong opposition, Congress abolished the National Resources Planning Board, an agency created by executive order in 1934, which, under a series of titles, had produced some first-rate research and resource reports. Similarly, Congress has been suspicious of, and in some instances outright hostile to, the role of the federal budget agencies and other presidential staff aides, when administrative spokesmen have appeared at budgetary or other legislative hearings.

These attitudes were somewhat alleviated, however, when in 1946, Congress created the Atomic Energy Commission and the Council of Economic Advisers and set up a joint committee of both houses to deal directly with each agency. Thus Congress was ensured a full partnership in these crucial areas. The relationship to the Council of Economic Advisers is especially significant because the CEA is one of the president's staff agencies and works closely with the OMB.

The Universities. Academic criticism of the institutionalized structure of the presidency is more searching than the criticism of Congress, and some of it goes back before 1936 when the Brownlow Committee began its work. A number of writers have questioned whether it was the constitutional intent to make the president the undisputed general manager of the federal government. *Both* Congress and the president, it is argued, are involved in administration, which is part of the price that must be paid for the benefits derived under the separation-of-powers doctrine. Moreover, some of the president's express powers, such as those of chief legislator and commander in chief of the armed forces, as well as his role as party leader, are vital to democratic government and might suffer from neglect if the president were to devote a disproportionate amount of his limited time to discharging his managerial responsibilities.

Other Criticism. There has also been some criticism of the administrative desirability of raising so many decisions in government to the presidential level. Many public administrators believe that the lower the level at which decisions may be made, the greater is the vitality of management and the speed with which problems will be solved. According to this view, administration is more a matter of cooperation than it is of authority; consequently, roles must be defined and decisions made at *all* levels in the hierarchy.

Another issue relates to what the Brownlow Committee called "a passion for anonymity" to describe a desirable quality in those serving as the president's chief assistants. Quietly sharing burdens and shunning the limelight, these men and women would be in close touch with the major policy areas of the government, keep a finger on crucial pulses, report to the president the things he ought to know, and help him and others to think through their decisions.

This concept of nonvisible administrative management, however, has its shortcomings. In a democracy, dealings are supposed to be in the open. Secrecy is an invitation to various forms of corruption and influence peddling, and the press takes a dim view of concealed action. Moreover, why should anonymous presidential assistants in effect decide issues that agency heads and program directors are presumably as adequately qualified to decide? The rebuttal was that the president can make his decisions only if he has direct knowledge of the issues; but this view also was challenged on the ground that the members of the cabinet and other agency heads whom he trusted could act as his agents just as easily as his anonymous assistants could.

Then there was criticism of the strain on the president's span of attention. When the organization around him began to proliferate to include agencies such as the National Security Agency, the Central Intelligence Agency, and the Office of Defense Mobilization, it began to appear that the president might be spending too much time on his immediate staff and neglecting other matters. To deal with the anonymous six special assistants provided in the Brownlow Report is one thing, but when the number of officials whom the president must see more or less regularly reaches a peak of 300, as it once did, that is something else again. This is more than any man's span of attention can encompass, especially when there are many nonadministrative responsibilities that he also must discharge.

Yet another adverse reaction concerned the high turnover rate among top policy executives. The characteristically short service of departmental secretaries and assistant secretaries might be due in part, at least, to the inadequate authority and challenge of their office. If all important matters are decided in the Executive Office of the President instead of at the cabinet or agency level, able executives in the departments and agencies are not likely to derive much satisfaction from their jobs. In a recent year, the average length of service of assistant secretaries was 24 months, and that of cabinet officials was around 32 months—just about long enough, it was noted, for an executive to learn his job. Some began to wonder whether the more the experts tried to secure coordination at the apex, the less likely coordination was to appear in the action agencies where most of the people work and where all services to the citizen are rendered.

Finally, those interested in the theory of administration and who know something of business management and comparative administration began to believe that "administrative management" as pursued in the federal government was proceeding on the basis of false assumptions. Like all Gaul, federal management was apparently being divided into three parts: planning, concentrated largely at the presidential level; decision making, also narrowly held at the presidential level; and administration, covering all the nondiscretionary responsibilities left to the departmental and action agencies after the president's staff had had all the fun.

If these assumptions are pursued, concluded these critics, the quality of the federal administration must deteriorate, for the present trend violates assumptions that practitioners have proved through their own experience: that administration is a unified process and decisions should be made as close to the scene of action as possible.

The Nixon Experience

The most serious and sustained effort to unify the national executive branch under the president occurred during the administration of Richard M. Nixon (1969–1974). This effort was flawed, however, because it was conceived not as a partnership, but as domination by the White House. While the winds of Watergate washed this effort away, it is instructive to look at what Nixon tried to do and why.

Nixon was a Republican president whose party was in a minority in both houses in Congress. He and his staff resented the semiautonomous character of much of the bureaucracy. They thus set out to forge a strategy that would enable them to control the bureaucracy while ignoring Congress.

After relying initially on department heads to manage the bureaucracy, Nixon and his staff concluded that the secretaries appointed originally were not loyal enough to the president and should be replaced. In the words of Nixon aide John Ehrlichmann, "When the President says 'jump,' the secretary should only ask, 'how high?'" The government was now going to be run from the White House. The new department heads would be political nonentities selected for their loyalty to the president. As Peter G. Peterson, a secretary of commerce known for strong argument in the inner councils of the administration, said, he was fired because "[his] calves were too thick and [he] could not click his heels."[22]

Another step in the Nixon strategy was budget reductions, discussed in more detail in Chapter 22. Nixon aides told a shocked Congress that the president had a right to reduce or eliminate any appropriation it made.

A third approach was to control the writing of

regulations by agencies. Regulations in welfare were extensively rewritten to reduce expenditures on the poor, while labor department regulations were rewritten to reduce federal controls in job training.[23]

A fourth measure crucial to the Nixon strategy was to politicize the career civil service. Positions just below the top in both line and staff agencies (for example, the assistant directors of OMB), which had been filled historically by civil servants, were now given to presidential appointees. These appointees then went after civil servants with a vengeance, transferring some, pressuring others to resign, and replacing them with loyal allies who were appointed only through subversion of the civil service system.[24] In fairness to the Nixon administration, there is little question that many key administrators did not share the president's policy preferences.[25]

Nixon and his aides saw the bureaucracy as the villain of the American political system, because bureaucrats had discretion to act on their own. But in the words of Peter Woll and Rochelle Jones,

---

The bureaucracy is at least as accountable and controlled as the original three branches. It sometimes exercises discretion, but so do the other branches. It is checked by and acts as a check upon the other branches. It is not elected, but is responsive to political constituencies, some of the components of which are elected. It is often rigid and wrong, but these traits are not exclusively those of bureaucrats. Presidents and congressmen too have been known to possess them.[26]

The Nixon attempt to dominate the federal government failed when the Watergate scandal toppled the president and his key aides. Its immediate impact was to make coordination among Congress, president, and the bureaucracy more difficult.[27] A suspicious Congress now examines presidential proposals for reorganization, budget impoundment, personnel appointments, and a host of other matters more carefully. After the Nixon experience, congressmen are much more suspicious and wary of presidential overtures.

Career civil servants are also careful and chary. Some of their concerns are discussed in the chapters on personnel. We can note here that the practice of politicizing high positions formerly held by civil servants continued and grew in the Carter administration. One veteran observer and former official, James Sundquist, believes that federal administrative capacity has declined as a result. "The more enterprising of the careerists tended to leave; others tended to avoid responsibility and identification with the party in power."[28] All of these measures reduce cooperation and coordination and the likelihood of getting the job done.

The 1980 National Academy Proposals

About the time the Reagan administration was preparing to take office, the National Academy of Public Administration issued a report entitled *A Presidency for the 1980s,* which had been two years in the making. Some of its features were warmly welcomed by the incoming administration, notably the wider use proposed for the president's cabinet as a coordinating device, greater concern for organizational and management questions in the OMB, and a reduction in the size of the White House staff. There were also excellent chapters on the departments and agencies and ways to involve career officials more actively in policy and leadership. Stress was also put on relations with Congress and the tendency of that body to legislate in great detail concerning internal matters that are the province of the president. "A president who attempts to manage the details of government from the center dooms himself to frustration and an image of ineffectiveness," said the academy report. Accordingly, "far greater weight should be given in recruitment and promotion to substantive and managerial competence." Since this report is the latest broad survey of the presidency and occupies a position similar to that of the Brownlow Committee of 1937 and the Hoover Commissions of 1949 and 1955, the entire report deserves careful study and discussion.

THE DILEMMA OF THE CHIEF EXECUTIVE

Can the chief executive always be trusted?[29] Should the president alone, for example, have the power to involve the United States in war? No individual, it is argued, is that trustworthy, a belief demonstrated by business executives who increasingly now prefer group decision to individual decision on questions of major concern. In the past, when autocratic power appeared in business, the results have almost always been disastrous, and the day of that power is now over.[30]

Final answers to the problem of overconcentrated power at the top of American government have not been found, but a number of alternatives have been offered. These include the following:

More extensive use of the cabinet. The cabinet might be allowed to play a more prominent role in decision making and planning and in coordination generally, as happened when Ronald Reagan became president. If this method works well in other countries—and by and large it does[31]—then there is reason to believe that it could become an equally successful device in the United States. Its record in several states, however, indicates that at least at the state level cabinet government makes policy coordination all but impossible.

A modified system of cabinet government. Since the time of Woodrow Wilson, at least, all presidents, and Ronald Reagan most of all, have "cultivated" Congress. The president and his cabinet officials all have special legislative assistants to handle routine relations with Congress. During recent administrations, the presidential liaison staffs were considerably strengthened. In addition, the president holds many informal briefing sessions with key members of Congress, and activist presidents are constantly on the telephone to the Hill. It has been suggested that this process might be in some degree institutionalized and made to include some of the best features of cabinet government as it is practiced in Britain, for example.

Greater responsibilities for political parties.[32] These organizations are not even mentioned in the federal Constitution but have evolved as a result of a demand inherent in the system of government that the Constitution created. As the work of govern-

ment becomes of increasing concern to the citizen, one or both of the major political parties might continue their evolution and try harder to carry out the programs they guarantee in campaign pledges. Such an attempt might even be good politics.

New modes of planning. Possibly something more than OMB, the Domestic Council, and the Council of Economic Advisers is needed as overall planning mechanisms. We return to this issue in Chapter 10.

Whatever solution is found, of course, is likely to be a combination of these remedies and others not yet conceived, and it will develop through the usual trial-and-error methods. Certainly much more is needed to overcome the problems of fragmentation, if the federal, state, and local governments are going to be able to meet the policy challenges of the economy, energy, and the environment, as well as the other foreign and domestic problems that face the country.

SUMMARY

We have shown that because of federalism, there are a variety of chief executives in the United States, ranging from "weak," or figurehead, mayors to presidents of the United States who in time of crisis have had enormous powers—greater even than executives in so-called responsible (cabinet) governments. A number of chief executives in the United States are efficient managers, like the managers of larger cities such as Cincinnati. They all recommend policy and depend upon the ups and downs of politics for their tenure. Some chief executives coordinate through their cabinets and delegation; some try to do most things themselves or rely upon staff agencies and departments of administration combining financial, personnel, and planning powers. Professionalization is strongest at the local and county levels. Popularity contests often decide state and national elections to the governorship or the presidency.

Since the short ballot and budgetary reforms commencing in the early 20th century, however, most higher executives in state and local government have had more coordinative and leadership powers, and hence more accountability for results, than was true under America's separation-of-powers doctrine in the 19th century. The civil service idea has gradually grown since the last quarter of the 19th century; but the coordination of elective and civil service programs is uneven and overall does not operate as smoothly as in countries such as France, Britain, Germany, Canada, and other Western democracies. There is more mobility from the private sector to elective office, and back again, than in the countries just mentioned, and hence elective office has not been made a career to the extent it has in those countries. Political parties are not so influential from the highest to the lowest levels of government. Finally, in the competition of legislatures and elected executives for control of administration, the pendulum has swung in one direction or another at different times. Overall, the responsibility of executives has increased during the past 50 years. This was also true in Washington until Watergate (circa 1973) when Congress began to interfere increasingly in internal administration. Under President Reagan, presidential influence began to increase in 1981.

NOTES

1. Bill Gilbert, *This City, This Man: The Cookingham Era in Kansas City* (Washington: International City Management Association [ICMA], 1977), p. 146.

2. Nowhere has this problem been more understandingly and forcefully dealt with than by Norton E. Long in *The Policy* (Chicago: Rand McNally, 1962). The first two chapters are especially pertinent.

3. For an objective appraisal, by a Canadian, consult J. A. Corry, *Elements of Democratic Government* (New York: Oxford University Press, 1947).

4. These statements were offered in a debate, carried on in the pages of *Public Administration Review,* between Harold Laski, the eminent British political scientist, and Don K. Price, who later became dean of the Littauer School of Public Administration at Harvard University. Price's original article appeared in *Public Administration Review* 3 (Autumn 1943): 317; Laski's article was in *Public Administra-*

tion Review 4 (Autumn 1944): 359; and Price's reply appeared in 4: 340.

5. For an introduction to the literature critical of the presidential system, see Henry Hazlitt, *A New Constitution Now* (New York: McGraw-Hill, 1942); Thomas K. Finletter, *Can Representative Government Do the Job?* (New York: Reynal & Hitchcock, 1945); W. Y. Elliott, *The Need for Constitutional Reform* (New York: Whittlesey House, 1935); and Woodrow Wilson, *Congressional Government* (1885; reprint ed., New York: Meridian Books, 1956).

6. William L. Morrow, *Public Administration: Politics and the Political System* (New York: Random House, 1975), pp. 111–112.

7. On the presidency, see Edward S. Corwin, *The President: Office and Powers,* 4th ed. (New York: New York University Press, 1958); Harold Laski, *The American Presidency* (New York: Harper & Row, 1940); Pendleton Herring, *Presidential Leadership* (New York: Farrar & Rinehart, 1940); Clinton Rossiter, *The American Presidency* (New York: Harcourt, Brace & World, 1956); Louis Brownlow, *The American Presidency* (Chicago: University of Chicago Press, 1949); Sidney Hyman, *The American Presidency* (New York: Harper & Row, 1954); Richard Neustadt, *Presidential Leadership* (New York: Wiley, 1980); and Thomas E. Cronin, *The State of the Presidency* (Boston: Little, Brown, 1980).

8. Joseph A. Schlesinger, "The Politics of the Executive," in *Politics in the American States,* ed. Herbert Jacob and Kenneth N. Vines, 2d ed. (Boston: Little, Brown, 1971).

9. Thad L. Beyle and J. Oliver Williams, eds., *The American Governor in Behavioral Perspective* (New York: Harper & Row, 1971), p. 2.

10. T. McN. Simpson, "President-To-Be" (Manuscript, 1977). ch. 2.

11. Deil S. Wright, "Executive Leadership in State Administration," *Midwest Journal of Political Science,* February 1967; and F. Ted Hebert, "State Service Executives and Administrative Reorganization" (Paper presented to the 1980 national meeting of the American Society for Public Administration [ASPA]).

12. *The Municipal Yearbook,* (Washington: ICMA, 1967).

13. Russell M. Ross and Kenneth F. Millsap, *The Relative Power Position of Mayors in Mayor Council Cities* (Iowa City: University of Iowa, Laboratory for Political Research, 1971), p. 16.

14. Jeffrey L. Pressman, "Preconditions for Mayoral Leadership," *American Political Science Review* 66 (June 1972): 511–524.

15. Russell D. Murphy, *Political Entrepreneurs and Urban Poverty* (Lexington, Mass.: Heath, 1971).

16. Pressman, "Preconditions."

17. Pressman, "Preconditions."

18. Chester Newland, *Professional Public Executives* (Washington: ASPA, 1980), p. 166.

19. President's Committee on Administrative Management, *Report of the President's Committee* (Washington: U.S. Government Printing Office, 1937).

20. See Herring, *Presidential Leadership.*

21. Commission on Organization of the Executive Branch of the Government, *General Management of the Executive Branch* (Washington: U.S. Government Printing Office, 1949); the second Hoover Commission, which reported in 1955, had little to say about the organization of the presidency and recommended no changes.

22. Richard P. Nathan, *The Plot That Failed: Nixon and the Administrative Presidency* (New York: Wiley, 1975), p. 68.

23. Nathan, *The Plot That Failed,* p. 75.

24. Frederick C. Mosher et al., *Watergate: Implications for Responsible Government* (New York: Harper & Row, 1974), pp. 63–76.

25. Joel D. Auerbach and Bert A. Rockman, "Clashing Beliefs Within the Executive Branch," *American Political Science Review* 70 (June 1976): 456–468.

26. Peter Woll and Rochelle Jones, "The Bureaucracy as a Check Upon the President," *The Bureaucrat,* April 1974, p. 19.

27. See Harvey C. Mansfield, Sr., *Congress Against the President* (New York: Praeger, 1975).

28. James L. Sundquist, "The Crisis of Competence in Our National Government," *Political Science Quarterly,* Summer 1980, pp. 202–203.

29. The Vietnam war brought this question to a focus. See, for example, Senator J. William Fulbright, Chairman of the Senate Foreign Relations Committee, *The Arrogance of Power* (New York: Vintage Books, 1966).

30. For an example, see T. A. Wise, "The Coup d'État at Interpublic," *Fortune,* February 1968. Shortly after this article appeared, the leading actor in this drama was forced to resign.

31. Even in the Soviet Union, a cabinetlike device, the Presidium, is one of the most successful features of government. This body deals with the coordination of domestic and foreign affairs simultaneously, encouraging the development of a wide strategy. On the experiences of some countries with a cabinet, see Marshall E. Dimock, *The New American Political Economy* (New York: Harper & Row, 1962), ch. 14.

32. A proposal discussed in the report of the Committee on Political Parties of the American Political Science Association, *Toward a More Responsible Two-Party System* (New York: Holt, Rinehart & Winston, 1950).

PART 3

PROGRAM MANAGEMENT

Andrea Beatty, city manager, Bellevue, Washington, meets with aides. (Photo courtesy of the city of Bellevue)

9

Managing and Leading

Of the various executive abilities, no one excited more anxious concern than that of placing the interests of our fellow-citizens in the hands of honest men, with understanding sufficient for their stations.

Thomas Jefferson

In this chapter we examine the nature of the manager's work, the skills a manager needs, different leadership styles, and the importance of communication in managerial leadership.

PRODUCTION MANAGEMENT IDENTIFIED

How does this group of nine chapters differ from those considered in Part 1 and Part 2? It is the difference between top management on a government-wide basis, and what is called program, line, or action management. In this part of the book we shall assume that the reader is a city manager, a department head, or the manager of a bureau such as social security, child welfare, census, or employment service—anything that has a discrete identity and that directly aids consumers. This, at the second level, is where most of the work of the world is done, in business as well as in government. Moreover, it is the skill, quality, and efficiency with which these consumer services operate that spell the main difference among countries, political systems, and success and survival. The level of line management, more than any other factor, determines the payoff. In the competition between capitalism and socialism, for example, it is at the level of program or production more than at any other level that long-range results are determined. In a sense, therefore, this group of chapters dealing with leadership, planning, organization, supervision, motivation, coordination, control, productivity, and communication is the very heart of our subject. Anyone who masters these concepts and integrates them in his mind is already a manager, and truly great managers are rare.

The successful manager is, above all, an integrator, one who sees that the different parts of an organization work together to accomplish a task. In this sense the manager is like a quarterback who directs his team to victory. The quarterback cannot win the game by himself, nor can the manager do his agency's or unit's job all by himself. The manager's job is to integrate the work of the other members of his organization so that goals are reached.

CASE STUDY: CHALLENGE AND RESPONSE

An example of such integration comes from the World War I experience of Ezio Pinza, who later become a famous opera singer and Broadway star. As an officer in the Italian army, Pinza was given the job of moving a large number of artillery pieces to a mountaintop, where they would face the opposing Austrian forces. To do the job, Pinza was assigned 200 soldiers, who were in a nearby rest camp. These soldiers bitterly resented the task, because they felt they had earned the right to a respite after months of hard fighting at the front. Even though they respected Pinza's competence and were helped by army trucks, they were not close to finishing the job on schedule. "There was no laughter, no singing, and very little progress despite the great show they put on at hauling and pulling." Pinza's superiors were becoming impatient; how was he going to persuade the men to pull together as an enthusiastic team? "Instead of issuing another futile order to keep pulling this or that gun upward, I did a little climbing myself to study the terrain, and a little figuring, and told the men, 'This gun has to be moved to that point over there, and it has to be done today. No one will leave until we do it, even if we have to keep at it through the night. But the moment the gun is where I want it, the day's work is finished and you can go back to the camp.'" The result was that the soldiers reached the goal an hour after lunch and went home. They used their brains, as well as their muscles, to do the job, and they laughed and sang. Pinza had done so well that he was sent all over the front whenever artillery had to be moved fast. Later on, he was a great singer; at this point, he showed he was a great *manager*.

WHO IS A MANAGER?

The best definition of a manager is anyone who thinks like a manager, that is, anyone who thinks consecutively, practically, and inspirationally and who sets a good example until the job is done. Such people succeed time after time. Others seem not to have the faintest idea of how to start.

Very few people have managerial-executive ability. Many have no interest in it. Among those who do, the main reason for their difference is their skill at synthesis, in the vernacular, their ability to make everything come together. In certain individuals their innate executive skills show up early in life. Others, equally successful, develop these skills over longer periods of time, frequently after intense self-discipline and concentration. Because the acid test of executive capacity is synthesis, formal measurement of managerial capability may be misleading and even injurious.

The qualities of a successful manager grow out of experience and cannot be judged by the number of degrees a person has. As a matter of fact, unless the person has a strong personality and character, formal education may prove a disservice to the potential manager, because such persons often substitute technique for purpose and a facade for competence.

The manager combines opposite traits and makes of them a unity. He is logical and also temperamental, tough and idealistic. Consider the following managerial qualities.

- The manager is able to analyze opportunities, problems, alliances, competitors, public relations, and the future. We examine these concerns in Chapter 10.
- The manager creates an organization, delegating step by step, while he does so. He lets his subordinates pick their subordinates. We study these concerns in Chapter 11.
- The manager challenges subordinates by giving them responsibility. He encourages initiative and innovation and supports those who make honest mistakes. He focuses on results when supervising his subordinates. These concerns are the subject of Chapter 12.
- The manager motivates his employees positively. He knows that giving credit for dedicated work is a powerful incentive, and he respects individual differences and idiosyncrasies. These matters are discussed in Chapter 13.
- The manager works hard to make his unit a team, knowing that work performance must be coordinated if the job is to be done effectively. Chapter 14 deals with this topic.
- The manager knows that he must be able to keep track of job performance if the work is to be done and if future work is to improve. Such concerns are dealt with in Chapters 15, 16, and 17.

The following case study presents a manager doing many of these things.

CASE STUDY: PRACTICAL INVENTION

LeRoy Harlow, city manager of Fargo, North Dakota, was inspecting the city's sewerage disposal plant. During his visit, he noted that an open space of 75 feet separated the main pump from the filtration building. Harlow found out from the plant superintendent that there was only one employee on the night shift and that he had to cross the open space once an hour. Concerned over the recent accidental death of an employee in another city department, Harlow asked whether the employee was in touch with any other city department during his shift, in case he was overcome by gas, fell down the stairs, or stumbled in the open space during a blizzard. The answer was no, the employee was all alone. Harlow then asked the superintendent whether he thought it would be a good idea to build a covered passage across the open space. The superintendent replied that it would cost too much. Then they both looked into the cost of laying several lengths of large, steel culvert pipe from door to door. The cost was much lower, so the pipe was laid. Arrangements were also made for the night-shift worker to call the police department once an hour. If the worker did not call, the police could send a patrol car to see whether he was all right.

In this situation, then, the manager countered a potential problem by putting together a solution that involved the sewerage disposal superintendent, the night-shift worker, and the police department. All worked together to avert a terrible accident.[1]

It is sometimes said that the best manager is hard-nosed. If hard-nosed means being shrewd, a good strategist, competitive, efficient, and economy-minded, combined with setting a good example, inspiring others, giving them credit, delegating responsibility and seeing others expand and grow, then hard-nosed is what a good manager should try to be. But another connotation ought to be avoided, that of bluffer, four-flusher, or bully. Such a person has little or no sense of ethics. Eventually he does the organization more harm than good. He lowers the organization's reputation, which it may take years to recover.

An example of a manager of outstanding capability combined with serious weakness is Billy Martin, manager of several major league baseball teams. After having directed the Texas Rangers and the New York Yankees, he took over the Oakland A's. In 1980 he brought the A's up from last place in their division to second place by emphasizing baseball fundamentals, aggressive tactics, and hustle. Unfortunately, he has had trouble drawing the line between assertiveness and fighting. In 1978, in the middle of a game he flew into a rage and wanted to punch his star hitter, Reggie Jackson. One of his numerous fistfights inside and outside bars cost him his job as Yankee manager. Martin's lack of self-control is the chief reason why his career as a manager has been so tempestuous.

DECISION MAKING

Every manager must make decisions every day in the course of his work, and he must have the authority to do so. Most managerial decisions are merely *routine,* others may be called *tactical,* more important ones are *strategic,* and those at the highest level may be *critical* in that the life of the program or even the future of the nation—as in certain decisions in the White House or the State Department—may be at stake.

Management in Action

Decision making is no mere intellectual exercise; it is management in action. For the most able managers, moreover, decision making is more than problem solving in the sense of stewing over a troublesome issue and neglecting other matters. Beyond a particular decision and of greater moment is the long-range strategy of accomplishing some social good. It may be parks, or playgrounds, or education, or greater production; but in a realistic sense, it is always something that has been clearly defined.

An illustration, taken from the recent experience of a New England town, underscores the need for astute managers. A developer proposed building a shopping complex in a small town. The town manager had surveys made by engineers and architects and found that if the shopping center were built, many downtown merchants would be put out of business, the demands on schools and highways would be greatly increased, and the center of town would rapidly wither and die. The town would pay greatly increased taxes for the new development while tax revenues from downtown merchants would dry up.

Having made his economic survey, the town manager next turned for advice to the environmental authorities at the regional and state levels and to the appropriate planning and zoning boards in the town and region. He consulted the school board and its administrators. The downtown merchants formed a protective association, which raised a war chest to fight the new shopping center. The taxpayers' association moved into the picture. Someone came up with the idea, which others characterized as crazy, of building a dome over the downtown shopping area, thereby saving heat and adding to the attractiveness of the central area of the town as a shopping center. A bus route was speedily organized. Many public hearings and protest meetings soon took place. The town manager brought in state and federal authorities. Throughout negotiations, the town manager acted like an executive, drawing on many experts who had specialized knowledge. He kept calm, realizing that if he made too many false moves he might be seeking employment elsewhere. Eventually, the developers lost and the long-range view prevailed.

Decision making is involved in the work of judges, researchers, model builders, and those concerned with game theory. In each situation the approach and the methods have something to contribute to the process of decision making. But beyond this, decision making also requires intuition and judgment gained from experience and from wide reading, observation, and reflection.

As former British Prime Minister Winston Churchill once said, "You don't have to have a lot of brains to make the right decision, *if you have all the facts. Where you need the brains is to get the facts on which to make the decision.*"[2] Churchill certainly did not mean that one has to get literally all the facts, but rather the most important facts relative to the decision.

Three Models

Three principal models relating to decision making in administration today are the *positivist,* the *incrementalist* (or strategic), and the *mixed-scanning.*[3]

Positivist. The positivist model was first prominently suggested by Nobel Prize winner Herbert Simon.[4] In developing this model, Simon ac-

knowledged his debt to Chester Barnard, an American business executive in the first third of this century who wrote one of the most influential books on management. Barnard believed that decisions fall into two main classes: positive decisions to do something—to direct action, to cease action, to prevent action—and negative decisions, which are decisions not to decide.[5] Simon developed a logic of administration in which he assumed that every executive action involves a decision aimed at advancing group goals and values. Employee cooperation is secured by appealing to their self-interest. When self-interest and hence employee cooperation have been aroused as a result of a decision on objectives, every administrative move thereafter becomes a calculus between relative advantage and disadvantage to employees, on the basis of which the employees cooperate or remain passive.

Incrementalist. Opposing this positivist view, Charles E. Lindblom, in an article entitled "The Art of Muddling Through,"[6] took the incrementalist position. He denied that positivism has anywhere near the degree of influence claimed for it and argued that the results would be less than desirable if it had. Decision, said Lindblom, is the result of a cumulative process. The method is largely by trial and error; mistakes are made and then corrected. Decision, therefore, is evolutionary and experimental. We discuss Lindblom's ideas at greater length in the next chapter, which deals with planning.

Mixed-Scanning. In proposing the mixed-scanning model, Amitai Etzioni tried to build a compromise on middle ground. Positivism, he said, assumes far too extreme a degree of control on the part of the decision maker, while incrementalism assumes too little. Etzioni believed that there are both fundamental and incremental decisions and that all must be viewed in relation to strategy. In effect, a decision should be seen as if through two cameras—hence the term mixed-scanning—one with a wide-angle lens and the other zeroing in on what must be seen in depth.

To the practical administrator making decisions as a supervisor, it seems obvious that there are various kinds and levels of decision. Who makes them and with what preparation is important. The lower down and the nearer the point of action most of them can be made, the better the results will be for the administrative process. The more experience in decision making supervisors can gain in their formative years, the more likely they are to succeed later in top management positions when policy issues and decisions concerning them occupy a greater proportion of their time. It should also be noted, moreover, that these major policy issues do not conveniently present themselves at top echelons exclusively; for, in fact, they permeate the organization. In a program for the benefit of a minority group, for example, it may be important how its members are treated in the administration of the program. Or the manner in which a bureau chief in a labor department handles labor relations in his own agency may determine his standing with outside labor groups. Even small things, a Chinese philosopher once said, have a way of becoming important when one stubs one's toe on them.

The following case deals with decision making. Which of the three models discussed above would be most useful in this case?

CASE STUDY: THE CONDITIONAL APPOINTMENT

John Steele, aged 42 and deputy commissioner of agriculture in the government of a rural state, was a troubled man. He had graduated with honors from the Agricultural School at Cornell, served as a county agent for four years, and then moved to the state university, where he had been in charge of the county agent program. As a county agent he had always been successful because he spent a lot of time talking with dairy farmers about better methods and getting them to take a more active part in county committees and other participatory programs run by the state Department of Agriculture. Under a liberal governor he had also been in charge of one of the offices of the soil-conservation program and had directed the regional planning office that reported to the state capital. He liked the state in which he worked, owned a home, had two teenaged children in school, and didn't want to move, sideways and out, that is; but he did want to move up.

Steele was troubled because the new state governor had asked him to come over and talk about another job. Steele knew what the prospective job was, all right. It was the post of commissioner of agriculture, the highest job in the department that the state could give. Not bad at 42. The trouble was that the governor was a conservative, and his ideas and Steele's were considerably at variance.

After a few pleasantries in the governor's office, the governor remarked that before offering his guest the job, he wanted to talk over some policy issues. "You know," he said, "that I'm pictured as a strong governor. I have definite ideas of policy, and I intend to see that they're carried out." He then explained in his suave, reassuring way that he liked and admired government career officials with executive ability and leadership qualities, one reason being that he himself had gained his money and reputation as a self-made businessman. "But as you know," he added, "I won't have anyone on my team who isn't prepared to follow my policies. I don't want to have to fire him. I want to avoid appointing him in the first place."

John Steele could see that he was in for serious cross-examination.

"Now, take this new law giving towns the right to give farmers a tax break by putting their farms under a 'use' category instead of a 'resale' category. I know you've worked on that program. You want to save the farms from the developers by taxing their land on the basis of income produced instead of on their resale value for out-of-state buyers." The governor then explained that he was in favor of the objective but not the means. "I'm going to try to get the legislature to change the law," he said, "and when I do, I want my commissioner to support me."

"What do you favor?" asked Steele, in one of his few chances to speak.

"I'm in favor of a land trust," replied the governor. "You know what that is, a scheme where a lot of people in the same locality get together, put their land in a trust, and agree not to sell to outsiders but only to the trust itself." He then explained that the present law was costly to the state because the state treasury had to pay the difference between what the municipality received from taxation according to use compared to the higher amount based on resale value. Also, said the governor, the trust idea was strictly private whereas the tax rebate idea tended toward government control of the economy.

"The other thing we might disagree on," continued the governor, without allowing Steele to say what he thought about the first issue, "is this. I don't like the socialistic tendency of these state, regional, and local planning boards; and I'd like to try to do away with them, with the possible exception of the local ones. I know you headed a regional board at one time, and I understand you did a good job of it. But I don't think the state and regional boards have the right to tell the local board what it can and cannot do. I have two objections. First thing you know, you'll have state planning. And second, local people ought to decide. If they want to have a developer come in and change their landscape, that's their business. I believe in self-determination.

"Think it over," said the governor, in his most ingratiating manner, "and let me know on Monday. I know that if you say you'll support my policies, you will. I don't know anyone in the state who'd make nearly so good an executive." So the two men shook hands, and Steele went home.

"Well," said his wife Martha. "I see he offered you the job."

"Do I look that glum?" replied her husband. Then Steele proceeded to tell his wife about the governor's proposition.

At the end, Martha said, "Do you think you could support him on the tax rebate issue and in curtailing the activities of the planning boards?"

"I hardly think so," replied her husband.

"Well, I'll tell you what you can do on Monday," said Martha. "You can say you'll support his programs if he gets his legislation through."

Steele interrupted, "But I'd have to appear before the legislative committees—that wouldn't work."

"Well, you could ask him if you wanted to," his wife said defensively. "The second thing you might do is tell him you want to stay in your present position. You're young yet, and you'll get another chance. After all, governors are elected for only two-year terms. The third thing you might do is agree to stay, at least for the present, and start looking around in other states or in Washington for a better job. But I don't favor that much because I like it here. I'm afraid I'm not much help," Martha apologized.

"Oh, yes you are," said her husband. "I'll bet by Monday I'll know exactly what I want to do."

In this case the mixed-scanning mode was applied. Steele decided to take the long-range view and refuse the job.

POSDCORB, THE FUNCTIONS OF MANAGEMENT

One of the first attempts to define the functions of the program manager was made by Luther Gulick and Lyndall Urwick during the 1930s in a volume which both edited, *Papers on the Science of Administration.*[7] After reviewing the ideas of Henri Fayol, Frederick Taylor and his disciples, and others, Gulick and Urwick formulated a list of seven functions that they considered to be the substance of the administrator's role. In recent times this list has been criticized as incomplete and unduly concerned with engineering concepts, but it serves to introduce the specifics of the subject. The word POSDCORB (Planning, Organizing, Staffing, Directing, Coordinating, [O], Reporting, Budgeting), invented to identify the various operational aspects of the work of a chief executive, is made up of the initials of the seven functions on the list.

1. *Planning* is working out in broad outline the things that need to be done and the methods for doing them to accomplish the purpose set for the enterprise.
2. *Organizing* is establishing the formal structure of authority through which work is subdivided, defined, and coordinated.
3. *Staffing* is bringing in and training the necessary personnel and maintaining favorable conditions of work.
4. *Directing* is the continuous task of making decisions and embodying them in specific and general orders and instructions and serving as the leader of the enterprise.
5. *Coordinating* is the all-important duty of interrelating the various parts of the work.
6. *Reporting* is keeping those to whom the executive is responsible informed as to what is going on. It includes keeping himself and his subordinates informed through records, research, and inspection.
7. *Budgeting* is allocating funds, fiscal planning, accounting, and control.

This list pays little attention to the human element, which later students of the subject have found to be important in administration; nor does it say much about economic policy or the public interest, neither of which can be ignored in government or in industrial administration today. Nevertheless, POSDCORB does identify the main steps in the operating process for which the chief executive is responsible. We shall examine each of these steps in future chapters.

EXECUTIVE TRAITS

Although POSDCORB is a useful list of the functions of management, it does not tell anything about the traits of character and skills that mark a successful executive.

First of all, as has been noted, is the manager's distinctive ability to create a synthesis of organizational resources to solve problems. Second, is his ability to synthesize all facets of his personality in such a way that he is competent to lead an organization at a particular *time* and in a particular *situation* in order to achieve its socially approved goals, whether they be business profits or carrying out a legislative mandate. A third ability is to perform so that the result can stand the test of future time as well as present time.

These abilities required of managers make it impossible for them to succeed by purely formal means. H. Edward Wrapp, a professor of business policy, warns that executives who go by the textbook are not good at synthesis or integration. More interested in form than content, says Wrapp, they would rather define, categorize, and quantify a job than accomplish it. Elaborate planning studies, reorganizations, and use of consultants are symptoms of this executive disease. The best managers develop in a turbulent, changing environment, in which they learn to deal calmly with the unexpected and become familiar with the management "laws" listed in Box 9.1. While these laws are obviously tongue-in-cheek proverbs, anyone who has worked in an organization for a while will recognize situations that the laws accurately describe. But since the "textbook" manager works in a more controlled environment with lengthy leadtime, where everything is carefully studied beforehand, he is unlikely to learn how to cope with the unexpected.[8]

Similarly, the skills that will make a successful executive cannot be accurately judged by formal means. It is questionable, for example, whether it makes sense for the prestigious Wharton Business School to reject students who have not mastered calculus. It seems more likely that Wharton will reject some outstanding future managers as a result. Likewise, it seems quite possible that the army's current requirement that officers must write good seminar papers or be retired before reaching the rank of lieutenant colonel will lead

Box 9.1

THE MANAGEMENT LAWS OF MURPHY AND HIS FRIENDS

MURPHY'S LAW
If anything can go wrong, it will—and at the worst possible moment.

HUNT'S LAW
Everything takes twice as long and costs 50 percent more than the estimates.

RUDIN'S LAW
In a crisis that forces choosing among alternatives, most people will choose the worst possible one.

CHISHOLM'S LAW
In any collection of data, the figures that are obviously correct contain the errors.

FINAGLE'S LAW
The information we have is not what we want, the information we want is not what we need, and the information we need is not available.

SOURCE: Reprinted, by permission of the publisher, from MUDDLING THROUGH: THE ART OF PROPERLY UNBUSINESSLIKE MANAGEMENT, by Roger A. Golde, © 1976 by AMACOM, a division of American Management Associations, p. 161. All rights reserved.

to the loss of talented field commanders. What if General George Patton, the brilliant World War II commander, had not done well at writing papers?[9]

Further evidence that the criterion of standardization is the wrong approach to evaluating performance and productivity is found in the researches of Chester Barnard, the principal proponent of the synthesis theory. According to him the most important factors determining success are nonrational. They lie in the areas of judgment, taste, and the proper thing to do. They are prophetic concerning the future. They are sensitive to public opinion. They are genuine, not ersatz.

The ability to synthesize is one of the four skills that management professor Ichak Adizes claims successful executives need.[10] One is production, or the necessary technical or functional knowledge to understand whether or not a job is being done correctly. Another skill is implementation, the ability to plan work and direct subordinates to do it. A third skill is entrepreneurship, or the ability to be a self-starter, to change goals and strategies when necessary. The last, which we have stressed, is synthesis, or integration, the process whereby individual strategies and goals become group and organizational goals. Adizes argues that the successful executive has skill in all areas. If he is deficient in one area, trouble is likely.

One type of trouble is encountered by the manager without production skills. Regardless of his other strengths, this manager will eventually flounder because he does not adequately understand the environment and/or technology in which he works. Likewise, those without entrepreneurial skill cannot adjust to change, and those who are not implementers will be unable to organize the agency well enough to achieve goals. Managers without integrative abilities will be in the worst shape of all.

Would not the ideal executive be the one who combines all four skills? Perhaps so, but since Adizes has found that managers who have all four skills in equal amounts are rare, he recommends team management and maximum delegation of authority to those with the skills to accomplish a job. Managers should take an inventory, he thinks, to understand better their strengths and weaknesses. In this way, they can develop weak areas or encourage subordinates to help them in those areas. Barnard also thought that teams as well as individuals provide the secret of efficiency. Members of a good team supplement one another, and they volunteer to do things not expected of them.

Perhaps the most valuable trait to be encouraged in managers is the ability to work on a team.

Box 9.2

A DIVERGENT VIEW

Admiral Hyman Rickover, manager of the Navy's nuclear submarine programs from the 1950s to 1982, has some stimulating and unconventional thoughts on management. Rickover is convinced that it is impossible to teach management in classes or from books and does not believe that there are generally applicable rules of management. Rather, he feels, the manager must first immerse himself in program details and technology so that he understands exactly what it is he is managing. There are far too many generalist managers in government (and business), states Rickover, who move from one type of agency to another without mastering the specifics of any one management.

Rickover offers a set of principles for achieving mastery in management:

First is *ownership.* A person who feels he does not *own* a job and will not remain in it indefinitely will not act in the long-range interest of the agency. "We need to make it challenging and rewarding for managers to remain in one organization for more than a few years." If a job is seen as a mere stepping stone, the organization will suffer.

Second is *responsibility.* Joint accountability and team management are anathema to Rickover because they mean to him that no one is responsible. "Unless the one person truly responsible can be identified when something goes wrong, then no one has been responsible."

Third is *attention to detail.* The tendency to avoid detail as one is promoted must be avoided. Otherwise, subordinates will not do so either. This is particularly true in technical areas " . . . when the details are ignored, the project fails; no infusion of lofty ideals or policy can then correct the situation."

At the same time, *priorities must be established* so that one does not become lost in trivial detail. "A tendency of human beings is to while away time with unimportant matters because these do not require mental effort or energy."

Fifth is *accurate information.* "I require regular, periodic reports . . . in plain English" from my subordinates. This involves "constant drudgery," but is an absolute necessity. This constant checking should be done in writing, so that one is not dependent on memory. This way, a permanent record will exist.

Facing the facts is also required. " . . . one must brutally make needed changes despite considerable costs and schedule delay. Figuratively, (the manager) must, if necessary, kill his own child, regardless of the consequences to himself. After all, he is the trustee for the government; he is not the owner."

Hard work is Rickover's primary admonition. The aspects of management discussed above are not easy to implement, and hard work yields benefits in itself. "A manager who does not work hard or devote extra effort can not expect his people to do so. . . . Hard work compensates for many shortcomings. You may not be the smartest or most knowledgeable person. But if you dedicate yourself to your job and put in the required effort, your people will follow your lead."

SOURCE: Adapted from Admiral Hyman Rickover, "Management in Government," *Management,* September 1979, pp. 16–19.

Teamwork relies on good will instead of authority. Its psychological base is the feeling it creates in subordinates that their personal growth and the organization's welfare are equally bound up together. Anything that looks like standardization, centralization, rules and regulations, and machinelike precision is therefore the enemy of this psychological truth.

Interestingly enough, in large organizations, the manager spends less than half of his time dealing with subordinates. He devotes much of the day to horizontal relationships. Rather than giving or receiving orders, he has to coordinate his activities with other organizational units. These units may lack authority over the manager, just as he lacks authority over them. They include groups to which he has "contracted out" assignments or groups that have contracted assignments out to him. Units within the police and traffic departments, for example, may have to work closely together and may swap assignments and resources. Other groups may control access to equipment and space that the manager wants to use. Agency officials who want to apply for a grant will work closely with the departmental grant officer.[11] These examples can be multiplied almost indefinitely. While we shall say more about techniques of coordination in Chapter 14, our point here is that the modern manager has to be an integrator *par excellence,* or he will never be able to accomplish the job.

The characteristics of teamwork strengthen the argument that executive performance cannot be judged by rigid standards. The supplementary aid and extra volunteer effort of team members are not recognized by classification of position and evaluation of technique. Furthermore, the skills of a team assembled for a particular purpose are not immediately transferable to a totally different situation without the team's undergoing a considerable period of regrouping and reorientation. That fact was Barnard's answer to the question why an efficient team of Bell Telephone executives was not moved into railroad management "to clean up the mess." He pointed out that skills may look transferable on paper, but subtle

rearrangements and modifications in the personalities of executives are constantly called forth by new stimuli. Just as there are differences among individuals, so each three-way relation among people, situations, and time is different.

Despite all the evidence that standardization has a chilling effect on organizational efficiency and morale, it is desirable to analyze managerial-executive traits for all action programs, whether at headquarters or in the field. But analysis should be made by the agency itself, not by a personnel or other central agency. Such analyses might be useful in peer evaluation and also in training. But like organization charts, most of the time they should be locked in a bottom drawer. There is no substitute for executives rating or "discovering" other executives. It may be not a neat and tidy method, but it works better than anything else.

LEADERSHIP

In administration, leadership is the principal means of overcoming program fragmentation, correcting the weaknesses of bureaucracy, substituting willing cooperation for rules authorized by top management and making it possible for people to enjoy their work as well as to earn a living. To achieve these ends, moreover, leadership must go beyond the routine variety to become entrepreneurial. It must be innovative, ready to break new ground, willing to experiment, and able to admit errors when experimental methods fail.

Even in highly technical fields, such as science and technology, leadership is necessary for program success. Professional musicians will attest to the importance of leadership in orchestral conducting. The great conductor Bruno Walter stated that technical knowledge of music is "a very small part" of the necessary skill of the conductor. Far more important is "how to handle people . . . how to influence musicians by word, by gesture or by looks . . .".[12]

There are many definitions of leadership, depending on the purpose and the professional predilections of the definer. With the role of the executive in mind, *leadership in administration means supplying the energy, the signals, and the example* needed to sustain cooperative activity in a program in which many individuals with formally assigned roles act to achieve a particular objective or set of objectives. Energy includes factors such as personality and values. Signals are communication, which may be silent as well as spoken, attitudinal as well as formalized in the written word. Supplying the example means active participation by the administrator as peer among peers. As Chris Chambliss, first baseman for the Atlanta Braves, said in 1980: "You can lead by example. I disagree with guys who want to lead by telling people what to do. Everybody here knows what to do. . . . It's a matter of doing things together."

Different Leadership Styles

Douglas McGregor, late professor of industrial management at the Massachusetts Institute of Technology, suggested two theories of leadership, X and Y. He stated that most contemporary organizations adhere to Theory X and operate according to a set of principles described as follows:[13]

1. People dislike work and will avoid it if possible.
2. Therefore, they must be threatened, coerced, and controlled if they are to work to fulfill organizational objectives.
3. People have little ambition, wish to be directed and to avoid responsibility, and desire security above everything else.

Organizations that subscribe to theory X implement these principles by outlining the one way to do a job, minimizing the amount of discretion allowed employees, and maximizing control over employees from the top. These procedures are certainly appropriate for a manager who believes in Theory $X;$ indeed, they are the only way to follow the principles of Theory X. Theory X advocates believe that employees use discretion only to

waste time. Employees are not naturally results-oriented, so the only way to ensure results is carefully to control all aspects of their conduct.

McGregor argues that management according to Theory X produces good results in very hard times when loss of a job means severe deprivation, such as losing one's house or even starving. But in times of affluence, unemployment insurance, and welfare, such basic subsistence needs may not be enough to motivate employees. As McGregor says, "Management cannot provide a man with self-respect, or with the respect of his fellows, or with the satisfaction of needs for self-fulfillment." But he goes on to say that management can encourage and enable its employees to seek these conditions for themselves, or it can thwart their efforts. Employees can be encouraged if managers subscribe to the principles of Theory $Y,$ which includes the following principles:

1. People do not dislike work.
2. Employees do not have to be threatened in order to make them work but can become self-directed.
3. Employees will be self-directed if, and only if, the work satisfies their ego and need for development.

President Dwight D. Eisenhower endorsed this positive approach when he said:

Leadership is a word and concept that has been more argued than almost any other I know. I am not one of the desk-pounding types that likes to stick out his jaw and look as if he is bossing the show. I would far rather get behind and, recognizing the frailties and the requirements of human nature, I would rather try to persuade a man to go along—because once I have persuaded him, he will stick. If I scare him, he will stay just as long as he is scared, and then he is gone.[14]

The distinction between Theory X and Theory Y is a useful way to begin thinking about differences in leadership styles. But most present-day research on leadership has advocated a contingency approach, tailoring techniques to fit the situation. These writers believe that one leadership style may work wonders in one kind of situation and be disastrous in another. Further, a manager is likely to have different types of employees. Some may like to be told in detail how to perform every aspect of a job, while others may chafe at such instructions. Other employees can be given an enormous amount of discretion and use it to do a job well, while still others would fail miserably if they were on their own in this way.

Robert Tannenbaum and Warren Schmidt point out that there are many leadership styles in between authoritarian and team leadership.[15] For example, the leader can work to persuade followers to accept his decision rather than simply give an order and leave it at that. Such an approach recognizes that subordinates are autonomous individuals who must feel they will receive some kind of benefit from the decision. Another approach is for the leader to present his ideas and invite discussion. In this way, followers can better understand the purpose of the decision, and the entire work group can explore the ramifications of the decision in more detail. A further option open to the leader is to present a tentative suggestion, subject to change, to the work group. While the leader himself will make the final decision, the opinions of subordinates may well lead him to change his initial decision.

Yet another approach is to present to the group a problem rather than a tentative solution and ask for its suggestions. Here, followers have a chance to set an agenda of proposed solutions, not just react to the leader's solution. The leader reserves the authority to choose one of the suggestions. Finally, the manager can define the limits and ask the group to make the decision. An example is a decision to establish a training program. The manager will allow followers to make the decision as a group so long as they stay within a specified budget and spend the funds on nothing but training. The group can establish the nature and format of the training program.

Note that each of these five alternatives falls in between the extremes of, on the one hand, ordering the group to perform an activity without asking for its advice and, on the other hand, allowing the group to set its own goals and action plans.

How does the leader know which alternative to pursue? Tannenbaum and Schmidt recommend first that he examine his own value system. Does he believe that he should make all decisions himself? Is he comfortable about sharing power with subordinates? If the answer to the second question is yes, he may well want to move toward greater participation. If it is no, he may be well advised to stay away from a more participatory approach.

Another crucial consideration is confidence in subordinates. If the leader feels that subordinates leave something to be desired in dependability and competence, he will probably not opt for a more participatory approach. But if he feels that they are dependable, he may well involve them to a much greater extent in decision making.

Likewise, the attitudes of subordinates about their proper role is crucial. If subordinates want to play more of a role in decision making, the leader can involve them more heavily. If they do not, he need not.

Finally, the particular situation must be considered. Most large organizations have a preferred managerial style. If, for example, one agency prefers individualistic, problem-solving leaders, the leader may be courting disaster if he encourages group participation. Or if the nature of the work performed is confidential, that fact may discourage group involvement. Likewise, if the group members are geographically separated, it may be hard to arrange for group participation in decisions. Time pressure may also discourage a more participatory approach. If these circumstances are not present, greater participation may be viewed as highly relevant. The successful leader, in the opinion of Tannenbaum and Schmidt, is aware of the various external and internal circumstances affecting the work situation and is able to pick the leadership style most appropriate to the task.[16]

Managers may evidence a considerable variation in style when going from one situation to another. The manager who favors the participatory approach may not always use it. If a decision must be made quickly, he will make it himself. If in a different situation he has not consulted in the past or invited participation, he may do so, on occasion, explaining the reason. Hence there is no loss in teamwork but a gain in prompt and decisive action. This contingency approach is relevant for dealing both with different types of individuals and with different types of situations.[17]

For example, consider two employees who left their offices to "visit" other offices. One employee did so because she was too intelligent for her job, which frequently bored her, but was a reasonable person. Her supervisor checked on her absences, made a facsimile time sheet spelling out what her pay would be if the visits were deducted, and showed it to the employee. The visits stopped, and the supervisor then began to discuss with the employee the possibility of trying for a more challenging assignment. The other "visitor" was a social butterfly who was not as bright as the first woman. The butterfly's manager simply tracked down the employee several times and ordered a return to work at once, which cured the employee of the visiting habit.[18]

Need For Entrepreneurial Leadership

Unlike pedestrian, routine, business-as-usual leadership, entrepreneurship in administration is a willingness, even an eagerness, to take the initiative to innovate, to take risks, whether the operation is creating a new enterprise, putting a new product on the market, improving a social process, or increasing the effectiveness and influence of a public program.[19] Entrepreneurship adds a new dimension of risk-taking innovation to the concept of leadership. The term appears with growing frequency in the vocabulary of American public administration.[20]

There is much evidence today of a growing need for entrepreneurial leadership in a complex society and its increasingly complex institutions. An example concerns the federal civil service. In a short study for the Brookings Institution, "Developing Leadership in Government," Douglass Cater, former Washington correspondent and later a special assistant to the president, makes

some interesting observations. Many career officials at the top levels of the civil service are "predominantly inbred." Many started their careers in the executive branch at a low level and a youthful age and progressed up through the ranks, in most instances, as specialists. Few have had planned opportunities to learn all the functions that now, as top executives, they are called upon to perform. If they are to fulfill the leadership requirements of these top positions, three things are necessary. They must be guided by subtle judgments that cannot be bound by hard and fast rules. They must have a more thorough understanding of roles, including their own. And they must be able to comprehend the whole range of government in order to appreciate their own part in it.[21]

From the standpoint of the members of an organization, people look to personal leaders "for the tangible focusing of their loyalty to the institution"; but today, "impersonal if not anonymous headship tends to prevail," and hence both in business and in government, the personal relationship is denied and loyalty is weakened.[22]

The sociologist Philip Selznick believes that among the responsibilities of leadership is the need to grasp and hold a true conception of the nature of the enterprise, including its long-run aims as shaped by long-run commitments; "leadership fails if it permits a retreat to the short run." Such a retreat is increasingly easy because of the growing reliance of society on technologies, for these are concerned with new and exciting ways of doing things, which divert attention from the ends involved. It is the obligation of leadership today to understand these relationships.[23]

COMMUNICATION AS LEADERSHIP

In its most general sense, communication is a signal that sets in motion an interaction, verbal or otherwise, between the sender and the receiver. Such communication may be a glance, an expression, a display of emotion, or total silence. Thus words, oral or written, are not a prerequisite of communication, although they may, of course, help to clarify the message.

The spoof in Box 9.3 satirizes an all-too-frequent phenomenon: bureaucratese. This kind of language makes communication much harder, if not impossible, yet many agencies seem addicted to it.

The aim of communication is to bring about a meeting of minds on common issues and understandings, but it is doubtful whether such a meeting can occur except where the parties have had sufficient common experiences to reach similar conclusions. In administration, the most important form of communication is frequently what has been called inwardness of communication, or the interchange of states of mind and attitudes among individuals and groups owing each other respect on the basis of equal status. The most meaningful communications are those occurring in daily intercourse and are face-to-face. This form of communication is especially important when new ideas are being explained for the first time. Finally, communication is usually more effective when the participants are of the same peer group than when they are of unequal status. To become really effective, therefore, communication must be part of a network of values, sympathies, and mutual understandings.[24]

Emotions and Facts

Emotions are more readily communicated than facts. The manager who remembers this can profit from it. People communicate not only through words but also through actions, facial expressions, bodily gestures, and the like. A subordinate who receives permission to do something from a boss who looks at him with contempt is not going to appreciate the boss's approval. Instead, the employee will remember the antagonistic look on the boss's face and respond with similar antagonism at a later date.

The manager strives not only to keep negative emotions out of communications but also to replace them with positive ones. A factual message will be communicated more effectively if the su-

pervisor can relate it to employees' personal interests. He might, for example, announce, "The productivity plan will yield individual bonuses if successful."

Negatively phrased communications such as "*Don't* delay in getting the job done," "*Don't* use that machine," and "*Don't* let anything fall out" are guaranteed to evoke negative emotions. There are few ways to make employees more resentful than by accentuating the negative. They will assume that the boss thinks they are untrustworthy boobs of the first order. Negative communications should not be made.

Precision

Communications should be precise, containing the answers to the questions who? what? when? and where? In communicating, the manager should keep in mind the *why,* or purpose, of the communication. This will help to make the who, what, when, and where clearer. Communications should be put in concrete terms, using examples where appropriate. Plain, everyday English rather than esoteric jargon or bureaucratese should be used.

Since correct communication is a difficult art, the manager should check to see if subordinates understand the communication. "Do you understand?" is inadequate. Employees may think they understand when they do not, or they may be embarrassed to say that they do not. The manager should *check* to see that employees understand what has been said or written. One way of doing so is to ask them to repeat what was said in their own words or to demonstrate what they thought the words meant. In this way, the manager can see whether any flaws in communications exist and should be corrected.

Unfortunately, many managers neglect this necessary step and then blame their subordinates when things go wrong. Business administration professors William F. Dowling, Jr., and Leonard Sayles offer the example of a busy manager who gave several instructions in a brief time to his secretary. One was to call another manager and re-

Box 9.3

NEED INSTANT EXPERTISE?

It has been reported that one of the reasons that the military departments have failed to get their proposals by Secretary McNamara has been the inability to couch their arguments in terms acceptable to the systems analysts, cost effectiveness experts, and "E-Ring" Ivy Leaguers. All of which seems hardly fair, since only a limited number of the uniformed have taken courses in Harvardese.

With this in view, the services might do well to borrow a page from the book of their counterparts at Canadian Forces Headquarters.

Circulating in the Defense Department in Ottawa is a new TIC (Tongue-In-Cheek) Aid for preparing speeches and briefings, etc. The new invention known as a buzzphrase generator gives its prime practitioners what amounts to instant expertise on matters pertaining to defense.

The buzzphrase generator consists of three columns of buzzwords numbered zero to nine:

Column I	Column 2	Column 3
0. integrated	0. management	0. options
1. total	1. organizational	1. flexibility
2. systematized	2. monitored	2. capability
3. parallel	3. reciprocal	3. mobility
4. functional	4. digital	4. programming
5. responsive	5. logistical	5. concept
6. optimal	6. transitional	6. time-phase
7. synchronized	7. incremental	7. projection
8. compatible	8. third-generation	8. hardware
9. balanced	9. policy	9. contingency

The procedure is simple. Think of any three-digit number at random. Then select the corresponding buzzword from each column. Put them together and WHAM! POW! ZAP! you sound just like you knew what you're talking about.

Take for instance the number 257. Take word two from column one, word five from column two, and word seven from column three. You now have "systematized logistical projection." You don't know what it means, but don't worry, neither do "they."

Would you prefer "balanced incremental flexibility"? Possibly "parallel reciprocal options." Or maybe "integrated transitional contingency." How about "functional third-generation hardware" and "optimal management mobility." Now that ought to do the trick.

The important thing is that the buzzphrase generator provides the user with the perfect aid for preparing anything on the subject of national defense. Automatically you have one thousand different combinations, all of which will give you that proper ring of decisive, progressive, knowledgeable authority.

. . . once you've mastered the art of the ringing declaration and become a connoisseur of convoluted phraseology, no one will ever take exception to your rationale.

With thus-broadened etymological horizons, your programs are assured. No one will have the remotest idea of what you're talking about and they're not about to admit it.

SOURCE: *Defense Digest*, November-December 1968, p. 519.

---

mind him how important it was that his current assignment be finished by a specific date. But then the manager said no, the secretary had better not say this because it might annoy the other manager. On returning from a week's trip out of the office, the manager found that his colleague had not finished the assignment, and he took his frustration out on the secretary. He caustically asked why she had not called the other manager to tell him to finish the job. The woman replied that she had called and said her boss was concerned and would appreciate whatever could be done. At those words, her boss collapsed with a groan, but he had only himself to blame. His instructions to his secretary were ambiguous, to put it mildly, and he never asked her to confirm that she knew what he wanted her to do.[25]

Two-way Communication

A one-way communication process exists where managers tell subordinates what to do but are not interested in suggestions of subordinates. Two-way communication exists when managers will not only listen to their subordinates but also actively solicit their advice. Managers should not feel magnanimous in so doing. Rather, they are drawing on the collective experience of their workers to enable themselves to make better managerial decisions. At the same time, they are indicating to employees that they are indeed members of a team, whose advice is appreciated and respected by the team leader.

Listening is *not* easy—it takes practice. Managers should remember to ask who? what? where? when? how? and why? For example, "Did you go to the meeting?" is not so useful a question as "What happened at the meeting?" Managers should be ready to listen when the sub-ordinate initiates the conversation. Some managers do not want to "waste the time" involved in listening, but they should view this time as an investment in improving communications, morale, and performance.

A good listener will often spot underlying causes of problems that may not be apparent at first. If a dependable employee suddenly begins to fall down on the job, the manager should not bawl him or her out and order improvement but ask what the matter is and listen carefully. This may take time, because the employee may be reluctant to divulge the problem, whether or not it is work-related. The manager should not only listen to the employee but also talk to others and observe and think about what might be causing the problem. That is the best way to identify the difficulty, whether it be some unpleasantness at work or off the job, and then try to do something about it.

For example, a draftsman in a public works department began to fall down on the job and to show hostility toward the manager. The manager patiently looked into the matter, listened carefully, and found out that the draftsman was angry because his desk had been moved and he felt cramped in his new location. This problem was speedily solved by moving the draftsman's desk back to its former location. A reprimand to this employee would have doubtlessly caused more hostility and even less achievement, whereas careful listening solved the problem.[26] It should be noted that advance consultation with the draftsman would probably have kept the problem from arising.

A *responsive* listener is one who has time for employee comments even when they may not seem directly related to the task at hand. Dowling and Sayles give the example of an employee who tells the boss that nothing seems to be going right today. The responsive boss notes that everybody has such days and asks what's gone wrong. The subordinate proceeds to explain. The *unresponsive* boss responds that the employee has been falling down on some aspect of the job and should master it right away, or he says that there is no time to listen to the employee. Such a response is a great mistake, for the recognition or attention the employee wanted can contribute greatly to morale. Simply restating what the worker has said makes him feel that the manager understands and thereby sympathizes with the problem, which is certainly true, if the manager is taking time out to listen.

There is no better way to destroy team spirit and end two-way communication in the organization than to refuse to listen. This can only hurt the organization's performance in the long run.[27]

SUMMARY

In this chapter we have analyzed management skills, decision making, leadership, and communication. The practical public administrator is not likely to be too much concerned with theories of leadership and communication if his program is of manageable size and he is experienced in his job. If his experience has been limited by his years, however, or if his job is so complex as to be hard to keep within bounds, then he will find helpful clues in some of the theories discussed in this chapter. In that situation, it makes a difference which of the various interpretations of leadership he is inclined to favor. In a possible synthesis and on empirical grounds, it would seem more useful and congenial to the requirements of public administration to see leadership as involving at least three things: personal competence, response to challenge, and the ability to work with and inspire people.

A sufficiently comprehensive view of entrepreneurial leadership might be the most useful approach of all. Problems in administration are solved by people with initiative and the wit to use it, who do not wait to receive specific orders before taking needed action. Innovation is as nec-

essary in human relations and in the running of an effective program as it is in such spectacular undertakings as putting men on distant planets. Enterprise means looking at the best method known at the time, assuming there is a better one, and then finding it. The enterprising administrator believes that the best way to cope with change is to anticipate it. He also knows that people have more fun and enjoy their work more, if they avoid ruts.

Moreover, an enterprising spirit is frequently infectious, and the more the individual lives on several planes, the more human he becomes. If he is sufficiently human, he might never deliberately seek leadership but simply gravitate into it when the need occurs because it's more fun.

NOTES

1. LeRoy Harlow, *Without Fear or Favor* (Salt Lake City: Brigham Young University Press, 1977).

2. Howard Jarvis, *I'm Mad as Hell* (New York: New York Times Books, 1979), p. 269.

3. Amitai Etzioni, "Mixed-Scanning: A 'Third' Approach to Decision Making," *Public Administration Review* 27 (December 1967): 385–392.

4. See, for example, "Administrative Decision Making," *Public Administration Review* 25 (March 1965): 31–37; Herbert Simon, *Administrative Behavior* (New York: Macmillan, 1947), preface and p. 36 ff.; Dwight Waldo, "Public Administration 1948–1968," *Journal of Politics,* May 1968.

5. Chester I. Barnard, *The Functions of the Executive* (Cambridge: Harvard University Press, 1938), p. 194.

6. Charles E. Lindblom, "The Art of Muddling Through," *Public Administration Review* 19 (Spring 1959): 79–99.

7. Luther H. Gulick and Lyndall Urwick, eds., *Papers on the Science of Administration* (New York: Institute of Public Administration, 1937).

8. H. Edward Wrapp, "A Plague of 'Professional' Managers," *New York Times,* 8 April 1979, Business Section, p. 9.

9. Andrew Hacker, "Creating American Inequality," *New York Review of Books,* 20 March 1980, pp. 20–28.

10. Ichak Adizes, "Mismanagement Styles," *California Management Review,* Winter 1976, pp. 5–20.

11. Leonard R. Sayles, *Managerial Behavior* (New York:

McGraw-Hill, 1964), pp. 38–45; and John J. Corson and R. Shale Paul, *Men Near the Top* (Baltimore: Johns Hopkins University Press, 1966), p. 43.

12. Robert Chesterman, ed., *Conversations with Conductors* (Totowa, N.J.: Roman and Littlefield, 1976), p. 22.

13. Douglas McGregor, *The Human Side of Enterprise* (New York: McGraw-Hill, 1960).

14. Dwight D. Eisenhower, Press Conference, 14 November 1956.

15. Robert Tannenbaum and Warren H. Schmidt, "How to Choose a Leadership Pattern," *Harvard Business Review,* March–April 1958.

16. James McGregor Burns finds the source and inspiration of leadership in the mutual needs, aspirations, and values of the people in the work group or, on a larger scale, in the circumstances surrounding the policy requirements of an entire country. In his *Leadership* (New York: Harper & Row, 1978), the main emphasis is on the political process. It deserves careful reading by future public administrators. Michael J. Fox, in his "Some Rules for Community Lawyers," *Clearinghouse Review* 14 (May 1980): 1–7, makes a number of points, which are generally relevant to any kind of leadership situation.

17. Victor Vroom and Philip Yetton, *Leadership and Decision Making* (Pittsburgh: University of Pittsburgh Press, 1973).

18. William F. Dowling, Jr., and Leonard R. Sayles, *How Managers Motivate* (New York: McGraw-Hill, 1971), pp. 140–141.

19. Joseph A. Schumpeter, *Business Cycles* (New York: McGraw-Hill, 1939), pp. 102–104; Marshall E. Dimock, *Administrative Vitality: The Conflict with Bureaucracy* (New York: Harper & Row, 1959), pt. 3.

20. See John Corson, "The Mastery of Management," *Public Administration Review* 25 (June 1965): 170.

21. Douglass Cater, "Developing Leadership in Government" (Washington: Brookings Institution, 1960), pp. 9, 20.

22. Ordway Tead, *The Art of Administration* (New York: McGraw-Hill, 1951), p. 139.

23. Philip Selznick, *Leadership in Administration: A Sociological Interpretation* (Evanston, Ill. and White Plains, N.Y.: Row, Peterson, 1957), pp. 81–82.

24. Tead, *The Art of Administration,* pp. 184–187.

25. Dowling and Sayles, *How Managers Motivate,* pp. 199–200.

26. Vincent W. Kafka and John W. Schaefer, *Open Management* (New York: Peter H. Wyden, 1975), p. 38.

27. See Barnard, *The Functions of the Executive,* pp. 175–180, for one of the most illuminating analyses ever made of organizational communication.

10

Planning and Policy Analysis

You can never plan the future by the past.

Edmund Burke

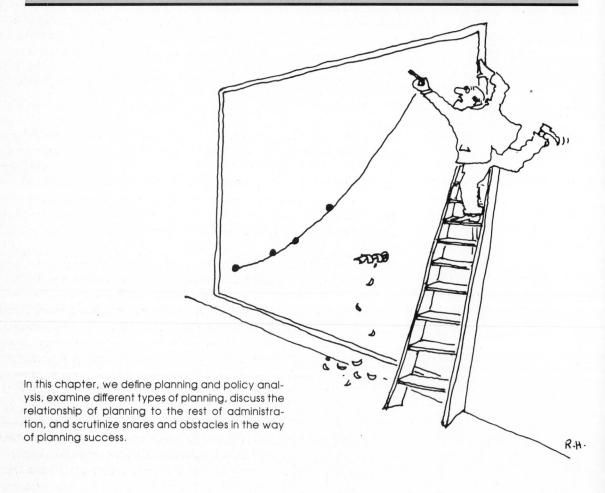

In this chapter, we define planning and policy analysis, examine different types of planning, discuss the relationship of planning to the rest of administration, and scrutinize snares and obstacles in the way of planning success.

Of the many functions of leadership and administrative direction, a central one is knowing what to plan for, how to plan it, and how to carry out the plan. In its broadest sense, planning is thinking before acting, establishing goals before setting out, and appreciating the limitations of planning as well as the essential need for it. Planning is not merely an idea, much less a vision of what might be. Rather, planning specifies a definite goal and prescribes the method and the mechanism by which concrete results may be achieved.[1] Planning is inseparable from administration.

We have included the term policy analysis in the title of this chapter because there is a close connection between it and planning, which is the older term and the one we shall concentrate upon. Policy analysis is similar to the case method of lawyers. It starts with a problem or situation, collects all the relevant facts, analyzes the alternative solutions or explanations, chooses the alternative that appears to have the maximum chance of success and the largest amount of rationality behind it, and indicates with varying degrees of explicitness how the particular objectives may best be achieved. Sometimes, however, this last step is eliminated entirely.

Policy analysis has become a popular concept, especially in political science. The reason is quite obvious. If one starts with the need for public policy development as a rational study, the next step is analysis. The third step, which logicians tend to divorce from analysis, is implementation. Public administrators find this formal separation of analysis and implementation less effective, practically, than keeping them together and interacting. Hence the preference for the term planning, which is dynamic and is meant to be instantly used in all manner of situations and as part of an overall, managerial strategy. The two concepts are so closely related, however, that developments in policy analysis are reported in periodicals such as the *Journal of Policy Studies* and *Policy Sciences,* both of which appeared in the 1970s.

PLANNING DEFINED

We define planning here as a process of interrelated steps, which we have diagrammed in Figure 10.1. The first step is identification of a problem, such as a high rate of fire loss or a low rate of reading achievement, relative to some standard, such as the national average. Once the problem has been pinpointed, broad goals, such as minimizing fire loss or increasing reading ability, can be set. Next, specific objectives can be designed to attain these goals. Over a period of several years, objectives for fire loss might include reducing the losses to 10 percent more than the national average the first year, 5 percent the second year, the same as the national average the third year, and 5 percent less than the national average the fourth year. For reading scores, the first-year goal might be to bring grades five through eight to within an average reading level of only one grade below actual grade, half a grade below in the second year, grade level in the third year, and half a grade level above grade in the fourth year.

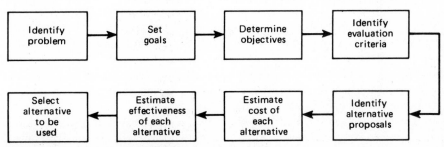

Figure 10.1   The Planning Process

Planning is not a cure-all, nor is it true that the more planning there is, the better the results of the program will be. It is the *quality* of planning that counts, rather than the extent and detail with which it is undertaken. Nor is planning a wholly rational process because, like leadership, it also depends on personality, values, and similarly non-measurable components. Planning is socially and culturally related to every issue and value of importance to human beings; it must, therefore, be practiced with political as well as administrative skill. Indeed, planning is a highly sophisticated area of executive responsibility.

In some quarters, planning is typically viewed as having a mysterious quality or as being dangerous because it is psychologically associated with the state planning characteristic of socialist and communist countries. In fact, there is nothing mysterious about planning, for it is based on a rational process, even if nonrational influences are involved. Where political ideologies are concerned, planning is a process, not an objective, and is immune to contamination from either the right or the left.

Planned and unplanned areas mixed up in the same society create imbalances harmful to the neglected areas and, in the long run, possibly harmful to the whole society. There is an interesting paradox here in that *planning is often needed merely to ensure that unplanned areas may safely be left alone*. For example, a small town in Oregon, whose residents fight hard to maintain its natural beauty, creates a planning board to prevent water pollution.

Modern Importance of Planning

The primary reason for the sustained importance of planning is that with every increase in social complexity, a corresponding emphasis on planning may be expected. Again, the quality of the process is more significant than its extent. In this reciprocal relationship, although feelings may be involved, the common element is rationality. It takes reasoning power to invent computerized industrial and administrative processes and at least an equal degree of intelligence to control, through

planning, the social consequences of this invention.

In a simple society, the processes of production are few and the relations among them can be comprehended by a single individual, perhaps even without taking notes. In an industrialized society, a single process may be so complex as to require the combined efforts of many people, few of whom can see the operation in one piece or the whole of its relation to the rest of the enterprise. Even a new woodstove company in Vermont discovered that it had to set up both a research and development unit and a management planning unit before it was two years old.

In a single undertaking, planning may involve less than a dozen factors and project into the future no more than a year or so. In other undertakings, much more information and time are required. The hardware used in modern defense—and much of industrial production as well—requires a lead time of 20 years. The building of an atomic power plant may take 10 years from start to finish; and even before the decision can be made to go ahead with it, factors such as cost feasibility in relation to other sources of power and anticipated rates of profit must be determined. In addition, the problems of safety to the community and of the possible pollution of river waters used for cooling must be extensively explored and solved. The question of taxes to be paid by the plant to the local community and to the state is a complex one with interesting ramifications, and these also must be studied in detail. Then the questions of whether the power produced shall be shared with public, cooperative, and private power plants and whether it shall be used wholly within the state or channelled into a larger regional system must be decided. All of this takes time, and if any factor is overlooked, the consequences can be disastrous. An accident like the one that closed down the Three Mile Island nuclear power plant in 1979 could affect thousands of people.

In other words, in a highly developed nation, even if there were no more planning than was absolutely essential, there would still be a great deal. It is paradoxical that even if planning were carried beyond the minimum in some instances, there would still be more freedom in the nation than would be possible if there were no planning at all. Planning begets more planning, a plan here may require a plan there. When International Business Machines (IBM) builds a great plant in the center of a rich farming area, for example, someone must decide whether local farmers are going to be taxed at the same rate per acre as IBM. If they are, then farming is likely to disappear from that community. Some would support this policy; but others, possibly looking further ahead, would regard it as a step in the wrong direction. Similarly, when a large industrial plant is built on the periphery of a good residential area, it becomes essential to adopt a zoning ordinance; if the company had built elsewhere, the restriction might not have become immediately necessary.

A second reason for the modern importance of planning—to the point where in the United States it is sometimes discussed more widely than management itself—has to do with the increasing size and technological sophistication of organizations.

For example, as will be seen in Chapter 17, to use a computer is to resort to artificial means, meaning simply that the computer is a machine rather than a human being. But because a computer is incapable of "thought" that has not been programmed into it, human considerations may be overlooked. An order from a retail grocer to his wholesaler is scanned by a computer, and an item that is out of stock is thrown out. Unless a human being notes this and arranges for a substitute, the retail grocer must place an additional order, or his customers, not finding what they want, may go elsewhere. To prevent the inconvenience and the possible loss of business—to say nothing of customer frustration— requires planning, not at one point, as formerly, but now at two, with the computer standing between them.

The conclusion is that *the more technological factors are introduced into management, the more must management redress the balance with respect to quality, through appropriate planning.* It is true that many automatic mechanical processes

do a better job than a human can—a mechanical dishwasher, for example—but it is also true that to operate the machines requires more-able, better-trained human beings than were ever needed before. This training also must be planned, which is one of the reasons that personnel administration has come to occupy so central a role in public administration.

A third reason for the modern importance of planning is its relation to national economic planning, which was a hotly disputed issue a generation ago. Today, when the issue has lost most of its heat, this kind of planning is largely a technical matter. All nations now plan their national economies, and most people agree on the necessity of doing so.

National economic planning is accomplished through a variety of methods; some of them are still occasionally at issue, notably the question of whether the function is to be accomplished through private or public agencies. Moreover, the methods of capitalism are not those of communism, especially where quality is concerned. One of the most interesting achievements is in France, where planning is carried on under a formal arrangement in which both the private and the public sectors work together.

As national economies expand, the problems of planning also increase. How much to plan becomes a less significant decision than how little, quantity is less important than quality, and the blueprint is less relevant than the style. In short, the most important aspect of planning today is the *degree of managerial sophistication brought to it.* This was the main point of the task force study on the Three Mile Island nuclear power plant accident, which strongly criticized the planning done by the electrical utility that ran the plant.

Planning in the Private Sector

In the private sector, the United States has undertaken more planning than any other country, and the American example is still studied by others, including Britain and Japan. Some of the main steps in the evolution of this activity are as follows:

In the 18th century Alexander Hamilton, among others, strongly advocated national planning under government leadership. Hamilton's plan of manufactures probably influenced and stimulated enterprise capitalism more than is generally appreciated.

Scientific industrial planning got its real start around 1912 when Frederick W. Taylor initiated the scientific management movement. At first applied to engineering, with an emphasis on rationality, planning soon spread to every step in the administrative process: plant layout, assembly line procedures, organization, personnel, coordination, sales, finance, cost control, and public relations. Taylor even advocated planning for securing cooperation and handling labor relations, which he considered the most important factor in production, although he admitted he didn't know much about it.[2]

Some of Taylor's heirs—men such as Harlow S. Person who had become leaders in the Taylor Society and helped to transform it into what is now called the Society for the Advancement of Management—refined Taylor's ideas and worked out in great detail the steps involved in industrial planning. Moreover, they eventually saw that *the same techniques applied in a single industry could also be used in national economic and public administration planning.*

Many of the leaders in the scientific management movement between 1906 and the end of World War II (1945) also played prominent roles in government. Perhaps if this fact were better known there would not have been so prejudiced an attitude toward scientific management among public administrators as has existed in recent years (a prejudice found in no other country, incidentally). Morris L. Cooke, a Pennsylvania businessman, who founded the Rural Electrification Administration (REA), was regarded as one of the half dozen top New Deal administrators. Henry Dennison, of Massachusetts, head of Dennison Manufacturing Company, one of the largest corporations, was a member of the National Re-

sources Planning Board under Franklin Roosevelt. Ordway Tead, distinguished editor of *Advanced Management,* the journal of the Society for the Advancement of Management (SAM) and long-time editor at Harper, was at one time an employee in Washington and for many years headed New York's Board of Higher Education. Harlow Person, mentioned earlier, helped found the Amos Tuck School and served for many years in the U.S. Department of Agriculture as planner and management adviser. Before the American Society for Public Administration (ASPA) was founded in 1939, many of those who transferred to that movement had been leaders in the SAM. They included Larry Appley (later head of the American Management Association), Arthur Flemming (later secretary of the Department of Health, Education and Welfare), Luther Gulick, John Corson, Marshall Dimock, and many others. Even today, some of the most penetrating articles on finance, personnel, organization, planning, productivity, and management philosophy are found in the early issues of *Advanced Management.*

Among those who constituted the original Taylor group, Harlow Person was outstanding because of his intellectual contributions. Rejecting the idea that most planning is by theorists and never gets beyond the ivory walls of their secluded studies, Person insisted that planning is a necessary part of operations. The sequence includes a fairly definite objective, some basic understanding of policies and principles derived therefrom, and finally the execution of planning through administration. In this process, action is divided into a pattern of definite and assignable parts *but flexibly enough so that changes can be made if a better method is found.* For example, in the Soil Conservation Service of the U.S. Department of Agriculture, local planning is done by committees elected by local farmers. This approach was adopted early in the history of the service, after an initial experience with centralized, Washington-based planning.

For purposes of analysis, several different varieties of administrative planning can be distinguished: *strategic* planning on the highest plane of the enterprise, *tactical* planning on the intermediate plane, *blueprint* planning at the level of detailed direction of execution, and *work* planning at the shop or agency level. Consequently, planning is everybody's business; it is very far from being the monopoly of the few at the top of the organization. Except where a worker is a victim of highly mechanized chain operations, employees have a large amount of discretion within the frame of specifications relating to quality, quantity, tolerances, suggested methods, standard times, and so on, to plan how they as individuals will handle particular jobs.[3]

Planning in Government

It is only since 1947 that planning in public administration has been much emphasized in the United States, and even then, until recently, progress has been slow. When the public administration profession turned its attention to the problems of developing countries and national economic development, there was a sharp increase of interest in planning in and by government, and the neglect began to be rapidly repaired.

Among the practitioners of public administration, freedom to plan is limited by the statutory requirements surrounding public programs and by centralized financial controls exercised at the top of government. An additional handicap has been that until very recently, public administration professors and practitioners alike have largely neglected the subject of defining objectives, which is a central step in administrative planning. For people in business, on the other hand, such a definition is a major concern because of its direct bearing on profits. The contrast becomes apparent when the space allocated to objectives is compared in textbooks on business management and public administration, respectively. In business, as much as a third of the text is devoted to the need to be clear about objectives, while in public administration, until a few years ago, the subject was almost wholly neglected.

INCREMENTAL PLANNING

The approach to planning we have been sketching is called ideal-rational by some writers. They go beyond the cautions and caveats we mention to conclude that planning as we define it is neither possible nor desirable. The economist Charles Lindblom says that government policymaking is inevitably a matter of "muddling through." Administrators, in Lindblom's view, have too little information, time, and intellectual capacity and too many political obstacles to make comprehensive, rational plans. Further, the values behind one policy may conflict with those behind another, making for contradictions. Decision makers may have to choose between accuracy or speed, employment or inflation, and better schools or lower taxes.

"Incremental" planning or policymaking, which adjusts policy rather than going off in dramatic new directions, is not only the norm, as far as Lindblom is concerned, but should be the norm. Lindblom states that policymaking is incremental, meaning that a new policy will be closely linked to current policies. For example, national energy policy in the early 1980s was based primarily on conservation and further exploitation of traditional energy sources rather than on intensive development of renewable sources such as the sun, wind, tide, and wood. Each participant in the policymaking process anticipates the moves of other participants and makes adjustments to them. This "very rough process" helps avert large-scale and lasting errors, according to Lindblom.[4]

Lindblom has definitely drawn attention to significant hazards in policymaking. Yet to endorse his views would be to surrender before many a battle began. Major technological breakthroughs such as development of the atomic bomb and landing on the moon indicate that massive research and development programs focusing on the energy crisis might well yield dramatic results. It is one thing to take into account the booby traps on the road before trying to plan for change and another to give up before the battle begins. Unless the United States can move in some dramatic new directions in the rest of this century our real standard of living will decline. This is neither desirable nor inevitable.

Lindblom's cautions should be carefully heeded. A plan that has no chance of being implemented may serve as inspiration in the future but is of no help in the present. And many of the comprehensive planners in the early 20th century fell into this error. It often seemed as if they would rather have no loaf than half a loaf. If compromise characterizes democracy, planners must learn to compromise.

Lively debate continues between Lindblom and his critics, which is all to the good.[5] Any thinking that contributes to an understanding of the potential contributors and the limitations of planning and policy analysis will be of help to working administrators.

NATIONAL ECONOMIC PLANNING

The three principal areas of planning in the United States are technological, economic, and managerial. The concern of this chapter with the first area is limited to its social and administrative consequences.

National economic planning, on the other hand, is of immediate relevance because public administration operates within its confines. Indeed, the policy patterns determined by national economic planning—when they have been embodied in legislative statutes—may be said to constitute a large part of the mandate of public administration.

It should be noted, however, that although Americans in business and industry were among the first to stress planning as a central aspect of scientific management, and on a worldwide basis the United States has held the lead in this area, at the same time where national economic planning is concerned, other nations have gone far ahead. American experience has been limited to the decade following 1933 when the National Resources Planning Board (NRPB) was working on

planning policy—but not action—and more recently, since the Council of Economic Advisers (CEA) was created by the Employment Act of 1946. The CEA has done outstanding work, but it is not national economic planning as that function is ordinarily understood.

The CEA is located in the Executive Office of the President and has the job of analyzing and forecasting national economic trends in areas such as inflation, unemployment, investment, and consumption. But the CEA is not a planning body. It carries out research and makes analyses, but it does not have the responsibility of developing a plan that would then be implemented on a national basis.

In the public sector, attention to planning—even on the policy and research side—developed much later than in industry, for the first big breakthrough occurred only in 1933 when the NRPB was created under the New Deal and operated successfully for the following decade. Nowhere, even today, have the philosophy and methods of planning in public administration been set forth better than in the NRPB's publication entitled *A Report on National Planning and Public Works.*[6] Professor Charles E. Merriam of the University of Chicago, who helped organize the NRPB, defined planning in public administration as the systematic, continuous, forward-looking application of the best intelligence available to programs of common affairs. Planning is a means, said Merriam, not an end; nor can it be separated from management because unless plans are put into effect, they remain in the realm of good intentions quietly filed away. The range of this agency's concern was wide and the quality of its work was high. Its administrators and researchers always insisted that its primary interest was in long-range planning, but several of its studies had an immediate and useful impact.

The 1935 study called *Regional Factors in National Planning and Development,* for example, led to regional planning units in all sectors of the country, often following the watershed model of the Tennessee Valley Authority (TVA). This not only brought planning nearer the people but it also laid a foundation for the whole ecology movement, which peaked a generation later.

One reason for neglect has to do with the need in planning to analyze facts so as to define the problem and develop alternative solutions. In the lower reaches of administration this process offered no difficulty, for practical people do it all the time. But at higher levels where major policy is determined, facts are characteristically less concrete and alternatives harder to identify. The result was, and still is, a tendency to move ahead but without much sense of direction.

In an outspoken, hard-hitting article, Michael D. Reagan analyzes the structural weaknesses involved in high-level policy decision in the United States and suggests improvements. Only in times of crisis, he notes, has the federal government planned and coordinated well. Thus, "Except during the wars of the twentieth century, our national style has been one of looseness, of pursuing private goals in the faith that God would watch over children, drunkards, and the United States of America." This is not enough. So instead of a system that suspends the normal workings of centrifugal forces in favor of a "constitutional dictatorship whenever a war or depression crisis occurs," there must be developed a process that will provide sustained strength for effective government even when crises are not at hand.[7]

Reagan suggests a number of ways to tighten up the planning and coordinating functions at the top levels of the federal government. From the administrative standpoint the most interesting is to extend the procedure laid down under the various reorganization acts passed by Congress. Fuzzy objectives, says Reagan, are partly the result of uncertainty as to just what is involved in complex government operations under the separation of powers. A possible remedy, therefore, would be to allow the president to effect substantive statutory changes simply by laying a proposal before Congress. If a majority does not object within a given time, it would become law. The burden of proof would then be shifted. Instead of the president having to round up a positive majority in favor of a given proposal, it would be the

responsibility of the opposition to round up a majority against it.

In contrast to Reagan's aversion to the methods of crisis government, Bertram Gross finds crisis useful as the principal means of developing the planning function all over the world.[8] He also believes that the degree to which results are achieved depends on the capacity of leading elites to respond to the challenge, their cultural values, and the availability of technical and managerial skills.

Gross notes the paradox, however, that the more successfully a given problem is solved through planning, the more likely it is that another will be created in consequence. Increasing life expectancy on a large scale, for example, creates pressures on food supply in a country such as India to the point where mass starvation may be the result. The problem is then a dual one of persuading the people to adopt birth control methods and to improve agricultural practices, and in both areas the rigidities of tradition may be a considerable obstacle.

Gross also expresses a profound skepticism as to the value of long-range national planning and even of clearly defining objectives. Plans may become a snare and a delusion because they seem to make concrete that which has not yet been achieved. Especially in developing countries, planning is apt to acquire a mystique, to become an escape mechanism. Consequently, he urges the kind of planning that can be immediately implemented. Long-range planning is useful, he seems to say, only if it goads nations to do the right things sooner than they otherwise might. In place of a rigid, sacrosanct projection developed through long-range planning, therefore, Gross sees *contingency* planning as more effective because it includes modifications of the original scheme to fall back on in case the original scheme fails.

Gross does not argue against rationality in projecting the future. But he believes that what goes under the designation of national planning, especially in developing countries, is not planning at all, for there is generally too wide a gulf between vision and performance, between fantasy and reality. Instead of setting goals that are too precise to be realistically achieved, he believes that progress is faster when a nation proceeds from one plateau of accomplishment to the next one at a little higher level and that the upward impetus derives more from crisis and necessity than from deliberately formulated plans. He also makes it plain that he trusts administrators with demonstrated abilities to produce results more than he trusts theorists and economists who can say what *should* be done but not *how* to do it.

Because of his multinational survey of planning, Gross speaks with some authority. It is possible, however, that his conclusions apply more to developing nations than to those where a higher degree of sophistication has been attained. His recommendations would certainly be unpopular in large American corporations, for example, where planning is designed to *forestall* crisis, a practice that American governments, after a series of memorable incidents, might do well to imitate. Gross's emphasis on planning geared to action, however, is a strong aspect of his findings.

PROGRAM PLANNING

The third area of planning, after technology and economy, is administration, which is of major concern here. What are its components and characteristics, and how does the administrator deal with them?

The field of administrative planning has become very large indeed, and each variety of planning is distinct from the others. Nevertheless, they have certain elements in common. Three obvious elements are that plans must be formulated, then decided upon, and finally executed. There are additional common characteristics.

Planning occurs in a given culture pattern, which conditions the goals that may be accomplished. The time factor is everywhere relevant. Planning is a political act because at the very least it involves power, pressure, conflict, and persuasion. Planning rarely means very much unless

it is closely tied in with action within the administrative process. When planning is regarded as having a kind of mystique, it often becomes an excuse for ignoring reality and winds up by doing nothing, except that a propaganda effort usually keeps this fact from the interested public. All planning is based on research; and the better and more complete the information available to the planner and the better these data are organized, the more effective will be the subsequent steps in the process. Not even the best of plans is self-executing. The administrator must first sell it internally to his employees and colleagues and then externally to his customers and clients, who include political leaders and voters. This is a sizeable list of common characteristics.

In public administration, there are as many forms of planning as there are levels of government: local, regional, state, national-regional, and national. Above that there is international-regional, functional (the International Labor Organization, for example, or UNESCO), and the United Nations itself. Within a single government, planning is by the legislative, judicial, and administrative branches, each of which has characteristic features of its own. Traditional planning is by political parties and pressure groups, both of which are part of the political-legislative-administrative process.

In the executive branch, planning in a department or agency occurs at several levels—top, middle, and first-line, at the very least, as well as at headquarters and in the field.

From the standpoint of the program manager or the chief executive, the three stages in administrative planning include the long range, the near future, and the detail, all of which must focus on a common goal. Planning is a cooperative process and occurs at all levels of administration. The quality of each component determines the quality of the entire administrative program.

Ultimately, all planning within a particular agency or program is coordinated into a master plan by the administrator, for planning is an aspect of all of his functions—organization, methods and processes, personnel, finance, delegation of authority, supervision, training, motivation, co-ordination, control, public relations, evaluation, and feedback, as well as avoiding administrative obsolescence among his subordinates and assis-tants. Consequently, planning touches all ingre-dients and all stages of the administrative process and neglects nothing of importance. The follow-ing case illustrates the point.

CASE STUDY: SAILING UNCHARTED WATERS

It was a year after the United States entered World War II. The War Shipping Administra-tion (WSA) occupied offices in the Commerce Department building in Washington. A meeting was being held in the office of the administrator of the Recruitment and Manning Organization (RMO) of WSA. Present at the conference were the administrator, the deputy administrator, the chief's administrative assistant, the head of re-cruitment, the chief of manning, the control offi-cer, and the director of the foreign division. At this point in the war, merchant ships were un-armed, sinkings from U-boat activity were alarm-ing but declining, and new ships were coming off the ways and would reach a rate of five a day two years later.

ADMINISTRATOR. As you know, we have an urgent need to provide welfare activities for the men of the merchant marine, for some of our Allied seamen in remote places too. We need to make a firm decision. First, we need to repatriate the men who are recovered from the sea. Second, when the men are ashore between voyages we need places where they can stay. We shall need to take over hotels in New York, San Francisco, cities on the Gulf Coast, and in other places in the United States. We shall have to pro-vide food and entertainment. In Western Europe, Murmansk, and the Far East we'll have to rent or erect facilities. It will be a big operation.

DEPUTY ADMINISTRATOR. It sounds as if it would double our present staff and more than dou-ble our appropriation from Congress.

ADMINISTRATOR. Yes, that is true. Besides, as you know, we'll have to create recovery centers, with psychiatrists in charge, for men suffer-ing from battle fatigue. This in itself will add greatly to our burden. Psychiatrists un-fortunately don't know much about man-agement, and hence I expect we'll have to put trained administrators in charge of these six rest homes.

ADMINISTRATIVE ASSISTANT. This doubling or tri-pling of our present burden might result in doing a poorer job of our main re-sponsibility.

ADMINISTRATOR. Yes, our main responsibility is to see that wherever our ships need to be manned we must have complete and trained crews available at all times. There must be no delays. The navy and army can't fight the war unless we have our merchant ships there on time to provide the needed ma-terials.

CHIEF OF MANNING. So the question is whether we take on the welfare activity or get someone else to do it?

ADMINISTRATOR. Exactly. It can be argued that organizationally we're in a position to ex-pand. We have the organization and so far we're on top of our job. But the opposing argument is that if we take time to expand, it will necessarily reduce our attention to the recruiting and manning job, and that's our prime responsibility.

HEAD OF RECRUITMENT. If we didn't do the new job ourselves, who else could do it?

ADMINISTRATOR. We'd create a welfare organi-zation called the United Seamen's Service

(USS). It would have headquarters in New York. It would have a board of directors and an executive committee. We'd get some able executives, such as Albert Lasker and Henry Kaiser, to go on the board. We in War Shipping would occupy the key positions on the board of directors and the executive committee. We could do this in a matter of days.

CONTROL OFFICER. Sooner than we could do it ourselves?

ADMINISTRATOR. Possibly. For one thing, we'd have less trouble getting space so the staff could be together in one place.

DEPUTY ADMINISTRATOR. Where would we get the executive to run the United Seamen's Service?

ADMINISTRATOR. We have a good welfare executive in mind already.

DIRECTOR OF THE FOREIGN DIVISION. Could you get him?

ADMINISTRATOR. In wartime? Of course.

ADMINISTRATIVE ASSISTANT. Where would you get the money?

ADMINISTRATOR. We'd raise $2 million and expect the shipping companies and the maritime unions to raise 1 million apiece.

DIRECTOR OF THE FOREIGN DIVISION. How long would this take?

ADMINISTRATOR. Maybe a month. In the meantime we'd get Congress to give us an emergency appropriation. The Bureau of the Budget has already said that they'd approve.

ADMINISTRATIVE ASSISTANT. If we did the job ourselves we'd be sure of a unified operation and Congress would give us all the money we need for an expanded activity. But if we turn the job over to a new agency, we'd still be a hard-hitting organization and that's the way we like it. There'd be no danger of neglecting our main job.

CHIEF OF MANNING. But the RMO would still run the psychiatric centers?

ADMINISTRATOR. Yes. And we'd also be responsible for repatriation because we have War Shipping officials and consular officials all over the world.

CONTROL OFFICER. Are you afraid of having too many functional heads to coordinate?

ADMINISTRATOR. No, not really. We have only six or seven at present and it wouldn't hurt to add one or two more.

CONTROL OFFICER. But the combined operation might result in the tail wagging the dog?

ADMINISTRATOR. If welfare became larger than recruitment and manning operations, I suppose that could happen. I've seen it happen many times before.

HEAD OF RECRUITMENT. Is that your main objection?

ADMINISTRATOR. No. I want to keep our priorities straight. Our main job is to see that there are no ship delays because of inadequate crews. Create a corporate device, with all of its flexibility, and in effect you double the sources of initiative.

CONTROL OFFICER. How would the United Seamen's Service finance itself after the initial start-up period?

ADMINISTRATOR. By public contribution. The United Fund that finances other wartime welfare activities. That might amount to $5 or 6 million for the Seamen's Service in a short time. Then if the United Fund didn't provide what's needed, we'd go to Congress for supplementals.

ADMINISTRATIVE ASSISTANT. It would be a serious matter if the USS didn't work in harmony with us. You know the tendency of all organizations to build empires?

ADMINISTRATOR. Yes, I certainly do. But if we occupy the key policy spots in the USS, I think we can prevent that.

DEPUTY ADMINISTRATOR. What do the ship operators and maritime unions think about devolving this responsibility?

ADMINISTRATOR. The unions are strongly for it. We'd give them the responsibility for maintaining order in the USS facilities. Then if some performer got drunk and started to break up the furniture, the union members would call a halt. Experience shows that they'd do it for their buddies when they might not do it for us.

CHIEF OF MANNING. And the operators?

ADMINISTRATOR. They're generally for a separate corporation, too. Some are a bit worried about giving the unions so large a piece of the action, but they are in a distinct minority. After all, this is wartime.

DEPUTY ADMINISTRATOR. What does Congress think of the plan?

ADMINISTRATOR. As you know, I've talked with the key members of Merchant Marine committees in both the House and Senate, and they're for the United Seamen's Service.

DIRECTOR OF THE FOREIGN DIVISION. Even though Congress wouldn't have direct control of it?

ADMINISTRATOR. Yes, they're in favor of winning the war, too.

Objectives at Different Action Levels

The planning function as it occurs at different levels of administration is taken up here.

Top-level planning is primarily concerned with economics, lower levels with technique. In this context, economics is broadly conceived to include the structure of the economy, the development of productive institutions, sustained growth, policy determinations, values, and the like. Technique is the knowledge of various technologies, such as agronomy and accounting, as well as the processes of administration. Both elements are present at all levels of planning, but at each level, the proportions of the mix are different.

Moreover, since the set of mind of top executives and those at the action level is different, the quality of planning—and, indeed, of everything involved in the administrative process—depends on the degree to which *top officials understand technique and action officials understand the economic implications of their work.* This is essentially a problem in communication, although other instruments, such as training programs, are also involved. If the proper mix is secured at each level of administration, then sustained communication is easier and so is cooperation. The result will be more unity, integration, coordination, and a more smoothly running program. In addition, top-level planning will be more practical and action-level planning more inspired. Administrators able to combine an understanding of economics with a skill in technique are in short supply and the demand is great.

A brief illustration will make the point. When the governors of nine U.S. states visited the Soviet Union in 1959 to observe Soviet administration at first hand, they found national education officials thinking of goals such as these: (1) the direction in which the Soviet economy was heading and the skills that would be needed; (2) the demand for new courses and training, if consumption was to be more emphasized; (3) the need to keep education from weakening the identification of educated individuals with the workers; and (4) how much larger a share of the gross national product should perhaps be allocated to education.

In the lower ranks of Soviet administration, a different set of objectives in education was evident: (1) the appropriate number of students in each classroom; (2) education for all, or possibly only for the brightest students; (3) the possibility of vocational schools; and (4) the best methods of training future teachers. When the governors participated in discussions with Soviet officials at this lower level, the subjects were so technical and practical that no ideological overtones were apparent. Except for the difference of language, Soviet and American technicians could have exchanged places and felt at home. This particular illustration shows, moreover, how ideological differences that are significant at the higher levels of policy determination become less so at the lower levels as universally applicable matters of technique are of greater interest.

Another observation is that the lower the level of administration, the more precise are the objectives; the higher the level, the vaguer are the objectives and the more likely the decisions are to have life-or-death consequences. A nation may win a war, for example, and yet lose the peace by behavior that costs it the respect of other nations or by sowing the dragon's teeth of a future war in which former allies line up on the other side.

These characteristic differences between planning at the higher and lower levels of administration mean that communication in both directions is crucial, for if lower-level hardheadedness can moderate top-level concerns with ideology and power, then wrong policy decisions are much less likely to occur. The popular aversion in the United States to the concept of ultimate authority is no doubt due in part to the fact that power and loneliness at the top are apt to affect a person's judgment.

Planning and Action

Planning is involved at all levels and in all stages of administration; consequently, everyone in the organization takes part in it, or should. People are more interested in their work when they help to determine the objectives, policies, and techniques that shape it. Participation makes people feel more important and more needed; it stretches their minds and causes a ripple of excitement that makes their work more satisfying.

The fact that planning is a pervasive function, however, does not dispose of the need to define its place in the organization. Indeed, one reason for the long neglect of planning in public administration in the United States was that the profession never came to grips with the organizational decision.

Administration is a flow of energy in a two-way process, from one level to another and back, from one phase of action to the next, always in motion, always interacting and drawing all elements into a single stream toward both immediate and long-range goals. The task of management at all levels is to see that this merging occurs.

In a thoughtful article on planning, Donald C. Stone, then assistant director of the U.S. Bureau of the Budget, distinguished between the planning of substantive programs on the one hand and of administrative facilities on the other.[9] The first variety is resource and program planning, based on technical research. The second is management planning, for it involves the development of sound organization, staffing methods, procedures and practices, and program direction and coordination. Stone acknowledged, however, that the line between programs and administrative planning is often a fine one and that the two must ultimately merge in action.

From the functional standpoint, planning is closely related to research, which occurs at all levels of public administration; but research by itself is no substitute for planning.[10] "Planning," said Harlow Person, "expresses no preference for a particular mode of research. It is concerned with variables; its problems vary, and therefore the modes of research vary."[11] Planning is also closely related to budgeting, the evaluation of results, and the measurement of performance. "A budget," remarks Robert A. Walker, "is indistinguishable from the planning process—the budget is itself a plan of work."[12]

If planning is to be of any practical use to the administrator, it must be an integrated part of the administrative process and not shoved off by itself as a separate staff function secure in its own ivory tower, as sometimes happens. For many years this question has been a matter of warm debate in management circles, with city and resource planners backing the idea of a separate profession and a detached status for planning and businessmen and public officials arguing more often for the integrated relationship. E. J. Coil, long the guiding force of the National Planning Association, once formulated ten propositions supporting the separate, professional approach to planning. He recognized the need for the planning staff to work closely with general management, but he regarded professional planning as a full-time job that should stay clear of special interests. He also believed that planners should be generalists rather than specialists.[13]

Such a separatist view is seldom heard today

even among professional city planners, for most administrators have come to share the view of the late Gordon Clapp, formerly chairman of the TVA and a leading figure in public administration. As a result of his TVA experience, Clapp believed that the distinction between those who plan and those who execute is inevitably a vague and shifting one; it would be hard if not impossible to diagram the planning unit in a single box on an organization chart; there should be as wide a distribution as possible of competence and responsiblity for *both* planning and execution among all departments of an agency; and in practice, the same person, staff, or department may participate at several points in the planning, formulation, and execution of a given project.[14]

The evidence seems to be that different kinds of organizational relationships are needed for different kinds of planning activity. City planning and national economic planning, for example, may justify a separate, detached unit tied in at the top of the organization to the office of the chief executive; but in business and government alike, program managers find that the more closely planning and action are related, the better are the results of the operation.

PLANNING PROSPECTS AND PROBLEMS

While it is difficult to spell out the precise impact of planning under differing conditions, there is no question but that planning activity is greatly on the increase. Thirty years ago, few agencies had the elaborate planning process that many of them have today. Likewise, larger state, county, and city governments—and even some medium-sized and smaller units—are more and more concerned with forecasting. Publication of books, articles, and manuals on planning by such organizations as the Urban Institute and the International City Management Association indicate that planning is here to stay and is spread throughout many of the United States' 80,000 local governments.

While this trend is positive, there are some hidden snares in planning. Planners have to be aware that the road over which policies are implemented is littered with boobytraps. The political scientist Eugene Bardach has studied policy implementation and come up with a counsel of caution. Many public policies, according to Bardach, do not achieve their stated objectives. Further, they take much longer to achieve anything than originally planned. Third, they cost more than planned or cost too much for the results achieved.

At the heart of these problems is the defensive nature of the implementation process. The various agencies and individuals involved engage in an enormous amount of maneuvering to avoid responsibility and blame. According to Bardach, if an interdepartmental policy is undertaken, each of the departments will want to look good, first of all, rather than achieve anything. Thus, if police, fire, and sanitation departments embark on a fire prevention program for high-crime areas, each unit will be primarily concerned that it not be blamed if the program fails. Employees of each department will produce documentation that they did their utmost to make the program work rather than going into the field and trying to make the program work. Agencies play a large number of games to protect themselves, all of which stand in the way of positive action. While Bardach is pessimistic about chances for improving programs in areas of human service such as health, education, and welfare, he does make some recommendations. They revolve around the addition of technically and politically skilled policy analysts to both legislatures and agencies to design plans to minimize the damages done by defensive games. His solution, then, is more and better planning if planning is to succeed. Bardach's warnings are well founded. Plans that ignore political and administrative realities are paper exercises, which will inevitably fail.[15]

Political scientist Fred A. Kramer has cautioned that planning contains certain characteristic assumptions, which can act as an ideology, blinding the planner to the reality of a situation and thus reducing the value of planning work.[16] Two aspects of this alleged ideology that concern Kramer are its emphases on quantification and social science theory. Kramer warns that stressing the quantitative may drive out qualitative considerations, which are all-important to the analysis. That is, a stress on the *numbers* of prisoners paroled under a program may be emphasized more than the *nature* of the guidance and counseling provided by the whole program. These qualitative considerations, which defy quantification, may well be the factors that determine the success or failure of the program.

Kramer's second point is that the social and economic theories behind a plan may be inaccurate and lead to unanticipated and unwanted events. An example is the social science theory behind the War on Poverty of the administration of Lyndon Johnson. Policymakers were amazed when the poor, instead of being worshipfully grateful, used antipoverty programs to denounce all levels of government while simultaneously demanding even more program support from them. Likewise, the social science theory that guided advocates of strategic bombing of the civilian population in both World War II and Vietnam was far off the mark. In both instances, enemy war production and morale *increased* as a result of the bombing.

Kramer's advice to the planner whose work is rejected by government officials is to use self-analysis. Perhaps the study was rejected because it did not meet the needs of the official. Maybe the planner did not spell out some implicit assumption of the study or neglected some aspect with which the official was familiar. Kramer concludes by stating that "[m]ore likely, the analysts probably did not spell out the weaknesses in their work because *their perspective—their implicit ideology*—made it impossible for them to see the weaknesses."[17]

Additional drawbacks have been identified by Hatry and his colleagues.[18] First, they point out, there is no consensus on what constitutes "good" systems analysis or planning. For example, a survey of Defense Department studies found no agreement on which studies were good, let alone *why* they were good. Public planning, then, is hardly a science comparable to physics or chemistry.

Second, planning may tend to justify ends over means. In their anxiety to achieve results, planners may be expedient about procedural matters, the types of concerns which lawyers, in contrast, tend to stress. And ethics may be of no concern. If it is true that exponents of results-oriented management tend to argue that the end justifies the means, this is a bias they should be aware of. Otherwise they will adopt the same stance as totalitarians determined to triumph regardless of other considerations. Again, planners who are aware of these biases can learn some necessary humility and self-restraint.

Economists Murray Weidenbaum and Linda Rockwood have pointed out that *comprehensive* planning efforts are in for trouble. They argue that it makes more sense to try smaller-scale planning in specific agencies rather than to mount a concerted and coordinated planning effort.[19] They cite the 1965–1971 rise and fall of federal Program Planning and Budgeting Systems, (PPBS),[20] a topic that will be explored in more detail in Chapter 22. This planning-oriented budgeting system was launched in too grandiose a fashion and collided head-on with existing planning and budgeting efforts. Weidenbaum and Rockwood conclude that even long-range, corporate, business planning has a poor record, so that hopes of installing such a system in government and seeing it succeed are doomed to disappointment.

These warnings have wisdom. Planning can accomplish much. But its own worst enemies may be the enthusiastic advocates who oversell its merits. Government agencies badly need much more results-oriented planning. But this planning must be flexible and realistic if it is to succeed. Someday comprehensively coordinated planning systems may be feasible, but there is more than enough work ahead in trying to design planning procedures for individual agencies.

SUMMARY

In this chapter we have defined both planning and policy analysis, demonstrated the essentiality of planning in industry and all modern institutions, distinguished the various forms of planning, suggested the strengths and weaknesses of each type, and dealt with the environment of planning. Several federal agencies plan with lead times of a mimimum of 20 years; perhaps this procedure will become more common.

NOTES

1. Harry P. Hatry, Louis Blair, Donald Fisk, and Wayne Kimmel, *Program Analysis for State and Local Governments* (Washington: Urban Institute, 1976), p. ix.

2. Edward H. Hempel, *Top Management Planning* (New York: Harper & Row, 1945), preface.

3. Harlow S. Person, "Planned Execution: The Issue of Scientific Management" and "Research and Planning as Functions of Administration and Management," in Albert Lepawsky, *Administration: The Art and Science of Organization and Management* (New York: Knopf, 1949), pp. 522–524, 535–536.

4. Charles E. Lindblom, "The Science of Muddling Through," *Public Administration Review* 19 (Spring 1959), 79–88.

5. See *Public Administration Review* 39 (November-December 1979): 517–555.

6. National Resources Planning Board, *A Report on National Planning and Public Works* (Washington: U.S. Government Printing Office, 1 December 1934). This agency was originally called the National Planning Committee. Its name was subsequently changed to National Resources Board, then to National Planning Board, and finally to National Resources Planning Board. It died quietly in 1943, when Congress refused to appropriate funds for its use. There were probably a number of underlying causes, including the end of the Depression of the 1930s, the fact that the nation was in World War II, and institutional jealousy and rivalry between the legislative and executive branches.

7. Michael D. Reagan, "Toward Improved National Policy Planning," *Public Administration Review* 23 (March 1963): 10–19.

8. Bertram Gross, "National Planning: Findings and Fallacies," *Public Administration Reivew* 25 (December 1965): 263–275.

9. Donald C. Stone, "Planning as an Administrative Process" (Paper presented to the National Conference on Planning, 12 May 1941).

10. John D. Millett, *Management in the Public Service* (New York: McGraw-Hill, 1954), pp. 73–75.

11. Harlow S. Person, "Planned Execution—The Issue of Scientific Management," *Advanced Management* 10 (December 1945).

12. Robert A. Walker, "The Relation of Budgeting to Program Planning," *Public Administration Review* 4 (Spring 1944): 97–102.

13. E. J. Coil, "Administrative Organization for Policy Planning," *Advanced Management* 4 (January 1939): 12–17.

14. Gordon R. Clapp, "Some Administrative Aspects of Regional Planning in the Tennessee Valley" (Address to the American Political Science Association and the American Society of Planning Officials, 30 December 1940). For a professional tribute to the late Gordon Clapp, see Harry L. Case, "Gordon R. Clapp: The Role of Faith, Purpose, and People in Administration," *Public Administration Review* 24 (June 1964): 86–91.

15. Eugene Bardach, *The Implementation Game* (Cambridge: Massachusetts Institute of Technology Press, 1977).

16. Fred A. Kramer, "Policy Analysis as Ideology," *Public Administration Review* 35 (September–October 1975): 509–517.

17. Kramer, p. 512.

18. Hatry et al., *Program Analysis for State and Local Governments,* pp. 58–59.

19. Murray Weidenbaum and Linda Rockwood, "Corporate Planning Versus Government Planning," *Public Interest* (Winter 1977), pp. 59–72.

20. See Allen Schick, "A Death in the Bureaucracy: The Demise of Federal PPB," *Public Administration Review* 33 (March–April 1973): 146–156.

11

Organization Guidelines and Practice

Order is a lovely thing.

Anna Hempstead Branch

In this chapter we examine the central role of an organizational framework, assess the implications of hierarchy for organizations, scrutinize the structure of different types of organizations, examine the costs and benefits of reorganization, and speculate on what the future holds for the shape of organizations.

Christopher Robin, owner of Winnie the Pooh, in books by A. A. Milne, once said that "organizing is what you do before you do something, so that when you do it, it's not all mixed up." Organization is the formal as well as the informal structure through which work flows. Not an end in itself, organization is a means; it is the framework of functions and relationships which results from the assignment of roles, the arrangement of methods of communication and cooperation, and the exercise of coordination at the leadership level.

Organization is basic in the administrative process, but it should nevertheless be kept in its proper place and should not be allowed to dominate all other aspects of administration. Because organization is everywhere greatly needed as the means to achieve social objectives, the organizational specialist has become a permanent figure in public administration all over the world. Departments of administration, for example, are increasingly common in state and local governments and in federal agencies, as we noted in Chapter 8. The widespread concern with organization is justified by the fact that every aspect of administration flows through it.

The reasons for the prominent role of organization in the administrative process are these. Wrong structure is a frustrating handicap to action. Organizational arrangements have long-range as well as short-range consequences, some of which may not become apparent for 5, 10, or even 20 years after they have been adopted. The objectives of a program are not likely to emerge clearly or to be pursued with energy unless the structure is right. And although organization is ordinarily conceived as an up-and-down relationship, it is also a lateral one; recognition of this fact is often the means of securing cooperation and avoiding program fragmentation.

Mary Parker Follett, one of the great figures in modern thinking about organization, argued that agencies often ask the wrong question when they are organizing. The question should always be For *what* is a person responsible?, not To *whom* is a person responsible? This stress on *results* is the proper emphasis in organization.[1]

PRINCIPLES OF ORGANIZATION

Several principles have been used in the 20th century to justify the structure of modern organizations. As we shall make clear throughout this chapter, however, it is best to regard these as mutable, or changeable, rather than eternal truths.[2]

Modern organizations are large and complex because of their intensive specialization of labor. Two centuries ago, craftsmen would perform a wide variety of tasks. Today, they are so specialized that a carpenter may not know what some of a plumber's most basic tools look like. At the turn of the century, one college professor might have taught courses in history, sociology, economics, and political science. Today, those courses are taught by four different specialists.

As Figure 11.1 indicates, government organizations have become exceedingly large, specialized, and complex. This pattern can be seen even in small towns, which may have a visiting-nurses' association, an ambulance service, a sanitarian to inspect liquid-waste removal and restaurants, and a dump for solid wastes. All of these institutions are concerned with public health, yet each one is so highly specialized that it requires different offices and individuals.

Hierarchy

It is difficult to find agencies that lack the vertical structure diagramed in Figure 11.1. This chart indicates that the office and office holder at the top have authority over those at the level immediately below and so on down to the bottom of the structure. This is a hierarchical structure; the term hierarchy derives from the Greek term for the ruling structure of religious organizations. (The term is still widely used for the organization of a number of religious bodies, including the Roman Catholic Church.)

Hierarchies are the result of the inability of one boss or office to supervise effectively a very large number of subordinates. Most organizations create a hierarchical structure to delegate author-

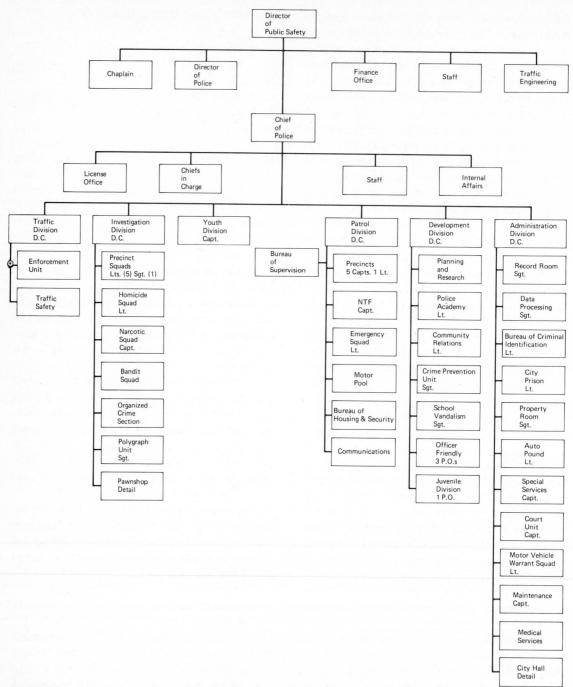

Figure 11.1 Present Organization of the Jersey City Police Department

ity to subordinates so that the situation becomes manageable. This problem is not new. After Moses led the Israelites out of Egypt, the Bible says, he became exhausted dealing with problems brought to him by his people. ("Moses sat to judge the people; and the people stood by Moses from the morning into the evening.") Jethro, Moses' father-in-law, is one of the earliest known management consultants. He took Moses aside and told him, "Thou wilt surely wear away, both thou and this people that is with thee, for . . . thou are not able to perform it [Moses' work] thyself alone." Jethro's solution was to urge the creation of a hierarchical structure, with trusted subordinates to be "rulers of thousands, and rulers of hundreds, rulers of fifties, and rulers of tens." Moses would issue orders to the managers immediately below him, and the orders would then flow down through the hierarchy. Moses would have more time to devote to big, crucial problems, while subordinates took care of matters that were narrower in scope. ("The hard causes they brought to Moses, but every small matter they judged themselves.")[3] Not only was Moses able to use his time better, but the people did not have to wait all day in long lines to see him.

Chain of Command

One of the implications of a hierarchical structure is that it has a chain of command that should be followed, whether one is moving up or down the hierarchy. One may suppose, for example, that Moses' hierarchy included a supervisor named Efraim three levels below Moses, as indicated in Figure 11.2. If Efraim wanted to bring a matter to the attention of authorities at higher levels, he was authorized to go only one level up, to Reuben, his immediate supervisor. If Reuben thought that the matter was important enough, he would report it to his boss, Aaron. The principle of the chain of command is based on authority and efficiency. If Efraim ran to Moses or Aaron whenever he thought he had an important matter to discuss, Reuben's authority would be undermined. He would have no real control over his subordinate.

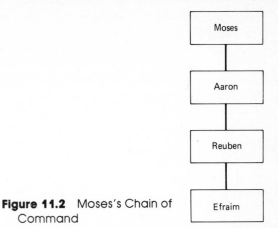

Figure 11.2 Moses's Chain of Command

This is the predicament in which a former coach of the Boston Celtics basketball team, Tom Heinsohn, found himself in 1978. Heinsohn, who was fired shortly thereafter, viewed his situation as one where "the coach is subverted. He takes a player aside and says, 'Lookit, I want you to dive on the floor for loose balls.' The player goes over his head to the owner or general manager, who's trying to satisfy the player's salary demands. The owner or general manager says, 'Lookit, don't worry about it. We'll talk to the coach.' . . . And the player winds up not diving on the floor for loose balls. A lot of coaches are getting frustrated. With the merest curtailing of the coach's authority out there, you don't have a team."[4]

Furthermore, the greater efficiency of the hierarchy, which saved Moses from exhaustion, would also be undermined, if Efraim brought to Moses' attention matters that could or should have been settled at lower levels.

The principle of the chain operates when one is descending the hierarchy as well. If Moses or Aaron were to communicate directly with Efraim, Reuben's authority would also be undermined. In effect, his superiors would be casting a vote of no confidence in his administrative abilities, which would quickly demoralize him and lessen his effectiveness. This practice would also add significantly to Moses' and Aaron's work load, which it was the purpose of the hierarchy to reduce.

Unity of Command. A corollary of the chain of command is unity of command, the principle that each employee should have only one boss. If the chain is strictly observed, each subordinate can have only one supervisor. Unity of command also holds for other employees at any one level in the organization. Each should have only one boss to promote efficiency and effectiveness. If several bosses are giving orders to one individual, the result is likely to be confusion. The subordinate will not be able to focus on doing one job because of commands to do another job. Further, the orders of different bosses may well be contradictory. If a police sergeant tells an officer to be very strict in handing out parking tickets, while the lieutenant tells the officer to ignore violators, stress and chaos can result.

Span of Control

A supervisor's span of control refers to the number of subordinates he has. If the head of a shift on a hospital floor supervises 12 nurses, his span of control is 12. If a police sergeant oversees 4 patrolmen, his span of control is 4. What are the spans of the director of public safety and chief of police in Figure 11.1? Many attempts have been made to determine the ideal span of control, which is a difficult task. Evidently, Moses' original span of control was too big for him to handle. On the other hand, a fire chief who has one deputy chief between him and the rest of the organization almost certainly has too narrow a span of control. Yet it is dangerous to be dogmatic when assessing variations within those extremes. Some police administration textbooks, for example, still give a number of 8 as the ideal span of control for a patrol sergeant. Since no recent research is cited to support this assertion, readers should be skeptical. Given the rapid rate of change in the modern world, the span of control has to be adjusted to altering conditions, including the capability of subordinates and the nature of the task to be performed.

Organization with large spans of control will have fewer hierarchical levels than organizations with the same number of employees with smaller spans of control. Figure 11.3 diagrams this phenomenon. An organization with fewer levels is called a relatively "flat" organization, one with more levels is a relatively "tall" organization. The relationship is a simple arithmetic one. Given the same number of employees, smaller spans of control lead inevitably to more levels. Given fewer levels, the span of control must be larger.

Tall organizations pay a price in time, because the more levels communications must clear, the longer it takes them to reach the top or bottom. If six subordinates have to approve the special instructions for April Fool's Day procedures, the instructions may not pass all the way through the hierarchy till April 2. Communications can move more quickly in flat organizations, but this does not mean people should strive to make all organizations flatter. They should be more concerned whether the span of control is appropriate at all levels in the organization. Former federal official and current public administration professor Rufus Miles states that "Wide span of control satisfies many constituencies; narrow span of control satisfies few. If the chief executive wishes to fend off . . . special pleaders, he is likely to prefer a small number of officials directly answerable to him; if he can take the time and wants to hear what they have to say, he will enlarge the range of important membership in his immediate family."[5]

A Critique

Hierarchy makes it possible to increase administrative efficiency by reducing personal contact between the top and the bottom. Max Weber, a path-breaking analyst of bureaucracy, argued that the essence of modern bureaucratic structures was their impersonal approach. Bound by rules and regulations, the bureaucrat is far better able to resist special pleading and demands for exceptions than are officials in prebureaucratic structures. (Weber claimed that true bureaucracy was a product of the specialized and secular civilization of the 19th century; before then, kings

Figure 11.3   Flatter and Taller Organizations

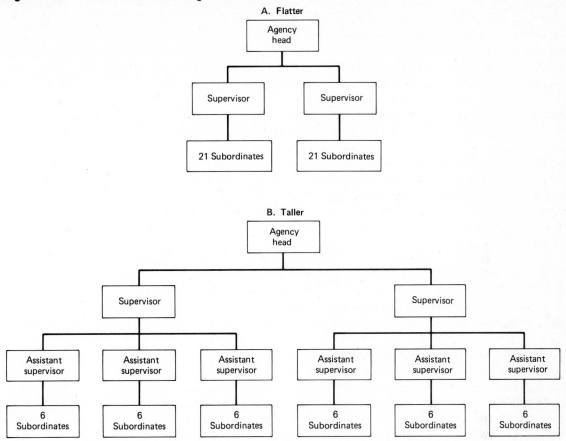

and religious leaders could and did regularly overrule bureaucrats.)[6]

Such an impersonalized system has costs as well as benefits. One is the obsession with status reflected in Box 11.1. Another is related by Dostoevsky, the great 19-century Russian novelist, who says in his *Notes from the Underground,* "I used to be in the government service. I was a spiteful official. I was rude and took pleasure in being so. . . . When petitioners used to come for information . . . I . . . felt intense enjoyment when I succeeded in making anybody unhappy. I almost always did succeed." Our point is not that the average bureaucrat behaves the way Dostoevsky did. Rather, large bureaucracies solve certain problems but have other problems all their own.

Control over some negative aspects of the behavior of tenured civil servants in a large and complex hierarchy may be much more difficult to achieve than it is in a smaller, "prebureaucratic" one.

The principles of the chain of command and unity of command do not always yield the best results. For example, what if a supervisor ignores excellent recommendations made by a subordinate? If Aaron ignores Reuben's warning that the supply of manna is about to run out, the people may starve. But how is this message going to reach Moses? The only way it can is for Reuben to ignore the chain of command and report his recommendation to the next higher level.

This problem is perennial, fabled in song and

Box 11.1

MEMORANDUM

FEDERAL ENERGY ADMINISTRATION
Washington, D.C. 20161

APR. 1 4 1975

OFFICE OF THE ASSISTANT ADMINISTRATOR

Memorandum For: FEA Senior Staff

Subject: Executive Position Titles

In the past few weeks the number of titles available to important FEA personnel has been drastically reduced. It is also understood that OMB will shortly place a freeze on the proliferation of FEA titles. In the interest of maintaining staff morale, it has been decided to make the remaining titles available on a limited basis for the next two weeks. Written requests and justifications for the remaining titles should be filed with the Deputy Associate Assistant Administrator for Management Nomenclature, telephone number, 961-8534.

Those titles currently in use are:

1. Administrator
2. Deputy Administrator
3. Assistant Administrator
4. Deputy Assistant Administrator
5. Associate Deputy Administrator
6. Associate Assistant Administrator
7. Deputy Associate Assistant Administrator

Those titles available for selection during the next two weeks are:

1. Associate Administrator
2. Deputy Associate Administrator
3. Assistant Associate Administrator
4. Deputy Assistant Associate Administrator
5. Assistant Deputy Associate Administrator
6. Assistant Deputy Administrator
7. Assistant Associate Deputy Administrator
8. Associate Assistant Deputy Administrator
9. Associate Deputy Assistant Administrator

Some offices have opted to call their Deputy Associate Assistant Administrators Office Directors. These persons, of course, are free to use the more formal title, Deputy Associate Assistant Administrator.

Although other titles are available, such as Deputy Associate Deputy Administrator, good form dictates evidence of such tendency. It is hoped that all desirous of titles will be satisfied with those listed above.

A memorandum describing titles available to the Office of General Counsel, Office of Congressional Affairs, Office of Communication and Public Affairs, Office of Private Grievance, and Office of Intergovernmental and Special Programs will be circulated within the next two weeks. The use of informal titles, such as Executive or Special Assistant, will remain flexible as in the past.

Leonard M. Pouliot
Assistant Administrator
Management and Administration

story. Iago, a subordinate of Othello in Shakespeare's play *Othello*, feeds Othello a diet of false information, which eventually causes Othello's death. Since Iago has also continued to discredit Cassio, his immediate supervisor, Othello has no way to discover Iago's falsehoods.

Corrupt officials throughout history have failed to report to their masters information that might point to their involvement in corruption, and they have punished subordinates who reported such incriminating evidence. Incompetent officials have rejected the excellent advice of subordinates on countless occasions. What, then, is the official to do? If the chain of command is dispensed with entirely, the organization will collapse under a weight of memoranda and crossed signals. Some kind of selective reception of subordinates who have broken the chain of command is necessary. If they are bringing routine matters to the top, they should be told to desist. But if they seem to have uncovered matters of great importance, which their immediate superiors have refused to send to the top, they should not be disciplined. Instead, a careful investigation should be made.

Justification for a supervisor to break the downward chain may be more ticklish. If the supervisor spots a potential crisis, which he has reason to believe his subordinate cannot handle without unnecessary loss of property or life, there may be reason to break the chain. But in more routine matters, the supervisor is destroying the incentive and ability of subordinates to grow in the job. If subordinates are not doing a good job, they should be given training. If that fails, they should be replaced. But except in a crisis that threatens the immediate physical well-being of employees or the life of the organization, the chain should be observed.

Unity of command is an even more troublesome principle to follow than the chain of command. It should be noted that Frederick W. Taylor, the leader of the scientific management movement, did not advocate unity of command.

Inflexible adherence to this principle will cause trouble. Firemen fighting a four-alarm fire will not disobey an order just because it comes from a supervisor other than their immediate boss. That person may be elsewhere in the thick of the fray and be unable to issue orders at that time.

Some writers have argued that the existence of separate line and staff units in large modern organizations makes it impossible to observe unity of command in any strict sense. *Line* units are operating units, which deliver services or regulate behavior. A classroom teacher, a police traffic officer, and a welfare case worker are all line employees. They directly serve the agency's clienteles whether they be schoolchildren, pedestrians, or welfare recipients. *Staff* units provide services to line units. Planning, budgeting, accounting, personnel, and purchasing office are staff units. Staff employees serve line employees; in a real sense, the line agencies are their "clientele."

The existence of separate staff units means that many line employees may well have more than one superior. Their extra superiors are the staff units whose procedures line employees must follow. For example, the personnel department may specify the procedure to be followed before a new employee can be hired, regardless of the opinion of the line employee. The accounting office may issue directions for forms that have to be followed, regardless of what the line supervisor thinks should be done. In any realistic sense, then, the existence of separate line and staff operations means that the principle of unity of command cannot be strictly followed.

Unity of command marks a great improvement in efficiency over situations where there is no organization chart and no clear lines of authority so that many different superiors are giving orders to the same (confused) subordinate. But the principle of unity of command must be interpreted flexibly if it is not to cause serious stumbling blocks to effective administration.

CENTRALIZATION-DECENTRALIZATION

Hierarchies differ greatly in the extent to which authority is centralized or decentralized. If Efraim, a fourth-level bureaucrat, had to have approval from higher levels for almost any action he wanted to take, he was working in a highly centralized organization. But if he had the authority to do almost anything he wanted without clearing it first, authority was much more decentralized.

Harvey Sherman, director of the Organization and Procedures Department of the Port of New York Authority, has pointed out there are many possible degrees of decentralization. In one situation, a subordinate may be able to take action without notifying the boss. In another, he may have to tell the boss what was done. In a third situation, the person may tell the boss what he plans to do and then do it unless the boss says not to. A fourth possibility is for the subordinate to let the boss know his plan and wait until approval is given to carry it out. A fifth option is that the subordinate can list alternatives and recommend one for the boss. Finally, the subordinate can report the facts to the boss, and the boss can issue an order later. The point here is that it is necessary to spell out what decentralization means in a specific organization, because the meaning will vary from one situation to another.[7]

Debates have raged for many years about whether organizations should be more centralized or decentralized. There is no general solution to this problem, for the need for centralization varies with the type of work to be carried out. The highly centralized organization reaps the benefits of control and uniformity at the cost of time and flexibility. The highly decentralized organization's costs and benefits are exactly the opposite.

The county extension service of the U.S. Department of Agriculture is an example of a highly decentralized organization. Each of the 3,000 counties has an extension office with personnel who serve farmers and other land users. The work such an office does in the urban northeast is very different from its work in the grain belt. Extension offices need not obtain clearance from the Agriculture Department's regional office to carry out most of their work; they just go ahead and do it.

Compared to the extension service, the U.S. Social Security Administration is much more centralized. Uniform policies are expected to be carried out in its regional and district offices. Applicants who ask for it can obtain a fat book listing thousands of different regulations governing the distribution of benefits. Local office workers are not able to overlook these rules, and an applicant who thinks the rules are not relevant in his or her case is going to have to go through a lengthy appeals procedure, perhaps taking the matter to court.

Which system—a more decentralized or more centralized one—is best? One cannot generalize. Instead, one has first to discover what the agency's goals are. If they are to serve clients depending on their needs in relation to local conditions, one would probably want to design a decentralized system similar to that of the Agriculture Department. If the goal is a uniform system, which would provide the same kinds of benefits to applicants in New Mexico as in New Jersey, one would probably want a centralized system similar to that of Social Security.

If the degree of decentralization is not appropriate, the costs can be high. Some colleges have a large, highly centralized registrar's office. Students who want to make an adjustment in their schedules may have to spend many hours appealing this change up through the hierarchy. Both employees and clients will lose much precious time over matters that could have been easily adjusted by a clerk in another registrar's office. Yet, if a registrar's office is so decentralized that clerks are making decisions that contradict each other and destroy any possibility of consistent and coordinated policy, the organization has become too decentralized to do its work effectively.

In deciding on the extent of centralization, then, the administrator has to ask which tasks should be performed and what specific benefits and costs for each will result from the particular degree of centralization chosen. The right degree is not easy to determine. Many governments and agencies go through cycles where more centralization is followed by less, as they try to adjust to changing demands and conditions. Nor is the

Figure 11.4 Four Ways to Organize a Department of Transportation

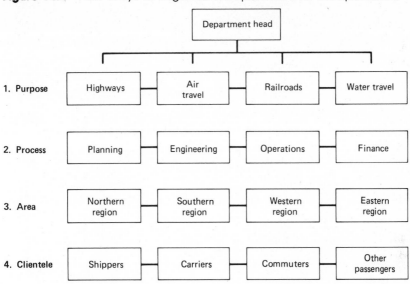

problem of achieving this balance limited to the United States. In June 1979, Chinese Finance Minister Zhang Jingfu argued that China needed decentralized financial administration: "There is the malady of too much control, over-tight management . . . confusion . . . and the waste of state funds."[8] After 25 years, it is probable that Zhang's successor will move to recentralize, using much the same language Zhang used to argue for decentralization.

FOUR PATTERNS OF DEPARTMENTAL ORGANIZATION

Regardless of whether a department is flat or tall, or centralized or decentralized, there are different ways to organize it.[9] Figure 11.4 demonstrates four different patterns of organization for a Department of Transportation. The first is organization by *purpose*. Each major division—highways, rail travel, air travel, and water travel—contains all the activities necessary to accomplish each type of travel.

The second pattern, organization by *process,* shown in Figure 11.4, groups activities by special skills. Here work is not organized by purpose, but by the specialized steps in the work process. These steps include, but are not limited to, planning, engineering, operations, and finance.

It is also possible to organize by *geographic area,* the third pattern, shown in Figure 11.5. According to this pattern, the department is organized around geographic boundaries.

Finally, organization may be by *clientele,* that is, the groups that the agency serves, whether

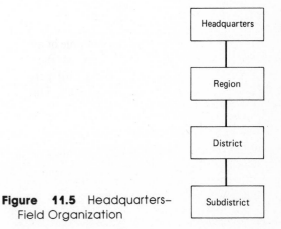

Figure 11.5 Headquarters–Field Organization

commuters, shippers, carriers, or other passengers.

It is possible to organize divisions of a department along these patterns, as well as the department as a whole. A department may mix its patterns, organizing some divisions on a process basis, for example, and others by clientele. Such combinations, in fact, are the rule, and not the exception, in American government.

What are the pros and cons of each type of organization? Organization by purpose makes it easier to hold subordinates accountable. If the organization is set up according to program goals, it will be easier to hold program managers responsible for results. Likewise, employees should be better able to see how their work relates to broader organizational goals instead of becoming bogged down in a particular specialized activity.

Yet the other patterns of organization have advantages as well. Organization by process may increase efficiency through specialization. An accounting division's machines could serve the entire department, for example, where a department organized strictly by purpose would allot machines to each division. This approach would probably make it necessary to buy more machines, which would not be used so intensively as they would be in a department organized by process.

Adherents of organizing by area claim that this pattern encourages the making and carrying out of policy that is more appropriate for the area. Appropriate kinds of police protection will differ enormously between high-crime and low-crime areas in the same city, for example. An orientation towards a particular area will lead to better understanding of the particular needs and problems found there. The costs of area organization, on the other hand, include inconsistency in policy between areas. There may also be extra financial cost as staffs and equipment are duplicated. Area organization costs more because it is a form of decentralization, emphasizing local needs. Centralized administration may not be so responsive, but it will be uniform and cheaper. One illustra-

tion involves a change in the Kansas City, Missouri, Public Works Department. This department formerly repaired potholes in a centrally planned manner, moving from one area to a contiguous one. In 1963, however, a new administration announced that all repair trucks would be dispatched to potholes by radio when citizens reported them. The new approach was responsive to citizen demands and was popular. The old approach was far more uniform, efficient, and effective. (Kansas City has since returned to the first approach.)

The benefit of organization by clientele is that it is easier to give consistent treatment by following through on all matters involving the client. A children's bureau, for example, can take steps to place a child in a foster home and arrange for medical care, special education, or whatever else might be needed. Otherwise the child might have to go to ten different agencies, starting from scratch in each one. The costs of organization by clientele are duplication and difficulty of coordination. An agency organized on the basis of clientele, such as a department for the aging, duplicates the work of organizations based on purpose such as a department of welfare and health, thus causing problems of coordination.

One lesson of this look at different patterns of organization is that organizers cannot have their cake and eat it too. Each pattern has certain costs and benefits. One cannot have maximum efficiency together with maximum effectiveness, nor responsiveness with uniformity and coordination. How individuals will respond to different types of organization depends ultimately on their values and how they believe organization affects policy.

HEADQUARTERS–FIELD RELATIONS

Almost all large government agencies maintain field offices to serve clients. If they did not, anyone who wanted to transact business with a federal agency would have to go to Washington. Likewise, those who wished to obtain state government services would have to go to the capital, and big-city residents wanting city services would have to go to the city hall. Instead, there are precinct police offices, regional offices of a state welfare department, and district offices of the Social Security Administration. There is a necessity to maintain field offices, but there is no necessary agreement about how they should be organized. This subject will be more fully analyzed in Chapter 14, dealing with coordination.

It should be noted that field organization is inevitably organization on the basis of area. Were it not, there would be no reason for a field organization. Some of the points that have been made about organizing departments on the basis of area apply to field organization. The hierarchy from headquarters to field may be flat or tall, centralized or decentralized. There are several different variations, even though most departments have the type of organizational chart found in Figure 11.5. The U.S. Department of Agriculture, as we have already noted, devolves great authority on the lowest levels, its 3,000 county offices. In other federal departments, such as Housing and Urban Development, authority is decentralized to 10 regional offices. The lowest levels lack substantial discretion, having to report back to the region before they can take action. The federal department of Health and Human Services, on the other hand, has never decentralized substantial authority to any level in the field, meaning that a region cannot take much action on its own. Similar variations exist in state and large city governments.

We shall return to headquarters-field relationships in Chapter 14, examining problems of coordinating the two.

IT ALL DEPENDS: CONTINGENCY ORGANIZATION

Harvey Sherman wrote a book called *It All Depends* to sum up his contingency approach.[10] Mary Parker Follett talked about "the law of the situation," meaning that action should be tailor-

made for a given situation.[11] Rather than follow a uniform general plan in matters of organization, organization should be on a contingency basis to find the most appropriate pattern.

Several examples follow to illustrate this crucial point. The first involves the Recruitment and Manning Organization (RMO) of the War Shipping Administration, a federal agency that one of the authors headed during World War II. Upon assuming his post, he discovered that the agency was not responsible for training merchant seamen. Some officials within the agency believed that it should incorporate training so that it could be reorganized more thoroughly on the basis of purpose. "Since training constituted such a small part of the total function and since it was only one source of supply [of merchant seamen], it should become an integral part of the RMO and administratively subordinate to it."[12] The department head found himself opposing this approach because, although he could see the theoretical value of the argument, he realized that there were strong practical reasons that made such a consolidation undesirable. "These practical reasons were that the training program was much older than the RMO and had developed a strong institutional life of its own. It would have resisted to the end any serious proposal to subordinate it to the new agency. Even more important than this, however, the training program was a large administrative undertaking in itself, and hence was more likely to succeed if its autonomy was maintained."[13]

A nice, neat theoretical approach, then, would have ignored the operating realities of the training program and reorganized it in a way that probably would have impaired its efficiency and effectiveness. "Thus the most plausible analysis is not always the most feasible. . . . All that glitters in the eye of the expert is not administrative gold."[14]

Another example involves a change that was made successfully. Harvey Sherman relates how the Port of New York Authority took over the bankrupt Hudson and Manhattan railroad.[15]

Three alternatives were considered for operating this new program. First, the Port Authority could make a contract with an outside agency to run the railroad. Second, it could assign the job to a line agency (new or existing) within the organization. Third, it could create a new subsidiary corporation within the Port Authority.

The solution adopted combined elements of different plans. A subsidiary corporation was set up to operate as much like a line department as possible and to contract out minor functions such as selling advertising displays. The law of the situation dictated this choice. Contracting out of major functions was rejected because a suitable qualified contractor would be hard to find, and the agency would not be able to ensure the standards that existed in its other operations. Direct assignment to a line department was rejected because it would be difficult to merge the railroad employees, with their different personnel systems and union contracts, with existing units. Further, it was feared that stringent federal railroad regulation might thus spread to the other operations of the department to which the railroad was assigned.

The decision to form a subsidiary corporation made it possible to continue railroad operations with minimal disruption, while Port Authority employees learned how to run a railroad. The arrangement also allowed the Port Authority to provide a new managerial climate, while allowing enough autonomy for the old personnel system and union contracts to continue.

Again, this solution was not nice and neat in the way textbook maxims sometimes are. But the important thing is that it worked, it achieved the desired results.

REORGANIZING? PROCEED WITH CAUTION

Reorganization may seem the best way to solve certain organizational problems. But a look at the record reveals that administrators should be extremely careful in deciding whether to reorganize.

They should also use great care in how they reorganize if they decide to do so. As Gaius Petronius Arbiter, setter of social protocol for the court of ancient Rome, remarked in A.D. 66: "I was to learn later in life that we tend to meet any new situation by reorganizing, and a wonderful method it can be for creating the illusion of progress while producing confusion, inefficiency, and demoralization."

Drastic and periodic reorganizations have drastic costs. It is far better to accept organizational change as a continuing process and to find the means of introducing innovations without disrupting programs and upsetting people by sudden and unexpected changes.

Take the example of the federal water pollution control agency in the period 1961–1970. This agency, which changed its name several times, was located in three federal departments—Health, Education and Welfare, Interior, and the Environmental Protection Agency. The constant restructuring of the agency meant that "5 to 8 years have been lost to environmental programs through reorganizations."[16]

Experience has shown that the disruptions often tend to outweigh the gains, which in any event are more often disappointing than not. People have established loyalties and identifications with the programs for which they work; they instinctively react against having their agency uprooted from one department and transferred to another; the whole experience is upsetting to them. When it was found that an agency mobilizes its interest-group support to fight a transfer, the strategy was developed of issuing the transfer order without notice, making the blow a sudden and unnerving one and the upsetting effect even worse.

As a result of these unfortunate experiences, many larger government agencies have now arranged reorganization procedures so that the process is a continuous one, a little here and a little there from time to time. It is common now for some central staff agency, such as a budget bureau or department of administrative services, to exercise a constant oversight of organization and to be available for consultation. In the larger federal agencies, staff specialists deal with questions of organization and take the initiative in suggesting alterations. In addition, of course, it is the responsibility of line executives themselves to watch the operations of their agencies and gradually to make organizational improvements. Thus, instead of the federal Office of Management and Budget (OMB) stepping in with an order to reorganize, today the program director, perhaps with OMB consultation, commonly arranges his own internal organizational changes. When a whole agency is to be moved, of course, the central staff agency is involved and, in addition, is often busy behind the scenes suggesting the rearrangement it thinks should be made. But when the time comes for action, the line official assumes the responsibility, as he should.

Here again, it is important that organizational changes should not be too frequent and that employees not be constantly stirred up. In the State Department, in the early 1950s, for example, after Henry Wriston studied the Foreign Service and recommended reorganizations, the term "wristonized" became a popular one to describe the almost constant reorganizations that took place in the department with a highly upsetting effect, and, apparently, little real improvement in the workings at Foggy Bottom.

ADAPTING TO CHANGE

Because the stakes in terms of effective operations are high, responsible officials must act with full awareness of what they are doing. Research and experience have suggested certain guidelines in this area.[17]

1. Symptoms and causes of organizational problems should be carefully analyzed. If they can be ascertained, it may become clear that reorganization is not the appropriate solution.
2. Proposals for change should be announced gradually so as not to stiffen instinctive opposition even before people have had a chance to consider the matter rationally.
3. No public announcement of change should be made until the members of the organization have been told of it in person by the responsible official. In this way rumor may be discouraged.
4. Flexibility should be built into the reorganization plan. The expectation that many modifications may occur as the causes of problems become clearer during reorganization should be clearly communicated.
5. Those who oppose a change should have an opportunity to express their reservations as early in the process as possible. Even though this procedure may give them a chance to organize opposition to whatever is being suggested, it is better to face such opposition before the move is publicly announced than later, when the unsettling effect may be even greater.
6. The aspects of reorganization affecting the work and arrangements of particular groups should be discussed with them privately, not in a general meeting of the whole agency.
7. These groups should have a chance to study proposed changes and to register their mature judgment before final action is taken even if the decision ultimately goes against them.
8. When change has been decided upon, it should be put into effect gradually so as to allow employees time to adjust. If gradual change is not possible, the reasons should be explained.
9. A monitoring mechanism should be set up to follow the implementation of reorganization. It should allow those involved in reorganization to communicate how changes are affecting them and what problems are being solved, or created, by reorganization.

In effect, organization is a way station on the road between stability and change, and the art is to maintain a balance between the two. Since the ultimate measure in public administration is the effect on society in many areas where change is both constant and revolutionary, the program executive often has a hard time deciding when reorganization is indicated and when it is not.

Sometimes there is no choice in the matter, as when a service is dropped, an activity discontinued, an area office closed, or a technological development makes some kind of automation possible in place of human effort. In each of these instances, employees are necessarily displaced and must be let go, employed elsewhere, or retrained for some other duty. A somewhat different circumstance is when some higher authority decides to consolidate services, medical programs that formerly were separate, for example; here also, the program manager has no choice in the matter.

But even in situations where change is not a factor, there remain problems of organization for the program manager that require a high order of judgment. Thus, how far down the line should he discuss and consult with his subordinates? The next level below or further? In determining internal arrangements, what is the administrator's effective span of control? Can he deal reasonably well with 5 people or with 50? Is it realistic to suppose, as personnel administrators commonly do, that the position is more important than the person and that the candidate for a job must fit a preexisting slot? Or should the job description be altered to take advantage of the abilities of the candidate? If so, to what extent is the program manager prepared to fight to secure the person he wants?

In addition, in examining his agency with a critical eye, does the administrator find duplication of effort in planning and other staff functions? If planning was done better, would it require additional staff personnel or perhaps fewer? Is it an advantage or a disadvantage to post an organization chart on the office wall for all to see, when in fact everyone knows it is disregarded in practice? Why use organization charts at all since most of them are no more than pretty pictures anyway? (One executive, when asked if he had an organization chart of his program, replied that he did but that he kept it under the blotter on his desk where no one but himself knew where it was.) Perhaps it would be more realistic to show organization on a flow chart of the kind used to illustrate the circulation of the blood.

Harold Seidman, a former federal official and current professor of public administration, has written the most trenchant and incisive critique of reorganization. He argues that whatever rele-

vance to federal organization such principles as span of control, chain of command, and departmentalization by purpose once had is now gone; in fact, the principles do a disservice since they help to perpetuate the "myth . . . that we can solve deep seated and intractable issues of substance by reorganization."[18] For example, an analysis of reorganizations of the U.S. Public Health Service concludes that "the fundamental facts of health politics remain unaffected by reorganizations. No amount of reorganization will produce agreement on goals in the health field or produce unity among doctors, hospital administrators, biomedical researchers, public health officials, nurses, or the many groups of specialists."[19]

In Seidman's opinion, the principles neglect the political realities of public organization. If people do not live in a nice, neat, orderly society, how realistic is it to expect a nice, neat, orderly governmental structure? Seidman argues that the most important characteristics of bureaucracy in a democracy are representativeness and responsiveness. In other words, agencies should reflect the interests of competing groups in U.S. society. If there is no administrative diversity and pluralism, have-not groups will suffer. When President Richard M. Nixon proposed reorganization, it is noteworthy that agencies such as the Office of Economic Opportunity (OEO), which was the foremost antipoverty agency, were designated for destruction. This is nothing new. The 1949 Hoover Commission recommended that the Farmer's Home Administration (FHA) be divided up between two other Department of Agriculture agencies because its functions overlapped theirs. However, the FHA was established to help small farmers with little political influence, while the record of the rest of the Department of Agriculture showed that it marched in step with the bigger, more conservative members of the American Farm Bureau Federation. Lumping FHA functions with those of other bureaus would have brought FHA functions to an end in this new and unfavorable environment. Seidman also notes that even "have" groups like bankers and scientists prefer particular organizational arrangements that do not follow the principles of reorganization.

The point here is that there is a lot more to organizational reality than is to be found in the principles. The creation of a neat and orderly bureaucracy will help some groups and agencies while it hurts others. Reorganizers should constantly be aware of the points raised by Seidman, who has provided a list of questions to ponder.

1. What is the nature of the interest-group constituency created or acquired as a result of the reorganization? To what extent will it influence policies and administration? Is it broadly based or is it narrow and opposed to some of the goals of the program?
2. What is the internal environment of the agency being given program responsibilities? Will it help, hinder, or ignore the program? Does a particular type of professional outlook that may regard certain programs unfavorably dominate?
3. Are safeguards ensuring that no group or class of people is excluded from the program provided? Are there any built-in obstacles to joint administration with related government programs?[20]

INDEPENDENT REGULATORY COMMISSIONS AND GOVERNMENT CORPORATIONS

The two forms of organization we are about to consider do not fit neatly into a conventional organizational mold. The regulatory commission is many-headed, with anywhere from 3 to 11 commissioners instead of a single chief. The government corporation is a separate legal entity with a board of directors and an executive chosen by the board. By contrast most of the so-called departmental agencies we have previously discussed have single heads and are part of a hierarchy leading to the chief executive. Both the commissions and the corporations are independent. Yet these two forms of organization are so numerous, so significant economically, politically, and financially, and so much involved in political controversy that they are almost daily in the local news. During the administration of Ronald Reagan, task forces were set up for the express purpose of reducing regulatory constraints or eliminating the agencies entirely.

A concern common to these organizations is accountability. Legislatures frequently favor these forms of organization because such forms increase their power and influence relative to that of the chief executive. Since the chief executive lacks direct control, these agencies are able to operate largely on their own, and some may not have to answer to anyone.

As different as government corporations and independent regulatory commissions are in theory and practice, they have this in common: they are unlike most conventional agencies. They are detached; they complicate the separation-of-powers doctrine; they complicate integration and control by their separateness; and they have peculiar problems of internal management as a result of their form.

Independent Regulatory Commissions

The major federal commissions include the Interstate Commerce Commission (ICC), Federal Trade Commission, Civil Aeronautics Board, Federal Energy Regulatory Commission, and Securities and Exchange Commission (SEC). Other such commissions are the National Labor Relations Board, Federal Maritime Commission, Board of Governors of the Federal Reserve System, Federal Communications Commission (FCC), Nuclear Regulatory Commission, Commodity Futures Trading Commission, Consumer Products Safety Commission, National Transportation Safety Board, Federal Labor Relations Authority, and Merit Systems Protection Board. To be noted, especially, is the fact that despite all the criticism of major regulation by commission, the number has increased markedly in the past 10 years.

Likewise, most state governments have numerous commissions to regulate utilities and other industry. Perhaps the most famous state commission is the Texas Railroad Commission, whose primary function is to regulate the amount of oil pumped out of the state's wells.

The underlying theory of the commissions was established in the Progressive era, at the end of the 19th century, and proceeds as follows. First, a business that is granted a monopoly has so much power that it should either be owned or regulated by the government. Regulation is preferable for two reasons: it would provide the business with better management than if the government ran it directly, and it reduces government's direct responsibility for management. Next, it is assumed that those who live in fear of government ownership will provide good service at a reasonable cost if independent officials are chosen as commissioners. The commission should be bipartisan. There should be term rather than permanent appointments, good salaries, and protection from partisan or interest-group encroachments. Then, the commissions should in effect act as the agent of the legislature. The legislature might study and decide, but it has enough work of its own to do, and hence the duty of regulation should be entrusted to experts. The commissioners, assisted by expert staffs, should hear and decide cases. The commission should set standards and enforce them. It should make investigations and educate the public as well as the legislature. The president should appoint commission members, but they should be subject to Senate approval.

The idea was that independent commissioners acting independently could be relied upon to decide in the public interest as well as in that of the regulated industry. High expectations were entertained concerning human nature and its motivation. In case of dispute the matter could be decided by the creating body, by administrative review within the commission, or by appeal to a court of law.

How has the system worked? In some instances such as the SEC and FCC, the system has apparently satisfied the regulated industry and most of the public. On the whole, however, Congress has become in recent years increasingly disenchanted with independent regulatory commissions. In addition, many economists have called

for a new formula, and the public administration profession has been critical of policy and organizational separateness, the loss of independence in some areas, and the weak internal management found generally in commissions.

In most instances the commissioners divide up the work functionally. One will deal with insurance or contracts and another with rates or licenses, for example, because that is their training. Hence there is splintering within the commission itself. In recent years Congress and the Office of Management and Budget, plus the General Accounting Office, have attempted to offset this splintering by giving the chairman enhanced managerial powers. However, frequently when this happens the other members seem to gang up and try to reduce the chairman's powers. As a result, in some instances there has been a net loss of administrative effectiveness rather than an appreciable net gain. When the president (or governor) tries to intervene and suggest or change policy, the result frequently is to raise the legislature's hackles and he desists. At the worst there is no communication whatever between the chief executive and commission members. Even the president's White House staff learns to keep hands off because once their overtures become known in Congress there is resentment and a charge of unfair influence.

When commissioners retire or are offered more lucrative jobs in the industry being regulated, they gravitate to law firms that deal with commission matters, giving another ground for undue influence. Congress has tried to stop this practice by placing a limitation on former members of commissions as well as on ex-lawmakers, but this limit is usually confined to two years. Hence one of the charges brought against independent regulatory commissions is that there are too many in-and-outers. Individuals join the commission, stay a short time, and expect to reap rich rewards because of the associations made.

Related to this problem is the fundamental problem of commissions, their alleged takeover in some instances by the very industries they are supposed to regulate. In most instances, the commission and the industry become close friends; so the commission becomes, in fact, a captive or creature of the industry. Captivity is caused by the collapse of the temporary alliance that originally created the commission. Most commissions are assertive and vigorous in their first years, but they gradually lose the interest-group allies that created them.[21] The industry, which has a strong, permanent interest in the commission, remains. For example, most state public utility commissions are accused of doing pretty much what the utilities they are supposed to regulate ask.[22]

More recently, the independent regulatory commissions have been the subject of a crusade called deregulation.[23] Many groups have become convinced that regulation of industry forces up prices. But the regulatory commissions have their champions as well as their detractors. The telephone companies prefer regulation to government ownership. So do the television networks, the nationwide trucking companies, the commercial airlines, and those other industries that prefer regulation to government takeover as has happened elsewhere throughout the world. Billions of dollars of investment are involved. Commissions dealing with transportation, communications, stock markets, and atomic energy sit astride the finance capitalism of the country. Some businesses, such as American Telephone and Telegraph, are considered the bellwether of good investments. As a result, businessmen may be opposed to regulation in general but are prepared to fight to maintain their particular form of regulation, if it is to their advantage.

One may consider the airline industry. Before the administration of Jimmy Carter the Federal Aviation Administration (FAA) set minimum rates for air travel. Under deregulation, such rate setting was greatly curtailed, and airlines engaged in price wars. As a result, the price for a flight from New York to Los Angeles was cut in half in the spring of 1980. Consumers loved it, but many of the airlines loathed such competition.

Future Policy What of the future? As long as the legislature and the chief executive fight each other, it is likely that the independent regulatory

commission will prove durable. Neither the legal profession nor the public administrators are in complete agreement about the the issues just discussed.[24] Even on the question of how complete a control the president or governor should have over policy matters there are widely varying shades of opinion. It may be supposed, for example, that the issue is whether railway or truck transportation would be more advantageous in light of the oil shortage. Is the president more competent to decide that issue than the commission? But if one opts for the commission, what then does Congress decide if the president lobbies for one solution and the ICC for the other? Is that tolerable? It happens all the time, either by the backstairs or openly to Congress and its committees.

What is to prevent undue influence from focusing on the president's advisers quite as much as on the commissioners? The answer depends upon one's views of pluralism: either the government should speak with one voice or citizens should permit the luxury of having several voices. Or, to change the metaphor, at what level should such decisions be made: at the departmental or commission level or by the president himself? About all that can be said safely concerning these issues is that generally public administrators are more favorable to consistency of policy than otherwise, and that lawyers and businessmen are in general more attached to a flexible or negotiating approach, leading to diversity and competition within the government.

Government Corporations

Government corporations usually provide a so-called business function. They predominate in transportation, utilities, banking, and municipal services. Such corporations are very old. India was using corporations as early as the 6th century B.C.; Rome, not much later. Starting in the 19th century, governments also used corporations; many local governments went into the utility business, operating their own electric and water companies. Twentieth century examples include the Tennessee Valley Authority (TVA) and the Port of New York Authority, both of which are behemoths with budgets in the billions.

It must not be thought, however, that corporations are used exclusively or even principally for operating billion-dollar ventures. Any county, state, or local administrator knows that from an administrative standpoint, what perplexes him is the spawning of literally thousands of special districts (also called public authorities) throughout the country. We have already discussed these local corporations in Chapter 5, which deals with intergovernmental relations. These are alongside, but administratively independent of, the formal framework of government. They are used for a variety of purposes.[25] Examples are toll roads, conservancy districts, irrigation projects, public housing, power projects, law enforcement regions, and land planning organizations. In fact, they cover almost the whole range of government activities.

Corporations are as flexible as bureaucracy is rigid. A corporation may be a mixed enterprise (part private and part public) as well as being wholly owned by the government. As a result, corporations may be used for a surprising number of purposes.

This flexibility calls attention to the developmental use of public corporations. They undertake tasks that regular departments may not be geared to accomplish so quickly. This situation is found in several state governments, where state legislatures set up a public authority, give it a sizable capital fund, allow it to finance new businesses for the state's economy, and repay the loans out of income from the borrower.

Another variation on this same theme is found in the U.S. Postal Service, created by Congress in 1970, which has about 700,000 employees. It superseded the Post Office Department created in the earliest days of the republic and headed by a Postmaster-General with cabinet rank. The U.S. Postal Service has a board and all the trappings of a corporation, but it is not called one. It was created to reduce the direct management responsibilities of the United States government and make the postal enterprise a paying one. It was

touted as a move to return to the private sector as many governmental functions as could be transferred in the public interest. Congress still maintained its ultimate responsibility for deficits and oversight, however, and a separate agency alongside the operating one, the Postal Rate Commission, was given responsibility for fixing rates and weighing the claims of the highly organized postal labor unions. Other examples are space-satellite communications systems financed partly by public funds but administered by private companies such as telephone companies and their competitors.

In effect, therefore, the United States government has as subsidiaries, companies that in magnitude rival those found in the country's largest business conglomerates. Many of them are banking institutions: the Export-Import Bank of Washington, Farm Credit Administration, Commodity Credit Corporation, Federal Crop Insurance Corporation, Federal Intermediate Credit Banks, Federal Land Banks, Federal Mortgage Association, and Federal Savings and Loan Insurance Corporation. Others, like the Federal Prison Industries, Inc., and the St. Lawrence Seaway Development Corporation, have other adjunct purposes.

The corporation entrusts policy decision to a board of directors but, as in private corporations, expects the appointed chief executive officer to recommend policies, budgets, key appointments, organizational changes, financial management, and periodic reviews of accomplishment and financial results. Armed with this mandate, the board believes that it can give the management a great deal of freedom to innovate and to manage. Committees of the board, such as the executive committee, keep tabs on the progress of work and assist in decisions, thus serving as a link to the larger board of directors. The corporation is not part of the larger civil service system of the government unless the legislature decides to make it so. There is greater freedom in purchasing, making contracts, and installing innovations in management. In short, the corporation makes its own decisions and is not part of the larger bureaucracy with its centralized controls. The board of directors in effect fills the role of the legislature; and so long as the legislature trusts the board, the corporation has greater freedom in all areas of management than would be true if it were part of the central establishment.[26]

Opponents of the public corporation have some strong objections. Multiplication of the number of units makes centralized planning and control more difficult for the party in power. The authority of the president or governor is reduced to the vanishing point. It is difficult to watch all the central departments of government, much less government corporations, regulatory commissions, and independent establishments. And, if the government is rationally run, the same advantages of efficiency and entrepreneurship can be achieved under integrated government as under proliferated government.

In the long run, therefore, continue the critics, it is wise to try to improve the management of the entire government instead of relying upon palliatives. Energies devoted to government corporations might be better invested in improvements for the public administration as a whole. The separate personnel system claimed for the corporation tends to treat old-line agencies unfairly because the government corporations are free to pay relatively higher salaries. The budgeting of government is made more difficult because the accounts of the corporations are attached to rather than being an integral part of the budget as a whole: this situation leads to a less accurate picture of overall governmental finances. Above all, accountability of these bodies to the elected representatives of the public is made difficult or impossible.

The extremes of independence to which special districts and those who direct them can go is illustrated by the 40-year career of New York's Robert Moses.

CASE STUDY: AN EMPIRE OF GOVERNMENT CORPORATIONS

In the 1920s, Moses was director of the Long Island State Park Commission, a special district designed to serve the population of metropolitan New York. He was able to persuade the state legislature to set up other special highway districts, which he also headed, to enable people to reach his parks. At one point, Moses was simultaneously head of many state and city agencies, including New York City departments of housing and parks, the Triborough Bridge and Tunnel Authority, the Henry Hudson Parkway Authority, and a host of others. He had accumulated so much power that he was able to keep New York mayor Fiorello LaGuardia waiting in his office, fuming with anger at Moses' tardiness, but unable to do anything about it. Once a visitor entered Moses' office and heard him call the speaker on the other end of the telephone "a goddam son of a bitch," before he hung up. When his visitor asked to whom Moses had been speaking, Moses replied that it was New York's Governor Thomas Dewey. Like LaGuardia, Dewey found it impossible to rid himself of Moses.

Moses was able to act this way with impunity because of the vast revenue produced by the tolls on his highways, bridges, and tunnels. He used them to lend money to the city of New York and to provide patronage jobs for followers of party chiefs. He thus cemented his support in city and state so strongly that he could operate independently of elected chief executives and legislatures. His power was impressive enough that onlookers wondered if he was about to emulate his biblical namesake by rolling back the waters of the Hudson River. Moses had admirers, to be sure, but his accomplishments did not include increased coordination of policy in New York government. He was rather head of a vast state within a state, which went in a direction all its own.[27]

Future Policy Weighing the opposing arguments on methods of regulation, one is inclined to fall back on the title of Harvey Sherman's book, *It All Depends*. It depends upon these factors: what the objective is at the particular time, whether the corporation is to be temporary or long-lived and whether alternative agencies are doing their job sufficiently well to satisfy the need. An emergency is different from a normal situation (which, incidentally, has been a figment of the imagination for a long time). It depends upon how one weighs the rival claims of uniformity and flexibility, strict accountability in a centralized system and a looser system in a pluralistic government.

It also depends upon the people at the top of the government who run it and make its decisions. Businessmen brought in to run government corporations (as illustrated by the TVA in its early days) may be more dedicated, experienced, and effective than those in older bureaus and departments of the general government. It depends upon how important one thinks it is to have uniformity in the civil service system or whether one favors a universal "system" at all. It depends upon how important it is to show a profit. It depends upon the caliber of competition coming from other countries. If they are taking over one export market after another, for example, there may be reason to innovate. It depends upon how favorable or unfavorable public opinion is toward what is trying to be accomplished.

The importance of this last point cannot be overemphasized. As experience in the federal government shows, it is relatively easy to infiltrate the authentic corporation and change it almost beyond recognition in a relatively short time. The hatchetmen were out to "get" the Reconstruction Finance Corporation (RFC), and they succeeded in the 1940s. But many times since then the government has wished that it still had this agency to cope with economic crises of one sort or another. Many federal officials remember Jesse Jones, the Texas financier who presided over the RFC's destinies for so long a period. Do citizens want to bring domineering figures into the government? Do they want accomplishment? If so, a republic can afford to innovate and take chances.

Perhaps this analysis is enough to demonstrate that there is no simple answer to either the use of the independent regulatory commission or the continued use of the government corporation as a device for transacting the public business. The answer lies in the realm of political economy, balancing the opposing considerations and finding the answers that prove beneficial for a time frame which includes the past, the present, and the kind of future the country desires.

SPECULATIONS ON ORGANIZATIONS OF THE FUTURE

A number of writers believe that future organizations will be much flatter than those of today. In addition, they think that organization will be increasingly less formal in other ways.[28]

These writers see the present knowledge explosion as the reason for this likely trend. There are more scientists alive today than all the dead scientists in the entire history of the human race. Every 10 years, the volume of published scientific research doubles, meaning that the quantity of research produced in the 1980s will equal the quantity produced in all previous history. An example of a technological change that has reorganized many agency operations is the computer, which we discuss in more detail in Chapter 17. Specialization has increased at a rapid rate, and workers have much more formal education than they did even 20 years ago. A master's degree has become increasingly necessary for many government positions.

Rapid change has become a way of life in American society. Demands for a better deal for women and minorities, the growth of government labor unions, the environmental movement, the energy crisis, and a host of other sudden and severe changes and demands for change have become the rule, not the exception. Life-styles and values seem to change overnight.

In such a society, it has been argued, hierarchical structures become increasingly less effective as a way to organize. The social psychologists Daniel Katz and Robert L. Kahn believe that hierarchies work best when jobs require little creativity, there are few demands for change, and demands on the organization are crystal clear.[29] But today organizations are under pressure to innovate, be flexible, and provide job satisfaction to employees. The environment in which they operate is increasingly complex and unpredictable, and so the hierarchical structure is less and less useful.

What will the new organizations look like? They will be flatter than the ones we find today, with more emphasis on lateral or horizontal cooperation for accomplishing the job. That is, not so many issues and problems will rise to higher levels of the hierarchy but will be settled lower down. To return to the Transportation Department sketched in Figure 11.4, the rail and water transport divisions will be more likely to settle a common problem involving a drawbridge over a river than they would have in the past.

Temporary work groups ("adhocracies," to use Alvin Toffler's term) will evolve in response to changing conditions.[30] They will work on a particular problem and then disband. The Apollo space program was composed of 100 of these project-management teams, coordinated by a person who lacked the formal authority to give orders. Yet this program was uniquely successful; men landed on the moon and returned safely to earth. Related to project management is matrix organization. Workers are organized laterally or horizontally to perform many jobs, even though they may still remain in their formal hierarchies. There will be more decentralization of work of all kinds.

While this forecast of coming organizational change is probably accurate, some of the more radical visions of the organizational future seem most unlikely to come to pass. Even though some writers argue that hierarchy is contrary to human nature,[31] it has been present since the beginning of recorded history. Flatter organizations, with more decentralization and more cooperation, will be seen more often. But hierarchy will not disappear.

SUMMARY

This chapter has dealt with some colorful and exciting issues, government "interference" and ownership, for example. The main purpose, however, was to show how principles of organization such as specialization, hierarchy, unity of command, span of control, and adaptation to change are the daily life of management. No enterprise runs solely on its organization, and many a good management team has been defeated by hopelessly rigid organization. Another area deserving intensive study is headquarters-field relations, because most of the actual delivery system is found there. One reason organizations are so much written about is that they look so tidy, scientific, and rational. Actually, if any one of these three assumptions is allowed too much play and not admixed with other factors, organization can become pretty deadly.

NOTES

1. Mary Parker Follett, "Responsibility in Business Management," in *Dynamic Administration: The Collected Papers of Mary Parker Follett,* ed. O. Henry Metcalf and Lyndall Urwick (New York: Macmillan, 1937).

2. See Harvey Sherman, *It All Depends: A Pragmatic Approach to Organization* (Tuscaloosa: University of Alabama Press, 1966), pp. 196–201.

3. *Exodus* 18: 13–26.

4. Roy Blount, Jr., "Heinsohn's Complaint," *New York Times,* 19 February 1979, p. 37.

5. Rufus E. Miles, Jr., "Considerations for a President Bent on Reorganization," *Public Administration* 37 (March-April 1977): 158.

6. Hans Garth and C. Wright Mills, *From Max Weber* (New York: Oxford University Press, 1946), pp. 196–198.

7. Sherman, *It All Depends,* pp. 83–84.

8. Randy H. Hamilton to the editor, *Public Administration Times,* 15 June 1979.

9. Sherman, *It All Depends*, pp. 30–38.

10. Sherman, *It All Depends*.

11. Mary Parker Follett, "The Giving of Orders" and "Leadership Theory and Practice," in *Dynamic Administration*, ed., Metcalf and Urwick.

12. Marshall E. Dimock, *The Executive in Action* (New York: Harper & Row, 1945), p. 167.

13. Dimock, *The Executive in Action*, p. 167.

14. Dimock, *The Executive in Action*, p. 171.

15. Sherman, *It All Depends*.

16. John F. Wall and Leonard B. Dworsky, *Problems of Executive Reorganization: The Federal EPA* (Ithaca, N.Y.: Cornell University Water Resources and Marine Sciences Center, 1971), p. 40.

17. Eli Ginsberg and Ewing W. Reilley, *Effecting Change in Large Organizations* (New York: Columbia University Press, 1957); Warren G. Bennis, Kenneth D. Benne, and Robert Chin, eds., *The Planning of Change* (New York: Holt, Rinehart & Winston, 1961); and Roger A. Colde, *Muddling Through* (New York: AMACOM, 1976).

18. Harold Seidman, *Politics, Position, and Power: The Dynamics of Federal Organization* (New York: Oxford University Press, 1975), p. 4. This book is indispensable for the serious student of federal organization.

19. George D. Greenberg, "Reorganization Reconsidered: The U.S. Public Health Service, 1960–1973," *Public Policy* (Fall 1975), pp. 513–514.

20. Seidman, *Politics, Position, and Power*, pp. 315–316.

21. Marver H. Bernstein, *Regulating Business by Independent Commissions* (Princeton, N.J.: Princeton University Press, 1955).

22. James W. Fesler, *The Independence of State Regulatory Agencies* (Chicago: Public Administration Service, 1942).

23. American Bar Association, Commission on Law and the Economy, *Federal Regulation: Roads to Reform* (Washington: American Bar Association, 1978).

24. See, for example, Marver Bernstein, *Regulating Business;* Emmette S. Redford, *American Government and the Economy* (New York: Macmillan, 1965); H. J. Friendly, *The Federal Administrative Agencies* (Cambridge: Harvard University Press, 1962); or Bernard Schwartz, *The Professor and the Commissions* (New York: Knopf, 1959).

25. Annemarie Hauck Walsh, *The Public's Business* (New York: Twentieth Century Fund, 1978) is the most thorough and searching critique of state and local public authorities.

26. Marshall E. Dimock, "Government Corporations: A Focus of Policy and Administration," *American Political Science Review*, I and II, 43 (October 1949): 899–921 and (December 1949): 1145–1164; David E. Lilienthal and Robert Marquis, "The Conduct of Business Enterprises in the Federal Government," *Harvard Law Review* 54 (February 1941): 545–601.

27. Robert A. Caro, *The Power Broker* (New York: Knopf, 1974) is a massive and monumental analysis of Moses' career.

28. These writers include Richard L. Chapman and Frederic N. Cleaveland, *Meeting the Needs of Tomorrow's Public Service* (Washington: National Academy of Public Administration, 1977); Warren G. Bennis and Phillip E. Slater, *The Temporary Society* (New York: Harper & Row, 1968); and George E. Berkley, *The Administrative Revolution* (Englewood Cliffs, N.J.: Prentice-Hall, 1971).

29. Daniel Katz and Robert L. Kahn, *The Social Psychology of Organizations* (New York: Wiley, 1966), p. 214.

30. Alvin Toffler, *Future Shock* (New York: Random House, 1970).

31. Lynton K. Caldwell, "Biology and Bureaucracy: The Coming Confrontation," *Public Administration Review* 40 (January-February 1980): 1–12.

12

Supervision: Leadership at Lower Levels

A man has just naturally got to have something to cuss around and boss, so's to keep himself from finding out he don't amount to nothing.

Donald Robert Perry Marquis

In this chapter, which is closely related to policy and leadership, we probe the job of the supervisor, examining his role at different levels within the organization, giving guidelines for more effective supervision, and setting forth different theoretical approaches to the subject.

In 1978, Congressman Elliott Levitas of Georgia succeeded in attaching an amendment to the Civil Service Reform Act. This amendment was an attempt to legislate good manners. It stipulated that federal employees with a "pattern of discourtesy" to clients would be subject to disciplinary measures. When interviewed in 1980, Levitas complained that some agencies were not paying attention to the amendment.[1] The congressman should not have been surprised. Effective disciplinary action of this sort can be taken only by the employee's supervisor. It cannot be legislated.

This is not to say that supervisors will always make perfect decisions. For example, we might question the appropriateness of the communication in Box 12.1. But there is no question that this *kind* of communication should come from the supervisor.

While organization provides the channels through which the work of a program flows, there must also be a way to provide the drive and the energy to *keep* it flowing so that the program will attain its objectives. This energy has its source in leadership and is translated by supervisors into action. The direction of the flow of work is based on decisions that must be made at every level in the organization, from the front office where major policy is decided to the action level where minor questions may also be important. In this total process, the guiding principle, the criterion by which every act of supervision is made, is the objectives of the program.

A supervisor is one who directs the work of others. A distinction is sometimes made between high-level executives with large responsibility for policy decisions and subordinate supervisors closer to the day-to-day work, whose influence on policy is only incidental. There is, to be sure, a difference in orientation among administrators at various organizational levels, but it must not be pushed too far or it will obscure the policy and leadership roles of supervisors at all levels.

In large government agencies, the three main levels of supervision are top, middle, and primary, or first-line, and it is at the middle and primary levels that most of the work of government is ac-

complished. It is also at these two levels that most college graduates beginning their careers in government make their first contact with the practice of public administration.

THE SUPERVISOR'S ROLE

The modern approach to administration is by delegation and decentralization, so as to avoid excessive rules, concentrated authority at the top, and other weaknesses of bureaucracy that cause a program to plod cautiously instead of moving with energy and determination. This delegation of authority is mainly to the supervisor and initially to the supervisor at the middle-management level.

Delegation

One mark of a good manager is the ability to delegate tasks. The temptation to try to do the job oneself can be overwhelming. In fact, management authority Louis A. Allen has enunciated the principle of operating priority, which states that "when called upon to perform both management work and operating work during the same period, a manager will tend to give first priority to operating work."[2] But this decision is a mistake, since the manager's job is to supervise others to do work. A manager wastes time by doing work subordinates should do and indirectly conveys a lack of confidence in subordinates' abilities to do the job, a surefire way to destroy morale.

A manager who feels that subordinates cannot do the job adequately must do everything possible to have these employees trained so that they can improve their performance. At the same time, the manager should indicate to employees that however the office was run in the past, more authority will now be delegated.

Delegating authority will develop the initiative and resourcefulness of subordinates and increase their respect for their superior. At the same time, the manager will be less likely to be surrounded by yes-men. A domineering supervisor attracts subordinates who agree with everything he says,

Box 12.1

MEMORANDUM

Internal Revenue Service
memorandum

date: **MAR 15 1979**

to: All Group Managers

from: Chief, Executive Branch CP:OIO:65

subject: Information Requests

   Recently an employee received and apparently answered a telephonic request for information.
   Calls from taxpayers for Information Requests should be referred to the Freedom of Information Reading Room at National Office.

   Please bring this to the attention of all your employees.

---

while driving away those with independence and creativity. Once the organization encounters a crisis, yes-men are worse than useless, because they prevent the supervisor from seeing how serious the situation is. What the manager needs in an emergency is a subordinate who will clearly sketch the dismal picture and help formulate a solution, no matter how drastic or unpopular.

Some managers detest delegation because they fear their subordinates will outshine them. For the same reason, they resolutely refuse to groom anyone to take their place while they are away from the job. In this way they hope to be seen as indispensable. What they fail to realize is that the most valuable managerial skill is developing talent, especially talent that may come to outshine them. In results-oriented organizations, managers' achievements in developing talent will be richly rewarded. By the same token, an organization may be reluctant to promote someone who

has not trained a successor. After all, who can do that supervisor's work if he is promoted? Finally, the manager will have more time to do managerial work if he has help from an assistant. Many, or most, managers complain that there is not time enough in the day to do everything. An assistant can make it possible to lengthen the day by sharing the burden.

Administrative Assistants. The job of administrative assistant is an attractive one for students entering the public service. A supervisor discovers so much value in an administrative assistant who can multiply his eyes and ears and at the same time deal with organizational, budgetary, and personnel matters the chief needs to know about that, not surprisingly, many secretaries have been reclassified by their bosses and given the designation administrative assistant. An honest executive will admit that he is multiplied about four-fold by acquiring a good assistant. This is especially true if each senses what the other is thinking or wanting done and each does what seems indicated without a word being spoken. A closely related position is that of executive assistant. The one difference here is that the administrative assistant usually deals with organization, budgets, and related matters, while the executive assistant may deal with a wider range of subjects, including negotiation. There is no hard and fast rule about this, however, and ultimately the role depends upon the personality, strengths and weaknesses, and style of the supervisor.

The Key Role of Middle Management. Where top management belongs in the office of the chief executive of a government or a major government agency, middle management is the responsibility of division and bureau chiefs in all agencies of government from the federal to the local. Probably no one has studied the subject more penetratingly than Mary Cushing Niles, who started her professional career in the scientific management movement and was once president of the Washington chapter of the Society for the Advancement of Management.[3] Indeed, Mary Niles is one of three remarkable women in the field of management scholarship, the others being Mary Parker Follett, who was one of the first to recognize the technique now referred to as group dynamics, and Lillian Gilbreth, who was an outstanding member of the scientific management movement.

In the administrative process, the forces of leadership flow upwards, downwards, and sideways, and all lines of communication meet in the middle; in many respects, therefore, middle managers are the key people in administration. It is they who transmit orders, decisions, and guidance from the top down, and, in turn, communicate problems, difficulties, viewpoints, complaints, and suggestions from the lower ranks to the top.

Also because of their position, *middle managers share in the burdens of their superiors in working out policy and grand strategy, and they are also close enough to first-line supervisors to*

understand their problems and points of view. The top manager is too far removed from most employees to exercise much direct influence on them. This influence must be channeled through the middle manager, who thus becomes the transmission line for interpreting policy, inspiring effort, and cultivating the favorable attitudes and sentiments that constitute loyalty.

Consequently, the middle manager, as Niles analyzes his role, is the focal point in the meeting of minds that is the basis of a happy working group. Just as senior officers see, hear, and analyze problems beyond the scope of internal administration, so do junior officers see, hear, and, in the main, deal with the problems of internal operations. Indeed, in its leadership, policy-interpreting, energizing, and coordinating role, middle management is the core around which most aspects of administration revolve.[4]

The middle manager is also a key person when an enterprise takes on a new activity and someone is needed to advise as to its organization and functioning and *see that it is geared to overall operations.* One may suppose, for example, that the Immigration Service wants to launch a big program in citizenship education, as it did immediately before World War II, as a means of helping aliens become naturalized and acquire American citizenship. When a new manager is appointed to head this program, an experienced middle manager may prove to be the one ideally suited for such as assignment, working with a chief who is an expert on the subject matter of the activity.

Orientation at the Primary Level. Peter Drucker, in his *Practice of Management,* entitled one of his chapters "Management by Objectives and Self-Control." In it he notes that the philosophy of the subject is the most important aspect of it. The term should not be used with "happy abandon," however, as in the case of a purchasing agent who wrote an article on purchasing in which it turned out that the essence of his "philosophy" was the need to make records in triplicate. By the philosophy of supervision Drucker means values, states of mind, attitudes toward people, and judgments as to how things add up.[5]

Supervision may be approached from two different standpoints: it may be centered on authority, the issuing of orders, and the application of rules; or it may be centered on the worker. The first approach is bureaucratic, the latter is based on human relations and is the more favored modern approach.

In industry, supervision became worker-centered when business managers eventually realized that to issue commands merely on the basis of authority and to hold the threat of dismissal over workers if they disobeyed, was a costly procedure in terms of realistically accomplishing tasks. In searching for a solution, a considerable amount of research was undertaken and a clue found in the fact that the higher in the hierarchy a given supervisor is located, the greater is the deference shown him by subordinates and also the more employees become tongue-tied and uneasy when he enters the room. Contrariwise, the closer the supervisor is to the work group, the more he becomes one of them, identifies with them, and is able to influence them. In terms of influence on employees, therefore, the role of the primary supervisor is in some respects more crucial than that of the middle manager.[6]

Subordinates commonly respond to the instructions of a supervisor with the mental query What does it mean to me? Not What am I going to get out of it? but What does it mean to me in my job? If the supervisor is to be effective, he can benefit by carefully considering the following guidelines.[7]

Person to Person

Focusing on the work rather than on the worker, skilled managers avoid unnecessary supervision, seeking instead to give the employee maximum discretion in deciding how to do the job. The chef who keeps telling the cooks to mix sauces with a certain motion regardless of the way they taste and the foreman who insists that workers lift gar-

bage cans with a particular motion regardless of their weight are authoritarians with little grasp of psychology. They have lost interest in results and become obsessed with matters of technique. Predictably, their subordinates will chafe under this unreasonably close supervision and become less productive.

Consultation. A sure recipe for disaster is to announce without consultation that some big changes are going to be made. The prospect of change usually causes anxiety and insecurity because to change is to venture into unknown territory. Employees will wonder if the way they have learned to do their jobs will be considered inadequate and whether, ultimately, they themselves will be declared unfit for further service. As a result, they will react negatively—directly or indirectly, consciously or unconsciously—decreasing their performance to a point where the new manager will end up in hot water. As Howard E. Ball, a veteran federal career employee, has written, "Never knowingly let your boss repeat a mistake already made by his predecessor [although] I have broken this rule . . . where the arrogance level of my supervisor was so high that I felt he had to go through the disaster and fully and directly experience the put down."[8]

Blame. Blaming subordinates for his mistakes is a sure way for a manager to lose the respect and loyalty of his workers. Yet how many times have we asked supervisors why they had not yet done something that was supposed to have been done yesterday, only to be told that their failure was due to a subordinate? A writer once called two editors to ask why they had not made a decision on a proposal he had made. One editor frankly acknowledged that he had goofed and made no excuses, while the other blamed his secretary. The poor impression made by the latter editor would surely have been aggravated even further had his secretary been present to hear this remark. Managers should never pass the buck, because admissions that they are to blame are unlikely to hurt them unless they fail constantly. Furthermore, buck-passing managers will soon have a completely disloyal and disrespectful staff.

Favoritism. Another constant concern of the manager is to avoid even the appearance of treating employees of equal status unequally. If subordinates come to believe that some of their number are favorites of the manager or are on an enemies' list, morale will quickly decline and performance will follow. For example, if one worker always receives desired assignments and equally qualified peers do not, trouble is bound to result. While it is not possible to treat equally qualified workers equally in every instance, a good manager will strive to do so.[9]

Anger. The supervisor who loses his temper becomes less effective. Operatic conductor Erich Leinsdorf relates how a star singer came up to him and told him he wanted to break his commitment to appear in several performances. "He probably expected and hoped to get into a fight with me, but I disappointed him by calmly admitting that I myself had wanted to get out but was unable to do so gracefully so I would see it through. He had no choice but to leave my room without a fight."[10] Since it takes two people to have a fight, if the supervisor refuses to fight, he may be able to defuse a tense situation and start moving toward a solution of the problem. As Thomas Jefferson said about George Washington, "His temper was naturally irritable and high toned; but reflection and resolution had obtained a firm and habitual ascendancy over it."

The foregoing is not to say that the supervisor should be some kind of saint who never gets angry. But he should express that anger in a more positive way than fighting. One alternative is to let the subordinate know the supervisor is angry, but to keep things in the first person. Instead of saying "You blew it and screwed everything up," the supervisor can say, "I am very upset that this work was not done." Having cleared the air and having let the subordinate know that he is angry,

the supervisor may now be able to guide the worker back on the track. A person can be angry without losing his temper and can channel that anger constructively to solve problems. But loss of self-control is unlikely to do anything but make a bad situation worse.

The point recalls an anecdote. A guest at a dinner given in Denver in honor of Marshall Ferdinard Foch, commander of the allied forces in World War I, said that there was nothing but wind in French politeness. Marshall Foch retorted: "Neither is there anything but wind in a pneumatic tire, yet it eases wonderfully the jolts along life's highway."

Reward. Managers give out rewards and punishment every working day. A word of praise, a sarcastic remark, permission to leave early, denial of a request for a raise, and listening to a distraught employee's problems are all rewards or punishments. While punishment is sometimes necessary, reward is a far more effective means of motivating workers.

Americans live in a punishment-oriented society, which endorses penalties as the best way to make sure crimes and undesired actions will not recur. But punishment is a problematical procedure to use in motivating employees and should be turned to only as a last resort. For one thing, punishable behavior is likely to happen again when the punisher is absent. Second, the punisher is perceived as the "bad guy": the whole relationship between subordinate and supervisor may be jeopardized. Third, punishment has many undesirable consequences. The subordinate can get even with the punishing superior in 1,000 different ways, whether slowing down work or slandering the manager in front of other employees. Fourth, it is impossible to enforce penalties fairly and evenhandedly. Just as some speeders are never caught, while others receive a ticket, some workers who should be punished are never caught. A feeling of being treated unfairly will rankle in a subordinate and may eventually cripple performance.

With all these problems, it makes sense to stress reward over punishment. Reward focuses on what the employee is doing right and contributes to a positive relationship with the manager. Praise ("Thanks for doing that," "That was an excellent job,") can be a highly effective reward, even better in some instances than monetary (pay raise), status (new title), or power (more authority) rewards. Since most people like rewards, they may modify their behavior so that they will continue to be rewarded.

Managers will do well to follow certain principles in giving rewards. One is to discover which rewards mean the most to which employees. Some will prefer money raises, others challenging assignments, others recognition. Each person is different, and the manager should analyze what makes each subordinate tick. A second principle to follow is rapid reward, so that the employee realizes just what is being rewarded. Do not defer rewards, or the subordinate will not be so highly motivated to repeat desirable behavior. Third, rewards should be given only when they are deserved. If employees find they are rewarded without having done anything to be rewarded for, they lose all incentive to improve. Fourth, having employees keep records of their own behavior can pay large dividends. This step at once rewards subordinates by indicating that the manager trusts them, and allows them to see that rewards are given on an objective, results-oriented basis. For example, employees could keep records to see how many units of work at what level of quality were finished.

Readers may balk at the advice that undesirable behavior should be ignored unless it jeopardizes the safety and health of other employees or clients. But occasionally it is useful to try this approach and to focus on reward to see if subordinate behavior can be modified. One of the authors once surprised two subordinates taking an unauthorized break. Instead of saying a word, he ignored the infraction, and these two dependable and productive workers continued their excellent work in the future. If unacceptable behavior persists, punishment can always be used as a last resort.

Discipline. Punishment is like surgery, a remedy to be tried only after other approaches have failed. Perhaps the most necessary reason for punishment is to show other employees that the person who does not obey the rules will not get away with it. Few things can infuriate a person so much as the feeling that he is being treated unfairly or invidiously. If someone else can disobey the rules, why not this person? Indeed, the record shows that tolerating one employee's absences, tardiness, or other infractions is likely to lead other employees to imitate the bad behavior.

A manager who contemplates taking a disciplinary action should ask whether the subordinate understood that a rule had been broken. If there has been a communication error or inadequate training, punishing the worker would have disastrous consequences. Supervisors should be especially careful when the violator is a new employee, who may be confused on beginning work in a new environment. Only when the manager can be sure that the employee definitely knew that a rule was being broken should disciplinary measures be taken.

In meting out discipline, the manager should seek to remove the cause of the violation wherever possible. For example, if smoking is forbidden in certain areas for safety considerations, it should be allowed in other well-publicized areas.

Before applying discipline, the manager must investigate the circumstances. Is this the subordinate's first infraction or the latest in a long line of similar occurrences? Was it done by accident or on purpose?

Again, the rule of fairness is critical. The manager should stress the facts, instead of rushing up to an employee and shouting, "How did you do this, you jackass?" One approach is to show an employee an error or point out a rule infraction and simply ask in a friendly tone what happened. The employee may be completely innocent of any blame for the error. But if not, the supervisor should not greet obviously lame excuses with derision. A remark to "cut the baloney and own up!" is only going to cause the employee to hate the manager. Instead, by patiently listening to the explanation and failing to express any irritation, the manager is much more likely to get improve-

ment. The manager can then say, "Let's review the procedure to make sure you understand it." In this way, the subordinate has been able to save face and avoid humiliation. At the same time, the appropriate behavior has been made crystal clear.

CASE STUDY: OUT IN THE WOODS

Ben Ladd frowned again. As head of the Mount Majestic district office of the state department of Environmental Protection, he had run up against many sticky situations, but he did not like the position he was in now. He was one week into the summer season, the period when he had the most work to do and the largest number of employees to do it. These additional employees were college students, who signed up for three months of summer work. With their help, Ben was to get the woods, trails, and campsites in the wilderness recreation area set up to last another year.

Ben was perturbed because half of his summer work force of six was not working the way he had expected. And it was a mystery to him why not, since all three were majoring in ecology and appeared to be highly motivated to do the work. Ben reviewed each of the three unsatisfactory workers in his mind. First was Abe Stein, who was exceptionally bright. Maybe *too* bright, for Abe was always trying to do things in his own way, rather than listening to Ben's instructions. Sometimes Abe came up with excellent ideas—Ben had already adopted two of his suggestions for repairs—but at other times he wasted time and material and had set work back two days when a bridge collapsed because he wouldn't listen to Ben. Personal relations between Ben and Abe were pleasant, but Abe did not give adequate weight to Ben's advice when making a decision.

Maria Sanchez offered a different challenge. Most of the time she was a crackerjack worker, productive and smart. Ben had not expected her to be able to keep up with the men because she

was the first woman to have such a summer job. She had held her own, but several times she had disappeared. When Ben located her, her mood was sullen. She talked about male chauvinism and sexual innuendoes directed at her by the men when Ben wasn't around. While she quickly snapped out of these moods, they pulled her work down below the expected standard. Perhaps, even more importantly, the five male summer employees had begun to ask why they couldn't take breaks as Maria did. Was she favored by Ben? One had even made a tongue-in-cheek remark about Ben's being romantically involved with Maria.

The last of the three was Tom Morey. Tom was as strong as an ox and could do an enormous amount of work. But he was not the brightest student who had ever worked for Ben, and his love of socializing was interfering with his work. You wouldn't think it was possible to run into people in the woods, but Tom could. He had already come across Seth Barlow, the only farmer within miles. And he had encountered the town road crew on its break and every camper within miles. (There were few campers now, but soon there would be multitudes.) The other guys didn't seem to mind because Tom worked so hard, but Ben didn't see how Tom was going to be able to do his share unless he curbed his on-the-job socializing.

In his musings, Ben noted that 20 years ago he could have fired all three workers and obtained superior replacements. He doubted this would be true today, for summer job opportunities had increased. Further, he felt that firing them was a last resort. All three had outstanding work ability. "It's up to me, as their boss, to see that they do the work. But how am I going to do it? And I certainly can't use the same approach for all three. Dealing with Maria is going to be the hardest, since I've never had a female subordinate in this type of work before. What I have going for me there is that she doesn't believe I'm biased against women. Abe is sharp as a tack, but how do I harness that brainpower? How do I keep him thinking, avoid turning him off, while getting him to listen so he doesn't make any more damn fool mistakes like that bridge disaster? Tom should be the easiest of the three, since I've dealt with somewhat similar problems before, but I've still got to be careful, since I don't yet know him all that well."

Ben got up, since it was five minutes to supper. In the dining room he asked Abe, Maria, and Tom to see him individually for half an hour each after dinner.

Question: The reader is Ben. What will the reader say or do to motivate each employee to do a better job? Why?

SELECTION AND TRAINING FOR SUPERVISION

Middle and first-line supervisors are so crucial to the effectiveness of government programs that much attention has been centered on them in recent years by the public personnel profession. "It is a shame," comments experienced personnel manager O. Glenn Stahl, "that many able technicians founder when they have supervisory responsibilities thrust upon them." Stahl is talking about a phenomenon described in a tongue-in-cheek best seller as the "Peter Principle." This principle states that people rise to the level of their incompetence. A good mechanic may be a disastrous service manager; a good teacher, a terrible principal, and so on.[11] Even though training for supervision is offered, Stahl notes that "it does not follow that supervisory behavior improves automatically as a result of it."[12] Stahl sees the most common shortcoming of supervisors selected by the civil service system as insensitivity in the area of human relations and lack of motivation. Consequently, most of the training of supervisors now being done in government—and it is extensive—concentrates on these weaknesses. Supervisory training is more than occasional participation in an executive development session; in fact, such training is a continuous process.[13]

It is worth noting that it is the primary and middle supervisors of today who will ultimately occupy the highest executive positions in the civil service, so it becomes crucial to try to develop the needed blend of qualities. As suggested, temperament and native ability are included in the complex; outlook and personality traits also play a part. The entrepreneurial, strategic type of supervisor able to delegate is the most effective variety, but even he benefits from some degree of training. Liking and understanding people is almost a fundamental necessity. A combination of toughness and the ability to say no when necessary with giving encouragement when subordinates are inclined to innovate and seek their own way of doing things is also essential. A good supervisor never tells a subordinate *how* to do things unless asked; he prefers to encourage the subordinate to use his own initiative, to be resourceful, and to focus on results.

SUPERVISION THEORY: DIFFERENT EMPHASES

If administration were a matter of merely establishing procedures whereby one decision after another could be made, much like an action before a court of law, then, of course, the desirable model for decision making would be bureaucracy. But today, most administration is less bureaucratic than it is entrepreneurial and strategic. To the supervisor, the model within which he works makes a difference.

The Bureaucratic Model

The bureaucratic model of supervision has many distinguishing characteristics, but in the eyes of the administrator, the principal one is probably its heavy reliance on rules. Every aspect of management must be reduced to formal organization, set procedures, iron-clad assignments of responsibility, and specific direction from the official next highest in the hierarchy.

Scientific management was on the verge of becoming dangerously rule-ridden when the human relations school of thought came to its rescue sometime after the close of World War II. Having discovered the advantages of planning before acting, scientific management had concluded that every aspect of action must be minutely planned down to the smallest detail. For the most part, this went under the heading of work planning, a process in which every step in a given operation was examined according to time-and-motion studies to determine the quickest and best way of accomplishing it. Such techniques are useful, to be sure, but to carry such measurements to extremes and to impose the one-best-way rule without discrimination, creates rules and procedures so rigid and inhuman as to alienate most of the members of an organization. Organized labor, for example, has revolted against this approach, reminding management that workers are not a commodity and do not wish to be regimented or treated as standardized, interchangeable parts. This passion for regulation in administration is similar to what occurs in legislatures. A person elected to a legislature often finds himself— somewhat to his own surprise—looking around for some subject on which he can introduce his "own" legislation. Surely that was one reason he was elected to office, he tells himself. He begins to assume that if some area is still not regulated by law, it should be.

The bureaucrat falls into the same habit of thought. When a question of policy is raised, the rule maker immediately assumes that since the same question might arise at some future time, no matter how remote, a rule must be promulgated. Indeed, to formulate rules becomes almost a disease. In the course of a study of a large-scale undertaking abroad, it was found that some 50 rule books applied to the technical side of a particular business, and another 50 to the procedural side, but that in practice, neither set was extensively used. In explanation, it was said that those who make and promulgate the rule books are paid for the job, and line officials felt they should not interfere with a professional occupation in which its practitioners take pride.[14] In such a situation, courtesy becomes the basis for the proliferating red tape of which the citizen complains.

To forestall these complications, and despite his professional pride, the supervisor must be on guard against the temptation to reduce the work of his subordinates to rule and rote. In addition, he and every other manager should periodically review existing rules and traditional procedures to discard what is no longer relevant. If they are not carefully controlled, rules constitute a form of creeping paralysis.

The tendency toward standardized procedures and multiplication of rules is now the main cause of criticism of bureaucracy by public officials themselves, such as those reported in the Brookings Institution study *The Image of the Federal Service*[15] and in replies to a questionnaire circulated in 1968 among top federal officials by the National Academy of Public Administration. Public officials want greater freedom to decide questions of method for themselves, and they believe that they should enjoy this freedom so long as they achieve the indicated objective and conform to law and the policies laid down by their superiors. They want to be trusted to think for themselves, to use ingenuity in accomplishing their goals. They react emotionally against the straitjacket of rigid rules and regulations, which are the harder to bear because so often they hinder rather than promote the program. Indeed, these are some of the reasons for a rather widespread antagonism to the civil service concept on the part of many public administrators. They are not necessarily against the merit system, but they believe a greater freedom of self-determination would encourage better program results.

It is sometimes wondered whether it would not be possible to follow Max Weber's prescription for bureaucracy and still remain enterprising and innovative; or whether, as a matter of fact, it is necessary to be enterprising at all. As the members of the Soviet bureaucratic apparatus keep saying in Vladimir Dudintsev's novel *Not By Bread Alone,* what does it matter that set procedures are slow and plodding? At least, these procedures work.[16] In the United States, at any rate, the answer is that for understandable historical reasons, few Americans willingly tolerate regimentation or the multitude and rigidity of the rules that accompany it.

The Newer Approach

Because of considerations such as these and a need to create more flexibility in management, the concept of administering by objectives was formulated and is now the dominant mode of supervision. One of the most eloquent pleas in its favor found anywhere in the literature of public administration is by Rufus Miles, whose views gain weight from the fact that he rose through the federal career service to the post of administrative assistant secretary of a cabinet department. In an article called "Administrative Adaptability to Political Change," Miles points out that

---

too many decisions are made at too high a level. Some decisions made at the Budget Bureau level ought to be made by the Secretary of a department and his staff; other decisions made at the Secretary's level might better be made at the next level below—the "operating agency" level; still others made at the operating agency level should most appropriately be made at the bureau level.[17]

This is no bureaucrat speaking but what John Corson calls an entrepreneur. It is the prescription that government agencies should follow if they would have their employees become excited about their jobs.

Is this term administering by objectives just a high-sounding phrase or perhaps merely an admonition? It might be either, except that when applied, the concept does, in fact, produce results. In a book titled *Management by Results,* Edward C. Schleh takes administering by objectives as the central theme of his analysis. The tendency in large-scale organization, he says, seems to be to reduce every aspect of administration to procedures that have been made as automatic as possible; now it is time to realize that outstanding achievement depends less on procedures than on the expansion of the individual, his abilities, and his personality.[18]

We have merely introduced the subject of administering by objectives here to explain its philosophy, leaving to Chapter 15 (on control) matters relating to the application of the concept and its evaluation.

Large organizations would have it made if they allowed their various operating division managers to proceed as though wholly free of overhead control and if these managers then made all decisions with the collective interest of the entire group foremost in mind. That is what some executives in big organizations have meant in the past when they counseled "centralize planning, decentralize execution." Today they go a step further and say, "When planning is centralized and execution decentralized, everyone in the organization must be involved in decision making and in the defining of objectives."

The advantage of this approach is that people have more fun when they share in the defining of objectives and in making planning and policy decisions and then follow through on them and on other related decisions than they do out of any other aspect of administration. The greater their interest and the higher their morale, the better are the results likely to be for the organization and its program. Routine, nondiscretionary work is dull and bureaucratic; but when decision is involved, work becomes alive and challenging.

Decisions may safely be allowed at the lower

levels of administration if the following conditions are met. (1) The people at those levels have already been involved in determining program objectives, thus understanding the frame of reference. (2) They are familiar with and accept the philosophy and strategy underlying the plan by which these objectives are to be attained. (3) Each person has a carefully defined role and understands its relation and dependence on the roles of others. (4) There is a real desire and willingness to assume responsibility and share the risks for the decisions they will make. (Many people lack this quality, which is a main reason that able executives are perennially scarce.) (5) And finally, adequate provision has been made for coordinating the work of the organization and evaluating results. A certain amount of slack in administration seems to encourage innovation, while too tight a rein discourages it.

With this orientation, supervisory work has a certain appeal not found elsewhere in management, for the focus is on people as well as processes, on human relations, the encouragement of morale, and the development of skills. All these concerns require an entrepreneurial approach that is challenging and full of satisfactions.

SUMMARY

In this chapter we have dealt primarily with delegation, the importance of middle management, and administering by objectives. In the final analysis, however, supervision is a philosophy, not a science. It is good human relations based upon respect for others, not an expression of the aggressive instincts of a martinet. The good supervisor shares his interest in top-level concerns such as objectives, policies, and difficulties with those he wants to inspire and work with. As Mary Parker Follett remarked, his influence is *with,* not *over,* other people.

NOTES

1. "Georgia Democrat Wants Manners in Government," *Danbury (Conn.) News-Times,* 21 January 1980, p. 4.

2. Louis A. Allen, *The Management Profession* (New York: McGraw-Hill, 1964), p. 77.

3. Mary Cushing Niles, *Middle Management,* rev. ed. (New York: Harper & Row, 1949).

4. Niles, *Middle Management,* pp. ix, 217, 251.

5. Peter H. Drucker, *The Practice of Management* (New York: Harper & Row, 1954), p. 136.

6. F. J. Roethlisberger and William J. Dickson, *Management and the Worker* (Cambridge: Harvard University Press, 1939), pp. 456–458.

7. An outstanding text on supervision, which deals with these and other matters, is William Dowling and Leonard Sayles, *How Managers Motivate* (New York: McGraw-Hill, 1978).

8. Howard A. Ball, "The Art of Disobedience," *The Bureaucrat* (Fall 1973), pp. 248–255.

9. James K. Van Fleet, *The 22 Biggest Mistakes Managers Make and How to Correct Them* (West Nyack, N.Y.: Parker Publishers, 1973), pp. 121–134.

10. Erich Leinsdorf, *Cadenza* (Boston: Houghton, Mifflin, 1976), p. 301.

11. Laurence J. Peter, *The Peter Principle* (New York: Morrow, 1969).

12. O. Glen Stahl, *Public Personnel Administration,* 7th ed. (New York: Harper & Row, 1976), p. 271.

13. Stahl, *Public Personnel Administration.*

14. Cited in Marshall E. Dimock, *Administrative Vitality: The Conflict with Bureaucracy* (New York: Harper & Row, 1959), pp. 229–231.

15. Franklin P. Kilpatrick, Milton C. Cummings, Jr., and M. Kent Jennings, *The Image of the Federal Service* (Washington: Brookings Institution, 1964).

16. Vladimir Dudintsev, *Not By Bread Alone* (New York: Dutton, 1957).

17. Rufus Miles, "Administrative Adaptability to Political Change," *Public Administration Review* 25 (September 1965), 224.

18. Edward C. Schleh, *Management by Results* (New York: McGraw-Hill, 1961).

13

If there is any one secret of success, it lies in the ability to get the other person's point of view and see things from his angle as well as your own.

Henry Ford

In this chapter, we examine the factors influencing motivation and morale in organization, consider the importance of the study of psychology for public administration, probe the sources of organizational conflict, and discuss ways to channel conflict constructively.

An organization experiencing a crisis in motivation and morale hired a consultant to look into the causes of the problem. The consultant asked a foreman his opinion of management. In a contemptuous tone, the employee stated, "They are treating us like a mushroom farm." The puzzled consultant asked for an explanation, and the foreman replied, "They keep us in the dark, feed us you-know-what, and then they can us."[1]

To administer by objectives means paying close attention to motivation and incentives and to individual and group morale within the organization. We define morale in an individual as his emotional condition relating to work and morale in a work group as the group's capacity to pull together persistently and consistently in pursuit of commonly defined objectives and purposes. An individual with low morale does not like his work; a work group with low morale is unlikely to do as much as one with high morale.

An example of how morale can fluctuate is described by Michael Straight, former deputy chairman of the National Endowment for the Arts. Upon assuming his office, Straight discovered that the endowment was under attack by a number of congressmen because it had paid a poet $500 for a poem that consisted of a single word. Straight describes an encounter with one congressional aide, who said, "Always glad to meet the enemy" and "If you think you are going to get any money for ballet dancers while the hog farmers of Iowa are in trouble, you are stupider than I think you are." The effect on the morale of Straight and his assistant was that they went to a bar until the working day was over. Straight's morale promptly improved when one senior congressman put his hand on Straight's shoulder and said, "Son, everyone is entitled to one mistake," even though he immediately followed up with the warning "and that one is yours."[2]

In a sense, the current interest in motivation and morale is a continuing development of what started in the 1920s and 1930s as the human-relations approach to management and may now be called the psychological approach. Although many support this idea, there are the skeptics who believe it tends sometimes to be sentimental and soft, overemphasizing psychology at the expense of group objectives and production. Like most aspects of public administration, therefore, the psychological approach has raised some basic controversies, creating fuzzy areas that need to be constantly reevaluated and refined.

ENVIRONMENTAL CONDITIONS

In a consideration of the psychological foundations of motivation and morale in management, certain environmental conditions provide the setting. The first of these is the *age of the enterprise,* for motivation and morale are ordinarily harder to sustain on an older project than on a newer one. A state government's Department of Public Works, because of its greater age, is unlikely to have as much enthusiasm among its employees as the state agency charged with energy development and conservation, which is only a few years old.

Despite the usual frustrations that often accompany the initiation of a new program, there is a certain challenge in newness that seems almost automatically to kindle effort and engender a cooperative spirit. This positive atmosphere is reinforced in a *time of crisis,* a notable aspect of federal administration during the New Deal, for example, and World War II. Unfortunately, this crisis atmosphere has been lacking in most civilian agencies of United States government since the end of World War II, meaning that the manager has to work harder to motivate his employees.

Most government programs are relatively old, and even if crises do enhance motivation and morale, they are ordinarily to be avoided. A key problem of management, therefore, is how to sustain motivation and morale under ordinary circumstances. One means is through *tangible rewards,* such as promotions or bonuses. In government, however, where the profit motive is largely lacking, group and individual accomplishment is harder to measure and to reward in financial terms than it is in industry. Moreover, in many government programs, such as research or police protection, the results of effort are less tangible than, say, in engineering or farming, and motivational factors may be equally hard to pin down.

Yet another environmental condition is the *anonymity* that usually surrounds the work of most public employees. In government programs, credit for success usually goes to politicians or officeholders, who occupy a more visible position than those who do the daily work. But credit and praise for work well done are high incentives, and since in government they are hard to provide for all to see, public administrators are again handicapped in a manner that industry is not.

Since these environmental conditions make it harder to sustain employee motivation and morale in government than in private employment, public administrators must look for assistance where they can find it. A good deal of comfort may be gained from the statement of a social psychologist that *"humans have an enormous capacity for acquiring motives."*[3] There is also help in the view of a sociologist that human nature is not wholly confined to the individual; it is also influenced, conditioned, and socialized by the group, to the point where there comes to be a group nature as well.[4] Carrying this idea a step further, later social psychologists have argued that human nature is essentially the "typical personality attributes of the members of a particular group."[5] Still others have noted that each group has its own "characteristic needs and demands and other characteristic ways of expressing and satisfying them. . . . Looked at in this way, there is not one human nature, but many—as many as there are cultures, societies, and social groups."[6]

These views stress the malleability, the possibility of development, and the strong influence of the group on human nature, thus offering clues to the means by which the managers of government programs may deal with the problem of motivation and morale, despite the environmental handicaps under which they operate.

MOTIVATION AND INCENTIVES

Motivation releases stimuli, which create drive, which in turn is reinforced by the offer of rewards of one kind or another. Leaving aside the question of which motives are instinctual and which are learned—of interest primarily to psychologists—it seems clear than most motivations involved in administration require some degree of thought and encouragement in order to create and sustain them.

Morale

The relation between motivation and morale is at once obvious: when motives are satisfied, the result is an agreeable state of mind. Morale may be an individual matter or a group condition. For the individual, high morale means being well adjusted, confident of the future, and highly motivated. As applied in administration, however, morale is more often a group condition, with the same connotation as the French term esprit de corps.[7] As applied in small-group theory, morale is usually a matter of simple virtues such as friendliness and cohesiveness.

Industrial psychologists regard morale as an index of productivity and job satisfaction. High individual and group productivity, they believe, correlates with high job satisfaction, and the combination of the two creates—and is in turn explained by—high group morale. Thus, Daniel Katz sees four indexes of morale as relating to job satisfaction: pride in the work group, intrinsic job satisfaction, involvement in the enterprise, and financial and job status satisfaction.[8] There is also a significant interrelation between morale and a generally favorable worker attitude toward the organization as a whole, including its goals and leadership.

There have been a number of attempts to measure morale according to criteria such as pride in group, confidence in attaining group goals, and respect for group leadership. Various scales of attitude have been devised, including an adaptation of the Thurstone scale, in which a choice may be made among statements such as, "I think [this employer] treats its employees better than any other one does."[9] In military circles, morale sometimes connotes efficiency or persistence in the face of opposition. Industrial management also takes account of these factors and constructs measuring devices to test morale on the basis of these relationships.

It is important to note that since organizations differ, what causes high morale in one type of organization may cause the opposite in another. An example is provided by Richard Gabriel, a retired U.S. Army colonel and present professor of political science.[10] Gabriel argues that in the 1950s the U.S. Army began to reorganize itself along certain lines of the business corporation. Lower-ranking officers, for example, were referred to as middle-tier managers. Officers were sent to business schools for training, and traditional military concepts were replaced with the concepts of corporate departmental management. Gabriel notes, however, that the mission of the military is fundamentally different from that of business. No one in General Electric or Xerox expects to lay down his life for the corporation, but the military may be called on to do just that. This fact, according to Gabriel, means that successful armies have to be premodern organizations with a deep

sense of the individual belonging to the group, a sharing of common values, and a uniqueness. This esprit de corps motivates soldiers to risk their lives in the group effort. Business training, on the other hand, exalts individual self-interest and maximization of profit, two totally different goals. This failure to provide training relevant to the military mission, in Gabriel's opinion, led to the following events in Vietnam.

1. The army tried to provide all its officers with an opportunity to command troops in the field. This meant that officers served only 6 months in combat, while ordinary soldiers served 12. Gabriel feels that this pattern caused morale to fall so far that 1,000 officers are estimated to have been killed by their own troops.
2. To economize, individuals rather than units were sent in as replacements. This approach, modeled after the auto industry's spare-parts replacement system, meant that combat units became composed of strangers, not men who knew each other well. As a result, mutinies and refusals to fight reached an alltime high.
3. Training programs contributed to 80 percent of the army's officers changing assignments in 1978. Officers became remote from their troops. In 1978, desertions, in an all-volunteer army, were the highest in peacetime history.

We do not endorse all of Gabriel's points or changes in a blanket fashion. Yet they indicate that procedures that contribute to high morale in one situation may be poison in another situation.

CASE STUDY: FOREIGN SERVICE WIVES

The assistant secretary for administration, U.S. Department of State, sat at his conference table facing four of his colleagues. The atmosphere was friendly and relaxed. In addition to the assistant secretary were the director of personnel, the chief budget officer, and a country expert, or desk man.

ASSISTANT SECRETARY. The chief wants our views on that provision in the pending Foreign

Service act that encourages the hiring of wives of foreign service officers. As you know, it's a long bill—200 pages—and although we've had a chance to work it over, it was introduced and pushed by two congressmen, largely at the instigation of the employees' associations. The provision we're concerned with says in effect that to encourage Foreign Service officers to stay in the service, improve their morale, and make the service more efficient, we shall try to find jobs for wives in the overseas posts where their husbands are stationed. The wives would be on the payroll of the Department of State. In effect, they would take the place of most of the local nationals the department has hired in the past.

DIRECTOR OF PERSONNEL. Are the jobs restricted to secretaries and the like?

ASSISTANT SECRETARY. No, anything that local foreign nationals have done in the past.

COUNTRY EXPERT. Won't this be resented by the host country?

ASSISTANT SECRETARY. Not if we watch our public relations. We'll try to do it over a period of time, as vacancies occur.

COUNTRY EXPERT. Do you think that will fool anyone? Americans are already accused of being more cloistered than, say, the Germans or some other nationalities that mix with natives more than we do.

BUDGET OFFICER. Will you pay them the same as the former foreign employees or will you add the 20 percent bonus that career officers get for overseas duty?

DIRECTOR OF PERSONNEL. The latter, probably. Otherwise, there'd be a row from the union representatives.

BUDGET OFFICER. So it would cost the taxpayers more?

ASSISTANT SECRETARY. Not a great deal more.

COUNTRY EXPERT. (facetiously) Instead of improving husband-wife relations as supposedly it would because they'd have something to talk about, might it not have just the opposite effect? Maybe they'd fight over policy or pay or something internal to administration.

PERSONNEL OFFICER. With their combined salaries, they could probably afford to hire additional household help and that might make the wives more relaxed.

COUNTRY EXPERT. But hasn't it been a long, historic policy of the United States govern-

ment not to give jobs to members of the same family when they work in the same agency?

BUDGET OFFICER. Yes, but that's been changing gradually. The emphasis is now placed on prohibitions against working in the same office.

COUNTRY EXPERT. You mean the wife might be a company chauffeur or something like that? Think of the possible entanglements.

PERSONNEL OFFICER. No, seriously, we in personnel and the traveling inspectors-general would see that the wives were put into suitable jobs, ones where there would be no conflict of interest.

COUNTRY EXPERT. Are the wives unhappy because they don't have enough to do? Are they bored? Why don't they study the country and make friends of the local population?

ASSISTANT SECRETARY. Some do, others are bored. And when that happens they want their husbands to return stateside and get other jobs.

COUNTRY EXPERT. I'm still worried about this cloistering bit. Also, it might provide an awkward precedent for other federal civil servants.

ASSISTANT SECRETARY. But we're different. We are Foreign Service, which is separate and distinct from civil service.

COUNTRY EXPERT. What you're saying, in effect, is that getting better-trained American employees would make the work they do more efficient. Then this added efficiency would make all the work done by the department overseas more efficient. Is that your logic?

ASSISTANT SECRETARY. Yes, that's part of it, but not all of the reasoning. We're mainly concerned with the improved morale of the husbands because their wives would be happier.

QUESTION: How would the reader decide this policy issue in a way that would maximize morale?

THE WORK CONCEPT

Since a main concern of management is to increase productivity by improving work satisfactions, the work concept becomes a matter of some interest. There are two principal views of the work concept. One holds that work constitutes most of the life activity of most people and should therefore be made as attractive and rewarding as possible. The second holds that work is something unpleasant, which has to be endured; but with great strides in modern technology, machines will eventually do man's work for him and he will have nothing to do but think. From the standpoint of management's interest in developing employee motivation and morale, which of these two views is adopted as a starting point will go far to determine the effectiveness of any attempt to increase work satisfactions. The first view is consistent with Theory *Y,* and the second with Theory *X,* both of which were described in Chapter 9.

In the work-as-punishment approach and the pleasure-pain calculus of 19th-century economists, work was considered as an evil or as something essentially unpleasant that one was paid to do. More recently, largely under the influence of psychologists and professional managers, the idea of work as essentially agreeable in its own right has been strengthened. Humanistic psychologists such as Abraham Maslow refer to work as "self-actualizing," and the growing number of those who favor the human-relations approach to management see work as potentially "creative." According to this view, work satisfactions and personality development are in a cause-and-effect relationship, and the bond between them is indissoluble.[11]

The human relations school regards work as a highly desirable challenge. "Most of us," comments one authority, "need . . . a dare, a challenge, a test to see what we amount to," an opportunity more likely to be provided by an organization having "a deep and abiding faith in the capacities of men and women than by one which is skeptical of such capacities and seeks to compensate for human weakness rather than capitalize on human strength."[12] The assumption here is that strong men and women do not need to be induced to work well, for the desire to accept the challenge of work is inherent; the role of management, therefore, is simply to liberate the will to work.

One may take the following example from veteran city manager Leroy Harlow, who asked two clerks in one department to come up with some ideas for making their work at the customer reception counter more efficient. "A few days later [they] had some ideas. . . . *They were excited* [emphasis added]. They had thought of two or three other changes. . . . We made the changes, which were really very simple. We got no complaints from the public. I estimate we reduced the energy expenditure of the counter help by 20 percent."[13]

Is this view myth or is it real? If it is true that self-actualization and self-fulfillment depend upon the individual testing himself in a chosen field, then this view of work is no myth. When it is further considered that humans are differentiated from other members of the animal kingdom by intellect, imagination, conceptual understanding, and the ability to look ahead, it is possible to conclude that people can become more human by developing these skills in a work situation.

"Behind every managerial decision or action," says Douglas McGregor, "are assumptions about human nature and human behavior." If it is supposed at the outset that the average human being is inherently averse to work and will avoid it if he can, that most people work only because they are coerced and threatened with punishment if they do not, and that they prefer to be told what to do because they lack ambition and would avoid responsibility, then management's approach to questions of motivation and morale may be less than effective. But if it is supposed that people need only the proper work conditions, insights, and opportunities to perform well without being bought or coerced, then factors such as morale, spirit, incentives, and pride in the service become of central significance and the results will bear their stamp.[14]

Among the increasing number of those who identify with the human-relations approach to management, however, it is beginning to be realized that there are limits to what can be achieved by this means. Thus, good human relations, said one authority, "cannot be either window dressing or deliberate manipulation. And it had better not be just sweetness and light. There is no reason why it should not have some spine and firmness."[15] O. Glenn Stahl, whose main interest is in personnel in public administration, has noted that " 'good human relations' has too often been misunderstood as such a complete substitute for autocratic and arbitrary supervision that it necessitates a surrender to mediocrity and even maudlin pandering to every employee's whim. A careful appraisal of basic emotional needs exposes this view as a gross misconception." He adds that the responsibility for sound human relations rests as much with those who are supervised as it does with the supervisor. "It is a two-way street."[16]

In short, if human employment is sharply restricted as machines take over, as appears likely, then people must learn how to "repersonalize" those who are deprived of work, in order to make them more human. Few people whose work motivations are low will be needed at all. And if the predictions of cybernetic specialists are correct, that leisure-time activity will become the lot of most people most of the time, then the achievement of what Maslow and others call self-actualization will become infinitely more complicated than it is today.

Applied Motivation Research

In certain respects, government employment has a distinct advantage over other forms of employment, including business, because of the motivations called forth by the public service itself. These include the satisfaction of working to help one's country, the appeal of being close to the center of power where important issues are decided, and the pleasure of working unselfishly for the benefit of all the people.

It is interesting to test a group of managers on what they believe motivates workers and then discover from the workers what in fact does motivate them. At the beginning of these studies, managers were frequently and surprisingly wrong. Thus, employers who rated financial incentive highest in motivating workers found that the workers themselves rank it only in third place. Employees who placed credit for work well done at the top of their scale of motivation discovered that in management's estimation it was only in seventh place. Employers and researchers alike have learned from the experience, and their assumptions are less often wrong.

It is hazardous to try to summarize the results of such extensive research, but some general conclusions may be indicated. For one thing, motivation turns out to be a much more complex subject than was at first supposed. An almost complete correlation between high productivity and high morale, for example, was once accepted as fact; but today it is questioned because of instances where productivity remained high while morale was low. Research generally confirms, however, the basic assumption that productivity is higher when supervisors are employee-oriented—providing their subordinates with opportunities for participation, decision making, and the like—than when they are production-oriented and authority is rigidly centralized.

In addition, studies by Katz and others at the University of Michigan have clarified some of the things that supervisors should and should not do if high morale is the objective. These studies also confirm that the further the supervisor is from the people in the shop or the office, the weaker is his personal influence likely to be; the more face-to-face his relations with his subordinates, the greater his influence.

A third finding, which might check any tendency of the human-relations school in management to become unduly soft and sentimental, is that employees apparently derive greater work satisfaction when standards of performance are high than when they are low and supervision is lax and indifferent. If this finding means what it seems to—that through either self-discipline or group discipline, most people feel more pride and security when standards are high rather than sloppy—the implications for the modern generation gap might be profound indeed.

In addition, the early findings of the so-called Hawthorne experiment, noted in an earlier chapter, have been confirmed: when workers are made to feel important by being shown various kinds of attention, their morale seems to improve, the quality of management-labor relations is enhanced, and productivity rises. To a degree, of course, the outcome depends on whether the workers are being merely manipulated or tested as though they were guinea pigs or whether management is following a sincere, employee-oriented policy of supervision. The Hawthorne experiment was a massive study of Western Electric's Hawthorne plant, located in the Chicago area, which took place in the 1920s and 1930s. It was carried out by a team of scientific management experts from Harvard. They wanted to probe in detail the effect on productivity of factors such as the level of lighting, heat, number and spacing of work breaks, and incentive plans. To their amazement, productivity in one section of the plant kept rising whether they turned the lights and heat up or down, gave more or fewer breaks, or whatever. The Harvard team concluded afterwards that what caused the rise in productivity was the workers' knowledge that the Harvard professors were observing them. This group of workers felt good that someone cared enough about them to pay some attention to them, to observe and interview them. The point of the Hawthorne experiment is not that productivity will go up if management brings in a study team, because the Harvard team's work in another section of the plant had no impact on production. The point is that emotions and feelings about nonphysical and nonmonetary aspects of employment are ex-

tremely important. Human relations at work must be paid attention to if the work is to be done correctly.

Finally, the democratic assumption has been borne out that when people are consulted and allowed to participate, then their interest, their initiative, and their creativity are notably improved. The more respected an individual feels himself to be, because of considerate treatment by his supervisor, the more likely he is to accept occasional bossing without resentment.

How employees rate their motivations tends to confirm the thesis that in the affluent society of the United States, money is less important than management once assumed. Relatively more important are motivations such as liking the work and the supervisor, feeling successful and respected, and being in a position where growth is possible. The personal, nonmonetary incentives tend to supersede the purely financial ones, according to Frederick Herzberg. Herzberg's research indicates that salary and fringe benefits, job security, work conditions, and interpersonal relations on the job do not cause high levels of motivation and job satisfaction. If these "maintenance" concerns are inadequate, however, a great deal of dissatisfaction will result. High motivation and job satisfaction depend on a sense of achievement, recognition, advancement, the work itself, the possibility of personal growth, and responsibility. These incentives do not cause much satisfaction if they are missing, but high levels of motivation are unlikely without them.[17] (In Chapter 19, we discuss how this conclusion affects the monetary assumptions underlying the Civil Service Reform Act of 1978.)

A 1978 survey of 100 employees in field offices of the federal Social Security Administration supports this viewpoint. The survey found that 96 percent of the employees felt they were highly motivated by "the feeling of achievement you get from doing your work well," and 94 percent were highly motivated by "your inner need to always try to do a good job."[18]

Pay remains important. A summary of recent

research on pay as an incentive concludes, "In the course of fifty years, we have moved from a firm belief in the concept of 'economic man' to an equally firm belief in 'social man' and 'self-actualizing man.' Research evidence suggests that both these extreme views are fallacious." The authors conclude that pay is a major incentive, but they cannot state without qualification that it is the most important work motivator.[19] The authors also conclude that for the best managers to be satisfied with their pay, differences in pay must be clearly linked to differences in performance.[20]

Organizational Development and Transactional Analysis

Organizational development (OD) is a process of planned change designed to modify the behavior of agency employees. There is a problem recognition phase, program planning, implementation, and evaluation. Crucial to our concern is the training aspect of OD, in which training groups called T-groups are given sensitivity training.

Developed by National Training Laboratories, T-groups usually include 9 to 15 people and a trainer, who is an outside consultant. The goal of the training is for the participants to gain a better understanding of their job-related feelings and the feelings of their coworkers. T-groups are not group therapy sessions but work-related training groups. Although the trainer guides the group, there is no structure, agenda, or set procedure. Trainees are encouraged to express their true feelings and ask others how they feel. The trainer's job is to focus on the way the group is working, individual relationships in the group, and issues facing the group.

Well-run T-groups can help foster improved job participation. If, with the trainer's help, trainees express themselves frankly without being punished, they may well be ready to participate more fully when on the job.

T-groups are no panacea. One drawback is that the typical T-group lasts only a week, which is only long enough for some kind of change to begin. T-groups should continue for a much longer period of time

Second, T-groups must involve all levels of the organization if they are to work. If middle managers undergo training but top managers do not, much less is likely to change than would if all managers underwent training.

Third, according to Henry Levinson, an industrial psychologist, T-groups focus too much on confrontation, hoping thereby to draw out the negative feelings of participants. Levinson urges greater use of other techniques as well because he thinks that confrontation alone quickly becomes a gimmick.[21]

Finally, while some researchers have found that T-group participants become more skilled in communication, leadership, group effectiveness, and acceptance of change than do matched groups that do not undergo sensitivity training, others have found a mixed bag of results.[22]

The related technique of transactional analysis (TA) can also be used in OD. This approach is based on the writing of psychoanalyst Eric Berne,[23] who argues that everyone behaves in three different ways: as parent, child and adult. Parent behavior is paternalistic and authoritarian; child behavior is impulsive and dependent; and adult behavior is factual and results-oriented. Every human relationship is a transaction between these different states. For example, a manager may say to a subordinate, "Give me that report by five o'clock," and the subordinate will reply, "Yes." This is a *complementary* transaction, between boss (parent) and subordinate (child), for it goes off without a hitch. But if the subordinate were to think or to reply, "Go to hell!," this would be a *crossed* transaction, with negative rather than positive results.

TA training attempts to have trainees recognize whether they are acting as parent, child, or adult at various times.

Organizations can become far more effective by avoiding games that use parent and child roles, such as "Kick me" (self-criticism); "Now I've got you, you son of a bitch!" (entrapment of someone else, forcing an admission of failure); and "Yes, but" (nothing you can say will influence me). When players of these negative games learn that a game cannot be continued if one of the players acts the adult role, great progress has been made.

Problems Common to All Training Techniques

Whether T-groups, TA, or other training approaches designed to change behavior are used, there will be certain limitations on their effects. These limitations must be pointed out so that the real benefits to be gained from training are not dissipated by disappointment.

First, substantial change takes quite a while. Behavior learned over many years cannot be modified overnight. Management Professor James A. Lee recommends that top management "double a behaviorial scientist's estimate of the time required for change and triple its own."[24]

Second, middle management needs guidance and support from top management in introducing change. A T-group alone is unlikely to change a manager who will not delegate authority. The manager's superiors will have to take steps such as asking the manager what subordinates think about a problem and stressing that the better the manager's subordinates are, the more highly the superiors will think of him as a manager. In short, training must be integrally related to management philosophy or no benefits will result. Training without follow-up will not be taken seriously by managers.

IMPLICATIONS FOR MANAGEMENT

In a superficial way, morale might be considered a by-product of enlightened managerial policies effectively pursued, but in fact it is more than that. Morale depends primarily on constant innovation. Increasingly, therefore, public administration is turning to psychology for help in determining the factors that enter into creativity, innovation, and incentives to achievement.

There has been some exciting research in this area. Maslow has worked on self-fulfillment,[25] David C. McClelland on the achievement motive,[26] and Arthur Koestler on creativity.[27] Their findings are now being widely applied in management analysis.[28] The implications of this research for management are nothing short of revolutionary when applied to motivation and morale in administration. Self-realization is now recognized as a matter less of molding human nature than of releasing potentials already there: management must provide the conditions, the environment, and the encouragement. McClelland's studies indicate that the achievement motive is a matter of degree, that the urge to excel is apparently widely prevalent in children and needs only to be recognized early and encouraged. It is the responsibility of management to carry this urge forward when young employees enter the organization. Creativity, says Koestler, is a matter of recognizing and encouraging what was once called the conceptual ability, which lies beneath the surface in people in all walks of life, from comedians to philosophers and scientists. It is frequently found among executives in the higher ranks of administration whose conceptual abilities have been developed to the point where the individual is imaginative, sensitive, philosophical, and able to use the subconscious to bring forth creative ideas of his own and to stimulate them in his associates. Of all the areas of motivation and morale, these studies of self-fulfillment, achievement, and creativity are the most exciting.

The range of possible applications of these new ideas in management is wide and varied. Sensitivity training (through role playing, for example), executive-development programs, suggestion systems, and recognition of outstanding performance are only a few; many more might be developed. Fortunately, since the human-relations approach in management began to gain speed during the 1950s, the changing atmosphere of expectations is resulting in the finding and use of new applications. Morale may not be wholly accepted as a scientific term, but as a result of this recent research, the fact of morale is likely to be more rather than less emphasized by management in the future.

Left to themselves, organizations tend to slow down. Established habit frustrates innovation and change. The parts of the enterprise become insulated each from the others and pull alone rather than in concert. Increasingly, people shun responsibility, becoming more interested in their pay checks than in accomplishment or the goals of the enterprise. And yet, as all the studies cited in this chapter show, people would *prefer* to find scope for their abilities. When management encourages motivation, the enterprise remains alert and so do those who work for it.

Thus, motivation is a central ingredient of the entrepreneurial spirit. To be human is to be an innovator. If motivations are lacking, sooner or later people invent new ones for new times and new conditions. They are interested in their work if their work is made interesting for them, and they may even make it interesting for themselves, for there are always some who reach out toward rather than shrink from work. People like the feeling of belonging if the group is sufficiently attractive. They like to cooperate and to lose themselves in a joint effort, and they also like privacy and an opportunity to develop the distinctive qualities of their own personality and character.

As applied in administration, this point of view is a complicated matter. Possibly it is unscientific, but that depends on how the term is defined. Is it workable? Some think it is. Among those who do is a growing number of hardheaded executives, in business and government alike.

CONFLICT AND COOPERATION

High motivation and morale are no guarantee of administrative harmony, for administration, as the largest part of the political process, is constantly the scene of struggle among competing interests. In public administration, the two principal kinds of conflict are the external, which results from the activities of interest groups, and the internal, which has its source within the ad-

ministrative process itself. Business executive Robert Townsend has said, "A good manager doesn't try to eliminate conflict; he tries to keep it from wasting the energies of his people," a statement that applies to public management as well.[29]

Regarding external conflict, interest groups are involved in politics, their initial focus on action; and when they succeed in getting their programs passed, they naturally turn their attention to the execution of them. Sooner or later, their influence becomes so internalized among government agencies that factions and competitions appear within the administration itself.

Some external conflicts have obscure roots. Louis Brownlow tells the story of a battle between two political factions in Fairlawn, New Jersey. He asked Nicholas Kuiken, leader of one faction, to explain why he and Jasper Van Hook, the leader of the other faction, could not get along. Kuiken replied that the reason was simple: Van Hook was a Flakkee and he was a Frisian. "It seemed that a few centuries earlier, when the Spanish were in control of the Low Countries and the Duke of Alva's soldiers were ravaging the country, the Frisians, who lived on the fringe of the northeast coast and its adjacent islands, accused the inhabitants of the island of Overflakkee of treacherously permitting the Spanish soldiers to enter their gates. Ever thereafter, said Mr. Kuiken, no Frisian has ever forgiven a Flakkee."[30]

External stresses are more likely to be most severe in areas of social and political conflict, such as labor relations or policy issues relating to the clash between capitalism and socialism. But no government undertaking is wholly immune. An agency that gathers and publishes statistics, for example, might be expected to be nonpolitical; but if a statistical series shows that the economic position of agriculture was declining, at a time when a high public official said publicly that it was improving, the agency may have to act to safeguard its integrity and its appropriations. In 1971, for example, the work of the federal Bureau of Labor Statistics received intense scrutiny by high administration officials. The bureau was reporting that unemployment was climbing during a recession, news that President Richard Nixon's key aides did not want to hear. The bureau's reports were reinterpreted and reissued by higher officials in the labor department to make the situation seem better.

These policy and power conflicts appear more openly in pluralistic, democratic nations, but even in authoritarian and communist regimes they may be at least as severe, though less visible, within the inner recesses of action programs. Democratic administration accepts open competition for government benefits on the ground that the struggle promotes freedom and participation; but even in authoritarian regimes, conflicts in public administration are never wholly absent, no matter how determined the effort to throttle them.

External conflict, however, is only part of the problem because, by its very nature, organization seems to constitute a seedbed of conflict. This viewpoint flows logically from "Miles's Law," which states: "Where you stand depends upon where you sit." Rufus Miles, a former federal official who is now an academic, formulated his law after reflecting on his work experience. The viewpoints of administrative officials depended on where they worked, he noticed, not who they were. For example, a budget examiner in the Bureau of the Budget had been critical of one agency's budget requests. Then he had an invitation to move to the agency as its budget director. Miles pointed out to the examiner that he would now have a much more supportive attitude toward the agency's budget. The budget examiner was shocked and protested that he would not change his views. Yet, he did—Miles was right.

Prominent among internal struggles are the competitions of skill groups, each claiming a right to top priority in administrative decisions. Equally numerous and hard to cope with are jurisdictional disputes among related agencies, engineering and agricultural programs, for example, or foreign office and foreign aid undertakings. At another level are the conflicts between line and staff officials, unskilled and highly trained employees, national and local officials, and specialists and generalists. Examples of such conflict are provided later in this chapter.

One of the most-needed skills of administrative leadership, therefore, is the ability to deal with conflict and convert it to the public good. The leader's objective is to secure cooperation without penalizing competition and dissent, to develop a style and reinforce it with a technique. To the extent that the executive can accomplish this purpose with the skill of the most gifted politician, he lays the ground for the coordination of his program, the subject of the chapters that immediately follow.

How the administrative leader reacts to conflict situations within his program depends a good deal on his grasp of the relationships between conflict and cooperation. Are they polarities or are they complementary parts of a single aspect of behavior? The issue is basic in political science.

During the past 50 years or so, many political scientists in the United States have tended to make the concept of struggle the central theme of political theory. Man seeks his own individual *atomistic* ends, it is argued, and so do interest groups. The purpose of the political state is to provide the forum in which conflicting interests fight for benefits of various kinds.

Marxist theory takes a different approach. Marxists see the state as the ruling mechanism of capitalist society. Once it has been captured by the proletariat, the mechanisms of the state, that is, public administration, may be used to promote cooperation and higher standards of living for all the people. Thereafter, strife and conflict will ultimately disappear. Hence the state, which Marxist theorists picture under capitalism as representing power and domination, is claimed under communism to represent only cooperation and good will.

What Is Involved in Conflict?

The influence of the theme of conflict in political science has become apparent in the literature of public administration.[31] The chief expression of conflict in public administration is probably competition over values and special interests. Other expressions may be equally appropriate, however, for the competitions between management and labor, for example, are often struggles if not battles; those between big corporations and independent businesses are at least collisions; and the goals of competing interest groups are often incompatible. In each situation, different interests, attitudes, assumptions, and premises are involved, and the resulting confrontation is more often one of conflict than of harmony.

The sociologist Philip Selznick has tried to explain conflict as it arises within administration itself and finds an answer in a preoccupation with internal conditions. In his book *Leadership in Administration*,[32] Selznick notes an undue respect for such things as the formal aspects of organization and the structure of decision making. The result is neglect of certain internal matters, such as the values and needs of the members of the organization, and too little attention paid to external matters, such as the value system implied in the wants and needs of citizens for whom, presumably, the program exists.

An example is the preoccupation found in some agencies with case load. If social workers in a welfare agency are expected to deal with so many clients (cases) a week and to resolve them in certain ways, internal tensions may develop. The caseworkers may come to be preoccupied with case "clearance" (moving so many files off the desk in a week) to the exclusion of the real needs of the clients. If one client is behaving somewhat strangely, for example, maybe he should be referred to a mental health clinic for an examination. But that will take a good deal of the caseworker's time and effort and could prove to be unnecessary. So nothing is done, and a few months later the client suffers a complete emotional breakdown. It is no wonder that social workers in such circumstances become extremely cynical about their work. They were trained as social work professionals and now are reduced to clerks, whose job it is to move paper and files from one place to another. Such a situation is bound to

produce conflict, whether overt or covert, within the organization.

Thus, Selznick sees the cult of efficiency to the neglect of client needs as the main reason for internal tensions in administration. Many of these tensions could be released if administration were recognized for what it is—a living, growing entity, guided by a proper attention to values and philosophy. In short, when administration is viewed as an end in itself instead of only a means to other ends, the common result is a degree of internal malaise that may increase to the point where it becomes more or less open conflict.

To keep the perspective clear and avoid overdoing the conflict theme in the belief that it is realistic, it should be appreciated at the outset that external conflict is far from being the only guide to the creation and operation of government programs. Indeed, much policy is made through the quiet interaction of employees within any program structure.

Resolving Conflict in Administration

The opposite of conflict is sometimes assumed to be cooperation, but that is not invariably so. Cooperation is people working together to the same end; it is a joint operation combining a number of individuals. Such a definition makes cooperation nearly synonymous with administration itself and allows for people working in a common understanding without necessarily eliminating all competition and conflict.

Competition is a long-standing characteristic of American society. People think and feel differently and the result gives zest to the life of the community and its institutions. A free society is one in which individuals and groups may advocate their beliefs and promote their interests by all lawful means. But along with this diversity has gone a high degree of consensus as to certain values that require cooperation to maintain: human dignity, equality of opportunity, and the right to improve one's status through competition and growth. Where disagreement occurs, it is on the methods by which these goals are to be attained.

The problem of the administrator, like that of the political philosopher, is not how to *eliminate* disagreement or even all conflict, but how to *guide* it to the end that wider human benefits may be attained along lines suggested by Selznick. Rather than a deadening uniformity of viewpoint, most people seek a basic accord that allows for individual differences. And to the degree that cooperation promotes this basic accord, it is opposed to conflict when that term means battle and violence of various kinds.

Accord Through Analysis and Integration: Mary Parker Follett

Mary Parker Follett, a political theorist and management consultant whose early ideas were largely responsible for the development of group dynamics, the human-relations approach in administration, noted that conflict can never be wholly avoided because it occurs everywhere. So why not put it to use? In an article entitled "Constructive Conflict,"[33] she explained how this can be done.

Of the three ways of resolving a dispute, said Follett, the first is for one side to obtain all of its demands by *dominating* the other, which is no real solution because the weaker side gains nothing and remains unsatisfied. The second method is through *compromise,* but this is no real solution, either, because neither side is wholly satisfied. The third method is to analyze the demands of each side into its components and then bring them together in an *integration* in which both sides are fully satisfied, because both have risen to a higher level of accord.

An integrative solution was used to solve the following problem. The building of a dairy cooperative was located on a hill, and as a result a conflict arose among dairy farmers unloading cans. Farmers coming up the hill thought they should be allowed to unload first, while farmers coming downhill wanted priority. The disagreement became rancorous. Yet when an outsider suggested that the platform be relocated so both groups could unload at once this integrative solution was quickly adopted.[34]

Another example involved a hotel executive, who was a grandfather of one of the authors. In the restaurant of one of his large New York City hotels, a bitter conflict between the two pastry chefs erupted. They were both excellent chefs but apparently could not abide each other, and each resented the work the other did. After talking to both chefs, the executive found out that one's love was cake making, the other's, pies and other types of pastry. The executive then gave each chef a new title: one was now cake chef and the other pie chef. Through this integrative solution they were able to work smoothly together.

Conflict resolved in this fashion is constructive because each side is satisfied and, if it is an important conflict, something new has been created that may be of social benefit.

This kind of integration is based on an objective revaluation *(sic)* of interests and desires so that they may be seen with a new eye and in new combinations. The parties to a dispute should never allow themselves to be bullied by an either-or dichotomy, said Follett, because generally something better than two given alternatives can be found. The first step is to bring the conflict into the open and identify its most significant aspects, separating them from the merely symbolic or dramatic aspects, which are so often unduly blown up by those who are emotionally involved. Ideological disputes must be discarded and attention directed to the factors that will lead to a higher accord. By means of such an analysis, "the whole demand, the real demand, which is being obscured by miscellaneous minor claims or by ineffective presentation," can be found.

The main obstacle to integration, said Follett, is the idea of "power over," which involves compulsion. Society can never wholly dispense with this ultimate sanction, but it can recognize and frequently follow the alternative idea, which is "influence with," a jointly developed relationship built on a cooperative rather than a coercive basis.

So long as there is the possibility of reciprocal action, "influence with" may be increased and integration achieved.

When direct orders *must* be resorted to, the *manner* in which they are given can be controlled. Follett notes that the time, the place, and the circumstances are important; a long-distance order is less effective than one delivered face-to-face, and desirable habit patterns and mental attitudes must be cultivated through training. The thought pattern of the individual who is constantly being bossed eventually hardens into an acceptance of bossing to the point where initiative and dynamism are lost.

The implications of this analysis for the administrator are that he should seek influence with, instead of power over, his subordinates. He should not fear conflict or try to repress it but rather bring it out into the open and, by analysis and integration, seek to direct the parties to the problem to a higher level of accord in which both sides benefit as well as the organization.[35]

CASE STUDY: PUTTING OUT A RAGING FIRE

Boomtown is a city of 120,000. The past few years have seen rapid expansion, from a small town with one major industry to an industrial center where new corporations move in monthly.

The city has a professional fire fighting force of 200, plus 1,200 volunteers organized into 20 companies. The combined equipment of all the Boomtown companies is more than adequate for a city of its size.

The paid department is currently headed by a 66-year-old veteran of 38 years service, who has held the position of chief for the past 10 years. This man began his career as a volunteer and is believed by the mayor to be popular among the volunteer companies.

The volunteer companies are supposed to be subject to the orders of the city chief. However, in the past some orders from the chief have been disobeyed. For example, volunteer company heads are no longer supposed to wear a white chief's hat at fires, but some still do. More important, when fire headquarters was short one pumper, the volunteer companies refused to lend one of theirs. On the other hand, volunteers and their families make up a potent voting bloc. Also, the city votes a lump sum of $300,000 to the volunteer companies each year.

Aside from the conflict between the paid and the volunteer firefighters, there are problems within the paid department. The chief has four assistant chiefs, who have no duties other than commanding each of the four platoons. They do not, for example, participate in budgetary planning. In fact, they do not even see the current budget, although it is unclear whether this situation is at their discretion or the chief's.

The city council does not adequately support the department chief financially. For example, equipment at the airport is inadequate and out of date. Also, the department does not have a complete file of information on buildings in the city. Appropriation requests for these items have not been granted.

The current president of the firefighters' union is regarded by many city officials as a troublemaker, more interested in grandstanding than in solving problems. Another union official is known for calling people names and issuing public insults. At a recent fire, his abuse of the mayor received more publicity in the newspaper than the job done by the firefighters in extinguishing the fire. It has been observed that the department and its union seem to be their own worst enemies.

The firefighters' union has voted a statement of no confidence in the chief. The mayor, the chief, and the union president have established a five-member panel composed of labor and fire-fighting professionals, whose purpose is "an objective review of management and labor policies and practices within the Fire Department."

QUESTION: The reader has been appointed to the panel. What recommendations would he make to reduce conflict within the department?

INTERNAL ASPECTS OF CONFLICT

It would be difficult to say whether the external or the internal aspects of conflict and cooperation are of greater importance for public administration in the United States. The external aspects of the matter relate to policy determination, planning on a wide scale, and decision making; these have been discussed in several preceding chapters. It remains here to deal with the internal aspects of the subject.

Skill-Group and Jurisdictional Infighting

Administration, Brooks Adams once remarked, is "the capacity of coordinating many, and often conflicting, social energies in a single organism, so adroitly that they shall operate as a unity."[36] Skill groups are by nature specialized, and today these specializations are progressively subdividing into increasingly smaller areas, as the knowledge of a constituent subject expands to the point where it constitutes a separate profession or even the subdivision of a profession.

For example, within a hospital run by a state government are many different skill groups: doctors, nurses, physical therapists, laboratory technicians, paramedics, nutritionists, radiologists, psychologists, and many others. Conflict among these groups is to be expected. Laboratory technicians may complain bitterly when doctors want test results back immediately without understanding circumstances that prevent such speed, such as a large work load and lack of equipment and staff. Likewise, busy nurses may chafe at suggestions from physical therapists that special attention be paid to "their" patients; and psychologists may be appalled at what nutritionists prescribe for patients and vice versa. A major problem of program management is to secure the cooperation of these skill groups and avoid the debilitating effects of jurisdictional disputes.

Among his many functions, the administrator is a broker of influence and a reconciler of opposing views and interests, those that impinge on his program from the outside as well as those that appear within it. In this function he has a dual responsibility: to anticipate and cope with conflict and competitions among his subordinates and to secure the cooperation needed for the success of his program and the larger programs of society.

An indispensable tool in the administrator's stock is a grasp of the essentials of group dynamics, which is the development of a consensus through concentration on points of agreement rather than on points of difference. So long as two sets of individuals believe themselves to be on different sides of an issue, there can be little progress toward agreement; but as soon as they begin to think of themselves as both of us together working toward a common goal, then conflict usually begins to change into cooperation. In addition, of course, there must be patience, an understanding of the other fellow's point of view, objectivity, and the avoidance of false pride, personal or institutional.

Persuading Specialists to Cooperate

Industrial psychologists Robert Tannenbaum, Irving Weschler, and Frederick Massarik offer a number of tips to the manager who wants to transform conflict into problem solving.[37] First, the manager can welcome the existence of differences rather than complaining about them. Second, he can listen carefully to all sides to gain an understanding of the issue rather than make a quick judgment. In this way, he will help all involved better to understand the other viewpoints. Next, the manager can clarify the issues. Is it facts, methods, goals, or values that are in contro-versy? In what kind of mix? Fourth, he can sug-gest procedures and ground rules for resolving differences. For example, if the difference is over goals, all parties can list their goals. Once these are clearly stated, they can be dealt with in a more realistic way. The manager can also stress maintaining the group relationship, emphasizing common purposes while group members are fight-ing over their differences. Finally, the manager can help communication. One way to do that is to make it easier for those with differing positions to meet more frequently, so that they will come to know one another better and be less likely to have distorted or stereotyped perceptions of one an-other.

In all of these actions, the manager encourages the free expression of feelings and ideas. He does not attempt to suppress conflict but to guide dif-ferences toward a solution that will benefit the organization as a whole.

These psychological insights offer one means of avoiding jurisdictional infighting, which, when uncurbed, causes program fragmentation and is a main obstacle to problem solving. Unfor-tunately, this type of conflict exists almost everywhere in government—nor is it limited to government, of course—and represents an im-measurable loss of social energy that might oth-erwise be directed to positive accomplishment. The tendency toward exclusiveness, which has been noted as a characteristic of bureaucracy, is also a characteristic of specialist and professional groups. Each group believes itself to be better than the next and disparages the competence of another group that might rival or compete with it.

The essence of executive work is problem solv-ing, and most problems present themselves as ac-tual or potential conflicts. The manager who can resolve these conflicts has earned his pay.

SUMMARY

We have dealt with three main aspects of psycho-logical insight in this chapter: how to excite mo-tivation and raise morale in government service, why crisis and conflict in administering govern-ment programs are to be expected, and why skill-group exclusiveness and insularity play so prom-inent a role in bureaucratic excess, frustrating the executive who seeks cooperation. More than any other, perhaps, this chapter has shown the inti-mate relation of management to politics and the debt both have to psychological research and its occasional breakthroughs.

NOTES

1. Elizabeth M. Fowler, "Books Offer Managerial Guid-ance," *New York Times*, 30 April 1980, p. D 13.

2. Michael Straight, *Twigs for an Eagle's Nest* (San Fran-cisco: Devon Press, 1979), p. 22.

3. Theodore M. Newcomb, *Social Psychology* (New York: Dryden Press, 1950), p. 144 [emphasis added].

4. C. H. Cooley, *Social Organization* (New York: Scribner, 1909), pp. 28–30.

5. R. T. LaPiere and P. R. Farnsworth, *Social Psychology*, 3d ed. (New York: McGraw-Hill, 1949), p. 221.

6. D. Krech and R. S. Crutchfield, *Theory and Problems of Social Psychology* (New York: McGraw-Hill, 1948), p. 47.

7. S. A. Stouffer, *The American Soldier* (Princeton, N.J.: Princeton University Press, 1949), p. 83.

8. Daniel Katz, *Productivity, Supervision and Morale in an Office Situation* (Ann Arbor: University of Michigan Press, Survey Research Center, 1950).

9. R. S. Uhrbrock, "Attitudes of 4,430 Employees," *Journal of Social Psychology* 5 (1934): 365–377.

10. Richard Gabriel, "What the Army Learned from Busi-ness," *New York Times*, 15 April 1979, Business Section, p. 9.

11. Abraham Maslow, *Motivation and Personality* (New York: Harper & Row, 1954).

12. James C. Worthy, *Big Business and Free Men* (New York: Harper & Row, 1959), p. 118.

13. Leroy F. Harlow, *Without Fear or Favor* (Salt Lake City: Brigham Young University Press, 1977), pp. 88–90.

14. Douglas McGregor, *The Human Side of Management* (New York: McGraw-Hill, 1960), p. 34.

15. Edward C. Bursk, ed., *Human Relations for Manage-ment* (New York: Harper & Row, 1958), p. viii.

16. O. Glenn Stahl, *Public Personnel Administration,* 7th ed. (New York: Harper & Row, 1976), p. 201.

17. Frederick Herzberg et al., *The Motivation to Work* (New York: Wiley, 1959). It should be noted that not all researchers have found the same pattern. See William F. Dowling and Leonard Sayles, *How Managers Motivate* (New York: McGraw-Hill, 1978), pp. 19, 280.

18. Richard E. Wasiniak, "What Really Motivates Workers?" *Management,* Summer 1980, pp. 15–17.

19. Lyman W. Porter and Edward E. Lawler, III, *Managerial Attitudes and Performance* (Homewood, Ill.: Irwin, 1968), p. 96.

20. Porter and Lawler, *Managerial Attitudes and Performance,* p. 158.

21. Henry Levinson, *The Great Jackass Fallacy* (Cambridge: Harvard University Press, 1973), pp. 160–162.

22. H. George Frederickson and Charles R. Wise, eds., *Public Administration and Public Policy* (Lexington, Mass.: Heath, 1977), pp. 46–48.

23. Eric Berne, *Games People Play* (New York: Grove Press, 1964).

24. James A. Lee, "Behavioral Theory vs. Reality," *Harvard Business Review,* March-April 1971, p. 157.

25. Maslow, *Motivation and Personality.*

26. David C. McClelland, *The Achievement Motive* (New York: Appleton-Century-Crofts, 1953).

27. Arthur Koestler, *The Act of Creation* (New York: Macmillan, 1964).

28. Ordway Tead, formerly social science editor at Harper & Row, was a pioneer in this. For applications in business, see Rensis Likert, *New Patterns of Management* (New York: McGraw-Hill, 1961); and for public administration, see Marshall E. Dimock, *Administrative Vitality* (New York: Harper & Row, 1959).

29. Robert Townsend, *Up the Organization* (Greenwich, Conn.: Crest Books, 1971), p. 21.

30. Louis Brownlow, *A Passion for Anonymity* (New York: Knopf, 1955), pp. 216–217.

31. See the following works: E. Pendleton Herring, *Group Representation Before Congress* (Baltimore: Johns Hopkins University Press, 1929) and *Public Administration and the Public Interest* (New York: McGraw-Hill, 1936); Avery Leiserson, *Administrative Regulation* (Chicago: University of Chicago Press, 1942); Bertram Gross, *The Legislative Struggle: A Study in Social Combat* (New York: McGraw-Hill, 1953), and *The Managing of Organizations,* 2 vols. (New York: Free Press, 1964).

32. Philip Selznick, *Leadership in Administration* (Evanston, Ill. and White Plains, N.Y.: Row, Peterson, 1957).

33. Mary Parker Follett, "Constructive Conflict," in *Dynamic Administration: The Collected Papers of Mary Parker Follett,* ed. Henry C. Metcalf and L. Urwick (New York: Harper & Row, 1941).

34. Follett, "Constructive Conflict." See also her book *Creative Experience* (London: Longmans, Green, 1924), p. 300.

35. For a further analysis of this interesting woman's views, see Gross, *The Managing of Organizations,* vol. 1, pp. 150–162.

36. Brooks Adams, *The Theory of Social Revolutions* (New York: Macmillan, 1913), p. 216.

37. Robert Tannenbaum, Irving Weschler, and Frederick Massarik, *Leadership and Organization* (New York: McGraw-Hill, 1961), pp. 112–115.

14

Coordination

We are the two halves of a pair of scissors, when apart, Pecksniff, but together we are something.

Charles Dickens, Martin Chuzzlewit

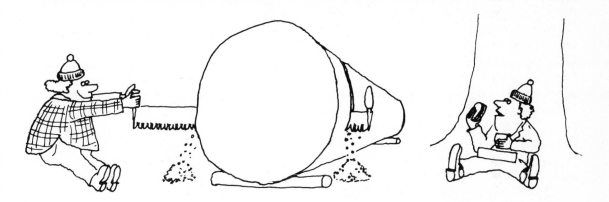

In this chapter, we examine the factors necessary for successful coordination of agency programs and headquarters-field relationships. It will be recalled that we dealt with a related aspect of this subject in Chapter 5, on intergovernmental relations. Coordination is one of the most difficult objectives to achieve in government. Some of the elements in program management as well as in intergovernmental relations are the same; but coordination, with which we shall now deal, is affected more by bureaucratic resistance than by strictly political considerations, such as, for example, states' rights.

In physiology, coordination is the combined action of a number of muscles in a complex movement. In public administration, the definition is not much different; coordination is the harmonious, combined action of agents or functions towards a given objective. What both definitions have in common is combined action in a complex situation. In all large-scale operations and in most countries, including those with authoritarian regimes, administrators find coordination one of their most difficult problems.

In small agencies and governments as well as in large ones, coordination is often difficult to achieve. For years, the principal of the New Castle, Colorado, elementary school asked the Highway Department to paint crosswalk signs on the road in front of the school. In May 1978, the Highway Department did just that. Unfortunately, the school had been moved to the other side of town the week before, and there were no longer any school children around to use the crosswalk.[1] Even seemingly simple matters may be overlooked, as Box 14.1 and Box 14.2 indicate.

The reason that administrative coordination is such a hard task is that it involves so many relationships at so many levels. Earlier chapters have discussed the coordination of separate governments in a system of administrative federalism, the coordination of the branches of government in the context of the separation of powers, and the coordination of political and career executives in the executive branch. And within administration itself, there is the coordination of the component parts of the organization, of line and staff officials and divisions, of labor and management, and of specialists and jurisdictions.

To refer to coordination in all of these relationships, however, is to use the term in a much broader sense than is customary in public administration. Although the larger aspects of coordination must be recognized, in the present chapter the term is used in a narrower sense and with a more specific application: first, as the coordination of administration in a single government or agency of government, and second, as the coordination of headquarters and field relationships.

MEANING AND ISSUES

The purpose of coordination is to synchronize action. A golfer may be intent on holding in his elbow as he swings his driver; but if that is all he is aware of, his drive may not get very far. If a batter thinks only of his stance at the plate, he may neglect to watch the trajectory of the ball as it approaches him. As these simple analogies show, to concentrate on one factor or agent to the neglect of others produces disappointing results, no matter how much energy may be brought to the situation. But the synchronous meshing of all elements produces favorable results, so long as ability is there to begin with.

The bearing of coordination on all other important areas of public administration may be briefly indicated. Thus, *cooperation* provides the foundation for effective coordination and leads to a consideration of that function, but it is by no means the whole of the matter. *Organization* determined by structural arrangements provides the arteries along which coordination flows, but organization by itself is not self-coordinating nor self-energizing. *Planning* indicates the objectives and the logical steps in an unfolding strategy of moves and procedures, but no plan is realized without coordination. *Leadership* and the direction of work, as in supervision, involves many things; but productivity will be limited unless coordination brings together that which is expected of each component in the overall operation. And *control,* the subject of the next chapter, involves coordination so closely that these two aspects of administration are often regarded as a single function; but coordination is more than control, which is merely the methods of evaluating costs and progress on a time schedule in terms of the objectives of the program.

Against this background, coordination is an active agent of administration, for, as in physiology, *energy and performance depend as much on the linkages involved in the total operation as they do on the energy contributed by each component part.* Jurisdictional disputes, discussed in the preceding chapter, are a case in point. If some 10 to

Box 14.1

MEMORANDUM

UNITED STATES INTERNATIONAL DEVELOPMENT COOPERATION AGENCY
AGENCY FOR INTERNATIONAL DEVELOPMENT
WASHINGTON D C 20523

ASSISTANT
ADMINISTRATOR

OCT 23 1979

Mr. Ray Kline
Deputy Administrator
General Services Administration
18th and F Streets, N.W.
Washington, D.C. 20405

Dear Mr. Kline:

The Agency for International Development has encountered a problem of some proportion which I bring directly to your attention as it will soon obtain in all Executive agencies and doubtless generate costs and embarrassment for the Government if not avoided.

We have found that the new, larger (8½" x 11") standard stationery prescribed by the Joint Congressional Committee on Printing which GSA is stocking for Government-wide use beginning January 1, 1980 is too large to fit the stationery drawers of many standard GSA desks. We discovered that earlier this month when we printed new letterhead necessitated by a recent reorganization, and converted to the larger stationery at the same time to avoid costs of a second conversion three months later.

We have found no single, easy solution of the problem but, rather, have been improvising -- exchanging desks for others in stock, providing desk-top holders and employing other costly devices.

Perhaps the Federal Supply Service can with this advance note of the general problem find some central way to avoid it for the Government as a whole.

Sincerely,

D. G. MacDonald
Bureau for Program and
Management Services

cc: Mr. Boulay, GSA

Box 14.2

MEMORANDUM

TO	FROM	DATE
SEE DISTRIBUTION	Chief of Staff, ADMINCEN	5 October 1976

1. The October Commander's Call will be held at 1530, 20 October 1976, in the Ballroom, FBH Officers' Club. The guest speaker will be Mr. Daniel J. Crowe, Indiana State Division of Addiction Services, who will discuss Industrial Alcoholism.

2. Following the presentation, there will be a question and answer session. At the conclusion of the question and answer session, there will be a "Happy Hour" in the Ballroom to afford everyone an opportunity to meet Mr. Crowe.

3. All officers, NCO's in grades E8 and E9, and interested civilians of ADMINCEN and FBH resident commands are invited and encouraged to attend.

FOR THE CHIEF OF STAFF:

H. M. SCHOENBERG
Captain, GS
Asst Chief of Staff

DISTRIBUTION:
1A
6A
CF:
FBH Officers' Club

---

20 percent of a given program's potential energy is consumed in infighting, the harmful social consequences may be much greater than the percentages would indicate.

Since coordination is a complex aspect of administration, a number of rather complex issues are involved. The first has to do with the *nature of the function.* The two sides of coordination are first, a state of mind, which is the human aspect, and second, a method, the juxtaposition of phys-

ical things and processes, which is the operational aspect. Neither taken alone constitutes effective coordination. The first grows out of the human-relations approach to administration which, as stated by Ordway Tead, means using coordination to bring about that "common understanding which is essential for unity of intention and which yields a shared realization of the social function of an enterprise."[2] The second, figuratively speaking, is turning the switch and meshing the gears to secure the structural integration that people will support because of a favorable state of mind. An example of the interdependence of both sides of coordination follows.

When racing driver A. J. Foyt stops during a race for gas and tire changes, his "pit crew" can do the job in 12 to 20 *seconds*. How? When Foyt pulls into the pit, Jim Pope jacks up the car with a quick-action platform jack. Cecil Taylor and Tony Foyt, A. J.'s father, change the two right-side tires in 10 to 20 seconds. (The right tires get more wear in racing and are usually the only ones changed.) Meanwhile, Steve Jordan is pumping methanol fuel into the car, while Billy Woodruff vents trapped air from the fuel tank. They finish their work within 20 seconds. Each man knows his tools and how to work with the other crew members. If any one failed to do his part, the job could not be finished. But because this team is so competent and coordinated, the task is finished in a brief time.

Consequently, coordination is not merely the mechanics of efficiency, for the human factor is at least as necessary as the mechanical or procedural means by which coordination is secured.

A second major issue involves a *conflict between authority and freedom,* one of the oldest concerns of political philosophy.[3] If coordination is too tightly imposed, people feel constrained and frustrated in the full use of their capacities; but if coordination is too loose, these same people may founder in incertitude. If directions, roles, and objectives are clear to everyone, and the freedom to innovate is also present, a middle position is achieved, which allows maximum freedom within the processes of the right degree of coordination to secure the desired goals. To some people, coordination suggests integration, which, if carried to excessive lengths, insists on extremes of conformity. But in fact, coordination is more like the behavior of ball players, who coordinate voluntarily whether the coach is present or not.

The third issue is the *relationship between coordination and size.* An example of this occurred when the research department of a large corporation worked for six months on improvements to an old product without once talking with the functional department heads who produced it originally.

Every increase in size magnifies the problems of coordination. People tend to transfer their feelings about size to the coordinating process itself; the objects of their dislike are mounting power, bureaucracy, the subjection of the individual to the organization, and perhaps a certain neglect of ethical awareness. It must be recognized, however, that size is now a fact of life, that even greater size is possibly in the offing, and that so long as people must live with size and feel helpless about changing its course, the only remedy is to coordinate as effectively as possible.

The fourth issue is *centralization,* which is often a function of size; indeed the two are commonly thought of together. But centralization has two aspects that should be distinguished: the institutional-geographic and the managerial-functional, with power an element common to both. The institutional-geographic aspect of centralization is the more common of the two, as in the centralization of government agencies in Washington or of government functions at the federal level as power shifts from the periphery to the center. An example is the requirement that Washington approve of all key state appointments, as established in the early days of the Social Security Administration. The managerial-functional aspect of centralization relates to administration itself and is more properly called integration, which is the opposite of devolution or delegation. That is, in the integration approach higher units do not give as much authority to lower ones. As with the issue of size, again, many people transfer their objections to the centralization of power to the coordinating process that power requires, and the response to coordination is negative.

The objection can be neutralized if the planning function is retained at the center, while the authority to execute is devolved as far down the line and out into the field as possible. Those who actually implement a policy—teachers, social workers, police, for example—must have the authority to do the job if it is to be done well.

The fifth issue relates to *unity,* usually expressed as unity of command or unity of leadership. This issue brings to mind President Harry S. Truman's oft-quoted aphorism, "The buck stops here." "Executive direction itself has to be at all times unitary, vigorous and firm."[4] There are compelling reasons for this belief, for without unity, coordination is weak, especially in complex organizations; people and divisions work at cross purposes; and little of social consequence is accomplished. Without unity, moreover, leadership is thwarted, communication is slow and incomplete, planning is haphazard, and a favorable relation between input and output is problematical.

Note that we have already discussed some aspects of this subject in Chapter 11.

Probably this question of the unity of the constituent parts of a program is one of the most misunderstood issues of public administration. Some supporters of the human-relations approach assume unity to be synonymous with authoritarianism. But, of course, it is not, because unity can be secured by voluntary action even better than by use of the bludgeon. There is no inherent conflict between the demands of unity of intent and those of pluralism and democracy. The quality of unity depends on how it is achieved and the degree of diversity and creativity that are deliberately encouraged in the operation as a whole. These are questions to ponder in the following case.

CASE STUDY: ACADEMIC INSULARITY

Jane Pierce thought back to last night's ballet program. All those dancers were always in the right place at the right time, working together to achieve a beautiful performance. Why couldn't the organization she had headed for a month get its act together to do the same?

As dean of a state university School of Management, Pierce was struck by the irony of it all. The faculty was responsible for teaching employees in private, public, and nonprofit organizations how to do a more effective job—yet, its members could not even coordinate efforts across departmental lines! For example, the departments of Management, Public Administration, and Nonprofit Administration each had separate courses in organizational behavior. Although the courses were 90 percent similar, the department heads had a swift and negative reaction to Jane's suggestion that a common core course be substituted. Also, each of the eight departments had a separate internship program, even though four of them (Public Administration, Management, Accounting, and Finance) currently had interns in

the same agency, the local branch of the Internal Revenue Service!

This fragmentation was destroying the original intent of the school—to expose students to a diversity of managerial approaches and environments. Students now seemed to be pushed to identify with one department rather than the school and immediately to become specialists. In fact, the departments of Public Administration and Nonprofit Administration had some vocal members who were talking about pulling out entirely and starting a school of their own.

Pierce had dealt with similar problems in industry, where she had been an executive vice president for administration. But there she had much greater authority to make decisions, hire and fire, reorganize, and reward employees. In academia, her authority was far more limited, so she would have to be very persuasive indeed.

Pierce thought about what she might be able to do with some of the disruptive influences in the school. Jake Carrey, chairman of Management, was a strong advocate of departmental independence, but only because he thought it strengthened the department and its graduates' job chances. Pierce made a note to set up a lunch with him and Jud Jones, the chairman of XYZ Corporation. Jones, who had just served four years as a cabinet officer in Washington, felt strongly that the best training for management was in a variety of fields, nonprofit and government as well as business. Jake was a reasonable person; exposure to Jones could help the situation.

Jack Broglio, head of Accounting, thought that departmental independence would increase his power. Pierce made a note to have a talk with him next week and to remind him that his continued service as chairman depended on her recommendation.

Ann Mobley, the chairperson of Nonprofit Administration, sincerely believed that her area was so different from the others that there could be no cooperation. Pierce planned to meet with Mobley and five graduates of Mobley's department, whom Pierce had met. The graduates were working in private business and felt that the training they had had was very helpful. So while the two areas were different, they were not totally opposite.

Ed Baines, chairman of Finance, did not cooperate because he did not get along personally with the other chairs. Baines was not popular, even within his own department. Pierce was fully prepared to replace him with Alma Zschau, who saw eye-to-eye with Pierce, when his term expired.

Dan Tobin, head of Public Administration, was consumed with the idea of establishing an Institute of Public Administration, and this goal was absorbing all his energies. Pierce would offer to give him seed money for the institute if he would work more closely with her.

The other chairpersons had their own problems. None of this would be easy. But the dean knew she had to do all she could to pull the school together.

ANATOMY OF COORDINATION

Coordination is a complex business because modern organizations are complex. In public administration, the federal government is the most complex organization of all, but the governments of the larger states and cities are a close second. In the anatomy of program administration, the place of coordination may be illustrated by a few examples.

Thus, a federal department such as Treasury or Agriculture may be so large as to number its employees in the tens of thousands; for the Postal Service Department the figure is more than half a million; and for Defense the total goes beyond a million for civilian employees alone. Moreover, only about 10 percent of these employees are stationed in Washington; some 90 percent are elsewhere in the nation and in foreign countries. In addition, it is a rare federal agency that operates a single program. If it does, it is one of the smaller ones. The more typical pattern is that of a congeries of programs under one roof. There may be only a few hierarchical levels at the Washington headquarters, but usually there are several. Each agency has at least a double function; the first is its mission, such as health, foreign relations, or commerce; the second is special skills, such as finance, personnel administration, or purchasing, to facilitate the achievement of its mandate. And finally, all large organizations rely on geography; operations are devolved from Washington to units in the states and local communities in a headquarters-field administrative relationship.

These geographical subdivisions of operating programs are almost as complex as the parent agencies in Washington. They may be determined according to regional, state, or local boundaries within the United States, but they may also be located in other countries, as in embassies, consulates, and military bases. In a field office, moreover, coordination must be internal within its own confines and external with the field offices of other federal agencies whose programs have similar concerns in some respect. (It was once found, for example, that 37 federal agencies operating in the field had some interest in fish.)

As President Franklin D. Roosevelt once wrote to his budget director,

---

I agree with the Secretary of the Interior. Please have it carried out so that fur-bearing animals remain in the Department of the Interior.

You might find out if any Alaska bears are still supervised by (a) War Department (b) Department of Agriculture (c) Department of Commerce. They have all had jurisdiction over Alaska bears in the past and many embarrassing situations have been created by the mating of a bear belonging to one department with a bear belonging to another department.

F.D.R.

P.S. I don't think the Navy is involved, but it may be. Check the Coast Guard. You can never tell![5]

Considering the diversity and complexity of these relationships, it is not to be expected that uniform methods of coordination would work equally well in all situations. There is a world of difference, for example, between the job of an ambassador in Paris and a chief forester in Utah. Perhaps a useful initial approach is through Tead's two-fold classification of coordination as state of mind and as method. This suggests a series of twelve related propositions as the starting point for effective coordination.

1. When authority is delegated, coordination must be increased to balance it and keep the delegated function in a live relationship to the whole.
2. Those who participate in the formulation of program objectives will the more willingly submit to coordination in carrying them out.
3. The clear assignment of roles and responsibilities facilitates coordination.
4. The executive who successfully rids himself of superfluous and detailed duties has more time to devote to coordination.
5. The more frequently the functional heads of a program come together in face-to-face encounters, the more dynamic coordination will be.
6. To sell coordination to his colleagues and subordinates is a responsibility of the line executive which he cannot delegate.

7. To achieve effective coordination is a strenuous, daily, time-consuming job.
8. Coordination must be lateral as well as vertical in the organization, and it must also extend outward to similar programs in ambassadorial relationships.
9. Coordination is necessary in particular segments as well as in the whole program because of the practical limits to the supervisor's span of control or attention.
10. The committee device is increasingly useful for coordinating purposes, for it brings plans and action together in the minds of those who have both kinds of responsibility, thus promoting balanced judgment.
11. Authority should be at least equal—and should sometimes even exceed—responsibility in order to secure dynamic coordination.
12. Significant delegations of authority must be regularly reevaluated.

It is doubtful if any effective coordinator ever had a one-track mind. He may sometimes wish he could concentrate on a particular problem until a satisfactory solution is found, but if he did that very much he would spend all his time doing so. Nor can functions be parceled out in such a way as to draw a clear-cut line between them: there are bound to be overlappings as one function shades off into the next. But this shading is the very area in which overall efficiency is secured, for it is here that the various parts of the program are blended into a unified whole. Consequently, the executive must pay special attention to these areas, mark them in his mind with a red flag, and keep a constant check on them.

The Law of the Situation

Some parts of each program need more coordination than others, depending on what Mary Parker Follett called the law of the situation, which is what each situation, by its nature, seems to require. In general, where detailed planning is needed, so is coordination more needed than in other areas. Consistency and close coordination are required in technical matters such as accounting, pricing, wage rates, vacations, and the like.

But in other operations such as providing a new service or responding to diverse community needs, rigid, detailed planning is inappropriate because not all the factors are known and the future may change the situation considerably; consequently, close coordination is less essential.[6]

This means that the administrator responsible for coordination must be sufficiently flexible and versatile to appreciate the requirements of each situation. Not only will this careful attention elicit the kind of coordination appropriate to the situation, but it will also take some of the curse off the coordinating function, which to some people seems nothing short of an arm-twister aimed at securing total conformity. Arm-twisting, where it occurs, is a mistaken use of function. Rather, it should be applied sparingly or not at all in situations where independence is part of the job and used with as much force as necessary where consistency, uniformity, or dependency seem to require it.

Let us suppose, for example, that a city manager is faced with the formidable task of installing a new water supply or a new sewerage system for the community. If the other departments are running smoothly, he will, in effect, turn over directing activity to the divisional heads until such time as he masters the new activity, even though that may take most of his time for a six-month period. What he loses in personal involvement may be more than offset by enhanced challenge to older department heads. Or let us suppose that the corrections commissioner in a state government is empowered by the legislature to establish a halfway house for juvenile offenders. This is a ticklish problem because if he is too lenient the offenders may escape, but if he is overly authoritarian the offenders will make little or no progress toward returning to useful employment in society. Under these circumstances he may focus his time and attention on the new project and temporarily transfer the bulk of responsibility to his associate commissioner. In both instances, flexibility is needed if the span of attention is to be adequate to the new challenge being addressed.

It takes a variety of techniques to produce the complete coordination of the components of an enterprise. In addition, there is the all-important question of the personal relationships that have been built up among those concerned. With a desire to achieve a common goal, a degree of mutual respect, and enough give-and-take, the result is usually a smoothly operating and relatively harmonious program. Where these elements are lacking, the administrative ulcer will be a common complaint.

Authority and Responsibility

The general rule applying to delegation and coordination is that authority and responsibility should be in substantial balance. The reason is that if an administrator is given a responsibility for a particular job, he should also be given the tools necessary to accomplish it. In practice, however, the degree of authority granted generally turns out to be less than the responsibility delegated.

The external constraints on managerial control and coordination in the public sector often distinguish it from the private sector. Business executives who become familiar with government are often appalled at the gap in government between authority and responsibility. The gap is often caused by the heritage of the civil service system, which we examine in later chapters. Civil service's concern for employee rights and an objective evaluation system have often hamstrung managers. Managers may lack control over employees and be unable to direct them to perform certain tasks necessary to carry out the job.

Another cause of the authority gap is the frequent centralization of staff functions, which allows the manager minimum control. Government managers may not only lack control over their employees, compared to their counterparts in business, but may be unable to control their budgets and obtain staff services. For example, let us suppose snow has been light this year, and the highway department wishes to transfer monies budgeted for snow removal to road repair. This proposal may require a major effort or may be refused by the central budget authority, as we shall see in Chapter 22. Likewise, managers who want to send employees out for training may be unable to do so.

Another reason for the authority gap has been touched on in the chapter on organization. Line managers must often share authority with staff managers, but rarely can they share responsibility. For example, a line manager cannot refuse to go along with an accounting system, hiring procedures, or budget appeal procedures. Even if these procedures make accomplishing the job much harder than it would be otherwise, the manager must learn to live with them.

Another set of causes, found in all types of organizations, are situations where the delegator is not sufficiently confident of himself to release any more of his authority than he must, or where he feels that since the ultimate responsibility is his, he should retain control of authority, or where he wishes to test a subordinate to determine his trustworthiness and resourcefulness.

Among these causes, probably the most telling is lack of self-confidence. The self-confident administrator is likely to delegate even more authority than is needed because it seems worth the gamble, and lucky gambles produce superior results. People who know they are trusted grow in the job, find better ways of doing what needs to be done, and search for new ways to make the program effective and useful to those it serves.

Coordination is partly a matter of securing clearances from superiors before action is taken. Every program involves some kind of work that impinges on that of other divisions, a fact that cannot be repeated too often. In most organizations, many decisions cut across the boundaries of two or more subdivisions of the enterprise. If mistakes are to be avoided, therefore, all aspects of every proposal relating to other parts of the program must be scrutinized by those who know what to look for. With confidence on both sides, those who receive delegated authority will reciprocate by knowing when to clear proposals and when to proceed on their own. Moreover, with a constant flow of information in both directions,

the problems of coordination are greatly simplified.

An example of this coordination is an incident in the building of the Interstate Highway System in 1967. A district engineer who was an expert on gradients routed the highway two miles longer than it would have been on a straight line in order to avoid a 7 percent grade at one point. The specifications read that a 5 percent grade was the desired norm. But in so doing, he overlooked the fact that by changing the route it would be difficult, if not impossible, to serve the third-largest city in the state. An outcry naturally arose. The congressional delegation was alerted and went into action. In the trade-off between the 7 percent grade and access to the city, the latter won.

The first step is for the functional heads of a program working on the same problem to confer at their own level and devise a solution before asking for approval at the next higher level, for this procedure encourages local initiative and relieves the burden on superiors. The more the executive can encourage his associates and subordinates to think independently and not merely mirror his ideas, the greater will be the inventiveness and the range of solutions; moreover, the results will usually be better than if he tries to monopolize the thinking for the entire organization.

Most subordinates, however, seem naturally to dislike consultation on the ground that it represents a kind of weakness, even though the higher official more often regards consultation as an accommodation to himself. Consequently, the higher official must lay the intellectual and emotional basis for consultation by his subordinates; he should teach them to recognize the situations in which they should consult for clearance and those in which they may appropriately proceed independently. A large part of this recognition, however, is a matter of intuition and the adjustment of personalities involved in the superior-subordinate relationship. But unless the relationship is clarified, subordinates will tend to consult only as a gesture to "the old man," discussing small, unimportant matters with him in some detail and deciding the larger ones for themselves.

Multiple Management

A growing trend in administration toward group decision and group coordination has come to be called multiple management. It is regarded not as an alternative to unified authority but as its complementary principle. Just as different areas of the human brain serve different purposes, in an organization also the functions of thinking, deciding, and coordinating are now being accomplished by layers and divisions. Among many other management functions, coordination occurs at all points and many levels of the enterprise, not merely at the top, as those who have not had the experience sometimes assume.

Multiple management is now extensively practiced in most large corporations in the United States. Exxon, the largest oil company in the United States and the top of the list of *Fortune*'s 500, has for the past 50 years been run by an executive committee of 11 members. The members meet daily, clear necessary matters with one another, go back to their respective offices, put on the new hat, and spend the rest of the day dealing with their assigned executive functions.

In public administration multiple management has been less widely adopted. The neglect is probably due to a pair of misunderstandings as to what multiple management entails. The first is a long-time aversion in public administration to committees as agents of execution. They are assumed to be appropriate for policy determination and quasi-judicial functions but not for the directing function. So rigid a rule is self-limiting and should be modified. The second misunderstanding is the common assumption in public administration that a committee must be formalized so that certain designated people meet together at stated intervals. The pattern is quite different in business management, where the practice is for division heads to huddle *not by prearrangement but when the law of the situation requires particular people to consult for particular purposes.*

This practical approach to the use of committees in administration avoids excessive bureaucratization and provides the dynamism needed in large-scale program management: huddles are ad hoc and formalization is dispensed with. Moreover, once this method has been accepted throughout the organization, it is a convenient means of coordinating at lower levels, which relieves the burden at the top; and since in most governments the tendency is to overload the top, the remedy should be welcome. Writers such as Ordway Tead and Peter Drucker make much of the advantages of multiple management through the use of the ad hoc huddle, and it should be far more extensively used in government than it is.

Interagency Coordination

Yet another use for the ad hoc group is in coordination among different agencies, an area of great weakness in public administration today, especially in the federal government. In coping with areas as diverse as urban problems, mental-health programs, conservation, or foreign affairs, the greatest loss of energy and effectiveness may be the result of a failure to coordinate the thinking, research, planning, and execution of separate programs that should work together if they are to achieve major solutions. As noted in earlier chapters, this kind of cross-referencing is still deficient at the top in the federal government, and the void could be at least partly filled by interagency coordination at the operating level, both at Washington headquarters and in the field.

A number of methods might be used at all levels of coordination. The standing interdepartmental committee has been employed in Washington with some occasional success, but it tends to become time-consuming and overly formalized. As former New York Governor Al Smith once said, "A committee is a group of men who individually can do nothing, but collectively can meet and decide that nothing can be done." Consequently, the ad hoc committee, which is more flexible and action-oriented, should be widely substituted.[7]

An interesting recent example is the Federal Committee on Pest Control, created in 1964 to find solutions to a problem that no agency, working by itself, could possibly devise. With representatives from the departments of Defense, Interior, Agriculture, and Health, Education and Welfare, the committee provided a small staff to plan and coordinate, and the results were immediately apparent. With a mandate "to recognize the need for balance between man and his environment that will be consistent with his total aesthetic and economic necessities and his social values,"[8] the committee was able to take a much larger view of the problem than any single agency could have done. Since its formation, the system has worked well, examples being the outlawing of DDT for spraying forests and the restrictions on defoliants used by electrical utilities on their rights-of-way.

If this coordinating device were more often used, many of the large problems of the people of the United States, which increasingly cut across many subjects and interests in complex interrelationships, might be more quickly dealt with; in addition, the current tendency toward program fragmentation in Washington might be checked.

Staff Meetings

Another essential device of coordination is the staff meeting, which is in fact widely used in public administration but often with lean results. Too frequently the regularly scheduled staff meeting in the boss's office is merely pro forma; the boss goes through some of the right motions but does not come to grips with real issues. Or the boss tries to solve all his problems in conference and holds the group together so long, discussing matters affecting only one or two of them, that the others become restless, fretting at the time wasted when their own desks are cluttered with the day's work. Then there is the kind of staff meeting in which the boss does all the talking and neither expects nor receives the participation of the members of the group, with the result that they may be enlightened, but he seldom is.

The proper functions of a staff meeting are as follows: to give the members a sense of the unity and interconnectedness of the work of the organization, to learn from the chief executive about new problems and developments affecting their

work, to solicit and enlist the thought and cooperation of the staff members in the solution of these problems, and to give department and division heads a chance to bring up questions that the boss should know about and that need his approval. (For an example of a staff meeting see Box 14.3.)

HEADQUARTERS-FIELD NETWORK

Larger agencies usually have distinct headquarters and field offices. The field offices serve a certain geographic area, whether neighborhood (police precinct office), several municipalities (state Welfare Department district office), or several states (federal Department of Transportation regional office).

Most aspects of coordination apply as much to federal and state field offices, where the bulk of program management occurs, as to headquarters offices in Washington and the state capitals. After all, most action is in the field. Ninety percent of federal employees work outside Washington. And, in most states, the majority of state employees work outside the state capital. In addition, however, the areal aspect of field administration creates distinctive problems of coordination that should have special attention. In some respects, the headquarters-field relationship is one of the most neglected areas in public administration; it is also the one from which some of the greatest gains might be achieved if more resourcefulness were devoted to it.

James W. Fesler, a political scientist who has studied the headquarters-field relationship closely, notes some major problems of federal coordination, stemming for the most part from the fact that control is still too centralized in Washington, thus limiting the freedom of program managers in the field.[9] The country is so large and diverse in character that centralization causes a serious loss of energy and initiative in actually accomplishing the work of government. Overcentralization also means too little planning and coordination at the lower levels; if more could be

Box 14.3

AGENCY TEAMWORK VITAL IN EMERGENCY PLANNING

By James L. Unterwegner
U.S. Depart. of Agriculture, Forest Service
Gifford Pinchot National Forest

Two months before the May 18 eruption of Mt. St. Helens, the forest disaster coordinator at the Gifford Pinchot National Forest began plans to provide a coordinated response to a possible emergency.

On March 20, the first earthquake activity in the vicinity of Mt. St. Helens was reported to the Gifford Pinchot National Forest office by the University of Washington. Others were reported on the following Saturday and Sunday. On Monday, March 24, earthquake activity began to build in frequency and magnitude and by Tuesday, geologists from the U.S. Geological Survey advised the forest officials that people should not spend the night in the vicinity of Spirit Lake, north of Mt. St. Helens.

These events led the forest disaster coordinator to contact key county, state and federal agencies and adjacent landowners and invite them to a meeting to review the current situation of activity generated by the mountain. A framework for an interagency contingency plan which would provide a coordinated response to an emergency was developed at the meeting. The plan called for an organization with direct interlinkage to prime response agencies including the sheriffs' offices, state police, state departments of highway, emergency services and natural resources, Pacific Power and Light Company, county commissioners and forest service. A core group, the Emergency Coordinating Center, would be located at the forest supervisor's office in Vancouver. The forest service would take the lead role. Key agencies would establish a hot line from the forest service headquarters with 24-hour service to their respective units so that, in the event of a major event on Mt. St. Helens, all key agencies could be notified and could implement their emergency plans.

Little did those attending the meeting know that on the very next day, March 27, the plan would be tested.

Sometime after 12:30 p.m., the first eruptive activity was reported on Mt. St. Helens. Immediately key contacts were made and soon individuals began appearing at the forest supervisor's office in Vancouver where the Emergency Coordinating Center was set up. Despite the brief amount of time available for preparation, the plan worked quite successfully.

Evacuation procedures were initiated to remove forest service personnel from the St. Helens Ranger Station at the head of Swift Reservoir. An airspace closure was requested to restrict aircraft near the mountain. Advisory warnings were issued to keep people out of the area, roadblocks were established and a public information system was implemented. As the volcano quieted, parts of the Emergency Coordinating Center were cut back.

At the onset of subsequent eruptions on May 18, 25 and June 5, the emergency plan was put back into action, utilizing the original groups, plus other representatives who became involved as needed. This added to the complexity of the total system necessary to administer each aspect of the volcano emergency.

No one can predict what lies ahead, nor for how many years the area may have to deal with eruptive activity from Mt. St. Helens. The coordinated response plan and the participants involved during the initial activities, however, are prepared for future emergencies.

done in state and regional offices, and especially in the key regional cities throughout the country, headquarters offices could devolve a greater freedom to field managers, which in turn would encourage a greater degree of coordination both within each agency and among agencies operating in the same area.

In Chapter 11, on organization, we examined alternative patterns of organization. An agency can be organized on a functional, or purpose, basis or on a geographic, or areal, basis. Fesler says that securing a balance between functional and areal coordination is now a perennial problem characteristic of all large-scale organizations, and constructive solutions must be found.

The overall problem may be clearly seen in these terms: a continental expanse of 3,000 miles, in addition to states as remote as Hawaii and Alaska and programs in most foreign countries; a distribution of federal field offices in every state and most communities of any size; a concentration of federal activities in large regional centers such as Boston, New York, Atlanta, Chicago, Denver, Los Angeles, and San Francisco; and scores of federal programs throughout this whole vast area, each with its own regional network and no formally recognized regional coordination (although, fortunately, a start has now been made). The terms include headquarters officials in Washington trying to maintain control over and achieve uniformity of procedures for distant outposts but often failing to allow for the degree of freedom needed in regional, state, and local centers if administration and coordination are to become as effective as all field officials realize they should be.

Nowhere, not even in large-scale, diversified corporation management, are the resulting problems so acute. Nor is it any real solution to say, as was once the practice, that the matter can easily be solved simply by following the principle of centralizing planning and policy decision at headquarters and decentralizing operating responsibility among the field establishments; for field officials rightly demand a part in policy planning and decision so as to represent local differences of circumstance and viewpoint. Indeed, if local respon-

sibility, individual initiative, and a high standard of resourcefulness are to be secured, then headquarters must allow a greater freedom in all areas of field administration.

Organization at Headquarters for Field Supervision

Another bothersome problem of the headquarters-field relationship, especially in multifunctional programs, is whether to concentrate or to disperse the authority of central-office officials to communicate with the field. A wide range of practice has been developed, usually on a trial-and-error basis and depending on the nature of the program, but no practice is satisfactory in every respect.

Where the top executive cannot bring himself to delegate authority and tries to do everything himself, he either personally prepares instructions to the field offices or has subordinates prepare them for his signature. If, on the other hand, he is the kind who prefers to delegate so as to clear time for the jobs that only he can do, then he may distinguish between communications through the line and those through the staff and allow staff instructions to flow out freely so long as they do not impinge on the authority of line officials in the field offices. In this situation, communications to line officials usually go from his own office. Or as a third alternative, he may appoint a director of field operations either in his own office or as the head of a separate division and require all communications, line and staff alike, to flow through that channel. These are the three main types of organization, but there are many variations and combinations.

Although there is no one best system that may be applied to all kinds of programs, there is doubtless a best system for every individual program. To discover what it is, however, may be a very confusing matter. Donald Stone, who was himself once the director of a field-operations office in a federal agency, has stated as an abstract proposition that "some operating official in the line of command must be responsible for the *whole* field program," and the italicized word is his.[10] When the various parts of a multifunctional program must be coordinated so as to make sense in the field, some one person at headquarters must be responsible for seeing that policy and instructions are consistent. But who is that person to be? the top person? a director of field operations? or a staff committee?

An illustration of the complexity of this problem is the experience of the War Production Board during World War II.[11] Because the WPB was a rush program, the administrator did not take time at the outset to study the problem; he might have saved time in the end if he had, for the agency tried everything in the book so far as headquarters-field organization was concerned. First, for field offices, the administrator agreed to accept space in each of the 12 Federal Reserve regions, irrespective of whether the areas were suitable to the work of his agency. This plan was a failure from the start. Then a crazy quilt pattern of organization developed in the field, pretty much hit or miss. This also failed. Next a Bureau of Field Operations was set up at headquarters. This gave way to a director of industry operations and finally to a system of dual hierarchy.

Dual Hierarchy

A difficulty in every far-flung organization, and the WPB was no exception, is to persuade staff officials in charge of such matters as finance, personnel, engineering, and the like and line or operating officials to work harmoniously together in a field office when one group is at least partially subordinate to the other but both report to different superiors at headquarters.

The theory of dual hierarchy, or dual supervision, which was developed to explain these relationships was first brought into prominence by Arthur W. Macmahon, J. D. Millett, and Gladys Ogden in the book *The Administration of Federal Work Relief.*[12] The theory rests on a distinction between specialist and generalist, between function and authority, and assumes a *dual line of supervision and control from the top down and a*

dual set of loyalties from the bottom up. The arrangement is similar to one worked out in the Forest Service, where parallel chains of operating and functional officials drop down through all levels of the service, which has long had a reputation as one of the better-managed agencies in Washington.[13]

When the War Production Board finally turned to dual hierarchy in the management of its field offices, the distinction between specialist and generalist was formalized in an arrangement under which the policymaking and policy-interpreting responsibilities in functional matters were reserved to the appropriate functional divisions in the Washington office, of which there were approximately 40. It was then agreed that these central-office officials should maintain routine relations with their functional subordinates in the field; at the same time, "administrative" authority and general coordinating responsibility was vested in regional directors.[14]

The Social Security Administration is an interesting illustration of an agency that insists on a high degree of centralization. Now part of the Department of Health and Human Services, the Social Security Administration was originally established as an independent agency and was notable in Washington for having successfully used a separate field-operations division with jurisdiction over procurement, budget, travel, space, communications, and personnel administration for 12 regional and 2 territorial offices. This division passed on all outgoing communications from any Washington unit to 2 or more regional offices and reviewed all business management activities to ensure their adherence to policy and administrative standards and to secure overall coordination.[15]

Generally speaking, however, this type of central organization for field supervision has not been favorably regarded by other federal agencies that have tried it, the WPB being only one among many. To combine policy-review responsibility with a concentration of housekeeping functions in a single headquarters division obviously creates a formidable aggregation of power in one place and limits the freedom and authority of program administrators. Jealousy and frustrations begin to appear. If the work piles up, the field operations division at headquarters becomes a bottleneck, and field men complain of unnecessary delays. On the other hand, there are certain advantages to the plan in that it unifies authority, acts as a "friend at court" for field officials vis-à-vis functional divisions at headquarters, and helps to coordinate the policies of manifold programs in the field.[16]

Yet another illustration of field relationships is the experience of the Office of Price Administration (OPA) during World War II in establishing field offices for its rationing program.[17] Originally, these offices were set up in each state, but they were later consolidated on a regional basis. Politics became a problem when many congressmen opposed the change on the ground that it would diminish the role of the states. But to the OPA, there was the advantage of being able to recruit a staff free from the influence of state politics, whose loyalties were more likely to be to the program itself.

The OPA also applied the dual-supervision arrangement. The chief administrative difficulty in field operations was to define the line of contact between field offices. From sheer necessity, multiple lines of supervision developed from the outset and continued throughout the history of the OPA. This arrangement seems to have been the reason that headquarters officials were willing to accept an integrated field office at the top, for it reserved to them the freedom they needed to discharge their own responsibilities for the direction of the program.[18] A similar organization for field supervision in the War Production Board, if created early enough, might have saved much grief in that agency also.

Coordination in the Field

A number of methods have been worked out to increase the freedom of action of officials responsible for the administration of federal programs in the field. Some of these have already been tried, others are still on the drawing board. Still others will doubtless have to be devised.

One proposal that has received a good deal of backing for some time but has not been widely practiced as yet is to establish recognized regional subcapitals, so to speak. This would mean setting up in all major areas of the country regional centers that would be formally and consistently recognized as centers of coordination; such centers would coordinate both individual programs and groups of programs and would include the work of every federal agency operating in each region.

This plan was suggested as early as 1935 in a report of the National Resources Planning Board.[19] Later, David B. Truman studied the matter and found that officials of the U.S. Department of Agriculture found a clear advantage when departmental and interdepartmental coordination centers were established in cities such as Chicago.[20] And James Fesler, in his studies of area and administration, has consistently noted the benefits to be derived from this solution. Yet as late as 1982, Congress has resisted such moves, because it wishes to maximize its power over programs.

The enormous growth in federal grants-in-aid to state and local governments in the 1960s and 1970s has exacerbated problems of headquarters-field coordination. The Advisory Commission on Intergovernmental Relations (ACIR) concludes that most attempts to coordinate the spending of federal grants have failed. Many federal agencies have gone in their own direction without trying for teamwork with related agencies. An example is the Model Cities program of 1966–1974, designed to coordinate urban grant activities. The federal Department of Housing and Urban Development (HUD), which funded the Model Cities grant, could not obtain full cooperation from other federal agencies, such as Health, Education and Welfare (now Health and Human Services), Transportation, and the Office of Economic Opportunity, which operated programs with a direct impact on Model Cities. In the words of a General Accounting Office report, "The lack of adequate federal coordination had plagued the program from the start."[21]

"For many, the decade ended with a feeling of disillusion and dissatisfaction. . . . the efficiency of planned, centrally coordinated, comprehensive approaches to policymaking and the provision of services have been challenged."[22] Many observers believe that the cause of lack of coordination lies in the political and not the managerial arena. Until Congress and the president set clear goals and commit resources to carry them out, little progress can be made. "If we want coordination, we must first agree on our national goals and priorities and commit the resources required for their accomplishment."[23]

During the administration of Richard M. Nixon (1969–1974), a number of steps were taken to improve coordination in the field. First, federal regions were standardized. This meant that state and local officials would have to travel to just one city to meet federal regional officials. Before, they might have had to go to a different city to talk to officials of each federal agency they were doing business with. Second, federal regional councils (FRCs) were established in each of the 10 regions. The FRCs, made up of representatives from each federal agency and state and local delegates, were designed to increase teamwork among all concerned. Unfortunately, they seem to have had little impact. For example, a survey of 404 administrators of federal-grant programs conducted in 1976 found that 90 percent of them felt that the FRCs had no appreciable effect on defining interprogram problems, development of strategies to solve interprogram problems, elimination of interprogram frictions and objections, and relations with state and local governments.[24] The ACIR has summed up by saying the FRCs "have made but limited progress. . . ."[25] Such failure was not inevitable, however. The federal government did not invest a great deal of resources or energy in FRCs. Lack of sufficient, experienced staff and rotation of the head of the FRCs do not seem to have improved coordina-

tion.[26] If the FRCs are reinvigorated and given more resources, they might be able to achieve a good deal more.

SUMMARY

There are many experiments, but alas few lasting improvements. And yet the stakes are high, because an ounce of coordination can save a great deal of money and buy a corresponding amount of improved service. In this chapter we have dealt prominently with the philosophy and techniques of coordination and with the vexing problem of real coordination.

In all areas of coordination, methods should remain flexible so that appropriate means may be used in appropriate circumstances. Coordination then becomes dynamic, not stereotyped and limited. Authority and responsibility should be as nearly equal as possible, accompanied by a mutual confidence that will encourage clearances with superiors and permit freedom to decide at the lower levels. Multiple management through the use of ad hoc committees should be more widely used, both within programs and among programs of an interagency basis. And staff meetings, if imaginatively and dexterously handled, can give substance to the philosophy of administering by objectives.

NOTES

1. "Colorado School Zone Is Lacking a School," *New York Times,* 15 May 1978, p. 34.

2. Ordway Tead, *The Art of Administration* (New York: McGraw-Hill, 1951), p. 194.

3. William H. Newman and Charles E. Summer, Jr., *The Process of Management: Concepts, Behavior, and Practice* (Englewood Cliffs, N.J.: Prentice-Hall, 1961), p. 407.

4. Tead, *The Art of Administration,* p. 191.

5. Memorandum for the director of the Bureau of the Budget, 20 July 1939. See Harold Seidman, *Politics, Position and Power* (New York: Oxford University Press, 1980), p. 101.

6. Newman and Summer, *The Process of Management,* pp. 408–409.

7. Harold Guetzkow discusses this device in "Interagency Committee Usage," *Public Administration Review* 10 (Summer 1950): 190.

8. *Federal Committee on Pest Control: What It Is; What It Does* (Washington: U.S. Government Printing Office, February 1967).

9. James W. Fesler, *Area and Administration* (Tuscaloosa: University of Alabama Press, 1949); and "Field Organization," in *Elements of Public Administration,* ed. Morstein Marx (Englewood Cliffs, N.J.: Prentice-Hall, 1946), ch. 9.

10. Donald C. Stone, "Washington-Field Relationships," in *Washington-Field Relationships in the Federal Service* (Washington: U.S. Dept. of Agriculture, Graduate School, 1942), p. 17.

11. William D. Carey, "Central-Field Relationships in the War Production Board," *Public Administration Review* 4 (Winter 1944): 31–42.

12. Arthur W. Macmahon, John D. Millett, and Gladys Ogden, *The Administration of Federal Work Relief* (Chicago: Public Administration Service, 1941), pp. 265–268.

13. Earl W. Loveridge and Peter Keplinger, "Washington-Field Relationships in the Forest Service," in *Washington-Field Relationships in the Federal Service*, p. 23.

14. Carey, "Central-Field Relationships in the War Production Board," pp. 37–38.

15. W.L. Mitchell, "Washington-Field Relations in the Social Security Board," in *Washington-Field Relationships in the Federal Service,* p. 35.

16. George F. Rohrlich, "Consolidation of Unemployment Insurance and the Problem of Centralization," *Public Administration Review* 4 (Winter 1944): 43–50.

17. Emmette S. Redford, *Field Administration of Wartime Rationing,* OPA Historical Reports on War Administration, General Publication no. 4 (Washington: U. S. Government Printing Office, 1947), p. 196.

18. In a review of Redford's book by John D. Millett, *Public Administration Review* 8 (Winter 1948): p. 68.

19. National Resources Planning Board, *Regional Factors in National Planning* (Washington: U.S. Government Printing Office, December 1935).

20. David B. Truman, *Administrative Decentralization* (Chicago: University of Chicago Press, 1940).

21. Advisory Commission on Intergovernmental Relations (ACIR), *Improving Federal Grants Management* (Washington: U.S. Government Printing Office, 1977), p. 72.

22. ACIR, p. 81.

23. ACIR, p. 83.

24. ACIR, p. 187.

25. ACIR, p. 198.

26. ACIR, p. 186.

15

Control: Philosophy and Methods

God grant me the serenity to accept the things I cannot change, the courage to change the things I can, and the wisdom to know the difference.

Reinhold Neibuhr

In this chapter we define managerial control, distinguish among different types of control, focus on the sensitive question of feedback and the installation of control systems, and evaluate the results of various systems.

Box 15.1

MEMORANDUM

CONFIDENTIAL

```
The markings on this page (the
last page of this report) repre-
sent the OVERALL security classi-
fication assigned to this report.
By itself this page is UNCLASSI-
FIED.
```

CONFIDENTIAL

Control is a central function of management because it is the means of measuring results, not only in terms of finished products or services, but also over periods of time. Control makes it possible to say at any given point, even daily: this is where we stand in relation to our planned objectives.

THE NATURE OF CONTROL

Control is, therefore, a dynamic concept, a powerful incentive, and in the hands of the program manager, an indispensable tool. Like so many key concepts in administration, such as organization and supervision, control is intrinsic to everything the program manager does, for it draws on and contributes to every aspect of the administrative process.

Like anything else, control can be overdone, as Box 15.1 indicates. President Lyndon B. Johnson overdid control, calling his aides when they went out for lunch, asking what they were eating and then whether they had added salt and pepper. This obsession with *dominance* is not what we regard as a productive use of control.[1]

CASE STUDY: SHIPPING

A good example of how central the control function may be occurred during World War II in the War Shipping Administration. The Recruitment and Manning Organization (RMO) of the WSA had as its objective avoiding ship delays as a result of inadequate crews. Its jurisdiction included Allied as well as American ships. New ships were being produced at the rate of five a day, and some of them were allotted to Norway, Greece, Britain, and other countries.

The key to the whole task was the Control Division of the RMO. First, the control officer needed to know exactly how many ships were required, were being launched, and were being sunk by enemy action. Then he needed to know how many seamen and in what skill classifications were in the labor force, how many experienced seamen could be recruited, and how many were being trained in maritime academies or required such training. Third, he needed to know where the ships were at all times and what their daily manpower requirements were. In order to have such knowledge, he had to have projections of ships and manpower losses resulting from enemy action. The work of every other unit in the RMO depended upon the accuracy and currency of this information.

How did the control officer operate? First, he tapped a great number of sources, United States as well as Allied, for accurate information. Second, he kept such data up-to-date. Third, he supplied this information where and when needed at an instant's notice. This last step was facilitated by staff conferences of division heads, in which the control officer received advice as well as gave it. Under the circumstances, the executive officer who headed the manpower program could expect to be no better than his control officer's efficiency enabled him to be. Even coordination and negotiation, which were his two main jobs, depended upon the effectiveness of current intelligence. Control, then, was the indispensable way in which program results were measured, making it possible to say "here is where we stand in relation to our planned objectives."

Control is an integral part of the theory and philosophy of administration, and it constitutes a dynamic aspect of public administration. For many people, however, control has unfortunate connotations, and, when misused, it can cause a serious loss of morale and lessened accomplishment. People tend to think of control as an external force imposed on them against their will. The temper of the modern age is such that the mere mention of control sometimes sets up resistance. Another use of the term implies condemnation, as when an accountant, for example, is chiefly interested in mistakes or fraud. There is also the connotation of higher authority, as in control by the central budget or accounting office. But none of these connotations is in line with the modern philosophy of control. Control should not be conceived of as a set of dictatorial devices to manage employees, but as an approach that helps those responsible for implementation of a plan to stay on the right track. Highway traffic lights are a means of control, and some drivers might not like them for this reason. But if traffic lights were done away with, chaos, terrible accidents, and traffic backed up for miles would result. Likewise,

implementing an action plan without adequate controls will result in failure.

Means of Control

Control has always been more emphasized in business management than in public administration, and the business community must be credited with developing the function as internal motivation rather than external pressure. As early as 1941, in a book called *Top Level Management Organization and Control,* the whole managerial process was interpreted in terms of control, much as some writers have used decision making or organization as the key managerial concept. The control philosophy has been further developed since then.[2]

Until the middle-1960s, the control concept was little employed in public administration, except in connection with top-level "control" agencies such as central budget, management, and personnel offices. A series of related steps is involved.

When the objectives of a program have been determined, initiative should be encouraged among those down the line. They must have constant and current information in order to measure progress. This information is an encouragement to all who participate in the program.

The sources of such information are many, including reports (the R in Luther Gulick's POSDCORB), accounting, statistics, and computer and information systems, discussed in Chapter 17; but the most important one is daily checking by supervisors on the degree of progress made toward predetermined goals. If management is to remain dynamic and resourceful, all such information must be in the hands of line executives, not stored away in some staff or "control" agency and made available only periodically as in end-of-the-year audits.

The information-control function must remain in the hands of line officials because deviations and innovations promote enterprise, and new ideas are stimulated by a constant flow of information. In all programs, it is the end results that count, and rigid conformity to procedures imposed from the outside seems to frustrate the state of mind that keeps constantly in view the ends of the program and devises better ways of promoting them.

This type of control is not limited to internal administration, however, for the legislature and the public also are entitled to receive reports on measurements of results and the progress of government programs, although their interest is often largely centered around overall results and adherence to statutory authority.

A necessary implication of this line of reasoning is that the controller, as he is called in business management, or the central budget office and the external auditor, the terms used in government, should never be permitted to dictate to administrators the manner in which they shall run their programs. These top agencies may have more detailed facts about the government as a whole and a wider range of information than the line executive has, and they should make such information widely and easily available. But they are not responsible for achieving program results

and, in any event, lack the necessary skills in that area.

This relationship between top budgeting and accounting agencies and line operating officials is a serious problem in all large organizations. Figure-minded individuals addicted to precision and tidiness, almost without consciously intending it, seem to become authoritarian and censorious.[3] Often they insist on having their own way about everything. When that is allowed to happen, program managers become frustrated, then immobilized, and finally fiercely hostile to the controls imposed.

Types of Control

Three types of control can be distinguished, each of which relates respectively to the concepts of input, activity, and results.[4]

Preliminary Control. Preliminary control focuses on inputs, whether people or things. Do personnel have the capacity to perform their jobs as expected? Are equipment, supplies, and material of the requisite quality to accomplish the job? Have adequate funds been budgeted for the proper expenditures to enable the agency to achieve its stated goals? We shall examine preliminary personnel controls in Chapter 18, where we discuss employee selection and placement. Likewise, Chapter 22 on budgeting is concerned with preliminary control.

Concurrent Control. Concurrent control focuses on activities carried out in the implementation of policy. We have already covered this topic in Chapter 12 on supervision.

Supervision is the means by which concurrent control is established and maintained. If employees are not doing their work properly, it is the supervisor's job to see that they do. Concurrent control is concerned with making sure workers perform the activities they are supposed to.

Feedback Control. Feedback control focuses on results; it is our principal concern in this chapter and the next two chapters. The classical example of a feedback device is a thermostat. A thermostat maintains a preset temperature. When the actual temperature starts to fall below the preset temperature, the thermostat activates the heating system until the actual temperature equals the preset temperature. In this illustration, the preset temperature is the *goal*. This goal is achieved by the thermostat's constant monitoring of the actual temperature and the corrective action the thermostat takes. Temperature is the *results,* which can be related back to the goal. Feedback control monitors performance to see if the desired results are being achieved. The job done by workers is measured by personnel performance appraisal, dealt with in Chapter 18. The efficiency of programs is measured by productivity analysis, examined in Chapter 16. Chapter 16's treatment of program evaluation examines the effectiveness of programs. Chapter 23 examines the audit, while Chapter 17 deals with management information systems and explains techniques that can be applied in all of these areas.

ASPECTS OF CONTROL SYSTEMS

The common aspects of all effective control systems are standards, information, and action. Standards are targets, such as 50 miles of paved roads, 100 applications processed, or 70 percent of third graders reading at or above the national average, which provide direction for the agency. They are derived from goals and objectives and are often synonymous with them. *Information* that reports actual performance is necessary before any corrections can be made. If a manager does not know that an employee or program is not meeting standards, he cannot do anything to change the situation. *Action* to correct the difference between standards and actual performance must be possible. If a manager is incapable, for whatever reason, of improving employee or program performance that is below par, no meaningful control system exists. If the manager knows

that performance does not equal results but cannot or will not take corrective action, all the standards and information in the world will not solve the problem. Standards, information, and action, then, are interrelated prerequisites for any control system.

Internal Controls

Internal controls are those that employers and agencies adopt as part of their own preferred values. The police officer who spends unpaid, off-duty time trying to solve a crime, the employee who refuses a perfectly legal and acceptable free lunch from clientele group representatives, and the worker for an alcoholic treatment program who does not have to leave the comfort of the office to spread the word about the program but does so anyway—these are all examples of government workers who have internalized results-oriented goals and controls. The best policy that management can follow with them is George Odiorne's advice: "Leave me alone as much as possible to do my job."[5]

An example is the 17 percent cutback of energy in the city of Los Angeles in 1974. After the December 1973 Arab oil embargo, the mayor and a group of civic leaders asked for cutbacks. Each group, such as residents and representatives of different types of business, was given a goal. No one was told how to achieve it. If Mr. X wanted to watch TV and turn the lights off, while Mrs. Y turned the TV off and kept the lights on, that was their choice. Similar examples occurred in the 1981 drought in the Northeast. Water consumption levels dropped without penalties of any kind being enforced.

External Controls

External controls, on the other hand, are those imposed on employees whether workers like them or not. Position controls, for example, can be used by the central budget office to prevent an agency from filling vacant jobs. Budgeting and account-

Box 15.2

A SIMPLIFIED CHECKLIST FOR CONTROL

GENERAL

1. Does the agency have a formal plan under which management responsibilities are clearly defined, reasonably aligned, and adequately documented by an up-to-date organization chart?
2. Are written policies and procedures readily available to all employees?
3. Are duties separated so that no single individual can control a series of related transactions from beginning to end?
4. At a minimum, are managers and supervisors offered training in the budget process, the personnel process, and the procurement process?

PROCUREMENT

1. Have the agency's procurement policies and procedures been spelled out in a manual?
2. Have managers and supervisors been told where and with whom the manual for their respective units is kept?
3. Does the procurement office have an established communications system to inform the requesting offices on:
   a. The lead time required for processing actions?
   b. The approvals required for different types of procurement?
4. Does the procurement office consolidate individual purchase requests from different offices to save money and avoid excess inventories?
5. Are procurement requests screened by the property office to see whether the agency can use existing items rather than buy new ones?
6. Is the receipt and inspection function separated from the ordering and payment functions?

PERSONNEL

1. Are new employees given an orientation?
2. Are time and attendance cards:
   a. Maintained only in the custody of an approved time and attendance clerk?
   b. Approved by the supervisor?
3. Are work reports:
   a. Sufficiently detailed to show time charges to assignments, leave, and administration?
   b. Reconciled with time and attendance cards?
4. Are hours reported for overtime pay periodically compared to an external record (e.g. a security station "In & Out" log)?
5. Are floor checks conducted periodically?
6. Do supervisors give employees assignments with deadlines so that their performance and progress can be monitored?
7. Do supervisors give employees assignments having no rigid deadline, which the employee can work on when there is a slow-down in tightly scheduled work?

TRAVEL

1. Are agency travel policies and procedures in writing?
2. Are travel claims and vouchers prepared in ink or typed?
3. Are transportation arrangements made or approved by a responsible individual other than the traveler?
4. Is use of government-owned cars prohibited for other than official business?

DATA PROCESSING

1. Is there a formal internal audit program for regular review and audit of data processing operations and procedures?
2. Does the organization provide for strict

separation of the programming, computer operation, and manual control duties?

3. Are data processing personnel prohibited from performing duties in other operating areas of the organization?

4. Is there a method of preventing unauthorized persons from gaining access to the data processing facility?

5. Is a log of program changes maintained, indicating the date on which the change went into operation, in such a manner as to provide an accurate chronological record of the system?

SOURCE: Management, January 1980, p. 13.

ing controls are designed to make sure money is spent for designated purposes and to prevent fraud. Box 15.2 is a checklist of these kinds of controls.

These controls are set by outside agencies, but other external controls would include time clocks, inspection systems, quotas for quantity of work to be done, and any other measures used by agency supervisors to check whether the job is being done.

Controls that have gone haywire are often responsible for red tape, which delays decisions. It is a good idea to have checks and balances in any agency, but too many checks and balances make it impossible to accomplish anything. If an action needs the approval of 10 government officials, rather than 2, it may take forever to finish the job.

External controls that are unpopular with agency employees are often ineffective.[6] Anthony Downs has proposed "laws" of imperfect control and counter control.[7] The first holds that it is impossible to control fully the goal-oriented behavior of employees in a large agency. The reasons for lack of control are the necessary discretion that has to be given to employees so they can do their work and the different values of different employers. If Bill Bureaucrat is convinced that a certain program is bound to fail, for example, the possibility of motivating him to devote his full efforts to it is slim.

Counter control is the inevitable reaction to attempts at tighter external control. Employees will work harder to find ways to evade tightened controls for which no reasonable grounds are apparent. In one government agency, for example, employees were required to fill out forms accounting for the way they spent their time in 20-minute blocks. While the intent of management was to motivate workers to use their time better, the employees saw it as regimentation. As a result, the system was counterproductive. Employees gathered on their work breaks to see who could fill out the most ludicrous listing of activities.[8]

Figure 15.1 outlines in diagram form some of the costs and benefits of internal versus external controls.

Insofar as it is possible, it is preferable to seek to motivate employees toward internal control and self-control rather than impose external controls. Yet it is not possible to do so in all situations and the kinds of external controls listed in Figure 15.1 are crucial to most organizations. If they can be restructured, so much the better; but they are needed regardless. This topic will be one of our chief concerns here and in the next two chapters.

MANAGEMENT BY OBJECTIVES

Management by objectives (MBO) is the modern approach to results-oriented management, as suggested in Chapter 10 on planning.

MBO is a comprehensive approach, which includes planning, implementation, and review, as Figure 15.2 indicates. In this chapter, we shall focus on the implementation and review phases of MBO since they are concerned with control.

The authors Wayne Kimmel, William Dougan, and John Hall define MBO as "an approach to the internal management of an organization in

Figure 15.1 Two Different Strategies of Control

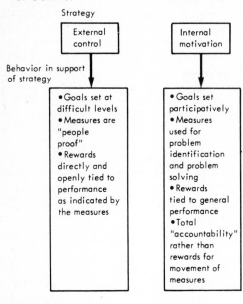

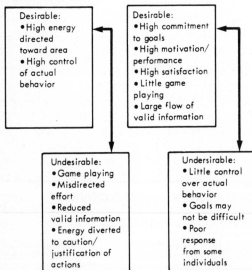

Figure 15.2 Principal Components of MBO

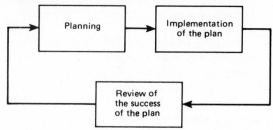

which individual managers set performance goals in terms of output or achievement rather than input or activity.... Beyond this activity, an MBO program may be as unique as the organization that uses it."[9]

Indeed, MBO is used for different reasons or combinations of reasons in different organizations. It can be used as an *evaluative technique* for employee or program performance, as an *incentive technique* to motivate employees, as a *system to enhance job satisfaction,* or as a means to attain *mutual understanding* among different levels of the organization.[10] A well-designed and implemented MBO system can perform all these functions, and in all of them the concern is with some aspect of control.

Implementing MBO

MBO is a flexible management approach, which can be introduced at any level of an organization and implemented in a variety of ways. There is no one best way to introduce MBO. For example, the author George Morrisey lists a half dozen alternatives, which range from across-the-board implementation to an individual manager's practicing MBO alone to set an example.[11] While there is no one best way, *commitment* to MBO is crucial. Managers who want to implement MBO must examine their own level of commitment and ask whether it will suffice to make the plan workable. At the same time, managers must gauge the support likely to be given by colleagues, whether peers, subordinates, or superiors. If they are unlikely to support MBO to the same extent as the manager, its chances for success will be adversely affected.

While MBO can be introduced at a number of different points, one survey of several hundred managers found that it was most likely to be accepted by them if introduced by top management. Such sponsorship indicates to managers that MBO is to be taken seriously because it is more than the passing fancy of just one part of the organization, such as the personnel department, which can be ignored without penalty.[12]

Preconditions

A substantial training effort is necessary if MBO is to succeed. Such training requires no weekend seminar but a prolonged period of several months. Special training sessions are a must, but most of the learning will come on the job, as managers seek to apply the principles of MBO and are instructed further in their efforts by the project director or trainers.

As a result of training, managers come to know the general principles of MBO and the way it fits into their agency before they can go into the nitty-gritty of fashioning and implementing specific objectives. A substantial amount of time during the training period should be allotted to both the costs and benefits of MBO. The training process should stress individual self-assessment of skills and judgments about the utility of MBO.[13] A common experience in agencies that fail to train managers in this way is for managers to wait passively for their superiors to set objectives for them instead of fixing the objectives themselves.

Several different steps are involved in the implementation process, as Figure 15.3 indicates.[14]

Preparing the Action Plan

Once an objective has been chosen, an action plan must be drawn up to implement it. The statement of the plan should be brief, but it should be broken down into different phases as well. One example of an action plan follows.

The city of Podunk Welfare Department finds

Figure 15.3 Implementing MBO

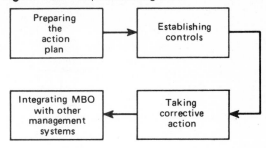

that a large number of welfare checks are going out to ineligible clients. It forms the following action plan to correct this problem. A new information system designed to end these errors is to be installed in six months, at a cost of $100,000 and 2,500 work hours of effort. The first step in the plan is to gain agreement and support for it within the agency. One week and 50 work hours of *specifically designated personnel* are allocated to this phase. Next, the design and installation of the new computer-based information system is allotted $50,000, 75 days, and 850 work hours. Third, training staff to use the new system will take 50 days, $35,000 and 1,000 work hours. Implementation of the new system is allotted $15,000, 35 days, and 500 work hours. The final step is review and evaluation, for which 13 days and 100 work hours are allocated.

Figure 15.4 outlines an action plan followed by the former U.S. Civil Service Commission to attain the objective of improving the accuracy of estimates of new employees hired by federal agencies. While the cost element is not included, steps, timetable, and individual responsibility are detailed in the figure.

In the examples just given, we have sketched a five-step implementation plan, which involves several tasks. These tasks include *programming,* or determining the steps to be followed to gain objectives; *scheduling,* or determining the amount of time necessary to accomplish each step; *budgeting,* or allotting resources—whether money, men or merchandise—necessary to attain each objective; and accountability, or assigning to each per-

Figure 15.4 U.S. Civil Service Commission Action Plan

Objective	Responsible office and individual	Oct.	Nov.	Dec.	Jan.	Feb.	Comment
7. A system, usable by any of the region's area offices, for improving the accuracy of agency new hire estimates.	Milwaukee (Belluzzo and Freeman)						CARE—S1–I 1, 2, 3; IV analysis CARE—S2–VI A2, B1
a. Initiate development by 10/7. b. Draft format, procedures, and letter to AO's by 10/25. c. Comments to lead AO by 11/8. d. Final recommendations to SD by 11/22. e. Published in MAR Guide Supplement by 12/6.							System development should include: —Study of reasons for inaccuracies. —Establishing accuracy criteria. —Format for comparing agency forecasts with actual hires. —A model quarterly letter to agencies displaying differences.
10. A model handout that directs the public to FJIC's for job information.	Dayton (O'Donnell)						CARE—S1–III analysis CARE—S2–III analysis MAR Guide, pages 8, 11, 12
a. Initiate development by 10/1. b. Draft to AO's by 10/21 c. Comments to lead AO by 11/7. d. Recommended text to SD by 11/21. e. Published in MAR Guide by 12/5.							Tells how to obtain Federal job information: FJIC/WATS addresses, telephone numbers; what to ask or say when inquiring; kind of information available. Intended as a "bridge" for distant or reticent publics. Should be low cost but attractive, and be written at 8th grade Fog Index level. Each AO will print its own handout.

SOURCE: *Civil Service Journal,* July/September 1975, p. 15.

son his share of responsibility for completing each step of the job.

Establishing Controls

Controls should follow the guideline, already noted, set forth by George S. Odiorne, a leading authority on MBO: "Leave me alone as much as possible to do my job."[15]

Morrisey notes that control is intended to warn people when they are going to get in trouble so that they have enough time to change direction to avoid disaster. For this reason, too much control should be avoided, for it is a waste of organizational resources. If managers are constantly looking over their subordinates' shoulders and telling them what to do, MBO does not have a chance to be established. Subordinates will never learn to do the work on their own, and managers will waste valuable time that could be put to productive effort elsewhere.

Control should focus on the most important concerns of the organization. For example, a health department should be more concerned with establishing controls for the cost and quality of its public inoculation programs than with working out elaborate controls to reduce the number of pencils and paper clips used each year.

Controls involve standards, discussed earlier in this chapter, which are accepted levels of performance, or yardsticks by which to measure achievement. Standards can be applied to almost any aspect of organizational input, activity, or output. Examples might include the amount of sewerage purified per work hour, the employee absentee rate, and the number of welfare client complaints dealt with per week. Some standards, such as those relating to employee morale, may be very difficult to measure, but Morrisey recommends that the attempt be made. Otherwise, there would be no criteria to gauge objectives-oriented performance and thus no way to tell early enough (when it is preventable) what is likely to go wrong. For example, if Dutch water engineers know that a certain amount of dike leakage is inevitable and easy to deal with, they know that it is not a critical problem. But if leakage exceeds a certain amount, they know a crisis is coming and must immediately be met. Without such standards, they could not adequately respond to leaks and would either ignore the crumbling of the dike or treat each leak as if it forecast a flood. In either situation, the consequences for agency efficiency and effectiveness should be obvious: The need for standards applies equally strongly, though usually not so dramatically, to every organization.

The whole point of establishing controls is to be able to take action to change course. One type of action is *self*-correcting. Competent and motivated individuals can adjust their own behavior when it is inadequate to achieve objectives *if* they are aware of the objectives and how they are doing in relation to them.

A second type is *operating* action. If problems develop, managers may step in and do the work themselves, or they may direct another employee to take over. Although such intervention may sometimes be necessary, managers should not do so if it is not. Otherwise, subordinates will never learn how to deal with a crisis and will thus never develop their full potential. One of the authors remembers well how his father, a motel manager, turned over the office to a new employee on his first day, walking out and leaving him alone on his shift after five minutes' instruction. This manager was willing to risk some mistakes so that the employee could learn how to handle by himself any situation that might arise. Perhaps the most important benefit of this action was its impression on the employee, who interpreted the manager's action as a vote of confidence in his ability to do the job.

A third type is *management* action. Here the manager reviews the *process* that has caused the discrepancy between the action plan and actual events. Was the discrepancy due to a fault in the planning process for the action plan, or did it arise from uncertainty, unexpected events, failure, or human error? This difficult determination is the measure of a manager, for the plan can only be implemented if the supervisor is able to determine why it went wrong and take steps to correct it.

John W. Humble, a British specialist in MBO,

has suggested the following checklist to be used in the implementation of MBO:

- Do managers have control information on all the key results they must achieve?
- Is it simple? relevant? timely? acceptable? a good basis for self-control?
- When did you last make a critical study of the information and control systems and paperwork?
- Is there too much information?
- Is it costing too much?[16]

Integrating MBO with Other Systems

A final crucial question remains. Is MBO integrated with other organizational procedures, or is it set up as a system that functions independently of personnel, budgeting, and other key areas of organizational decision making? As business administration scholars Stephen J. Carroll, Jr., and Henry L. Tosi have put it, "Unless the MBO program is integrated with other organizational procedures and systems, it will be viewed as something outside normal operating procedure and will receive inadequate attention. In addition, it will create a source of conflict, as it is likely that action required by the MBO program will contradict other procedures and requirements."[17] Carroll and Tosi note that unless other organizational subsystems, such as data processing, forecasting, and budgeting, are tied into MBO, MBO will lack the data it needs to operate. Conversely, they observe that "the more that the MBO system is made interdependent with other subsystems of the organization, the more the use of MBO will be reinforced and will become a natural aspect of management."[18]

An illustration of this point is the manager who restructured the work system in his office so that 39 employees were able to accomplish what had previously been done by 44. For this reason, he did not ask for replacements when 5 employees quit or retired. But when the manager was told that he would be paid less because he now supervised less than 40 employees, he immediately asked for 5 more employees and gave them busy work. Thus, failure to integrate MBO with personnel department procedures wiped out all the gains made possible by MBO.[19]

The Results of MBO

What is the record of MBO? A survey of studies of MBO's impact in private-sector organizations concludes that "MBO has some research support. On the other hand, there seems to be varying success with MBO in organizations with the possibility that only a minority of MBO attempts have proved viable. The level of success appears to vary with managerial commitment to the program and with other factors associated with effective organizational practices."[20]

There is no such thing as a perfect, self-implementing plan. Those MBO plans that are carried out in the way just described will have more results than those that are not. While detailed studies of the impact on program of governmental MBO have not been made, the information available is consistent with our thesis. Let us take, for example, the federal MBO efforts of the administrations of Richard Nixon and Gerald Ford in 1973–1976. Various studies indicate that MBO had little effect on federal management. That is not surprising, since neither middle managers of line agencies nor examiners of the central budget agency (Office of Management and Budget) were involved or committed to the new system. Had they been, and had MBO been a real priority of department heads, the story might have been different.

Political scientist James Swiss has found that federal MBO was viewed by top government executives as an effective means of increasing their power over lower levels in their departments. Department secretaries supported MBO, not because it led to greater efficiency, but because it gave them greater power. And secretarial support was the most important single factor in determining the likelihood of success for MBO.[21]

A number of state agencies and divisions within these agencies have used MBO. New York State's central budget office uses MBO in framing the budget.[22] Some state officials, such as Dennis E. Butler, personnel director of the Pennsylvania Department of Environmental Resources, are enthusiastic supporters of MBO. "It's the only way to run a railroad. At least, it's far ahead of what's in second place," said Butler in 1973.[23] Unfortunately, objective studies of his and other departments' experience with MBO are not yet to be found, so we cannot endorse Butler's comment without reservations.

Many municipalities have adopted MBO. New Orleans, Louisiana, installed it in 1973; other local governments employing MBO include Little Rock, Arkansas; Overland Park, Kansas; Fort Worth, Texas; Virginia Beach, Virginia; Pasadena, California; St. Petersburg, Florida; and Seattle, Washington. Cities ranging in size from New York to Gobbler's Nob have experimented with MBO.

For example, Fort Worth set up MBO in 1972 and tied it directly to the budgetary process. Budget examiners now review budget requests in light of the statements of objectives provided with the requests. The examiners make recommendations based on their opinion of whether objectives are realistic and whether the departments have the resources to reach their objectives. A slow and careful approach has been taken in implementing MBO, rather than trying to establish it across the board in one year as a crash program, according to Budget Director William B. Gordon.[24]

In Fort Worth, department heads meet quarterly with the city manager, who is the city's chief executive. Gordon claims this process has enabled all involved to see the problem areas better. Communications between department heads and the manager have improved as well. MBO has enabled city officials to identify duplication of effort and program results. Drawbacks include the tendency of some departments to get lost in a paperwork shuffle because they focus on MBO process rather than purpose. Gordon also notes that "it is extremely difficult to make MBO type decisions in a political environment." Gordon claims that department heads are "generally enthusiastic about MBO" because it was implemented gradually rather than being imposed by overnight edicts from above.

This example is intended more as an illustration of local government use of MBO than a conclusive summary of its impact at the local level.

Certain Problems and How to Minimize Them

A basic problem in implementing MBO is verifying whether or not objectives have been attained. Since 1976 the New York City Highway Department has installed MBO on an experimental basis.[25] One of the objectives of its MBO action plan is to fill a certain number of potholes per month, but department managers have no way to run an independent check to see if the number of holes reported filled have indeed been filled. Even more difficult to ascertain is the quality of the job done. Will the repair last a year or just a month? Short of doubling the number of department employees by creating a huge force of inspectors, there is no completely satisfactory way for managers to verify reports.

The history of administration is replete with false reports of program effectiveness. Harun al-Rashid, a Turkish sultan of the eighth century, used to disguise himself and walk around the capital to check on the status of public works and to find out what ordinary citizens thought about his administration. South Vietnamese officials soon became aware that the U.S. Department of Defense thrived on statistical reports of the war during the 1960s, and the South Vietnamese manufactured data that would make U.S. officials happy.

These examples can be multiplied a hundredfold, for they illustrate a classic stumbling block in administration, which has no easy solution. If employees participate in setting goals and believe that these goals are appropriate, they will be less likely to file misleading reports. But if the goals are merely dictated from above, workers will use their ingenuity to beat the system and protect themselves. The New York City MBO experi-

ment attempts to decentralize power, thus giving managers at all levels more authority to carry out their duties.

MBO does not come free of charge, unfortunately. A substantial number of resources, particularly employee work hours, must be invested in it. To ensure that unnecessary expenditure is minimized, the procedures recommended for estimating the period of time necessary to acquire a fully functioning MBO system should be followed. For time is money. The extra cost of MBO should be viewed as an investment that will more than pay for itself in increased effectiveness, but there is no point in covering up the fact that the investment costs resources. In manager Bruce Faulkner's words, "it won't work if there is no staff to run it. . . . [MBO] has functioned well where there has been a heavy dose of planning staff time injected to coordinate, promote, and move it along and has not functioned well when and where staff attention to these functions has been minimal."[26]

Morrisey warns that there will be a "disenchantment period" after MBO efforts are begun.[27] This period usually occurs after about six months, when the novelty of MBO has disappeared. Some objectives now look as if they will not be achieved, and managers realize that MBO is a long-term approach, not a panacea that yields quick results.

Disenchantment can be minimized by several approaches, which should be part of any MBO implementation plan. MBO is a dynamic process in which action plans should constantly be adjusted on the basis of the latest data available. Means and methods of making such adjustments include group progress reviews scheduled as an integral part of MBO, a no-holds-barred dialogue with top executives, and problem-solving "clinics" conducted by managers. While these regular reappraisals will not make everyone happy, they should reduce disappointment with MBO.

An additional problem encountered by MBO is faulty communications, found especially in large organizations. Often managers will hear from an outside source such as a reporter or legislator about a problem in the organization, or they will find out on Tuesday that there is a problem that should have been solved by Monday at the latest. What can be done to implement action plans under such conditions?

Morrisey stresses that regularly scheduled progress reviews between superior and subordinate will help to dispel much of the communication distortion.[28] This periodic review is essential to MBO if the plan is to be successfully implemented because only through such reviews can each party gather the information it needs.

Carroll and Tosi emphasize that many managers do not provide enough feedback to their subordinates. These managers hold staff meetings and consider them adequate progress reviews, but their subordinates rarely do. Superiors must tell each subordinate on a one-to-one basis how they feel about the individual's work; otherwise, subordinates will not have all the information they need. This evaluation cannot be done in a group session because it might seem critical or could embarrass the subordinate, since coworkers are looking on. Progress review must be personalized if it is to be a truly effective, two-way communication.[29] In this way, MBO sets up its own communication channels to avoid being trapped by the faulty communication system in the organization. If this system were to follow MBO principles, communication would improve markedly.

A classic problem that can plague MBO is what Odiorne calls the quantitative fallacy. This weakness compels the victim to ignore phenomena that cannot be quantified. One firm that introduced MBO gave out awards for achievement at year's end, recognizing only those with precisely measurable results. Ignored were a great improvement in company-community relations and a general drop in employee hostility to management. Furthermore, the manager who received the most MBO awards had broken faith with union leaders, who consequently vowed revenge for next year. That same manager fired two promising subordinates whose competence threatened him and neglected equipment maintenance in order to show "savings." The quantitative fallacy caused top management to reward a manager who was in fact crippling the organization.[30]

A final problem to be aware of in implementing MBO is the necessity to limit the number of objectives to a critical few. Public administration professor David S. Brown has advocated, tongue in cheek, the SLO, or System of Limited Objectives.[31] Only high-priority items should be included; otherwise, management, lost in a sea of paper, will equate objectives involving use of paper clips with objectives involving the prevention of polio. That happened in the Wisconsin Department of Health and Social Services. When the number of objectives being monitored declined because some had been achieved, a search was begun to find new ones. "As a result, objectives have occasionally been established which are only of secondary importance."[32] Quantity must never be confused with quality.

It would be extraordinarily unusual to install a new management system without a hitch. If managers are told that they will have to manage in a new manner, they are going to resist some or all of these changes, consciously or unconsciously. In fact, the better the job of management they have done or think they have done, the more likely they will be to resist a new system such as MBO. After all, if they think they are doing a good job, why should they want to change?[33] Managerial resistance to MBO should be anticipated so that it can be dealt with. Otherwise, the implementation of MBO is going to be all blood, sweat, toil, and tears. Some commonly encountered reasons for managerial resistance to MBO are catalogued below.[34]

A full-fledged, formally structured MBO system requires training for those who will use it, as we have previously mentioned. Managers cannot simply implement the system overnight. And veteran managers may resent having to be trained to work in the new system. Carroll and Tosi found that managerial complaints such as "I've always managed this way. Why do I have to spend time in training? ... My people know what is expected" were commonplace.[35] The best way to deal with these complaints is to explain to the managers, in the training sessions themselves, what the benefits of MBO are likely to be for both them and the organization. At the same time, the flexibility of MBO should be stressed. If an action plan is not working, managerial advice can lead to changes in the plan. If managers understand that MBO will give them much more discretion and freedom in managing, they will be more likely to take this particular problem in stride.

Another frequent cause of managerial resistance involves the manager's relationships with subordinates. For example, a manager may argue that subordinates are not competent enough to implement MBO. But if the underlying causes of managerial resistance can be analyzed, it may be found that the real reason for resistance is the manager's fear of losing control. Managers may feel that they are no longer real managers if their subordinates exercise greatly increased discretion under MBO. This kind of problem is not easily solved. Perhaps the best way to try to sell MBO to managers is to ask them to see the results achieved by MBO after the system has run for a while. Managers should be reminded that they will gain much of the credit if the effectiveness and efficiency of their employees improve as a result of MBO. Unfortunately, some long-term, veteran managers will probably not be able to make this shift. A whole life's habits are not easily discarded in late middle age. But many managers will be able to make the change, even if it takes time.

One study of several hundred managers found that they felt forced to endorse what they considered unrealistic or inappropriate objectives.[36] The managers felt that if they expressed their true feelings, top management would think they could not, or did not want to, handle the job and would downgrade them accordingly. Managers also felt handicapped, compared to MBO planners, in determining objectives and action plans. It is easy to see how this situation occurred. Change usually causes anxiety because the stable structure of the past is taken away. If this anxiety—which need be only short-lived when installing MBO—is compounded by faulty communication, MBO is in trouble. In the situation just cited, management either did not try or tried unsuccessfully to create an atmosphere that would allow for frank talk among managers and MBO planners. A

manager who feels that an action plan will not work should be encouraged to explain why. If the manager is afraid to state these reasons, MBO will not be able to yield the dividends it is designed to give. Establishing such an atmosphere is easier said than done; but one crucial step is making clear, by actions as well as words, that candor will be rewarded, not punished.

Nathaniel Hawthorne, one of America's greatest novelists, once wrote, "It is the iron rule in our day to require an object and a purpose in life. . . . No life now wanders like an unfettered stream; there is a millwheel for the tiniest rivulet to turn. We go all wrong, by too strenuous a resolution to go all right."[37] It is possible to overdo anything. Yet our *work* needs an object and purpose to guide it and a means of control, or it will go all wrong. MBO is such a means.

SUMMARY

We have seen that what is called control is vastly more than that. It is information, which is essential to everything else; it is a navigational chart of trends and constant comparison with earlier periods; it is essential to tactics and strategy; and if properly used, it is a powerful morale builder. Just as there are many purposes served by control systems, so also are there various subtypes. Among these we singled out managing by objectives for rather full treatment because it is in line with the modern tendency to bring everyone into the act and hence build teamwork and morale.

NOTES

1. See Martin Landau and Russell Stout, Jr., "To Manage Is Not to Control: Or the Folly of Type II Errors," *Public Administration Review* 39 (March-April 1979): 148–156.

2. See Paul E. Holden, Lounsbury S. Fish, and Hubert L. Smith, *Top Level Management Organization and Control* (Palo Alto, Calif.: Stanford University Press, 1941); also, Edward C. Schleh, *Management by Results, the Dynamics of Profitable Management* (New York: McGraw-Hill, 1961); and Robert C. Anthony, *Planning and Control Systems: A Framework for Analysis* (Boston: Harvard Business School, 1965).

3. E. P. Learned, D. N. Ulrich, and R. D. Booz, *Executive Action* (Boston: Harvard Business School, 1951), ch. 8.

4. See James H. Donnelly et al., *Fundamentals of Management* (Dallas: Business Publications, 1978), pp. 131–149.

5. George S. Odiorne, "M.B.O. in State Government," *Public Administration Review* (January-February, 1976): 31.

6. Cortland Commann and David A. Nadler, "Fit Control Systems to Your Managerial Style," *Harvard Business Review* (January-February, 1976).

7. Anthony Downs, *Inside Bureaucracy* (Boston: Little, Brown, 1967).

8. Commann and Nadler, "Fit Control Systems to Your Managerial Style."

9. Wayne A. Kimmel, William R. Dougan, and John R. Hall, *Municipal Management and Budget Methods: An Evaluation of Policy Related Research, Final Report, vol. 1: Summary and Synthesis* (Washington: Urban Institute, 1974).

10. Kimmel, Dougan, and Hall, *Municipal Management*, pp. 29–30.

11. George L. Morrisey, *Management by Objectives and Results in the Public Sector* (Reading, Mass.: Addison-Wesley, 1976), pp. 203–207.

12. J. M. Ivanevich, J. H. Donnelly, and L. Lyon, "A Study of the Impact of MBO on Perceived Need Satisfaction," *Personnel Psychology* 23 (1970): 139–151.

13. Stephen J. Carroll, Jr., and Henry L. Tosi, Jr., *Management by Objectives* (New York: Macmillan, 1973), pp. 52–54.

14. The rest of this section is based primarily on Morrisey, *Management by Objectives and Results in the Public Sector*, pp. 105–169.

15. Odiorne, "M.B.O. in State Government."

16. John W. Humble, *MBO in Action* (New York: McGraw-Hill, 1970), p. 283.

17. Carroll and Tosi, *Management by Objectives*, p. 107.

18. Carroll and Tosi, *Management by Objectives*, p. 108.

19. George S. Odiorne, *Management Decisions by Objectives* (Englewood Cliffs, N.J.: Prentice-Hall, 1969), p. 140.

20. H. George Frederickson and Charles R. Wise, eds., *Public Administration and Public Policy* (Lexington, Mass.: Heath, 1977), p. 49. Claims such as those of Fred Luthans that "the literature does contain a fair number of success stories of MBO in the public sector" (in his "How to Apply MBO," *Public Personnel Management*, March-April 1976, p. 85) turn out to be based largely on superficial or hortatory studies.

21. Joel Havemann, "OMB's MBO," *National Journal*, 27 April 1974, pp. 609–618; Ralph C. Bledsoe, "Is MBO Working in the Public Sector?" *The Bureaucrat*, Occasional Papers Service, 1975, pp. 15–16; and Richard Rose, "Implementation and Evaporation: The Record of MBO," *Public Administration Review* 37 (January-February 1977): 64–71; and Richard Rose, *Managing Presidential Objectives* (New York: Free Press, 1976). Swiss's research is not yet published.

22. James Ramsey and Merlin M. Hackbart, *Innovations in State Budgeting* (Lexington: University of Kentucky, Center for Public Affairs, 1978), p. 12.

23. Dennis E. Butler, "The Evolution of MBO in a State Governmental Agency," in Morrisey, *Management by Objectives and Results in the Public Sector*, pp. 249–260.

24. William B. Gordon to Douglas Fox, 26 October 1976.

25. Steven R. Weisman, "New Management System Tightens Beame's Control," *New York Times*, 27 September 1976, p. 1.

26. Bruce Faulkner, "Policy Execution Using MBO: Lessons from a State Human Services Agency" (Paper presented at the National Conference of the American Society for Public Administration, 1974).

27. Morrisey, *Management by Objectives and Results in the Public Sector*, p. 197.

28. Morrisey, *Management by Objectives and Results in the Public Sector*, pp. 213–225.

29. Carroll and Tosi, *Management by Objectives*, p. 58.

30. George S. Odiorne, *Management and the Activity Trap* (New York: Harper & Row, 1974), pp. 122–27.

31. David S. Brown, "MBO: Promise and Problems," *The Bureaucrat* 2 (Winter 1974): 413–420.

32. Faulkner, "Policy Execution Using MBO," p. 31.

33. Faulkner, "Policy Execution Using MBO," p. 28.

34. Carroll and Tosi, *Management by Objectives*, pp. 49–52, is the source for these common troubles.

35. Carroll and Tosi, *Management Objectives*, p. 49.

36. Carroll and Tosi, *Management Objectives*, p. 68, footnote 6.

37. Nathaniel Hawthorne, *The Marble Faun*.

16

Program Evaluation and Productivity

Nothing can be produced out of nothing.

Diogenes Laertius

In this chapter, we examine approaches to evaluating program effectiveness and efficiency and point out their costs and benefits as means of program control.

Henry Ford once hired an efficiency expert to evaluate his automobile company. After a few weeks, the expert made his report. It was highly favorable, except for one thing. "It's that man down the hall," said the expert. "Every time I go by his office he's just sitting there with his feet on his desk. He's wasting your money." "That man," replied Ford, "once had an idea that saved us millions of dollars. At the time, I believe his feet were planted right where they are now."

There is a large body of literature on evaluation concepts and procedures and many definitions of the term. But most definitions probe the impact of a program using predetermined criteria of success.[1] These criteria, whether objectives or other evaluation criteria, provide the yardstick by which to measure program effectiveness. When we speak of effectiveness, we mean the extent to which a program achieves its stated goals.

What is the difference between the review process in management by objectives (MBO), discussed in the preceding chapter, and evaluation? The MBO review process is a form of *monitoring* intended to document whether goals are being attained. Evaluation goes beyond monitoring to try to determine if a program has caused the results observed or to identify the particular aspects of the program that have caused success or failure.[2] For example, monitoring would indicate that the Grand Teton Dam had burst and flooded the countryside, whereas evaluation would try to explain why it had burst. Program evaluation is a more elaborate process than the usual MBO review. Because this evaluation is more careful, costly, and cumbersome, it is not likely to be part of a monthly review, though it may well use the same information as the review. Furthermore, MBO reviews often focus on the work of individual managers, who set their own objectives. Program evaluation focuses on the total program.

IMPLEMENTING EVALUATION

Deciding the type of evaluation procedure to use is a bit like shopping for a new car. A bewildering array of alternatives, with different price tags and features, confronts the shopper. The specialist Harry P. Hatry has even referred to one alternative as the "Cadillac."[3] This section examines several of these alternative approaches to evaluation.

The Controlled Experiment[4]

The experimental approach to evaluation is likely to give the most accurate picture of program accomplishment. Not surprisingly, it is also the most expensive and most difficult method of evaluation.

The distinctive approach of the controlled experiment is the division of program clientele into two or more groups. Typically, the first, or *controlled,* group will have a service, for example, trash collection or education, performed just as it has been in the past. The second, or *experimental,* group will be served in a new and different manner. At the end of a specified period, an investigation of the results of the two approaches will be made. It can then be determined which procedure picked up more litter or which group of students learned more. In this way, a judgment can be made about the quality of the alternatives.

For the experimental approach to work, the control and experimental groups have to be roughly equivalent. That is, it makes no sense to have a control group of very bright students contrasted with an experimental group of average or below-average students. The bright students will almost certainly do better than the other group, regardless of the type of teaching method used. Likewise, if different approaches to garbage collection are applied in neighborhoods with greatly differing topography, such as flat ground and straight streets versus twisting and tortuous terrain, the results will be meaningless.

In implementing this approach, steps should be taken in the following order. First, the control and experimental groups should be selected in a scientifically random manner. Such selection will ensure that they are indeed comparable. (Random selection involves choosing a group in a manner that gives each person considered an equally good chance to be selected. The simplest method is drawing names out of a hat, and there are several other more sophisticated and less clumsy methods.)[5] Next, the preexperiment performance of each group should be measured according to the evaluation criteria, for example, reading-skill level or cleanliness of streets, established for the program. Third, the experimental program, for example, teaching children with color TV as well as with traditional methods, is applied to the experimental but not the control group.

Fourth, the experiment must be carefully monitored to detect anything that might bias the results. For example, program personnel working on the experiment might be very much for or against it compared to control-group personnel. This kind of attitude must be changed through conferences with the personnel. But if sufficient change is impossible or comes too late, the problem must be acknowledged in the evaluation so that the two groups are not judged to have been equally insulated from extraneous events. Fifth, the performance of each group should be measured according to the evaluation criteria, after the experiment has run its course. This is the crucial and critical phase of the experiment. If the results attained by the experimental group are better than those of the control group, a promising new program approach may be in the works. If the opposite is true, it is time to go back to the drawing board.

But before one can come to such definite conclusions, two further checks are in order. First, the preexperimental performance of each group should be compared to the postexperimental performance. This is the reason the preexperimental data were gathered in the first place. After all, even if the different groups are very similar, they will not be identical, so that a record of their exact performance is needed to make precise comparisons. For example, the conclusion that the experimental program produced a 5 percent decrease in fire department response time would be false if the squad in the experimental program already had a 6 percent faster response time than the squad in the control program.

The final check to be made is a search for causes of different performance between experimental and control groups that lie outside the program. For example, if the traffic accident rate declines in an experimental area where a major road has been closed for repairs, the closed road, and not a new traffic enforcement program, may be responsible for the decline.

The experimental approach is a complex task. It is not for amateurs untrained in procedures of experimental design, including statistical measurement and random selection. Likewise, higher cost and many problems investigated in later sections are associated with the controlled experiment. But it is the best of the evaluation procedures because it is the only one that allows precise estimation of program impact.

The Quasi-Experiment

Quasi-experimental design is the next best thing to the controlled experiment. The quasi-experiment can be used when meaningful control or random selection are not possible. For example, parents or teachers may object to students being reshuffled into control and experimental groups, just as government employees may not want to be transferred.

Carol Weiss, an authority on evaluation, has argued that quasi-experimental designs are more than poorly executed experimental designs.[6] Instead, they have a definite logic, admitting what they do and do not control for. Thus evaluators who proceed carefully can draw conclusions. One type of quasi-experiment is the nonequivalent control design,[7] which does not require random selection of subjects. Rather, it may utilize volunteers or self-selection. A drug treatment program, for instance, may ask for volunteers to try a new method of treatment. The volunteers would then be compared with a selected group, chosen from those in the program who did not volunteer. To get around the lack of random selection of each group, the groups would be matched as closely as possible on various performance measures, whether written tests or staff appraisals.

The volunteer and nonvolunteer groups, which are called comparison groups, would then be compared much as a control and experimental group would be.

As indicated, there are a number of shortcomings in the quasi-experiment, but a good quasi-experiment is inferior only to experimental procedure. For, as we shall see later, several other methods of evaluation do not involve anything like this kind of direct comparison.

Nonexperimental Approaches[8]

While all of the nonexperimental approaches examined here are based on comparisons of the results of new programs, they do not involve anything similar to a comparison of control and experimental groups. While inferior to the controlled experiment, they are much less difficult and costly to run and far better than no evaluation at all.

One approach is *before-and-after program comparison.* It compares program results before a new program was implemented and immediately afterwards. Changes in program results should be carefully scrutinized to see if conditions other than the new program caused them. After this step, an estimation of actual program impact can be made. Such an evaluation procedure was applied to Pennsylvania state prison vocational education programs in 1970. It was discovered after comparing preprison and postprison jobs and earnings that prison education had little or no effect.[9] The program was not achieving any positive results.

A second method is *time-trend projection of preprogram data versus actual postprogram data.* Unless some unanticipated events have intervened, the difference between actual program results and what was likely to have happened under the old program is assumed to be due to the new program. Table 16.1 illustrates the use of this approach in the Indianapolis Police Department. The program under examination involved having police officers drive patrol cars at all times, whether on or off duty, to see if crime would be deterred.

A third nonexperimental method is *comparisons with other jurisdictions not served by the program.* If a city health department initiates a new method of inoculation of the public against polio, it can compare its program results with those of other jurisdictions not using the program. If the city is found to be inoculating fewer people per cost-dollar than other cities, it may be time to redesign the program. Such an evaluation was made for the State of Connecticut after it implemented a strict traffic enforcement project in the 1950s. When traffic fatalities declined, evaluators measured the record in other states to make sure that something other than the new program had not caused the decline. The results, depicted in Figure 16.1, show that the program did have a positive impact.

Data Collection

Hatry calls data collection the "dirty job" of evaluation,[10] but he notes that it is a crucial task that cannot be done haphazardly if the evaluation is to be a success. There are many possible sources of data, some of which we examine here.

Existing Records. The evaluator can draw on much data already in existence such as pupil reading scores or police arrest records. Usually, however, it is necessary to dig further, putting together different information sources to come up with details on program cost, residence of clientele by neighborhood, and so on.

Unfortunately for the evaluator, procedures used in gathering data often change, so that reports from different years may not be directly comparable. The federal Census Bureau, for example, delights in changing the boundaries of its "census tracts" (neighborhoods within cities) from census to census, making it very difficult for analysts to measure the changes that have taken place in these neighborhoods.

Interviews. Existing records will usually provide only a fraction of the data needed for evaluation. More often than not, the evaluator will have to

TABLE 16.1   Summary of Indianapolis Police Fleet Plan Effects and Costs

A. Reported crime, clearance rates and traffic accident records, 1969–70.[a] Compared with projections based on previous trends

	Projected result without fleet plan[b]	Actual result with fleet plan	Percent difference
Reported crime (in numbers)			
Total crime	21,978	22,451	+ 3
Larceny	9,458	10,996	+16[c]
Burglary	6,281	6,308	0
Robbery	1,294	1,207	− 7
Outdoor crime index	7,467	6,431	−14[c]
Purse snatching	306	241	−21[c]
Street robbery	820	762	− 7
Theft from auto	2,420	2,378	− 2
Auto theft	3,921	3,050	−22[c]
Clearance rates (in percent)			
Total crime	21	22	+ 5
Larceny	17	20	+18
Burglary	20	17	−15
Robbery	27	27	0
Auto theft	23	26	+13
Vehicle accidents (in numbers)			
Total accidents	10,846	9,356	−14[c]
Killed	60	40	−33[c]
Injured	4,197	4,000	− 5

B. Cost of fleet plan operation[d]

Initial investment	$650,000
Subsequent annual cost	
Equipment replacement	$200,000
Operating expense	250,000
Total	$450,000

[a] Based on the "Fleet-Plan year" comprising September, October, and November of 1969, and January, February, March, April, and May of 1970.

[b] Projection based on trends from 1963 through 1969, using months of "Fleet-Plan year."

[c] Indicates that change is significant according to standard statistical test.

[d] Full year cost; not Fleet-Plan year.

SOURCE: Donald M. Fisk, *The Indianapolis Police Fleet Plan* (Washington: Urban Institute, 1970), p. 2.

Figure 16.1 Connecticut and Control State Traffic Fatalities (per 100,000 Population), 1952–59

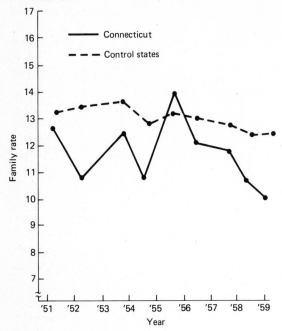

Note: Speeding crackdown program was introduced in FY 1955–56.

arrange to interview systematically certain categories of people.

One category is *persons who have left a government program.* Interviews are the only way to find out the long-term effect of the program on these individuals, since agencies usually do not keep records on their "alumni."

Another category is *those who use (or do not use) government services.* First, factual information can be gathered ("Do you use service X? How frequently? When?"). Second, and perhaps even more important, are questions framed to measure citizens' perception of the adequacy of certain services ("Does the sanitation department do a good job of garbage collection in your neighborhood? Explain."").

In both situations, scientifically selected random samples of residents or clientele must be made, or the survey is likely to be inaccurate.

This is no job for the dilettante. Better that the survey not be done than that it produce a false picture. It is possible to conduct such surveys by telephone, which is much easier and less expensive for the agency.[11] Surveys administered face to face are superior to mail questionnaires, which are unlikely to be so accurate. They are never answered by 100 percent of the sample, which causes results to be biased. In most situations, no more than 100 people need to be interviewed to produce accurate findings.[12]

Professional Ratings. Outside specialists can be called in to rate an agency's performance. Agencies hiring such professionals should be sure to make them explain their reasons for feeling as they do. Vague statements that the agency is doing a good, mediocre, or bad job are useless. Statements that, for example, fire response time compares in a certain way to the national average are far more valuable. In fact, a rating system should ideally be established before the raters come in. They could then use this system to indicate, for example, whether police behavior toward all ethnic groups is the same.

The Relevance of Evaluation

Hatry and his colleagues note than an effective evaluation will have to have the same kind of support from the department head or higher government officials that a successful planning effort needs.[13] Planning studies must be assigned to units that can carry them out objectively, be relevant to the needs of officials, be adequately staffed and supported, be carefully monitored while in progress, and be thoroughly reviewed and actually used, when reported. All of these conditions must also apply if an evaluation is to be useful.

Evaluations of programs are most useful if the following criteria are met:

1. When decision makers have to determine whether a program should continue, be modified, or end,

an evaluation is highly desirable. Of course, the decision makers have to be serious about the decision. We are not talking about a pro forma review, such as the periodic federal tax "reforms," which usually end up sheltering the income of the very wealthy through numerous loopholes.

2. It must be determined whether the evaluation can be made and made in time for the decision makers to use it in making up their minds. If adequate data and sufficient resources for the evaluation are lacking, the evaluation cannot be undertaken.

3. Evaluations should focus on certain types of programs. These include large, expensive programs, programs that appear to be operating in a substandard manner, new programs, and programs touted for expansion. Evaluation is likely to have more impact on such programs than on older, medium-sized ones that seem to be running well. Since evaluation is costly, it should concentrate on programs in which savings and enhancement of effectiveness are likely to be the greatest.

As authority Wayne A. Kimmell and his colleagues have put it, "Local managers should remember that program evaluation, like anything else, is not infinitely valuable. . . . Not all government programs can or should be evaluated."[14]

THE USE OF OUTPUT-ORIENTED EVALUATION IN U.S. GOVERNMENT

Evaluative studies of federal programs have increased greatly since 1969, when the administration of Richard M. Nixon began. After the great expansion of programs that took place under the administration of Lyndon B. Johnson, program expansion slowed and Congress, the president, and the agencies took a look at what some of these programs were accomplishing. Congress, for example, required that agencies evaluate programs authorized by such acts as the Energy Reorganization Act of 1974, the School Lunch and Child Nutrition Act Amendments of 1973, and the Rangeland and Renewable Resources Planning Act of 1973. Legislation in 1970 and 1974 called for extensive program evaluation to be per-

formed by the General Accounting Office (GAO), which is the audit arm of Congress, a topic we discuss in further detail in Chapter 23.[15] Federal evaluations have encompassed productivity in the Postal Service, federal strike forces against crime, and alternative approaches to welfare.[16]

But while much has been learned about the likely impact of variations in welfare programs, the floundering U.S. welfare system remains intact. As Joseph S. Wholey wrote in 1972, "After investment of significant resources and effort, not one federal agency has an overall evaluation system and few programs are able to make any use of the evaluations produced."[17] Interviewed in 1976, Wholey saw little reason to change his earlier opinion.[18] He felt that the technical and especially the political problems we examine in later sections of this chapter had prevented the use of evaluation. Evaluations were being run, but few agencies were using evaluation reports to modify their programs. A 1977 survey of evaluation use at all three levels of government found no "example of a study whose negative finding resulted in the abolition of a program."[19]

While federal use of evaluations to date may be dismally deficient, interest in evaluation is growing. There is a growing interest in sunset laws, which mandate the end of a program after so many years unless it is reauthorized by the legislature after an evaluation has been conducted. Similarly, President Jimmy Carter implemented zero-base budgeting, which incorporates program evaluation in the budgetary process and which we discuss in Chapter 22.

State Government

State government use of evaluation has also increased greatly since 1969. The use of state zero-base budgeting in promoting evaluation is examined in Chapter 22 and state performance auditing[20] in Chapter 23. Suffice it to say here that both state legislatures and agencies have become increasingly concerned with evaluation.

Local Government

Many attempts at evaluation have been used in the 80,000 local governments. In a 1976 article, Wholey lists a number of effective evaluations, including one that stopped an attempt to end the Cincinnati police paraprofessional program and another that led to better performance by the Washington, D.C., sanitation department.[21] Savannah, Georgia, has implemented an extensive evaluation of city services to determine if all neighborhoods are treated equally.[22] Rockford, Illinois, St. Petersburg, Florida, and Nashville, Tennessee, have used a common evaluation approach to recreation programs, while Palo Alto, California, has evaluated its police department.[23]

One area in which local government is taking an increasing interest is measuring and evaluating educational programs. In the winter of 1977, the parents of a recent high school graduate from Copiague, New York, sued the school district for $1 million because their son could not read. New York City schools announced in April 1977 that they were going to require that higher reading, writing, and arithmetic standards be met before a high school diploma would be awarded. Student performance relative to these standards would be measured by a written test.[24]

While interest in, and use of, evaluation is increasing at the local level, Kimmel and his colleagues noted in 1974 that there was "a very limited body of evidence *from research and formal study* on the utility, impact and effectiveness of conducting program evaluation."[25] As Wholey said in December 1976, "For many years evaluators have been meeting in conferences. . . . I'd like to see an evaluation conference in which all the papers have the same title: 'How Evaluation Was Used in Improving the Programs in Our Agency.'"[26] Such a desire, of course, indicates that evaluations are not yet heavily used.

MINIMIZING EVALUATION PROBLEMS

All of the problems and examples discussed in this section apply equally strongly to experimen-tal as well as to nonexperimental designs, but the emphasis is on nonexperimental approaches.

Goal Statement

One problem with the statement of goals is lack of clarity. Pamela Horst and her colleagues have identified as "vaporous wishes" goals such as "adequate quality of life" and "improved mental health," which were never followed up with much more specific criteria. (Such criteria for the goal of mental health might include ability to hold a job outside of a mental-health institution or improved family relationships.) In addition, Horst commonly encountered terms such as *outreach capability* and *upgraded job skills,* but rarely were adequate definitions and measures provided for them. The evaluator cannot evaluate when there are no stated criteria of evaluation.[27]

To avoid this problem, evaluators should be in on the design of a program from the beginning. Political problems are also involved in stating goals; we shall discuss these problems later. A number of other problems relative to goal statement exist. Rarely, for instance, do agencies or programs have only one goal. Multiple goals are the rule, not the exception. This raises the question of how the evaluator separates these goals from one another and determines priorities. Perhaps the best way to assign a priority rating to a goal is to research the legislative history of the program and to ask government officials what their priorities are. But if a consensus is lacking, this task will not be easy. Separating closely related goals, such as reduction of odor emanating from sewerage-treatment plants and reduction of germs from the same plants, is a task for which there is no substitute for hard work and ingenuity.

The way goals change over time also causes complications. The submarine service of the U.S. Navy is now largely a nuclear-missile system, whereas up until the 1950s its function was to sink enemy ships. Comparisons between the submarine service of 1956 and 1976 will be extremely misleading if these changes in goals and functions are not carefully considered.

Evaluation Criteria

The search for quantitative measures can produce inappropriate measures of evaluation.

What are the most satisfactory indexes of output for a given agency? How does one measure how many crimes have been deterred by a police force or how much a child has learned in school as distinct from the other environments of family, peers, and media? Unfortunately, for many programs, there is either no way or only very costly ways that require an analysis over several years to measure results. There is no way to minimize this difficulty. Perhaps the best that can be hoped for is to make government officials aware of this technical problem and thus avoid inappropriate or inimical approaches to evaluation. An example of such counterproductive steps is the practice some cities follow of awarding bonuses to patrol officers on the basis of the number of arrests made. Such a system could easily result in scores of false arrests or arrests for minor offenses, rather than in measures that would serve to deter or cut down serious crime.[28] There are no shortcuts or substitutes for careful analysis and confrontation of the difficulties inherent in defining output measures.

Agency Resistance

Perhaps the most important political obstacle to evaluation comes from the agency itself. Aaron Wildavsky has argued that the very concept of evaluation, denoting change, may be incompatible with organizations, which denote stability. It is certainly not difficult to find example after example of agency resistance to evaluation, which is difficult to explain on any other ground.

For instance, a study of federal funding of local police departments in the New England states found that police officials believed that the concept of evaluation was unimportant or nonsensical.[29] The police believed that only those with extensive experience in police work could make rational decisions, based on their intuitive knowledge. Former Secretary of Defense Robert McNamara ran into a similar problem during the 1962 blockade of Cuba, when he asked the head

of the navy how he was going to conduct the blockade. Admiral Anderson replied by holding up a copy of navy procedures to be followed in such a case. McNamara replied, "I don't give a damn what John Paul Jones would have done! What are *you* going to do?" Here we have in a nutshell the difference between agency adherence to traditions and intuition and the approach of the output-oriented evaluator.

Edward Suchman has noted how many agencies prefer "pseudo-evaluations," which make them look good to probing output-oriented evaluations.[30] Variations on this theme include the *eyewash,* which selects for evaluation only the aspects of a program that look good on the surface. Another approach is the *whitewash,* or cover-up of the real nature of a program. The Nazis tried in 1945 to impress world public opinion by inviting three observers to visit a concentration camp especially spruced up for the occasion. Large numbers of inmates were hidden from view, and inmates who would repeat what the Nazis wanted them to say were selected as guides for the observers. This whole farcical "inspection" tour viewed nothing that was representative of the reality of the camps and won high grades from the naive observers.[31]

The *submarine* is an attempt to destroy or torpedo a program unpopular in the agency, regardless of the program's accomplishments. It is a hatchet job, which overlooks the positive achievements and focuses on the shortcomings of a program.

Another variation is *posturing,* which points to the use of evaluation as a "gesture" of objectivity. Most evaluations used in government today fall into this category because they are not output oriented. "We have evaluated our program and found that it meets professional standards" is a comment that usually begs the question. The real question should be, "So what if we meet professional standards? Are these standards meaningful, and if so, how do they affect program results?"

A final ploy is *postponement.* Needed action is delayed through the pretense of seeking the "facts." One of the authors once went through a year of frustration while the administrative officials at the college where he worked decided to fill a position they had previously authorized only after they had made an evaluation of the entire department's programs. This move was clearly designed to punish the department rather than to accomplish any useful purpose.

Having detailed a host of obstacles posed by agency resistance to evaluation, what can be done to combat such hindrances to results-oriented management? The overall strategy is to try to convince agency personnel that evaluation will work for them because the better the job they do, the more recognition and budget resources they are likely to receive.

While such salesmanship makes sense, it will not always work. Low-performance agencies will see nothing to gain by it. And other agencies may not be willing to sell their bureaucratic souls for a mess of increased appropriations. The U.S. military's leadership greatly preferred Defense Secretary Melvin Laird (1969-1973) to Secretary McNamara (1961-1968). They felt as they did even though budget pickings were much leaner under Laird than McNamara. While they prospered under McNamara, they had to prosper on his terms. He demanded evaluation and justification before he would endorse proposals by the professional military. Under Laird's tenure, however, the services were allowed to cut up their smaller budget pie pretty much the way they wanted to.

Public administration professor Bruce Rocheleau studied the impact of evaluation in 14 mental-health agencies in Florida.[32] His findings were paradoxical, since he discovered both substantial support for and opposition to evaluation within the agencies. While agency personnel agreed with many of the evaluators' recommendations, they felt that it would be political suicide to try to carry out some of them. Rocheleau found that the key factor in effective evaluation is authority, or the ability to evoke compliance in others. In this instance, authority was based on good personal relationships between the evaluator and program directors. This goodwill was built up by the evaluator's assuming service jobs such as data gathering and replying to information requests from local, state, and national funding agencies. On the other hand, evaluators had to be careful while performing these tasks not to be sidetracked from their job of evaluation.

Attitude of Top Officials

Equally critical if evaluation is to work is a commitment by top management. Department heads must make clear their commitment to evaluation, assign adequate resources to the task, monitor efforts, and act on evaluation recommendations.[33]

None of these suggestions is a cure-all. Different opinions and beliefs will always combine to kill certain recommendations of evaluators. The Nixon administration, for example, ignored the recommendations of advisory commissions set up to investigate marijuana and pornography, just as the Johnson administration ignored the finding of both the Advisory Commission on Civil Disorders and the Douglas Commission on Urban Problems. In none of these instances did the recommendations of the commissions jibe with the political preferences of high officials and their perception of how the adoption of such recommendations would affect their political party at the polls.

Sometimes the results of evaluations are ignored in the attempt to see a proposed bill become law. For example, President Nixon's proposal for welfare reform included a work requirement provision, which he privately admitted would accomplish no useful purpose, since all studies showed that the vast majority of welfare recipients (including mothers of small children) could not work. Yet Nixon kept this questionable provision in his bill to ensure conservative support for it in Congress. While the bill did not become law, its chances would probably have been even dimmer without this counterproductive or useless requirement.[34] But while there are no sure ways to persuade officials to accept evaluation reports, the steps we recommend will minimize such problems insofar as they can be minimized.

The Evaluator's Own Attitude

A final problem is the intrusion of the evaluator's own values into the report. Two equally competent evaluators might be led by their values to different recommendations. As evaluation specialist Carol Weiss has noted,

---

Different people looking at the same data can come up with different conclusions in the tradition of the "fully-only" school of analysis. "Fully 25 percent of the students . . ." boasts the promoter, "only 25 percent of the students . . ." sighs the detractor.[35]

Keeping a Sense of Proportion

Evaluation is only one aspect of management, as is policy analysis or planning, which we looked at in Chapter 10. Several careful observers have warned us what happens when the integrative aspects of management are lost in an obsession with evaluation. Hale Champion, a state manager who went to Washington to work in the Department of Health, Education and Welfare (HEW) during the Carter administration of 1977-1981, has the following to say:

Enormous effort went into making decisions automatically by the data, verified before there had been any experience with these programs and evaluated afterward in terms of the numbers, without looking at the problem in a more common, direct, reportorial, experiential way—in a manager's way. . . . HEW is still staggeringly far from paying much attention to management, to what people can do in shaping solutions to problems. . . . people who are trying to bring about social improvement in this country have been preoccupied with data. . . . I would like to reintroduce the notion that management is a risk-taking, judgmental enterprise requiring many skills but fundamentally depending on the character and opinions and abilities of the people involved in it.[36]

Allen Schick, a well-known commentator on trends in public administration, remarked in the late 1970s that most analysis and evaluation is irrelevant. "There is an enormous and growing mismatch between the production and use of policy studies,"[37] says Schick. In the words of Erwin Hargrove, who studied U.S. Department of Labor evaluation efforts, "Too often evaluation research is a program in itself which proceeds quite apart from the implementation of policy."[38] The manager interested in evaluation must not lose sight of the forest for the trees. If evaluation becomes a program or an end in itself, management cannot be improved.

PRODUCTIVITY IMPROVEMENT

The word productive has a positive ring. People talk about how productive Smith was, or conversely, how a failed effort was unproductive. Yet many workers have come to be suspicious of the term productivity, because they believe it to be a euphemism or cover-up for forcing them to work harder without additional compensation. Our concern in this section is the explanation of the positive aspects of productivity. Unfortunately, productivity is often used as a label for any number of practices that are not consistent with our definition, and the reader should bear this in mind. As we shall see, many of the things labeled productivity are not productivity as we use the term.

Defining Productivity

Productivity is synonymous with efficiency. It is defined here as the relationship between inputs used to produce a service and the outputs or results of that service. Productivity increases can be simply defined as either accomplishing a job with less, or doing more or better work with the same resources. If two men and one truck can pick up as much garbage in the same time, and with the same result in sanitary or cleanliness standards, as four men and two trucks did previously, one would say that productivity has increased. Likewise, if the four men and two trucks increase the amount of garbage they haul this year with the same results, compared to last year, their productivity has also increased.

To put it more technically, productivity is the total of an organization's outputs divided by inputs for a given year. This relationship can be stated as a percentage. For example, if an organization manufactured 10,000 widgets with 700 man-years of labor in 1978, productivity during 1978 would be 10,000 widgets divided by 700, or a ratio of 14:3. If the same firm had produced 11,000 widgets of the same quality with 900 man-years in 1977, its productivity for that year would be 11,000 divided by 900, or a ratio of 12:2. In this instance, productivity has increased from 1977 to 1978 by 16.9 percent, a figure we arrive at by

$$\frac{10000}{700} \div \frac{11000}{900} \, .$$

In other words, each unit of input (man-years) produced more output (widgets) in 1978 than it did in 1977.[39]

In productivity measurement, one year is usually selected as a base year against which to measure the record of future years. In the example just given, 1977 might become the base year for the next decade.

John W. Kendrick has written that the "broadest and most useful concept of productivity is one in which output is related to *all* associated inputs, in real terms—labor, capital, and purchased materials, supplies and outside services, combined (weighted) in proportion to their relative costs in a basic period."[40]

The most important thing to remember about productivity is that it is concerned with the output or results of activity, not with activity itself.[41] As one professor criticized for working only nine hours a week in the classroom responded, he could be likened to a bull. The time that he and bull spent on the job was much less important than the quality of their output.[42]

One has to remember that productivity is only a technical measure of the relationship between inputs and outputs. It does not tell whether the goals set for the program or the outputs achieved are wise or appropriate ones. For example, the Nazis devised a diabolical device for occupying the time of some concentration camp prisoners. They forced the prisoners to dig large holes—and then fill them in again. If one were to assemble productivity figures for this activity, they would be as meaningless as the activity itself. Likewise, if the productivity of file clerks involved in Medicare billing increases because the Medicare program itself is encouraging unnecessary use of medical facilities, such an increase is of very limited value. Productivity, then, is only a means to an end itself. Productivity stresses efficiency in attaining a goal, not the effectiveness of the goal.

Productivity Becomes Popular

Productivity is now enjoying a period of renewed popularity. In 1970, President Nixon set up a National Commission on Productivity largely because productivity increases in the United States economy slowed down after 1965. Politicians, government officials, and many private citizens have become concerned with government productivity now that one-third of the average citizen's income is paid in taxes to federal, state, and local government. "At long last," as former New York Deputy Mayor Edward K. Hamilton puts it, "the public seems to care about productivity."[43]

At the same time, productivity improvement is unlikely ever to be the predominant concern of citizens.

In the early 1970s, the Harris poll asked, "What kind of people should work in government and what qualities ought they to have?" While 24 percent of those polled cited efficiency, this quality only came in eighth. Ranked higher were qualities such as honesty, a desire to help people, courage, and concern for freedom. While voters want efficiency in government, they value other considerations even more highly.[44]

Improving Productivity[45]

The following steps are recommended for implementing productivity improvement. If the program is to work, employees should be consulted and their ideas carefully solicited. Further, they should receive bonus awards and credit toward promotion if their ideas are adopted. In this way they will become part of a productivity team rather than recalcitrant resisters of results-oriented management. An example showing the value of this approach is that of the Georgia Highway Department employee who suggested to Governor Jimmy Carter's budget team that grass on the sides of the highway be mowed only 30 feet from the center line of the road. Previously, tractors had mowed down into drainage ditches, which destroyed natural vegetation, caused erosion, and caused tractors to turn over. The suggestion was adopted and cut maintenance costs by 15 percent, earning the employee a cash bonus award. No top executive would have been likely to come up with this idea. Productivity was enhanced by involving lower-level employees in the process.[46]

Step One. The productivity planning process begins by preparing basic policy statements that will clearly explain the goals of productivity to employees and seek their participation in the program. Productivity should be explained as an approach designed to gain more output from inputs. To stave off immediate strong resistance, it should be carefully explained *in writing* that productivity will not lead to layoffs. Otherwise, a job action or strike may ensue; at the very least, the work atmosphere will be poisoned with suspicion and hostility. Any reductions in the work force made possible by productivity measures can usually be made through normal turnover, as employees quit, retire, or are transferred to other divisions. After they leave, their job positions can be eliminated. (There is, for example, a normal turnover of 5 percent annually in federal civilian employment.) Hand in hand with assurances that layoffs will not take place should go the announcement of a plan in which employees will share in savings caused by productivity improvement. It can also be pointed out that improved performance reports are likely to improve the agency's likelihood of being granted the budget requests it makes. Just as the most able people are

the busiest because they are given more and more responsibility, so an agency is given more resources to do a job if it demonstrates a record and capacity for work achievement.

Step Two. Having clarified the goals of productivity and having sought to involve employees in the process, the next step is to work on *priorities* for analysis. Productivity managers should be cautious here, because *crash programs are usually crashing failures.* Attempts to apply a new approach across the board do not work.[47] Time is needed to explain a new system to employees, and manpower and equipment must be devoted to the productivity analysis. A comprehensive approach is likely to cause confusion and chaos as the entire organization wrestles with productivity. It is far better to start in one of several selected areas, examining programs that are relatively easy to measure. For example, a municipal manager would be well advised to start productivity improvement in the public works or sanitation departments. Measures relating to the amount of garbage picked up or the miles of streets washed, cleared of snow, or paved can be developed. These tangible achievements are easier to analyze than the services provided by the schools or the police department. It makes sense to begin with public works and learn by experience and then to go on to schools and police.

It also makes sense, in all situations, to start first with more routine and uncomplicated operations such as police traffic-law enforcement rather than more complex programs such as drug-abuse control.

The following criteria can be useful in determining which priority areas to select for productivity improvement. First, operations that use a large share of an agency's budget or employees will yield a far greater return than smaller operations if productivity gains are made. Gains among public-works road crews are likely to exceed gains made by garage mechanics in the same department because the road crews make up the bulk of the work force.

Second, divisions that have large backlogs of

work, such as welfare recipients yet to be visited at home or buildings yet to be inspected for fire risks, are divisions that may not be working well. Perhaps more resources are needed, but chances are that productivity could be dramatically improved in such situations.

Step Three. Bureaus with obvious management problems, such as dissension in the ranks or low morale, or operational problems, such as snow not plowed until several hours after the storm is over, are good candidates for productivity studies. Improvements will be visible and known and will provide positive incentive for further changes.

Step Four. Evaluators should consider carefully new technologies, a machine to collect leaves, for example, or automated processes such as computer programs, which could boost program output. Of course, cost is a factor here, and the consideration must be careful for that reason alone. If the equipment costs more than it could possibly return in productivity gains, it is not worth the investment.

Step Five. Supervisors should be evaluated on the basis of their receptivity to new ideas and their ability to follow through on productivity improvement. Those who can carry the ball should be promoted and given additional responsibility. They are the key to the success of the program, especially for their ability to sell it to their subordinates.

Development of a program with proven results will make productivity more acceptable in other programs that are more difficult to measure. At the same time, open-mindedness and humility on the part of the productivity analyst are needed. Productivity gains and methods used in one area, such as the teaching of reading, may not apply in another area, such as the teaching of arithmetic. One is reminded of the Louisiana logger who compiled an enviable record and then moved to the Maine woods to try his luck. He was very productive and began to feel superior to his Maine colleagues until the winter came. Then his pro-

ductivity declined drastically because he could not cope with the rigors of cutting and hauling wood in ice, snow, and mud.

Step Six. To implement the productivity approaches discussed in this chapter, employees must be trained.[48] They must be aware not only of the goals of the program in general but also of the detailed nitty-gritty of what is expected of them. This training may include mundane and menial steps, which are nonetheless essential. New procedures must be carefully gone over with employees. They cannot just be given a ball and told to run with it. Rather, they need instruction in the methods of the new game—whether it is a different approach to record keeping, recreation, or urban renewal. In addition, supervisors should be instructed in the various productivity study techniques and procedures so that they know what is going on and can explain the program adequately to their subordinates. A short briefing or a memo is no substitute for this kind of training, without which a productivity program will flounder.

The process of educating managers to identify their needs and the information necessary for better management is slow and difficult. Managers need to know how to extract from a productivity report what is relevant for them to do a better job of management. Some examples of productivity studies that managers must be trained to interpret are given in the following sections on work measurement.

A key figure in the productivity program's success is its director. In larger organizations, this should be a position with no other responsibilities. Candidates for the job should include the productivity-oriented supervisors mentioned above. The director will be responsible for selecting productivity analysts, establishing a reporting system, setting reporting criteria, monitoring the program to keep it on the track, and identifying areas for future analysis.

Step Seven. In the initial stages of the project, key staff members may have to be brought in from outside the organization. The specialized skills for productivity analysis are unlikely to be found internally. Productivity specialists who can work full time and not be lost in daily routine are needed. At the same time, an internal analytical capability, building on productivity-oriented supervisors, should be developed for the long haul. These in-house people should also become full-time analysts if they are capable of doing the work. Nothing can be more futile and frustrating than to expect them to perform both their old jobs and productivity analysis at once.

Step Eight. Once the system has been fully installed, however, care must be taken to avoid dual management. At some point the usual line managers must be given a unified responsibility or otherwise there will be, in effect, dual management, a source of confusion, conflict, and loss of vitality.

Step Nine. A timetable, which specifies target dates for the attainment of each productivity objective, must be established. It should include periodic evaluation sessions with management, supervisors, and productivity analysts to review accomplishments and adjust objectives and target dates accordingly. This procedure and structure will enable management to know what productivity improvement is accomplishing, decide whether a project needs more resources, and determine whether the project should be continued. If a fire department, for example, finds it can handle fires with a crew only three-fourths the size it previously used in one station house, it can continue with this productivity improvement. But if the smaller crew is found unequal to the task, this approach will have to be abandoned.

Step Ten. The final, and perhaps most crucial, element of the productivity program is its reporting and control system. This system should produce monthly reports (some analysts recommend weekly reports) on the performance of each unit or division. This commitment to regular monthly reports is absolutely necessary if the program is

to work. Regular reports signal that management is truly committed to productivity improvement; they convey that productivity is a *permanent* program, rather than a one-shot or sporadic review. And information must be gathered at regular short intervals if management is to monitor trends, spot problems, and start to work on them as soon as they develop. Without this routine and regularized reporting, productivity programs cannot proceed.

Productivity Measurement[49]

One commonly used approach to productivity improvements is called *work measurement,* and we shall examine it in some detail here, to give the reader a feeling for one procedure. One concept to this approach is the *work standard,* or the time required by a well-trained employee to complete an assignment that is of acceptable quality. If the work standard for picking up 100 garbage cans is one hour, the employee who takes 75 minutes to do the job has a performance that is 80 percent of standard. Box 16.1 lists areas in which work standards have been developed.

In calculating the work standard, the analyst must be sure to include not only the time necessary to do the work without interruption *(normal time),* but also allowances for unavoidable delays such as fatigue, telephone calls, or employee trips to the bathroom. Such allowances usually average between 10 percent and 15 percent of normal time. The total time assigned to the job as a work standard is called *standard time.*

Standard time values are expressed in terms of units of work accomplished. For instance, garbage-collection time could be measured by applying the following standard-time values to the work unit: (1) standard hours per route mile (a measure of travel time between stops), (2) standard hours per site (a measure of pickup time), and (3) standard hours per nonroute mile (a measure of travel time to and from garage and disposal site). It is often useful to express standard time by a single easily measurable limit of output, such as standard hours per cubic yard collected.

Box 16.1

PRODUCTIVITY STANDARDS

Following is a list of local government activities illustrating the kinds of work standards that have been developed:

Law enforcement—Fingerprint classification, traffic or parking citation standards.

Probation activities—Caseloads for investigation, review and supervision of probation cases.

Health and welfare—Caseload standards, hospital laundry operations, claims processing.

Solid waste collection—Pickup times, tonnage standards, collection tasks, vehicle maintenance and repairs.

Street maintenance—Pothole repairs, sanding, plowing, sweeping, snow removal.

Building maintenance—Janitorial tasks (sweeping, cleaning, etc.).

Utilities—Water meter repairs (in the shop or in the field), meter reading tasks.

Inspections—Buildings, restaurants, wiring and safety, weights and measures.

Clerical—Transcription, typing (especially for special repetitive forms, e.g. medical, welfare or police records).

Data processing—Entry of data onto cards or tape, verification.

Library services—Cataloging.

Parks and recreation—Park maintenance activities such as pruning, raking, grass cutting.

There are many means of work measurement. They include numerous techniques, some of which are listed below:

1. *Time study.* Direct observation of a task and the recording of the time it takes constitutes a time study. The analyst must make important judgments here, determining the amount of delay and interruption that must be estimated and added to normal time to get standard time. Table 16.2 illustrates a time study done for the routes of readers of water meters.
2. *Predetermined time values.* A prescribed time is assigned to each action involved in a task, such as a reach or a typewriter stroke. Unlike the time study, no judgment is involved in rating employee performance because the method draws from a large previous study to determine very precise values.
3. *Time log.* Each employee lists beginning and ending time for an action in a log book. For example, a clerk notes that he spent the 48 minutes between 8:04 and 8:52 filling 130 invoices. If the analyst

works closely with employees and supervisors, time logs can be accurate to within 5 percent.

4. *Work sampling.* Work sampling is done at random intervals to determine allocation of employee time to different tasks. Table 16.3 is an example of a work-sampling study.
5. *Standard data.* A storage bank of time data used in previous studies of types of work commonly found throughout government provides standard data.
6. *Historical record.* The agency's past experience in using inputs to produce a given output is reviewed.

What is the manager to make of this myriad of methods? The following guidelines are not infallible but may be of help in selecting an approach.

1. Time study and predetermined time values can be used in most local government operations. The former is less time consuming, but the latter is useful for high-volume and repetitive work and

TABLE 16.2 Meter Reading Routing

	Time requirements (in minutes)				
	Route 1	Route 2	Route 3	Route 4	Route 5
Nonroute travel	30	40	57	65	15
Time per stop					
Inroute travel	0.35	0.40	0.45	0.35	0.55
Read meter	0.65	0.65	0.65	0.65	0.65
Total per stop	1.00	1.05	1.10	1.00	1.20
Workload balancing					
Total available time	480	480	480	480	480
—nonroute travel	30	40	57	65	15
Net available time	450	440	423	415	465
Meters assigned (Net available time ÷ total time per stop)	450	419	385	415	388

TABLE 16.3 Work Schedule for Parks Maintenance Grounds Keeper*

Time	Work task	Measured work hours	Standard hours
8:00 A.M.	Check in, get equipment	0.08	0.08
8:05	Travel to park site	0.25	0.25
8:20	Unload equipment	0.08	0.03
8:25	Police 6 acres grass areas	1.08	1.05
9:30	Rest break	0.25	—
9:45	Mow 4 acres grass areas	2.25	2.08
12:00 P.M.	Lunch	—	—
12:30	Mow 2 acres grass areas	1.00	1.04
1:30	Clean 2 restrooms	0.75	0.68
2:15	Rest break	0.25	—
2:30	Grade and line baseball diamond	1.58	1.60
4:05	Load equipment	0.08	0.03
4:10	Travel to district office	0.25	0.25
4:25	Unload equipment, check out	0.08	0.08
4:30	Off duty		
	Total hours*	8.00	7.17
	Utilization 89.6 percent		

*Figures are rounded.

does not require measurement of employee performance while on the job.

2. Work sampling does not require as much analytical effort as the first two techniques, but it is also not as precise a measurement. This technique is useful to determine the percentage of time spent on a particular task, such as telephone inquiries or time spent by mechanics waiting for parts.

3. Time logs are best used for low- or medium-volume jobs, jobs with a long processing cycle, or varied work fragmented among a number of employees. They are most easily applied to clerical operations.

4. Time data from historical records can be used for work scheduling and input allocation, but they should not be used for measuring employee performance. Time study and predetermined time values alone would be accurate for that purpose.

Work standards can be useful in improving productivity in a number of areas. One is the calculation of staffing needs. In a hospital admitting room, for instance, work loads fluctuate greatly from one time period to another. On Friday and Saturday nights, for example, admissions run much higher than they do Monday through Thursday. Friday night shifts may be understaffed and Monday shifts overstaffed. Adjustments can be made in staff assignments to cover expected work load as a result of such a study.

Another area where work standards can be applied is in setting up balanced routes for functions such as meter reading and garbage pickup. Different crews can be assigned different routes that should take about the same time, and more productive readers can be rewarded. Table 16.2 shows how this can be calculated for meter readers.

Daily work scheduling can also be improved through work standards. Since employees who are scheduled for only six hours of work in an eight-hour day are using only 75 percent of the time even if they perform with 100 percent efficiency when they do work, maximum possible use is preferable. Table 16.3 shows a planned work schedule for a parks grounds keeper; the schedule aims for 90 percent utilization.

Performance reporting is perhaps the most beneficial by-product of work standards. This approach usually involves a manpower use report comparing hours worked by the unit to standard hours set for tasks performed. Such reports include the following:

1. Available hours, including overtime, part-time help, and personnel borrowed from other agencies, as well as hours lost because of vacancies, leave, or loaned personnel. These factors must be included or subtracted to obtain an accurate reading.

2. Unmeasured hours, such as training, conferences, supervision, or unscheduled work, must be included. These must be subtracted to obtain accurate work standards.

3. Measured hours spent on each job should be arranged separately, if possible, so that use of time for each task can be calculated.

Manpower performance should fluctuate between 85 percent and 100 percent because of different levels of personal skill and variations in work pace and volume. Performance lower than 85 percent indicates that a productivity analysis would be useful. When a service is provided on a demand basis, such as a hospital admissions office or a library reference desk, it makes sense to search for other tasks for these employees to do in their slack periods.

Units consistently achieving over 110 percent work standards performance should be carefully analyzed, since they may well be overstaffed, not performing work properly, or working under inaccurate standards.

Quality and Local Condition Factors

Performance reporting is perhaps of greatest value as a safeguard against declining service quality or effectiveness. For example, if employees take shortcuts to maintain production quantity, quality is likely to fall. But the consequences of decline may not be visible for a long time, as is true in the work of a building inspector. A poorly built building may collapse years after the inspector has. Performance reporting can provide an early warning that something is amiss and lead to corrections before the house caves in.

Since the discussion up to this point has stressed quantitative work factors such as hours worked and number of personnel, we need to emphasize that productivity gains are meaningful only if the work done is at least of the same quality as that done before the productivity campaign began. Some productivity publicists like to label certain practices as productivity gains when they are nothing of the kind. An example is a sanitation department that used to pick up trash from people's back porches or garages. If it decides to increase tonnage picked up per shift, it can require residents to leave their garbage by the curbside for pickup. This should result in increased tonnage hauled, since workers will save time by not going to the porch or garage and can apply this time to curbside pickup. But in this situation if more trash is hauled, we cannot say that worker productivity has increased. *Rather, some of the burden has been shifted on to other shoulders,* in this instance those of the residents who must now carry their trash from the porch to the curb.[50]

To measure productivity, one must measure the same activity that occurred before the study began. Otherwise, the two situations cannot be compared and no conclusions about productivity can be made. Government official and taxpayer alike must beware of public relations panegyrics and be sure that a claimed productivity increase is not really just the result of shifting a burden. This warning does not mean that shifting a burden might not be desirable or a good way to save money. It could be both, and it could be decided on as a wise public policy. But it is not the same as a productivity increase. *Money is saved at the cost of a decline in the quality of the service provided when burdens are shifted.*

A focus on quality must go hand in hand with careful consideration of local characteristics that can affect productivity. When studying and interpreting the work of the public schools, relevant information about quality or output would include student performance on achievement tests in such subjects as reading and math. Suppose two fifth-grade classes in a school differ drastically in student scores. Should the teachers with high-scoring students be given praise for high

productivity and those with low-scoring students be dismissed? Not necessarily, because the conditions peculiar to each class may make direct comparisons inappropriate. Perhaps the students in the high-scoring class are from middle-class professional families while the low-scoring class is made up of students from poor families. Scores of studies show that the poor are likely to do worse in school than the middle class, probably because the poor receive relatively less intellectual stimulation and encouragement to succeed academically at home. Thus, productivity studies must consider these and similar circumstances before blindly rushing in and concluding that School A is doing a better job than School B.[51]

The need for care in drawing conclusions does not mean that productivity analysts must throw up their hands and declare that the job is impossible. For example, productivity measurement in the two classes would be better spent in internal rather than external comparisons. Are students *in the same class* doing better or worse than they did in the past? Even if student composition has changed, there are plenty of ways for skilled productivity statisticians to take this change into account and come up with a valid conclusion that output has risen, stayed the same, or fallen.

A finished productivity measurement presentation might look like Table 16.4, which surveys solid waste pickup productivity. Note that Table 16.4 includes input costs, work-load measures, and output measures. In this example, tons of solid waste is the work-load measure, while street cleanliness and population satisfaction with the program are used to calculate output. Cost is expressed both in current cost and in terms of the base year, which controls for inflation. With these data, the analyst can make conclusions about how much input was expended per work-load unit and what the true measure of productivity is, by dividing items 1-3 in Table 16.4 by costs and then calculating the change from 1970 to 1971. It should be noted that while more tonnage was hauled in the latter year, streets were not so clean, and costs rose. Thus, while work-load productivity rose 3 percent, output productivity declined 14 percent in 1970 dollars. In other words, increased

TABLE 16.4 Illustrative Productivity Measurement Presentation: Solid Waste Collection Example

Data	1970	1971	Change
1. Tons of solid waste collected	90,000	100,000	10,000
2. Average street cleanliness rating[a]	2.9	2.6	−0.3
3. Percent of survey population expressing satisfaction with collection[b]	85	85	−5
4. Cost (current)	$1,200,000	$1,500,000	+$300,000
5. Costs (1970 dollars)	$1,200,000	$1,300,000	+$100,000
Productivity measures			
6. Workload per dollar (unadjusted dollars)	75 tons per thousand $	67 tons per thousand $	−11%
7. Workload productivity (1970 dollars)	75 tons per thousand $	77 tons per thousand $	+3%
8. Output index: $\dfrac{(1) \times (2) \times (3)}{(4)}$ (unadjusted dollars)	0.185	0.139	−25%
9. Productivity index: $\dfrac{(1) \times (2) \times (3)}{(5)}$ (1970 dollars)	0.185	0.160	+14%

[a] Such rating procedures are currently in use in the District of Columbia. The rating in line 2 is presumed to be based on a scale of "1" to "4," with "4" being the cleanest.

[b] The figures in line 7 indicate some improvement in efficiency, but line 6 suggests that cost increases such as wages have more than exceeded the efficiency gains. Productivity has gone down even further on the basis of decreases in the street cleanliness ratings and decreased citizen satisfaction. However, such indices have to be studied carefully and interpreted according to local circumstances to be fairly understood.

SOURCE: Harry P. Hatry and Donald M. Fisk, *Improving Productivity and Productivity Measurement in Local Governments* (Washington: The National Commission on Productivity, 1971), p. 19.

productivity quantity occurred along with *decreased* quality. In this instance, of course, local conditions, such as more trash, might be the cause. The productivity analyst must carefully consider these conditions before rendering a final verdict on the success of the program. (For an example, see Box 16.2.)

PRODUCTIVITY ACCOMPLISHMENTS IN GOVERNMENT

Productivity has been studied and used more intensively as a means of evaluation at the federal level of government than at the state and local levels. For this reason, we examine a federal productivity effort in the case study in this chapter. There are, however, plenty of state and local productivity efforts, some of which we examine in this section.

In their 1974 study, John P. Ross and Jesse Burkhead argue that even "studies of federal government productivity have been relatively unsophisticated as compared with the work that has been done in the private sector,"[52] but that "compared to the work done on local government productivity, federal efforts appear to be a mature area of endeavor."[53] But since Ross and Burkhead wrote these words, teams of productivity analysts have worked to try to increase sophistication in productivity in all three levels of government.

Federal Productivity Efforts

As mentioned earlier, President Nixon established a National Commission on Productivity in 1970. At the same time, federal agencies were directed by the Office of Management and Budget (OMB) to begin analysis of program productivity possibilities. The seriousness of these efforts is re-

Box 16.2

PRODUCTIVITY COMES FROM PEOPLE, NOT FROM MACHINES: AN INTERVIEW WITH MAJOR GENERAL LYNWOOD E. CLARK, U.S.A.F.

Major General Lynwood E. Clark began his military career in 1949 as an aviation cadet and in 1961 graduated from the Armed Forces Staff College in Norfolk, Virginia. A much decorated command pilot and fighter gunnery instructor, he has served all over the world and seen combat in Korea and Vietnam. In 1967 he was assigned to Headquarters, U.S.A.F. as an operations officer and served with distinction in command posts in Idaho, Taipei, Okinawa, and Hawaii before coming to San Antonio.

The San Antonio Air Logistics Center, Kelly Air Force Base, Texas, has recently been the focus of national attention as a result of its dramatically increased productivity. Since General Lynwood E. Clark assumed command in 1977, Kelly has received the Air Force Organizational Excellence Award and the 1980 National Award for Excellence in Productivity Improvement of the American Institute of Industrial Engineers. It has also been designated an Exemplary Practice in Federal Productivity by the Office of Personnel Management.

One of five similar centers in the Air Force Logistics Command, Kelly Air Force Base provides worldwide support to air force aircraft, engines, support systems, and components, including purchase, storage, distribution, and maintenance. The base is organized into seven directorates and employs 16,500 persons; 15,300 of them are civilians and 9,000 are of Hispanic heritage.

Under General Clark's leadership, Kelly Air Force Base has used such management techniques as orthodox job enrichment (OJE), management by objective, and a strong labor standards improvement program to raise productivity substantially. The Maintenance Directorate, for example, produced 30,000 more engine components, overhauled more than twice the number of aircraft, and produced 23 percent more commodity items in 1978 than 1977. At the same time, the directorate achieved a decline in defect com-

plaints, a 90 percent rating for on-time delivery, and improved levels of quality control.

An important component of the Kelly productivity effort is management's commitment to a vigorous employee-relations program. Structured competition, formal recognition programs for performance, and a high priority employee "hotline" have resulted in reduced sick leave rates, smoother union-management relations, and improved worker morale. In response to management's firm support of affirmative action principles, EEO (Equal Employment Opportunity) complaints have decreased by 50 percent.

Q. Since your arrival at Kelly Air Force Base, you've launched a number of programs to increase productivity. One that stands out is the Orthodox Job Enrichment program. What is OJE, why did you choose the OJE approach, and how did you carry it out?

A. Let me say first that what works for one organization or person may not work for another. When I arrived here, I had to find out what the problems were and what motivated the people involved before I could begin. Orthodox job enrichment offered a structured approach to solving problems that touched a great number of people and a very complex pattern of organization where normal techniques of leadership might not work. With OJE, I was able to get things moving across the barriers between our directorates. That had been a major problem here.

OJE involves improving the work environment and the quality of work through redesigning jobs to make individual workers more responsible and the work less fragmented. It provides a structured approach for managers to tackle problems, whether they're problems in morale or in the production process. It trains managers to do this and brings them together as problem-solving teams. There's no magic in OJE—I've used the term on occasion that it's snake oil—but it does offer structure. At first, I attempted to apply OJE principles informally, across the board, with a minimum of training, but this approach didn't prove very effective. OJE worked best when we went through the whole hierarchy of training, the entire procedure. That structure was needed to get people working. It forced supervisors and employees to sit down and talk about problems, as opposed to thinking the other guy was doing something about it and losing the problem in the interface. When OJE was done thoroughly, people recognized its value and it was successful.

One area where OJE worked especially well was in the J-79 engine teardown unit. Our success was bred primarily by a group of people who were bored and disillusioned with their jobs because they didn't feel recognized. They were the also-rans, and they needed an opportunity to spread their wings, to feel more productive and undertake more complex tasks. We improved the work environment and restructured some of those jobs to increase worker involvement in the total project. We got our managers meeting together. The proof of the pudding is that under OJE they came up with some darned good ideas on how to improve the tear-down process and how to salvage parts. Morale is good. Some of those people, the ones who demonstrated excellent performance, have been promoted to higher grade levels in jobs where they feel they're doing something more important.

Q. What about your labor standards improvement program? How did you decide to cut 10 percent from nonengineered job standards and 15 percent from engineered job standards?

A. I wish you hadn't asked me that. We reached out and grabbed those figures out of the air. Frankly, we took a chance—calculated, of course. I had been in the shops and watched the people in their work environment. You can tell when people are really busy or just busy-busy or not busy at all. I felt it was a reasonable risk to make those cuts. I knew one thing: if we cut too deep, heads would pop up, and people would say, "Help, I can't do my job," or else certain items would not be produced on time. As it turned out, not a single head popped up. So I have to draw one conclusion: we didn't cut them quite far enough.

But there's a point where you can become counter-productive. If people begin to believe you're running a sweatshop, then you're going to have a rebellion. When we cut standards we launched some recognition programs to make people feel that increased productivity through better efficiency paid off in a sense of accomplishment. The productivity award received by our Directorate of Maintenance from the American Institute of Industrial Engineers was an outgrowth of that effort. With malice aforethought, determination, and intent, we went out to get that award for a group of people who had done very, very well. We put together a brochure and did a lot of horntooting (advertising). They deserved it. That's why we did it.

Q. Were people afraid that increased productivity would lead to lay-offs?

A. In cutting standards we had to assure people that we would bring in extra work. One reason I had confidence in the program was that I knew from my previous assignment in an operational command that there was lots of work that had been stacked in the back shelves awaiting space in the depots' overhaul lines. We hustled for that work. In fact, in 1979 we arrived at nearly 800,000 extra manhours, and a significant proportion of that went to increasing air force readiness. We brought in extra airplanes, some of which nobody else would touch, extra pieces that needed repair, extra engines. That does everybody a favor. It gives us more work and puts more serviceable items on the shelves in our combat units. That's what we're in business for—to support our operational forces.

But basically people wanted greater productivity. Some of them were very bored. I talked to literally hundreds of our employees, asking them what they felt about Kelly and their jobs and what they would do to improve things. I found a significant number wanted more work. They didn't have enough to keep them busy and dreaded coming in the gate because they knew they'd be bored. Now they don't have to wait for the day to end.

Q. When you were formulating ideas for your productivity effort, where did you look first?

A. I went to the people. I went to the situation. I spent a lot of time in the shops. I'd worked in the maintenance area of an operational unit on Okinawa, so I understood what people were doing and talked their language to some degree. I found—and I'm referring to our Mexican-American employees now—that they're patriotic, very proud of their association with Kelly Field. After you've broken the ice, they'll tell you honestly what the problems are. In some organizations, people try to hide problems, but that wasn't the case here. Also, we have a very stable, very experienced workforce at Kelly. If you give them a problem, take the rules away from them and just get out of their way, they'll solve it for you.

Sometimes when you talk to people, you learn some non-job-related things which later turn out to be very useful. For instance, the people here enjoy a park. When you're giving them something in return for their hard work, you might want to upgrade the park. I've been all over the world and, with the exception

of this place, I wouldn't spend a nickel on a park because most people merely look at it as they drive by. But that's not true here. You'll find hundreds of people in our on-base park almost any day and close to 1,000 on weekends. When we wanted to thank our employees for their efforts, we built pavilions for them and latrines and extra barbecue pits and kept the grass up. For our people, that's a good investment. That's the kind of thing a manager has to find out if he or she is going to motivate people.

Another thing: I always check the interfaces between units. I don't care where you are, there's inevitably a disconnection at the interface. If you know where to look for the problem, you don't waste time at the middle of the organization. Instead you determine how the interface needs to be accomplished and get the people there talking to each other. That way, they believe they're solving the problem, and they're happy. You've stuck your nose right in the middle of their business, and they don't resent it—too much.

Q. How do you keep productivity up, after the initial excitement's worn off?

A. You have to go back in and remotivate people frequently. Frankly, if we did something like OJE over again, that would be demotivating to them. They've already had OJE, they know the rules, and they would be bored. You use something different and establish a rhythm of change.

And, once again, you have to know your people, you have to maintain contact with them. We seem to go through cycles here. For a while we'll work on one aspect of employee relations and give it a big push. We'll interview and listen to grievances and complaints. Then it seems to die off and something else comes up as a problem. Right now, hot weather is an issue. We're pushing hard on the cooling problems that exist and putting more effort into it than rightfully it's owed from a priority standpoint—but again, it pays off in keeping people happy. And I think that's the bottom line. Productivity comes from people, not machines. You can spend millions of dollars to get a 1 percent increase in efficiency by putting in new machines, but by convincing people that they can do the job more easily, more efficiently, better, and with pride, you can get a 10 or 15 percent increase.

Q. Do you have any special ways of handling red tape?

A. I do, but I don't recommend them because you get in trouble all the time. And I am in trouble continuously. Let me put it this way. I don't break rules, but I sure as the devil stretch them to the maximum degree in order to get the job done. And I encourage our people to do the same. Now, after the air force writes a rule or regulation, as it comes down the line each intervening level of commands adds a little twist to it, and pretty soon you have an end-product which you have to implement, but which sometimes is not too sensible. The normal thing to do is salute smartly and proceed as directed in that particular regulation. But I have tried to convince people here that they ought to challenge that. I don't suggest that they break the rule, but rather that they challenge it and show the people back up the line how the job can be done more effectively if all the trash and trivia are removed. We also try to get permission to deviate from certain procedures on an interim basis until they can be corrected or improved.

In a way, it's a test of patience more than anything else. You need patience to see whether the ideas you have will be accepted or, if they're not, what it is you can do to say it a different way another day. Finally people get so sick of hearing you that they say, "All right, go ahead and do it."

Q. You seem to be someone who takes risks. How do you encourage the people you work with to take risks?

A. By protecting them. One of the reasons I can take risks is that my boss works very hard to protect me. He's great to work for. You've got to be willing to stand up and take all the brickbats that are thrown. Otherwise your people won't stick their necks out, and you can't blame them. It took a long time for the employees here to gain enough confidence to take chances and start doing things that needed doing.

Q. How do you use competition to increase productivity?

A. Generally speaking, if you have a competition, people enjoy it. There are exceptions, of course, but the majority will get in there and hustle. If they feel they affect the outcome, they'll hustle for sure. If they think they're not influencing it or have little influence, it won't mean much to them. You've got to make sure the competition is something they can touch and feel. You also have to protect some of the weaker ones. If you have a weak section because of poor supervision or poor training or a tougher job, you've got to modify the rules so that they stand a chance of winning. Competition can be counter-productive if you're always losing. Also, I think you have to change the competition from time to time because people become bored with the same game.

One important incentive to our people is a Hall of Fame competition among the Resource Control Centers, which are organizational units in the production area. Units with similar functions compete against each other for recognition. Productivity is only part of it. Other factors involved are quality and leave rates. We also have performance awards for individuals.

And then there's Tourneyfest—that one even shocked me. It started in our Materiel Management Directorate—I just watched in amazement. Basically Tourneyfest is a competition among employees in anything they want to do. If they play checkers, darts, tiddlywinks, tennis, or even make wine, they are encouraged to compete—after work and on weekends, of course. The idea was so effective that I stole it and applied it to the whole base. Now we have a yearly competition that lasts from late February through the playoffs during our Family Festival in June. If you don't believe people get excited about it, you should see some of our Kelly workers who have never been inside the fences past Friday lining up to get on the softball field. But just as important, Tourneyfest got people who work together talking to each other. It's not directly related to work—except that the directorates compete against each other—but it builds esprit de corps and individual morale, and makes for a happier, more productive workforce.

Q. Every now and then I hear it claimed that productivity has suffered from affirmative action programs. Could you address this issue?

A. The EEO program here has paid off because the majority of our people believe it's doing some good for them. Our workforce is 63 percent minority, so it's understandable that if our employees feel we're concerned about EEO and treat them fairly, they're more productive. Now, in any group there are a few exceptions, people who use the EEO program either to subvert the merit system or to promote themselves in an unfair way, but all in all, the organized effort to improve the lot of minorities is worth every bit of time invested. We press hard here for EEO, and it has helped us get the kind of cooperation and performance we're looking for.

Q. What are your strengths as a manager?

A. Oh, probably persistence. And a bit of the chance taking that we talked about earlier. I feel secure in my job, my boss is very supportive, and I've always been a chance-taker, so part of my competition is to compete against myself. Obviously there are times I make mistakes, but my ego isn't so big that I have to win

Clark's Management Agenda

1. identify problems and inefficiencies
2. encourage friendly competition
3. encourage innovation
4. be patient and persistent
5. maintain involvement with the total operation—but delegate
6. handpick key people, whenever possible
7. know your people
8. assign specific tasks to specific people and avoid committees
9. balance discipline and reward
10. take care of your people

every time. I care whether I'm successful, but if I'm not, I scratch that one off the books and try something different.

I guess another factor is that I enjoy people. I like them, I believe they're basically good. I also believe that they want to work and that if you take the stumbling blocks away from them, they'll do a tremendous job. As a result, they probably work better for me than they would for somebody who didn't enjoy them, who felt they were tools or playthings.

Q. What do you look for when you hire staff? Experience?

A. Yes, but experience can be hard to determine. I look for people who are leaning forward in the chair wanting to get at the job. You can take someone like that and steer him or her to significant accomplishments. You allow for a little toe-stubbing (mistakes), but ultimately you can turn that person loose to accomplish things. With someone who's hesitant and has no confidence, you spend most of your time pushing. More than experience, I look for an attitude that says, "I really want to get in there and do something."

For more information on Kelly AFB productivity, write OPM's Productivity Resource Center, Box 14080, Washington, DC 20044.

SOURCE: Abby Rosenthal in *Management*, Fall 1980, p. 6.

flected in OMB requirements that every federal agency of more than 200 employees must report annually on progress made in productivity.

A study begun in 1971 by OMB, the General Accounting Office and the Civil Service Commission produced a measure of productivity covering 64 percent of the civilian work force, or 1.8 million employees in 24 major functional areas with similar tasks, as, for example, records management.[54] This study group later added the General Services Administration and acquired semipermanent status under the title of Joint Financial Management Improvement Program.

The 1977 *Annual Report* of the National Center for Productivity and Quality of Working Life stated that federal productivity rose at an average annual rate of 1.2 percent from 1967 to 1976. There were wide variations among functions, ranging from an increase of 8.2 percent in communications to a decline of 2 percent in printing and duplication. Many federal line agencies, as well as the OMB, the GAO, and the National Center for Productivity, continue to press for productivity improvement at the federal level.[55]

Productivity in the States

A 1975 study of state government productivity efforts concluded that the states had a long way to go before they could adequately gauge the efficiency and effectiveness of their programs.[56] Researchers examined state budget documents and other reports and then surveyed 32 states with questionnaires. Of the 32, 11 had only "barely adequate" effectiveness measures, while 10 had "adequate or quite adequate" efficiency measures. Since then, a large number of states have embarked on productivity improvement efforts. All too often, however, these efforts seem designed for public relations rather than results. That is, they lack followup and make questionable assertions about saving. An example is Wisconsin, identified by a 1976 study as one of the two states making the most comprehensive productivity-improvement efforts.[57] A 1977 report claimed that $47 million in productivity gains was

"targeted" by agencies in this program between 1973 and 1976. Yet the report documented only $2.1 million in savings.[58] Examples included $25,000 in the Department of Motor Vehicles, a saving made possible by replacing 2.5 clerks with a letter-sorting machine. Apparently the machine cost nothing, since each clerk's salary and fringe benefits must have come to $10,000 a year. Likewise, an investment of $247,000 for a new air heating and cooling system in one building, which saved $131,000 per year in fuel, was counted as a $131,000 gain. The reader has to raise questions about such claims.

Productivity in Local Governments

Hundreds of local governments are experimenting with productivity. One may examine the record of several cities studied in depth by administrative scholar and former New York City Budget Director Frederick O'R. Hayes.[59]

Dallas, Texas, has made gains by concentrating on areas with high potential for payoff and low likelihood of employee resistance. Examples include the following:

1. The cost of cleaning public buildings was lowered from $2 per square foot in 1971 to $0.96 in 1975, while improving building cleanliness at the same time. Savings were accomplished by a new training program, standardization of equipment and supplies, and continued reexamination of policies. As an example of this last practice, it was found cheaper to replace flooring more frequently than to wax it.

2. Massive reductions were made in use of energy for cooling, heating, and lighting. Many offices were found to have more lighting than needed, so lighting could be reduced. Likewise, by putting building cleaning crews on a day schedule, air conditioning could be turned off at night. One large city building cut energy costs 55 percent through these and related measures.

3. A study of Dallas Fire Department deployment enabled four new fire stations to be manned by the transfer of existing fire companies, saving more than $600,000 a year.[60]

Milwaukee, Wisconsin, has been using productivity improvement methods since the early 1950s, longer than any other big city in the country. Accomplishments include the following:

1. Reorganization of garbage collection in 1971 saved $3.8 million annually in 1974 prices. These savings resulted from a combination of pickups of combustible and noncombustible trash, more efficient scheduling, two-way radios enabling trucks to eliminate checking in and out of headquarters, and a host of other innovations.
2. A $500,000 annual saving in the repair and maintenance of water pipelines was achieved. Overly large crew sizes and overly specialized position classifications were changed to make response and repair faster and far more efficient.
3. Building inspection functions of the Health, Building, Fire, Water, and Public Works departments were consolidated into one Building Department, at an annual savings of $270,000 a year.[61]

Phoenix, Arizona, estimates that it saves more than $7 million annually through work measurement and related studies that have been implemented. In addition, reorganization of such functions as garbage collection, park maintenance, and street repair has saved millions. Hayes concludes that "few cities in the country have done as much to improve productivity and have been as successful in doing so as Phoenix."[62]

Productivity has failed in such places as Detroit, Michigan and Nassau County, New York. The Hayes study finds that productivity improvement tends to be most successful in areas where public employee unions are relatively weak or passive, as in Phoenix and Dallas. But since these unions are definitely *not* weak in Milwaukee, one may conclude that productivity improvement is indeed possible at the local level.

THE OTHER SIDE: CRITICISMS AND PROBLEMS

This chapter has implicitly suggested productivity studies as a means of improving program efficiency and effectiveness. Nevertheless, some cogent critics of productivity conclude that it is only of marginal value or is even counterproductive. Frederick C. Thayer has written what is probably the most trenchant criticism of today's efforts to study productivity.[63]

Thayer argues first that tying wage and salary increases to productivity gains is a self-defeating effort since productivity gains will be canceled out by increased wages. That is true if workers receive the entire productivity dividend, so these dividends must be split between management and labor. Examples of such a division of the gains have been given above.

Thayer is on firmer ground when he contends that suitable productivity standards cannot be devised for service employment. We have already examined this subject and noted some of the difficulties.

The quantitative fallacy mentioned in the previous chapter has roots in, but is a distortion of, scientific management. This distortion must be assiduously avoided by managers. Measurement was the essence of Taylor's system. One could not only measure the factors, but also measure the way they were put together. These two assumptions were true only if it was also assumed that there are two kinds of measurement, quantitative and qualitative. Measurable productivity is not the only method of evaluating management. The nonmeasurable may be a greater source of efficiency than the measurable. Also, it was recognized that if measurement is carried to extremes it may result in a revolt of workers and managers, jeopardizing all previous efficiencies attained heretofore.

Anything that involves comparison is likely to be a useful tool in judging effectiveness. The reason for this, as already suggested, is that to overlook vital factors may be disastrous, or at least gravely distorting. However, a comparison of the same organization over a time period may yield a clue that is worth investigating. Similarly, to study a common element, such as a hospital bed, may explain why one agency does a better job than another. Such study is never conclusive, however, because measuring consumer satisfaction is difficult, and near and future effects may be in sharp conflict. Also, leadership is a dynamic, evolving quality, and its significance depends somewhat upon where it is measured over a time scale. The potential may be decidedly better or worse than the instant photograph.

Since the influence of time and side effects are always present in every situation, it becomes impossible to measure all of the elements entering into productivity and effectiveness. This problem is exacerbated by the modern tendency to feed everything into a computer.

When the totality of elements is not considered and judgments are made on the fictitious assumption that the method is scientific and fair, the human reaction is strong to the point of becoming irrational. There is a tendency to turn against the system and toward the labor union and the informal office clique, both of which militate against the ability of managers to manage. The outstanding talent of the manager is his ability to secure cooperation, dedication, and drive. Rating individuals and organizations on less than all the elements involved has a chilling effect on these qualities.

Productivity should be one of several criteria for judging individuals and programs. The criteria are likely to be more defensible when comparing situations in the same governmental function or area, but they may be seriously distorted if an attempt is made to apply them across the board to all diverse governmental functions.

Productivity should never be judged, in the last analysis, by a "system." Nor should decisions be made by the personnel office. In the last analysis they should be made by the line executive or line executives acting together.

Far more important than productivity are the terms potential, trend, and motivation. They are never completely measurable and possibly never will be.

Thayer also discusses the social costs of productivity. While productivity improvement may work well for one organization, he argues, one cost will be an increase in the number of unemployed workers in the society as a whole. There is

real social utility in big sanitation crews in cities with large, low-income and low-skill populations because otherwise these workers would be unemployed. On the other hand, an affluent suburb can be tougher about cost effectiveness without putting its own residents out of work. Thayer is saying that there are more important human values than efficiency and that the ability to support oneself is one of them. This criticism cannot be easily sloughed off, yet job training to increase skills seems to be a better approach to this difficulty than does continuing the practice of featherbedding. At the same time, it must be admitted that job-training programs for the unskilled have not netted impressive results in gaining better jobs for trainees. On the other hand, unemployment might diminish or disappear in an economy geared to greater productivity.

Thayer's strongest criticism of productivity studies is that it tends to turn administrators into heartless beasts who treat their employees like machines. Thayer thinks that the inevitable result of this approach would be a speedup by management in work done to the point where workers become alienated from their work instead of enjoying it and being proud of their accomplishments. He cites the example of the automobile plant in Lordstown, Ohio, where workers often quaff a quart of wine during the lunch break so that they become numb enough to finish their shift. These workers are surrounded by productivity experts determined to push one more car per hour through the assembly line. One result is that cars produced in Lordstown have had to be returned at a staggering rate for repairs.

Thayer believes that the speedup is the inevitable result of productivity without close cooperation between management and labor. Not that developing such cooperation is easy. But without it, productivity efforts will either fail or not be worth the work involved because of the social costs they generate.

CUTBACK MANAGEMENT

Increases in program effectiveness and efficiency will not be enough to save all government programs in a period of declining resources and economic growth. Just as President Ronald Reagan proposed and secured extensive cuts in federal programs in the first year of his tenure, governors and local chief executives are doing the same. One scholar has dubbed this hard necessity "cutback management," saying, "when all else fails . . . cutbacks are called for."[64] This step involves difficult decisions about priorities and the willingness to terminate contracts and employees. These steps must be taken, however, by managers in many places in the 1980s since the standard of living in the United States and the willingness to pay higher taxes for government services, discussed in chapters 21 and 24, are declining. Improvement in productivity cannot solve all problems of scarce resources. Nevertheless the 1980s will provide the most positive environment for productivity improvement since the Great Depression of the 1930s. One of the effects will be to add a far greater financial strain on the 50 state governments and local governments of all sizes, where Uncle Sam has long been the banker. Since state and local governments are three times the size of federal government, this situation might give quite a fillip to public administration at state and local levels.

SUMMARY

The two main subjects dealt with in this chapter, evaluation and productivity, could possibly prove valuable to readers irrespective of their entering government employment. The two subjects grow logically out of our discussion of control systems, which led up to this chapter. Further, this and the next chapter provide a solid and useful background for those that will follow later on public finance, budgeting, accounting, and the like.

The terms efficiency and economy, which triggered the public administration movement of the early 1900s, tended to go into eclipse shortly after World War II, only to reappear in a new guise under different titles. If resources continue to shrink and population expands, and if financial stringency should continue to be the order of the

day, the challenge of the next generation of public administrators might be to reconcile and so far as possible harmonize the rival claims of efficiency and human sensitivity and aspiration.

NOTES

1. Wayne A. Kimmel et al., *Municipal Management and Budget Methods: An Evaluation of Policy-Related Research, Final Report,* Vol. 1: *Summary and Synthesis* (Washington: Urban Institute, 1974), p. 39.

2. John D. Waller et al., *Monitoring for Government Agencies* (Washington: Urban Institute, 1976), pp. 7–8.

3. Harry P. Hatry et al., *Practical Program Evaluation for State and Local Government Officials* (Washington: Urban Institute, 1973), p. 56.

4. This subsection is based primarily on Hatry, *Practical Program Evaluation,* pp. 56–62 and "Program Evaluation," ch. 15 in Barry Bozeman, *Public Administration and Policy Analysis* (New York: St. Martin's Press, 1979). See also Carol A. Weiss, *Evaluation Research* (Englewood Cliffs, N.J.: Prentice-Hall, 1972); and Peter H. Rossi and Walter Williams, *Evaluating Social Programs* (New York: Seminar Press, 1972).

5. John Madge, *The Tools of Social Science* (Garden City, N.Y.: Doubleday Anchor Books, 1965), pp. 232–235.

6. Weiss, *Evaluation Research,* p. 68.

7. Weiss, *Evaluation Research,* pp. 69–72, and Bozeman, *Public Administration and Policy Analysis.*

8. This subsection is based primarily on Hatry, *Practical Program Evaluation,* pp. 39–56, 62–70.

9. Hatry, *Practical Program Evaluation,* p. 44.

10. Hatry, *Practical Program Evaluation,* p. 71.

11. Joseph S. Wholey, "The Role of the Evaluation and the Evaluator in Improving Public Programs," *Public Administration Review* 36 (November–December 1976): 681.

12. Executive Office of the President, U.S. Bureau of the Budget, *Household Survey, 1969* (Washington: U.S. Government Printing Office, 1969).

13. Hatry, *Practical Program Evaluation,* pp. 107–126.

14. Kimmel, *Municipal Management and Budget Methods,* p. 47.

15. Joel Havemann, "Congress Tries to Break Ground Zero in Evaluating Federal Programs," *National Journal,* 22 May 1976, p. 708.

16. See Joseph A. Pechman and P. Michael Timpane, eds.,

Work Incentives and Income Guarantees: The New Jersey Negative Income Tax Experiment (Washington: Brookings Institution, 1975).

17. Joseph S. Wholey, "What Can We Actually Get from Program Evaluation?" *Policy Sciences* 3 (1972): 361–369.

18. Havemann, "Congress Tries to Break Ground," p. 710.

19. James E. Prather and Frank K. Gibson, "The Failure of Social Programs," *Public Administration Review* 37 (September–October 1977): 562.

20. Richard Brown and Ray D. Pethtel, "A Matter of Facts: State Legislative Performance Auditing," *Public Administration Review* 34 (July–August 1974): 325.

21. Wholey, "The Role of the Evaluation," p. 681.

22. Frank Wise, Jr., "Toward Equity of Results Achieved: One Approach," *Public Management,* August 1976, pp. 9–12. Wise was assistant city manager of Savannah at the time.

23. "Measuring Basic City Services," *Search,* May–August, 1974, pp. 8–10. (*Search* is a periodical newsletter of the Urban Institute [see Appendix].)

24. Leonard Buder, "High School Graduation Standards to Be Stiffened by New York City," *New York Times,* 25 April 1977, p. 1.

25. Kimmel, *Municipal Management and Budget Methods,* p. 38.

26. Wholey, "The Role of the Evaluation," p. 682.

27. Pamela Horst et al., "Program Evaluation and the Federal Evaluator," *Public Administration Review* 34 (July–August 1974): 300–308.

28. An excellent treatment of this problem is V. F. Ridgway, "Dysfunctional Consequences of Performance Measurements," *Administrative Science Quarterly* 1 (September 1956): 240–247.

29. Aaron Wildavsky, "The Self-Evaluating Organization," *Public Administration Review* 32 (September–October 1972): 509–520; Laurence W. O'Connell and Susan O. White, "Politics and Evaluation in LEAA: New England States" (Paper presented at the Annual Meeting of the American Political Science Association, New Orleans, 1973).

30. Edward A. Suchman, "Action for What?" in Weiss, *Evaluation Research,* pp. 52–84.

31. Richard Petrow, *The Bitter Years* (New York: Morrow, 1974), pp. 300–313.

32. Bruce Rocheleau, "Evaluation, Accountability, and Responsiveness in Administration," *Midwest Review of Public Administration,* October 1975, pp. 163–172.

33. Cf. Hatry, *Practical Program Evaluation,* pp. 107–123.

34. Daniel P. Moynihan, *The Politics of a Guaranteed Income* (New York: Random House, 1973).

35. Weiss, *Evaluation Research,* p. 32.

36. Hale Champion, "Husbanding the Public Dollar," in *Proposition 13 and Its Consequences for Public Management,* ed. Selma Mushkin (Washington: Public Affairs Press, 1978), pp. 4–5.

37. Allen Schick, "Beyond Analysis," *Public Administration Review* 37 (May–June 1977): 262.

38. Erwin C. Hargrove, "The Bureaucratic Politics of Evaluation: A Case Study of the Department of Labor," *Public Administration Review* 40 (March–April, 1980): 150–159.

39. Thomas D. Morris et al., "Productivity Measures in the Federal Government," *Public Administration Review* 32 (November–December 1972): 754.

40. John W. Kendrick, "Public Capital Expenditures and Budgeting for Productivity Advance," *Public Administration Review* 32 (November–December 1972): 804.

41. Morris, "Productivity Measures."

42. Lyle C. Fitch, "Remarks," *Public Administration Review* 32 (November–December 1972): 843.

43. Edward K. Hamilton, "Productivity: The New York City Approach," *Public Administration Review* 32 (November–December 1972): 786.

44. Gerald Christenson, "Fragmentation in Government—A Challenge for State Planning," in *State Planning Issues* (Lexington, Ky.: Council of State Governments, 1975), p. 1.

45. This section is based primarily on Daron K. Butler and Jay G. Stanford's fine *Checklist for Planning and Implementing a Productivity Improvement Program in Governmental Units,* Intergovernmental Brief (Austin: Texas Advisory Commission on Intergovernmental Relations, June 1976).

46. Jimmy Carter, "Making Government Work Better," *National Journal,* 9 October 1976, pp. 1448–1449.

47. A relevant example is that of planning-programming-budgeting (PPB), implemented across the board in the federal government, several states, and several large cities in the 1960s, but pretty much abandoned today. PPB is gone largely because it was comprehensively mandated instead of tried out on a pilot basis.

48. These remarks on training are based on Herb Simon, "Policy Implications and Implementation Issues in Creating a Productivity Program," in *Public Productivity: The State of the Art,* Papers from the Tenth Annual Conference on Management Analysis in State and Local Government (Windsor Locks, Conn., October 1973), pp. 28–39.

49. This section is based primarily on Patrick Manion, *Improving Municipal Productivity: Work Measurement for Better Management* (Washington: U.S. Government Printing Office, November 1975).

50. See Harry P. Hatry, "Issues in Productivity Measurement for Local Governments," *Public Administration Review* 32 (November–December 1972), p. 777.

51. Hatry, "Issues in Productivity Measurement," pp. 774–778.

52. John P. Ross and Jesse Burkhead, *Productivity in the Local Government Sector* (Lexington, Mass.: Lexington Books, 1974), p. 78.

53. Ross and Burkhead, *Productivity in the Local Government Sector,* p. 83.

54. Peter G. Peterson, "Productivity in Government and the American Economy," *Public Administration Review* 32 (November–December 1972): 741; and Neal R. Peirce, "Productivity Is Slogan for Taming Spiraling Expenses," *National Journal,* 12 April 1975, p. 538.

55. National Center for Productivity and Quality of Working Life, *Annual Report* (Washington: U.S. Government Printing Office, 1977), pp. 72–76.

56. National Center for Productivity and Quality of Working Life, *The Status of Productivity Measurement in State Government: An Initial Examination* (Washington: U.S. Government Printing Office, 1975).

57. Edgar G. Crane, Barry Lentz, and Jay Shafritz, *State Government Productivity: The Environment for Improvement* (New York: Praeger, 1976), p. 48.

58. Wisconsin Department of Administration, "Survey of State Agencies Management Improvements," January 1977, p. 1.

59. Frederick O'R. Hayes, *Productivity in Local Government* (Lexington, Mass.: Heath, 1977).

60. Hayes, *Productivity,* pp. 20–37.

61. Hayes, *Productivity,* pp. 57–69.

62. Hayes, *Productivity,* p. 167.

63. Frederick C. Thayer, "Productivity: Taylorism Revisited (Round Three)," *Public Administration Review* 32 (November–December 1972): 833–39.

64. Charles H. Levine, ed., *Managing Fiscal Stress: The Crisis in the Public Sector* (Chatham, N.J.: Chatham House Publishers, 1980), p. 11; see also Elizabeth A. Kellar, ed., *Managing With Less* (Washington: International City Management Association, 1979), a more practically oriented volume.

17

Information Systems and Data Banks

And now I see with eye serene
The very pulse of the machine.

William Wordsworth

In this chapter we deal with communication in administration. Information transmission and retrieval, which involves computers, data banks, and statistical skills, is a rapidly expanding field.

An anecdote presents several scientists huddled around the new supercomputer. With bated breath, one asks the computer, "Does God exist?" After some lights flash, the computer answers, "He does now."

The anecdote testifies to changes that may be referred to as the computer revolution. This revolution, which began shortly after World War II in the United States, is now in full stride. But although the computer is dramatic and significant in its own right, it is nevertheless only one element in a much larger movement known as management information systems.

A bewildering array of new terms has come flooding in on layman and official alike, as for example, electronic or automatic data processing (EDP and ADP), operations research, cybernetics, systems analysis, and data banks. The origins of this larger movement are complex, for they lie in science, technology, and the requirements of defense. At the core is management's ever-increasing need for information, which is not only met by technology, but also stimulated by the growth of technology in all fields in a reciprocal relationship. To deal with problems of size and technology, which press in on all sides, the manager must have more information than he has ever needed before, and he must have it quickly.

It is still too soon to judge the social, political, and economic consequences of this upheaval in the field of information; but there is no doubt of its lasting effect on public administration. As a tool of management, information systems offer vast new potentialities. And for the manager himself, he may not have to be a mathematician or an ADP expert in his own right, but he will have to know enough about machine theory and technique to be able to deal with the experts in that area. For generations, managers have had to understand the work of lawyers, doctors, statisticians, accountants, and other professional specialists; the expert in automatic data processing has now been added to the list.

THE DEMAND FOR MANAGEMENT INFORMATION SYSTEMS

An interest in management information systems began, somewhat tentatively, at the end of World War II as the potentialities of ADP were progressively developed to the point where they became practical. As the machines were perfected, the demand grew. By 1976, a virtual explosion had occurred: the federal government alone had acquired and installed more than 10,000 computers, all 50 state governments had at least 1, and so did the larger cities and school systems.[1] Well over half of all local governments with 10,000 or more population used computers, while almost all local governments of 100,000 or more did. Computer expenses averaged 1 percent of the budget, an investment most localities thought well worthwhile.[2]

Since management information systems are concerned with more than computers, it will be useful to explore what is involved. In the relationship between automatic data processing and modern budget personnel, accounting, and other management systems, ADP is the mechanized means of collecting and organizing information, which these systems then use, along with other material, to develop long-range programs. It is true that both ADP and these systems use quantitative methods and may be called formal systems, but from a managerial standpoint, ADP is an adjunct to such systems. Systems analysis, as noted earlier, is used in many fields, including science, the social sciences, and now in management. Operations research and cybernetics are managerial methods for analyzing complex factors involved in program operations, thus helping to clarify possible managerial alternative courses of action.

All of these functions are related, all involve information, and all are involved in the larger area of management information systems, but ADP is the only one confined to information gathering and retrieval. Moreover, it is neutral with regard to the use made of these data.

The Rationale of Management Information Systems

What are some of the reasons that management information systems have come to play so important a role in large-scale management in recent years?

Management information needs have risen sharply and will continue to rise as the pace of change accelerates. These needs must be met if business enterprises are to remain competitive and government is to respond to the challenges with which it is increasingly confronted. Since World War II, developments in science and technology have been in the forefront of this era of change.

The impetus for the development of information through the use of science and technology was the demands of war, plus the plentiful supply of federal funds for government and private research. Research and development funds (R&D) have steadily increased to a figure in 1979 of about $51 billion a year.[3] Some two thirds of all R&D in the United States is financed by government, and of this, 70 percent is spent by private industrial and educational institutions.

In the mid-1970s and early 1980s there was a steady decline in the proportion of funds devoted to R&D. Some experts felt that this decrease was directly linked to falling productivity. Whether this is so or not, R&D needs greater support if society is to meet the grave challenges it faces in the rest of this century.

In older information systems, methods were crude and slow. Reports were often received too late to be of any real value, and the information they contained was not always tailored to the administrator's needs because these needs had not been clearly defined. Too often what was offered in the way of information was diffused, fragmented, and unrelated.

A present-day example of such a failure in management information systems led to the Boston Red Sox losing one of their top players in 1981. Although the contract stated that players must be offered new contracts by December 20, the Red Sox did not mail out a contract to star catcher Carlton Fisk until December 22. As a result, Fisk was declared a free agent. He later signed with the Chicago White Sox.

Such methods cannot be tolerated today, for, more than ever, managers now need timely, accurate, and reliable information as the basis of executive action. No information system can be forced on those who do not wish to use it, but ingrained resistances to change can be overcome when the practical advantages are understood and the technical skills to handle the equipment involved are made available. Designing a management information system is no easy task, but the stakes are large. It is a concerted undertaking, for many disciplines must be represented, and the focus must be on action. The ultimate test is action: time must be saved so as to permit better planning, programming, decision making, and evaluation.

Communications and Feedback

When managerial decisions have been made, communicated, and put into effect, the feedback is the relaying back of information, again through communications, to the manager, enabling him to combine, reconsider, and possibly alter present courses of action. As new information in the form of feedback comes in, then current plans, methods, and procedures may be altered so as to remain relevant to action. This procedure is sometimes called management by exception and is closely related to concepts of administration discussed earlier, notably the control function. Feedback, therefore, is a vital element in directing the work of organizations. It is also involved in general systems theory, operations research, cybernetics, and other analytical methods referred to in earlier chapters.

Many disciplines have contributed to the basic theory of management information systems. An influential writer in this area was Norbert Wiener who, in *The Human Use of Human Beings*,[4] used a biological analogy. The human brain, said Wiener, constantly receives messages, or communications, from the body, and this information is absorbed, integrated, and then used to direct bodily responses. Here is a constant flow of communication in which the nervous system integrates messages relating to goal and achievement, thus facilitating continuous adjustments on the basis of pertinent current information. The analogy cannot be pushed too far, however, because the nervous system is a "closed" system, and administration is an "open" one. Moreover, administration includes a wide range of variables—external and internal, valuational and sensory, long-range and immediate—and hence is a far more complicated process than the relation among brain, nervous system, and bodily response. But although the analogy is more suggestive than fully congruent, it does reinforce what has already been noted in previous chapters regarding the central role of communication theory in administration.

Both business and government look increasingly to formalized systems to produce the information necessary to make decisions, operate economically and efficiently, and plan for the future.

The development of modern information systems had a new start when it became possible for communications systems to transmit large volumes of data and for the modern computer to process that data speedily for the purpose of solving specific problems. Prospects for the future growth of information technology stagger the imagination. Computer speeds are continuing to increase, storage capacity has been enlarged, processing costs are declining, the sharing of computers is on the rise, and so is the simultaneous use of computers through remote, direct-access terminals. Computer facilities are becoming economically available to an ever-increasing number of users, and the demand for their services is accelerating.

Management must be prepared to profit from these developments, for those who fail to take advantage of the opportunities offered will operate under a handicap. For government, an outstanding advantage of this new technology relates to budgetary control: if the budget must be altered at any time so as to respond to changing economic conditions, the necessary information can now be made immediately available to chief executives and legislatures.

The Computer

Human beings have definite limitations as processors of data. Machines can process much data far better than man. Automatic data processing has been defined as "data processing performed by a system of electronic or electrical machines so interconnected or interacting as to reduce to a minimum the need for human assistance or intervention."[5] The computer is such a machine, capable of accepting information, applying prescribed processes to it, and supplying the results of its computations.[6]

When computers function badly, the result can be near catastrophic. In June 1980, the computer at North American Air Defense Command Headquarters inside Cheyenne Mountain, Colorado, sent a message that the Soviet Union had launched a missile attack on the United States. As a result, bomber crews started their engines, submarine missile crews were put on alert, and ground missile crews readied themselves to fire. But after three minutes the alert was called off, when it was discovered that the computer had made a mistake. The cause of the error lay in a defective chip in an integrated circuit, an item that cost 46 cents.[7]

As noted earlier, the computer is part of a much larger development of information systems, with both parallel and converging lines of thought and practice. But since the computer is the center as well as the symbol of this whole complex, it will be helpful to try to understand its evolution, without, however, going into technical detail.[8]

The use of a card by means of which instructions may be introduced into a machine developed in Europe between 1812 and 1880. It is associated with the names of Joseph Marie Jacquard, Gottfried Wilhelm von Leibnitz, and Charles P. Babbage. By 1833, Babbage had conceived a general-purpose computer seemingly capable of solving any type of mathematical problem. It was not until 100 years later, however, that this so-called analytical engine actually evolved into a successful machine such as Babbage had contemplated.

Meanwhile in the United States, the need of the federal government for machines to solve its tabulating problems was the impetus to further experimentation. Hollerith, a statistician, spent seven and a half years developing the Hollerith machine, which constituted another large step forward. Cards were manually inserted into the sorting slot of the machine, and sorting was at the rate of from 50 to 80 cards a minute. Research on this project was started in connection with the census of 1880, but the machine was not operative until 1886.

By 1937, Dr. Howard H. Aiken had invented the "automatic-sequence-controlled calculator," known as the Mark I. It was capable of following a sequence of instructions punched into a tape. Later models (Mark II, III, and IV) were equipped with magnetic tape for input and output and electronic relays for calculating processes. During World War II, such machines were used in areas such as ballistics, aeronautics, and nuclear physics.

In 1947, the electronic numerical integrator and calculator was developed at the University of Pennsylvania; this was the first machine to use electron tubes for the calculating process.

By 1951, assembly-line production of computers had been introduced by Sperry-Rand, followed by National Cash Register and International Business Machines. These computers used vacuum tubes, relays, and mercury-delay lines in their operations.

By the late 1950s, these large machines had been replaced with smaller ones using transistors and diodes; these "second-generation" models also had increased memory capacities.

By the mid-1960s, high-speed, buffered channels were in use, with outside limits of 100,000 characters per second.

Today, "third-generation" computers using integrated circuits are capable of processing speeds ranging in some instances down to a few billionths of a second, and their memories are larger. Moreover, "computer families" range in size from the very small to the very large, all operating in response to the same set of instructions. Mass random storage available to a single system may be as large as several hundred billion characters; telecommunication systems may be attached; and the range of speeds is wide, permitting a better adaptation of equipment capability to job requirements.

Today, minicomputers and microcomputers are entering many private households. In 1981, a fairly sophisticated computer could be bought for under $1,000 and used in homes and schools in many ways.

Five characteristics apply to the spectacular development of ADP: (1) the acquisition, handling, and manipulation of data are done almost wholly by machines; (2) the work is accomplished with a minimum of human intervention; (3) because of interconnections, machines are capable of interacting in a variety of sequential steps; (4) because the system controls itself, the whole process is carried out under set rules firmly established in advance; and (5) the operations of the machine appear to be simultaneous, although in fact they are not. Consequently, the concepts and even the vocabulary of computer technology suggest analogies to public administration as a body of knowledge.

Two basic computer terms are hardware and software. Hardware refers to the machinery involved in ADP: sorters, terminals, central processing units, and other related machines. Software is the programming put into the computer and everything else relating to instructing the machinery what to do. It is imperative to keep up with not only the latest hardware, but also the latest software. Increasingly complex and sophisticated programs maximize the usefulness of hardware. Jurisdictions that use outdated software cannot get the most from their hardware.

If the point is not obvious by now, let us state it explicitly: young people being trained in public administration today must develop a basic working knowledge of computer hardware and software. They do not need to be experts, but they must know the basic concepts. The same is true for two other aids in processing data—statistics and accounting.

Uses of the Computer

In government, computers were first used to perform routine clerical operations, and they still are, as in preparing payrolls, checkwriting, bookkeeping, purchasing operations, and the like. Later they came into wide use for control purposes: accounting, auditing, cost analysis, and, more recently, scanning income tax returns.

In industry, and only to a lesser extent in government, today's computers are so completely automated that they are capable of operating other machines. Examples are the processing of metals, such as copper and aluminum, where machines are superior to human supervision in automating the production cycle and exercising quality control. The computer is also increasingly employed for strategic calculations, making possible, for example, the application of game theory in business competition and even in the higher ranges of international relations. As these uses and capabilities expand, some people anticipate the time when men will no longer be required to make their own decisions, for the machines can do it better than they can. These newer uses of the computer have created the possibility, however, that the content of the information furnished may be overlooked or downgraded by attention to the manner in which it is supplied.

The two basic and related distinguishing characteristics of ADP are, first, to provide quick and reliable information to managers to guide their actions and, second, to store information, indeed, an almost infinite amount of information because of the memory banks and their feasible interrelations. It is because of these storage capacities that government hopes eventually to develop data banks for everyday administration.

In an understandable enthusiasm for what is possible, however, a certain limiting condition must not be overlooked: new interconnections among seemingly different elements may produce "new" knowledge, but nothing comes from a computer that was not put into it by human beings in the form of raw data; consequently, there are always the questions: Are the right questions asked? and Are the data accurate, relevant, and complete?

It seems likely now that in some, perhaps many, areas of public policy and administration, a combination of ADP and operations research will create a tendency to stress game theory and strategic decision more now than in the past. One of the best brief analyses of this alliance is in a publication of the International City Management Association called *Program Development and Administration*.[9] Thus, an infinite number of models may be developed for public administration purposes to solve problems relating to inventory, routing, waiting time, replacement and maintenance, and the like. And since, like public administration itself, operations research is problem oriented, it is also capable, in combination with ADP, of solving problems such as linear programming, dynamic programming, factor analysis, queuing theory, decision theory, game theory, and others based on a host of statistical techniques.

Linear programming is used when the structure of a given problem is such that one of its variable factors varies in direct ratio to another, as in cost and quantity, output and input, and the like. Queuing theory deals with problems such as arrival and departure times in a bus terminal and is concerned with waiting times, excess capacity, bottlenecks, and the efficient use of scarce resources. With population congestion now so widespread, the application of queuing theory is a useful technique.

Simulation techniques are another area of application. Once a mathematical model has been constructed and the coefficients specified, then various outputs in terms of manpower and equipment are systematically varied as the model is repeatedly tested to develop information concerning the average equipment and manpower needed to produce a given number of outputs.

In this application of these techniques, however, the public administrator should recognize two provisos. First, no matter how sophisticated the model and the techniques, they will be no better than the selection of variables to be included in the analysis; these must be consonant with comparable variables in the "real" world, or the results obtained will be either unreliable or of limited value. Second, the public administrator must be *more than passably* conversant with the techniques employed before he can adequately supervise the expert; but at the same time, no technique, however complex, can altogether replace the judgment of the able executive.[10]

While ADP can be an enormously helpful analytical tool, this capability for analysis has been downplayed in government. Government computers, especially at the state and local level, have been used predominantly for clerical functions. That is, they have been used "to mechanize limited, well-understood procedures, or portions of a procedure, that have a high volume of routine operations."[11] This use of the computer as an adding machine or file cabinet neglects its potential to create models and provide analysis that may be of great help in dealing with problems.

A Trial Balance

Stanley Kubrick's film *2001: A Space Odyssey* features a computer that can reason on its own. The computer, HAL, has a nervous breakdown and attempts to kill all human beings within reach. Such a nightmare is merely the most extreme kind of preoccupation with the computer.

Thousands of news stories, articles, and television programs have centered on the revolutionary impact of the computer, and opinions range all the way from total endorsement to warnings similar to those in George Orwell's novel *1984*. As might be supposed, the public administrator finds himself caught somewhere between these two extremes: appreciative of what the computer revolution has to offer but concerned with possible misuse as well. An example of such misuse came to light in the late 1960s, when it was discovered that the U.S. Army had data on 30 million Americans in its computers. Without any authorization from Congress, the army had consolidated information from other government agencies and nongovernment sources, compiling the names of a vast number of people whom someone, somewhere, had at one point or another suspected of subversion. While Congress eventually ordered most of these computer tapes erased, the technical ease with which information can be stored and transferred is a tremendous tool for tyrants. Recent excesses of the Central Intelligence Agency and the Federal Bureau of Investigation in gathering information, when coupled with the capacity of the computer, must make citizens nervous.

Some people complain that widespread use of computers and identification numbers, such as social security numbers, assigned to individuals, are dehumanizing. Many have protested that they are human beings, not numbers or part of some machine. But Michael Herbert Dengler of Minneapolis is ready for the computer age. In 1978, he went to court to change his name legally to the number 1069, saying that numbers "describe what is inherent in me." Dengler's request was refused by the county judge, who stated that "to allow the use of a number instead of a name would only provide additional nourishment upon which the illness of dehumanization is able to feed and grow to the point where it is totally incurable."[12]

There seems little question that computers and ADP are now permanent fixtures in Western culture and that the capabilities of computers may be expected to expand. Most people would agree that there can never be an oversupply of information or of information readily and quickly available for the solution of problems. Knowledge has expanded so rapidly in all fields and society has become so complex that no one can any longer know everything about a given field. In fact, no one can any longer know everything about even a specialized field, such as chemistry or economics. Information is needed for research, research is needed for analysis, analysis for goals, and goals for administration. Information promotes goal definition, choices among alternative methods of reaching them, work performance, the exercise of control, the evaluation of results, and citizen interest and participation. In producing the needed information in all of these processes, the computer is merely a tool; it is no more dangerous than any other tool when properly used.

The computer is not, however, a sacred cow, although interest in it is so great, and it is being so assiduously promoted—partly, of course, for its news value—that people may fall into the habit of regarding it as a kind of cultural idol. No doubt most people will eventually recover their sense of balance and their sense of humor. Moreover, when computers are classified as public utilities and brought within the range of all, as is already beginning to happen, the fear that they engender while their use is still limited to large businesses and governments, will tend to be alleviated. Exaggerated expectations often lead to exaggerated disillusionment, and some businesses and government agencies are already going through this experience with the computer. But the reason is that buyers were oversold at the start and failed to recognize the limitations of the tool, as well as its capabilities.[13]

More important than the capabilities of the computer, perhaps, are some of the results of its use in management. Some executives may unwittingly fall into the lazy habit of assuming that a precise answer is a complete one and will fail to do the additional thinking needed in determining goals, making choices, and giving due weight to the human element in management. Theoretically, therefore, the computer elite could suffer the same fate that *Punch* magazine predicted for the British civil service if, by itself, it were to try to rule the nation: first it would be appreciated, then tolerated, and finally hung to the nearest lamp post.

As every scientist knows, the danger of exploitation does not lie in science itself but in man's proclivity to worship that which is new and not fully understood. In effect, therefore, uninformed citizens make undue obeisance, not realizing that

their own native wisdom may be equal to that of the experts. As Max Weber and other have appreciated, authority is not merely a matter of competence and position, for it may also become something of a myth, the myth of omnicompetence. In a democratic society, such a myth is as dangerous as hereditary privilege.

A second possible hazard in the use of the computer in management is overcentralization because expanding public information systems will certainly mean greater concentrations of that information in fewer places. Worldwide satellite communications systems and eventually the use of the laser will conduct information to a few central sources, notably Washington. There will be access to this information, but it will be costly and hence limited. And yet, as Elmer Staats, U.S. comptroller general (1966-1981), has remarked, "The information system should be planned centrally to avoid fragmented, disparate systems that will ultimately have to be redesigned."[14]

Therefore, caution must be exercised lest public administration eventually be divided into three parts: planning and decision making by a top few; all matters relating to money and organization controlled by budget officials; and the remainder, called administration, mechanically executed on guidelines emerging from computers. Although this is not likely to happen, it requires no paranoid fantasy to realize that it might; if it did, then the qualities of unity and enterprise that have been sought for program administration in recent years would go by the board.

The third area of concern has to do with middle management, the demise of which is foreseen by several students of "the shape of things to come." What these trend projections overlook, however, is that most administrative skill in securing production and program results resides in these middle-management, line officials, who in fact occupy strategic positions in the fabric of management. If this group were to disappear as the use of machines expands, most administrators would no longer need to think and administration would lose its inner unity and drive. A focus on human relations in management would also disappear except at the highest, elite levels. If history is a reliable guide, the result would eventually be harmful to society, no matter how pure the intentions and motivations of this particular technological elite might be.

The long-range solution to these problems lies in a deliberate effort to absorb the new computer technology into the larger synthesis that the public administration profession seems now to be making, instead of allowing the computer to become dominant over other essential elements in management. As one scholar suggests, "Given the growing and powerful capabilities of information technology, and in view of the increasing complexity of problems facing government at all levels, the public executive has no alternative but to learn something about and use scientific and systematic program evaluation."[15]

DATA BANKS

A resource many administrators would like to attain is the development of data banks. Conveniently located pools of information would be invaluable for old and new programs alike. The information exists, but access to it is difficult. For example, how does an agency such as the National Aeronautics and Space Administration handle such administrative problems as coordinating tracing stations all over the world? How much is reliably known about how to persuade diverse skill groups, lacking even common vocabularies, to work together? How does productivity differ from management by objectives, and which is preferable for control? What are average minimal needs in certain kinds of programs, and what are the determining factors? When an agency divides its functions among two components, as some do, under the headings of "program" and "administration," what are the resulting strengths and weaknesses? These questions are but a small sample of those asked almost daily by busy administrators, and it would seem that in an age when information is so meticulously gathered, something like data banks might be developed.

Unresolved Problems

The difficulties of codifying such information are more complex, of course, in some areas than in others, but there is already enough profitable experience with the problem to show that the attempt might be worth the effort. The requirements are money, imagination, and a vast amount of systematic research.

An area of marked success since World War II is in the preparation of scientific abstracts. The United States, the Soviet Union, and several other nations where science has been highly developed, have undertaken programs of collation and translation, reducing whole fields of knowledge to photostats, microfilm, and tapes, which can be made available, relatively inexpensively, even to small college and university libraries. In some areas of science, both U.S. and Soviet scientists claim to have access to all important information, in the original or in translation. The same process of abstraction is now widely undertaken in medicine. In library administration, it has become an advanced art.

It is true that science and medicine are fairly precise fields and their subject matter disposes them to orderly analysis. But although thousands of learned articles are involved, the task of bringing them together and making them widely available has turned out to be feasible. In areas of public administration where the subject matter is similarly adapted to such codification, therefore, no insuperable obstacle appears, if enough money, trained personnel, the needed technology, and the right kind of administration can be provided. The prospects for government programs involving science are, of course, brighter than for most.

In other fields, the difficulties are greater. The State Department could use complete data on developing countries and on the different political, economic, and social systems of all nations, plus a rundown of their resources and their economic and population growth potentials. Some recent progress has been made in this direction, but the complexity of the undertaking is formidable, if only because, as yet, the needed agreement as to categories and systems is lacking. The complexities are at least equal in the field of social welfare, for programs relating to housing, urban decay, delinquency, city planning, waste disposal, and many more.

If the creation of data banks is still difficult for substantive areas such as these, the problem of codifying data relating to administration is even more formidable. There may be one best method in a particular kind of surgery, but who is to say what the best method is in budgeting or in personnel administration, where the variables are greater and considerations relating to environment and values differ from one culture to the next?

In each situation there is the problem of categories, for if these are too hastily determined, the results become unreliable. To set them up in the field of public administration will be a long and complex job, for no preexisting framework is seemingly of universal application. If data banks are to be created in this field, therefore, presumably the initiative must come from intrepid pioneers working within national and local frames of reference, and there will have to be widespread experimentation and collation before the final step can be taken to make the categories universal. In such matters, integration occurs *after* the fact, for the schema do not exist in isolation *before* the fact. The researcher must create his own guidelines as he proceeds.

Nevertheless, such practical difficulties are no excuse for not making the attempt to deal with them. Collation must start somewhere. False starts, to be rectified by later modifications of the research scheme, are inherent in the process. If the indiscriminate use, without careful questioning, of assumptions and predictions is avoided, and a combination of rigorous analysis corrected by hindsight is insisted on, then ultimately and cumulatively the effort may prove widely rewarding.

The moment is right to encourage such an effort because with computers increasingly available, vast amounts of data may now be stored in their memories. Computers may also be used to help determine the main categories that emerge from inductive procedures. By a system of gradual refinement that would have been inconceivable a few years ago, the essential schematic framework may be made to appear. Through the rigorous use of the principle of comparability, the ordering process may begin to take shape.

Ordering Data in Public Administration

That the ordering of administrative data is feasible has already been demonstrated through the development of methodologies that have been widely applied and should facilitate the eventual installation of data banks.

One of these methods is the so-called capture-and-record technique, which began in public administration in the 1930s. Under the aegis of the Committee on Public Administration of the Social Science Research Council, there began a systematic attempt to study, as participant-observer, actual administrative situations and to record them for later use and analysis. The underlying assumption was that public administration should be inductively approached and that a vast amount of data is needed before convincing generalizations can safely be made.

In pursuance of this objective, a number of first-class studies were undertaken during the early period of the New Deal and are still highly regarded for having captured the feel of administration.[16] They dealt with actual administrative situations. Instead of starting with limited hypotheses and assumptions, they were inductive and empirical, resembling in method the patient research by which every science must provide a sufficient factual basis for the formulation of principles and eventually a philosophy. In their participant-observer methodology, these early studies also resembled the field methods of anthropologists, who concentrate on particular communities, live among the people, and record what happens with as little bias and preconception as is humanly possible. In short, the authors of these public administration studies were not trying to prove anything or to reinforce their own theoretical concepts, but to report what they found and to suggest what conclusions seemed indicated.

During this same period of the 1930s, busy administrators such as Secretary of the Interior Harold Ickes, David Lilienthal of the Tennessee Valley Authority, and others were inspired to keep diaries describing their own day-to-day decisions and the consequences thereof. In addition, colloquies of public officials were arranged, such as that of the Brookings Institution reported by Marver H. Bernstein in *The Job of the Federal Executive.*[17] These sessions were widely recorded by stenotype, and the transcripts became, in effect, the material of potential data banks for later consultation by scholars and government officials.

Activity of this kind has been much less common since 1960 than it was earlier, which is perhaps an unfortunate oversight. The limiting factor has been financial, plus the growing popularity of studies based upon more highly refined models. If data banks are to develop for the benefit of public administration, however, it would seem that more of the earlier, anthropological type of study would have to be undertaken.

Another major method of collecting empirical data is the case study. Starting a little later than the capture-and-record studies, the case approach has had a continuous existence, is gaining momentum, and is now found in many countries.

In the United States, the leader in the case method has been the Inter-University Case Program, financed by foundations and a number of participating universities and directed by a competent staff. The original organization, called the Committee on Public Administration Case Studies, was created in 1948 and in 1951 was succeeded by the present Inter-University Case Series. The first compilation of cases was brought together in 1952 by Harold Stein, a member of the program staff, under the title *Public Administration and Policy Development.*[18] More than

100 monographs have now been produced, covering all aspects of public administration at all levels of government. Edwin A. Bock, the director of the program, has also prepared a separate volume especially for the use of state and local officials.[19] Another important contribution is that of the Harvard Case Clearing House, which has accumulated thousands of cases.

As a result of these efforts, the public administration profession now has convincing proof of the value of the case method for the systematic collection of data on which to base reliable generalization; and, of course, the methodology is invaluable in the establishment of data banks, now so widely in demand.

Considering the whole of the information-systems revolution of the past generation, therefore, it is perhaps not too sanguine to suggest that before long the public administrator will have easy access to current, reliable data that will place him in as favorable a position in the practice of his profession as the physician or the engineer are in theirs; and, indeed, his profession resembles theirs in many ways. No inherent element prevents information systems from being made available to program directors as well as to central staff agencies. Although expense is, of course, a major factor, it is necessary only to review how television has developed from local to worldwide diffusion. We then realize that in less time than is now supposed, data banks can be made widely available, even to public officials remote from the center and occupying the lowest ranks of the organizational pyramid. Moreover, when difficulties of vocabulary have been overcome and data are interpreted in terms the layman can readily assimilate, the result will be a wider public understanding of government, of its programs and problems, and of its role in society.

If public administrators were so naive as to search for complete solutions by simply consulting data banks, however, the results would be disappointing if not unfortunate, for factors such as values and sentiments must also be considered before valid decisions are possible. But if the computer revolution is regarded as a challenge to the public administrator to become more independent and more fully in command of the problems with which he must deal, then the profession might take the next long step in devising the solutions that modern complexities demand.

CASE STUDY: DEVELOPING EXECUTIVE SKILLS BY THE STATISTICAL METHOD

State personnel officer Michelle Ross recently interviewed the personnel manager of a large multinational corporation that has long enjoyed a reputation for picking and developing executive potential. To protect his identity we shall call him William James. What follows is a true account of what transpired between these two.

William James said, yes, his company spent two and a half times the national average spent by 30 businesses that are doing research on executive skills under an arrangement in which these 30 firms pool their research findings. No one knows for sure, said James, the extent to which individual potential is inborn or developed through experience. There may be three main types of skill: conceptual, technical, and social. This breakdown, however, may be too generalized. Instead of developing a list of traits that are assumed to be universal, James's company decided to rely upon *biographies* and *statistical comparisons*. This step was based on concrete evidence that skills can be developed if reliable data are secured dealing with the company's future replacement needs and the potential of each individual in the group being considered for promotion. James said that his company's methodology had been influenced by the ideas found in a book by M. Joseph Docher and Vivienne Marquis, *The Development of Executive Talent*.[20] Technical skills are more easily developed through formal education than are conceptual skills or skills in human relations. Conceptual skills are more difficult to isolate and test because they relate to mind set, temperament, and character. Social skills may also be taught, but if they depend too largely on imitation rather than values, they may not approach scientific precision.

The essence of his company's plan, said James, was to discover reliable statistical differences between two control groups involved in the comparison. The choice of the statistical method was based upon five related steps. The first was to study the present management group to discover what the company's future needs would be. The second was to decide who was capable of filling those future needs. The third was to develop a replacement table outlining who would take over the vacancies as they occurred. The fourth was to determine, on the basis of biographies, the training and experience needs of those persons who were believed to have the potential for moving up. The final step was to develop tailor-made programs for those candidates.

James pointed out that during World War II the army had discovered that biographical differences between successful and nonsuccessful officers gave valuable information for selecting candidates from among enlisted men for development into future officers.

Hence the statistical formula: develop statistically significant data that will show *differences* between successful executives and those who have not succeeded, that is, who would not be promoted. At this point the control groups become necessary. If there are *enough* kinds of determinable factors, and values, or weights, can be assigned according to the frequency of occurrences of *differences* between the executives and a matched sample of nonexecutives, and if the data on a candidate give him a score comparable to those of the present executive group, the assumption is justified that such a candidate will match an executive being replaced in terms of potential. Furthermore, this approach makes it possible to include test scores or any other data that can be objectively obtained.

We have already established to our own satisfaction that this statistical method works reliably for certain lower-level forms of employment, such as foremen, salesmen, and those who use intangible skills rather than specific work that can be observed or inspected, stated James.

How does a person prepare for the big jump to a higher post? James mentioned two ways. One is learning by doing—we call this process training. The other is by participating in training programs we operate in our company, in which we are particularly intent on developing the individual's conceptual skill.

Earlier, you mentioned the importance of social skills, said Ross. Just how important are they?

Very, replied James. Such skills are one of the three guidelines we have: recognize the importance of the individual, accept the concept of cooperative effort, and understand the place of organized groups. Our top executives are teams, not prima donnas. We believe that a good executive makes a smoothly functioning team out of people with different skills and backgrounds and that his most important function is to reconcile, coordinate, compromise, and appraise the various viewpoints and talents under his direction to the end that each individual contributes his full measure to the business at hand.

These statistical comparisons you speak of, do you feed a lot of data into computers? asked Ross.

We could, and we sometimes do, replied James. But we also use other methods of checking the results thus produced. We can never be sure we've fed in things that have equal weight. Also, at times our intuitions and experiences seem to be more reliable than our unweighted scores. It's like adding apples and oranges. The computer is *one* tool, not the only tool, by any means. We're afraid that if we use computers too exclusively, we may stop thinking as sharply as we need to.

Questions:

1. What is your reaction to the methodology used in testing people's potential to be executives?
2. Are you satisfied with using the existing, successful group of executives as the standard of comparison? If not, what workable alternative is there?
3. Would you expect this method to throw reliable light on executive traits in general? (The company, after trial, thought it did.)
4. Do you think this private sector approach would work in government?
5. Do you agree with what was said about computers? Would you use them exclusively for scoring?

SUMMARY

In this chapter we have dealt primarily with computers and data banks, the information revolution. Theoretically, if people had all the facts at their fingertips, their potential for controlling the environment and their well-being would be almost limitless. But who sifts the facts, makes the decisions, and puts plans into effect? Executives. Managers. The rationale is that they will have more time to think. In 50 or 100 years from now it will be interesting to see how this prediction has stood up. In the 1960s when the National Conference Board (a prestigious business research organization) commissioned a predictive study of government in the year 2000, the main conclusion of that study was that the communications revolution would alter public management and in doing so solve stubborn problems heretofore insufficiently addressed. This change would occur, in part at least, because of the availability of a wealth of analyzed facts, alternatives, costs, methods, and all the rest that were formerly not available. The National Conference Board also predicted that after the computer revolution had been in process for a few years, everything would be different. Fine talk. Possibly true. But the best minds with the best intentions had better be in control of the machine or management might on occasion prove as powerless as the merchant whose order didn't arrive because the computer broke down.

NOTES

1. *Data Management* 14 (February 1976): 39.

2. Kenneth L. Kraemer and John Leslie King, *Computers and Local Government* (New York: Praeger, 1977), vol. 1, *A Manager's Guide,* p. 23.

3. *Statistical Abstract of the United States,* 100th ed. (Washington: U.S. Dept. of Commerce, U.S. Bureau of the Census, 1979), p. 621.

4. Norbert Wiener, *The Human Use of Human Beings,* rev. ed. (New York: Doubleday, 1954).

5. U.S., Bureau of the Budget, *Automatic Data Processing Glossary* (Washington: U.S. Government Printing Office, 1962), p. 40.

6. Charles J. Sippl, *Computer Dictionary and Handbook* (Indianapolis: Howard W. Sams, 1966), p. 67.

7. "Two False Alerts Traced to 46¢ Item," *New York Times,* 18 June 1980, p. 14.

8. Public Automated Systems Service, *Automatic Data Processing in Municipal Government* (Chicago: Public Administration Service, 1965).

9. Dennis J. Palumbo, *Program Development and Administration* (Chicago: International City Management Association, 1965).

10. Palumbo, *Program Development and Administration,* p. 65 [italics in original].

11. Geoffrey Y. Cornog, "Change, Management, and Electronic Data Processing in State and Local Government," in Geoffrey Y. Cornog et al., *EDP Systems in Public Management* (Chicago: Rand McNally, 1968), p. 8. See also Harold Hovey, "Some Perspectives on Data Processing in State Government," in *Computer Systems and Public Administrators,* ed. Richard A. Bassler and Norman L. Enger (Alexandria, Va.: College Readings, 1976).

12. "Judge Refuses Man's Request to Let Him Become a Number," *New York Times,* 14 February 1978, p. 31.

13. Maurice F. Ronayne, "'Leads' to Pertinent ADP Literature for the Public Administrator," *Public Administration Review* 24 (June–July 1964): 119–125.

14. Elmer Staats, "Management Information Needs in an Era of Change" (Address before the Washington Chapter, National Association of Accountants, Washington, 20 September 1967), p. 17.

15. Palumbo, *Program Development and Administration,* p. 65.

16. These studies were all published by the Public Administration Service, Chicago. Among them are Arthur W. Macmahon, John D. Millett, and Gladys Ogden, *The Administration of Federal Work Relief* (1941); John M. Gaus and Leon O. Woolcott, *Public Administration and the United States Department of Agriculture* (1940): Robert H. Connery, *The Administration of an N.R.A. Code* (1938); and V. O. Key, Jr., *The Administration of Federal Grants to States* (1937).

17. Marver H. Bernstein, *The Job of the Federal Executive* (Washington: Brookings Institution, 1958).

18. Harold Stein, ed., *Public Administration and Policy Development: A Case Book* (New York: Harcourt Brace & World, 1952).

19. Edwin A. Bock, ed., *State and Local Government: A Case Book* (Tuscaloosa: University of Alabama Press, 1963).

20. M. Joseph Docher and Vivienne Marquis, *The Development of Executive Talent* (New York: AMACOM, 1952).

PART 4

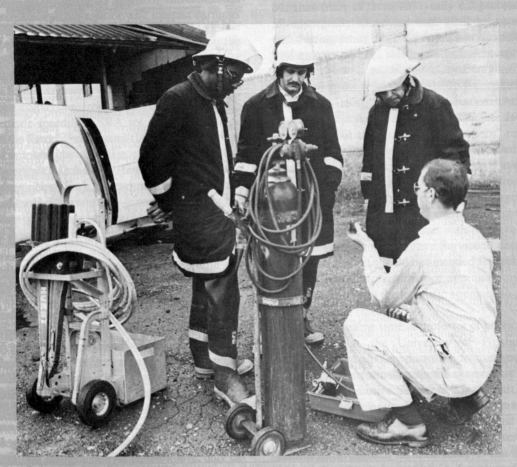

Rescue workers gather for a training session. (Photo courtesy of the Port Authority of New York & New Jersey)

18

Working for Government

Management is, in the end, the most creative of all the arts, for its medium is human talent itself.

Robert McNamara

In this chapter, we first deal with vocational opportunities in the public service. We then consider, by use of the interview method, the classic concerns and present-day challenges of a career as a personnel officer.

DIMENSIONS OF THE PUBLIC SECTOR

Various governments in the United States employ zoo keepers, railroad engineers, nuclear physicists, professional chefs, and executioners, as well as butchers, bakers, and candlestick makers. This is the human side of government. It presents the public service executive with most of his opportunities and challenges. If government becomes lethargic and excessively bureaucratic, the basic remedy must be sought in human nature, not machinery. On the other hand, if government becomes dynamic and full of energy, as it sometimes does, then the explanation must likewise be sought in human nature, specifically in motivation and morale.

There are five good reasons why we start by considering the size of public employment. First, it gives a sense of career perspectives. Second, it throws light on the claim that government is overgrown and needs to be reduced to size. Third, it clarifies the functions of government. Fourth, it is a good way of approaching the question of why American government has such difficulty coordinating and cooperating. And finally it points to the great diversity of skills the manager is somehow supposed to bring together and make coalesce.

The statistics of government employment are rarely, if ever, completely up to date. Also, there is some understandable doubt as to what to include and what to leave out. For example, is the postal service, administered by a public corporation, "government," or is it not? Are the armed forces governmental or is there some reason for putting them in a distinctive category?

According to recent estimates, government employment may be analyzed as follows:[1]

Total Civilian Employment (federal, state, local)— 16.5 million. This figure is approximately 18 percent of the total U.S. labor force. Uniformed military number another 2 million plus.

Government Distribution—State and local employment exceeds federal employment by a ratio of five to one.

State and Local Employment—13.6 million at the end of 1980.

Federal Employment—2.9 million (1980). At the end of 1980 federal departments and agencies employed a direct civilian *and* military work force of about 5 million with an annual cost of $120 billion.

State Employment—3.7 million (1980).

Local Employment—9.9 million (1980).

Perspectives are increased by considering *recent trends,* some of which are illustrated by Figure 18.1.

Federal, State, Local Employment. State and local employment have increased sharply in recent years while federal civilian employment has shown some decline.

State and Local Employment. Total employment increased more than 130 percent in the 20-year period 1958–1978.

Federal Employment. Of total federal employment 60 percent is in defense, foreign relations, and the postal service. That leaves only 40 percent in what is commonly called the bureaucracy. This last figure amounted to 1.2 million in 1978.

Public and Private Employment. Total private em-

Figure 18.1 How Government Employment Has Grown

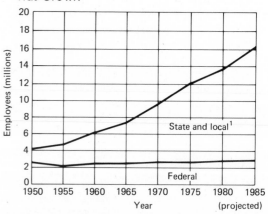

[1]Includes public education.

SOURCE: U.S. Department of Labor, Bureau of Labor Statistics, *Government Occupations,* Bulletin 1955–42 (Washington: U.S. Government Printing Office, 1978), p. 2.

ployment increased 47.7 percent in the 20-year period 1958–1978. State and local employment expanded by more than 130 percent during the same period.

Although the administration of Ronald Reagan was determined to reduce public employment, by 1982 no substantial changes in the above figures had been made.

A final way of rounding out the analysis is to consider *major functions.*

In a recent year (1978) when the federal government's actual purchase of goods and services amounted to $145 billion, two thirds of this was for *defense.*

Education accounts for the single, largest, peacetime activity, with 42 percent of all public employees being found there.

Health care accounts for another 10 percent, meaning that health and education total more than half of public service employment. Welfare activities were 3 percent. From careful reading of the above, it comes as no surprise that only 12 percent of federal employment is found in Washington, the rest being widely distributed throughout the country. Also to be expected is that the largest industrial states, California and New York, accounted for a fifth of total government employment. But it should be noted that in the least populous states the *ratio* of public employment to total population figures is higher than in more populous states.

On the basis of the above, the Committee for Economic Development (CED) study *Improving Management of the Public Work Force: The Challenge to State and Local Government* remarked in 1978:

The fact is that although the federal government collects and distributes enormous amounts of tax money, the preponderance of government administration (about 80 percent of nondefense purchases of goods and services) takes place at state and local levels.[2]

The federal government is like a bank or a holding company. The bulk of line administration takes place in the field.

Structural Analysis of Employment

In understanding government manpower in the United States, it is desirable to recognize that there are many forms of employment. The largest by far is the civil service. This term is used in at least two ways: first, descriptively to characterize any employment that is professionalized, and second—the more common way—to mean a legal system in which the legislative body lays down rules for hiring, promotion, and the like and where people have "permanence," that is, where they cannot be fired except for limited reasons stated in law.

We shall deal with civil service more fully soon, but at this point we offer an overview of relationships in the different levels of government. (Box 18.1 should be examined along with the following remarks.)

Federal Government. The first distinction is between "political," which involves elective office, and "appointive," which involves choice by someone higher in authority.

Civil service positions peak at GS 18. Above GS 18 a new nomenclature begins for cabinet and other politically appointive officials such as undersecretaries and assistant secretaries, agency heads, bureau chiefs, members of commissions and independent agencies. There are Schedule I-V positions in this group, beginning at around $50,000 a year, where GS 18 leaves off.

In the federal government, the president and vice president are elected, and the cabinet heads are appointed by the president to help make policy. The undersecretaries and assistant secretaries of departments are appointive and also have policy duties; below them is the permanent civil service, which is more than 98 percent of total employees.

There are exceptions to the civil service. These are so-called excepted positions, which are political appointments and not under civil service. They are often used in starting new programs. Their use in the federal government has varied by periods, tending to be less in recent years. In ad-

Box 18.1

STRUCTURE FOR PERSONNEL MANAGEMENT

Government personnel policy should not be restricted to any one class of employees. Rather, it should promote the personal development and effective use of all the people employed by government. However, appropriate policies and practices may vary according to the different roles and responsibilities of government employees.

- **Top Policy Makers.** Elected officials are selected directly by the public and usually appoint other top personnel to serve at their pleasure. The principal criterion guiding the selection and behavior of top policy officials is appropriately political. Nevertheless, public personnel policy should not neglect the development and best use of the analytic and managerial abilities and time of those in policy positions.
- **Professional Managers.** People in managerial positions bear the principal responsibility for the operation of government. They should be guided by, and judged primarily on, criteria of professional capability

and performance. The conditions of their employment (hiring, compensation, assignment, promotion, and discharge) should be largely insulated from political considerations. At the same time, they should be subject to the direction of, and accountable to, top policy makers. An approach that balances these professional and political needs is required. Certain classes of professional, technical, and confidential employees should be treated similarly.

- **Other Employees.** A more formal personnel structure is required for the other employees of government, who constitute the greatest proportion of the public work force. At this level, in particular, the laws and regulations of civil service and so-called merit systems have become rigid to the detriment of performance, and the advent of collective bargaining has tended to cause confusion and tension with more traditional personnel procedures.

SOURCE: *Improving Management of the Public Work Force: The Challenge to State and Local Government* (New York: Committee for Economic Development, 1978), p. 18.

---

tion, there are contract appointments, consultancies, and temporary positions, all of which are outside the permanent civil service.

Military personnel are not considered part of the civil service. However, working alongside them are thousands of civil servants doing so-called civilian work, making this category the single largest group of civil servants in the U.S. government.

In Congress, there are 100 elected senators and 438 elected members of the House of Representatives. Counting the personal staffs of members, however, plus the staffs of committees

of both houses, the appointive employees outnumber the elected members by a ratio of more than 30 to 1. This tendency began with the passage of the Legislative Organization Act of 1946 and has accelerated in recent years. Between 1970 and 1980, for example, the total staffs of members and committees increased from around 11,000 to almost 17,000. As might be expected, there were twice as many in the House of Representatives as in the Senate.[3]

In the judiciary, the judges of the Supreme Court, the courts of appeal, and the district courts are appointive and have life tenure, forming a kind of civil service of their own. In addition there is a larger number of strictly "administrative" officers. These are so numerous, in fact, that in the federal government and in a growing number of the 50 states they are organized into a professionalized Administrative Service. They work in and outside the courts, some being U.S. marshals and the like, and tie into the Justice Department. Others do administrative work reporting to the judges themselves. Total employment in the judicial branch of the U.S. government in 1980 was 15,200.[4]

State government. The configuration in the 50 states is similar to that of the federal government. Many states, however, have been reluctant to adopt the term civil service for a variety of reasons: some because they disliked the term, others because they saw faults in the federal civil service they wanted to avoid, others because political parties and partisan appointments predominated. By contrast, some states have been in advance of the federal government in their attachment to and improvement of the civil service system.

The hierarchy in the executive branch is the governor and other elective officers such as attorney-general, the appointive and elected department heads, civil servants, and excepted positions.

The increase in staffing, noted earlier for Congress, applies also to state legislatures and courts. In a recent six-year period, for example, there was an increase of 600 percent for committee staffs alone.[5]

Local Government. The city, town, or county may or may not have a formal civil service system; only the larger communities are likely to. Therefore, some department heads are under civil service and some are political appointees. The rest of the employees may or may not be under civil service, again depending primarily on the size of the community. Partly because of size and partly because service is closer to the citizens, local governments, by and large, have the best public administration to be found anywhere in the United States.

Diversity of Positions

It has often been said that somewhere or other in government employment every kind of job is to be found. Since this statement does not explain where the *concentrations* of employment are to be found, Box 18.2 gives a hint about the range of employment opportunities, while Table 18.1 lists federal pay rates. State and local governments pay less.

It is also possible to compare parallels between concentrations in private industry and government employment by occupation, as shown in Table 18.2.[6] In other words, industry led slightly in the percentage of managers and outdistanced government in blue-collar workers. Government led in professional workers by a large margin and also had a larger percentage of clerical and service workers.

Comparing federal and state-local distributions, one finds the federal government leading in national defense and international relations by a wide margin; it also leads in the postal service and in natural resources. State and local governments enjoy a wide margin in education, police protection, highways, and general control. There is not much disparity in health care and financial administration, except that the federal government is higher in the latter.

At all levels, but especially at the federal level, an acute shortage of high-ranking executives and professionals has developed in recent times. This trend is caused primarily by the fact that large numbers of capable people were recruited in the 1930s and 1940s (New Deal and World War II) and have reached retirement. So formidable was this replacement obligation that first the U.S. Civil Service Commission and later the Office of Personnel Management, which replaced it, could be said to be almost panicky at the prospect.

PERSONNEL MANAGEMENT: A CHALLENGING PROFESSION

The transition from the broader employment opportunities we have been discussing to those of a

Box 18.2

REPRESENTATIVE VOCATIONAL OPPORTUNITIES IN THE PUBLIC SERVICE (FEDERAL, STATE, LOCAL, AS OF 1979)

A survey of 62 common job classes in the public sector:

account clerk	dentist	physician
accountant (4 grades)	electrician	plumber
admin. analyst	engineering aide (junior)	police lieutenant
admin. analyst (senior)	fire captain	police patrolman
admin. trainee	fire fighter	police sergeant
attorney (3 grades)	fire lieutenant	psychiatric social worker
auditor (2 grades)	heavy equipment operator	public health physician
automotive mechanic	information representative	real property appraiser
bacteriologist	job analyst (2 grades)	recreation leader
carpenter	keypunch operator	sanitarian
case work supervisor	laborer	social case worker
chemist	librarian (junior)	stationary fireman
city planner	librarian	stenographer
civil engineer (3 grades)	machine records executive	tabulating machine operator
clerk	medical records librarian	telephone operator
clinical lab. technologist	nurse (2 grades)	typist
computer operator	nursing assistant	veterinarian
computer programmer		

SOURCE: *Pay Rates in the Public Service* (Washington: International Personnel Management Association, 1979).

principal staff agency, personnel management, is really not great. Both are concerned with the human factor in government, about which much has yet to be learned.

In the following conversation we talked with a woman who was the director of personnel in one of the 50 states. We assumed that a good way to gain a sense of personnel management is to talk with a person who is considered a success at it.

One of the first things she told us is that no two states are exactly alike and that the larger ones differ from the smaller. She also admitted that she has a management point of view, which, until a few years ago, was not common.

The Function of the Personnel Chief

Q. How many people are there in the personnel management profession for the public sector in the United States?

A. According to the Bureau of the Census and the U.S. Labor Department there are now almost 100,000.

Q. One hundred thousand for 16 million employees at all levels of government—not a bad ratio.

A. In addition there are administrative assistants who do much personnel work and also budget people and those who handle politi-

TABLE 18.1 Federal Pay and Jobs

There are 550 different white-collar occupations within the 18 general schedule grades in the federal government. Here are current pay scales for typical jobs in each of those grades.

Grade	Example of type of job	Average pay	Lowest pay	Top pay
1	File clerk	$ 7,293	$ 7,210	$ 9,125
2	Beginning typist	$ 8,308	$ 8,128	$10,327
3	Beginning personnel clerk	$ 9,570	$ 8,952	$11,634
4	Beginning computer operator	$11,163	$10,049	$13,064
5	Beginning accountant	$12,754	$11,243	$14,618
6	Midlevel computer operator	$14,434	$12,531	$16,293
7	Midlevel chemist	$15,738	$13,925	$18,101
8	Experienced secretary	$17,898	$15,423	$20,049
9	Beginning attorney	$19,103	$17,035	$22,147
10	Electronics technician	$21,261	$18,760	$24,385
11	Experienced auditor	$23,263	$20,611	$26,794
12	Experienced accountant	$27,963	$24,703	$32,110
13	Personnel director	$33,607	$29,375	$38,186
14	Experienced attorney	$39,651	$34,713	$45,126
15	Chief chemist	$46,754	$40,832	$50,113
16–18	Top career officials	$49,867(est.)	$47,889	$50,113

How to apply. For information about federal jobs and how to apply, visit, write or call your nearest Federal Job Information Center. It's listed in the telephone white pages under "U.S. Government" in most metropolitan areas. If you don't find a listing, contact the local state employment office or call or write your congressman.

SOURCE: U.S. Office of Personnel Management, 1980.

cal appointments. Yes, the ratio is not too bad, but it is growing.

Q. Parkinson's Law? (We were making the tongue-in-cheek observation that work expands to fill the time available for its completion.)

A. Perhaps, but it is also because legislatures pass more and more laws in areas where they assign us the responsibility.

Q. Such as?

A. Social security, occupational safety, pensions, labor relations.

Q. To the point where you sometimes wonder if you're stressing the central function?

A. If you mean understanding people singly and in groups and improving morale, yes.

Q. How are these 100,000 personnel experts distributed?

TABLE 18.2 Types of Jobs, in Percentages

Occupation	Government	Private
Managers-administrators	8	10
Professional-technical workers	36	11
Clerical workers	24	18
Blue-collar workers	14	39
Service workers	18	13

A. About half are found in the 50 state governments. The federal government has 25,000 to 30,000. The new OPM (Office of Personnel Management) created under the Civil Service Reform Act of 1978 has 8,000. Defense has more personnel people than anyone else, but it also has more employees than anyone else. The balance of the 100,000 work for local governments; except in large cities, local personnel agencies are quite small.

Q. Isn't there a danger that central personnel agencies like your own might become too large? They might try to regiment too much.

A. Agreed. But it is also argued that if they aren't large enough, the merit system will be undermined by partisan appointments.

Q. Can numbers alone guarantee that?

A. Of course not.

Q. Do you have professional associations?

A. Yes, lots of them. The International Personnel Management Association, in Chicago, has quite an extensive publication program. But so does PAS (Public Administration Service) and ICMA (International City Management Association) and a number of others.

Q. Is there much mixing between the private and public sectors?

A. Yes, a lot. We read each other's stuff and there is also considerable movement back and forth between the corporate and governmental areas.

Growth of the Profession

Q. When did the personnel field begin to blossom?

A. With the coming of the New Deal. And this both in private and public employment.

Q. The Wagner Act of 1935?

A. Yes, that had a lot to do with it. But social security, two years earlier, gave the expansion its impetus. The U.S. Employment Service was created. The Wage and Hour Division of the U.S. Department of Labor was started. Unemployment insurance also began in the early 1930s.

Q. What was the state of preparation at this time? Were there outstanding thinkers in this field?

A. Fortunately, there were. One was an Englishman, Elton Mayo, who came to the United States and wrote on the human problems of business and society as a whole. Another was an American woman, Mary Parker Follett, who went to England, came back to the United States, and wrote books on getting along together in groups; she was a political scientist and one of the greatest. There were others; F. J. Roethlisberger of Hawthorne experiment fame, for instance, Ordway Tead, Eric Fromm, and Douglas MacGregor. America has an enviable reputation in the field of personnel theory.

Q. Hawthorne? That was the one where in Western Electric they found out that the more attention to and interest in people you show, the better they will put forth?

A. Yes, they like to be treated like human beings. And they like to develop some feeling of identity and being important.

Q. Well, all this large number of 100,000. Are they all professionals?

A. Not if you mean are they all executives. Quite a large number have clerical designations.

Q. Is there a lot of specialization?

A. Yes, in some areas, such as position classification, preparing new kinds of examinations, the legal aspects of the work, investigations and hearings, and the like.

Q. Too much specialization?

A. When it tends toward stratification and bureaucratic rigidity, yes. Such things are supposed to be the opposite of what we're trying to attain.

Preparation for Personnel Work

Q. Now the crucial question: What is the best way to prepare for a personnel career?

A. There is no one best way.

Q. Why not psychology?

A. We once thought so. Certainly motivation, drives, personality development, are primarily the psychologist's interest. But in recent years training in psychology has changed.

Q. For the worse?

A. Yes, when it results in being interested in only clinical results. I mean by that measurement. People are treated as statistical units or interesting specimens to be experimented with. We have too many psychologists of that kind.[7]

Q. Then you are opposed to psychology majors?

A. Not at all. But I want the kind who think like managers and have some warmth and feeling about them.

Q. Where else do personnel managers come from?

A. Nowadays the largest number come out of management itself. They may study public administration or any one of a number of things, like history or law, or English and science, go to work for the government, discover that their interest lies in personnel matters, and thereafter get more education.

Q. Is there a type of person who does well in personnel?

A. Unquestionably. He is interested in people, likes them, understands them or tries to, relates to them and gains their confidence. He is sympathetic and objective at the same time, reads omnivorously and constantly expands his knowledge. He is down-to-earth, not the armchair type, and has good judgment.

Q. The kind someone like the governor would enjoy talking to?

A. Yes, or a top businessman who thinks he's pretty good.

Q. No place for the thinker?

A. Oh, to be sure. We need as many types as are found in the programs we service.

Q. You spoke earlier about the smaller county and local governments having little formal personnel organization. Could you explain that a bit further?

A. Yes. In 1980 the federal Office of Personnel Management and the Council of State Governments made a survey. They found that between 40 and 50 percent of the cities and counties surveyed lacked the professional leadership of a full-time personnel director.

Q. Then who does handle personnel matters in these small governments?

A. That's the trouble—no one has a clear responsibility. Various kinds of officials in small county governments are handling this matter for the locality, and they resist efforts to turn this responsibility over to trained personnel people. Accordingly, a great challenge of administration in small governments is to stress the importance of administrators who can coordinate the efforts of local personnel. The report concluded, "We've spent too much time and concern on big government and not enough on the most common kind of city administration, one with 100 employees and less." One of the problems of local government is that the local council is made up of part-timers, who do not look to the future of the town, just at policies and programs vital while they are in office. And so they look at personnel systems as just so much more bureaucracy.

The Range of Personnel Functions

Q. Do you have a checklist of personnel functions?

A. Yes, but I hesitate to get at the crux of the matter in this fashion. The personnel director needs a philosophy of his job. By that I mean a comprehension of how everything fits together as a whole.

I would give first place to *recruitment* of qualified people. Second is the *classification* of jobs and roles within the organization structure so as to know what to recruit for. Next is to determine *salary scales* in order to attract employees of the ability needed. Fourth is to determine *competence,* or merit, either by written examinations or by merely gaining an accurate insight into the work experience of the individual and his future motivation. Fifth is to determine a *promotion* policy; for if able people are not promoted, they will quit the service or remain frustrated; and if mediocre people are promoted merely because of seniority, the program will suffer. And sixth is to *train* employees in order to develop new skills, refresh people who have been on the job so long that they need a new outlook, guide professional people in developing administrative skills, and prepare for top leadership in the program.

Q. Are there other functions?

A. Yes. *Counseling* is a common function in most personnel systems. You get better results by treating employees as individuals instead of as impersonal production units. This is probably the greatest opportunity for innovation in the whole of personnel work. Then there is the important question of *retirement* benefits. Closely related to it is the matter of *fringe* benefits. Government employment is a package, and its attractiveness cannot be judged by salary alone. I refer here to such things as life insurance, health insurance, paid vacations, recreation associations—the list is constantly expanding.

Then there is *productivity* analysis, which is used as the basis of pay, position, and promotion. Employees need to be weeded out, demoted, and transferred when they are not meeting required standards or need to be disciplined. There is the whole question of *labor relations,* which in some ways has become the most taxing and challenging area of all. Labor relations and personnel work, though at higher levels they are separated, cannot be kept independent of each other at the program level of management. I might add, as Table 18.3 indicates, that there is substantial reform activity in these areas in many states.

Q. How about equality of treatment?

A. Just treatment is the cornerstone of good personnel work. It takes the positive form of equality of opportunity. Also equal work for equal pay. In a good personnel system women should be treated as equitably as men. Color, race, national origin—in all such matters the personnel director and employers should be colorblind. If the idea of merit did nothing else, it would be worthwhile for its insistence upon this. (Chapter 20 deals with this problem at greater length.)

Q. How about codes of ethics?

A. Yes, they are often a good idea. If people set their own standards, they often do not require negative sanctions in the form of punishment to keep them in line.

Pay Policy

Q. I gather that compensation is one of your crucial areas?

A. Yes, to be sure. This is one of the areas in which there has been the most improvement in the past decade. The idea of comparability of pay for positions of the same difficulty in the private and public sectors has now been acknowledged. Top salaries are as high in some state and local governments as in the federal pay scale. With all the fringe benefits that public employment now provides, the economic incentive to work in public administration is now as satisfactory as in the private sector and the professions, except in top management.

Q. Could you be a bit more specific?

A. The *Public Sector Compensation Report,*[8] prepared by the American Management Association, brought out some interesting points in 1980. These are summarized as follows:

- Virtually every participating government in the survey now provides employees with basic hospital, medical, dental, and group life insurance.
- Average salary for a mayor ranges from $19,300 for cities with less than 50,000 to $42,000 for 200,000 or over. Compensation for fire commissioners ranges from $22,000 to $35,800; for police commissioner, $22,800 to $37,500.
- Coverage for long-term disability is provided by about 35 percent of the participants in each of the city and county governments, with the employer paying the complete premium in almost every instance.
- A mandatory retirement age is in effect in 61 percent of the cities and 47 percent of the counties, with 70 years of age stipulated by more than two out of three of the respondents.

Q. This report, I take it, dealt primarily with state and local governments? The tops in federal civil service, I believe, is around $50,000?

A. Yes. For civil servants, that is; for political appointees it is higher.

Q. Why are salaries in the executive and judicial branches of the federal government tied to congressional compensation? I believe they are supposed to go no higher than legislative salaries?

A. Yes, this has long been true. But it is changing. A Brookings Institution publication called *The Rewards of Public Service: Compensating Top Federal Officials* argued in 1980 that the traditional linkage between congressional salaries and those of other federal officials is an impediment to intelligent paysetting and should be abolished.[9]

This study dealt with the pay and benefits of top federal officials—the 2,500 congressmen, judges, cabinet members, and senior civil servants who run the federal establishment. They took a close look at how top-level salary determination affects the pay and benefits of 30,000 other employees at lower levels in the executive branch.

Q. They concluded that the congressional ceiling should be taken off?

A. Yes. Any difficulty Congress has in adjusting compensation for its own members should not be a stumbling block for others. Job requirements and the relevant labor markets differ greatly among the three branches of government. Judicial salaries should be equated with other legal salaries, top civil service salaries with comparable salaries in business. The current system of reviewing every four years the pay of top officials by the Commission on Executive, Legislative, and Judicial Salaries is an awkward, political, and irrational method of trying to fix salaries in the executive and judicial branches.

Q. Then in some cases, you would favor paying top civil servants—those in the new Senior Executive Service—more than congressmen or even politically appointed cabinet officers?

A. Yes, and more than judges, if that is necessary. Pay what it takes to get the best executives. Business finds it pays. The TVA (Tennessee Valley Authority) did it in its early years. I consider it good business.

Q. You say that in progressive cities and states the levels of salaries compare favorably with those at the federal level?

A. Yes, and in some cases, such as some school systems, New York or California, for example, or some manager governments, it may be even higher for some top positions.

Q. How about people in your field? Personnel management?

A. The same applies here. An employment security interviewer, for example, earned be-

TABLE 18.3 State and Local Government Reform

Governments in 32 states are pursuing civil service reform programs in the areas of

	Senior executive service	Merit pay	Labor relations	Performance appraisal system	Decentralization of personnel functions	Protection for "whistle blowers"	Veterans' preference and benefits
Alabama							
Alaska			•				
American Samoa							
Arizona			•				
Arkansas		•		•			
California			•			•	•
Colorado	•			•	•	•	
Connecticut	•	•				•	
Delaware							
District of Columbia							
Florida	•		•		•		
Georgia	•			•			
Guam							
Hawaii		•		•		•	•
Idaho		•				•	
Illinois		•	•	•			•
Indiana							
Iowa	•						•
Kansas				•	•		•

302

TABLE 18.3 *(continued)*

	Goverments in 32 states are pursuing civil service reform programs in the areas of						
	Senior executive service	Merit pay	Labor relations	Performance appraisal system	Decentralization of personnel functions	Protection for "whistle blowers"	Veterans' preference and benefits
South Carolina							
South Dakota							
Tennessee				•			
Texas						•	
Trust Territory							
Utah						•	
Vermont		•		•			
Virginia					•		
Virgin Islands							
Washington	•	•		•			
West Virginia							
Wisconsin	•				•		•
Wyoming							

SOURCE: U.S. Office of Personnel Management, "Civil Service Reform: A Report on the First Year," January 1980, p. 24.

tween $18,000 and $21,000 in the top 1978 state salary, which compares favorably with what someone could do in Washington.

Q. What kind of a degree does it take to be an employment security interviewer?

A. A bachelor's or master's degree.

Q. The salary would be higher now?

A. Yes, a recent study showed it would be at least 10 percent higher in 1980.

Q. Are there any jobs at the state level that are more or less different from those at the federal level?

A. Yes, I would say so. There is a lot of vocational rehabilitation, for example, also civil defense, conservation, corrections, probation and parole, employment service, hospital administration, and forestry. Then there is a whole new area that has come to be called human services. I don't say that the federal government has no such jobs; often it doesn't have such a concentration of them in the areas I've mentioned.

Various Kinds of Appointment

Q. Do you think everyone should be under civil service?

A. No, that would be too rigid. We need some flexibility here.

Q. You mean like heads of departments and cabinet officers, who are appointed by the president or governor, often with the approval of the Senate?

A. Yes. Under our system their job is to see that the policies of the winning political party and winning chief executive are carried out.

Q. And assistant secretaries?

A. Yes, they ought to be political appointees, too, though I would add that in recent years, especially at the federal level, there have come to be too many of them. They tend to interfere with the management responsibilities of program executives too much. They make the higher ranges of civil service less attractive.

Q. You mean they're not as well qualified to run programs as the higher career officials?

A. Often. And invariably they are less experienced.

Q. What other kinds of appointments are there?

A. The nomenclature differs. In general, though, there are contract employees, who are appointed for a particular job and time period and are outside the formal civil service system. Then there are consultants, who are also contract employees. Finally, there are temporary employees—say for a summer, or something like that. And there are "excepted" employees, for example, the dollar-a-year businessmen. Usually they are used in time of crisis, like depression or war. And some of them hold high positions.

Q. Do you favor their use?

A. In exceptional cases, yes, but I think it ought to be watched pretty carefully.

Q. Do you think swapping people between the private and public sectors is a good idea?

A. Yes, I think there ought to be lateral mobility. But again I think it ought to be based upon demonstrated ability and not merely a way of rewarding party faithful for ringing doorbells.

Q. Are patronage and spoils politics a problem in American government?

A. Yes. I think they are less of a problem than they used to be, but I think they will always be a difficulty even in the best governed states.

Q. Why is that?

A. There are various forms of unmerited appointment—the doorbell ringer who may be a good politician but can't do the job he's appointed to, the unqualified person who is appointed as a personal favor, the person who is kept out of employment because of race or religion or something else.

Q. Then I gather you favor mobility and flexibility but are opposed to political hacks or anything that violates the principle of fairness. Equality of treatment?

A. Yes, there are two kinds of antisocial behavior that weaken administration and government's reputation. Some are acts of commission and others of omission.

Q. Have you had any bad experiences of this kind?

A. Yes, who hasn't? Once a high official tried to put a plant in my personnel office who would favor only those of a particular religious denomination. I put an end to that but only after threatening an exposé. Another time some prison officials were fired because of brutal treatment and an attempt was made to find jobs for them in probation and parole. And again, the political party that had lost out in the last election tried to stack the deck with last-minute appointments for unqualified employees. I'm glad to say our review procedure stopped that. Also the threat of airing the matter in the press.

Q. When you openly oppose such things don't you run some risks?

A. Yes, but my view is that only by taking risks can you make progress. And if you lose out on grounds of principle there is someone elsewhere who will reward you for your courage.

Q. Do women make good executives?

A. Yes, some of the best.

Q. In some fields, such as education and social work, or in all?

A. Some have proved that they can succeed in any field.

Q. Do you favor feminine militancy?

A. Yes, when it is needed, but by now I think women have made their point.

Critical Areas

Q. One hears a lot of criticism of examining procedures in civil service. Also, when one talks to government administrators one frequently finds that position classification is carried to extreme lengths and hampers effective management. Do you think there is any ground for such criticisms?

A. Yes, this is an important check on our

impressions. But remember, the rule in examining technique is that you must also rate the rater. He or she is subject to prejudice and other human failings, as well.

Q. We should think it might be hard to judge whether a candidate has supervisory or managerial potential, even with all the methods you use.

A. Agreed. We never reach perfection. But we do try to be as fair and as insightful as possible.

Q. In the final analysis, is fairness the hard core of the merit system?

A. Yes, I think it is. If I were to reduce it to one word that word would be equity or the adjective equitable.

Position Classification

Q. You mentioned earlier that position classification has become a controversial area of public personnel administration.

A. Yes. The reason for this is that it pits the bureaucratic instincts of the personnel expert against the managerial instincts of the general manager. The first seeks complete specificity, which may lead to rigidity, whereas the program manager wants flexibility in order to develop teamwork. I happen to have here a takeoff on the absurdities of classification. Maybe you'd like to see it. [See Box 18.3.]

Q. Yes. I see what you mean.

A. Nevertheless, position classification is a good and necessary thing. A leading authority, Lawrence Appley, who used to work in the federal government and later headed the American Management Association, makes classification analysis the cornerstone of his thinking. If everyone from the top down had his duties and parameters carefully analyzed, the groundwork would be laid for doing a complete job. Teamwork and efficiency would be furthered, almost assured, as in any well-formulated plan. Everyone would know what his or her mandate is, and

Box 18.3

MEMORANDUM FOR THE DIRECTOR OF PERSONNEL

Proposed — Allocation of a position titled Director of Personnel, Industrial and Agrarian Priorities, GS-14

Description of duties and responsibilities:

1. Without direct or intermediate supervision, and with a broad latitude for independent judgment and discretion, the incumbent directs, controls, and regulates the movement of interstate commerce, representing a cross-section of the wealth of the American economy.

2. On the basis of personal judgment founded on past experience, the incumbent integrates the variable factors in an evolving situation and on the basis of rapid cogitation formulates a binding decision relative to the priority of flow in interstate and intrastate commerce both animate and inanimate. These decisions are irreversible and not subject to appellate review by a higher authority nor can they be reversed by the legal determination of any echelon of our judicial complex.

3. The decisions of the incumbent are important since they effect with great finality the movement of agricultural products, forest products, minerals, manufactured goods, machine tools, construction equipment, military personnel, defense materials, raw materials and products, finished goods, and semifinished products; and they affect small business, large business, public utilities, and government agencies.

4. In the effective implementation of these responsibilities the incumbent must exercise initiative, ingenuity, imagination, intelligence, industry, and discerning versatility. The incumbent must be able to deal effectively with all types of personalities and all levels of education, from college presidents and industrial tycoons to truck drivers. Above all, the incumbent must possess decisiveness and the ability to implement motivation on the part of others consistent with the decision the incumbent has indicated. An erroneous judgment or a failure to properly appraise the nuance of an unfolding development could create a complex obfuscation of personnel and equipment generating an untold loss of mental equilibrium on the parts of innumerable personnel in American industry who are responsible for the formulation of day-to-day policy and guidance implementation of the conveyance of transportation both intrastate and interstate.

5. In short, at highway construction projects where only one-way traffic is possible, this son-of-a-bitch waves a red flag and tells which vehicle to go first.

(Anonymous)

SOURCE: Reprinted with permission from *Public Administration Review* © 1973 by The American Society for Public Administration, 1225 Connecticut Avenue, N.W. Washington, D.C. All rights reserved.

hence there would be no fumbling and no gaps in operations. It is not position classification that people complain about, but carrying a good idea too far. When carried to excess it results in bureaucratic disease.

Position classification is based upon *classes* of positions needed. Each class is comprised of *jobs*. Each type of job is approximately equal in difficulty and degree of skill needed. This allows valid comparisons not only within a single program but across the board into other programs where the same need exists. For example, the person who does radiology for a Veterans' Administration hospital may be compared with one who does like work in the U.S. Public Health Service. The resulting system makes it possible to use a common examination and a common *register* to fill a number of positions throughout the government and treat all persons equally. Finally, there is a *grade,* a subcategory of the class, which determines wage and salary scales within the grade. In sum, every civil servant employee works within a given class, at compensation determined by his grade, and according to a specific job description.

Q. This sounds logical enough. It seems to incorporate the working principles of scientific management. What, then, are the difficulties?

A. The program manager criticizes the position classification system as rigidly subdividing work to the point of fragmentation, thereby causing great difficulties of leadership and cooperation. The danger is that employees may develop mindsets that assume that so long as they do certain routine things, they need do no more. But if the program is to operate with flexibility and drive, everyone must do more. The interplay of roles is what produces efficiency and program results. If everyone did only what his position legally requires, the consequence would be to add to manpower needs unnecessarily. Morale would be lowered. Some people would wind up reading newspapers on "company" time.

Leadership may be defined as getting experts to cooperate. They will not do this if they think only of their little bailiwick. They need to understand what is going on around them in adjoining positions, and they should voluntarily seek to contribute to the holistic result. Their higher motivations come from their feeling that they are part of a larger enterprise. They tend to become dull and lacking in motivation when they are sequestered, insulated from the group activity.

Q. I think I see what you are driving at. You are saying in effect that management needs to combine what seem to be opposites. It is not either-or but both-and. The greatest efficiency occurs where jobs and roles overlap.

A. Right.

Q. Why can't position classifiers be educated to see this?

A. We try. But it is a difficult thing to accomplish. People who are attracted to position classification like to think of themselves as experts. They fall into the habit of thinking that the more they subdivide work the more scientific their accomplishments are. Being extremely orderly, they fight to make classification an end and not a means to an end.

Q. Give me an example.

A. A program manager puts in a request for a person who will do a certain job. His idea is to keep down the number of employees and emphasize quality instead. But the personnel agency responds to this request by offering to authorize two jobs instead of one, both at a lower level of competence and compensation. Who is to have his way? The program executive says he can get better results and save taxpayer dollars at the same time. The personnel expert says he knows more about this than the executive, that it will take two people instead of one to do the job the executive is planning.

Q. Who wins?

A. The program executive if he is stubborn enough. But first he must win over the higher officials of the personnel agency.

Q. Does business have this problem too?

A. Yes, to some extent. But not as often. Businessmen are more profit-minded, and they are more inclined to let the line executive have his way when there is disagreement.

Q. What you are saying, then, is that one of the objectives of good personnel management is to reduce bureaucratic excess but that personnel agencies are not without bureaucratic problems, too?

A. Yes, especially in this area we are talking about. Of all personnel experts, the classifier has a mind set that is most likely to result in neat little bundles. If classifiers are not made alert to their excesses, their work becomes a game. Their degree of concentration is like that of a man adding figures or an organization expert drawing charts.

The CED Challenge

Q. Incidentally, did you see the 1978 challenge of the Committee for Economic Development entitled *Improving Management of the Public Work Force: The Challenge to State and Local Government*?[10] I'm always impressed by things they say because they are a liberal group of businessmen who have a sincere interest in improving American government.

A. Yes, I agree with you, the CED is a first-rate organization. I did see the report.

Q. What do you think of it?

A. I agree with everything they say. The negative attitude that some civil service reformers adopt, for example, and cling to tenaciously. I have a copy here: Recruitment is slow, unimaginative, and unaggressive; selection procedures inhibit the hiring of the most qualified; job vacancies go unfilled. But most of all I like this: "Rigid classification systems impede efficient assignment of work." In addition, managers and supervisors lack authority to reward superior performance and discipline or fire nonperformers; promotion and salary increases are often based upon criteria unrelated to future performance. I like this, too, because much too often we who are in personnel management fail to look far enough ahead.

The Basic Challenge

Q. Can you summarize in a few words your philosophy of personnel work? What makes it appealing to you?

A. I think the personnel expert has to keep constantly in mind that he seeks influence with rather than power over the program executives. His is a staff function, not a program or directing function. He gives advice. He has no right to insist that he always have his own way. In every instance the personnel person must work with the line official, not dominate him.

Q. Do you always succeed in this self-limiting injunction?

A. No, like any expert we sometimes get carried away. We sometimes feel so strongly about principle that we resort to manipulation to assure our dominance.

Q. This is why you believe the personnel manager should be above all else management-minded?

A. Yes, that is exactly why I believe as I do.

Q. What else have you learned from experience?

A. Well, for one thing, there are five tests of a good personnel organization. It should link individual and group goals—perhaps that is the most important one. It should have built-in renewal systems. It should stress innovation. It should rely upon a results climate that concentrates upon performance instead of high-sounding sentiments. Finally, if it does not improve the quality of work life, none of the other objectives are defensible.

Q. Anything else?

A. Yes, we must outgrow the *control* frame of mind and really live the *service* motif. I wonder if personnelists, as they are now called, unfortunately, realize the daily frustrations of operating managers. When, for example, there is a one-year grant and it takes six months to fill jobs through the normal merit system procedures. Or when you have an employee performance problem and no one is providing the advice. Can you blame operators for reorganizing around the problem? I think one of the best ways of making personnel experts realize the faults of their own system is to have to suffer, themselves, from the defects of their own system. I take pleasure in rubbing their noses in it.

Q. What do you say to young people when they ask you if they should go into the personnel field? What is your sales-pitch?

A. I'm not sure I can answer that in a few well-chosen words. But I'll try. Of all the careers provided by the public service, none, perhaps, has a wider appeal to college-trained individuals entering the labor market than personnel management. The first reason for this is that there is a universal need for experts in this field, ranging from the White House at the highest level to the local government or medium-sized program office in the field. Second, the demand has increased as much in the private sector as in the public. Third, the main area of higher education in which incentives and human relations are dealt with is social psychology. Beginning three quarters of a century ago, and growing out of psychology and sociology, the study of social psychology became a field of its own. Moreover, it is now relied upon in political science, public administration, economics and business administration, and engineering and social welfare more than any "borrowed" subject. Recently, however, perhaps because so many psychologists are trained in clinical, quantitative measurement, their selection for personnel work has not been as popular as it once was. Instead, management types are often preferred.

Ask a personnel expert why his career appeals to him and he will probably mention the following:

- Human nature has more fascination, as a lifelong interest, than any other aspect of life.
- It is the human factor, more than quantitative factors, that determines efficiency and survival.
- There is a natural tendency for all organizations, especially large public ones, to become excessively bureaucratic. The main

way to prevent their becoming rigid and dysfunctional is to keep the human element alive and vital.
- The largest unsolved problems in the whole range of human knowledge lie in the area of human relations.
- With the growth of labor relations, social security, and other record-keeping programs in the 1930s, the need for personnel experts has grown more rapidly than other staff functions, such as finance, organization, law, or public relations.
- The more computerized technological society becomes, the greater amount of attention must be given to human factors if alienation and disequilibrium are not to result.
- Leadership and cooperation being two of the main ingredients of programmatic success, the personnel manager is looked to primarily for advice.
- People trained in personnel frequently make good executives for general administration.
- There is a good deal of opportunity for mobility and personal promotions in work of this kind.
- The concept of personnel management has considerably expanded since Leonard White wrote his pioneering text, *Public Administration,* in 1926 with the result that the well-equipped personnel specialist occupies a strategic position in the whole of management. Of necessity he must be concerned with goals, plans, organization, budgets, supervision, evaluation, and control because he cannot do an effective job unless he understands and is a part of all of these.

Q. How do you guard against the temptation to dominate?

A. A number of things seem to work. First, require personnel people to gain experience as line (program) managers early in their careers. Second, alternate their experience in personnel work with work in other areas that they ought to know about firsthand. Third, avoid overspecialization, even in large programs. Make them advisers, not operators. In general, try to recruit personalities who have the same interests as general managers, and guard against purists, Puritans, nitpickers, and sadists.

SUMMARY

We have done two things in this chapter—provided the facts concerning government employment at all three levels, while making some comparisons with the private sector, and listened to a skilled personnel chief at the state level get at the heart of personnel administration as a worthy and growing profession. Her summary was so good, and eloquent, that we have nothing to add to what she said.

NOTES

1. Sources as of November 1980: U.S., Department of Labor, Bureau of Labor Statistics, Office of Personnel Management.

2. Committee for Economic Development (CED), *Improving Management of the Public Work Force: The Challenge to State and Local Government* (New York, November 1978), p. 6.

3. *The Legislative Branch: The Next Billion Dollar Bureaucracy* (New York: Tax Foundation, 1976); Harrison W. Fox, Jr., and Susan Webb Hammond, *Congressional Staffs: The Invisible Force in American Lawmaking* (New York: Free Press, 1977).

4. Source: U.S., Department of Labor, Bureau of Labor Statistics. See also Mark W. Cannon, "Administrative Change and the Supreme Court," *Judicature, Journal of the American Judicature Society* 57 (March 1974): 334–341.

5. Randy Huwa and Alan Rosenthal, *Politicians and Professionals, Interactions Between Committee and Staff in State Legislatures* (New Brunswick, N.J.: Rutgers University, Center for State Legislative Research and Service, 1977), p. 1; James J. Heaphey, ed., "Symposium: Public Administration and Legislatures," *Public Administration Review* 35 (September–October 1975).

6. CED, *Improving Management of the Public Work Force,* p. 6.

7. On the question of insights versus tested clinical proof, L. L. Thurstone, the psychologist who specialized in factorial analysis of executive traits, once stated to one of the authors: "The experienced executive with long experience knows far more about what works than we psychologists can ever learn in our scientific experiments—we can only test what is testable and that is only a relatively small part of the whole of management. What is more, you must always provide the hypothesis."

8. *Public Sector Compensation Report* (New York: AMACOM, 1980).

9. *The Rewards of Public Service: Compensating Top Federal Officials* (Washington: Brookings Institution, 1980).

10. CED, *Improving Management of the Public Work Force.*

19

Strengthening the Public Service

Train up a child in the way he should go: and when he is old he will not depart from it.

Proverbs XXII, 6.

In this chapter, we examine personnel training and development, with special emphasis on the landmark federal Civil Service Reform Act of 1978.

In the best of all worlds, a college student attracted to government service would like an opportunity to take part in an intern program as a means of entry, to be assured that his merit and industry would be rewarded by rising to higher ranks, to know that there is adequate provision for a skilled executive corps, to be able to transfer without loss from one level of government to another, and to look forward to training opportunities at all stages of his career. All of this has been provided for in legislation passed within recent years, though, as we shall see, much more remains to be accomplished.[1] We shall deal with these areas of concern in this chapter, underscoring a landmark legislation, the Civil Service Reform Act of 1978.

The issues underlying any piece of legislation are stubborn and continuing and are never fully dealt with by a stroke of the pen. Among them are questions such as these: How does one measure merit? Who deserves to be promoted? How does one draw a balance between general management skills and professionalization in a substantive field? Is accomplishment individual or group?[2]

LANDMARK LEGISLATION

Notable achievements in the form of landmark legislation are these.

Crossgovernment Mobility

The Intergovernmental Personnel Act (IPA) of 1970 (P.L. 90–648) strengthened the personnel resources of state and local governments and cooperative grant-in-aid programs by encouraging temporary tours of duty at a different level and by assisting in training programs and the setting of standards. Full mobility has not been achieved by any means, however, and hence the law has disappointed the hopes of many of its initial sponsors. Nevertheless, recent additional responsibilities under the act include the Presidential Management Intern Program and the lead role in government agency support for improved state and local productivity.

Federal Civil Service Reform

The Civil Service Reform Act of 1978 (CSRA) did at least half a dozen important things. It created a single-headed Office of Personnel Management (OPM) in place of the plural-headed U.S. Civil Service Commission (CSC). It established a Senior Executive Service (SES), a Merit Systems Protection Board (MSPB) to deal with violations of the merit system, and a Federal Labor Relations Authority (LRA). It strengthened the Equal Employment Opportunity Commission (EEOC) and set up an Office of Government Ethics as an independent agency within OPM. In addition, the act moved the administration of intergovernmental personnel relations into OPM and authorized comprehensive research, training, and intern programs affecting all levels of government.[3]

Career Service

The Classification Act of 1949 created the supergrades, initiating what most people regarded as a true career service in government. Like other laws about personnel, however, its beginnings go back to the 1930s or even earlier.[4]

Training Programs

The Government Employees Training Act of 1958 resulted in the creation of a Bureau of Executive Manpower in the Civil Service Commission.[5]

Industry-Government Comparability

The Federal Salary Reform Act of 1962 is another landmark. It established the principle of equal pay for substantially equal work in private industry and in government. As for internships, there are a large number of these in state and local governments. There is also a White House Fellows program, which originated with the

American Political Science Association, and a Judicial Fellows program, which was the brainchild of the National Academy of Public Administration. Both are government supported.

Perhaps enough has been said to demonstrate that the legislative mandate for updated personnel management is now complete. It is the accomplishment of almost 100 years, beginning with the Pendleton Act of 1883 and burgeoning in interest and concern in the 1930s and again in the 1960-1980 period. The public administration profession, as might be expected, took the lead in this development. In fully two thirds of the 50 state governments, developments of proportional magnitude were occurring at the same time.

OFFICE OF PERSONNEL MANAGEMENT

In May 1977 President Jimmy Carter established the federal personnel management project to study problems in the civil service and recommend solutions. The project confirmed that (1) repair of the civil service system could not be accomplished through patchwork and (2) changes in the civil service organizational structure were required. On March 2, 1978, Carter proposed legislation to revise the system and seven months later Congress enacted Public Law 95-454. Congress also approved the president's Reorganization Plans 1 and 2 of 1978, effective January 1, 1979, which further changed the management of federal personnel.[6]

OPM became the primary agency for the president in carrying out his responsibilities for managing the federal work force. It is responsible for executing, administering, and enforcing the civil service rules and regulations and the laws governing the civil service. Implementation of the CSRA began in January 1979, involved major efforts during 1980-1981, and will have its ultimate impact in the 1985-1990 period. Like any major new enterprise, its features may, of course, be amended and altered as experience accumulates. See Figure 19.1.

Reduced to its simplest form, OPM has four main functions:

- It serves as the "president's arm" for federal personnel management and overall relations with other involved agencies.
- It helps agencies make effective use of personnel resources the better to accomplish their missions and programs, and it sets standards and reviews results.
- It promotes or directly administers a sizeable research and development (R&D) and training program.
- It deals with the main substantive matters involved in personnel management, such as staffing, compensation, individual and group productivity, executive personnel, and intergovernmental personnel programs.

OPM may participate in MSPB proceedings or seek judicial review only if, in the OPM director's view, MSPB has erred and its decision would have substantial impacts on civil service law and effectiveness.

A year after its creation the OPM had 8,000 employees, only 600 fewer than the CSC in its last full year of operation. Many of these, of course, had been inherited from the CSC. Other reasons for OPM's relatively large size are these:

1. OPM has a major research effort. It takes the form of developing new courses in its training programs relating to civil service reform subjects—performance appraisals, merit pay decisions, SES performance award decisions, and others. OPM offers these and other courses in its training centers and has made them available to other agencies for their training programs.

2. OPM does extensive self-evaluation. This evaluation is in addition to that done by the General Accounting Office (GAO), the Congressional Budget Office, the Office of Management and Budget, White House staff, assistant secretaries for Administration, directors of personnel in agencies, and the National Academy of Public Administration. The plan includes making surveys of federal

Figure 19.1 United States Office of Personnel Management

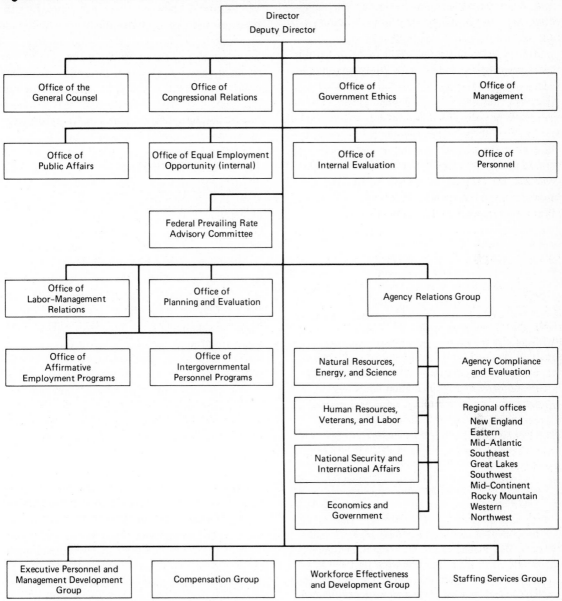

employee attitudes, organizational assessments, case studies, and special studies.

3. OPM has developed and issued new regulations to implement CSRA provisions, such as appointment of veterans, probationary periods for new

supervisors, performance appraisals, conversion to SES, and many other matters.

A GAO evaluation report issued in 1980 stated: "Implementation of CSRA is a major undertaking. It will take several years for the central features to be installed and operating. We believe that, overall, OPM has made good progress. . . . OPM sees its role as leadership in all phases of personnel management in the executive branch, in integrating personnel with the line management of agency programs, and in promoting productivity and better management in all types of government programs."[7]

In line with the determination to overcome the faults of the earlier system, a major purpose stated in the 1978 legislation was to provide more freedom for program (line) managers. A careful reading of the law reveals that finding the balance between decentralization and central control will be the main issue of OPM trusteeship. An example follows.

- The law provides greater flexibility for federal operating managers in managing human resources, new tools to motivate subordinate supervisors and employees, a comprehensive personnel system for executives, and an organization structure better equipped to carry out government programs.
- At the same time, the law expressly states that the filling of positions and other personnel matters should be "delegated in appropriate cases" to the agencies but that "central control and oversight" should be maintained in OPM.
- Further, "in appropriate instances" pay increases should be based on quality of performance rather than length of service. (Words such as appropriate are flexible; they mean that the decision might be one way or the other in future times.)
- The 1980 GAO appraisal tried to reconcile this seeming difficulty in these words: "The critical component of civil service reform is that it makes clear that managers are responsbile for directing the efforts of the people who work for them in accomplishing program goals. The law provides the tools managers need to create a work environment conducive to better productivity and improved employee morale."[8]

Performance Appraisal and Merit Pay

Instead of being given automatic pay increases based upon length of service, the middle manage-ment group consisting of General Service grades 13, 14, and 15 now has their pay figured on the basis of individual performance calculated on measurable productivity as a result of the Civil Service Reform Act of 1978. In the federal government these grades are a large and influential group, an estimated 72,500 persons as of the first full year of operation, 1980. This was a revolutionary change, based upon similar practices in the corporate world. Let us see what this entailed by getting a closer look at the anatomy of the federal job classification scheme.

In accordance with the Classification Act of 1949 and its amendments, all employees, except blue collar workers, fall into grades 1–18 in the General Service (GS) designation. There used to be a dual classification, GS and Professional, but the Professional was eliminated. Under the 1978 legislation, in the GS 13–15 group, the agency itself may designate a person General Management (GM) in order to underscore the importance of management leadership. There are presently around 125,000 GMs in this category. Above them, as we shall see presently, is the Senior Executive Service (SES) group, covering grades 16–18, numbering some 7,000 out of a 9,000 figure originally intended by the 1978 legislation. There are six salary gradations in the SES. The reason for these changes was to increase career leadership in government by providing incentives.

For the supervisors and managers the act provided that instead of step increases there should be established a special fund with which to pay those most meritorious. These funds come from (1) half the comparability increases the employees would otherwise have received and (2) the monies the employees would have received had they continued under the former system of step increases. Funds distributed to agencies by OPM are determined by merit pay calculations for each grade. Each agency then must award between 95 and 105 percent of merit pay funds each year unless OPM grants an exception. Under this system an "exceptional" employee receives twice what a "fully satisfactory" employee does, and persons who receive "minimally satisfactory" or "unsatisfactory" receive no increase. Differences in ratings thus translate into differences in merit pay.

Every system designed by operating agencies must relate critical elements to duties performed. Evaluations are based on critical elements individually and in toto. Implicit in the process is the importance of the accuracy of the employee's written description of his duties, for this is the starting point in terms of the individual's performance. "Critical element" is not defined in the law. OPM defines it as any requirement of the job that is sufficiently important that inadequate performance of it outweighs acceptable or better performance in other aspects of the job. It is possible to have three performance appraisal systems in a single agency: one for SES; one for GS 13–15; and a third for all others, namely those below GS 13.

Under the 1978 legislation it is easier to take action against a poor performer. "Unacceptable performance" is defined as failure to meet one or more critical elements of an employee's performance standard. Separations or demotions are upheld if supported by "substantial evidence."

In defining performance standards for managers some of the same yardsticks are those employed by industry: goal setting, from the top down; top management involvement and line management involvement at all levels of the organization; and establishing systems that meet the needs of the agency, are useful to managers, and are accepted by and motivate the people affected. Finally, in evaluating managers, the results of the operation as a whole as well as the contribution of each participant are considered as evidence.

In addition to merit pay, the act also provides for cash awards as an incentive to managers, a feature that industry commonly employs. These awards are clearly differentiated from basic pay and merit increases. Merit pay is a one-time pay increase given for unusual accomplishment. It has no connection with cost-of-living increases. Congress undertakes to make these monies available even when there is retrenchment in government programs as a whole.

Lessons Learned from Implementation

A major objective of the 1978 act was to give operating managers greater freedom to manage. Quite naturally, therefore, the operating departments and agencies were in many instances quick to seize their new opportunities.[9] They were working against deadlines. First they had to organize teams to apply the reform. Then they had to deal with lower-paid employees and the GS 13–15 group (1980 salary range: $29,395-$50,112.50). Even before this organization took place, however, many of them had taken initial steps to create the Senior Executive Service, a corps of around 8,000 top executives created by the act to provide top career leadership. Finally, as so often happens, the field service, through lack of central encouragement, tagged along in fourth place, although numerically, and in terms of delivery systems, it is far more numerous and more directly involved with citizens than the other three services.

Even if the act should accomplish nothing else, the initial benefits of implementation probably justify its enactment. For the first time in years the government as a whole was forced to think about management. How the departments did so differs considerably, but the best results were obtained when managers and personnel people, supported by professionals and workers within the department, were organized into teams, met regularly for weeks at a time, and came forth with a plan of internal personnel management that was adapted to the department's special needs. No two departments are the same and not even two programs within the same department are the same. Selective service, for example, had 375 civilian employees; the Department of the Navy, 300,000.

The second major lesson learned from this exercise is that the degree of management improvement depends upon the support given by top management and the personality and approach of the top personnel officer. Those inclined toward authoritarianism won grudging compliance; those who secured universal participation found that morale rose.

The third major lesson was that analyses of these matters occupy the time of top officials to the point where other things need to be temporarily neglected. Accordingly major exercises of this kind cannot be contemplated too frequently.

One of the outstanding accomplishments, for which it received a merit award from the president, occurred in the Department of Justice. This department had always been one of the more poorly managed in Washington. Lawyers inherently seem to dislike management. Some bureaus, such as the Federal Bureau of Investigation (FBI), have long resisted outside supervision, even from the attorney general. Immigration and Naturalization differs from the FBI and other Justice Department units. The improvements in cohesion and morale were so marked under the new personnel system that the award was well deserved.

The Department of Commerce also scored a significant success. One of the oldest and most respected bureaus, the Bureau of Standards is manned by scientists and lawyers who are fascinated by invention but have little or no interest in group activity. By contrast, the International Trade Administration is the reverse, outgoing and public relations-oriented. But before the installation was through, there was a perceptible change in the attitudes of all bureaus, including those of Standards and of Science and Technology.

The Merit Systems Protection Board

The MSPB is a quasi-judicial board, the OPM a staff agency like any large personnel office. Under a three-member, bipartisan board, the MSPB may stop personnel actions in federal agencies for varying periods of time. It may order corrective action, decide cases on appeal involving prohibited practices, and impose disciplinary action or remove or discipline employees. It may conduct special studies of civil service and other merit systems. It reports directly to Congress.

The MSPB also has the authority to *review the rules and regulations of OPM*. It is similar to a regulatory agency where the promotional and review functions have been divided between a commission and a court. Its clout is considerably augmented by the creation of a special counsel, who has authority that is separate from that of the MSPB board and that in some cases exceeds the board's authority. His powers are described as investigations of personnel practices, including reprisals against whistle blowers (informers), prohibited political activity and cases involving discrimination. He also has prosecutory functions and may institute corrective action, including action in areas where the special counsel *believes there is a pattern of prohibited personnel practices involving matters not otherwise appealable to the MSPB*. In short, the MSPB-special counsel system is one administered by administrative judges. It is the newest and latest example of the American predilection for judicial supremacy. See Box 19.1.

How will it work? It is still too early to say with any degree of finality. What is known is that the MSPB had to be organized and built from scratch. It had a backlog of 5,000 cases that had to be dealt with during the first full year of operation. To do this and still handle new cases, the MSPB had to appoint a large number of administrative judges, had to simplify and streamline hearing and deciding functions, and had to establish general policies and precedents that would stand the test of time.

THE FEDERAL SENIOR EXECUTIVE SERVICE

The SES, which was established by the Civil Service Reform Act of 1978, consisted initially of about 8,000 federal executives, a figure provided for in the act itself. The purpose was to create an executive corps, comparable to that in business or the military, that would provide more leadership

Box 19.1

MERIT PRINCIPLES
AS ENUNCIATED BY THE CONGRESS IN THE
INTERGOVERNMENTAL PERSONNEL ACT OF 1970

1. Recruiting, selecting, and advancing employees on the basis of their relative ability, knowledge, and skills, including open consideration of qualified applicants for initial appointment
2. Providing equitable and adequate compensation
3. Training employees, as needed, to assure high-quality performance
4. Retaining employees on the basis of the adequacy of their performance and separating employees whose inadequate performance cannot be corrected

5. Assuring fair treatment of applicants and employees in all aspects of personnel administration without regard to political affiliation, race, color, national origin, sex, or religious creed and with proper regard for their privacy and constitutional rights as citizens
6. Assuring that employees are protected against coercion for partisan political purposes and are prohibited from using their official authority for the purpose of interfering with or affecting the result of an election or nomination for office

SOURCE: U.S. Office of Personnel Management

drive to the country's largest work force. It was assumed that the larger the work force, the more important its leadership is, especially at the top. These persons should be able to be moved about as needed, as in industry. Or to put it in civil service language, they are given rank in person instead of in position; the idea is that individuals are fitted into slots instead of functions being developed around individuals. The idea also is that some persons are so proficient as executives that it is a safe bet they will succeed in almost any program they head, from agriculture to zoology.

This assumption is not true of the entire SES, however, as we shall see, nor are the most gifted of executives invariably successful. For example, one of the authors discovered, as early as the 1930s, that in the country's largest corporations, such as American Telephone and Telegraph, General Motors, and General Electric, top executives who had ventured into Washington positions referred to this experience as "the graveyard

of lost reputations"[10]; they did not succeed because the field, the environment, or their own attitudes were wrong. Hence the idea of executive infallibility is a myth, but it is an idea worth applying to government much more widely than it has been.

Main Provisions of SES

Title IV of the Civil Service Reform Act of 1978 sets forth the chief provisions of the Senior Executive Service:

The total number of SES positions, governmentwide, at any given time may not exceed 105 percent of the total number of positions authorized by the OPM for the two-year period.

The number in any one agency depends upon that agency's needs. This number is arrived at after consultation with the OPM, which may adjust the allocation upward or downward during the two-year period.

The initial cadre was drawn from those holding GS 16 through Executive Level IV positions. (These latter consisted of those above GS 18.)

Those under the superseded *supergrade manager* category and those who were designated as being in *scientific manager* positions were both put into the new, distinctive pool. This was a decision to combine, so far as possible, the managerial and professional categories so as to expand the executive scope of both groups.

An overall limit of 10,777 was set on SES and GS supergrade positions.

There are two kinds of positions: (1) *career-reserved*, which may be filled only by career appointees, and (2) *general*, which have a limited term for limited emergencies.

There are four types of appointments: (1) *career*, which is selection by merit staffing process and requires OPM approval; (2) *noncareer*, which is selection without merit staffing process; (3) *limited-term*, which is nonrenewable appointment for up to three years to a GS position that will then expire; and (4) *limited-emergency*, which is nonrenewable for up to 18 months to GS positions that must be filled urgently. Categories #3 and #4 may not exceed 5 percent of total SES positions, governmentwide.

Entry. The qualification standards for entry into the SES are established by the operating agency itself in accordance with OPM guidelines. For the career appointments the agency recruits and evaluates candidates using executive resource boards; there is a one-year probationary period for initial career appointments; and veterans' preference is not applicable to SES. No more than 30 percent of SES positions may be filled (when the act went into effect) by individuals with less than five years of current continuous service immediately prior to initial appointment to SES. For other types of appointment (noncareer, limited-term, and limited-emergency) the agencies determine the qualifications of candidates.

Reassignments and Transfers Within SES. There is a 15-day limitation on reassignment to an SES position within the same agency and a 120-day limitation of reassignment of a career executive when there is a new agency head or a new noncareer supervisor. Finally, executives may elect to transfer to another agency that wishes to employ them, but they may not be transferred involuntarily.

The safeguards surrounding these positions are somewhat tighter than those found in the private sector. This is to protect the autonomy of individuals and agencies and to provide checks on partisan (nonmerit) influences.

Financial Provisions. There are five or more levels of basic pay. The president announces the new levels annually. Agency heads set the basic pay of individual executives within levels. There may be only one pay adjustment per executive per year; and finally, if a career executive's basic pay is to be reduced, he must be given 15 days' notice.

Performance Awards. Career executives may be awarded a lump sum payment once a year for fully successful performance up to 20 percent of basic pay (another practice borrowed from business practice). Five percent of SES executives per year may be given the rank of meritorious executive and receive a one-time, lump sum payment of $10,000 (another industry practice). Another 1 percent may be designated distinguished executive and receive a one-time, lump sum payment of $20,000. Career executives may receive these ranks only once within a five-year period (this differs from industry). The agency nominates, the OPM recommends, and the president makes the actual award. The outside compensation limit was initially set at $66,000, consisting of basic pay, performance awards, and rank payment.

As in universities and some private companies, career executives are given sabbaticals—up to 11 months in any 10-year period, with full compensation, for study or other approved purposes. To be eligible, career executives must have seven years of service, two years in the SES. They must not be eligible for retirement and must agree to remain in service two years after the sabbatical.

There is no limit on the amount of leave accumulation members of the SES may acquire.

It will be seen, therefore, that there are some strong incentives operating here, not all of which, by any means, are strictly monetary. Others relate to prestige, recognition, sabbatical leave, and the like. But the basic idea is that persons of talent respond to monetary emoluments more than to anything else.

Accomplishments of SES

Among those who have examined the early history of the SES, there is wide agreement on the following points:

The opportunity was chosen eagerly by most of those eligible (more than 95 percent).

The conversion from supergrade to the SES was made speedily. CSRA set July 13, 1979, as the date for conversion, and the initial conversion was completed by that date.

It seems clear that to date the SES operates on a departmental basis instead of governmentwide; there is a long way to go.

The percentage limitations unquestionably work hardships on certain agencies such as National Aeronautics and Space Administration, which is primarily an engineering-scientific undertaking relying on experts.

A GAO study in 1980 found that inequity results from the fact that persons in several different levels of responsibility received the same pay ($50,112.50). If continued, this inequity would undoubtedly affect retention, recruitment, and incentive for advancement.

The GAO also discovered that there was potential for inequity in the bonus system; career executives in agencies that have a high level of noncareer executives have a better chance than those in agencies that do not. (As stated above, only career executives qualify for bonuses.)

Long-term prospects are hard to predict because presidential transition periods are always difficult times for everyone, especially for a new personnel system. Toward the end of 1981 there is no question that morale in the SES and in the federal civil service generally was very low. Said the *National Journal,* in a piece entitled "SES—From Civil Service Showpiece to Incipient Failure in Two Years,"

Morale is slumping and top bureaucrats in the Senior Executive Service complain of low compensation, and their political bosses find the new system hardly less rigid than the old one.

On the plus side, however, the article did bring out that from 1971 to 1977, only 6.7 percent of all supergrade vacancies were filled by persons transferring from other agencies, whereas in the first quarter of 1981 this figure had risen to 13.3 percent.[11]

In a progress report entitled "Civil Service Reform: 1978–1981," a panel of the National Academy of Public Administration, in October 1981, concluded that they had "serious concern" relating to merit protection. The report also called attention to the tendency of OPM to "second guess" the operating agencies; it noted the Office of Management and Budget or some other agency ought to be designated for general oversight; it mentioned wide dissatisfaction with the development of the Senior Executive Service to date; it stated that the act should be amended as it relates to merit pay and performance appraisal; and it raised objections to the legalistic approach to government labor relations.

About the same time, a professor of public administration at the University of Pittsburgh called the act "a policy disaster," focusing much of his fire on performance appraisal merit pay and the Senior Executive Service.[12] Another article, entitled "Obstacles to Effective Management," perceived a "crisis atmosphere" and focused primarily on employee attitudes toward civil service reform as revealed by attitude surveys. The long-expected academic reaction to civil service reform was clearly underway![13]

What do the government labor unions, discussed in more detail in the next chapter, say about SES? It varies. Sometimes they express distrust, talking about a privileged or superior class, unjustifiably high salaries, and the need for more opportunity to participate in management. Other times they state that leadership is necessary; there is no danger so long as advancement is fair to everyone; they would rather have recruitment from within the organization than from outside; and they could probably cope with "arrogant" individuals if they became "overbearing."

PARALLEL DEVELOPMENTS IN STATE GOVERNMENT

In 1980, five states had a senior executive service and another seven were seriously considering establishing one. State governments have in many instances advanced rapidly on the executive career front and some of their efforts are older and more successful than the federal government's program. This is especially true where there has been a strong citizen movement to improve the quality of state government by reorganization, budget reform, and other such moves toward effectiveness. It is also true where there are strong centers of teaching and research in public administration. Fifty years ago there were a dozen such centers; now every state has at least one. Some of the larger states, such as New York, which was one of the first, and California, whose educational system grew more rapidly than that of any other state, have been in the limelight. But smaller states, less well known nationally, have often done as much as their larger neighbors.

The New York program, centering originally in New York City, Syracuse, and Albany, goes back to the work of the New York Bureau of Municipal Research (which became the Institute of Public Administration) shortly after the turn of the century. Nelson Rockefeller, who served several terms as governor and whose main interest was always public administration, did a great deal to promote executive development opportunities in the 1960s and 1970s. During the New Deal it used to be said that if a person wanted to find a good executive for the Wage-Hour Divi-

sion, Employment Service, or most anything else, the place to turn was to New York State. The history of the New Deal shows what a large proportion of successful administrators were conscripted from New York State.

The California executive development program, which is the best known of any recent state system, began in 1963. Modified 10 years later, it has attracted much favorable attention. Called the California Career Executive Assignment Program, it calls attention to the flexibility and governmentwide character that the federal SES has yet to achieve. A study of this state program made by the National Academy of Public Administration in 1979 concluded that the program has functioned satisfactorily on the whole. It has reduced patronage appointments and at the same time provided junior executives possessing program and managerial expertise. It has not, however, proved a big drawing card for new talent at the highest level.

One last example is Vermont, one of the smallest states, where university attention to public administration and personnel management has been closely linked to governmental improvement. Examples are a "little Hoover Commission" staffed from the universities, the installation of one of the first Cabinet systems of government, and a department of administration, which included a personnel division. Cooperative executive development programs linking state government and the universities began in the 1960s.

It is unlikely, therefore, that the CSRA of 1978 and the organizations created by it will "seduce" the states and that the states will slavishly follow its example. What seems more likely is that enterprising states will set out to demonstrate how the federal government can improve its own system.

TRAINING PROGRAMS FOR EXECUTIVES

Training has been a major part of personnel management in the United States for half a century.[14] It has its ups and downs, but in general its impetus has been sustained. Likewise in the private sector, where one organization earned so much money on executive development programs that it was able to finance a big building in New York City.

Many kinds of training take place in public administration, of course, almost from entry to near retirement, but the aspect of training that one hears most about is the one on which we shall concentrate here, executive training. This breaks down, in turn, into training of junior, or future, executives and refresher courses for full-fledged executives themselves. The initial step begins even earlier, in the colleges and universities. The following case study indicates that instituting changes in training procedures may not be the easiest thing in the world, even if the would-be agent for change is highly respected.

CASE STUDY: ROADBLOCKS

Vice Admiral James B. Stockdale resigned his position as head of the Naval War College in 1979 to become president of the Citadel. The Citadel is a South Carolina military college, established in 1842, which calls itself the West Point of the South. Many of its alumni have gone on to outstanding military careers.

Admiral Stockdale had spent almost eight years in North Vietnamese prisons as a prisoner of war, where he organized resistance to his Vietnamese captors. He was also a scholarly humanist, who had taught moral philosophy and liberalized the curriculum at the Naval War College. Upon his arrival at the Citadel, Stockdale became concerned with hazing procedures for freshmen, or "knobs." In the spring a drunken senior who menaced knobs with a loaded pistol was expelled by Stockdale. Stockdale also asked the board to end the practice of "bracing" (an exaggerated and rigid posture of attention) required of knobs during meals. The board refused to do so and ordered the cadet expelled by Stockdale reinstated. Another Stockdale recommendation, to remove some of the control of hazing from students to end abuse, was also rejected. As Stockdale put it, "I'm not opposed to hazing. Hell, I understand. . . . I learned that in Hanoi, but you have to have a throttle on the system. . . . You would have thought I was tampering with America."

Stockdale had hoped to liberalize the Citadel's curriculum, stressing the humanities, as he had done at the Naval War College. He stated, "A liberally educated person meets new ideas with curiosity and fascination. An illiberally educated person meets new ideas with fear." The admiral never got a chance to put this new curriculum into effect. After failing to get the board's approval for a proposed administrative reorganization, Stockdale resigned. His parting words were, "The place is locked in pre-Civil War concrete."

A step between the universities and formal public employment is supplied by a number of internship programs. These constitute a kind of apprenticeship. Intern opportunities in public administration are of several kinds. They are found at all levels, federal, state, and local. Most are financed by public funds, others by private. Virtually all of them are competitive and the interested candidate has to apply and pass certain kinds of tests and interviews. Another characteristic is that internships are now found in all three branches of government—executive, legislative, and judicial. The oldest and best known are the White House and Judicial Fellows internships. Since the Civil Service Reform Act of 1978, the Office of Personnel Management is the principal administrator of internship programs for the federal service and indirectly for state and local governments, in the form of grants-in-aid. This process has been greatly speeded since passage of the Federal Service Entrance Examination (FSEE) in 1955 and its recent replacement, the Professional and Administrative Career Examination (PACE). In this wide, threshhold examination, expressly for college students, the successful candidate serves in an intern capacity initially, where, as in industry, he and his employer form some idea of where the individual ought to be heading. The National Institute of Public Affairs (NIPA), which is privately funded, is the oldest internship program. It commenced with the New Deal and is now affiliated with the National Academy of Public Administration in Washington.

It will be recalled that one of the provisions of the Civil Service Reform Act of 1978 deals with the training function. The apex of the federal executive training programs had been established earlier, in 1968, at Charlottesville, Virginia, in the form of the Federal Executive Institute (FEI). Supporting it are a number of other federal training centers in Oak Ridge, Tennessee; King's Point, New York; and Berkeley, California; covering the entire United States. As in industry, training is now big business in American governments.

Why do executives need to be trained? There are at least six good reasons. First, the development of good executives cannot be left to chance—they need encouragement. Second, many professionals in subject-matter fields such as engineering and health need to be broadened to cope with managerial techniques and philosophies. Third, new developments are constantly occurring in the social sciences, which need to be communicated to junior and senior executives. Fourth, managers need to learn increasingly about public policy and decision making, and off-the-job training provides the means. Fifth, executives in one field need to familiarize themselves with knowledge in related fields in order to improve their cooperation and effectiveness. Finally, executives need to be "refreshed," have their sights lifted, so to speak, which entails their temporary absence from day-to-day administration. Of all the subdivisions of personnel work, training perhaps puts more of a demand on those concerned than any other; it requires more innovation and resourcefulness if it is to succeed.

A Worldwide Need

Other countries, almost without exception, have recognized the need for creative training programs.[15] In France, for example, there is L'École Nationale d'Administration, which is world-famous and which has a virtual monopoly on access to and training for higher positions in the government. In Britain there is the Civil Service College and the Administrative Staff College. Among third-world countries there is the Indian Institute of Public Administration.

Germany was one of the first countries to emphasize formal training of public executives, and it still enjoys an enviable reputation. In developing countries, the establishment of training schools for government executives is acknowledged as one of the first and most salient needs; otherwise governments cannot effectively plan and administer all the programs needed in their stages of development. The Soviet Union and other communist countries have had to establish hierarchies of training programs in order to produce the cadre of executives needed for monumental duties.

In the United States formalized training programs for government executives began even earlier than those of the federal government itself. Examples are the Institute of Public Administration in New York City, the Maxwell School of Syracuse University, the School of Public Administration at the University of Southern California, the executive training program at the University of Minnesota in the early 1930s, and the program at Harvard University now called the John F. Kennedy School. In the South, where training has always been emphasized, similar developments were occurring: the public administration program at the University of Alabama; the multifaceted training programs at the University of Virginia, the University of Kentucky, and the University of Georgia; and the Lyndon B. Johnson School at the University of Texas, which has resources of considerable magnitude.

More recently some universities have established schools of management, combining business and public administration. Examples are found at Cornell University, Northwestern University, Yale University, and American University in Washington, D.C. At the national level they are all bound together by the National Association of Schools of Public Affairs and Administration (NASPAA), which has its headquarters in Washington. The 1978 directory of this organization contained information on 176 colleges and universities with programs in public administration and public affairs.

The United Nations, created in 1948, has established executive training centers in a number of regions, such as Turkey, Egypt, and South America. It has founded the United Nations University in Tokyo.

Stages in American Development

A thumbnail sketch of the sequence of developments in the United States federal government follows.

The so-called Brownlow Committee on Administrative Management of 1937 stressed career executive leadership, prepared a study on public personnel, and recommended grouping all executive positions into two categories, one specifically political and policymaking and the other nonpolitical and administrative. Between 1933 and 1935, Luther Gulick, later one of the members of the Brownlow Committee, directed the work of the Commission on Better Government Personnel, which published more studies of this subject than any venture before or since.

Following the Brownlow Committee of 1937, the first Hoover Commission on executive organization and the second Hoover Commission of 1955, especially, stressed the need for executive development programs administered by the government. In 1955 the U.S. Civil Service Commis-

sion proposed to create *generalist administrators* with mobility. In 1967, a Bureau of Executive Manpower was established within the CSC. This step led to the creation of the Federal Executive Institute.

The Training Act of 1958 authorized a comprehensive training program for all grades. By the year 1966, there were 65,000 employees enrolled in these programs, and a year later 2,000 interagency courses were being offered.

In terms of legislation, therefore, it will be seen that the two key dates are 1958 (the Training Act) and 1967 (the Bureau of Executive Manpower). During the administration of Richard Nixon further proposals emerged to extend executive training, but after the Watergate scandal no action was forthcoming.

Finally, now that training is a major division within OPM, and the success of the Senior Executive Service and everything else in the 1978 legislation depends upon it, a rapid intensification of training programs may reasonably be expected.

Methods Employed

It is hazardous to generalize on the methods employed by executive training programs because they differ not only among themselves but over time periods; if one method is not satisfactory another is tried.[16] Shortly after the FEI was launched, for example, the unofficial view was that "behavioral science" was emphasized almost to the exclusion of anything else. Later the approach was broadened. At one point the American Management Association (AMA) used graphics, films and sound equipment almost exclusively. Other programs have used simulation, group dynamics, sensitivity training, and case studies. There have been waves of experimentation in training as well as in management theories and techniques. It is, therefore, safer to focus on the atmosphere and general objectives of such programs, not exclusively on techniques.

An executive development program is often held elsewhere than in the work environment; and room, board, and privacy are provided. The directing staff is usually furnished by the sponsoring agency, but the teaching staff is commonly drawn from among outsiders, and frequently a large proportion are from the universities. These programs may last for a weekend, as for some top business corporations, or they may last for three months or longer, as do programs of the Administrative Staff College in Britain, the École Nationale d'Administration in France, or some of the programs operated by the Harvard Graduate School of Business in countries such as India.

Certain common assumptions underlie residential programs of this kind. It is recognized, for example, that a crucial moment in executive training is when a person is about to be promoted from middle to top management, usually when he is in his early forties. And the results are more satisfactory when the rising executive's superior also enrolls in a training program so that he will understand what executive development has to offer and not feel threatened by his juniors.

It is further recognized that a more lasting impact can be made on trainees if the program is conducted at some remote place free of telephone and family interruptions, and with opportunities for relaxation, contemplation, discussion, and reading. In content, these courses concentrate on administrative philosophy and method, and on policy determination and decision making, with policy relatively more emphasized than the techniques of management. Although teaching methods are various, a common element is group dynamics, that is, studying, thinking, discussing, and deciding together as a balanced team in which all major specialties are represented.

The objectives of executive development programs are equally various. In some instances the objectives are only informational, to make participants familiar with a new technique or to teach them more about policy analysis. In other instances they are merely to compare notes and exchange experiences with one's peers. In still other instances they are for participants to get away from the familiar environmental grind and do some fresh thinking.

Among these various objectives, the most am-

bitious is to change the outlook of the individual so as to have a lasting effect on his personality and his approach to his work. If he is excessively bureaucratic in outlook at the beginning of the course, he becomes entrepreneurial; if he is figure minded, he learns to appreciate the importance of psychology and motivation. Such changes take time and ideal conditions must prevail; but some institutions, notably the Administrative Staff College in Britain, believe that a well-run training program can in fact bring about visible changes in a person's personality and effectiveness. Although there is no magic in the program and its environment, they can nevertheless provide the initial push to the receptive individual, following which he himself determines the degree of change in his own personality.

When a Task Force of Career Development reported on its investigations in 1967, it outlined a number of objectives for residential training centers operated by the federal government.[17]

1. foster a sense of *common purpose,* increase mutual understanding, and stimulate approaches to common problems among top-level career executives
2. review the interrelationships of government, business, education, and other institutions to increase versatility in achieving desirable *national goals*
3. provide top-level career executives with opportunities to explore current aspects of the governmental process with an emphasis on emerging *intergovernmental* configurations
4. widen a knowledge of *world affairs* and explore methods for improving the administration of overseas programs
5. afford top-level career executives with opportunities to further their understanding about the *total governmental environment* as it affects their work and decisions
6. provide a forum for the discussion of governmental programs on an *interagency basis* for top careerists having special but related interests
7. foster executive attitudes that place a high value on *inventiveness,* consideration of a widening range of administrative alternatives, and significant risk taking to achieve difficult public objectives

Being fully aware of the growing number of career officials whose start was in a professional specialization, the task force report also emphasized that these people "need extensive professional training and experience (in administration), ability to develop policy and programs, and a sure hand on the levers by which their programs can be enthusiastically and forcefully moved."[18]

Overall Appraisal

Internships, merit pay for productivity, Executive Career Service, training—what we have been dealing with is a balanced and positive program. Will it work? It must be made to work. What are some of the main criticisms one hears since enactment of the Civil Service Reform Act of 1978?

On the plus side, Washington has become more management-conscious. Many departments and agencies have profited from a new-found teamwork. There begins to be evidence that managers will be given more freedom and flexibility. There might, in time, be a real transfer of talent laterally within a single government level, such as the federal government, or even among levels, that is, federal, state, and local governments. This of course is the ideal because it affords government more talent and the individual wider horizons of opportunity.

Possible trouble areas have already been suggested or implied. A major one is the discontent of the middle-management group with individual productivity assessment and corresponding variations in pay. Critics object to a pay pool that others control, arguing that bias and favoritism would be hard to prevent. Some doubt whether individual accomplishment can be measured quantitatively but believe that peer review and the judgment of higher supervisory officials is possibly more reliable. They point to fierce personal competitions and animosities in industry and say they want to avoid that in government. They argue that effort is primarily a group or team matter and not the work of separate individuals. The methods used by this disaffected group of middle managers provide an interesting insight

into office politics. A new club was formed, the 42 club, so named because it is the total of grades 13, 14, and 15. This club began to work covertly and sometimes openly to change the objectionable provisions of the 1978 law. Few doubted their eventual success. They argued for equity (treatment equal to that for the higher grades), which in the American culture has an almost irresistible appeal.

Another question to consider is: Are there really "critical" factors that can safely be used to reward and punish people for their productivity or lack of it? Take the matter of what makes a good executive, for example. Psychologists say they think they have isolated certain factors that produce success—verbal skills, ability to reach the heart of problems quickly, a clear idea of alternatives, ability to think conceptually, ability to get along with others, leadership skills, and the ability to put everything together in terms of completing a job. Some of these factors are rather fuzzy and are difficult to measure precisely. But it must be acknowledged that no reputable expert, practitioner or researcher, contends that he understands all that enters into executive success. So much depends upon time, place, and immeasurable conditions such as health or getting along with one's spouse. If they are right, then perhaps public opinion will eventually decide that the Civil Service Reform Act of 1978 attempted to go too far toward precision. Why it did so is clear: first, to justify the term merit by making it more concrete and, second, to give the almost 3 million federal employees stronger incentives to do outstanding work.

But how about incentives? Are they principally matters of money and prestige? Industry apparently thinks so, but government is not industry. Moreover, there is a good deal of evidence to support the contention that the hard-nosed, tough captains of industry, who seem to be insensitive to human feelings, do more harm than good, not only to their firms but to the capitalist ideology.

The incentive that counts most in government employment is a sense of working for all the people, a public-service ethic based upon altruism and helping the country.[19] Businesspersons who have worked in the government stress this difference more than any other. Other incentives are the challenge of the job, a sense of accomplishment, a feeling of fraternity, being at the center of things and feeling stimulated to grow, having more control over one's life and leisure than is possible in many businesses and professions, and a sense of honor that comes from acting unselfishly. The good manager, like the good professional, is one who derives most of his satisfaction from a challenging job well done.

SUMMARY

This chapter has been devoted to the 1978 Civil Service Reform Act, including the Office of Personnel Administration; the Merit Systems Protection Board; and the major programs spawned by the legislation, notably performance appraisal, merit pay, and the Senior Executive Service. It is still too soon to judge with any degree of objectivity how a system emphasizing improved management is going to work out. Will it clash with OMB's jurisdiction and, as seems likely, wind up playing second fiddle?

In the most comprehensive assessment of the 1978 act to date, the Merit Systems Protection Board found midway in 1981 that OPM had lost its prime role and suzerainty in federal personnel affairs. It also found that the largest problems lying ahead are divided authority, cost and time consumed in administering the programs, performance appraisal, and labor-management relations.[20] By September 1981, the exodus from the higher reaches of the Federal Service had reached 51.8 percent of eligibles, whereas the corresponding figure from 1978 was only 22 percent.[21]

It is quite possible that 5 to 10 years from now certain features of the new organization formed in 1978 will be largely unrecognizable. It might even be superseded by something else. But what seems just as certain is that the effort to make personnel measures more effective will continue

to receive central attention. When asked how the U.S. military potential compares with that of the Soviet Union, the chairman of the joint chiefs of staff replied, in 1980, "Technically it's O.K., but in terms of morale, I'm not so sure." And morale is the dominant factor.

NOTES

1. Chester A. Newland, ed., *Professional Public Executives* (Washington: American Society for Public Administration, 1980), ch. 1.

2. President's Commission for a National Agenda for the Eighties, Panel on the Electoral and Democratic Process, *Democratic Process Eighties* (Washington: U.S. Government Printing Office, 1980), pp. 76–81; *Civil Service Reform Implementation: A Report of Progress* (Washington: National Academy of Public Administration [NAPA], September 1980), pp. 10–13.

3. *Civil Service Reform: A Report of the First Year* (Washington: Office of Personnel Management, January 1980).

4. Leonard D. White, *Government Career Service* (Chicago: University of Chicago Press, 1935); Commission on Organization of the Executive Branch (Hoover Commission), *Personnel and Civil Service* (Washington: U.S. Government Printing Office, 1955); Commission on Public Service Personnel, *Better Government Personnel* (New York: McGraw-Hill, 1935).

5. Roger Jones, "Developments in Federal Manpower: A Federal Perspective," in *Professional Public Executives,* ed. Newland, pp. 143–155.

6. Alan K. Campbell, "Civil Service Reform: A New Commitment," *Public Administration Review* 38 (March-April 1978): 101. See also U.S. President's Reorganization Project: Personnel Management Project, vol. 1, *Final Staff Report* (Washington: U.S. Government Printing Office, 1977).

7. Comptroller General of the United States, *Civil Service Reform: Where It Stands Today*, 13 May 1980, p. 1.

8. Comptroller General, *Civil Service Reform, p. 1.*

9. *Report of the Task Force on Performance Appraisal and Merit Pay* (Washington: National Academy of Public Administration, 1981).

10. Marshall E. Dimock and Howard K. Hyde, *Bureaucracy and Trusteeship in Large Corporations* (Washington: U.S. Government Printing Office, 1941). Also Marshall E. Dimock, *Administrative Vitality: The Conflict with Bureaucracy* (New York: Harper & Row, 1959).

11. William J. Lanquette, "SES—From Civil Service Show-piece to Incipient Failure in Two Years," *National Journal*, 18 July 1981, p. 1296.

12. Thomas D. Lynch and Gerald T. Gabris, "Obstacles to Effective Management," *The Bureaucrat* (Washington, D.C., Spring 1981), pp. 8–14.

13. Fred C. Thayer, "Civil Service Reform and Performance Appraisal: A Policy Disaster," *Public Personnel Management Journal* 10 (1981): 20–28.

14. Marshall E. Dimock, "Executive Development After Ten Years," in *Professional Public Executives,* ed. Newland, pp. 60–70.

15. Brian Chapman, *The Profession of Government: The Public Service in Europe* (Westport, Conn.: Greenwood Press, 1980), p. 59. Ezra N. Suleiman, *Politics, Power, and Bureaucracy in France* (Princeton, N.J.: Princeton University Press, 1974).

16. John J. Corson, "Equipping Men for Career Growth in the Public Service," *Public Administration Review* 23 (March 1963): 1–9; Richard L. Chapman and Frederic N. Cleaveland, *Meeting the Needs of Tomorrow's Public Service* (Washington: NAPA, 1973).

17. U.S., Civil Service Commission, Presidential Task Force on Career Development, *Investment for Tomorrow* (Washington: U.S. Government Printing Office, 1967), p. 26 [Italics added].

18. U.S. Civil Service Commission, *Investment for Tomorrow,* p. 27.

19. Marshall E. Dimock, "The Potential Incentives of Public Employment," *American Political Science Review* 37 (August 1933): 259–262.

20. U.S., Merit Systems Protection Board, *Report on the Significant Actions of the Office of Personnel Management* [OPM] *During 1980* (Washington, June 1981), p. 13.

21. "Is the Federal Service Dying of Pensionitis?" *U.S. News and World Report,* 7 September 1981, p. 22. Data from the OPM.

20

Labor Relations, Affirmative Action, and Employee Political Participation

All your strength is in your union.
Henry Wadsworth Longfellow, **Hiawatha**

In this chapter, we deal with labor-management legislation and its enforcement under the Civil Service Reform Act, affirmative action to protect minority rights, and the regulation of employees' partisan political activities under the Hatch Act and its amendments.

Robert Krause, personnel director of the city of Miami in 1981, once remarked to one of the authors that in the 1960s he was thinking of leaving the field of personnel administration. "I had completed the last classification scheme I ever wanted to work on," said Krause, "and the work just didn't excite me any more."

Why, then, did he stay? "Almost immediately after, municipal unions became much more militant. And federal affirmative-action programs burst on the scene. Personnel work today may be frustrating at times, but it certainly isn't boring!"

RISE TO POWER OF GOVERNMENT UNIONS

Labor relations in government came late—mostly within the past 20 years—but it is now one of the most interesting and explosive areas of public administration. To take one example, government employee unions could make or break the Civil Service Reform Act. Equally, with the right kind of statesmanship on both sides, union activity and collective bargaining could improve human relations and administrative efficiency to the degree that the merit system, unaided, has been unable to accomplish in 100 years. In another example, labor's influence in lobbying, party conventions, and general elections could become so powerful that attempts might be made to restrict such activities by major legislation; on the other hand, it is not inconceivable that labor's influence could become so great that it would have a political party of its own, as in Britain. Or to take still a third example, the National Education Association, which is not a labor union but which because of competition from a rival American Federation of Labor-Congress of Industrial Organizations (AFL-CIO) union acts increasingly like one, has been witnessing many strikes among its members in small towns and villages as well as large cities throughout the country. Often these strikes are prohibited by law, but they take place anyway. They involve more than salaries and financial issues; they deal with freedom to act like profes-

sional teachers as regards curriculum, class size, choice of textbooks, and ways to teach. What if there were a general strike of teachers? Or a strike in which organized firemen or policemen were allied? Labor relations is a matter of high politics.

Federal Unions

As of late 1980, 61 percent of all federal employees were organized, almost 1.46 million, not including postal employees, who for decades had formed the most numerous and most politically effective union.[1] The remarkable thing about this statistic, however, is that in 1964, the corresponding overall figure was only 6 percent, the 1969 figure was 28 percent, and the 1974 figure was 49 percent. In contrast, about 23 percent of the nongovernment sector was organized by unions in 1981.[2] According to the Bureau of Labor Statistics, the federal government now ranks 14th in terms of *degree* of organization, *in the economy as a whole,* coming just below electrical machinery, fabricated metals, and mining out of 34 industries entering into the analysis.[3]

Shortly after the administration of Ronald Reagan came into power in 1980, Jane P. McMichael, legislative director of the American Federation of Government Employees (AFGE), with 700,000 members, said, "Federal employees are beginning to stand up for themselves. . . . They are not as passive as they used to be."[4] This action took the form of increasing the number of their legislative representatives on the Hill. "They're more sophisticated, more professional in contacting members of Congress than some other groups are," said the chairman of the House committee on civil service.[5] Then he pointed out that when President Jimmy Carter tried to reduce cost-of-living bonuses in 1980, one of the most conservative members of the House "carried the ball" and defeated the president's move.[6]

What accounts for this rapid growth of federal union activity? Was it perhaps that there have been three main periods of labor growth in the United States? First came the craft unions, then the industrial unions, and finally the unions in service areas, which government more nearly resembles.[7] This growth may be a reason. But against this explanation is the fact that state and local unionism grew much earlier and faster than federal unionism, and all are equally exposed to the same social movements. Perhaps it was because there was a series of liberal-democratic presidents with majorities in both Houses of Congress? If so, how does one explain that President Richard Nixon and President John Kennedy, though unlike, were the two who most contributed to union growth by the executive orders they issued?[8] Another explanation is that as early as 1912 the Lloyd-LaFollette Act gave federal workers the right to "petition" Congress and accorded postal workers the right to organize associations so long as they did not affiliate with any outside group. Since that time this work force of around three fifths of a million workers, scattered over the entire country, has naturally had a political influence envied by others. All of these reasons, and others, doubtless contributed to the result.

The Federal Labor Relations Authority

Title VII of the Civil Service Reform Act of 1978 created the Federal Labor Relations Authority (FLRA), with three members, who serve five-year terms, plus a general counsel, who acts as prosecutor of complaints. It was deliberately modeled after the National Labor Relations Board (NLRB), which grew out of the Wagner Act of 1935, "Labor's Magna Carta."

The objectives of the legislation are set forth in Section 7101 of the 1978 act. First, labor unions and collective bargaining are in the public interest. Second, experience in both the private and public sectors shows the following to be relevant: unions and collective bargaining contribute to the effective conduct of the public business, safeguard the public interest, and facilitate and encourage the amicable settlement of disputes between employer and employee in matters affecting conditions of employment. By far the most interesting

and long-range objective, however, is this: the efficient operation of the government requires progressive work practice and the highest standards of employee performance. This strongly worded statement struck a positive note. Labor relations exists not merely to settle disputes that might slow down work or inconvenience the public. Labor relations is designed to achieve better labor-management cooperation.

The 1978 act clearly established collective bargaining and set up a labor relations board to deal with disputes. The act did not, however, include jurisdiction over compensation and fringe benefits. Its main thrust, therefore, was to determine the appropriate bargaining unit, supervise elections, resolve issues and decide appeals concerning such matters, conduct hearings regarding unfair labor practices, issue orders to cease and desist, and turn to court enforcement if necessary. The act also transferred to FLRA the so-called Federal Service Impasse Panel, which acts as a last resort if ordinary methods do not work.

Evaluating the Results

The setting up of the FLRA clearly left unsettled some important questions, which in an area so complex is to be expected. What is perhaps the main one has been suggested: how far Congress might go in delegating the pay and fringe package. Congress clearly has power to delegate, but will it do so in this area that affects appropriations and taxes so significantly? It would likely be loath to give the whole authority to the Office of Personnel Management (OPM). What seems even more unlikely is that it would give the question of pay to scores of action agencies of various kinds.

Equally important is the question of labor-management cooperation. The two sides of this issue make equally strong appeals. Management ought not to allow labor unions to invade their management prerogatives or have their administrators join unions because managers need independence, flexibility, and final authority if they are to be effective. Equally the more managers sit down with organized labor and devise improvements that increase efficiency and morale, the more successful labor relations is and the more everyone benefits, especially union leaders, who, like everyone else, have constituents.

An interesting illustration of what may be anticipated in labor relations arose early in the life of the FLRA. It is the so-called *Fort Dix* case. During the course of negotiations between the Army-Air Force Exchange Service and a local AFL-CIO union, the union made the following proposal: *In the event of a disciplinary suspension or removal, the grievant will exhaust the review procedure contained in this agreement, i.e. grievance and arbitration before the suspension or removal is effective. Further, the employee will remain in a pay status until a final determination is rendered.* The employer (government) refused to consider the proposal, saying that it was a nonnegotiable infringement on management's inherent right to discipline employees. In addition, they submitted that in line with an executive order of the president (E.O.11491), union proposals that interfered with management's reserved authority to act or that unreasonably delayed that authority were equally nonnegotiable.

Much to the government agency's consternation, the FLRA ruled that the matter *was* negotiable. This decision was based on the ground that the intent of the Civil Service Reform Act (CSRA) was not to prevent delay but merely to protect management's right to act *at all*. The FLRA did not say that the proposal had to be accepted, merely that the two parties must negotiate in good faith. The matter has not been finally settled in the highest courts. The Office of Personnel Management and the Justice Department appealed the decision.

But even if the courts were to reverse the FLRA decision, says the assistant director for labor-management relations in the OPM, it seems clear that hereafter there will be (1) more constraints on management's freedom to act; (2) more complexity, more legal issues and litigations, more challenges to management decisions,

and more costs and delays; and (3) more likelihood that disputes will escalate to higher echelons of decision and that management flexibility will be reduced.[9]

Among the reasons given for this pessimistic view are the following. The administrative apparatus is complex, including as it does the Merit Systems Protection Board and its general counsel as well as the FLRA and its general counsel. Also, the greatly increased scope of matters that may now go to arbitrators enlarges the role of the courts. The proliferation of third parties involved in the legislation means that more decisions will be made outside the agency one manages.

Interestingly, it has also been remarked that for years the character of the federal work force has been changing: workers are younger, better educated, more interested in achieving personal satisfaction and personal goals, less patient, and less accepting of authority.[10]

If flexibility and management authority are to be retained, says an OPM official, more attention must be given to management-labor participation. Management and workers must learn to pull together toward efficiency and effectiveness. Management cannot afford to stand passively by. There should be more intelligence, preparation, and desire to achieve results in advance of negotiation and a recognition that the parties have interests in common. Further, although each party identifies strongly with its own interests, the parties should learn to know and respect each other's goals.[11]

This analysis of labor-management relations is concluded on this rather amusing note:

---

unions are political organisms, and union officials are politicians; they win or lose elections. Like all politicians, they want to look good, and they want their names and pictures before their constituents. Bureaucrats may be faceless, but union officials are not.[12]

The official gets over his facelessness when he states, "Management must be strong and management-oriented."[13] It must have a coherent labor policy and pursue it fearlessly and consistently.

State and Local Labor Relations

State and local governments have been almost a generation ahead of the federal government in their experience with labor organizing, collective bargaining, and settlement of disputes. As might be expected, the larger cities took the lead. There were more union members in the cities, the police and fire departments were larger, and the teachers were more militant than they usually are in small towns. The number and variety of "labor troubles" has been impressive in recent years and continues to grow. But, as also might be expected, state and local government have more to teach the federal government about remedies and methods than the reverse.[14]

Three fourths of the states have collective bargaining laws or weaker facsimiles, work-and-confer laws. Wisconsin, in 1959, was the first state to make collective bargaining apply to both state and local governments. Only a few states have work-and-confer laws, in which management has the final authority irrespective of the bargaining. Full-fledged collective bargaining laws provide for negotiations that have broad application, on such matters as salaries and wages, hours of work, fringe benefits, and cooperative consultations. As noted earlier, the right to strike is rarely provided, but, as also noted, strikes occur at all levels. About one tenth of all the states now have limited-right-to-strike laws, and bills have been introduced into Congress, as well as elsewhere, to extend this right. Much depends upon public opinion. The attitude is less favorable toward "crisis" or "emergency" services, such as fire and police, and it seems to be changing toward teachers and postal workers, who are by far the most numerous of nonmilitary public personnel.

The most widely used methods to avoid the resort to strikes include *comprehensive collective bargaining agreements*. These are like contracts for given periods of time, in which each side has its rights and duties clearly set forth. Since they are participatory and voluntary, agreements of this kind are the cornerstone of remedial action.

Other remedies are not dissimilar to those found in the private sector. *Mediation* involves a third party, who tries to bring the two sides together. *Fact-finding,* used increasingly in teacher disputes, consists of laying the facts bare and giving the citizens and their representatives, such as school boards, a chance to judge the merits of a case. *Arbitration* is stronger than the two just mentioned. It involves an outside arbitrator, chosen by both sides, and trusts the arbitrator's impartial weighing of the facts and the arguments. Highly experienced agencies such as the American Arbitration Association and a large cadre of professional arbitrators are available for such work, and arbitration is increasingly a resort. Compliance with decisions has been remarkably good. There are two main kinds of arbitration; in one the parties agree to be bound by the finding in advance, in the other they do not. Increasingly the former kind is being used; the reason is, apparently, that organized labor is generally reassured by the process and wants to avoid the possible negative reaction of the public if the strike weapon is used. *Labor relations boards* are like the federal board and are usually found in larger states or cities. *Impasse panels* are best known in federal practice, where even the State Department has one. Something like them, however, is found in a few state and local jurisdictions. Finally, there are the court system, management operation during a strike by higher officers, calling in the national or state guard, and, as the ultimate recourse, martial law.

Some Proposed Guidelines of Public Policy

An excellent study by the Committee for Economic Development (CED), with a standing committee on government relations, came up with a statesmanlike set of guidelines in 1978.

- An impartial public-employee relations board should be established to oversee the structure and procedures for labor relations in both the state and local governments.

- The process of bargaining in government should be structured so that the public is kept fully informed.
- Legal prohibition of strikes does not address the question of how to deal with illegal work stoppages.
- Managers should be given greater authority over such key personnel matters as recruiting, hiring, training, assigning, promoting, disciplining, compensating, and firing employees. Managers should be involved in collective bargaining with the employees for whom they are responsible.
- Promotion to supervisory positions should be based on managerial competence rather than other criteria, and supervisors should not be given the bargaining rights enjoyed by their subordinates.
- Comparability of compensation between the public and private sectors should be applied to total compensation.
- Employees themselves are a prime and important source of knowledge and energy for improving operations; there is room for experimenting with new forms of work organization.
- Prescriptions for change or improvement should be adapted to local circumstances.
- The diffusion of responsibility for personnel matters among civil service commissions, personnel boards and departments, and labor relations boards creates unnecessary problems of coordination and even competition among staffs.
- The executive branch should be responsible for representing government in labor relations and should be granted wide latitude by the legislative body.
- Governments should counteract the dangers of overreliance on the courts in public labor relations.[15]

Since some strikes are inevitable, the CED sought to broaden the range of remedies available for settling disputes. Prominent attention was given to fact-finding by neutral third parties; arbitration in which there is agreement in advance to abide by the finding of the impartial third party; mediation, which takes the form of conciliation; and public referendum by placing the issue on a ballot for formal vote. Eight states, as remarked earlier, were discovered to have granted

the right to strike in certain classes of cases. In a 10-year period there had been a 17-fold increase in unauthorized strikes in other jurisdictions. The CED, therefore, recommended that all states should lay plans to sustain essential public services in health, safety, and welfare when a complete impasse has been reached.

The approach of the CED might be capsulized as "leadership and new perspectives." Rigid bureaucratic pronouncements are no solution. Collective bargaining is apparently here to stay, but it is at best an adversary encounter. It needs to be supplemented by more innovative and human contrivances in management and organization.

Returning again to the political and long-range effects of labor's growing power on American government and life, it should be noted that the government unions, as contrasted with those in the private sector, are by far the more powerful within the AFL-CIO, in terms of membership, resources, and growth potential. The largest of any government union is the American Federation of State, County, and Municipal Employees (AFSCME), which includes public works' and utilities' employees, police personnel, and clerical, social service, and sanitation employees. Altogether, there are well over 1.5 million local employees in municipal unions. They, the teachers' unions, and the postal unions are all grass-roots organizations, which means that they have an enormous political potential.[16]

Following the passage of the Wagner Act in 1935, it was observed that as the labor force rapidly accelerated in numbers and power, younger and better-educated leaders flowed into the top circles of the AFL and the CIO. There seemed to be an innate recognition that with power comes a corresponding obligation to handle policy and management in a skilled and statesmanlike way. Many of these new recruits came from the economics departments of universities, as, for example, John R. Commons from Wisconsin and John M. Clark from Columbia. Soon, as industry was quick to recognize, labor's bargaining manpower became equal to its own. This development was evidence that the leadership of labor, like that of other bureaucracies, periodically needs renewal, an intake of fresh, highly educated manpower.[17]

Labor's need for statesmanship bears importantly on several of the questions analyzed in this book. An example is training programs dealt with in the preceding chapter. Organized labor has a choice of actively supporting these programs with enrollees and instructors or "going it alone," which is the inclination of bureaucracy. An even larger area of potential good is the training of labor leaders in business and public administration. If there is to be "co-direction," meaning a wider participation in policy and administration, labor, no less than management, needs to be trained. This focus, therefore, has an important bearing on the future of representative democracy in the United States, and today this cooperative enterprise is nowhere near as adequate as it needs to be.[18]

AFFIRMATIVE ACTION

"There probably isn't a single jurisdiction in the country that doesn't discriminate in its employment practices against minorities and especially women, to some degree. The question is who are the worst violators."[19] Since this nation as a whole practiced discrimination against minority groups and women in the job market, it is not surprising that government did the same. True, after the Civil War blacks found more opportunity working for the federal government than they did in the private sector, but few minority employees were found in middle management, and almost none in top management.

Affirmative-Action Programs

As a result of the civil rights movement of the 1960s and the women's movement, which followed it, a number of steps were taken to reduce discrimination in government hiring and promotional practices. Affirmative-action programs were so named to distinguish them from past programs prohibiting discrimination. The new programs took positive steps requiring government to recruit minorities and women and to eliminate discrimination in all aspects of personnel practice.[20]

Federal action directly affected state and local governments, since affirmative-action requirements were directly tied to federal grants-in-aid (discussed earlier in Chapter 6).

Numerous presidential executive orders, acts of Congress, and court cases have defined the affirmative-action programs. One key act was the 1972 Equal Employment Opportunity Act. Passage of this legislation meant that discrimination on the basis of race, religion, or sex violates federal law, and applicants and employees can go to court to sue for relief if they have exhausted all their administrative appeals.

Under affirmative-action programs, agencies have been given numerical goals to aim for in hiring or promoting minorities and women. To ensure that goals are met, agencies must keep figures on the number of employees by sex and ethnic group.

As one can imagine, this whole area has been one of controversy. Some critics have argued that goals amount to the same thing as quotas. To say that a person should hire so many women and blacks, Hispanics, or others is a form of reverse discrimination, in the critics' opinion, which makes things worse. By accepting the right to discriminate in favor of minorities, Americans have embedded the practice of discrimination in law—a terrible mistake that will boomerang and return the country to the days of legal segregation.

Others argue that after hundreds of years of discrimination, only a program like affirmative action can turn things around. They note that programs prior to affirmative action yielded little or no results.

The whole process of determining goals is fraught with perplexities. Should the goal, for example, reflect local, regional, or national ethnic composition? What relation should it have to training and skills of minorities and women? Should unskilled applicants be hired and trained on the job?

How can one determine whether an agency had been discriminatory? If the agency's employees are skilled professionals and if the agency's salaries are not competitive with those in other bureaus in the same field of work, capable minority employees, who are in high demand, will not be attracted by a job in this agency. Does lack of minority employees then mean, ipso facto, that the agency discriminated?

These and countless other problems bedevil affirmative-action efforts. Through 1980, the federal courts held that such programs were constitutional[21] in the face of challenges by critics who argued that reverse discrimination was an affront to the Constitution. The whole idea of goals or quotas is repugnant to many Americans, but the historical record makes it clear that discrimination has been an enormous blot on American society and government. Affirmative action will redress some mistaken policies, make some errors, and no doubt will remain a source of controversy to the end of this century. The most celebrated case, of course, is the *Bakke* Supreme Court decision of 1978, involving a white applicant to medical school in California. The court squarely upheld affirmative action.[22] (In effect, the Supreme Court confirmed the necessity of quotas for minorities but also satisfied the other side by saying that college admission procedures should protect whites as well and not result in reverse discrimination.)

Equal Employment Opportunity Commission

There has been an equal-employment opportunity program in Washington since the passage of the 1964 Civil Rights Act. Under the provisions of the Civil Service Reform Act of 1978 the equal-employment jurisdiction formerly centered in the U.S. Civil Service Commission was transferred to the new Equal Employment Opportunity Commission (EEOC).

It should be noted first that equal opportunity is a central part of labor relations; in the American setting there is possibly no other issue that

bulks larger. Second, equal opportunity and a civil service system are pretty much interchangeable conceptions. Third, it will be immediately grasped that the jurisdiction of EEOC and the Merit Systems Protection Board (MSPB) overlap directly. Not surprisingly this overlap has led to complicated and thorough efforts to coordinate the two jurisdictions. Fourth, the widened scope of EEOC underscores its importance; legislation by Congress now applies to discrimination on the basis of age, handicapped condition, and sex (the equal-pay-for-equal-work doctrine), as well as to discrimination on the original bases of color, national origin, religion, social status, educational identification, and other sources of social prejudice. The EEOC is defended as unifying the country and giving the doctrine of equality practical effect; at the same time it is blamed for adding to judicialized contention and significantly slowing down administrative processes.

Since the enactment of the CSRA, the EEOC program has operated as before under a chairman, small board, and field organization.[23] It has been primarily concerned with developing Uniform Selection Guidelines in cooperation with the OPM. It has carried on special training and recruitment programs and has cleared up the backlog of more than 4,000 cases inherited from the old Civil Service Commission. It has introduced a one-step investigatory procedure in place of a two-part procedure, and it has dealt with its overlap with MSPB by setting up a three-member review committee, one from each side and the third a public member, when conflicts arise.[24]

Under the 1964-1978 legislation, Congress vested initial jurisdiction over the equal-employment controversies in government itself in the various departmental agencies. The underlying idea was that if the several operating agencies worked out their own problems, they would have a more sincere interest in equality of opportunity than if this responsibility were centralized in one place at the apex.

The minority-recruitment program, provided for in the Civil Service Reform Act of 1978, puts teeth into this resolve. Each agency, says the act, must conduct a minority-recruitment program, with OPM oversight, to eliminate underrepresentation of minorities within categories of civil service employment. EEOC is to make determinations of underrepresentation and establish guidelines for minority-recruitment programs.

As in so many areas we have examined, the question that bulks large in the future is whether constructive means based on human relations can be found to supplement and make less necessary the "sanctions" approach, which is represented by constant appeals to the courts. These appeals are often long, costly, and upsetting to orderly enforcement. With so much progress already made, perhaps in future conciliation will tend to replace judicial compulsion.

POLITICAL PARTICIPATION: THE HATCH ACTS

Should government employees be allowed the same constitutional rights as others to partake in partisan political activities? Or because of their privileged position in the government should their rights be somewhat restricted? The first Hatch Act was passed in 1939 and broadened in 1940. Another passed Congress in 1976, when it was vetoed by President Gerald Ford. President Carter declared for a liberalization of the restrictive legislation in 1977, but the issue is still hotly debated.

The First Amendment to the federal Constitution ensures everyone the right to freedom of speech, press, assembly, and petition. The Hatch Act of 1939, which was called An Act to Prevent Pernicious Political Activities, declared:

No officer or employee in the executive branch of the Federal Government, or any agency or department thereof, *shall take an active part in political management of political campaigns.* All such persons shall retain the right to vote as they may choose and to express their opinions on all political questions.

"Little Hatch Acts" resembling the federal one have been passed in many of the 50 states.

Three further points need emphasis. First, the act reaches those beyond the merit system, per se, and includes all nonpolicymaking officers whether in the merit system or not. Second, the OPM may designate certain localities in the Washington area where federal employees are in a majority and give them the right to stand as candidates and to take sides concerning independent candidates. Third, the act allows political activity when there are nonpartisan elections or when there are constitutional and referenda questions not associated with partisan political parties.

The arguments in favor of Hatch Act policy are similar to the views of those who fear collective bargaining and labor union activity generally. Civil servants are supposed to be neutral, not partisan. The 16.5 million public employees in the United States constitute roughly a fifth of the voters for president and more than a fourth for members of the lower house of Congress. This figure of course does not include employees' families. This viewpoint was well expressed in a Supreme Court decision in a 1973 case, *United States Civil Service Commission* v. *National Association of Letter Carriers, AFL-CIO*:

—employees . . . should administer the law in accordance with the will of Congress, rather than in accordance with their own or the will of a political party. They are expected to enforce the law and execute the programs of the Government without bias or favoritism for or against any political party or group or the members thereof.[25]

The division in the court was 6 to 3; earlier, in a 1947 case, it had been much closer, 4 to 3.[26]

The unions' arguments in opposition to the Hatch Act are the ones that might be expected. The prohibition is so broad and undefined as to be unconstitutional. What is there in "taking an active part in . . . political campaigns" that denies advocacy and persuasion? How can a union be militant if its political activities are interfered with in any way? Besides, the government employee knows more about government than anyone else and consequently he may be expected to have a greater interest in issues and candidates than anyone else.

Several attempts have been made in recent years to abolish the Hatch Act but without success. The argument is that the legislation was once necessary and congruent but is so no longer. It does not touch and never was intended to discourage campaign spending. Both business and government give money through individuals or alternative organizations created for that purpose and exempted from regulatory legislation. It is argued that the greater power of corporations over financial resources must be matched by the smaller contributions of millions of members in organized labor.

A POSSIBLE PROGNOSIS

It will be interesting to see how labor relations and public personnel management develop in the years ahead. The government unions, as we have seen, have a clout they have never had before. In the United States, however, labor's predominant disposition has always been conservative. Except for a short period when the CIO was in the making during the incumbency of John L. Lewis, who seceded from the AF of L and formed an industrial union of his own, labor has been strikingly apolitical compared with European labor movements. American unions are as distrustful of government as conservative businessmen because their power lies in collective bargaining and strikes. Their independence and autonomy are due to economic, not political, sanctions. To them, the government is primarily a means of providing education, social services, and other forms of assistance that supplement but do not replace the bargaining situation.

One possibility is that organized labor groups will try to manipulate the public personnel system described in this group of chapters to their own advantage. They may try to put management more under judicial authority instead of granting it more freedom. They may choose to fight and adopt contentious tactics instead of using existing opportunities for cooperation and responsible involvement in appropriate areas of planning and operation. Much will probably depend upon the

degree of awareness on the part of labor and management and, equally, upon what is needed to improve and sustain the United States' competitive position relative to the outside world.

A thoughtful piece produced by the CED underscores the importance of the points just mentioned.

- Many public managers must deal with complexity and constraints more formidable than any found in most business organizations. This is partly to be expected because of the political nature of government.
- The constraints of most governments are unnecessarily paralyzing. Controls established to guard against political favoritism and graft now pose the equally ominous danger of crippling public service operations.
- Elected officials and the public cannot expect managers to exercise greater authority than they have been delegated from the top.
- If top policy makers cannot reach accord themselves on the direction of policy *or the general means of implementation* in line agencies, it is unreasonable to expect managers to develop such authority on their own.

This study concludes by admonishing schools of management and public policy to recognize the growing importance of personnel management. Their present-day challenge is to make complex organizations function effectively. They need a broad, human approach, one that will synthesize the legal, political, economic, managerial, and ethical aspects of personnel management and the potential storminess of trade union relations.[27]

SUMMARY

New dimensions have been added to national politics and public administration as a whole because of the growing power and institutionalization of government unions. In management, the acid question is whether this development will prove vexing to management or whether managers will be able to improve performance by involving the rank and file more closely in their work.[28] The possible implications for the political process are even more impressive. The air controllers' strike of the first year of the administration of Ronald Reagan (1981) will not soon be forgotten. The issues were so complex. Should the controllers have been classified as public employees in the first place, or would it have been better to have made them employees of the corporate airport administration? In another issue, in half a dozen states, a manager's union has been organized; and in some states, managers are "bargaining" with the state legislature over wages, status, and other matters. Is this development good public policy or bad? In the past, almost everyone, without a moment's hesitation, would say "bad." It will be an interesting period as the country approaches 1984!

NOTES

1. Anthony F. Ingrassia, "Labor-Management Relations for the Federal Government," *Management,* Fall 1980, p. 11.

2. "Federal Workers Brace to Fend Off Reagan," *U.S. News and World Report,* 23 February 1981, p. 79.

3. Ingrassia, "Labor-Management Relations," p. 11.

4. "Federal Workers Brace," p. 79.

5. "Federal Workers Brace."

6. "Federal Workers Brace." This would have saved 750 million dollars.

7. Gus Tyler, "Why They Organize?" in "A Symposium: Collective Bargaining in the Public Sector, A Reappraisal," ed. Felix Nigro, *Public Administration Review* 32 (March-April 1972): 99.

8. Thomas R. Colosi and Steven B. Rynecki, *Federal Legislation for Public Sector Collective Bargaining* (Chicago: International Personnel Management Association, 1975).

9. Ingrassia, "Labor-Management Relations," p. 11ff.

10. Ingrassia, "Labor-Management Relations," p. 12.

11. Ingrassia, "Labor-Management Relations," p. 13.

12. Ingrassia, "Labor-Management Relations."

13. Ingrassia, "Labor-Management Relations."

14. Advisory Committee on Intergovernmental Relations, *Labor-Management Policies for State and Local Governments* (Washington: U.S. Government Printing Office, 1969); Tim Bornstein, "Perspectives on Change in Local Collective Bargaining," in *Public Sector Labor Relations at the Crossroads* (Amherst: University of Massachusetts, School of Business Administration, 1977).

15. *Improving Management of the Public Work Force: The Challenge in State and Local Government* (New York: Committee for Economic Development, November 1978), ch. 4.

16. *Local Government Personnel Administration* (Washington: International City Management Association, 1975), ch. 10. This chapter is a thorough analysis in concrete and detailed form of the steps to be taken in collective bargaining and impasse resolution. See also Jerry Wurf, "Merit: A Union View," *Public Administration Review* 34 (September-October 1974): 36–45, by a president of the American Federation of State, County, and Municipal Employees.

17. David T. Stanley, *Managing Local Government Under Union Pressure* (Washington: Brookings Institution, 1972).

18. Marshall E. Dimock, *The New American Political Economy* (New York: Harper & Row, 1962), pts. 1 and 2.

19. Morton H. Sklar, *Civil Rights Under the General Revenue Sharing Program* (Washington: Catholic Law School, Center for National Policy Studies, 1975), p. 5.

20. Selma J. Mushkin, *What Achieves Affirmative Action in Cities?* (Washington: Georgetown University, Public Services Laboratory, 1975).

21. Carl F. Goodman, "Equal Employment Opportunity: Preferential Quotas and Unrepresented Third Parties," *Georgetown Law Journal* 44 (May 1976). Leading case: *Washington, Mayor of Washington, D.C., et al. v. Davis,* 426 U.S. 229, 96 S.Ct. 2040 (1976).

22. *Regents of the University of California* v. *Bakke,* 438 U.S. 265, 98 S.Ct. 2733 (1978) discussed (with opinions) in *New York Times,* 29 June 1978.

23. *EEOC: The Transformation of an Agency* (Washington: U.S. Equal Employment Opportunity Commission, July 1978).

24. "E.E.O.C.'s Improved Case Management System," *Management* 1 (Fall 1980): 14–15.

25. 413 U.S. 548 (1973).

26. *United Public Workers* v. *Mitchell,* 350 U.S. 75 (1947).

27. *Improving Management of the Public Work Force,* p. 95. This study makes so much sense that it would be desirable to assign it for class report.

28. Richard E. Walton, "Work Innovations in the United States," *Harvard Business Review,* 57 (July–August 1979): 88–98.

PART **5**

FINANCIAL MANAGEMENT

Anthony Milano, secretary of the Connecticut Office of Policy and Management and chief state budgetary officer in 1982, outlines the trends and prospects for state finances. (Photo courtesy of T. Dean Caple)

21

Public Finance

On February 15, 1981, the Gallup Poll released a survey indicating that the public believes that 48¢ of every dollar spent by the federal government is wasted.
Public Administration Times, *1 March 1981, p. 5.*

We deal here with the classic problems of public finance: revenues, expenditures, debts, effect on the economy, public opinion, and taxpayer revolts. The administrator is the one who knows the most at first hand about such things; he is looked to for pol- icy improvements and efficiencies and savings that will make all of the work of government more effective. This discussion lays the basis for chapters on budgeting, auditing, and accounting—at all three levels.

Since American government does much more that it used to, U.S. citizens spend much more money on government. The gross national product (GNP) is the grand total of all economic activity in a country, comprising all goods and services produced. In 1929, *all* American governments—federal, state, and local—spent a total of 10 percent of the GNP. By 1978, this figure had risen to 32.5 percent of GNP, or almost one third of the total economic activity of the nation.[1] These percentages speak volumes about the expansion of American government. But as the quotation prefacing this chapter indicates, many people in the United States are disgruntled about the amount of taxes they have to pay. As we shall see later, a tax "revolt" began in the late 1970s. In the summer of 1981, President Ronald Reagan succeeded in pushing $37 billion worth of tax cuts through Congress. Popular resistance to taxation is of the utmost importance for students of public finance.

RECENT TRENDS IN PUBLIC FINANCE

A budget is a statement of spending and revenue relationships. The governmental budget share of the GNP has grown from 26.5 percent in 1954 to 32.5 percent in 1978. Further, *all levels of government have grown at rates exceeding that of the economy as a whole.*[2] Since the money to pay for this growth had to come from somewhere, it is not surprising to learn that the tax burden of the statistically "average" family *doubled* between 1953 and 1974. In 1953, the average family paid 11.8 percent of its income in direct federal, state, and local taxes. By 1974, the figure had risen to 23.4 percent, a 98.3 percent increase. Small wonder, then, that tax lawyer Richard N. Servaas instructed his family to include the following message in his obituary: "The deceased requested that, to eliminate the middle man, memorials be sent directly to the Internal Revenue Service."[3]

We shall examine the causes of these enormous increases in spending and revenue in the sections that follow, dealing with the federal, state, and local governments in turn. For the mo-

ment, one example will illustrate the post-World War II growth of government. A majority of U.S. citizens live within 10 miles of the interstate highway system, a 50,000-mile network of roads built since 1956 at a cost for construction and maintenance of more than $100 billion.

Another indicator of increased spending is governmental debt. To pay for capital (large nonrecurring) expenditures such as buildings, state and local debt rose from $39 billion to $257 billion, from 1954 through 1977,[4] or about 13 percent of the 1977 GNP. At the same time, the federal government's debt rose from $226.6 billion in 1955 to $771.5 billion in 1978,[5] about 37 percent of the GNP. By 1981 it was a trillion dollars. Anticipating an increase in the federal debt, Congress authorized an increase in the debt limit to $985 billion in February 1981 and to one trillion dollars in September 1981. Later in this chapter we shall discuss the implications of debt policy. At present our message is that government spending, absolutely and relatively, has increased at a rapid rate since the 1950s. This fundamental fact is the foundation of this chapter.

PUBLIC OPINION OF PUBLIC FINANCE

"On February 15, 1981, the Gallup Poll released a survey indicating that the public believes that 48¢ of every dollar spent by the federal government is wasted. This was the median judgment. When the same question was asked in respect to state and local government expenditures, the median estimate of waste was 29¢ and 23¢, respectively."[6]

The Advisory Commission on Intergovernmental Relations (ACIR), described in Chapter 5, has been asking Americans since 1972 which level of government they think gives them the most for their money. In 1972, most picked the federal government, with local government second, and state government last. This pattern persisted each year until 1979, when local government replaced the federal government in the top spot. Likewise, the local property tax, which was the most unpopular single tax from 1972 to 1978, lost that designation in the 1979 poll to the federal income tax.[7]

This change in public opinion almost certainly reflects dramatic changes in tax policy, which have recently taken place and which we shall explore in the following sections.

THE FEDERAL GOVERNMENT

The story of U.S. public finance in the 20th century is the growth of the federal government's spending and revenues relative to state and local government. In 1929, state and local governments outspent the federal government three to one, as Table 21.1 indicates. By 1954, a great change had occurred: The federal government was spending more than two and a half times as much as state and local governments. In 1978, it spent more than twice as much as state and local government.

What are the causes of this enormous expansion? They are the demands for increased services, which it was most politically or legally feasible to meet at the federal level.

Federal Spending

One area in which federal spending has increased enormously is national defense. In 1930, the U.S. Army consisted of a skeleton crew scattered across various posts in the country; its cavalry units still used horses. In 1980, the army was a

TABLE 21.1   Spending by Level of Government, in Billions of Dollars*

Year	Federal	State and local
1929	$2.6	$7.6
1954	$69.8	$27.2
1978	$461.0	$223.2

*Federal data include expenditures for grants-in-aid to state and local governments. These amounts have been excluded from state and local expenditures.

SOURCE: *Facts and Figures on Government Finance* (New York: Tax Foundation, Inc., 1979), p. 33.

million strong, with personnel and equipment all over the world. No wonder, then, that the total defense budget had increased almost *180 times* in this 50-year period, far outstripping the rate of inflation. By 1981 it was the highest in U.S. history. No nation can become a military superpower, as the United States did after 1940, without spending a great deal of money.

Another area of great growth is that of social security taxes and payments, which grew from 1.2 percent of the GNP in 1954 to 5.4 percent in 1974. And, as we noted in Chapter 5, there has been an enormous increase in federal grants to state and local government. Total grant dollars jumped from 0.8 percent of the GNP in 1951 to 3.1 percent in 1974.[8]

These are some of the areas of most notable growth, but they do not begin to cover services provided by the federal government that were not available or that have increased greatly since 1945. The federal government sponsors alcoholism-treatment programs; runs railroads; provides job training; and contracts out billions of dollars in research projects, including studies of sexual attraction among fish.

What caused this remarkable expansion in the federal role? While different theories have been propounded, the expansion of government spending is probably due both to the unparalleled period of economic prosperity, which ran from the 1960s through the 1970s, and the simultaneously growing decentralization of political authority in the United States. The first factor encouraged proponents of spending to argue that the country was rich and could afford to spend more. The second factor made it possible for many different interest groups to demand services and receive them, since the will and power in Congress to say no ceased to exist after the huge Democratic majorities elected in 1964. The "great society" domestic programs passed in the administration of Lyndon B. Johnson in the 1960s have come to be fabulously expensive, as have similar programs passed in the 1970s. This costliness is often due to including provision for inflation in these so-called entitlement programs. An example is Medicaid, the federal grant program to the needy. In the 1960s, it cost less than a billion dollars a year; by 1981, the figure had risen to more than *20* billion. Medicaid and social security payments increase along with the inflation rate, automatically swelling government spending.

After such enormous growth, it was not surprising that newly elected President Ronald Reagan urged large federal spending cuts in the spring of 1981. Many federal officials, including some of the congressmen who voted for the entitlement programs, are now concerned that the country is spending too much on them. At the same time, the military budget, which declined relative to domestic spending in the 1970s, has increased dramatically under the Reagan administration, with the result that curbing the growth of the federal government as a whole is going to be extremely difficult.

Federal Revenue

What are the principal revenue sources of the federal government? Figure 21.1 diagrams them. As the figure's title indicates, individual income tax and social security payments now dominate the federal revenues. Corporation income taxes and social security taxes have almost exactly switched positions, 1954–1976, while sales taxes and customs have declined in importance.

As we have noted, the principal federal revenue source, the individual income tax, is now the most unpopular tax in the United States, and with good reason. In times of inflation, taxpayers are moved into higher tax brackets, even though they are not earning any more in real purchasing power. Some nations, including Canada, "index" taxes by making adjustments for inflation so that taxpayers do not pay a higher proportion of their income in taxes just because of inflation.

Federal Authority and the National Debt

As we have already noted, all three levels of government have a great deal of debt. There is a fundamental distinction between the legal authority of the federal government to go into debt, how-

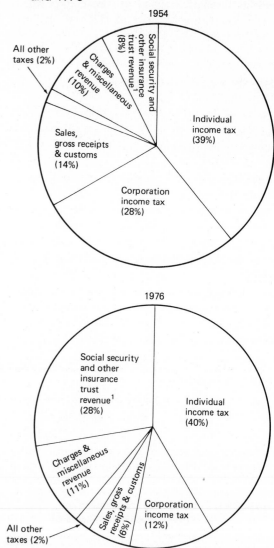

Figure 21.1 Federal Individual Income Tax and Social Security Tax Now Dominate the Federal Revenue System, Fiscal Years 1954 and 1976

[1]Mainly Social Security receipts (26% of total revenue in 1976).

SOURCE: Advisory Commission on Intergovernmental Relations.

ever, and the authority of other governments to do so. The federal government is in a more flexible position to incur debt because there are no constitutional and fewer legal restrictions on its ability to do so than is true at other levels.

As Figure 21.2 indicates, the national debt skyrocketed between 1966 and 1978. This increase was due primarily to two factors, the cost of the war in Vietnam and expanded social welfare programs. Budget deficits, which have to be added to the debt and financed by bonds, averaged over $30 billion a year in the 1970s. Economists differ on whether a large national debt is a bad thing. Some point out that in the period of England's greatest influence, the 19th century, its debt was greater than its GNP. They then argue that since the current U.S. debt is only a little over one third of the GNP, the country is in no danger. Other economists warn that citizens are mortgaging their grandchildren's future; that the interest of $54 billion, now the third largest expenditure in the future budget, is a serious and avoidable cost, which should be whittled down. Some economists have argued that there is no need to worry about the debt because citizens owe it to themselves instead of to foreign bondholders. Others voice alarm at the increase in foreign-owned bonds to the point where foreigners more than quadrupled their share of bonds (from 5 percent to 22 percent) between 1960 and 1980.[9]

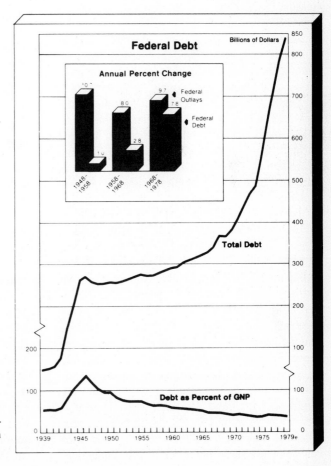

Figure 21.2 Federal Debt

SOURCE: The Conference Board, *Federal Debt,* Economic Road Maps, nos. 1850–1851, March 1979.

Uncontrollable Items in the Budget

President Jimmy Carter pledged during the 1976 election campaign to balance the federal budget by 1981 and thus reduce the rate of growth of the debt, but he was unable to achieve that goal largely because much of the budget has become "uncontrollable."

What is an "uncontrollable" budget item? It is an outlay over which neither Congress nor the executive branch can exercise effective control during a fiscal year under existing law.[10] Current estimates place *three quarters* or more of the federal budget in the uncontrollable area. There are a number of different kinds of uncontrollable items.

One kind is interest payments on the national debt. These payments are mandated, for good reason: failure to pay would destroy the credit of the U.S. government.

Another kind is payments due from prior-year contracts and obligations. The federal government cannot legally break contracts any more than private individuals can.

Legislation has made subsidies of the Postal Service and General Revenue Sharing and farm-price supports uncontrollable. Benefits financed through trust funds, such as social security and retirement, and through general revenues, such as veterans' benefits and Medicaid, are also uncontrollable.

Trust funds and other earmarked revenues are all *special* funds, which must be distinguished from *general* funds, at all levels of government. The distinction is crucial to any understanding of public finance in America. Revenues that are put into the general fund can be spent for *any* legal expenditure—gold-plated birdbaths, elephant racetracks, or statues of Benedict Arnold—so long as those authorized to spend the money approve. Special funds, on the other hand, can only be spent for explicitly designated purposes. Federal special funds include social security and the Highway Trust Fund. Highway Trust Fund dollars can be spent only for specifically listed transportation functions. Federal budget authorities could not use these funds for health, education, welfare, or any other function unless Congress abolished or amended the fund. The same is true for social security revenues; they can be applied only to specific social security benefits. It is to be noted that the revenues for both funds are raised through special taxes on those who will presumably receive benefits from these funds: workers who may retire or become ill and motor vehicle drivers.

A vast number of special funds exists at all three levels of government. The local library may have a special fund, as may the water or sewer department. State governments have their own highway trust funds and may have funds for their public college and university operations. We shall examine some of the implications of these funds in the next chapter.

The uncontrollable items mean that the president and Congress, in any given budget year, are dealing with the tip of the iceberg. They could, of course, change the laws that have made many of these outlays uncontrollable, but to do so would be to begin a protracted conflict that could not be settled in any one budget year.

Off-Budget Agencies

Another fundamental fact of federal finance is so-called off-budget agencies, whose financial transactions have been excluded by law from overall budget totals.[11] A 1977 estimate indicated that were these agencies' budgets to be included in the overall figures, fiscal year (FY) 1978 expenditures would have risen from $460 billion to $520 billion.[12]

Almost all of the off-budget agencies dispense loans. They guarantee to pay back a loan if the borrower defaults. Such agencies include the Rural Electrification Administration, the Export-Import Bank, the Federal Home Loan Bank Board, and the Federal National Mortgage Association. A 1979 study showed that these agencies had outstanding loan guarantees of $200 billion. As Robert J. Samuelson noted, "The Carter administration plans to spend $532 billion in fiscal 1980, but nowhere in that total will you find a $500 million program to assist sick steel firms. Or $140 million to help fishermen buy new vessels. Or $1 billion to encourage businesses to locate in rural areas. . . . Yet, these programs . . . are as real as the Washington monument."[13]

Large as the federal budget is, then, it *understates* the enormous amount of federal activity in the economy. This fact should be kept in mind as we turn to the financial picture of state and local governments.

STATE GOVERNMENTS

While state government spending and revenue growth has not matched that of the federal government, it has still been substantial. Table 21.2 traces this trend. Even when the double-digit inflation of the 1970s is taken into account, growth has still been substantial.

A specific example makes the meaning of these numbers come alive. In 1960 New York State had 35,000 full-time students in its public colleges. By 1970, it had 117,000 students. The number of university employees quadrupled to 31,000 while the annual budget rose from $55 million to $450 million.[14]

And while New Yorkers paid a per capita average of $60 of their 1950 income in state taxes, this figure rose to $338 in 1970.[15]

Table 21.3 shows aggregate revenue sources for the states. It should be noted that where the federal government relies preponderantly on individual income and social security taxes, state governments have a more balanced revenue mix. The sales tax is the most important revenue source, yet income taxes are also crucial. In addition, various fees and charges, ranging from college tuition to motor vehicle licenses and registration, total more than one fifth of revenues. These are *nontax* revenues and have crucial importance in financing state government.

How do the states spend this revenue? Table 21.4 lists the principal areas of expense, which amount to almost 80 percent of total state expenditure. It should be noted, as we observed in Chapter 5, how much of state spending is for grants to local government.

Self-Imposed Restrictions

State budgeting takes place in a different context from that of the federal government. Most states have laws requiring that the state operating budget be balanced, that is, that expenditures equal

TABLE 21.2 State Government Debt and Revenues from Own Sources, in Billions of Dollars

Year	Revenue	Gross debt
1902	$.183	$.230
1950	$16.4	$5.2
1960	$26.0	$18.5
1970	$68.6	$42.0
1977	$155.8	$90.2

SOURCE: *Facts and Figures on Government Finance,* 1979, p. 166.

TABLE 21.3 1977 State Own-Source Revenues by Type, in Billions of Dollars*

Total revenue	Individual income tax	Corporation income tax	General sales and gross receipts taxes	Selection sales and gross receipts taxes	Death and gift taxes	Miscellaneous	Fees and charges	Insurance trust
155.8	25.5	9.2	30.9	21.5	1.8	7.6	33.6	24.7

*Intergovernmental grants are excluded from this table because they are discusssed in Chapter 5.
SOURCE: *Facts and Figures on Governmental Finance,* 1979, p. 182.

TABLE 21.4   Selected Areas of State Spending, 1977*

	Education	Highways	Welfare	Hospitals	Aid to local government	Debt interest	Total
In billions of dollars	27.0	17.5	22.6	8.6	61.0	11.1	191
As % of total	15.5	9.2	12.5	4.5	31.5	6	100

*Note that these figures include federal grant monies.

SOURCE: *Facts and Figures on Government Finance,* 1979, pp. 173–179.

revenues. Deficit spending of the kind in which the federal government indulges is prohibited, although bonds can be floated to pay off the capital budget items. (The federal government does not have a separate capital budget.) For this reason, the states have to be more careful to raise revenue to pay for expenditures than does the federal government.

State spending is also restricted in many other ways by state constitutions and statutes, something which is not true at the federal level. Tennessee and New Jersey, for example, limit increases in state spending to the percentage of growth reflected, respectively, in the state economy and in personal income.[16] Other states may limit spending in specific policy areas. Many states (especially after 1978, as we shall see in the section on local finance) do not have the flexibility of the federal government in increasing expenditures.

While no estimates of total state budget uncontrollability were available to the authors, much of state government spending is de facto uncontrollable. Connecticut's late Governor Ella Grasso complained in 1980 that two thirds of her budget was uncontrollable. Areas of uncontrollability include interest payments on debt, trust fund disbursements, federal mandates, and areas where spending cuts will cause equivalent cuts in federal aid. While the legal flexibility of state governments may be greater than that of the federal government, the political popularity of many programs works to make the legal authority to cut budgets an academic issue.

State Diversity

So far we have lumped together all 50 U.S. state governments, from Alabama to Wyoming. As the reader might well suspect, to do so disguises the diversity of state public finance.

The states differ among themselves in the types of revenue systems they use. For example, Oregon raises 58 percent of its tax revenue from the individual income tax, while Texas and eight other states have no such tax. Oil-rich Alaska repealed its income tax in 1980. New Hampshire is the only state in the union that has neither an income tax nor a sales tax. Oklahoma has a 2 percent sales tax, while Connecticut has 7 percent. Arkansas charges its corporations 1 percent for their first $3,000 of income and nothing thereafter; Minnesota charges its corporations 12 percent of their total earnings. Delaware collected a total of $772 in taxes per capita in 1978, while New Hampshire collected $283.[17] We could go on and on, but the point should be clear: each state revenue system is unique and will remain unique so long as the states possess a measure of independence. It is now an article of political faith in the 10 states without an individual income tax, for example, that such a tax not be levied. While fiscal pressures will probably force some of these states to exact such a tax in the 1980s, elected officials will stubbornly resist it to the last minute, knowing full well that it will not be popular with the voters.

The variations in revenue patterns reflect variations in spending. California and New York have created vast and costly college and university systems, while New Jersey lies near the bottom of the state pile in its support of higher education. All three are high-income states, so the difference cannot be explained by variations in available taxable wealth.

Another element in diversity is the relationship between state-local spending and available revenue resources. One standard way of measuring this "tax effort" is to compute total spending paid per $1,000 of personal income. The average personal income in a state such as New Jersey, for example, is far greater than it is in Mississippi or Arkansas. To compare these states on the amount of money spent per capita is misleading because poor states will find it much harder to spend the same amount of money per capita that rich states do.

To gain an accurate picture of tax effort one has to include local with state spending, since state-local revenue systems vary so greatly. When this is done, some interesting discoveries appear. Excluding inflation-ravaged Alaska and Hawaii, whose aggregate figures are not comparable with those of the continental United States, one finds that wealthy states such as New Jersey and Connecticut are down near the bottom in tax effort. In 1977, for example, Connecticut spent $156.10 in aggregate state and local expenditures per $1,000 of personal income. Mississippi, the poorest state in the union measured on a personal income basis, spent $228.04. Montana made the greatest effort, with $250.36, and Indiana the least, with $153.99.[18]

One crucial distinction among the states that makes comparisons difficult is how they divide functions and payment for these functions with their local governments. At one end of the scale is Hawaii, whose state government picks up 80 percent of the combined spending and revenue total of state and local government. (Among other things, primary and secondary education is a state, not a local, function in Hawaii.) Nevada, on the other hand, let its local governments pick up 52.4 percent of the tab in 1977. States where the state government paid for less than half of

total expenditures in 1977 included California, Nevada, Colorado, Wyoming, Florida, Nebraska, Missouri, Ohio, and New York. States where the state paid more than 70 percent of the tab included Delaware, Kentucky, North Carolina, South Carolina, Alaska, and Hawaii.[19]

The state finance picture, then, is one of growth, diversification of revenue sources, and enormous diversity in spending and revenue patterns.

LOCAL GOVERNMENT

Local government taxing and spending once dwarfed the other two levels of government, as Table 21.5 shows. This is no longer true: local government now raises less revenue from its own sources than the other two levels of government. (In 1977 state government, once last in this category, raised $1.40 for each $1.00 raised by local government.)[20]

Yet it would be fallacious to leap to the assumption that local governments are less important today than at the turn of the century. The opposite is true: they now do far more than they ever have. They accompany citizens from the cradle's birth certificate to the grave's death certificate, both filed with local government clerks. They build day care and senior citizen centers, libraries, parks, zoos, schools, and roads. They provide health, welfare, mass transportation, job training, police and fire protection, and a host of other services.

TABLE 21.5 Federal, State, and Local Expenditures, in Billions of Dollars*

Year	Total	Federal	State	Local
1902	1,660	572	179	909
1977	759,686	483,283	153,930	122,473

*Grants are counted as expenditures of the first disbursing unit.

SOURCE: *Facts and Figures on Government Finance*, 1979, p. 17.

While they are no longer the leading source of revenue in American public finance, they still spend more on domestic government services than any other level. As we have seen in Chapter 5, when intergovernmental grants are credited to the level of government that spends them, local government is the leader in domestic spending. In 1977, local governments spent $195 billion and the states spent $129 billion. The federal government spent $174 billion, after subtracting budget items relating to international affairs such as defense, veterans' benefits, and interest on the national debt.[21] And most of the domestic expenditures of the federal government that are not grants are social security checks mailed to recipients.

As we saw in Chapter 18, local goverment is the labor-intensive level of government, which delivers services, whether snow plowing, cleaning up palm trees after hurricanes, or teaching school children. For this reason it has the bulk of governmental employees. In 1977, local governments employed more than 9 million workers, while state governments employed 3.5 million, and the federal government 2.8 million civilians and 2.2 million military personnel.[22] Local government is more vigorous than ever, even though it no longer is the dominant fiscal partner. What are the revenue and expenditure patterns and trends affecting the 80,000 local U.S. governments in the 1980s?

Local Spending

Public primary and secondary education is the biggest single expenditure of local government. In 1977, 36 percent of all local government spending was for schools. Seventy-five billion dollars was spent for 2.6 million teachers, backed by 2.4 million other educational employees, to educate 45 million students. Other large expenditure items, none of which approach education, were utilities ($20 billion), police and fire ($13 billion), welfare ($11 billion), health and hospitals ($11 billion), and highways ($9 billion).[23]

One major grievance of local governments is that many new expenditures or revenue restrictions have been forced on them by the federal and state governments. These requirements, commonly called mandates, include a number of different kinds of action. Examples are the removal of certain types of property from the local property tax base or adoption of new, uniform standards for police personnel. A 1977 survey found that the average state mandated 35 of a possible 77 items onto local government but that only 6 states required state compensation for certain types of mandates.[24] Growing concern with this problem has led a number of other states to investigate the matter.[25] Much needs to be done; the mandate, which has an effect diametrically opposed to the grant-in-aid, is "frequently adopted with little or no information as to the costs being passed on to others or the tax burden necessary to provide these services."[26]

When long-standing state restrictions on the size of local debt and type of taxes allowed are considered, many localities are in a double bind. Most states limit the indebtedness of their local governments to a percentage of the total value of taxable property, for example, while others bar localities from leveling sales or income taxes. Between mandates and revenue restrictions, localities may have a tortuous time making ends meet.

Because of state and federal mandates, much of local government budgets are uncontrollable. Most states, for example, require their local governments to operate school systems. Given other elements of uncontrollability, such as interest payments on debt and pension fund payments, local governments probably have the most uncontrollable budgets of all three levels of the American system.

A final word: there is even more diversity in spending among the 80,000 local governments in America than there is among the 50 state governments. In fact, the differences are so great that recent court decisions in California, New Jersey, New York, and Connecticut have ruled that it is a denial of due process to finance education through local taxes.[27]

Local Revenues

Table 21.6 details the revenue sources of local government in 1902 and 1977. The single most important source is still the property tax, levied principally on land and buildings. It should be noted, though, how this tax has declined as a percentage of total revenue. Various user charges, whether for dog licenses, recreation programs, sanitation tests, parking meters, school lunches, or hundreds of other items, pyramid into a large amount of revenue. In addition, miscellaneous revenue such as rents, sales, and interest earnings contribute to the total.[28]

While the property-tax share of total revenue has declined greatly, its share of *tax* revenue has slipped only slightly, from 88.6 percent in 1902 to 80.6 percent in 1977. It still remains the overwhelmingly prevalent local tax. To be sure, there are state and regional variations. The New England states raised 99 percent of their local tax revenues in 1977 through property taxes, while the Middle Atlantic states of Delaware, Maryland, New York, New Jersey, and Pennsylvania raised only 75 percent that way. Jonesboro, Georgia, has no property tax and raises most of its revenue through a tax on beer. Alabama raised only 40 percent and Louisiana 50 percent of local taxes through the property tax, but no other state fell below 65 percent.[29]

The most frequent criticism of this popular tax is that it is inequitably administered. Great variations in the assessed value of property are found among jurisdictions. For example, an outhouse in Pompous Plains might be assessed at twice the value of one in Mudville, even though the structures and communities are very similar. An excellent study of the property tax in Boston found that rental properties in the black ghetto were assessed at far higher rates, proportionately, than properties elsewhere in the city. In other areas, industrial and commercial properties may be "under assessed."[30] One authority argues that the property tax is in fact a progressive tax, one that puts a higher burden on the wealthy than on the poor and average-income family, and that it is the administration of the system that is the problem.[31] In response to this criticism, a number of experts and politicians have called for statewide, equalized assessment and administration of the property tax. Several states, including Georgia, Nebraska, Arizona, and New Mexico, have already done so.[32]

Current Crises in Local Finance

Local government has long been the storm center of American public finance. One reason is that local government is more accessible to the citizenry. Through referenda, budget decisions of governmental bodies at the local level in most jurisdictions can be overturned far more easily than they can at the state or national level. In the Western states, as we shall see, where it is equally easy to challenge state government financial decisions, similar phenomena are found.

Another reason that local finance is a storm center is the perilous financial condition of some of the older cities of the Northeast and Middle

TABLE 21.6   Total Local Revenues, from Own Sources

	Year	Property tax	Sales and gross receipts	Income	License and other	Charges and miscellaneous	Utility	Liquor stores	Insurance trust	Total
Amount in	1902	624	0	0	80	94	60	0	0	858
billions of	1977	60,275	8,232	3,752	2,534	27,237	14,191	368	2,783	119,373
dollars										
As % of	1902	72.0	2.2	.3	3.1	8.8	12.2	.2	1.2	100
total	1977	50.5	6.9	3.1	2.1	22.8	11.9	.3	2.3	100

SOURCE: *Facts and Figures on Government Finance,* 1979, p. 243.

West. New York and Cleveland both collapsed financially in the 1970s, and Newark, New Jersey, is kept going by a constant infusion of special state and federal revenue. These and other cities have lost much of their business base and middle-class population to the suburbs, yet they have to provide more services to the poor who have replaced wealthier citizens, and now pay much more to their politically powerful, unionized employees. All is not bleak, however; a 1979 study

of 66 cities between 50,000 and 900,000 in population found 54 of them to be in excellent health. The study concluded that state and federal aid and sound financial management were the key determinants in maintaining fiscal health.[33] The combined weight of state and federal regulation and local demands will make local finance in the 1980s a place for the wise and strong. Good financial management at the local level is possible, but it will not be easy, a theme we shall return to in the last chapter. Adding to the burdens of local financial managers is the tax revolt described in the next section.

Will This 1913 Critique of Local Finance Come True in the 1980s?

GOING! GOING!! GONE!!!

The City Hall Sold at Public Auction

SOURCE: Henry H. Klein, *Bankrupting a Great City* (N.Y.: Vanity (self-published), 1913).

Proposition 13: Local Tax Revolt

In June 1978, California voters approved a state initiative limiting the amount of local property taxes that could be collected. The initiative, listed as Proposition 13 on the ballot, rolled back assessments to their 1975 levels and restricted increases to 2 percent per year as long as property was owned by the same person. In addition, it prohibited taxes from exceeding 1 percent of the property's full value. The effect? The total revenue of California local governments was cut by 22 percent. Since then, Howard Jarvis, one of the leaders behind Proposition 13, has gone across the country to rally similar efforts in other states. Why was Proposition 13 passed? What has its impact been? How likely is it to spread to other states?

Several circumstances combined to bring about the California tax revolt. Property-tax rates were high; they were rising rapidly (the efficient assessment system in California quickly adjusts assessments to reflect changing property values); the state government had a $5 billion surplus, which was growing; and the state constitution is one of 23 that allow statewide propositions to be placed on the ballot by citizen initiative petitions.[34]

This combination of circumstances was uncommon. For example, other high-tax states, including New York, New Jersey, Alaska, and Massachusetts, did not have a state surplus, much less such a huge one. Further, none but Alaska allow for direct, voter-petition, constitutional initiative, and none have assessment systems so efficient as California's. It is interesting to note that Idaho and Nevada, two Western states with property-tax situations similar to California's, were the only states where voters approved Proposition 13-type initiatives between June 1978 and 1 January 1981. (In November 1980, Massachusetts voters passed a statutory restriction, which the legislature can modify if it desires.)

The immediate impact of the passage of Proposition 13 was to cut local property tax revenues by 57 percent and total local revenue by 22 percent. Stunned city and county officials predicted the breakdown of local government, but that has not come to pass. The huge state surplus was redistributed to local governments, cushioning the blow. ("Jarvis II," a 1980 initiative to cut the state income tax, was decisively defeated.) By November 1978, less than 1 percent of 1.4 million state and local employees had been laid off as a result of Proposition 13. In some cities, services formerly paid for by taxes, such as school bus transportation, are paid for by fees. Inglewood, for example, now bills property owners for putting out major fires, basing this charge on the amount of water used.[35] Some agencies, such as libraries and flood-control districts, were hit relatively hard, but the state aid legislation kept schools and police and fire departments at previous levels.[36]

As of 1 January 1980, the most noticeable effects were the increased financial dependence of local government upon the state government and the decline of the property tax as a revenue source. Interestingly enough, conservative professor Donald G. Hagman has attacked right-wingers such as William Buckley and Milton Friedman for supporting Proposition 13. He argues that the property tax is visible and hard to pay and thus keeps the public aware of the tax burden it is bearing. Further, since it is a local government tax, it strengthens the level of government closest to the voters and most amenable to their control. Proposition 13, according to Hagman and

many local government officials, will seriously damage grass-roots government and hand power over to the federal and state governments.[37] Paradoxically, Proposition 13 may cost California federal aid, since much of that aid is based on the taxing or spending contribution made by local government to different program areas.[38]

The electorate in 24 states voted in November 1978 and 1980 on various measures designed to provide tax relief. Constitutional amendments restricting state government *spending,* not tax increases, were passed in 5 states and defeated in 2. Amendments providing property tax relief by changing the administration, base, or assessment procedures used passed in 6 states and were defeated in 1. Proposition 13-type measures were passed in 2 states, as already mentioned, and defeated in 8.

While additional states have also passed property tax relief measures, they have been of a different kind. One count tallied 22 states making property tax reductions in 1979. These measures ranged from limited actions, such as cuts in aid for the elderly or disabled, to across-the-board rebates.[39]

One analyst concludes from the 1978 voting patterns that voters were concerned mostly with the control of *state* government spending.[40] Proposition 4, a California restriction on state and local spending passed in November 1979, underscores this argument, as does the passage in 1979 of state spending limits in 8 states. In addition, 1979 saw cuts in state income taxes in 18 states and cuts in state sales taxes in 15 states.[41]

There is no question, then, that Proposition 13 struck a sympathetic chord among U.S. taxpayers. There is also no question that the *type* of tax relief provided by Proposition 13 is different from that adopted in the vast majority of instances since June 1978. These measures either concentrate on spending restrictions or are more flexible tax restrictions, which do not focus so squarely on that bastion of local tax revenue, the property tax.

After devoting unparalleled financial resources to government, Americans began in the late 1970s and early 1980s to reverse this trend. In

1979, 30 state legislatures called for a convention to consider an amendment to the Constitution requiring a balanced budget. The Rand Corporation announced in December 1979 that the rate of increase of government spending slowed from 11 percent between 1969 and 1975 to 9.4 percent between 1975 and 1979. In the study director's words, "these tax limitation laws (such as Proposition 13) are just voter verification of something that has been going on for some time."[42]

Other data are even more revealing. The percentage of the GNP devoted to government declined from an all-time high of 34.8 percent in 1975 to 32.5 percent in 1978.[43] Both the federal and the combined state and local shares declined. Does this trend indicate that government spending has peaked and that U.S. citizens will now prepare to live with less from government? We shall return to this question in the final chapter of the book.

SUMMARY

For federal, state, and local government, we have presented the picture of income, outgo, and debt, leading to taxpayer revolts and attempts to amend constitutions. The administrator is caught in the middle. If the "meat-ax" approach is to be moderated, the administrator must come up with an acceptable program that satisfies the parties.

NOTES

1. *Facts and Figures on Government Finance* (New York: Tax Foundation, 1979), p. 33.

2. Advisory Commission on Intergovernmental Relations (ACIR), *Trends in Fiscal Federalism* (Washington: U.S. Government Printing Office, 1975), p. 2.

3. "Tax Lawyer, in Death, Provides for Short Cut," *New York Times,* 13 January 1980, p. 27.

4. *Facts and Figures,* pp. 221, 253.

5. *Federal Debt: Economic Road Maps, Nos. 1850-1851* (New York: Conference Board, 1979).

6. *Public Administration Times,* 1 March 1981, p. 5.

7. ACIR, *Changing Public Attitudes on Government and Taxes* (Washington: U.S. Government Printing Office, 1979).

8. ACIR, *Trends in Fiscal Federalism,* pp. 1–2.

9. *Federal Debt; New York Times,* 22 February 1981, p. F 19.

10. *Facts and Figures,* p. 8.

11. *Facts and Figures,* p. 20.

12. *Monthly Tax Features* (New York: Tax Foundation, September 1977), p. 3.

13. Robert J. Samuelson, "Taking Out a Loan Guarantee," *National Journal,* 27 January 1979, p. 151.

14. Mark Lawton, "Three Case Studies in Budgeting," *Empire,* June–July 1979, p. 38.

15. *Facts and Figures,* p. 190.

16. *Intergovernmental Perspective,* Fall 1978, p. 10.

17. *Facts and Figures,* pp. 180–190.

18. *Facts and Figures,* p. 144.

19. ACIR, *Significant Features of Fiscal Federalism, 1978–79 Edition* (Washington: U.S. Government Printing Office, 1979), p. 14.

20. ACIR, *Significant Features,* p. 3.

21. *Facts and Figures,* pp. 85, 166, 229.

22. *Facts and Figures,* pp. 24–25.

23. *Facts and Figures,* p. 236.

24. ACIR, *State Mandating of Local Expenditures* (Washington: U.S. Government Printing Office, 1978).

25. *Intergovernmental Perspective,* Fall 1979, p. 4.

26. ACIR, *State Mandating,* p. 8.

27. See George E. Berkley and Douglas M. Fox, *80,000 Governments* (Boston: Allyn & Bacon, 1978), pp. 221–222, 266.

28. Lennox L. Moak and Albert M. Hillhouse, *Concepts and Practices in Local Government Finance* (Chicago: Municipal Finance Officers Association, 1975), pp. 160–161.

29. ACIR, *Significant Features,* pp. 55, 59.

30. Diane B. Paul, *The Politics of the Property Tax* (Lexington, Mass.: Heath, 1975).

31. Henry J. Aaron, *Who Pays the Property Tax?* (Washington: Brookings Institution, 1975).

32. Moak and Hillhouse, *Concepts and Practices,* p. 132.

33. James Howell and Charles Stamm, *Urban Fiscal Stress* (Lexington, Mass.: Lexington Books, 1974).

34. Richard L. Lucier, "Gauging the Strength and Meaning of the 1978 Tax Revolt," *Public Administration Review* 39 August 1979): 372–373.

35. "Proposition 13, in 5 Months, Has Not Spurred Major Spending Cutbacks," *New York Times*, 7 November 1978, p. 17.

36. Robert Lindsay, "Dire Predictions on Proposition 13 Have Not Materialized," *New York Times*, 7 March 1979, p. 21.

37. Donald G. Hagman, "Proposition 13: A Prostitution of Conservative Principles," *Tax Review*, September 1978, pp. 1–4.

38. U.S., General Accounting Office, *Will Federal Assistance to California Be Affected by Proposition 13?* (Washington: U.S. Government Printing Office, 1978).

39. John Herbers, "States Grant Billions in Tax Relief to the Middle Class and Business," *New York Times*, 5 August 1979, p. 1.

40. Lucier, "Gauging the . . . 1978 Tax Revolt."

41. John Herbers, "Study Turns Up Surprises on Fiscal Shape of Cities," *New York Times*, 21 March 1979, p. 1.

42. "Study Finds Relative Drop in Government Spending," *New York Times*, 2 December 1979, p. 33.

43. *Facts and Figures*, p. 33.

22

The Budgetary Process

The budget is the World Series of Government.[1]
Henry Maier, Mayor of Milwaukee

In this chapter we scrutinize the stages of the budgetary process, examine the different types of budget systems, and assess the implication of each for public finance. We deal with the theory, history, types, evolution, strengths and weaknesses, and many uses of budgets, at all three levels of government; and we give prominence to the line-item executive, performance, program, zero-base, and other budetary experiments and improvements of recent years.

The word *budget* derives from the Middle English word for pouch or purse. "In Britain the term was used to describe the leather bag in which the Chancellor of the Exchequer carried to Parliament the statement of the Government's needs and resources."[2]

Such a statement provides information on the finances of an organization, including its sources of revenue, items of expense, and the purpose to which those items are put. Thomas D. Lynch, a former federal budget analyst, has noted that "the one common subject in any budget discussion is money. Other subjects are important, but they are mentioned in relationship to money or are translated into money."[3]

Sydney Duncombe, who has been budget director in two states, has noted that a budget is a work plan with a dollar sign attached. It is also a means of control, of making sure that scarce dollars are not overspent.

The line-item budget has an input-oriented approach, which groups items purchased, rented, or hired (all of which are called objects of expenditure) as shown in Table 22.1. It should be noted that each line lists an item or items; that arrangement is how the line-item budget got its name. The line-item budget does not provide any information on the activities of the organization or their results, as we have defined these terms.

TABLE 22.1 Proposed Street Maintenance Input Budget, City of Harmony Department of Transportation, 1977

Street maintenance	$10,950,662
Salaries and wages	6,230,162
Equipment	
7 Trucks	300,000
3 Steamrollers	150,000
Other	850,000
Maintenance of equipment	910,000
Supplies	
Asphalt	1,570,000
Other	520,000
Miscellaneous	420,500

EVOLUTION OF THE LINE-ITEM BUDGET

The line-item budget as used in the United States dates only from the late 19th century. Before that date, government agencies were given a lump-sum appropriation, which did not list specific objects of expenditure. Some agencies today, including the Bridgeport, Connecticut, library, with a budget of more than $1 million, still receive lump sums. Federal military and foreign-aid agencies also receive a form of lump-sum budgeting enabling them to indulge in covert and unauthorized spending. For example, Philippine, Thai, and South Korean troops were sent to Vietnam to aid U.S. and South Vietnamese forces in the 1960s. Only in 1969 and 1970 was it discovered that the Defense Department had given secret subsidies to these countries. The Central Intelligence Agency (CIA) has used covert financing to carry out thousands of projects, including aid to Thai troops in Laos during the Vietnam war and broadcasting radio propaganda to Eastern Europe. While Congress has moved to tighten controls in this area, military and paramilitary agencies still have wide discretion in spending funds for unauthorized projects. For as long as agencies are given lump-sum budgets, there can be no real control over their spending.[4]

In some governments, objects of expenditure are so broad that de facto lump-sum spending exists. Connecticut state government agencies, for example, usually have only a few, very large line items, such as personnel expenses, so that funds can easily be moved around within the agency.

The line-item budget was originally proposed as a control device by reform groups. Lump-sum budgets enabled party officials and government employees to spend money for purposes other than what was originally intended because there was no system of accountability. In the words of George Washington Plunkitt, a New York City party leader at the turn of the century, "I seen my opportunities and I took 'em." Appropriations often went into someone's personal pockets or were spent for purposes not intended by the legislature. An early study sponsored by the New

York Bureau of Municipal Research stationed observers to count the number of employees leaving the Streets Department warehouse and the paving materials each carried. The bureau then announced that it was impossible for those personnel and supplies to have exhausted the department's appropriation. Some of the money must have been siphoned off to another area, but exactly where it went was impossible to discern with the lump-sum budget.

Thanks to similar exposés and a political campaign for change, few lump-sum budgets remain today. The line-item budget is overwhelmingly predominant in American governments. To probe the process of budgeting in the United States, we must necessarily examine the line-item budget because the two are nearly synonymous.

In the 19th century, the chief executive was on the sidelines in the budgetary process. At all levels of government, agencies dealt directly with the legislature's budgetary component. What this arrangement amounted to, in fact, was a lack of planning, coordination and control in the budgetary process. Luther Gulick, one of the outstanding figures in American public administration, argues that what existed before the executive budget does not even meet our definition of budgeting. "You cannot imagine the chaos at every level of government. Expenditure plans were no plans at all. Individual issues would be decided at the initiative of outside pressure groups or legislative committees, all without coordination. When the government ran out of money, someone would agitate for a new tax. Meanwhile, the Treasury would borrow money. Nobody knew what a budget was except a few scholars who followed British government."[5]

In 1907, the Bureau of Municipal Research helped formulate a budget for the New York City Board of Health. This revolutionary, line-item document outlined expenditures for a year in advance and stipulated that no money could be spent unless the purposes for which it was intended were clearly stated in the budget. Subsequently, the executive-centered, line-item budget spread throughout the country, and it is the rule today.

STEPS OF THE BUDGET CYCLE

There are different types of budgetary systems, most of which share the following characteristics. First, estimates of revenue to be received are made by the central budget office. Second, the initial and basic responsibility for preparation of the bureau's budget rests with the bureau itself. The chief officials, in conjunction with the budget officers, draw up a list of items—salaries, equipment, services, and the like—and their projected costs for the next fiscal period. Third, this information is reviewed by the central budget office, which submits it along with its suggestions to the chief executive. Fourth, the chief executive, after studying all the materials sent, makes budget recommendations to the legislature. Fifth, the legislature appropriates money for the agency as it sees fit, for it is not usually bound by the recommendations it receives. Sixth, the funds go to the central budget office, which allots them to the agencies. Seventh, the agencies themselves spend the funds. Finally, auditors check back to see if funds were spent properly. Figure 22.1 diagrams this cycle for the federal government. In this chapter we discuss the first seven steps in the budgetary process; we examine auditing in Chapter 23. The first five steps relate to budget formulation, the last three to budget execution.

Step 1: Revenue Estimation

The crucial step of revenue estimation sets the boundaries for the budgetary process. A general rule of American government is that any revenue raised is spent. Few governments try to save substantial sums, although most try to avoid imposing *new* or increased taxes. If it is estimated that revenue will not be sufficient to pay for new, proposed programs, it is unlikely that these programs will be funded. (This is at least true at the state and local level; less so at the federal level, for reasons discussed in the previous chapter.) The government body with the authority to estimate revenues can use this authority in different ways. It can deliberately overestimate or underestimate, as well as issue technically unbiased estimates.

Figure 22.1 Major Steps in the Federal Budget Process

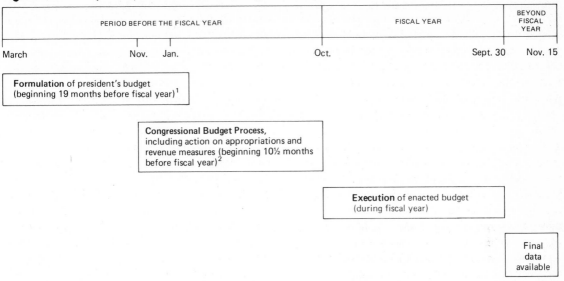

[1]The President's budget is transmitted to Congress within fifteen days after Congress convenes.

[2]If appropriation action is not completed by September 30, Congress enacts temporary appropriation (for example, continuing resolution).

SOURCE: Office of Management and Budget

And since estimation is not an exact science, it can claim that the best possible job was done even if the estimate is way off.

Chief executives facing tight budgets are tempted to overestimate revenues so that they can claim the budget will be balanced. Illinois Governor Richard Ogilvie even issued a budget in the 1970s that would be balanced only if Congress passed two new laws providing money to Illinois.[6] Ogilvie won his gamble, but many governors have lost out when at the end of the fiscal year their chickens come home to roost. Deficits must then be made up in the next fiscal year. But since they can be moved up one year, it is common to find state and local chief executives keeping taxes down while spending wildly during elections, only to raise taxes and cut the budget after the election. This situation often confronts newly elected chief executives, who discover that the cupboard is bare and that they will have to start off their administrations by raising taxes.

Another pattern is for the chief executive to overestimate spending and underestimate reve-

nue. When a surplus then appears at the end of the fiscal year, he can proclaim his fiscal-management abilities to one and all.

Step 2: Budget Formulation— Administrative Agencies

Because budgeting begins (and ends) within the operating agencies, line officials will always have an important role in the budgetary process. The agencies *set the agenda* to which the other participants in budget formulation then react. This fundamental fact must not be forgotten, for it explains why program managers will have a key role in budgeting.

As we have noted earlier, all programs do not have equal weight. Those with the strongest clientele and support in the legislature, for example, will do better than others. What we describe here and in steps three through seven are some general patterns which we do not claim will hold in all cases.

The paramount position of agency employees

is based in part on numbers. There are far more line-agency employees than there are staff-agency employees to oversee them. No one else is likely to know the budget of an agency so well as its own budget officers. The budget officer, in fact, is often legally responsible for agency action, giving him or her additional incentive to know every nook and cranny of the budget.[7]

Agency budget officials can pursue a number of strategies to try to obtain what they want in formulating the budget. The following discussion is meant to suggest, not exhaust, these strategies.

Agencies almost always want to maintain their spending levels, and they often desire to expand budgets. It is usually necessary for the administrator to seek larger budgets not only because of population growth and inflation, but also because of the need to satisfy several "audiences"—the agency's employees, the agency's clientele groups, and the officials who review the budget requests. Requests for more funds underline the significance and protect the status of agency employees, assure clientele groups that new and higher standards are being pursued, and ease the burdens felt by reviewing officials in dealing with programs about which they may have little or no knowledge. If an agency does not ask for more money, it may well have its budget cut on the grounds that it does not need the money it requested. Thus, for all these reasons, it is necessary to pad the budget somewhat.

Padding, or asking for more money than the agency needs, is a time-honored strategy. It is done in the anticipation of cuts by officials at steps three to six, outlined further on. Likewise, these officials often *expect* bureaucrats to pad their budgets and cut accordingly. Sometimes an agency that has not padded its budget suffers for its honesty. An example is the Connecticut state college system. In 1979 it submitted a request for a 7.3 percent budget hike, while the University of Connecticut and the state community colleges asked for a bigger increase. All requests were cut by the Board of Higher Education, but the state colleges fared worst because their initial request was less than that of the other units in higher education.

Another strategy is the opposite of padding; it has assumed more and more importance as the "uncontrollable" portion of the budget, mentioned in Chapter 21, grows. To take the U.S. Department of Agriculture's food stamp program, if Agriculture has an overall departmental budget limit imposed on it, department budget officials can make a low estimate of the costs of this mandated program for the coming fiscal year. That way they can justify inclusion of a controllable program. Later, if food-stamp costs rise, Congress *must* appropriate the money to pay for this uncontrollable item.[8]

Another favorite strategy has been called the Washington Monument game. In 1971, the National Park Service announced that if its budget were cut, it would have to close the Washington Monument to tourists. Such a move would cause such colossal consternation among tourists and tourist groups that it would be politically unthinkable. In this way, the agency tried to avert potential cuts. On the local level, school boards often play this game by threatening to eliminate sports and school bus programs.

The umbrella game is yet another strategy. A new chief executive, whether mayor, governor, or president, who comes in with new program initiatives, is welcomed by alert bureaucrats, who can say they are implementing this new executive priority, which should not be cut. As the budget officer of one federal department said, "Sure, if the President comes out with an environmental message, you begin to reclassify all the programs you can as 'environmental' and beef them up. . . . Of course it's transparent, but the President *wants* us to play that game. He wants to show the environmentalists he's on their side."[9]

Another strategy is related to the existence of special funds, discussed in Chapter 21. Special funds range from social security to a local library endowment; they may be crucial revenue sources for certain agencies. While agencies do not estimate general-fund revenue, they do make estimates of their special-fund revenues. One strategy that agencies can follow here is to underestimate such revenue through very conservative estimating. The lower estimates can then be used to justify a claim on general-fund money to make up the difference. A study of Georgia State government in the 1960s concluded that "if the key to budget padding is indeed to be found, the major technique must lie in underestimating funds, for it is here that the largest adjustments took place."[10]

A study of school-district budgets found another strategy, labeled marginal mobilizing. The author argues that organizations devote most of their efforts to those income sources that will yield the highest return. That means that in affluent school districts, which have an expanding tax base, school officials will devote their attention to cultivating local parent and taxpayer support to try to raise more money. Contrariwise, in districts with a declining tax base, more effort is put into attaining grants from state and local government for additional revenue. In both kinds of districts, administrators have "mobilized on the margin" in their budget-formulation efforts, looking for the area in which their efforts will yield maximum returns.[11]

The common thread in these agency strategies is the attempts to maintain and sometimes expand the budgetary "base," or the current appropriation. A number of writers have argued that budgeting in the United States is incremental; that is, all participants in the budgetary process accept the base as their starting point and make relatively minor adjustments in it. They concentrate their scrutiny instead on proposed new programs, which are not part of their base. Aaron Wildavsky, perhaps the best-known recent authority on public budgeting, has stated that an agency's budget is "almost never actively reviewed as a whole every year in the sense of reconsidering the value of all existing programs as compared to all possible alternatives. Instead, it is based on last year's budget, with special attention given to a relatively narrow range of increases or decreases. Thus the men who make the budget are concerned with relatively small increments to an existing base."[12]

This statement certainly holds for most public budgets, and it is the reason why zero-base budgeting, which we examine later in this chapter,

has been proposed as an improvement in public finance. But we need to note here that the budgetary process is a dynamic one. First, relatively minor changes in a department's budget from year to year may mask dramatic changes for programs and divisions within that department.[13] For example, the budget devoted to recreation and public use within the U.S. Forest Service doubled every three years from 1957 to 1973, a period of low, overall inflation compared to the later 1970s.[14] Second, a major study makes another point well worth considering: "Changes in budgetary decisions are not necessarily small, nor are they necessarily predictable as a function of a previous budgetary base."[15] Indeed, they could not be small, or the trends in growth of public spending described in the previous chapter would not be true. Third, when much of the budget is uncontrollable, how can the thinking of budget makers about increments and bases be translated into meaningful action?[16] With these qualifications, then, we agree with Wildavsky. Most budget-making activity focuses on relatively minor adjustments to the base. But these adjustments may be dramatic ones for particular programs, which can grow like Topsy or be eliminated.

Step 3: The Central Budget Office and Budget Formulation

Once the various operating divisions of an agency or department have drawn up their budget requests, the requests are usually forwarded to the department's budget office or officer. Once the office has assembled its final budget request, this document moves to the government's central budget office, a staff agency concerned with overall spending and revenue patterns. At the federal level, this agency is the Office of Management and Budget (OMB), which has more than 400 budget analysts. In the states, various titles are used: Budget Office (Mississippi); Finance Division (Arizona); State Comptroller's Office (Iowa); Office for Policy and Management (Kentucky); and Office of Planning and Fiscal Management (Washington) are but a few. Federal OMB is a presidential agency; likewise, many state budget offices are located within the organization of the governor's office. Most of those that are not so placed are perceived by participants in state politics as existing to help the governor to put the budget together. In a few states, however, the governor lacks this influence over the central budget office.

In local government, the title is likely to be Department of Finance, headed by a director of finance. As one can imagine, though, there are enormous variations among the 80,000 local governments. School and special districts may have nomenclature similar to the states; many towns entrust this task to a part-time Board of Finance; and the most humble hamlets will give this job to the elected chief executive, who may not even have a secretary to help put the budget together. Regardless of title and staff resources, however, all these offices have the responsibility of collating agency requests into a comprehensive document and then submitting it to the chief executive for scrutiny. (The smallest governments efficiently combine steps three and four.)

Just as the strategies of line-agency bureaucrats are based on a desire to maintain and expand the base, the strategies of central budget-office officials are in large part a reaction to this strategy. Budget officers who made a habit of *increasing* agency budget requests would soon be in trouble with the chief executive and legislature. Another related constraint is that budget officials have to be concerned about *revenues* as well as spending. Almost all state and local governments are legally required to submit balanced budgets, in which revenues equal expenditures. There is no such requirement at the federal level, as we noted in the previous chapter, but OMB officials are greatly concerned with the revenue-spending relationship. Line-agency bureaucrats may make revenue estimates for their special funds, but they are not centrally concerned with the problem of revenues, while central budget officials can never forget the revenue issue. Concern with revenues is reflected in central budget-office priorities and strategies.

Research on the budgetary process in Cleveland, Detroit, and Pittsburgh, all cities of more than 500,000 population, produced a simulation model of a budgetary system with characteristics common to these three cities. In the three cities, the problem in budget making that confronts the budget office is to produce a budget that is in balance, maintains existing service levels, provides, if possible, for employee wage raises, and avoids tax increases. When the budget office is convinced that it is necessary to cut costs, there are well-defined priorities. Maintenance and equipment are the first to go; operating expenses, supplies, and materials are next. Only after all the foregoing have been trimmed are salaries and wages reduced.[17]

A study of Oakland, California, agency requests for personnel positions, for example, found that central budget officials used standard rules in making budget decisions. These decisions rules can be classified into three categories: orientation, trade-off, and slash.[18]

Orientation rules give clues on how to approach department requests. If the department lacks status and influence, its budget should be carefully scrutinized and then cut. If it is a powerful pachyderm rather than a political pygmy, it is best to use a nail file rather than a meat axe, thus avoiding cuts that the agency has the power to restore. Other Oakland orientation rules included disregarding work-load data, which were believed to be inflated, and comparing the agency with other jurisdictions. For example, the Oakland library had more bookbinders than the much larger Los Angeles library had, a proportion that did not help the former's request.

Trade-off rules mean that the budget examiner has to give up something in turn for cutting personnel positions. The examiners might trade, for example, a higher-priced job for a lower-priced one or a position for overtime money. Or the examiner might trade equipment for personnel or give the agency a certain position if the agency promises to eliminate the position later on. Agencies the analyst has to trade with have more political influence or might be able to make an excellent case based on need.

Slash rules are those that lead the examiner to cut positions without making a quid pro quo exchange. Examples include cutting requests for new personnel or eliminating positions vacant for some time. It should be noticed that for Oakland and in the study of the three large cities, budget offices are most reluctant to lay off government employees. The political reasons are substantial: employees and their families vote and are organized into unions. Layoffs will spark enormous protest, so it is best to follow the procedures outlined above to avoid trouble.

Central budget officers are outnumbered and often too small in number, which puts them at a disadvantage vis-à-vis agency budget offices. Even large cities have relatively small budget staffs; a study of four New England cities found that "the absence of skilled and highly trained professionals was the rule . . . ," a fact that exacerbates the situation.[19] Likewise, state government budget staffs are small; in 1975, only 13 states employed 20 or more budget officers. An example is Washington State, where 14 budget officers examined a $4.7 billion budget in 1973. Since they had only two months for the task, they each had to review over $8 million worth of requests a day. A leading authority on state budgeting argues that talented central budget officers tend to be lured away by higher salaries to line agencies. Thus, in Washington State, central budget examiners had an average of 6 years of experience, while agency finance directors had 15.[20]

The same pattern is found at the federal level. There are seven budget examiners in OMB, for example, to examine the $20 billion Department of Agriculture budget. The average cabinet-level department has 450 to 500 budget people on its payroll, more than OMB's total budget staff. And in the words of Leonard Reed, contributing editor of *The Washington Monthly*, " . . . they are not there to help OMB find out where the bodies are buried."[21]

Another danger confronting central budget examiners at all levels of government is cooptation by the agencies they scrutinize. The examiner may come to identify with the agency and thus fail to do the job of objectively examining its requests. As we have mentioned as true in state government, there is also a tendency for OMB staff to move to line agencies, in some instances because they have come to identify with the agency.[22] For all these reasons, Leonard Reed concludes that "OMB is the lightweight and the agencies are the heavyweights in the battle of the budget."[23]

Special problems beset state and local budget examiners. One problem has been a tendency to ignore federal and state grants to their governments. Grant funds are often considered somebody else's money and are not given as careful scrutiny as programs financed by general-fund revenues. Likewise, special-fund revenues tend to receive a once-over-lightly treatment.[24]

Another area where less than thorough treatment tends to be given is the capital budget. State and local governments, unlike the federal government, divide their budgets into capital and operating budgets. The operating budget is for the personnel, equipment, and supplies needed to run an agency in any one fiscal year.

The capital budget is for large expenditures that do not recur annually, such as buildings or expensive equipment like a computer. Because of the high cost of these items, they are usually financed by floating bonds, which are paid off over a 20- or 30-year period. A 1975 study found that only half of the 50 state budget offices review capital-outlay projections and that 30 states do not treat operating and capital budgets as a single budget. That means that these states cannot have an integrated and comprehensive budget plan.[25] This pattern is probably even more prevalent in the 80,000 local governments.

Different types of accounting systems may allow central budgeters to play different budget games, which make the overall financial picture seem more rosy. The *cash* method of accounting records revenue when it is received and expenditures when they are paid. Transactions are recorded on the date when cash changes hands. For example, the cash method records a home owner's property tax on the day it is paid, whether it is paid early or late. Likewise, a government's purchase of a typewriter is recorded on the day the government pays for it. A cash system is easy to administer, and the cash balance is easily determined. But there is an enormous disadvantage: cash accounting makes accountability impossible because spending and revenue cannot be related to the budget and its fiscal year. If the home owner pays the property tax late, it will be recorded in the *next* fiscal year.

The *accrual* method of accounting records revenue when it is earned or billed and expenditures when they are obligated. A local government with an accrual accounting system records revenue when it sends out its property tax bills and records spending when it obligates itself to buy something. All transactions are thus entered in the budget's fiscal year, an arrangement that permits accountability. This important advantage is balanced by some disadvantages: there may be a long delay in receiving revenue, or revenue may not be received at all, even though the accrual system lists it on the books. If property tax payments come in late, for example, the government's bank account might show a deficit, although the accrual system might list a surplus. For this reason, a *modified accrual* system is recommended for government by accounting authorities. Such combinations and hybrids are so frequent as to be regarded as normal.

Modified accrual accounting systems accumulate expenditures and report revenues in cash. This approach, recommended for government agencies by professional accounting associations, is the most conservative of the systems we examine here. Spending is accrued when government incurs the liability to pay for a line item, while revenues must be received before they can be entered. Such a system forces governments to live within their means.

A modified cash accounting system is the reverse of the modified accrual system. Revenues are accrued and spending is on a cash basis. Such an approach, characterized by Connecticut state auditor Leo V. Donohue as "the worst of all possible worlds," makes possible a maximum of manipulation.[26] Revenues not yet received during the fiscal year can be listed against cash transactions. Both Connecticut State government and New York City have used this approach, which is contrary to accepted accounting principles, to maximize the revenue statement and minimize the spending statement.

Central budget offices are not patsies. They can be formidable foes for agencies that want particular programs, especially in times of economic retrenchment. But, as we have shown here, they have heavy handicaps in controlling government budgeting.

Step 4: The Chief Executive in Budget Formulation

All chief executives except the city and county manager are elected to office. The president, governors, and mayors (or other elected local executives) thus come to their jobs via a very different route than that followed by the career employees who dominate steps one and two of the budgetary process. Chief executives who want to be reelected do not wish to make budgetary decisions that offend public opinion and interest groups to the extent that such decisions will interfere with their chances for reelection. For example, Connecticut governors and gubernatorial candidates have adamantly opposed an income tax since 1971, believing that it is not politically acceptable. California Governor Jerry Brown, who originally opposed Proposition 13, enthusiastically embraced it after it passed by an overwhelming majority in 1978.

S. Kenneth Howard, who has been budget director in two states, has written that governors "usually limit themselves to suggesting general dollar ceilings and issuing broad statements of policy directives that help agency heads very little in setting their own priorities."[27]

A survey of eight states found that in only three did the governor issue instructions to increase or decrease funding for specific programs or provide a total ceiling for agency requests.

Even in these three states, detailed guidance about limitations on specific line items in the budget was not issued.[28]

One way for local chief executives to reduce tax increase is to starve the capital budget. All funds will go to the operating budget, and badly needed capital expenditures will simply be deferred. Another, opposite tactic is to move items that should be in the operating budget into the capital budget. Before New York City's financial collapse in 1975, employees of many departments were paid their salaries from the capital budget. That meant that operating expenses were paid by issuing long-term, interest-bearing bonds. Mayors John Lindsay and Abraham Beame both followed this strategy; Lindsay got away with it. His successor, Beame, was caught in the collapse of this financial house of cards.

One study of governors with diametrically different approaches to controlling the budget found that neither succeeded very well. Delaware Governor Peterson told department heads that 5 percent of the budget would be for new programs for which departments would compete. His successor, Governor Tribbitt, imposed rigid spending ceilings. But agency officials merely rearranged old budget items in new ways. Peterson encouraged agency heads to press for new programs. The resulting rush of requests made it hard for Peterson to impose a ceiling. In Tribbitt's case, the rigid ceilings he imposed prevented him from weighing program alternatives because bureaucrats worked out budgets at their own level. Thus, Tribbitt's approach prevented requests for new programs from reaching the governor. The price of expenditure control was loss of program control.[29] It is no surprise, then, that the governor's position in the budgetary policymaking process has been compared to that of a blind man on top of a mountain who is trying to affect its height and mass by moving pebbles near the summit. Although this simile is exaggerated, because a governor determined either to raise or to lower expenditures may well have some impact, gubernatorial constraints are more obvious than any gubernatorial freedom of action or power.[30]

Governors do not differ in this respect from most other chief executives. President Jimmy Carter campaigned on a pledge to balance the federal budget by 1981. Economic and political pressures became too great for him to achieve this goal. Carter also tried and failed to change the budget significantly through zero-base budgeting, which we shall examine in the next chapter.

Step 5: The Legislature in Budget Formulation

The predominant power in legislatures in the Western world is the power of the purse. English parliamentary history is the history of the legislature gradually gaining budgetary power from the king. In the United States all bureaucrats and chief executives must come to the legislature, whether Congress, the state assembly, the city council, a town meeting, or the governing board of special and school districts, to plead their budgetary cases.

At the same time, most legislatures are handicapped relative to both bureaucrats and chief executives. Most legislators are part-time lawmakers, who are paid little and have little or no support staff. With some exceptions, state legislators are usually not paid a living wage, and many lack offices and secretaries. The situation is even worse at the local level, where councilmen are often paid nothing.

Adding further complications is the legislator's paramount priority, the district that sent him or her to the legislature. Legislators often have little interest in programs and spending beyond their districts. Indeed, many think only in terms of the patronage—jobs, contracts, and favors—that they can deliver to their constituents.

Since the turnover rate among state and local legislators is very high, their ignorance rate is also high. Legislators who have spent two or four years familiarizing themselves with government often retire because of low wages or they lose their bids for reelection.

While all these factors handicap legislators, they do not mean that the legislature is fated to sit on the sidelines forever. There are examples of legislatures that play an assertive role in budgeting. A study of 14 Michigan cities, ranging in population from 25,000 to 200,000, found that local legislatures examined budgets carefully, asked many questions, and required extensive justification for budget requests. Some councils even directly opposed the trend of spending proposed by the agencies and the chief executive and reversed it. The authors conclude that the legislature has considerable influence of its own.[31] We believe that this kind of council activism is more the exception than the rule because we have seen too many legislators fumble through budgets to find something they could grasp and use as a basis for action. One local legislator held up action on a school budget for an hour to complain about an appropriation of $18 for golf balls for the high school golf team. Another legislator thought that since an appropriation for a pickup truck, in his opinion, was priced too high, the school budget should be cut by 10 percent. The truck was evidence of wasteful ways in budgeting. These examples reveal the bewilderment of legislators confronting a budget and their attempts by inappropriate means to make the document understandable. Of course, these legislators could become more active and expert in budgetary decision making if they wanted to, but most legislators seem not to want to.

Another obstacle to legislature control of budgeting is the fragmentation of the budgetary process. Gone are the days when a strong leader controlled one house of Congress or the state legislature. And even then, this dominant figure would have to bargain with the leadership of the other house. While there may be domination by one person in some local legislatures, most legislatures representing large jurisdictions (cities and counties over 100,000) are not ruled in such an authoritarian fashion.

To take Congress first, while recent changes are described in the next section, the congressional procedure has been for committees dealing with substantive areas—such as Armed Services, Labor, and Education—to *authorize* a certain

level of spending for the next fiscal year. But this is far from the last word in the budgetary process. The Appropriations Committee looks at the authorization and decides how much actually to *appropriate*. Since this figure is usually less than the authorization, the appropriations committees share power with the substantive committees. Anyone who reads that Congress has authorized $5 million for left-handed monkey wrenches has read only the first, not the final, chapter in congressional budget making. And it should be remembered that the House and Senate have to hammer out a compromise in their appropriations bills before sending them on to the president.

In state government, the same dynamic tension between substantive and appropriations committees often exists. While many state legislatures have joint upper house–lower house committees, power is often fragmented. Since there are usually fewer state legislators than federal senators (100) or representatives (438), an individual state legislator may have more influence over particular budget line items. At the local level, with even smaller legislatures, power may be fragmented even further.

This situation means that it is almost impossible for the legislature to come up with a coherent, coordinated, and consistent budget. The result is usually a mélange of compromises, some of which may be contradictory. For example, for years Congress has appropriated funds subsidizing mortages, enabling middle-class people to leave the city for the suburbs, and funds subsidizing the construction of apartments designed to attract the middle class back to the city.

Federal Government. A look at the federal legislature, whose members are well paid, work full time, and have large personal, committee, and institutional staffs of professionals, will illustrate some of the other problems that beset budget handling in legislatures.

In the 1960s and early 1970s there was growing concern among Congressmen that their control over the budget was slipping. Congress had passed laws making much of the budget uncontrollable, and executive agencies, as described in step one, seemed very much in the saddle.

These apprehensions came to a head after President Richard Nixon refused to spend billions of dollars appropriated by Congress, a matter we probe in more detail in step six. Nixon and his budgeters argued that they were moving to curb deficits and inflation. Many congressmen and senators denounced Nixon's actions, and political and legal steps to reverse them were taken. At the same time, Congress changed its budgetary process in 1974, a tacit admission that it agreed with some of the president's complaints. The chief changes included a requirement that a resolution setting target figures for total spending, tax, and debt levels be approved before Congress could appropriate funds for specific programs. New House and Senate committees were established to frame the resolutions, and the timetable outlined in Box 22.1 was instituted. A professionally staffed Congressional Budget Office (CBO) was established. The target figures would guide, but not bind, Congress, and most *new* (though not existing) forms of off-budget spending would be subject to the regular appropriations process. The president's authority to impound funds was made subject to congressional approval.

Many expert observers doubted Congress would keep within the target guidelines. Congress actually deserves a positive report card. To the surprise of many, Congress did keep within the limits set in fiscal year 1976. It did so by taking action such as cutting back on personnel fringe benefits and defense procurement. Never before had such a conference report on a military budget been defeated.[32] While there were some encroachments upon the figures approved in resolutions and some failure to observe deadlines, the new process has improved Congress's approach. A key change has been the 200 professional staffers in the CBO, who have given Congress the capacity to analyze executive budget requests, a capacity

Box 22.1

CONGRESSIONAL BUDGET TIMETABLE

Nov. 10	Current services budget submitted
15 days after Congress convenes	President's budget submitted
March 15	Committees submit budget reports to Budget Committees
April 1	Congressional Budget Office sends report to Budget Committees
April 15	Budget Committees report first budget resolution to House and Senate
May 15	All authorization bills reported
May 15	Final action on first budget resolution
7 days after Labor Day	Final action on appropriations bills
Sept. 15	Final action on second budget resolution
Sept. 25	Final action on budget reconciliation measure
Oct. 1	Fiscal year begins

SOURCE: Congressional Budget Office

it lacked before. Yet the change has hardly ended the fragmentation found within the national legislature. Congress remains a long way from having any kind of centralized, unified approach to the budgetary process. The change that has occurred is the recognition that some attention must be paid to the relationship of the budget totals to the economy and federal revenues; otherwise the nation will be in for increasing trouble. It is a positive step forward, but just one step. Much more remains to be done if Congress is truly to coordinate the budgetary process.

State and Local Government: Problems of Legislative Control. A common problem of legislative control is failure to make clear the legislative intent regarding spending. If the legislature fails to issue clear guidelines, the agencies and central budget office may be able to act contrary to actual legislative intent. If there are few or no instructions to the welfare department, for example, the department may be able to spend its budget as it wants. A study found that in Idaho, for example, legislative intent is so undefined that executive officials are unable to determine if a problem in that area exists.[33]

Another restriction found in some state and local legislatures is a ban on increasing appropriations to a level higher than that recommended by the chief executive or whatever body submits proposals to the legislature. The Maryland legislature, for example, can only cut gubernatorial proposals, not increase them. The Nebraska legislature needs a two-thirds margin to raise appropriations. Many local legislatures cannot increase appropriations beyond the level recommended to them, though almost all can reduce appropriations below the recommended level.

Supplemental spending, appropriated after the initial budget decision, is common practice at all levels of government. At all levels, supplemental funds are issued more hastily and with less careful analysis than is true for original budget bills. One study of state budgeting concluded that supplementals mean that as far as agency budgets are concerned "there is no reward for correct budgetary decision making and there is no real penalty for wrong budgetary decision making."[34]

A final frustration for legislative financiers is the fragmentation of funds into different budgets. We have already noted the existence of separate, uncoordinated operating and capital budgets, an arrangement that impedes legislative budget planning and control. This separation will probably continue to exist for some time because many legislators and interest groups want a separate capital budget. Because of its political "costlessness," achieved by pushing the date when bills are due into the future, the capital budget has an appeal to many politicians. It becomes a kind of political grab bag in which every group can find a project because it receives less scrutiny from the legislature than the operating budget. Thus, facilities may become divorced from programs. An example is building schools—after many years of fighting—at a time when the student population starts to decrease.

One proof of legislative exertion in the budgetary process will come when legislatures insist that operating and capital budgets be reviewed in relationship to each other. Until that day, legislatures will be exerting only part of their potential influence over budgets.

Step 6: Budget Execution

Once the legislature has finished its budget deliberations and the chief executive has signed the budget bill, the process of *formulating* the budget is over. But the budgetary process is far from over. Next, the appropriated monies go to the central budget office, which periodically allots them to the agencies. This fact gives the central budget office a continuing measure of control over spending.

Alloting Appropriations to the Agencies. Allotments (the term used in the federal government is apportionment) are usually distributed on a quarterly basis, allowing the budget office to adjust spending if revenues start to slip.[35] The purposes of allotments are to ensure that funds are spent properly and that spending is timed to meet requirements that vary widely for certain activities, such as snow removal or maintenance of outside swimming pools.[36]

Central budget-office discretion to withhold allotments is often limited. A 1974 survey of 44 states found that 27 imposed restrictions on executive ability to withhold funds. In Georgia, North Carolina, Oregon, South Carolina, and Utah, reductions must be uniform—all agencies must be cut by the same percentage. Some states exempt certain agencies, others require legislative concurrence in cuts, and others limit the cuts to a fixed percentage maximum (for example, 25 percent in Maryland and West Virginia and 15 percent in Montana). In the other 17 states, however, the central budget office has far more authority to cut.[37]

The federal and many local governments have similar authority to adjust spending when revenues slip. Sometimes presidents will impose a hiring freeze, not allowing vacant jobs to be filled. The federal government, all states but Missouri, and many local governments have a system of position controls operated by the central budget agency. These controls identify the authorized number of employees by agency and position. An agency has to file a request with the budget office before it can fill a position. This gives the central budget office a measure of discretion beyond formally withholding allotments, for it can save a good deal of money by simply failing to act on position requests. This is the pattern in Connecticut State government, where many position requests simply become bogged down in the budget office in tight fiscal times.

Even when revenues are more than adequate to cover spending, agencies operating under an allotment system must submit detailed spending plans to receive their allotments. The central budget office must then approve this plan before the allotment is disbursed to the agency. This system of pre-auditing expenditures, as it is called, gives additional authority to the central budget office. Budgeters may alter the plan to achieve compliance with legislative intent or ensure efficiency.

The specific criteria defining efficiency or interest vary greatly from government to government, unlike the discretion to withhold funds to prevent a deficit. California and Maryland, for example, give the budget office great authority over allotments, while South Dakota and Oklahoma give it none at all. But even in states where there is no such formal authority, the governor may informally ask department heads to refuse part of their allotments. Connecticut Governor Thomas Meskill did so in the early 1970s, achieving in fact what the letter of the law prohibited. Another approach that the budget office can follow to save money even when deficits do not threaten is to reduce the amount of allotments for the first three quarters. The Department of Public Works, for example, could be allotted 20 percent of its total appropriation rather than 25 percent, for each of the first three quarters. The central budget office might argue that this is the most efficient way to proceed. In the last quarter, it could then be refused the remaining 40 percent and be given a lesser sum on the grounds that it could not possibly spend all that money in one quarter. Or it could be given all 40 percent in the expectation that all of the money could not possibly be spent and that a good portion of it would have to revert to the general fund at fiscal year's end.

While central budget offices often have substantial control over agency spending, a few sources of agency power should be noted. First, much of the budget is uncontrollable and cannot be withheld, even under the threat of impending deficits. Second, budget controls often fail to control *programs*. As the Governor's Economy Committee in Delaware concluded, "funds appropriated for an object/line item can legally be spent for almost any purpose, and there is no meaningful way of relating expenditure to accomplishment."[38] A few dollars may be saved, while programs go on unexamined by the central budget office.

Impounding. Withholding of federal appropriations by the president is called impounding. Since World War II, presidents have refused to spend appropriations for weapons systems, flood-control projects, urban renewal, highways, model cities, and a host of other programs. Impoundment is nothing new. In 1803, President Thomas Jefferson refused to spend $50,000 for Mississippi River gunboats. Presidents and Congress have long fought over whether the president has the constitutional authority to impound funds. Presidents have argued that they are acting to carry out specific statutory directives, such as fighting inflation, making sure state welfare spending is maintained at stipulated levels, or withholding funds when racial discrimination is practiced.[39]

The Nixon administration (1969–1974) offered a new and different justification for sharply increasing the rate of impoundment. Officials justified impounding funds for programs incompatible with the president's priorities. In spring, 1971, for example, $12 billion (mostly for highway and urban spending) was impounded.[40] This aggressive impounding policy, which was accelerated after Nixon's 1972 reelection, collapsed only two years later. Why? First, Nixon became politically weak as a result of the Watergate scandal and had to back off on some of the impoundments to try to gain support in Congress. Second, Congress became incensed and passed anti-impoundment provisions in the 1974 Budget Reform Act, discussed in a previous section. Third, federal courts overruled several of the impoundments—those for health, education, and water-pollution-control funds, among others. The Nixon administration lost 25 of 30 court cases by September of 1973. The courts had never been so directly involved in the question of impoundment before, and they ruled that the administration's rationale was untenable. Since 1974, presidents have been able to continue to impound funds, but Congress can veto these impoundments if it so desires.

Step 7: Budget Execution: Agency Spending

After these lengthy and labyrinthine procedures, the agencies have their money. Yet spending it may be the most complex and complicated part of the budgetary process. That is so even when we

do not delve into the intricacies of purchasing procedures, personnel hiring, and bidding for contracts, matters we shall not take up here. Agencies want to be sure to spend all the money they receive; if they do not, instead of being rewarded for economy, they are likely to have their next budget slashed on the grounds that they could not spend all the money received in the last budget. This fact explains the frantic rush to spend every cent of the last quarter's allotment, which occurs in many agencies.

Most agencies retain a good deal of discretion when it comes to spending money. There are good reasons for that. First, if they had no discretion, they would be unable to act in many situations. They could not cope with changing conditions and would be trapped by the rigidity of the budget system. For example, let us suppose that snow-plowing funds are not needed because there is no snow. Then spring rains cause road damage, for which no funds exist. It is logical to spend the snow-removal money to fix the roads. Second, there are too many bureaucratic budgeters to be controlled by the central budget office. Third, when an agency has political support from the legislature and powerful interest groups, it may be able to ignore the legal authority of the budget office in many situations.

One strategy agencies can follow to maximize control is "multipocket budgeting." Agencies may have different revenue sources such as general-fund money, special funds, grants, and user fees. If they use those revenues with the greatest number of restrictions first, they will have those with the fewest restrictions left later on in the fiscal year. For example, if a school system has received a federal grant to pay teachers for instructing handicapped children, school budgeters will want to start that program moving at once. "An administrator has more flexibility when he obligates his more restricted funds for items in his regular program and reserves general purpose funds for activities which cannot be funded through special grants or programs."[41] In this way, an agency makes the most of its discretion to spend.

Bureaucrats may have many options open to

them in spending money, some of which may contradict legislative or chief executive interest. We shall examine two crucial areas—those of transfers and reprogramming—below and then discuss several other areas of bureaucratic option.

Transfers. Louis Fisher's superb studies of the federal budgetary process make clear that Congress has long given agencies authority to take funds appropriated for one class of appropriations and apply them to another.

For example, Defense Department and foreign-aid appropriations "are particularly generous in permitting the transfer of funds from one program to another."[42] In 1970, after the U.S. invasion of Cambodia, the Nixon administration borrowed $100 million in foreign-aid monies assigned to Greece, Turkey, Taiwan, and Vietnam and spent it for Cambodia instead.[43]

Federal funds may also be transformed over time as well as among classes of appropriations. Congress allows appropriations to "remain available until expended" for a number of purposes, including capital projects. This "no-year" money does not return to the treasury at the end of the fiscal year. In fiscal year 1972, for example, almost $300 billion in unspent authority carried over into the next fiscal year.[44]

In state government, the authority to transfer money *within* agency budgets is granted in 40 states and *between* agencies in another 19. Restrictions on agency ability to transfer money are also a general rule. Some states limit transfers to a maximum percentage of the specific line item. For example, the Public Works Department might be able to transfer 50 percent of its line item for trucks to the sand and salt line item, but no more. In other states, a specific dollar maximum per line item ($10,000 in Vermont, for example) is the rule. Transfers usually require the approval of the central budget officer or governor.[45] While comparable data on local government authority is lacking, most local governments also have provision for transfers.

These legal restrictions may not restrict agencies greatly in fact, however. Certainly there is a high volume of transfers (2 percent of the budget

in Georgia and 4.5 percent in Delaware, for example). These transfers may amount to 25 percent of the legislatively approved increase in spending.

Transfers in the states are not only routine, they are not random. A common practice is to transfer funds from the general salary and wage line items to cover spending for a particular project. One social service administrator transferred funds from institutional to outpatient care over a three-year period, remarking that "it was easier than requesting or justifying a new program."[46] A study of eight states found that in five of them more than half the agency heads transferred appropriations. The authors concluded that the only way to reduce transfers is a legislative ban, which exists only in Missouri, or tremendous affluence, found in oil-rich Texas, which makes transfers unnecessary.[47] Transfers, then, give bureaucrats a great deal of budgetary discretion.

Reprogramming. Reprogramming resembles transfers, with two differences. First, funds are not shifted from one account to another. Instead, the purpose to which the funds are applied can be changed. Second, no statutory authority is needed for reprogramming. Rather, there is an informal clearance procedure. At the federal level, agencies clear reprogramming with congressional committees. Reprogramming is allowed as a means of retaining flexibility in the face of changing conditions, "such as unforeseen requirements, changes in operating conditions, incorrect price estimates, wage rate adjustments, legislation enacted subsequent to appropriation action, and the like."[48] Between 1956 and 1972, military reprogramming averaged $2.6 billion a year.[49] The Defense Department, Veterans' Administration, and Department of Interior reprogram with regularity.

The leading authority on the topic concludes that "it is a peculiar fact that budget estimates are scrutinized . . . often undergoing intensive review—and yet no comparable review exists for the billions of dollars that are reprogrammed after the appropriations bill becomes law."[50] While Congress has tightened up on reprogramming in recent years, the practice still exists and affords federal bureaucrats substantial discretion.

Reprogramming is also found in state government. One imaginative example involved reprogramming within salary line items. In a Delaware department, employees rotated in and out of a single, high-paying supervisory position. Each acted as supervisor for a day, and all retained the higher wage, because personnel regulations permitted employees voluntarily taking demotions to remain at higher pay rates.

One strategy reprogrammers use is the foot-in-the-door technique. The Delaware Highway Department, for example, redistributed funds from authorized projects to unauthorized new projects, which the department desired. As a result, neither the authorized nor the unauthorized project had enough funding to be finished. Once the projects were started, however, the department could ask for money to finish them by arguing that the money spent so far would be totally wasted were the projects left unfinished. After all, what good is half a bridge?[51] The eight-state survey mentioned earlier found that a majority of agency heads in each state preprogrammed funds. The study's author concludes that state reprogramming is even more significant than transfers because there are fewer controls over the former than the latter. And since large state agencies are more likely to reprogram than smaller ones, central budget-office and legislative controls over the most important departments are lacking in this crucial area.[52]

Other Areas of Agency Discretion. The Defense Department often signs contracts for military weapons systems whose costs greatly exceed the original estimates. The department has argued that it has discretionary authority to pay the extra amount if the president rules that to do so is in the national interest.[53] Even if Congress does not buy that argument for a specific plane or tank, it is still stuck in a political mire. Having sunk billions of dollars into a weapons system, it cannot easily walk away from those committed funds. The pressure to spend more to obtain something rather than nothing may be irresistible.

In state government, accounting sleight of hand may be used to direct general-fund monies into special-fund accounts. That way the agency can hold on to the money, rather than having to return it to the general fund at year's end. If pre-audit controls are weak, this ploy can be carried out by improperly coding reimbursement forms. When general-fund monies are transferred from one department to another to reimburse the second agency for services rendered, they may end up in a special fund. We shall look at these practices from the auditor's perspective in Chapter 23; suffice it to say here that agencies that follow this and related practices are not acting within the spirit and perhaps not even within the letter of the law. Such practices are apparently widespread.[54]

BEYOND THE LINE-ITEM BUDGET

The line-item budget says what a government has purchased but nothing else. What does it do with its purchases and what are the results? The line-item system is excellent for *detailed* control, but not the kind of *management* control we discussed in Chapter 15. The exasperated outburst of a Flint, Michigan, city councilman may be considered a typical reaction: "Flint looks like hell. The budget is the size of three telephone books; no one can read it, let alone understand it."[55]

While the line-item budget represents an enormous managerial advance over lump-sum appropriations, it cannot tell anything about activities or results. Here we discuss three budget systems that attempt to do just that.

The Performance Budget

Performance budgeting was advocated as early as 1914 by the New York Bureau of Municipal Research, and it was strongly recommended by the 1949 Hoover Commission study of the federal government. The Hoover Commission said that performance budgeting would focus "upon the general character and relative importance of the work to be done, or upon the service to be rendered, rather than upon things to be acquired. . . ."[56]

Performance budgeting is concerned with the efficient use of personnel and other agency resources to accomplish the agency's job. To achieve these ends, performance budgets use activity classifications, performance measurements, and performance reports.

Activity Classifications. Functional classifications list "a group of related activities . . . for which a governmental unit is responsible."[57] An example is health care. This function can be broken down into certain *activities,* such as home health care, sewer and septic tank inspection, and mass innoculation campaigns. Table 22.2 illustrates a fire-prevention activity classification with relevant expenditure figures. As Allen Schick notes, there is no universal classification scheme that everyone agrees on. Rather, there are many ways to classify multifunctional activities. Dental-care instruction in school could be listed under either the health or education function, for example. Likewise, a hospital could be classified as a single activity, as part of a large medical program, or divided into subactivities, such as surgery, outpatient care, and the like.[58]

Performance Measurements. We have already examined performance measurements in Chapter

TABLE 22.2 A Performance Budget

CENTER CITY EXPENDITURE REQUEST FORM

DEPARTMENT: FIRE

Fire prevention	Actual 1963–64	Adopted 1964–65	Revised 1964–65	Budget 1965–66
Costs	$	$	$	$
Fixed costs—administration[a]	12.460	13,085	13,000	13,650
Fixed costs—fire prevention unit[b]	24,085	27,825	27,875	29,295
Variable costs—fire companies[c]	33,070	36,790	35,740	44,385
	$69,615	$77,700	$76,615	$87,330
Manpower (man-hours)				
Administration	4,160	4,160	4,160	4,160
Fire prevention unit	7,488	8,320	8,320	8,320
Fire companies	19,564	20,440	19,855	23,360
	31,212	32,920	22,335	35,840
Inspections performed (number)				
Fire prevention unit	9,634	10,500	10,100	10,500
Fire companies	94,493	102,200	99,280	116,800
	104,127	112,700	109,380	127,300
Unit costs ($/inspection)				
Fire prevention unit	2.50	2.65	2.76	2.79
Fire companies	.35	.36	.36	.38

[a] Fixed costs—administration. Revised expenditure for the current year based on full staffing. Next year's estimate is also based on full staffing and 5% pay raise.

[b] Fixed costs—fire prevention unit. Same estimating basis as administration.

[c] Variable costs—fire companies. Revised expenditures for the current year are based on the number of inspections to be delivered by the fire companies, and paid for at the rate of $.36 per inspection. Inspection rates are estimated at $.38 per inspection for next year's expected workload of 116,800 company inspections.

SOURCE: Edward A. Lehan, *The Practice of Municipal Budgeting* (Kingston: University of Rhode Island, 1975).

16 on productivity. Here the concern is the relationship of inputs to activities, with an emphasis on the unit costs in performance budgeting. For example, this part of the performance budget can list what it costs the hospital laundry per pound of laundry. Table 22.2 contains such unit cost figures for fire-prevention inspections.

Performance Reports. Reports are a look back at what an agency did with its budget. A report compares the goals and costs projected in the budget with actual accomplishments and costs. Such a report can be used to evaluate goals and the procedures followed to reach these goals. The reader should note that these reports are the budgetary equivalent of the Management by Objectives (MBO) program reviews we examined in Chapter 15.

Evaluating Budgets for Performance Criteria. We define a performance budget as a budget that uses activity classifications and performance measurements as its basic organizing principles. Other related criteria are commonly found in performance budgets. One criterion is the inclusion of narrative information describing the work involved in a program. Such a presentation immediately gives the reader a sense of what a particular activity is all about.

Another criterion is activity or work-load data, such as are arrayed in Table 22.2 and which indicate the number of man hours worked, inspections performed, and patients served. Such information is a useful aid. Ideally, however, a performance budget should include unit-cost data, not just activity data. The purpose of the performance data is to increase efficiency, and unit-cost information is necessary in any such type of analysis. It is necessary to know what a pound of laundry costs in order to be able to make meaningful comparisons between laundries.

Performance Budgeting: The Record. Performance budgeting has met with some acceptance at all three levels of American government, but it has a long way to go before it can challenge the line-item budget in popularity. Many budgets are "hybrids," Schick's term for line-item budgets that contain some aspects of performance budgeting but that do not meet all the requirements for performance budgets.[59] Many budgets, for example, may contain narrative information. But that may be as far as they go. Others may contain some work load data, as does Table 22.2, but that may be as far as they go.

A 1970 survey, using far less rigorous criteria, found that only 7 of the 50 state governments could be considered to have performance budgets.[60] But many more have some elements of performance budgeting. A 1975 survey of 49 states found that 31 central budget offices conducted productivity analyses, an increase of 17 since 1970.[61] At the federal level, some agencies took the advice of the Hoover Commission, but most to this day do not have performance budgets. While a 1974 survey of 88 cities of more than 50,000 found that they averaged a score of 59 percent on 7 indicators of performance budgeting,[62] most of the 80,000 local governments cannot be considered to have performance budgets.

The Planning-Programming Budgeting System

The Planning-Programming Budgeting System (PPBS) is the most ambitious of the results-oriented approaches we examine in this chapter. It combines long-range planning (up to five years into the future) with results-oriented programs and evaluation. Governmental PPBS had its origins in the Defense Department in the early 1960s, when President Lyndon Johnson was so much impressed by its work that in 1965 he directed that the PPBS be used in all federal agencies. At the same time, a number of states and localities adopted the PPBS.

PPBS budgeters follow the same kind of planning process outlined in Chapter 10. The programs that result from this process should then be evaluated by the approaches discussed in Chapter 16. Such evaluation, as noted in Chapter 23, is often referred to as a *performance audit*. The term is confusing, since performance budgeting is oriented toward activities and work load while performance auditing is oriented toward results.

The ABCs of PPBS. Expert observer Allen Schick argues that if the control function predominates in line-item budgeting and management function in performance budgeting, then *planning* predominates in the PPBS.[63] Planning, as we have noted in Chapter 10, refers to the process of setting goals for programs.

Under the PPBS, the objectives of every government program must be defined as precisely as possible for the budgetary period of a year, as indicated in Box 22.2. In addition, objectives should be defined for longer periods—five years or more. In this process, complete data must be provided as to costs, benefits, and feasibility; on this basis, a choice must be made among alternative courses of action. Once the decision has been made and the money budgeted and appropriated, then at various stages thereafter, accomplishment must

be evaluated on the basis of complete cost and benefit analysis. Hence, the PPBS is a system based on rigorous analysis, which seeks to discover the relative advantage of given solutions compared with other alternatives.

The four main elements are (1) clear goals for the government and its programs, (2) the identification of future-year implications, (3) the analysis of all pertinent costs, and (4) the systematic analysis of alternative courses of action and anticipated outcomes.

In 1965, President Johnson, impressed with the record of the PPBS, ordered it implemented in all federal agencies, from the Department of Agriculture to the Treasury Department. Federal PPBS was instituted across the board with a bang, but it died with a whimper in 1971. Schick concludes that its demise was due to multiple wounds: lack of preparation, inadequate support and resources, lack of skilled manpower, and a clash of perspectives between PPBS implementers and traditional budgeters. But the PPBS did

Box 22.2

PROPOSED STREET MAINTENANCE RESULTS BUDGET
CITY OF HARMONY DEPARTMENT OF TRANSPORTATION, 1977

PROGRAM GOALS

Assist in providing for the safe and expeditious use of public streets and alleys through a regular street maintenance program, minimize danger to life and property through the control of irrigation and storm water, and assist in maintaining acceptable aesthetic standards for public streets and alleys.

PROGRAM OBJECTIVES HIGHLIGHTS

1. Reduce street flooding 10 percent from last year's levels (criterion: number of square feet flooded to a depth of six or more inches × minutes flooded)..... $457,832.00

2. Reduce dwelling flooding 10 percent from last year's levels (criterion: amount of estimated property damage).... $119,830.00

3. Reduce automobile damage from potholes by 10 percent from last year's levels. . . . $384,296.00

4. Increase traffic flow on class A streets 5 percent from last year's levels through prompt repair. . . . $872,419.00

5. Increase aesthetic standards by 10 percent (criterion: citizen questionnaire). . . . $82,117.00

not die, in his opinion, because of subversion by the line agencies, most of which gave it a serious try. Schick concludes that the PPBS was doomed by the failure of the federal Bureau of the Budget (now OMB), the central budget agency, to give it adequate support.[64]

While the overall effort foundered, there were successes in various federal agencies. Thomas Lynch's study of the PPBS in the Department of Transportation concluded that the Coast Guard "took quite seriously the presidential order to develop a PPB system,"[65] using it as a decision-making tool in planning for aids to navigation. According to Lynch, some federal agencies, including the Coast Guard, continue to use the PPBS today even after its general demise.

State Government. The PPBS was adopted by a number of states, including New York, Pennsylvania, California, Wisconsin, Florida, and Hawaii. In some states, such as New York, the PPBS was dropped shortly after it was introduced. New York State budgeter Stephen M. Fletcher concluded that the scope and depth of the PPBS was too ambitious to be applied in New York; he also thought that the same reasons listed by Schick for the death of the federal PPBS applied in New York State. New York did not completely abandon results-oriented budgeting but switched to a narrower approach with selected, specific, priority areas for analysis.[66] A 1975 survey found that in 32 states the central budget staff conducts program-effectiveness analysis, an increase of 24 since 1970.[67]

Other states have stuck with the PPBS. One of these is Pennsylvania, which Schick designated in 1971 as the state that had taken the PPBS the furthest.[68] Yet a 1974 study concluded that only about half the Pennsylvania budget is governed by PPBS criteria. Stated objectives are not specific enough to be measured, so that evaluation of results is impossible. A case study of the Department of Education concluded that most budgetary decisions are made in the same manner they were made before the PPBS was introduced.[69]

A more-optimistic conclusion is found in a 1977 study, which concludes that results-oriented approaches are employed in Pennsylvania, if not so comprehensively or ambitiously as originally hoped. In many instances, analysts in the governor's budget office reported using output data as the primary basis on which at least part of their recommendations were made. The study concludes that progress toward a results orientation has been made even if optimal goals have not been reached.[70]

While the PPBS on the state level has not achieved revolutionary change, the system is still used in a number of states. A 1977 survey identified 11 states that use the PPBS. This study claims that the PPBS led to changes in line-agency decision making in a number of instances, but unfortunately it fails to provide details illustrative of these changes. The study also found that the governor and the central budget staff are the key factors in determining whether the PPBS will be adopted. If the governor wants it, the PPBS will be initiated; if not, it will not be.[71]

Local Government. A 1972 survey of 214 cities and 120 counties found that 22 percent of the former and 17 percent of the latter reported using at least some elements of the PPBS.[72] It has been used also in a large number of school systems, since federal- and state-aid program officials pressed for its use. A 1971 estimate by Harry Hatry concluded that "perhaps between 50 and 100 of the approximately 1,000 city and county governments of more than 50,000 population have made some significant use of the PPBS."[73] No doubt that is true, as a budget official of Orange County, California, insisted to one of the authors in 1974. A 1974 survey of 88 cities of more than 50,000 population examined the extent to which eight characteristics of the PPBS were found. The cities averaged 40 percent of the eight characteristics, ranging from a high of 60 percent for systems-analysis techniques to a low of 16 percent for long-range forecasts.[74] Unfortunately, data are lacking on the actual use of these components in decision making. We suspect there exists a discrepancy between analysis and its use similar to that found in state governments.

Zero-Base Budgeting[75]

In zero-base budgeting (ZBB) the budget base is not to be regarded as a given that should not be analyzed. President Carter, an advocate of ZBB who implemented it in the federal government, has defined ZBB as follows: "Under this novel concept, every dollar requested for expenditure during the next budget period must be justified, including current expenditures that are to continue. It also provides for examining the effectiveness of each activity at various funding levels."[76]

After Carter was elected governor of Georgia in 1970, he happened to read an article on ZBB by business consultant Peter A. Pyhrr. Intrigued by Pyhrr's arguments, Carter called him down to Georgia to set up ZBB for the Georgia government. Pyhrr divides ZBB into two basic steps, developing "decision packages" and ranking them. We shall examine this approach first and then look at a simplified alternative procedure.

Developing Decision Packages. A decision package describes an activity or function in terms of its goals, its performance measures, its costs and benefits, the consequences of not performing it, and alternatives to it. Box 22.3 is an actual decision package for the Georgia State Highway Patrol's field operations. It should be noted that there are specific statements for each of the items listed above.

Like MBO, ZBB is a decentralizing approach, which delegates to managers the task of putting decision packages together. Decision packages can deal with people, projects, programs, services, costs, and expenditures so long as they focus on *what is being achieved* by these personnel and items. For example, a people-centered decision package might focus on the principals for two neighboring elementary schools. It would focus on what they accomplish and it could raise for consideration alternatives such as eliminating one principal and turning over both schools to the remaining principal.

Box 22.3 illustrates a program-centered decision package. *Services* such as ambulance costs paid for by a welfare department, *cost overruns*

beyond the amount projected, and *line-item expenditures* such as travel or consultant fees could all become the subjects of decision packages. ZBB, then, is a flexible tool for managers, adaptable to a wide variety of uses.

1. *Description of Purpose or Goals.* The goal statement of a decision package should always be specific to the function performed. That is, the purpose of a state police laboratory is to identify the victims or criminals in various crimes, not to prevent crime and apprehend criminals. This broader goal is the goal of the entire state police force, and it is not useful in analyzing the activities of one of its components.

2. *Description of Activities.* The description of program activities answers the questions What will you do? and How will you do it? As Box 22.3 indicates, this section shows the approaches, activities, and kinds of employees and equipment recommended to do a job.

3. *Consequences of Not Performing the Activity.* This sections is undoubtedly the most painful for a line-agency manager to fill out, and he is thus likely to forecast the downfall of the country if the activity should be eliminated. Both line managers and ZBB analysts for a central staff agency should mull this entry over very carefully, for it is the package item most likely to be deliberately or inadvertently inaccurate.

4. *Performance Measures.* Performance measures or evaluative criteria have already been identified as crucially important. Item 10 in Box 22.3 lists the measures used in the Georgia State Highway Patrol decision package.

5. *Costs.* It is difficult to know just how much cost information to provide. Some information is absolutely necessary for managers to make a rational decision, but some is detail that may not be necessary. Monthly cost figures, for example, become quite burdensome and are not essential to do the job. They may be useful, but they are not useful enough to justify the added effort for most activities. Yet in some very expensive new projects, they may be considered essential. No easy rule of thumb can be given.

6. *Benefits.* Benefits are usually more difficult to measure than costs. One reason for this is that they often include qualitative judgments, such as beauty of the environment, as well as countable

Box 22.3

GEORGIA STATE HIGHWAY PATROL DECISION PACKAGE

(1) Package Name

Georgia State Highway Patrol–Field Operation (1 of 5)

(6) Statement of Purpose

To patrol the rural and public roads and highways throughout the State, to prevent, detect and investigate criminal acts, and to arrest and apprehend those charged with committing criminal offenses appertaining thereto, and to safeguard the lives and property of the public.

(7) Description of Actions (Operations)

Patrol the rural roads of the State and respond to civil unrest. Operate 45 patrol posts 365 days per year; utilizing a staff of 64 radio-operators, 45 clerk dispatchers, 45 sergeants, 45 corporals and 382 troopers for a total staff of 581.

- Replace 47 trooper positions with clerk dispatchers or radio operators to perform office duty, at a savings of $180 thousand.

- Reduce obligated and other service hours (for example: putting mail boxes at each station, rather than having 45 troopers spend one hour each day picking up the mail from the post office, saves 16 thousand man hours per year)—implement in FY 1972 rather than waiting until FY 1973.

- Increase preventative patrol 14% over the FY 1971 level.

(8) Achievements from Actions

Troopers already patrolling the roads can react faster to accidents and emergencies than if they were performing their other duties. The increased free patrol time will improve trooper service, plus reduce the time required by troopers to answer emergency calls—thus increasing even more the free patrol time available.

(9) Consequences of not Approving Package

The State would not have a patrol force to patrol the rural areas nor would local law enforcement agencies have access to a statewide law enforcement communication network.

(10) Quantitative Package Measures	FY 1971	FY 1972	FY 1973	(11) Resources Required ($ in Thousands)	FY 1971	FY 1972	FY 1973	% FY 73/72
Operate Station Hours	280	286	286	Operational	7005	7846	7131	91
Obligated Service Hours	191	163	163	Grants				
Other Service Hours	175	113	113	Capital Outlay	110			
Preventive Patrol Hours	526	703	600	Lease Rentals				
Total Hours Available	1172	1265	1162	Total	7115	7846	7131	91
(Hours in thousands)				People (Positions)	586	631	581	92

(12) Alternatives (Different Levels of Effort) and Cost

(2 of 5) Reassign 34 troopers from license pickup duties to the State Patrol. By changing the license pickup method, only 20,610 hours of obligated service will be transferred with these 34 troopers, providing a net gain of 49,464 hours for preventive patrol (cost $417K)

(3 of 5) Fifty State Troopers for 103 thousand hours of preventive patrol (cost $501K)

(4 of 5) Pay Troopers for overtime rather than giving compensatory time-off—equivalent to 20 troopers, provides 41,229 hours of additional preventive patrol (cost $173K)

(5 of 5) Upgrade 45 Trooper positions to corporal positions (cost $25K)

(Note: Approval of all packages would increase free patrol time 42% at a 5% increase in cost over FY 1972, and increase free patrol time 90% at a 16% increase in cost over FY 1971).

(13) Alternatives (Different Ways of Performing the Same Function, Activity, or Operation)

Abolish the Georgia State Patrol and let local jurisdictions provide traffic law enforcement in the rural areas. Not feasible because: (1) Local jurisdictions would be deprived of the statewide communication system. (2) The mobility of todays population, made possible by the motor vehicle, makes it impossible for local jurisdictions to deal with traffic law enforcement problems effectively. (3) In cases of civil disorder or natural disaster, there would not be trained force available to augment local effort other than the National Guard.

considerations. The benefits listed in item 8, "Achievements from Action," of Box 22.3 illustrate the less-precise nature of benefit forecasting. At the same time, these projected achievements are concrete enough to be measured and evaluated in the future.

7. *Alternatives.* Pyhrr states that "the key to zero-base budgeting lies in the identification and evaluation of alternatives for each activity."[77] He further recommends considering two different types of alternatives for each decision package. The first identifies different ways to do the job. One of these is selected for the decision package as the best way, while the others are listed with brief explanations for their rejection. Box 22.3 illustrates (in item 13) such a listing of alternatives for one governmental activity.

The second kind of alternative involves different levels of effort needed to perform the function. These involve a minimum level and other, more ambitious levels. *Each additional level should be identified as a separate decision package,* as is done in item 12 of Box 22.3.

Why should managers identify different levels of effort rather than recommend the levels they think appropriate? The rationale behind this procedure lies in the fact that line managers usually know the results of their programs better than

other budgetary decision makers. By breaking programs into specific packages, they may avoid the complete elimination of certain functions, which would occur if only one package were identified. Chief executives and legislators usually make across-the-board slashes or increases in agency budgets. For example, if the overall budget is to be cut 5 percent, most agencies will be cut at a level close to this figure. But if the budget decision makers realize fully the consequences of cuts, they may not want to chop across the board. Rather than eliminate entire functions or programs, they can reduce current levels of effort in a selective way.

Ranking Decision Packages. Ranking forces management to ask how much it should spend on each function and where it should spend it. The ranking process accomplishes these steps by listing all the decision packages in order of decreasing benefits to be derived from them.

Like MBO, the ranking process begins at the bottom of the bureaucracy. Managers at the lowest level rank their packages in order of priority and present them to their immediate superiors, who repeat this process all the way up the line.

Not every decision package can be reviewed by the top management of a large organization. Rather, there must be some consolidation of packages. At the same time, management must be careful not to overconsolidate. How can this balance be achieved?

Pyhrr recommends that management focus its review efforts on lower-ranked activities. To do so, a cutoff spending total must be established at each organizational level. Then, only the decision packages that did not make the cutoff would be reviewed in detail and ranked. Packages retained would be listed but not reviewed in this probing fashion. Furthermore, to keep down the accumulating number of decision packages, the expenditure cutoff total has to be increased at each successive level. For example, a cutoff point of 60 percent of the present year's budget can be set for the lowest organizational level, while the next level will allow 70 percent, and the final level 80 percent. This phasing prevents too great an accumulation of decision packages for review at each successive level and effectively *decentralizes* much of the decision-making process.

In applying this approach, ZBB managers and analysts must be very careful not to become overly mechanical. A cutoff point of 60 percent can easily panic line-agency managers. *The point of the process is to concentrate management's time on the low-priority packages, not to cut the budget by an arbitrary fixed figure.* Careful communication and reassurance must be carried out if terror and resistance are not to result. The purpose of the cutoff point is simply to make ZBB manageable.

Besides reviewing only the lowest-ranked packages, management must be careful to keep the number of budget decision-making levels down. But it should not reduce them so much that all ranking decisions are made only at very low levels because top managers will find it difficult and time-consuming to rank decisions made at those levels. A compromise is necessary and will probably have to be arrived at by trial and error in each organization.

Who should rank packages, and how should it be done? As is also true for MBO, Pyhrr recommends that packages be ranked first at the organizational level where they are originally developed. Where lower-level ranking can be done by the manager in charge, higher-level ranking should be done by a committee made up of managers whose packages are involved. After all, top managers will not be intimately familiar with all these packages and will thus need the advice of subordinates in committee to make sensible decisions.

In a large organization, such as a state government, the chief executives cannot review all the decision packages. For example, Jimmy Carter faced 10,000 decision packages while governor of Georgia. He focused his review on policy questions, major budget increases and decreases, new programs, and some special problem areas. Carter was actually reviewing and making final decisions on packages and rankings put together by line managers and budget division staff. They set the agenda for him to make the final decisions.[78]

PPBS and ZBB as Tools. Pyhrr defines PPBS as a "macroeconomic tool for centralized decision making on major policy issues and basic fund allocation," while ZBB "provides the microeconomic tool to transform these objectives into an efficient operating plan and budget and allows managers to evaluate the effect of various funding levels on programs and program elements so that limited resources can be more effectively allocated."[79] This microeconomic tool focuses particularly on efficiency, something that Pyhrr says the PPBS neglects. The PPBS also fails to provide line managers with tools for program implementation or any mechanism to evaluate the effect of different funding levels on programs. In short, ZBB is an operational tool for line managers, whereas the PPBS is a planning tool for staff analysts and top management.

In the words of public administration professor and consultant John Rehfuss: "ZBB is really a bottom-up process, just the opposite of PPBS. It isn't a planning tool—it is a management, cost/

efficient process. What ZBB really does is develop the skills and expand the views of lower level management and give them control of their budget process."[80]

Simplified ZBB. As one writer has said, "There is no 'right' ZBB format. A framework can be designed to meet the needs of the implementing government."[81] We now turn to an alternative, Joseph Wholey's proposal for simplified ZBB. Wholey's approach asks agency division managers to identify their lowest-priority functions, which would be cut if they were forced to take a 10–15 percent budget reduction. At the same time, other decision packages for new or expanded programs are submitted. This approach is designed to overcome many of the technical problems discussed earlier.

Wholey argues that focusing on a 10–15 percent cut keeps the budget dialogue within bounds of political feasibility. Further, it reduces the vast flow of paperwork. Wholey claims the approach has been used successfully in Arlington County, Virginia. Agencies submitted their organization charts, a list of authorized personnel positions and vacancies, current fiscal-year program costs, and a list of low-priority programs that would save 10 percent of the budget if cut. The legislature then met with department heads over two months to gain knowledge of their programs through a lengthy dialogue. The legislature was able to identify and reduce services it considered to be of low priority, such as an ineffective, police foot-patrol operation. In this instance, crime reports and citizen-opinion surveys indicated the program was not accomplishing very much. In other instances, not nearly so much program information was needed to reach decisions.

Decision packages were prepared only when real decisions were likely, thereby reducing the flood of paperwork that the Pyhrr method produces. (And the following fiscal year, paperwork declined significantly.) Nor was an explicit ranking of priorities made. Wholey claims that implicit priorities became clear as budget decisions were made. He also claims that because line-

agency managers were closely involved, they did not play games to evade the legislature's intent, committed themselves to specific tasks in return for budgets above 90 percent of their original requests, and felt fairly treated, even while 100 county personnel positions were eliminated. Many agency initiatives were included in the formal budget proposal, which was enacted almost intact.

Wholey claims that simplified ZBB is useful not only for stable or contracting budgets, but for expanding ones. He gives the example of the Washington Metropolitan Area Transit Authority (METRO). Its use of the approach in drawing up its 1978 fiscal-year budget resulted in a 10 percent budget reduction. Wholey believes these were cuts of low-priority items, not "meat-ax," across-the-board slashes. Again, he thinks the key to success was the involvement of division managers in the process from the beginning.[82]

Another variation on ZBB, which resembles Wholey's approach in many ways, merits brief mention here. *Target budgeting* holds total spending equal to total anticipated revenue. The central budget office then sets a spending target for each agency within this grand total. The agency target is based on current expenditures, anticipated program changes, and judgments about possible reductions. In this way, an already balanced budget is produced.

The agencies are then instructed to prepare a detailed, line-item budget, which does not exceed the target amount. It sets priorities for "reduction packages" to be cut if the budget is reduced by 5 percent and for "improvement packages," which could not be included in the target amount. For all packages, a service-impact statement is provided.

The budget office then makes final recommendations by adding or subtracting packages, based on service-impact statements and revised revenue estimates. In the opinion of one of its advocates, Dallas budget director Dean Vanderbilt, target budgeting does not require the extensive program analysis or quantitative performance indicators of performance budgeting, the PPBS, or ZBB. But when such analysis is available, the service-impact statement provides an excellent means for using it in the budgetary process.[83]

ZBB: The Record. Administration sources made several claims for ZBB as it operated in the Carter administration. One was the claim that $530 million, or about 0.1 percent of the total budget, had been cut from the 1980 fiscal-year budget.[84] Second, in May 1978, the OMB concluded that managerial participation and communication had increased substantially as a result of ZBB. It also listed cuts made possible by ZBB, including the elimination of 32 positions in the Labor Department. More than 9,500 managers prepared 25,000 decision packages.[85]

Since federal ZBB has indeed been a decentralized process, there seems little question that it has been a useful lesson for agencies in ranking programs and consulting more managers than usual in the budgetary process. A collection of articles by agency managers, which appeared in 1978, lends support to this point.[86]

ZBB has not, however, caused any significant change in spending. The Brookings Institution concluded in 1978 that ZBB brought about "virtually no" reductions in the 1979 budget and that new spending programs were "decided outside" the budgetary process.[87] Further, during the same year, interviews with budget officials in all 12 cabinet departments found that almost all of them were not forced carefully to restructure their budgets. As one said, "Zero, shmero. It's incremental budgeting." In January 1978, when OMB director James McIntyre listed three small programs cut by ZBB, departmental budget officials said that two of the three would have been cut anyway. These two totalled $37.4 million to the other program's $5 million.[88] It should be noted, however, that by an action of the Office of Management and Budget occurring on 7 August 1981, the federal use of ZBB was officially abolished, on the ground that ZBB "had not achieved significant results in holding down federal government spending."

After Jimmy Carter's initiation of ZBB for Georgia in 1971, the technique spread to another 11 states by 1976. In addition, another 6 used some but not all of the techniques associated with ZBB, while 3 more decided not to use ZBB because they had just introduced the PPBS, which they felt would accomplish the same ends.[89]

The states that use ZBB, however, apply it differently. For example, in California, Rhode Island, and Tennessee, decision packages are either not used or are used alongside the traditional, line-item system. Moreover, while some states, including Georgia, require that the first decision package be set at a level just adequate barely to sustain the program, others, such as Illinois (90 percent) or Montana (80 percent), set a given percentage of the current budget as the level for the first decision packages. Third, priority rankings are found in all states but California, which applies ZBB selectively rather than across the board.

Schick and Robert Keith conclude that state ZBB does not really require that the budget be built up from nothing each year but that it shift "the bulk of budget preparation from increments above the budget base to decrements below the base."[90] In other words, as used in the states, ZBB seems designed primarily to halt large increases in spending.

One state, New Mexico, has tried and abandoned ZBB. Schick thinks that the two principal causes for this relinquishment were the enormous paperwork generated by ZBB and a failure to take ZBB seriously after a huge (and temporary) budget surplus came into being.[91] It should also be noted that New Mexico ZBB was instituted by the legislature, without equal enthusiasm from the executive branch.[92]

Determining the results of ZBB is extremely difficult. As Schick has remarked, no one knows quite how to take before-and-after snapshots of budgets.[93] There are too many factors, such as changing economic trends and political variables, to make easy judgments about what ZBB produces. For example, while the budget of the Office of the Secretary of the Commonwealth of Massachusetts declined by 10 percent in two years of ZBB, that does not mean that it would not have dropped 10 percent without ZBB.

More likely to be true are claims such as that made by Texas Budget Director Charles Travis: "ZBB itself doesn't save money. What it does is to provide better information for the decision makers." Similarly, a 1974 study of Georgia budget analysts found that state employees understood the workings of government better as a result of ZBB. The study concluded that ZBB had improved the quality of management information and brought about greater involvement in the budgetary process by lower-level personnel. (Only 2 of 13 Georgia government department heads thought that ZBB "may" have reallocated resources, while only 7 of 32 Georgia budget analysts felt ZBB caused "some" shifting of financial resources.)[94]

ZBB in Local Government. ZBB has also been used in a number of local governments, including Wilmington, Delaware; Garland, Texas; and Yonkers, New York. At present, however, a survey of local ZBB practices comparable to the one of state practices is lacking. In its place, there are only inflated claims offered without evidence.

Prospects for Moving Beyond the Line-Item Budget

A look at the historical ebb and flow of budget systems in the United States raises the strong possibility that ZBB may just be the latest of several budgetary fads. Performance budgeting and the PPBS had their respective days in the sun in the 1950s and 1960s. Their champions pronounced inexorable and ineluctable growth for them, only to see them abandoned by the local, state, or federal governments that had initially embraced them.

What caused this fickleness? At bottom, oversell of the potential benefits and failure to mention the real costs and likely problems involved killed these budget systems. For example, it is no surprise that the PPBS did not last in the federal government. Instead of being gradually refined and introduced in a few agencies at a time, it was implemented across the range of the entire federal bureaucracy in 1965. When the OMB announced in spring 1977 that ZBB would be installed across the board in the federal government in time to produce the fiscal-year 1979 budget, old budget hands smiled wryly and wondered why budget innovators never seem to look record. A five-year introductory period, in which all agencies have used the new system once by the end of the fifth year, seems more sensible.

A second point is that a new budget system without detailed evaluations or performance audits is a meaningless exercise. That is, ranking packages or alternatives without examining the reasons given for ranking them means that the system still rests on untested assertions. Without evaluation, myths and assumptions are decked out in fancy new garments but remain just as impenetrable as ever.

Third, and most crucial, political decision makers have to be shown how these new budget systems can help them to keep expenses down or do jobs most effectively. A careful and *truthful* selling job is crucial if new budget systems are to be used. Otherwise, activities- and results-oriented budgeting, no matter how much needed, will remain in the world of public relations instead of becoming a political reality.

SUMMARY

We have covered the principal characteristics of the budgetary process, with the exception of the postaudit, which we examine in Chapter 23. The budgetary process is *complex*. It includes a number of phases and participants; the observer almost needs a program to follow and understand the budgetary game. As a corollary to this complexity, power in budgeting is *fragmented,* although we have shown that the agencies themselves are first among equals. As a result, "we should recognize that the budget cannot be used as an instrument for 'steering' government."[95]

There are a few outstanding features of the

budget in modern life. For the nation as a whole the following applies: the budget is *political*—it distributes political values to the few or the many; the budget is a main tool of *economic stability*—it may cause inflation or check it, depending upon how it is combined with other factors; and the budget is a *workplan*—if armaments are in short supply or if environmental needs predominate, the budget reflects the priority of decision. In the long run public opinion is the arbiter. Also at the top level (the macroeconomic) budgeting involves teamwork. The eight steps underscore this point: estimates, program formulation, budget review, the chief executive's input, legislative action, central allocation to agencies, utilization of the funds, and auditing. The line executive figures continuously in all these eight steps. His success depends upon persuasion as well as his practical ability to produce tangible results. Some budgets reflect legislative hegemony, others are chiefly controlled by the executive; ideally they should be cooperative. Some budgets make objectives and policies stand out boldly; others are a mass of detail that even accountants and auditors puzzle over.

The budgetary process will have to be dramatically changed before it becomes a tool for central, rational direction of public finance. Some attempts to do so are examined in the following chapter. Finally, there is a great deal of *variety* among the three levels of major government and 80,000 local governments. Different accounting systems, assignments of authority, and real power are common.

NOTES

1. Thomas D. Lynch, *Public Budgeting in America* (Englewood Cliffs, N.J.: Prentice-Hall, 1979), p. 2.

2. Jesse Burkhead, *Government Budgeting* (New York: Wiley, 1956), p. 2.

3. Lynch, *Public Budgeting in America*, p. 2.

4. Louis Fisher, "Presidential Spending Discretion and Congressional Controls" (Paper presented to the American Political Science Association meeting, 1971), p. 15. See also

his *Presidential Spending Power* (Princeton, N.J.: Princeton University Press, 1975).

5. Michael V. Gershowitz, "Gulick Sees Growth in Planning Function," *Public Administration Times*, 15 January 1980, p. 5.

6. George E. Hale, "Budgetary Politics in the States" (Manuscript), 1978.

7. Lynch, *Public Budgeting in America*, p. 93.

8. Leonard Reed, "The Budget Game and How to Win It," *Washington Monthly*, January 1979, p. 30.

9. Reed, "The Budget Game," p. 30.

10. George E. Hale and Scott R. Douglass, "The Politics of Budget Execution," *Administration and Society*, November 1977, p. 370. See also John F. Hulpke and Donald A. Watne, "Budgeting Behavior: If, When, and How Selected School Districts Hide Money," *Public Administration Review* 36 (November-December 1976): 667–674.

11. David O. Porter, *The Politics of Budgeting Federal Aid: Resource Mobilization by Local School Districts* (Berkeley, Calif.: Sage, 1973), pp. 9–10.

12. Aaron Wildavsky, *The Politics of the Budgetary Process*, 3d ed. (Boston: Little, Brown, 1980), p. 15.

13. Peter B. Natchez and Irvin C. Bupp, "Policy and Priority in the Budgetary Process," *American Political Science Review*, September 1973, pp. 951–963; and Ross Hopkins, "Further Research on Appropriations: A Closer Look at One Agency" (Paper, 1975).

14. Hopkins, "Further Research on Appropriations," p. 4.

15. Randall B. Ripley and Grace A. Franklin, *Policy-Making in the Federal Executive Branch* (New York: Free Press, 1975), p. 174.

16. John R. Gist, "Increment and Base in the Congressional Appropriations Process," *American Journal of Political Science*, May 1977.

17. John P. Crecine, *Governmental Problem-Solving: A Computer Simulation of Municipal Budgeting* (Chicago: Rand McNally, 1969), pp. 39, 73, and 218–219. See also Donald Gerwin, *Budgeting Public Funds: The Decision Process in an Urban School District* (Madison: University of Wisconsin Press, 1969), pp. 148–149.

18. Frank J. Thompson, *Personnel Policy in the City* (Berkeley: University of California Press, 1975), pp. 24–25.

19. David A. Caputo, "Normative and Empirical Implications of Budgetary Process" (Paper delivered at the American Political Science Association meeting), pp. 15–16.

20. Hale, "Budgetary Politics in the States," pp. 72–73.

21. Reed, "The Budget Game," p. 27.

22. Reed, "The Budget Game," p. 26.

23. Reed, "The Budget Game," p. 33.

24. Hale, "Budgetary Politics in the States," pp. 76–77.

25. Hale, "Budgetary Politics in the States," pp. 77–78.

26. Leo V. Donohue to Douglas Fox in conversation, 30 January 1980.

27. S. Kenneth Howard, *Changing State Budgeting* (Lexington, Ky.: Council of State Governments, 1973), p. 272.

28. Hale, "Budgetary Politics in the States," pp. 40–41.

29. George E. Hale, "Executive Leadership Versus Budgetary Behavior," *Administration and Society,* August 1977.

30. Thomas J. Anton, "Roles and Symbols in the Determination of State Expenditures," *Midwest Journal of Political Science,* February 1967, pp. 27–43.

31. Lewis B. Friedman, *Budgeting Municipal Expenditures* (New York: Praeger, 1975), p. 161.

32. James Reston, "Budget Reform: The Quiet Revolution on Capitol Hill," *New York Times,* 21 September 1975, p. E 17.

33. Jon L. Mills, "State Governments in the United States: Budget Preparation and Execution" (Manuscript, 1975), p. 38.

34. Ronald J. Hrebenar, "Washington State Budgeting" (Ph.D. diss., University of Washington, 1973), p. 169.

35. Hale, "Budgetary Politics in the States," p. 143. Vermont is the only state without an allotment system.

36. Richard W. Lindholm et al., "The Budgetary Process," in *Management Policies in Local Government Finance,* ed. J. Richard Aronson and Eli Schwartz (Washington: International City Management Association [ICMA], 1975), p. 86.

37. Mills, "State Governments," p. 30.

38. Hale, "Budgetary Politics in the States," p. 144.

39. Fisher, "Presidential Spending Discretion," pp. 14–17.

40. Fisher, "Presidential Spending Discretion," p. 16.

41. Porter, *The Politics of Budgeting Federal Aid,* p. 9.

42. Fisher, "Presidential Spending Discretion," p. 8.

43. Fisher, "Presidential Spending Discretion."

44. Fisher, "Presidential Spending Discretion," p. 13.

45. Mills, "State Governments," pp. 32–33.

46. Hale and Douglass, "The Politics of Budget Execution," pp. 371–372.

47. Hale, "Budgetary Politics in the States," p. 161.

48. U.S., Congress, House, *House Report 493,* 84th Cong., 1st sess., 5 May 1955, p. 8.

49. Louis Fisher, "Reprogramming of Funds by the Defense Department," *Journal of Politics,* February 1974, p. 87.

50. Fisher, "Reprogramming of Funds," p. 96.

51. Hale and Douglass, "The Politics of Budgetary Execution," pp. 372–374.

52. Hale, "Budgetary Politics in the States," pp. 161-162. We have no comparable information on local government.

53. Fisher, "Presidential Spending Discretion," p. 21.

54. Hale and Douglass, "The Politics of Budgetary Execution," pp. 370–371.

55. Brian W. Rapp and Frank M. Patitucci, *Managing Local Government for Improved Performance* (Boulder, Colo.: Westview Press, 1977), p. 347.

56. U.S. Commission on the Organization of the Executive Branch of the Government, *Budgeting and Accounting* (Washington: U.S. Government Printing Office, 1949), p. 8.

57. Lennox L. Moak and Kathryn W. Killian, *A Manual of Technique for the Preparation, Consideration, Adoption, and Administration of Operating Budgets* (Chicago: Municipal Finance Officers Association, 1963), p. 15.

58. Allen Schick, *Budget Innovation in the States* (Washington: Brookings Institution, 1971), p. 45.

59. Schick, *Budget Innovation,* pp. 52–53.

60. Schick, *Budget Innovation,* p. 57.

61. Robert D. Lee, Jr., and Raymond J. Staffeldt, "Executive and Legislative Use of Policy Analysis in the State Budgetary Process: Survey Results," *Policy Analysis,* Summer 1977, p. 397.

62. Lewis A. Friedman, "Control, Management, and Planning: An Empirical Examination," *Public Administration Review,* 35 (November–December 1975): 625–628.

63. Schick, *Budget Innovation,* p. 5.

64. Allen Schick, "A Death in the Bureaucracy: The Demise of Federal PPB," *Public Administration Review* 33 (March–April 1973): 146–156.

65. Thomas D. Lynch, *Policy Analysis in Public Policymaking* (Lexington, Mass.: Heath, 1975), p. 49.

66. Stephen M. Fletcher, "From PPBS to PAR in the Empire State," *State Government,* Summer 1972, pp. 198–202.

67. Lee and Staffeldt, "Executive and Legislative Use of Policy Analysis," p. 397.

68. Schick, "A Death in the Bureaucracy," p. 153.

69. Eli B. Silverman and Francis C. Gatti, Jr., "PPB on the

State Level: The Case of Pennsylvania," *The Bureaucrat* 4 (July 1975): 117–146.

70. James E. Skok, "Sustaining PPBS in State Government, *The Bureaucrat* 6 (Fall 1977): 50–63.

71. James Ramsey and Merlin M. Hackbart, *Innovations in State Budgeting* (Lexington: University of Kentucky, 1978); see their "Budgeting: Inducements and Impediments to Innovations," *State Government*, Spring 1977, pp. 65–69.

72. *Local Government Budgeting, Program Planning, and Evaluation*, Urban Data Service Report (Washington, ICMA, May 1972).

73. Harry P. Hatry, "Status of PPB in Local and State Governments in the United States," *Policy Sciences* 2 (1971): 178.

74. Friedman, "Control, Management, and Planning," p. 625.

75. ZBB is discussed in greater detail in Chapter 7 of Douglas M. Fox, *Managing the Public's Interest* (New York: Holt, Rinehart & Winston, 1979).

76. Edwin L. Dale, Jr., "ZBB and Sunset: What's the Difference?" *New York Times*, 7 August 1976, Business Section, p. 1.

77. Peter A. Pyhrr, *Zero-Base Budgeting* (New York: Wiley, 1973), p. 6.

78. Pyhrr, *Zero-Base Budgeting*, p. 97.

79. Pyhrr, *Zero-Base Budgeting*, p. 153.

80. John Rehfuss to Douglas M. Fox, 26 October 1977.

81. Edward J. Clynch, "Zero-Base Budgeting in Practice: An Assessment," *International Journal of Public Administration*, 1979, p. 45.

82. Joseph S. Wholey, *Zero-Base Budgeting and Program Evaluation* (Lexington, Mass.: Lexington Books, 1978), pp. 18–44.

83. Dean H. Vanderbilt, "Budgeting in Local Government: Where Are We Now?", *Public Administration Review* 37 (September–October 1977): 539.

84. Steven Rattner, "Gains from ZBB," *New York Times*, 15 January 1979, p. 37.

85. "OMB Assesses ZBB in Year-End Report," *Public Administration Times*, June 1978, p. 1; and "OMB Says ZBB Had a 'Good Start,'" *Congressional Quarterly Weekly Report*, 6 May 1978, p. 1139.

86. In *The Bureaucrat*, Spring 1978.

87. "OMB Assesses ZBB."

88. Joel Havemann, "The Budget—A Tax Cut, Little Else," *National Journal*, January 28, 1978.

89. Council of State Governments, *ZBB in the States* (Lexington, Ky.: 1976), pp. 4, 12.

90. Council of State Governments, *ZBB in the States* p. 5.

91. John D. LaFaver, "ZBB in New Mexico," *State Government* 47 (Spring 1974): 109–118.

92. LaFaver, "ZBB in New Mexico."

93. Allen Schick in conversation with Douglas M. Fox, 13 May 1977.

94. George S. Minmeier, *An Evaluation of ZBB in Governmental Institutions* (Atlanta: Georgia State University, School of Business Administration, 1975).

95. Hale, "Budgetary Politics in the States," p. 187.

23

The Audit

All goddam auditors ought to be in the bottom of hell.[1]
Gen. George S. Patton

In this chapter we examine different types of audits, the relationship of auditors to government agencies, and the crucial role of audits in ensuring the accountability of government. The word *audit* is derived from the Latin verb meaning to hear, and it originally referred to an oral report to a Roman official. In modern public administration, the audit is the last stage of the budget cycle. It is an examination of records or search for other evidence for purposes of evaluation. This definition will be filled out below when we examine different types of audits in turn. For now, let us emphasize the point that the audit is a crucial tool in ensuring the accountability of governmental officials, a topic we have discussed in previous chapters.

Auditing goes as far back in history as the accounting systems of which it is a part. The civilizations of the Middle East had rudimentary accounting systems 5,000 years ago, and surprise audits of provincial accounts were carried out in Persia 2,500 years ago. While the auditor in ancient Israel was the second most important official in government, ancient Greece employed slaves as auditors. The assumption was that statements from slaves, who could be tortured, would be more accurate than those of citizens, who could not be.[2]

Auditors who do a thorough job are not the most popular of government officials. More than a few program managers probably wish that auditors could still be tortured. As an old audit joke has it, the following are the two greatest lies ever told. Auditor to agency head: "I'm here to help you." Agency head to auditor: "I appreciate that and I'll cooperate in any way I can."

Most audits are postaudits, occurring at the end of the budgetary cycle, usually at the end of the fiscal year. But it is also possible to pre-audit expenditures, that is, to require that proposed expenditures be reviewed for approval before any money can be spent, a process we discussed in Chapter 22.

TYPES OF AUDITS

Audits can be divided into the same threefold typology we have used in earlier chapters, emphasizing inputs, activities, or results. We begin by examining the input-oriented audit.

Inputs: The Financial/Compliance Audit[3]

The financial/compliance audit is the audit equivalent of the line-item budget. The financial aspect of this audit involves examination of accounts to determine how reliable financial statements are. If the books do not balance, even though budget and accounting documents say they do, then the agency's financial statements are not reliable. The compliance aspect of the audit is concerned with the legality of spending actions. Was money spent according to the various laws and regulations of federal, state, and local governments, or were these requirements ignored? For example, were competitive bidding laws observed, or were contract approvals granted by appropriate officials as required by law?

While the financial and compliance aspects of auditing can be carried out separately, it is more efficient to perform them together. Most state and federal audit requirements mandate both aspects of auditing.

Auditing is an involved procedure. The auditor begins by examining accounting systems and methods, usually designing a plan with the governmental client. In this way, the scope of the audit is agreed on, and the client will be more likely to accept audit findings.

If the auditor finds a situation like the following, he will have to raise some questions. One auditor asked a small-town public works director for his records. The director went to his car and produced a number of paper bags. When asked by the auditor if he kept his records in the bags, the director answered no. It turned out the records were written *on* the bags. "I got no records when I got this job and I can burn these bags when I leave without any questions asked."

Before donning a green eyeshade and looking at the accounts, the auditor must be sure just which funds and activities are to be examined. The structure and jurisdiction of government varies from one locale to another. For example, in Flatula, the water and sewer system may be run by the city, but in Pristine Heights it may be run by an independent special district. To determine which funds to examine, the local government auditor must review the government's charter and ordinances. Likewise, at the state and federal levels, the auditor has to ascertain whether certain funds are actually under the control of the agency. Some state universities, for example, have funds contributed by alumni over which the state board of higher education has no control.

After preparing a work schedule and detailed set of instructions for the audit staff who are to perform the audit, the auditor should examine the internal control system. Accounting controls are those designed to prevent waste and fraud and to ensure accuracy of data. The only time that auditors attract attention from the mass media is on the very rare occasions when they uncover a particularly juicy scandal, such as one involving antipoverty-agency officials who become rich fighting poverty. (Auditors are leery of pronouncing agencies guilty of fraud. Instead, they turn their material over to government prosecutors for possible legal action.)

An example of a weakness in accounting control is the modified cash accounting system discussed in Chapter 22, which allows revenues and expenditures to be pushed from one fiscal year to the next. After New York City suffered a financial breakdown in 1975, analysts pointed out that the city had often included the first month of the new fiscal year's revenues in the preceding fiscal year. This gave the city a revenue statement based on 13 months, while only 12 months of expenditures were listed against the revenues.

"The only time that auditors get much attention from the mass media is . . . when they uncover a particularly juicy scandal . . ."

SOURCE: Peter F. Rousmaniere, *Local Government Auditing* (New York: COMP, 1979), p. 16. Paul Marshall, artist. Reproduced by permission of the Council on Municipal Performance, New York.

While many governments play this game from time to time, governments such as New York's, which became addicted to it, will eventually suffer greatly. As a character in Charles Dickens' *David Copperfield* notes, when he spent 19 pounds 6 shillings and had an income of 20 pounds, the result was happiness. When he spent more than 20, the result was misery. The same is true for state and local governments over the long haul (but not, as we have seen, for the money-minting federal government).

Administrative controls that relate to the compliance audit are concerned primarily with three goals: promoting adherence to stated policy, maintaining administrative efficiency, and ensuring that the law is obeyed. An example of failure of administrative control is the unauthorized pooling of restricted funds into a central cash account. It may be supposed that Stalwart State's Bureau of Libraries has spent more money than was appropriated for its overall budget. The agency's head then decides to mix the Cyrenius Booth Library Birdbath Fund monies in with the rest of the budget, since the fund had a big surplus during the year, in order to cover the overall agency deficit. Since the Booth Fund is restricted to birdbath expenditures, a properly functioning set of administrative controls will prevent this kind of abuse.

The alert auditor will also be responsive to *potential* abuses of control. One principle of control is segregation of duties, so that no one individual controls all phases of the processing of a transaction. If the director of an adult education program, for example, collects all registration fees, processes them, does the bookkeeping, deposits the money in the bank, and expresses a strong preference for cash, the potential for abuse is high. A system of checks and balances reduces this potential for abuse.

The auditor concludes the audit by issuing a report, which draws conclusions about the fairness in presentation of material covering financial and compliance concerns. Financial statements are said to be fair if they are consistent with generally *a*ccepted *a*ccounting *p*rinciples (GAAP).

(GAAFR is the term for GAAP concerned with governments.) Approximately half the states require or recommend that their local governments adopt such a set of principles.

Activities: The Efficiency Audit

The nomenclature for activities and results-oriented audits is extremely confusing at present. Many writers do not even distinguish between the two approaches, as we do here. Further, the most commonly used term, *performance audit,* is naturally associated by readers with the performance *budget.* But a performance audit may well be results-oriented, while a performance budget focuses on activities. Adding to the confusion are several other terms in use, such as management, operations, and program audit. There is no telling in advance what they may denote in a particular situation.

We have chosen to call the activity-oriented audit an efficiency audit, since activity-oriented analysis is concerned with efficiency. The efficiency audit is functionally identical to a workload or activities evaluation. The only difference is that the efficiency audit is done by audit-office staff as a regular part of the budgetary cycle.

The reader should note that we are not discussing efficiency or performance audits as substitutes for the financial/compliance audit. The financial/compliance audit is an absolutely essential foundation on which these other audits must be built. Nor should the reader confuse efficiency audits that examine financial data with the financial audit. A financial audit and an efficiency audit both could examine the area of recreation-staff overtime pay. But the former would limit itself to the accurate computation and recording of overtime pay, while the latter would ask who approved it, whether it was necessary and efficiently structured, and whether it might be incorporated with regular work hours.

Efficiency Audit Standards. The auditor has to have the kind of standards to justify his criteria

of efficiency such as those examined in Chapter 16. Such standards might include the following:[4]

1. legislative statement of goals and objectives
2. professional organizations' statements of policies on performance levels (for example, those of the National Library Association for libraries)
3. comparison with past performance of the agency
4. generally accepted criteria, such as the elimination of backlogs of work and duplication of effort
5. management's statement of its goals and objectives

If the last criterion is lacking, the auditor should ask management to work with him to develop such criteria before the audit begins. Just as working out a financial/compliance audit plan with the agency will make acceptance of audit findings far easier, the auditor needs to come to a similar kind of agreement with management if efficiency audit findings are to be accepted.

Methods.[5] An auditor who wants to carry out an efficiency audit must do much more than check

" . . . an efficiency audit must do much more than check the records of financial transactions."

SOURCE: Peter F. Rousmaniere, *Local Government Auditing* (New York: COMP, 1979), p. 16. Paul Marshall, artist. Reproduced by permission of the Council on Municipal Performance, New York.

the records of financial transactions. An audit of a purchasing department, for example, might examine the following:

1. the way decisions about the quantity and quality of materials to be purchased are made
2. the procedures followed to obtain the best price
3. the methods of determining whether the correct quantity and quality are received

To carry out an examination of these three steps, the auditor will want to follow several procedures. He can evaluate the internal reports that management uses to keep track of the purchasing process. Are these reports adequate for the purpose? For example, has the department carefully inventoried all its current holdings, and is it aware what that inventory shows? A 1977 audit of the New York City Board of Education's bureau of supplies found a 40-year supply of eight-cent postcards, outdated years before.[6]

Physical inspections can also be useful. A walk through the warehouse may indicate that employees are idle or that useful materials are being thrown away. An auditor once went to a state Motor Vehicles Department office to find that the employee in charge of the information desk seemed to be asleep since her arms were on the desk and her head resting on them. When asked a question, she did respond, but in a brusque and annoyed manner. In his report, the auditor mentioned this incident.

Another approach could be to follow one transaction from beginning to end, to see if procedures are efficient or employees capable of doing their jobs. If turnaround time for processing a certain form seems inordinately long, perhaps the form itself or the process that it moves through can be redesigned to expedite matters. And if trucks repaired at the town garage return for additional repairs more frequently than the national norm for such equipment, perhaps the mechanics need additional training in maintaining such vehicles.

Interviews with employees can be extremely useful sources of information for auditors. Employees may have excellent ideas for improvement of efficiency, which, for one reason or another, they have not been able to convey to their supervisors. In addition, they can point out many facets of agency operation that the auditor would find it very difficult to learn otherwise. For example, an employee might mention that a particular unit of the office is inefficient, compared to other units, but is a favorite of the office manager's, who does not insist that its performance be improved. Or an employee might note that some procedures described in the office manual are not followed. To gain the confidence of employees, auditors should be sure both to protect their anonymity and not to be overly critical of the office in writing recommendations.

Results: The Performance Audit

The auditing techniques used in the performance audit are identical to those used in the efficiency audit. The difference is in focus: here the auditor is concerned with the results of agency activities in achieving their legislative purpose, not the activities in themselves. The standards to be followed are identical with those described in Chapter 16, on evaluation. A number of cities now have auditors who wear hard hats, for they have to inspect the city's bridges to be sure that they will stand up under the weight of traffic. These auditors are not accountants, but engineers, who determined in 1977 that the rate of maintenance of city bridges does not appear to be keeping up with the rate of deterioration.[7]

A performance auditor in another state probed the use of a surgical technique called gastrostomy, which is used in mental-retardation centers. This stomach surgery permits continuous feeding of profoundly retarded children. The auditor discovered that one mental-retardation hospital performed more such operations than the sum total done in all the other hospitals in the county. He also discovered that it reduced the life span of some children by 50 percent.

We could list additional examples, but the point is that auditors are now looking at what government actually accomplishes, at results, not dollars alone. And there is growing emphasis on this type of audit. There is also often strong dislike of the performance audit among those being audited, who may share General Patton's opinion of what should be done with auditors. South Carolina's commissioner of social services, for example, denounced an audit of his department, and after much acrimony, resigned in response to it.[8]

For that reason Kansas legislative auditor Richard E. Brown warns that performance auditors have to be very careful as they go about their work. The performance-audit staff, for example, needs strong political support to function, or it will be disembowelled by the agencies and their interest-group allies. In Brown's words, the audit report, if it is consequential, is likely to be controversial.[9] Such controversy can overwhelm auditors without support. That is another reason why an audit plan agreed upon in advance by the agency and auditor is so important. With such a plan, there can be no argument about the scope of the audit.

At the same time, Brown cautions auditors not to lobby legislators or elected executives to support audit conclusions. The job of the auditor is to clarify compliance with legislative intent, not to write it. The lobbying auditor runs the risk of being asked by the elected official to let that official write or modify the auditor's report. Once that happens, the auditor will lose all credibility as an objective public servant and thus all the influence he once had.

Performance probes are not for the parsimonious or penurious. Local and state audits may take four to six months and $30,000 to $75,000 in 1979 dollars to complete. A recent list of 12 federal audits found that each cost over $189,000, with one totaling $818,000.[10] Auditors have to educate elected officials who want audit results immediately to this fact.

CASE STUDY: A STATE PERFORMANCE AUDIT

On March 25, 1977, the Connecticut State Auditors of Public Accounts issued their first performance audit, a critical review of the work of the state Department of Education. The department earned a low grade on this report since the auditors claimed it had failed to fulfill numerous statutory duties assigned to it. These included providing leadership and promoting the improvement of education, supervising education, engaging in research and evaluation, publishing curriculum guides, keeping informed on the condition of local schools, and engaging in planning. The audit report summed up its findings by concluding that "the department . . . appears to lack the spirit, the will, and the dedicated commitment to lead in a drive for quality education." Less than 3 percent of the billion dollars in state aid to local education was monitored by the department, said the auditors.

The audit report stunned and stupefied the Department of Education, which issued a rebuttal in July. The commissioner of education circulated two critical analyses of the audit report, labeling it inadequate. The state Board of Education also asked the governor and legislature for $145,000 in extra funds to measure the job local schools were doing. The request prompted one legislator to ask why the department now needed money to implement a law that had been on the books for several years. Further, the board asked the co-chairmen of the legislature's Education Committee to request $4,000 to audit the audit report. The Legislative Management Committee rejected this request in November 1977, saying that the audit was a sensible report.

Some two years later, the commissioner of education announced a five-year master plan for local schools, setting measurable performance objectives (for example, a 5 percent increase in the number of students who score 75 or better on a basic reading and math test). The commissioner conceded that the plan was an outgrowth of the 1977 audit report.

The plan and related actions of the department were given an outstanding grade by the auditors in December 1980. State auditor Leo V. Donohue stated, "It's extremely significant in that the board [of education] has implemented almost all of our recommendations. What was a very nega-

tive situation back in 1977 has turned into a very positive one now." Fellow state auditor Henry Becker agreed, adding that the auditors would continue to examine the Department of Education. "I would assume that sometime in the next few years we will be going back there and doing another review, mostly because this is a big spending area."

AUDIT STRUCTURES AND PROCEDURES

In this section, we shall examine some of the audit mechanisms found at the federal, state, and local levels of American government. Here we must distinguish between the internal audits carried out by employees of the line agency itself and external audits performed by auditors from outside the agency. Most of the discussion below will concentrate on the external audit.

The Federal Government

Internal Audits. There is proportionately more internal auditing done in federal agencies than at the state and local levels, and recent events make it likely that this pattern will continue. Following the lead of the military departments, the other cabinet-level departments established offices of the inspector general between 1976 and 1978 to carry out an augmented audit function.

One of the key lobbyists for the establishment of these new offices was the external federal auditor, the General Accounting Office (GAO), which we discuss in much greater detail in the next section. One GAO study, for example, found that 133 federal agencies, with annual budgets totaling more than $20 billion, had received no internal auditing over a three-year period. John J. Adair, the GAO auditor who conducted the study, stated, "I knew things were bad, but I was still surprised at the large number of units that admitted their lack of financial coverage."[11] The new inspectors general will have their work cut

out for them, for in some agencies audits occurred only once every *15 years,* using audit resources then available.

Since the internal-audit function has been performed more diligently, on the average, on the federal level than at the state and local levels, one may wonder whether there is a natural antipathy of agencies to self-audits. Certainly, as the record we discuss below shows, external audits have pointed to many problems that internal audits have ignored.

External Audits. The GAO was established in 1921 as both the federal external auditor and as an agency of *Congress,* not the executive. Most authorities on auditing argue that the external audit must be *independent* of the executive, and that is certainly true at the federal level. From the beginning, the GAO was concerned with much more than accounting. In fact, only one of its heads, called the comptroller general (CG), has been an accountant.

The GAO has often been unpopular with presidents. Franklin Roosevelt relished the retirement of the first comptroller general, in 1936. In 1974, after Vice President Spiro Agnew resigned, the GAO stated that the Secret Service bodyguard detailed to Agnew was unauthorized by law. President Richard Nixon discontinued the bodyguard service shortly thereafter.

In fall 1977, the GAO had more than 4,000 professional employees, 60 percent of whom were originally trained in accounting. Another 16 percent were trained in business and public management, while others were lawyers, mathematicians, engineers, social scientists, computer specialists, and policy-area (e.g., personnel or transportation) specialists. In the same year, GAO estimated that 10 percent of its audits were of the financial/compliance type, 41 percent were efficiency audits, and 49 percent were performance audits.[12]

The Evolution of the GAO. Frederick C. Mosher, author of an important study of the GAO, divides its history into three periods. In the first period, 1921–1945, the financial/compliance audit approach was stressed. In the second, 1954–1966, more emphasis was placed on efficiency/economy audits. In the third, 1966 to the present, the GAO has stressed performance auditing. During its history, the GAO has moved from hostility to cooperation with the executive branch, trying to persuade the executive to work with it to improve management. There is no question that the GAO is a powerful and respected agency of the government in the 1980s. At the same time, its power has definite limits.

The GAO's legal authority includes provisions to audit agency programs on a financial/compliance basis, for efficiency, and for results. In addition, the comptroller general has the authority to give advice and render decisions on the interpretation of financial legislation. The CG resolves disputes between agencies and businesses regarding contracts, and these decisions are binding. The accumulated decisions of the CG are "very nearly the Bible . . . on law in the Federal government."[13]

Two fifths of the legal cases that the GAO confronts are in the area of procurement law. Disappointed bidders, federal agency heads, congressmen, and state and local governments all bring complaints and inquiries to the GAO concerning government contracts.

Another area of substantial work is the interpretation of statutes dealing with the authority of agencies to spend money on programs and projects. A third area is that of rulings on pay, rights, and benefits of federal personnel. Besides these grants of legal authority, the GAO also determines the accounting standards and principles that federal agencies must follow.

The GAO, then, has a substantial amount of legal authority, more than that enjoyed by any state or local external auditor, to our knowledge. Yet this formal authority does not automatically translate into real power, as we note below.

Political Constraints on the GAO. The GAO is a congressional agency, which means that if a number of congressmen do not like what it does, it will be in trouble. A good example of this situation occurred when the GAO began an aggressive investigation of defense contracts in the 1960s. The chairman of the House Government Operations Committee, which oversees the GAO's work, was Congressman Chet Holifield. Holifield's California district included many defense plants, and he became upset at the GAO's probing in this area. The result was that in the defense industry GAO was forced to back off and be less aggressive, regardless of what it found to be true.[14]

At the same time, since Congress is not a monolith, the GAO found itself criticized by other senators and congressmen because it was not aggressive enough. And when CG Elmer Staats, in office 1966–1981, asked for subpoena power to obtain records from contractors, Congress failed to grant him this authority.

Congressional failure to give the GAO carte blanche to acquire relevant documents means that agencies such as the Defense Department can refuse to provide the GAO with their inspector general reports on the grounds that these documents are strictly for internal use.[15] In April 1980, Congress passed legislation granting increased authority to the GAO to acquire agency and contract records. It is too soon, however, to predict the practical effect of this legislation, the GAO Act of 1980.

Any criticism of the GAO for not being a vigorous enough watchdog ignores the fact that "you can't afford stepping on sensitive toes," as CG Staats put it in 1979.[16] That is the reason the GAO delays issuing its reports until everyone involved has been consulted, a practice that infuriates some of its critics. Erasmus Kloman, an authority on the GAO, said in 1979 that "an awful lot of what [GAO] puts out is powerful statements of the obvious. But I don't like blaming this on the GAO. Congress sets the duties. . . ."[17]

Perhaps the most fundamental limitation on the GAO or any auditor is that audit-report recommendations are not self-enforcing. The chief executive or legislature has to want to accept and implement such recommendations, or nothing will come of them. As we have seen, Congressman Holifield did not accept the GAO's logic in its defense contracting investigations.

What conclusions can we draw about the GAO's power, then? The GAO's influence is very difficult to measure. One reason is that agencies may be reluctant to follow GAO recommendations because to do so might seem to constitute an admission of guilt. Another is that agencies will often move to correct matters before the final report is written, so that no mention of such problems will appear in the report.

At times the GAO will make dramatic use of its authority, as it did in 1970 when it declared that money appropriated by Congress for the so-called Philadelphia-plan job-training program could not be spent because the legislation conflicted with the Civil Rights Act and was thus illegal. While the Supreme Court later reversed the GAO ruling, this legal authority is envied by most auditors.

We can conclude, then, that the GAO is an influential agency, which has concerned itself increasingly with agency-program results. Its ultimate impact depends on the support it is given by Congress.

State Governments

Internal Audits. Not so much internal auditing is done, proportionately, in state government departments as in the federal government. The principal reason for this difference seems to be that state governments do not require internal auditing to the extent that the federal government does. As a rough rule of thumb, the larger the state department is, and the larger share of its budget that comes from federal grants, the more likely it is to have its own internal auditing procedures. But there are exceptions, and no definitive summary of patterns in the 50 states exists.

External Audits. The external-auditing function is found in a number of different situations among the 50 states. In 1974 the external-audit function was located in the legislature in 35 states and in the executive branch in 15 states. (Thirteen of the 15 executive external auditors were "independent" executive officials, such as the comptroller of New York State, who are elected to office for a fixed term.) The trend has been for the states to turn the audit function over to the legislature. In 1951, there were only 8 legislatures with the external-audit function.[18]

Another trend, similar to the history of the GAO, has been an increasing concern with efficiency and performance audits. A 1972 survey of 22 states found that 14 auditors were carrying out these two types of audits.[19] Just five years later, another study cited 16 states where performance audits were regularly conducted.[20] Other states, such as Connecticut, carry out performance audits on an occasional basis. In a number of states, the legislature has reserved to itself the right to carry out performance audits, forbidding elected executive officials to do so.

As has been true with the GAO, more and more states are dropping the requirement that the auditor be an accountant. In Hawaii, the auditor is an economist; in Kansas and Illinois, the auditor's training has been in public management.[21]

Recent reports have cited numerous performance audits that have led to program changes, ranging from the reduction of the fire department at the Wisconsin State Veterans' Home to 56 changes in Montana's workman's compensation program.[22]

A major force behind the increasing emphasis on state efficiency and performance audits has been the federal GAO. Since more than $90 billion was dispensed by the federal government in grants to state and local governments during fiscal year 1981, it is no surprise that the GAO has become increasingly concerned about what is being done with this money. Many grants now explicitly give the GAO the authority to audit the recipient's records. In addition, the GAO began in 1971 to work cooperatively with state and local government auditors to improve intergovernmental audit standards. One principal method of working for this change has been to run conferences and workshops in which federal, state, and local officials and certified public accounts (CPAs) meet to discuss cooperation on joint problems.[23] Much work still remains to be done, however. For example, Connecticut's auditors resigned from the GAO-sponsored New England Regional Audit Forum because they could see no appreciable benefit to be gained from remaining in it. When they reported to the GAO that a Connecticut governor had illegally spent funds allocated to the New England Regional Commission, the GAO ignored this information. Despite such problems, though, the states have traveled a long way down the road of efficiency and performance audits. As is true at other levels of government, state auditors' reports are not self-enforcing. In November 1979, New York State Comptroller Edward V. Regan complained that New York City had failed to carry out the recommendations of state auditors. Referring to one area that was audited, Regan's deputy said, "Unfortunately, the system exists mainly on paper."[24]

Local Government

Internal Audits. Local governments typically do even less internal auditing, proportionately, than state governments. Some of the biggest city and county governments' biggest departments carry out internal audits, but these are the exceptions. In most local governments, the only auditor who visits agencies is an external auditor.

External Audits. There are several types of external audits in local government. The oldest type, still found in some small towns, is a committee appointed by the local legislature to review accounts and file a report. Since the members of these committees often lacked any accounting expertise, they were a bureaucrat's dream audit and are therefore increasingly hard to find today.[25]

The very largest cities, such as New York, Chicago, Philadelphia, and Detroit, as well as some medium-sized cities, such as Richmond, Virginia, have their own external-audit departments, often called the comptroller's or controller's office.

One fundamental fact of local government already alluded to is the legal supremacy of state government over its localities. A number of state governments use this legal control to require audits of local government by state employees. States that follow this policy include New Jersey, Ohio, and Louisiana.

By far the most common pattern in local auditing is the hiring of a private firm of accountants to conduct the audit. There is usually some kind of state-imposed certifying or licensing requirement for accountants who want to do this work. Typically, they are required to be CPAs. The advantage of this procedure is that the locality does not have to pay the cost of maintaining a permanent, full-time audit office. In small towns, this cost would be disproportionate to the benefits gained. At the same time, the locality usually gets a one-shot audit rather than the continuing audit process that a full-time office would provide. Like their state and federal counterparts, more and more local auditors are looking at efficiency and performance. Previous examples in this chapter cited the work of New York City auditors. Another example is that of Portland, Oregon, which has carried out extensive efficiency audits, looking into such areas as the Water Bureau's use of manpower, inventory control, and meter-reading procedures.[26] Compared to federal and state governments, however, these types of auditing are the exception, not the rule, in local government.

As is true for state government, the GAO has been much interested in federal grants to local government. In fact, one of the conditions set in the rescue of New York City from bankruptcy in

1975 was a provision that the loan and grant aid given to the city by the federal government be carefully monitored by the GAO. The GAO has had a team of auditors in New York since 1975 doing just that, and it has issued several reports, some of them sharply critical of city financial-management procedures.

THE INDEPENDENCE OF THE AUDITOR

Many audit authorities stress the concept of the independence of the auditor, including it in their definition of the audit. Just what does this term mean? CPA Kenneth S. Caldwell talks about "a degree of independence from the client agency or from the executive branch which is responsible for managing the government, which is not possessed by organizational units located in the executive branch who may perform internal audit ... functions."[27] Caldwell characterizes most of the external-audit arrangements we have discussed as ensuring independence, whether the audit agency is made up of elected auditors or legislative auditors or is a private accounting firm. There is some reason to conclude that the last of those three arrangements is less independent than the first two, regardless of the integrity or competence of the firms involved.

The major drawback of the contracting out of local government auditing revolves around the questions of continuity and independence. The local legislature can have a new auditor each year if it wishes—a very different situation from the one found at the federal and state levels, and in the largest cities. One of the authors once studied a small New Jersey town where the auditor made numerous recommendations for major changes in financial procedures. The local legislators, party officials, and department heads were displeased with these recommendations, and a new auditor was given the contract the next year. Even though none of the changes recommended by the first auditor had been implemented, the new auditor suggested that only one minor change be made. His work was deemed satisfactory, and he continues to hold the contract. Local auditors do not enjoy

the same legal independence as their federal and state equivalents. Congress and state governments cannot routinely fire the GAO or state legislative or elected auditors.

PROBLEMS IN GOVERNMENT AUDITING

The GAO and other authorities have identified a number of problems in state and local audits. One is the use of different standards and criteria among accounting systems. A related problem is duplication of audits. Examples abound of state and local agencies that are audited several times a year, by different auditors, all of whom use different standards. One agency that received federal grants had to respond to 25 different audit questionnaires![28] If a common set of standards could be agreed on, and one agency could serve as a clearinghouse, this kind of duplication of effort could be reduced, and audit-staff efforts could be redirected toward other important areas. The GAO has tried to promote such reforms since the early 1970s. It issued, in conjunction with other federal agencies, criteria for a "single audit" in 1980.

Another problem, already touched on in this chapter, is that "most [audit] staffs are too small to do all that is asked of them."[29] Nor are there enough CPA firms to do the work. Even if all duplication were to be eliminated, many audit staffs could not hope to audit the agencies under their jurisdiction on a biennial, much less an annual, basis. Both this problem and the first one discussed earlier have their roots in the political process. If auditors could generate more political support, legislators could easily appropriate more funds for audit staff. The crux of the problem is that if the auditor is doing the job he should, he will automatically generate political opposition and thus make increased budget for staff less likely. The reaction of the Queens Children's Psychiatric Center in Bellerose, New York, to an audit is typical: "There is no more validity in employing an auditor to evaluate the treatment of programs of a hospital than there would be in employing a physician to audit the financial affairs of a bank." This written reply also asked, "Is there a mortal behind those glinting steel-rimmed glasses, prone to fatigue, subject to error, perhaps afflicted with a hangover? Do those ominous attaché cases, with their shiny snaplocks and their aura of omniscience, sometimes contain only a salami sandwich?"[30] The center will not support additional funds for audit staff, we can be sure.

A final problem is the clash between compliance and efficiency or performance audits. Legal requirements enforced by auditors can destroy attempts to improve financial management because laws have not been adjusted to the realities of modern financial management. A ludicrous example occurred in Seattle when the city restructured its budget along organizational lines. This switch was designed to establish clear areas of responsibility and accountability for city managers. The state auditors intervened and determined that this approach was not compatible with state statutes. The result is that the state auditor might destroy Seattle's ability to hold individual managers accountable for a specific portion of the budget.[31]

These and other problems have to be addressed, and one place to address them is in the schools using this textbook. Roger Mansfield, a local government manager, argues that "lack of concern for governmental accounting and financial reporting by the academic community is easily substantiated by the conspicuous absence of classes being offered on that subject by schools and colleges of public administration across the country."[32] Students planning a career in government should take such courses, even if they have to go out of their way to do so.

SUMMARY

The three types of audit emphasize input, activities, and results. The input audit, another name for which is the financial/compliance audit, might be called basic; it examines all accounts to determine whether they are reliable and legal. It has its own methods, which we explained in some detail. The second type, the activity-oriented audit, is concerned with efficiency, which is something more than honesty and legality. It is concerned, among other things, with legislatively stated goals and objectives. The third type of audit, stressing results, is also management-oriented because it is focused on results and not merely the activities that lead up to them. For some time now in government, as well as in industry, auditing philosophy and techniques have increasingly related themselves to management philosophy and methods. That is one reason why Congress has entered more and more into areas that a short time ago were thought the preserve of the chief executive.

We also dealt with the difference between the pre-audit and the postaudit, stressed the independence of the auditor, and counseled everyone entering management to know the rudiments of accounting/auditing, as one should comprehend the rudiments of law.

NOTES

1. Frederick C. Mosher, *Program Budgeting* (Chicago: Public Administration Service, 1954), p. 191.

2. Jay W. Lorsch et al., *Understanding Management* (New York: Harper & Row, 1978), p. 121.

3. This section is based primarily on Peter F. Rousmaniere's excellent *Local Government Auditing* (New York: Council on Municipal Performance, 1979).

4. Rousmaniere, *Local Government Auditing*, p. 20.

5. This section and the following one are based largely on Ellsworth H. Morse, Jr., "Performance and Operational Auditing," *The Journal of Accountancy*, June 1971, pp. 41–46.

6. Ralph Blumenthal, "Auditors in Hard Hats," *New York Times*, 2 December 1977, p. B 1.

7. Blumenthal, "Auditors in Hard Hats."

8. Richard E. Brown, ed., *The Effectiveness of Legislative Program Review* (New Brunswick, N.J.: Transaction Books, 1979), p. 148.

9. Richard E. Brown, "Legislative Performance Auditing: Its Goals and Pitfalls," *State Government*, Winter, 1979, p. 33.

10. Erasmus H. Kloman, ed., *Cases in Accountability: The*

Work of the G.A.O. (Boulder, Colo.: Westview Press, 1979), p. 7.

11. Deborah Rankin, "Report Finds U.S. Agencies Unaudited," *New York Times,* 12 June 1978, p. D 1.

12. Frederick C. Mosher, *The G.A.O.* (Boulder, Colo: Westview Press, 1979), p. 179.

13. Mosher, *The G.A.O., p. 206.*

14. Richard F. Kaufman, "The One-Eyed Watchdog of Congress," *Washington Monthly,* February 1971, pp. 55–60.

15. Joseph Pois, "Trends in General Accounting Office Audits," in *The New Political Economy*, ed. Bruce L. R. Smith (New York: Macmillan, 1975), p. 259. See also Pois's excellent full-length treatment of the GAO, *Watchdog on the Potomac* (Washington: American University Press, 1979), pp. 115–150.

16. A. O. Sulzberger, Jr., "The Watchdog for Congress Losing Its Bite, Critics Say," *New York Times,* 2 December 1979, p. E 5.

17. Sulzberger, "The Watchdog for Congress."

18. Edgar C. Crane, *Legislative Review of Government Programs* (New York: Praeger, 1977), p. 28.

19. Mortimer A. Dittenhofer, "Progress in State Auditing," *State Government,* Spring 1973, p. 129.

20. Crane, *Legislative Review.* A 1977 GAO mail questionnaire survey found that 50 of 86 state audit agencies performed efficiency and results audits, but we are sure this is an exaggeration. (*Directory of State Audit Organizations,* GAO, 1977), p. 2.

21. Crane, *Legislative Review,* p. 30.

22. Brown, *The Effectiveness of Legislative Program Review,* p. 32; Raymond Pethtel and Richard E. Brown, eds., *Legislative Review of State Programs' Performance* (New Brunswick, N.J.: Rutgers University, Eagleton Institute, 1972), p. 12.

23. U.S., General Accounting Office, *What G.A.O. Is Doing To Improve Governmental Auditing Standards* (Washington: U.S. Government Printing Office, 1973).

24. Ronald Smothers, "New York City Charged with Failure to Act on Recommendations in Audits," *New York Times,* 26 November 1979, p. B 8.

25. Lennox L. Moak and Albert M. Hillhouse, *Concepts and Practices in Local Government Finance* (Chicago: Municipal Finance Officers Association, 1975), p. 362.

26. Andrew Kukura, "The Performance Audit Program of the City of Portland, Oregon" (Paper presented to the National Conference of the American Society of Public Administration, Chicago, March 1975).

27. Kenneth S. Caldwell, "Operational Auditing in State and Local Government," *Governmental Finance,* November 1975, p. 40.

28. *What G.A.O. Is Doing,* p. 14.

29. *What G.A.O. Is Doing,* p. 15.

30. Robert D. McFadden, "Audit of an Audit Spoofs Levitt's Staff as Liability," *New York Times,* 4 April 1976, p. 1.

31. Roger Mansfield, "The Financial Reporting Practices of Government: A Time for Reflection," *Public Administration Review* 39 (March-April 1979): 158.

32. Mansfield, "The Financial Reporting Practices of Government," p. 161.

PART **6**

CONCLUSION

A planning session held in the offices of the Port Authority of New York & New Jersey at the World Trade Center. (Photo courtesy of the Port Authority of New York & New Jersey)

24

The Challenge of the 1980s

If you do not think about the future, you cannot have one.
John Galsworthy

In this windup chapter we mention some of the problems facing the country, summarize the argument of the book, and single out some of the structural problems of government deserving serious attention.

No one knows for sure, of course, what is going to happen in times of crisis or normality when the electorate and the government are called upon to deal with issues developed in this book—issues such as achieving better coordination, for instance, or improved planning or better budgeting or personnel policy. Public opinion is too uncertain a factor. In past times it has seemed to be lethargic in times of crisis, or contrariwise, disposed to adventure when the provocation seemed slight. Public opinion may be "right" over long periods of time, as Rousseaueans believe, but in the short run public opinion often appears as fickle as someone who collects beaux.

Let us project four alternative scenarios for the United States during the 10 years ahead and gain some idea what might happen to public administration if one or more of the four proved to be accurate:

Alternative No. 1. The United States becomes embroiled in a major war.

Alternative No. 2. The 1980–1982 recession becomes a worldwide depression and lasts several years.

Alternative No. 3. There is an upturn in economic conditions by the end of 1982, and a majority of the electorate still supports further retrenchment in government.

Alternative No. 4. There is an economic upturn in 1982 and a swing of the political pendulum, with the result that some programs either cut or eliminated by the administration of Ronald Reagan are restored.

Much speedy action would be taken under the first alternative. The experience of two world wars in this century makes that certain. Congress and the president would work together; special agencies would be set up for war production, manpower, shipping, rationing, and the like. The authoritarianism found in previous wars would be greatly intensified because of the nature of the new weapons. In short, there would be plenty of change.

Under the second alternative (depression), there would also be much change but of a different order. New banking, public works, and labor-intensive programs would be set up to give people employment. The emphasis would shift from profits to payrolls. The old formula would be dragged out and refurbished. The more purchasing power there is, the more industry can produce; the more industry produces, the more employment there is; the more production there is, the more business, farmers, workers, and everyone concerned profits. If government needs to do more, directly or indirectly, to bring this about, national well-being justifies it. If banks and the stock market closed, as they did in the 1929–1933 period, the response would be pretty much the same irrespective of whether Democrats or Republicans were in power. As far as public administration is concerned, the big demand would be for program managers, as it was in the New Deal and in every recession since then.

Alternatives three and four are a bit tricky. Under the third, the trick would be to cut the military budget, social security, and what few monster appropriations remained after two years of retrenchment without inciting violent public protest such as demonstrations and street fighting. As in the past, such measures would call forth a concentration on the law-enforcement machinery of government, with an accompanying increase of expense in money and personnel. Under the fourth alternative, the public administration services that would be most affected would be education, health, and human services in general. The tax burden would be gradually shifted back to the federal government. Farmers and small businessmen, for example, would argue that it cost them less and they gained more under the old system than under the new (states' rights and block grants).

Before we leave this game, a final question seems in order. What in public administration is likely to be emphasized irrespective of which alternative happens to come up at the roulette table? On the basis of trends already under way, the best guess is that it would be efficiency, cooperation, and innovation. The voters want change. The way they have been voting tested leaders out of office in recent years is evidence of that. Voters want efficiency because they want lower taxes and more for that money. They want cooperation because bureaucratic infighting has become a national disgrace. And they want innovation because so many strategies have been tried and found wanting that the risk involved in trying something new becomes less inhibiting than it was formerly.

The public in public administration means government, and administration is skill in accomplishing things. Consequently, the modes of thinking of the administrator are ideal for contributing to a nation's problem solving. On that assumption, the logic in this concluding chapter runs as follows: The necessary condition for solving problems is a restoration of confidence in government. Citizens should next address the shortcomings in the nation's capacity to govern. In dealing with this question realistically, they would discover that administration is the most concrete and durable of all forms of governmental operation because it, alone, is the final step in the delivery system. Their primary focus, therefore, should be upon rapidly improving the art and science of administration in order that public confidence may be restored.

Acting upon this logical progression of ideas, we first try to summarize what we have learned about this art and science, with a few suggestions as to how it might be improved. Second we tackle the problem, again in summary fashion, of how the capacity to govern might be more realistically related to the solution of pressing national problems.

The problem is not unlike that of the dairy farmer who buys the best cows he can afford, purchases the best tools and technology available, only to find that his net earnings at year's end are hardly sufficient to maintain his family in reasonable circumstances. On closer examination he discovers that he has been neglecting his management and land. With his eyes focused on technology, he has been failing to consider input and output with sufficient realism. Working 18 hours a day, he has not been able to put everything together into a broad perspective.

THE DURABLE VITALITY OF ADMINISTRATION

The vitality of public administration comes not merely from individual genius and group creativity but from adequate perspective. What is needed is a sound theory, a workable philosophy, a grasp of surrounding factors not immediately within one's control. The vigilant businessman, for example, becomes aware of monopoly in surrounding areas as well as competition in his own. Similarly, the art and science of public administration cannot afford to concentrate solely on internal efficiency and productivity to the neglect of the legal and institutional framework in which the manager carries on his specialty. To free himself to make his efforts vital he must address himself to public opinion, law, pressure groups, legislation, judicialization, and other areas of representative government that limit or release his efforts in the public interest.

Another ingredient of this dynamic philosophy is awareness that time and situation make necessary constant modification and adaptation of methods one has discovered to work in the past. Hence, public administration is not only durable, but, like everything else in life, it needs updating to remain viable through being responsive. That is the true significance of the "new" public administration.

Summary of the Book

Insightful knowledge of management is needed as much by citizens as by those in management positions. That is a main justification for emphasizing the philosophy and techniques of management as much as we have here. Everyone manages in one way or another. Accordingly, if management is regarded as taking resources and fashioning them in a manner to realize so far as possible one's aptitudes and aspirations, management philosophy becomes far more than the techniques found productive in organizational activity. We would not go so far as to argue that without management skill one never realizes one's potentials or dreams. Artists and other geniuses know otherwise. But in general it may be said that those who think like managers are more likely to realize self-fulfilment and have more time left over for other adventures. Seeing how things fit together makes it possible to organize around one's individual characteristics and desires. Such organization involves a combination of rationality and temperament, logic and aesthetics, brainpower and values.

Parts 1 and 2 of this text showed how public administration operates in a political atmosphere in which there is a division of labor and a corresponding need for teamwork. No one begins at the top. But managerial and executive traits are observable early in a person's career. The political atmosphere involves knowledge of policy as well as getting along with others and developing leadership. There is a solid area of sameness in private and public administration, and equally there are distinct differences in incentives, freedoms, and environmental conditioning. Crucial areas of cooperation are the intergovernmental area, the branches of government, line and staff personnel, the headquarters-field area, chief executives and aides, and political and career executives.

Running through all this organizational structure are two elements that we stressed. The first is the law, which sets tasks, the metes and bounds of authority, and the substance and procedural requirements of due process. The other is ethics, which is a combination of prohibitions against antisocial activity and positive values, which are the source of drive and aspiration.

If there were not some who aspire to top management and chief executive positions, democracy could hardly survive against its harsher competitors. But in a democracy, power is "influence with," not "power over."

Part 3 undertook to be concrete about how the directing function unfolds and what one needs to know to be a program director. This is the nitty-gritty in which most of the government's trillion dollars is spent every year. The interrelation and flow of the manager's work starts with leadership and executive traits, moves next to policy analysis and planning, uses knowledge of the fascinating

field of organization, which basically facilitates or impedes vitality, and then deals with supervision. If energy is to be developed, for example, three elements are basic in directing that development: administering by objectives, understanding and applying motivation to secure morale, and coping with conflict. The next step in this unfolding process is coordination and control. Under the American system, control is probably too much emphasized, and coordination is not given its due.

Finally, as part of control and also as of vital interest to representative government, one must learn to evaluate productivity and draw upon information systems and data banks to feed the engines of modern management.

Part 4 aimed at bringing out the importance of the human element: the kinds of jobs, how to prepare for them, and what personnel management attempts to achieve. It wound up with labor relations, protection of minority rights, and the way to handle the controversial question of freedom to take part in the electoral process without abusing one's "inside" position.

The government as a whole also deals with finance, as Part 5 demonstrated, and it is also at the center of the public's recent absorption in the cost of government. Budgeting is a form of planning, as useful to the individual as to public administration programs. The individual, like the public official, needs a basic knowledge of accounts, audits, and purchasing. Finance underlies everyone's concern for inflation, balance of payments, and ultimately a nation's standard of living.

Compressing this summary still further, one who manages is politically minded, target-setting, policy-attuned, organizationally adept, able to secure cooperation and morale, a developer of others, and financially provident. As Teddy Roosevelt would say, that is not a bad prescription for a red-blooded, adventuresome type.

Promising Avenues of Exploration

A separate study in itself would be an exploration of all the interesting new developments that academic specialists in public administration have been suggesting.

There are already clear indications of a strong return to the private-public nexus dealt with in Chapter 3. Around the time of World War II, business and the economy had been officially recognized as a main field of political science by the American Political Science Association. Later it was eliminated. But now prominent consideration is being given to it again. There are at least three main advantages to such consideration: learning from comparative private-public experience, overcoming prejudice, and laying a foundation in higher education for better business-government teamwork at the national level of government. The countries that are best off economically today, Japan and Germany, owe their success in no small part to the effective teamwork the private and public sectors have developed.[1]

Another area recently emphasized by Luther Gulick is the cross-fertilization between science (especially biology and genetics) and public administration. This pioneer in public administration notes recent discoveries concerning the behavior of cells in symbiotic relationships, in which the organism has a built-in need to team up with others. Human organization, he says, is not wholly mechanical in structure, but consists of *organs of life*. In instances of transplants, organizations, like the human body, may reject the new body. Thus it is more difficult to reorganize an ongoing agency than to create a new one in its place.[2]

Around the year 2000, says Dwight Waldo, intellectual leaders in public administration will be concerned with five concepts, two of which are not much mentioned today. These are legitimacy, authority, knowledge, control, and confidence. The first and last of these terms are particularly intriguing. We mentioned confidence earlier in introducing this discussion. Waldo then goes on in his valedictory remarks at Syracuse University to ask a virtual barrage of enticing questions. How does one decide upon and negotiate trade-offs between hard and soft values? How can one achieve the proper mix of professionalism and expertise? How does one deal with unionism in the public sector? How can the values and mechanisms of centralization and decentralization be balanced? How can one deal with problems of racial-ethnic and sexual equality? How can the demands of the present and near future be balanced against the needs of a more distant future? How can one develop less-authoritarian and bureaucratic organizations without unwittingly creating confusion or even chaos? And finally, how is it possible to cope with increasing ethical complexity?[3]

Any one of these questions might be worthy of a lifetime of research. Also, it is easier to ask questions than to answer them. But Waldo's brainstorm illustrates the fact that with crisis there is evidence of fundamental philosophical thinking.

If it is objected that such speculations are rather "way out," the reply is that public administration is concrete and stable enough to withstand any amount of speculation because in the last analysis it is the practice not the teaching that accounts for its staying qualities.

THE CAPACITY TO GOVERN

If it may fairly be concluded that academic public administration is in relatively good health, then the next question is whether the health of the surrounding governing structure is equally good.

Under the administration of Jimmy Carter, a Presidential Commission on National Agenda for the Eighties issued a report, which concluded that much needs to be done to put the store in order. Public confidence in government has been rapidly declining. Between 1966 and 1979, public confidence in nine major institutions dropped from 43 percent to 23 percent, Congress's score fell from 42 percent to 18 percent, and confidence in the executive establishment during the same 13-year period declined from 41 percent to 17 percent.[4]

There is a basic problem of fragmentation, reported the presidential commission. Fragmentation is defined as a reduced capacity to resolve the throng of conflicting demands from various interest groups, constituents, and lobbies so as to define policies that can be supported by the majority. Fragmentation results in breaking down into semiautonomous units that act to further the interests of particular groups in society. Alienation arises when political institutions are unable to respond adequately to the welter of troublesome problems confronting the nation. Such response usually takes the form of long delays in action of any kind, which is perhaps more unnerving than any other form of dysfunction.[5]

We have seen that government needs to be made an effective instrument of economic well-being because it has a number of vital functions that no other human organization is capable of wholly providing. These functions take the form of planning and instituting fiscal, monetary, and other equilibrating policies, which sustain production without runaway inflation.

Government also helps maintain a favorable balance of trade and payments, conducts the nation's political and economic relations on a world basis that provides stability and balance, and maintains a legal system that distributes income fairly so as to ensure purchasing power and capital for replacement and growth. But none of these activities is likely to flourish without a skillful public administration deeply concerned, as other branches of the government should be, with production, stability, equity, and full employ-duction, stability, equity, and full employment.

Hence, the servant, the administrator, must see that his master, the government as a whole, improves, because his delivery system is effective. He knows how to organize himself and he shares this knowledge and ability with the rest of government.[6]

The 1980 presidential commission focused on the major issues, saying, "although continuous inflation, increased unemployment, and rising energy costs have created significant problems for the American public, another major problem is a sense of foreboding about the future. By 1985, will inflation continue to plague us? Will gasoline sell for $3 per gallon? Indeed, will gasoline and other fuels be rationed? Will millions of Americans be thrown out of work because of competition from imported products? Will our standards of living increase only slowly or even decrease for the average American? Does the nation face a decade of tense struggle among various interest groups maneuvering to maintain their slice of the economic pie?"[7]

Without being unduly pessimistic, the commission's list might be spelled out a bit further in order to show the breadth and scope of the administrator's concern. Thus, in addition to the energy crunch and inflation, there are the underlying problems of lowered productivity and the gross national product, the lowered value of the dollar and the unfavorable balance of trade caused in part by the costs of war and defense, and the decline of the motor car industry and consequent wide unemployment. Other matters of concern are the conflict between environmental policies and industry costs, the cost of government and the burden of national debt, the shrinking acreage in good farm lands, atomic energy and disposal of dangerous wastes, and unemployment, especially among minority groups. The list might also include problems of crime and the use of dangerous drugs, the financing of education, the rising expense of health care, the expansion of social welfare activities during periods of economic downturn, labor-management relations in both the private and the public sectors, and the interrupted flow of grants from the federal to state and local governments. Additional items are the decline in research expenditures, management planning problems in state and federal governments, the tendency of public service employment to be less attractive than formerly, public transportation problems, and urban blight. Problems are endless—the supply of new capital for areas such as shale conversion, the protection of wilderness areas, antitrust policy and consumer protection, policies for welfare and the senior citizen, problems of immigration and absorption of the displaced populations, foreign affairs and peace, aid to developing countries. The list could be further extended. Our reason for including it at all is that such a list immediately calls attention to the need for overall policy and the demands on the program administrator for policy formulation as well as improved execution in an interdependent world.

Structural Weaknesses of U.S. Government

The first results of the National Academy of Public Administration's extended study of the United States' capacity to govern was a report on the presidency. It would be impractical to attempt a summary of all the recommendations found in *A Presidency for the 1980s*.[8] Certain statements and conclusions, however, deserve emphasis because of their direct bearing on the present discussion. The commission recognized that, managerially, the president has little time to do much directly himself. Accordingly, he needs to delegate. The best way to delegate would be to use the cabinet more extensively and accord the president's department heads the same right they have in business practice, that is, to take part in policy formation as well as having a definite area of operating authority.

It is possible that now that the Reagan administration operates on the basis of this cabinet coordination system, the plan will receive a thorough testing. If business practice is any indicator, this system may greatly improve the operation of the executive branch, compared with the use of excessive, anonymous staffs surrounding the presidency, which has resulted from a generation of experimentation.

The academy study also strongly endorsed giving more authority to the heads of operating programs and supporting the Senior Executive Service, from which the necessary leadership must be obtained.[9]

The report of the President's Commission on a National Agenda for the Eighties develops what might be called a complete program because it deals broadly with all important segments of the political process. In line with the commission's focus on the problem of fragmentation, the study deals intensively with the decline of political parties as responsible agencies for policy formation, with the need to reorganize and improve the man-

agement of Congress, and with a detailed and highly constructive discussion of the presidency and the executive branch, winding up with a good chapter on the administration of the judiciary. The entire report of around 90 pages deserves careful reading; it also has a useful bibliography.[10]

This broad view of the political process is indicated at all times because everything administration does is conditioned by the framework within which it operates. It is almost literally true that administration, which is 95 percent of government employment, cannot rise higher (or at least much higher) than the effectiveness of the remaining parts of the government.

A brief summary of the difficulties that need to be overcome would include the electoral process, legislative-executive relations, and the coordination of the executive and administrative functions. Let us attempt this summary as concisely as possible.

The political process has become deficient in several important respects. Congress and the president do not work together as they should. This lack of coordination results in procrastination and near frustration in matters as important as energy legislation, approving treaties, and acting swiftly to head off debilitating inflation. The resulting impairment is as serious as it would be in a person who has circulatory difficulties. The political parties have become less responsible rather than more so. They do not present clear alternatives and assurances of making good on their word. It seems at times that one should vote for the presidential candidate who espouses the opposite of what one favors because in practice he will almost surely do the opposite of what he has promised in the election.

Vast sums are spent on elections. Candidates for the presidency and the House of Representatives seem always to be running for reelection instead of doing the far-sighted things the country needs. Partisan politics has become single-issue politics. The factionalism that the *Federalist Papers* warned against from pressure-group divisions has split the country apart. Citizens spend more time on abortion issues than on rebuilding slums or finding employment for minorities. Congress continually splinters itself as it creates more and more subcommittees to validate the basic assumption of Parkinson's Law, that work expands to occupy the time assigned to it.

In consequence the larger thrusts of public policy tend to lose energy rather than gain it. Congress and the president contend with each other to see which can create the largest staff organization studying overlapping problems. This rivalry in turn results in each devoting so much time to staff subordinates that there is precious little time left over for collaboration among the principals. Such collaboration is not sought because the machinery for consultation and teamwork presently does not exist in adequate measure. The result is a splintering of attention to major problems and a pulling in opposite directions when Congress and the president need to work together.

Another effect of this tug-of-war, as noted earlier, is to cut off the bureaucracy from adequate coordination with either the lawmaking branch or its parent executive branch. Increasingly the imperial presidency is being replaced by an imperial Congress.

Without adequate direction from either Congress or the president, the highest executives of the civil service can hardly be expected to develop leadership and sustained drive. As noted earlier in Chapter 7, on administrative law, program managers are tied in knots by legal red tape and by a nervous Congress that interferes with them at too many points.

A simple remedy that has been proposed—and it might go far to improve the situation—would be to persuade the leadership in Congress and the president in office to confer about proposed legislation and changes in policy before these changes are made public. The Reagan administration during its first year in office (1981) made more rapid strides toward frequent and effective face-to-face contacts with Congress than any previous administration in the history of the nation. There is no question that premature publicity

continually irks members of Congress and tends to elicit their instinctive opposition.

In recent years collaboration has increased between the president and Congress in certain areas such as atomic energy, the Central Intelligence Agency, and tax policy. Possibly this increase has laid a sufficient foundation so that every future president will find collaboration necessary and it will not depend as it does now on the vagaries of the president's personality. Presidential-congressional relationships might increase to the point where they will be institutionalized, and there might be more individuals with understanding in positions of leadership and fewer with chips on their shoulders. There might be fewer instances when executive privilege is claimed with little apparent justification.

Other suggested means of securing face-to-face contacts are not lacking. But recognition of the need to provide a social basis for official relationships appears to be inadequate to date.

As for the organization surrounding the president, there is need for broadening leadership in the executive branch through cabinet coordination and staff planning. This is an area, as suggested earlier, where big government can learn workable methods from big business. The chief executive is and should be a symbol and a molder of public opinion. It is not feasible for him to try to make every decision personally. On the other hand, the staff surrounding the president is too large and has become "politicized." Everything is measured by the effects of policies on the outcome of the next election. Apparently it is not realized that the people (as all public opinion polls reveal) prefer to vote for programs and not the polemics of the occupant of the White House.

Now that the permanent civil service has been provided with a Senior Executive Service, the way has been prepared for direct communication between the president and those to whom the implementation of policy decisions has been largely entrusted. But here again there will be no real magnification of leadership potential until face-to-face communications have been established. It is like star field runners in football waiting at the line until the quarterback calls the signal. What is needed, as the psychologists constantly point out, is communication and trust. The larger the organization, the more coordination must be emphasized if energies are to be vitalized.

Speaking at the 1980 spring meeting of the National Academy of Public Administration, one of the present authors suggested a method of ensuring top-level and program coordination:

have an inner Cabinet consisting of as many departmental heads as are needed and the availability of strong executives to serve on the team. This might be an inner Cabinet of four to six individuals, all good executives. One chieftain would deal with the economy, another with foreign affairs, another with defense, another with environment and conservation, still another with finance. In this small group the interplay of policy and objectives amongst the main areas of the political economy would hold promise of securing a realistic synthesis of policy and administration which no other expedient could provide.[11]

The author then went on to recommend that a team of Senior Civil Servants be designated as liaison with the inner cabinet, attend their sessions, and be prepared to take action thereafter. This method has been used with considerable success in Canada.

Policy Planning at the State and Local Levels

Although the policy problems of the federal government are global and hence more formidable, it is increasingly recognized in the Washington-based Council of State Planning Agencies that much more in the way of top-level coordination is needed if states also are to become more competent in solving their problems. The council is an affiliate of the National Governors' Council, which has been exceedingly active in recent years.

Policy planning has been a misnomer for making compliance reports for federal funds. The state plan for family planning and childrens' services that require the governor's signature, to take one example, consume so large a proportion of

top-planning time that new initiatives are hard to achieve. In other areas, such as regulatory planning (land use and the coastal zone), the situation is equally cumbersome.

One approach, of course, is to take something that has no credibility and associate it with a process of high credibility, the budget. On this subject alone seven volumes were prepared in 1979; they discuss state planning in general and refer to planning and budget consolidation.[12] These books are an indication of the degree of activity found at the state level.

Although it is possible for policy planning and budget consolidations to achieve a modicum of success, the danger is that planning of a higher order is likely to succumb to the budget process. One often hears state management-planning officials remark that consolidation of the two activities is the only way they can obtain more budget analysts. Another result is that adding planning to budgeting may make budgeting so complex that it may collapse of its own weight.

If these difficulties are to be overcome, there must be developed a concept of state policy planning that focuses on *strategic* planning. The Council of State Planning Agencies addresses this challenging concept in Series 2 on State Planning, with the volumes *Concepts of State Planning, Evaluation of State Planning, Statewide Policy Instruments, Financial Planning for State Government,* and *State Planning in Action,* all published in 1977.

At this rate of development—10 volumes on state planning between 1977 and 1979, a two-year period—the states may yet set an example for the federal government. But that will happen only if top officials enlighten the public as to what they are trying to achieve and only if they can prevail upon state legislatures for increased support not only of their studies but of the instrumentation they recommend. At present, unfortunately, sending out governors' policy themes to agencies *prior* to the budget is still considered extremely innovative. On balance, however, these activities of the Council of State Planning Agencies point the direction in which public administration must go if stubborn problems are to be resolved one at a time.

At the local level, policy planning of the comprehensive type is a mixed bag. Some progressive cities are doing a good job, as are some county governments. But like those of the state governments to which they are accountable, the requirements imposed by federal agencies are a serious burden. The most common agencies are those for budgets, city planning, and zoning. Other areas suffer because of the large number of agencies involved and the fact that local units frequently obtain their funds from different sources in Washington or the state capitol. There is frequently so much insulation between related programs that constant reorganization rather than strategic planning comes to be relied upon. Further, as illustrated by the experiences of New York City, Cleveland, and other large cities that have had serious financial crises in recent years, the facts of the situation are often insufficiently coalesced to come to the attention of the mayor and the city council.

In this respect the cities that have managers are much better off. Management planning is centralized in the city manager. If he is resourceful he can usually obtain the funds with which to plan all aspects of the community's business. Once the plans have been formulated they are more likely to be put into operation immediately because of the centralization of authority and responsibility in the manager.

One of the lessons common to all levels of government is that strategic planning can be a means of overcoming the lacunae and resistances that are inherent in the separation of powers. There are many ways of finding the facts, organizing them, and sifting them to arrive at the best course of action. Not all of these means are confined to people on the government payroll. There are city leagues of prominent citizens, private foundations, organizations such as the Committee for Economic Development, and especially the colleges and universities. Many of the latter now have public administration programs that carry

on research, governmental research centers, and separate public policy programs. Their chief virtues are independence and greater freedom to innovate and make constructive criticisms. Often by contract arrangements they can be induced to undertake studies that formal government agencies would be hard pressed to do at all or as well. There need to be stronger links between academia and public administration operations as well as between the government and the power centers in the national economy.

Strategic Role of the Line Executive

The best way to make a true synthesis of the ingredients of public administration is to stress the work of the program executive. Said a National Academy of Public Administration speaker in 1979, "Our schools of public administration should focus primarily on training line executives. Instead of piling one technical course on various aspects of management on top of each other, we should teach a few courses on the administrative process and broaden the interests and substantive knowledge of future administrators. History, economics, law, and a substantive field should be part of every student's preparation."[13]

The executive is paid to obtain results. In formulating his objective he should play an active role in determining goals and in drafting legislation. He does this best by face-to-face relations with his legislative committee and by direct dealing with the higher executive.

The skills he has to sell no one else can offer. He alone fixes targets, establishes policies, makes use of incentives, delegates clear-cut tasks, and coordinates as he goes along. The executive also adjusts to external forces and influences, makes allies, sees that the time schedule is maintained, is careful to stay within the limits of the law and its protections of civil rights, and leads by example. He is a hard worker, who gives credit and praise, spends a good deal of time on public relations, measures his results, and develops his subordinates.

One of the most important of these areas is public relations, that is, public opinion and dealings with the public.

In one of the wisest and most sophisticated treatises ever written by an American political scientist, entitled *Public Opinion and American Democracy,* V. O. Key, Jr., described public opinion as the interaction between what he called political influentials and the mass of common people.[14] Moreover, when democracy decays, he added, the reason is less the cupidity of the masses than the fact that the influentials make mass public opinion the scapegoat for their own shortcomings. In other words, the public is less often wrong than its leaders are.

Gradually, administrators in many fields—government, business, education, and others—have learned that the public and its attitudes and opinions are so influential as to constitute virtually an integral part of the administrative process. In the long run, the public gains what it wants and cannot be prevented from doing so. Of all the elements entering into a philosophy of administrative behavior, the contributions of the public are the most significant. Public relations is less a manipulation of public opinion than it is a faithful response to what the public wishes. And if an appreciation of the influence of the ordinary citizen should become the operative foundation for all aspects of administration, it would contribute more than any other factor to tangible results and good will. The administrator who understands these relationships avoids the role of elitist manipulator, for both intellectually and emotionally he is attached to the philosophical assumptions of popular government. He knows that institutions come from the people, their needs and their values, and that the relationships between people and institutions are important to both.

When administrators in a popular government ignore the need for active public participation in the conduct of public affairs, tensions are generated and administration loses its effectiveness. The result is frustration and public apathy. If, however, the people are encouraged to participate and to advance communally held wants and ideals, then their sense of morality stimulates them to cooperate, and the governmental process becomes more effective.

The energy residing in the people themselves may turn in one of two main directions. First, when tensions are generated, governments and public administration may periodically be taken by surprise when the public asserts itself and changes leaders and the direction they are taking. Second, when public administrators understand the potency of communal aspiration, the people can work actively with their elected representatives and expert administrators. In consequence the work of government becomes distinguished rather than halting and ordinary.[15]

The very call to serve a larger interest, says Stephen K. Bailey, "evokes a degree of selflessness and nobility on the part of public servants beyond the capacity of cynics to recognize or to believe." At the same time, an awareness of the dilemmas and paradoxes of policy formation and decision making requires a spirit of humility on the part of the administrator and a willingness to defer to the view of others through compromise. These qualities are "the priceless attributes of the life-style" of the administrator in a free society. It should be noted, however, that humility is not obsequiousness nor a willingness to compromise in a spirit of weak affability. Rather humility is ultimately a form of moral toughness, for it involves self-discipline and the sublimation of persistent inner claims for personal recognition, power, and status. Thus charity is the "principle above principles."[16]

With this observation on the need to be independent and concerned, this chapter on "futures" may be brought to a conclusion.

- There is no problem confronting the country that cannot be solved if citizens and administrators alike give it enough study. A richer cultural experience might be forthcoming in the process.
- Professional standards and professional conduct, like that long espoused by the International City

Management Association and more recently by the American Society for Public Administration and the National Academy of Public Administration, are a means of bringing such study about.

- Active participation in the political process and in the formation of public policy is the likely means of changing public attitudes toward government to something more promising.
- A lifetime of study and reflection is characteristic of the best public administrators, who are honored and who serve as models to emulate.
- The ideal public administrator is the one who grows by speaking out and taking calculated risks.
- Everyone ultimately makes his own synthesis of the elements, processes, and values that will advance the art and science of public administration.

There is nothing profound in any of these propositions. Commonplace as they are, in the consciousness of concerned citizens and dedicated public administrators, they could turn things around.

Some challenges suggest a disputatious image and hence are rather unpleasant. Others appeal to the imagination and untapped resources. The challenges to public administration in the final quarter of the 20th century are mostly of this latter kind. There is a wealth of experience and wisdom to draw upon in the ideas we have been considering, and with a bit of spunk and resolve the tapping should not be too difficult.

NOTES

1. Robert Ball and George Williamson, "The Coming Speed-Up in the German Economy," *Fortune*, 10 April 1978; "Japanese Managers Tell How Their System Works," *Fortune*, November 1977, p. 126; Sanford Rose, "Secrets of Japan's Prowess," *Fortune*, 30 January 1978.

2. Luther H. Gulick, *Perspectives in Public Administration: Past, Present, and Future* (Greenvale, N.Y.: Long Island University, 19 December 1979), pamphlet.

3. Dwight Waldo, *The Enterprise of Public Administration* (Novato, Calif.: Chandler & Sharp, 1980), chs. 10 and 11.

4. President's Commission for a National Agenda for the Eighties, *The Electoral and Democratic Process in the Eighties,* pp. 2–3.

5. President's Commission, *The Electoral and Democratic Process*, p. 3.

6. This, in effect, is what the National Academy of Public Administration decided to do, in 1979, when it launched a 10-year study of America's capacity to govern.

7. President's Commission, *The Electoral and Democratic Process*, p. 3.

8. *A Presidency for the 1980s* (Washington: National Academy of Public Administration, 1980).

9. *A Presidency for the 1980s*, ch. 5.

10. President's Commission, *The Electoral and Democratic Process*.

11. Marshall E. Dimock, "Public Administration in the 1980s" (Occasional Paper, National Academy of Public Administration, Washington, 1980).

12. These studies may be secured from the Council of State Planning Agencies, 444 Capitol Street, Washington, D.C. 20001. One of them is *Economic Development: The Challenge of the 1980s*. Others are *State Taxation and Economic Development, Innovations in Development Finance, The Working Poor: Toward a State Agenda, Inflation and Unemployment: Surviving the 1980s, Venture Capital and Urban Development*, and *Development Politics: Private Development and the Public Interest*.

13. Dimock, "Public Administration in the 1980s."

14. V. O. Key, Jr., *Public Opinion and American Democracy* (New York: Knopf, 1961), p. 557.

15. John Dewey, *The Public and Its Government* (New York: Holt, 1927), pp. 53, 128–151.

16. Stephen K. Bailey, "Ethics and the Public Service," *Public Administration Review* 24 (December 1964): 237.

APPENDIX

A LIST OF ORGANIZATIONS CONCERNED WITH PUBLIC ADMINISTRATION

Advisory Commission on Intergovernmental Relations, Washington, D.C. 20575. The ACIR, described in Chapter 5, is the major research source in this policy area.

American Institute of Planners, 1776 Massachusetts Ave., N.W., Washington, D.C. 20036. This is an important association of public planning officials.

American Society for Public Administration, 1120 G Street, N.W., Washington, D.C. 20005. This generalist organization, which had 20,000 members in 1980, draws from federal, state, and local government, as well as from academia and the nonprofit sector. This most important general-purpose group for public administration has active state and regional chapters. We strongly urge anyone in the field to join ASPA.

Council of State Governments, P.O. Box 11910, Lexington, Ky. 40511. The council publishes *The Book of the States* and other important research relating to state government.

Institute of Public Administration, 55 West 44 St., New York, N.Y. 10036. This is a research group of long standing.

International City Management Association, 1140 Connecticut Ave., N.W., Washington, D.C. 20036. The professional organization of America's city managers, ICMA publishes a variety of books on many public management topics. Individuals who are not city managers can join as associate members.

International Personnel Management Association, 1850 K St., N.W., Washington, D.C. 20006. This is the national association of professional public personnel managers. State and regional chapters hold regular meetings.

Municipal Finance Officers Association, 180 N. Michigan Ave., Chicago, Ill. 60601. This is the national professional association of local budget officials.

National Academy of Public Administration, 1120 G Street, N.W., Washington, D.C. 20005. This national organization is privately financed and self-perpetuating, with an outside limit of 300 members drawn from all parts of the country. Created in 1967, it gives high-level advice to governments, operating through panels for research and consultation.

National Association of Counties, 1735 New York Ave., N.W., Washington, D.C. 20036. This is the national organization of county officials.

National Association of Schools of Public Affairs and Administration, 1120 G Street, N.W., Washington, D.C. 20005. This national association has a membership of over two hundred schools and colleges focusing on graduate preparation in public administration. Commencing as the Council on Graduate Education for Public Administration in the 1950s, in 1970 it underwent a reorganization. This association intensively studies academic measures designed to prepare persons for, or improve their performance in, the public service.

National Association of State Budget Officials, Iron Works Pike, Lexington, Ky. 40511. This is the national professional association of state budget officials.

National Civil Service League, 1825 K. St., N.W., Washington, D.C. 20006. This organization is dedicated to civil service reform.

National Conference of State Legislatures, 1405 Curtis St., Denver, Colo. 80202. This is the organization of state legislatures.

National Governors Assocation, 444 No. Capitol St., Washington, D.C. 20001. This is the association of state governors.

National League of Cities, 1620 I St., N.W., Washington, D.C. 20006. This is the major association of smaller cities.

National Municipal League, 47 East 68 St., New

York, N.Y. 10021. This association has been dedicated to improving urban governments for over a century.

Public Administration Service, 1313 East 60 St., Chicago, Ill. 60637. This venerable organization provides consulting services and issues research reports on a variety of topics.

United States Conference of Mayors, 1620 I St., Washington, D.C. 20006. This is the association of mayors of larger cities.

Urban Institute, 2100 M. St., N.W., Washington, D.C. 20037. This federally funded research organization has published many excellent guides for public administrators.

ANNOTATED BIBLIOGRAPHY

CHAPTER 1

The reader may gain a sense of public administration and discover its scope and coverage in many ways. One way is to read Woodrow Wilson's 1887 essay on this subject, which is generally acknowledged as the starting point of U.S. public administration. "The Study of Public Administration" is found in *Political Science Quarterly* 2 (June 1887), reprinted in 56 (December 1941): 481–506. One or more of the following are recommended: John M. Gaus, Leonard D. White, and Marshall E. Dimock, *The Frontiers of Public Administration* (Chicago: University of Chicago Press, 1936); Roscoe Martin, ed., *New Horizons in Public Administration* (Tuscaloosa: University of Alabama Press, 1945); Dwight Waldo, *The Administrative State* (New York: Ronald, 1948); and *The Study of Public Administration* (New York: Doubleday, 1948); or Frank Marini, ed., *Toward a New Public Administration: The Minnowbrook Perspective* (New York: Intext, 1971). Also recommended are the excellent "Introduction" in Harold Stein, ed., *Public Administration and Policy Development: A Casebook* (New

York: Harcourt Brace Jovanovich 1952); Robert Presthus, *Behavioral Approaches to Public Administration* (Tuscaloosa: University of Alabama Press, 1965); and Herbert A. Simon, *Administrative Behavior: A Study of Decision-Making Processes in Administrative Organizations,* 2d ed. (New York: Free Press, 1957).

On substantive problems and policy making the reader might consult Charles E. Lindblom, *The Policy-Making Process* (Englewood Cliffs, N.J.: Prentice-Hall, 1968) or *Politics and Markets: The World's Political-Economic Systems* (New York: Basic Books, 1977); also Emmette S. Redford, *American Government and the Economy* (New York: Macmillan, 1965) and *Ideal and Practice in Public Administration* (Tuscaloosa: University of Alabama Press, 1966). On trends, fully discussed in Chapter 24 of this book, a good overall treatment is found in *Public Administration Review* 36 (September-October 1976), Special Bicentennial Issue: American Public Administration in Three Centuries.

CHAPTER 2

A good case study is often a good method of translating the theoretical into the practical. An interview such as that found in this chapter is similar to a case study in that it presents a profile of a particular administrator and allows the reader to grasp the administrator's insights and experiences with a minimum of words. In R. J. Novogrod, Marshall E. Dimock: *Casebook in Public Administration* (New York: Holt, Rinehart & Winston, 1969), there are a number of interview profiles of such administrators as the comptroller-general of the United States, a state governor, a Job Corps director, a civil rights administrator, a school superintendent, and the Metropolitan Transportation Authority chairman.

Other cases, which may be called situational cases, are longer and stress negotiation, decision making, and directing activities. Both these cases and those included in the *Casebook,* however, usually make considerable use of the interview method. The greatest storehouse of public administration cases is found in

the Inter-University Case Program. Some early cases have been compiled in Harold Stein, ed., *Public Administration and Policy Development* (New York: Harcourt Brace Jovanovich 1952). Scores of individual cases continue to appear from time to time. Such cases make excellent independent reading, material for class reports or discussion, and grist for term papers. Other collections include F. M. G. Willson, ed., *Administrators in Action: British Case Studies* (Toronto: University of Toronto Press, 1961); Frederick C. Mosher, ed., *Governmental Reorganization: Cases and Commentary* (Indianapolis, Ind.: Bobbs-Merrill, 1967); John D. Glover and Ralph M. Hower, *The Administrator: Cases on Human Relations in Industry,* 5th ed. (Homewood, Ill.; Irwin, 1973); Robert T. Golembiewski and Michael White, *Cases in Public Management,* 3d ed. (Chicago: Rand-McNally, 1980); and Marc Holzer, *Cases in Public Administration* (New York: Harper & Row, 1981).

Additional case studies are included in the following books: Arthur W. Macmahon, John D. Millett, and Gladys Ogden, *The Administration of Work Relief* (Chicago: Public Administration Service, 1941); Marshall E. Dimock, *The Executive in Action* (New York: Harper & Row, 1945); Herbert Kaufman, *The Forest Ranger: A Study in Administrative Behavior* (Baltimore: Johns Hopkins Press, 1960); Nelson McGeary, *Gifford Pinchot: Forester, Politician* (Princeton, N.J.: Princeton University Press, 1960); and Graham T. Allison, *Essence of Decision: Explain-*

ing the Cuban Missile Crisis (Boston: Little, Brown, 1971).

We deal with executive leadership in Chapter 8; at this stage the reader may be interested in a study by Lawrence A. Appley, a former Washington official who later headed the American Management Associations. *Management in Action* (New York: American Management Associations, 1956) or Melville Dalton, *Men Who Manage* (New York: Wiley, 1959).

CHAPTER 3

In addition to the basic sources mentioned in the footnotes, the following studies are worth consulting: Luther M. Gulick and L. Urwick, eds., *Papers on the Science of Administration* (New York: Institute of Public Administration, 1937); Ordway Tead, *The Art of Administration* (New York: McGraw-Hill, 1951); Rensis Likert, *New Patterns of Management* (New York: McGraw-Hill, 1961); and Frederick W. Taylor, *The Principles of Scientific Management* (New York: Harper & Row, 1974).

Perhaps the most authoritative book on large-scale management so far published is Peter F. Drucker, *Management: Tasks, Responsibilities, Practices* (New

York: Harper & Row, 1973). Public administration is discussed in E. N. Gladden, *History of Public Administration,* 2 vols. (London: F. Cass, 1973); and Frederick C. Mosher, *American Public Administration: Past, Present, Future* (Tuscaloosa: University of Alabama Press, 1975).

On retiring from Syracuse University, Dwight Waldo, a creative thinker in public administration, incorporated his thoughts into *The Enterprise of Public Administration* (Novato, Calif.: Chandler & Sharp, 1980). Waldo deals extensively with various competing theories and provides historical perspective. The book includes some helpful reading suggestions.

CHAPTER 4

The relation of politics and public policy to public administration has been one of the most rapidly growing fields of social science in recent years. Outstanding examples of books dealing with the subject are Francis E. Rourke, *Bureaucratic Power in National Politics,* 3d ed. (Boston: Little, Brown, 1978); and Harold Seidman, *Politics, Position and Power: The Dynamics of Federal Organization,* 3d ed. (New York: Oxford University Press, 1980).

An introduction to the topic focusing on subnational government is Douglas M. Fox, *The Politics of City and State Bureaucracy* (Santa Monica, Calif.: Goodyear Publishers, 1974).

One of the first American scholars to assume that administration is an integral part of government as a whole was W. F. Willoughby, of Johns Hopkins University and the Brookings Institution. An appraisal of his influence and approach is found in an article by Marshall E. Dimock, "W. F. Willoughby and the Administrative Universal," *Public Administration Review* 35 (September–October 1975). Pendleton Her-

ring, a Willoughby protégé, who had already established himself as a "realistic" political scientist, wrote *Public Administration and the Public Interest* (New York: McGraw-Hill, 1936). This was followed by Avery Leiserson, *Administrative Regulation: A Study in Representation of Interests* (Chicago: University of Chicago Press, 1942).

A former Washington official, Paul H. Appleby, who started his career as a journalist and later became head of the Maxwell School at Syracuse University, wrote *Policy and Administration* (Tuscaloosa: University of Alabama Press, 1949), following his *Big Democracy* (New York: Knopf, 1945). One of the most systematic pioneers in public policy was Harold D. Lasswell. With Daniel Lerner he wrote *The Policy Sciences: Recent Developments in Scope and Method* (Palo Alto, Calif.: Stanford University Press, 1952) and followed this by his *A Preview of the Policy Sciences* (New York: Elsevier-Dutton, 1971).

Other significant books are Charles E. Lindblom, *The Policy-Making Process* (Englewood Cliffs, N.J.:

Prentice-Hall, 1968); Larry L. Wade and R. L. Curry, Jr., *A Logic of Public Policy: Aspects of Political Economy* (Belmont, Calif.: Wadsworth, 1970); Larry L. Wade, *The Elements of Public Policy* (Columbus, Ohio: Merrill, 1972): Thomas Dye, *Under-* *standing Public Policy,* 2d ed. (Englewood Cliffs, N.J.: Prentice-Hall, 1975); and Charles O. Jones, *An Introduction to the Study of Public Policy,* 2d ed. (Belmont, Calif.: Wadsworth, 1977).

CHAPTER 5

Perhaps the best short introduction to federal-state-local intergovernmental relations (IGR) is Michael D. Reagan and John G. Sanzone, *The New Federalism,* 2d ed. (New York: Oxford University Press, 1981). The authors' position favoring the federal government adds spice to the debate rather than weakens the book. Two current textbooks are Parris N. Glendening and Mavis Mann Reeves, *Pragmatic Federalism* (Pacific Palisades, Calif.: Palisades Publishers, 1977), and Deil S. Wright, *Understanding Intergovernmental Relations* (North Scituate, Mass.: Duxbury Press, 1978). The latter probes vertical IGR more deeply but neglects to cover horizontal IGR, which the former does. The best single analysis of the politics of IGR, even though somewhat dated, is Donald H. Haider, *When Governments Come to Washington* (New York: Free Press, 1974). A 1937 classic still worth reading is V. O. Key's *The Administration of Federal Grants to States* (New York: Johnson Reprint Corp., 1972).

Probably the single most influential postwar analysis of IGR is Morton Grodzin's *The American System* (Chicago: Rand McNally, 1966), which stresses cooperation in IGR, symbolized by the marble cake analogy. Grodzin's most prominent student, Daniel J. Elazar, has written a fascinating analysis, *American Federalism: A View From the States,* 2d ed. (New York: Crowell, 1972).

The Advisory Commission on Intergovernmental Relations (ACIR) has published numerous trenchant analyses of IGR. Indispensable are *General Revenue Sharing: An ACIR Re-Evaluation,* A-48, 1974; *Block Grants: A Comparative Analysis,* A-60, 1977; *Categorical Grants: Their Role and Design,* A-52, 1978; and ACIR's quarterly publication, *Intergovernmental Perspective.* ACIR's address is Washington, D.C. 20575. David B. Walker, assistant director of ACIR and the most prolific writer in the agency, has summed up his views in *Toward a Functioning Federalism* (Cambridge, Mass.: Winthrop, 1981).

On horizontal IGR, see Douglas M. Fox and George E. Berkley, *80,000 Governments* (Boston: Allyn & Bacon, 1978), for an introduction. Michael M. Danielson et al. probe the topic in more depth in *One Nation, So Many Governments* (Lexington, Mass.: Heath, 1977). A forceful dissent from the conventional wisdom deploring the growth of special districts is Robert B. Hawkins, Jr., *Self Government by District* (Palo Alto, Calif.: Hoover Institute, 1976). The best single analysis of the forces attempting to create a metropolitanwide government is National Academy of Public Administration, *Multi-Tiered Metropolitan Government* (Washington: NAPA, 1977).

Perhaps the best book on grantsmanship is Virginia White, *Grants* (New York: Plenum, 1975).

CHAPTER 6

Most students enjoy reading and reporting on leading cases of the Supreme Court of the United States and the highest state courts when they understand how to read and report on cases as class exercises or in preparing term papers. There is an excellent brief discussion of this question in Kenneth Davis, *Administrative Law and Government* (St. Paul, Minn.: West Publishing, 1960), pp. 7–9. James Hart, in his *Introduction to Administrative Law With Selected Cases,* 2d ed. (New York: Appleton, Century, Crofts, 1950) deals more fully and even more interestingly with this subject in his "Introduction" and especially pages 15–22.

One of the best analytical-philosophical approaches to the content of this chapter is found in J. Roland Pennock, *Administration and the Rule of Law* (New York: Holt, 1941). The trend toward recombining public administration and administrative law is reflected in Ernest Gellhorn and Glen O. Robinson, "Perspectives on Administrative Law," *Columbia Law Review* 75 (1975): 771; and Robert Stewart,

"The Reformation of American Administrative Law," *Harvard Law Review* 88 (1975): p. 1117.

Background books on administrative procedure acts are found in Lloyd Musolf, *Federal Examiners and the Conflict of Law and Administration* (Baltimore: Johns Hopkins University Press, 1953); Ferrel Heady, *Administrative Procedure Legislation in the United States* (Ann Arbor, Mich.: University of Michigan Press, 1952); Robert S. Lorch, *Democratic Process and Administrative Law* (Detroit: Wayne State University Press, 1969); and V. M. Barnett, Jr., "Judicialization of the Administrative Process," *Public Administration Review* 8 (Spring 1948): 128.

There is a vast literature on regulation. Among the best books are Marver Bernstein, *Regulating Business by Independent Commission* (Princeton, N.J.: Princeton University Press, 1955); H. J. Friendly, *The Federal Administrative Agencies* (Cambridge: Harvard University Press, 1962); and W. L. Cary, *Politics and the Regulatory Agencies* (New York: McGraw-Hill, 1967). On the role of Congress in legislation, see Freeman J. Leiper, *The Political Process: Executive Bureau-Legislative Committee Relations,* rev. ed. (New York: Random House, 1965) and Joseph E. Harris, *Congressional Control of Administration* (Washington: Brookings Institution, 1964).

CHAPTER 7

On the subject of morality, which underlies ethical behavior, an excellent source is Paul H. Appleby, *Morality and Administration in Democratic Government* (Baton Rouge: Louisiana State Press, 1952). Perhaps the best essay on this subject, to date, is Stephen K. Bailey's "Ethics and the Public Service," *Public Administration Review* 24 (December 1964): 234–243. One of the pioneers in this field, W. A. R. Leys, has written *Ethics for Policy Decisions: The Art of Asking Deliberative Questions* (Engelwood Cliffs, N.J.: Prentice-Hall, 1952). A humanist psychologist, Abraham Maslow, is editor of a volume, *New Knowledge in Human Values* (New York: Harper & Row, 1959). Another good book is Abraham Kaplan, *American*

Ethics and Public Policy (New York: Oxford University Press, 1963). Alice M. Rivlin and Michael P. Timpane have produced *Ethical and Legal Issues of Social Experimentation* (Washington: Brookings Institution, 1975).

The Ethics in Government Act of 1978 is Public Law 95-251 (October 26, 1978). Excellent illustrative material on croneyism and high-level influence is found in David A. Frier, *Conflict of Interest in the Eisenhower Administration* (Ames: Iowa State University Press, 1969). The National Academy of Public Administration sponsored *Watergate: Implications for Responsible Government* (New York: Basic Books, 1974).

CHAPTER 8

There has been a recent significant harvest in the field of the chief executive. The institution of the American presidency is "unique," said the President's Commission for a National Agenda for the Eighties in *A National Agenda for the Eighties* (Washington: U.S. Government Printing Office, 1980), pp. 98-99. About the same time, the National Academy of Public Administration brought out a two-year study, *A Presidency for the 1980's* (Washington: NAPA, 1980), in which the theme was "The President Needs Help." There are so many facets of this problem that it deserves extended study. At the state level, the National Governors' Association produced *The Guidebook for New Governors* (1979) and *Perspectives on Being Governor* (1981), both distributed by the NGA in Washington, D.C. Rounding out the picture, at the munic-

ipal level, the International City Management Association, through its Committee on Future Horizons, published *New Worlds of Service* in October, 1979 (Washington: ICMA, 1979).

A landmark in the history of writing on the executive function is Louis W. Koenig, formerly of the U.S. Bureau of the Budget, *The Chief Executive* (New York: Harcourt Brace Jovanovich, 1964). A former dean of the Maxwell School and former university president, Harlan Cleveland, published *The Future Executive: A Guide for Tomorrow's Manager* (New York: Harper & Row, 1972). More recently, Chester A. Newland, who headed the Federal Executive Institute in Charlottesville, Virginia, wrote a wide-ranging essay, "Professional Public Executives and Public Administration Agendas," in the book he edited, *Professional Public Executives* (Washington: American Society for Public Administration, 1980), pp. 1–30. In the same collection, see Donald C. Stone "Notes on the Governmental Executive: His Role and His Methods."

CHAPTER 9

Putting it all together is an apt description of leadership in program management. Harlan Cleveland writes on this subject in "The Get-it-all-together Profession," *Public Administration Review* 39 (July–August 1979): 306–309. John J. Corson pioneered the Old Age and Survivors' Program in Washington during the 1930s and is considered one of the best line administrators Washington has ever seen. He wrote "The Mastery of Management," *Public Administration Review* 25 (June 1965); a similar article, except that it emphasizes renewal, is Marshall E. Dimock, "Revitalized Program Management," *Public Administration Review* 38 (May–June 1978). A factorial analysis of what is involved in management (compared to law) is found in Dimock's *Law and Dynamic Administration* (New York: Praeger, 1980), pp. 52–67. On the practical side of management (where the pay-off occurs) some of the best leads are Edward C. Schleh, *Managing By Results: The Dyamics of Profitable Management* (New York: McGraw-Hill, 1961); Peter Drucker, *The Practice of Management* (New York: Harper & Row, 1954); and Leonard R. Sayles, *Managerial Behavior* (New York: McGraw-Hill, 1964). John J. Corson and R. Shale Paul draw an accurate profile of line administrators in *Men Near the Top: Filling Posts in the Federal Service* (Baltimore:

Johns Hopkins Press, 1966). Recently, among behaviorists, there has been a preference for the term "implementation." George C. Edwards's book *Implementing Public Policy* (Washington: Congressional Quarterly Press, 1980) is an example.

On leadership, there are some good recent and good older references. James McGregor Burns wrote *Leadership* (New York: Harper & Row, 1978), tying administration into the political process. Some other books directly related to management are F. E. Fiedler, *A Theory of Leadership Effectiveness* (New York: McGraw-Hill, 1967); Harry Levinson, The *Exceptional Executive* (Cambridge, Mass.: Harvard University Press, 1968); and Robert Dubin et al., *Leadership and Productivity* (New York: Intext, 1965). Chris Argyris has written *Executive Leadership: An Appraisal of a Manager in Action* (New York: Harper & Row, 1953) and *Personality and Organization* (New York: Harper & Row, 1957). On Mary Parker Follett, one of the pioneers, see *Dynamic Administration,* Henry C. Metcalf and L. Urwick, eds. (New York: Harper & Row, 1941). From sociology, one of the best volumes is Philip Selznick, *Leadership in Administration* (Evanston, Ill. & White Plains, N.Y.: Row, Peterson, 1957).

CHAPTER 10

Planning, which has never been particularly popular in the United States since the Cold War began, has become identified in the public mind with policy analysis. Pierre Clavel and Harvey Jacobs cite as an example of this convergence the emergence of the United States' urban policy in the 1970s, which pleased the planners and developed a large constituency. In their review article "Planning and Urban Policy," *Public Administration Review* 41 (January–February 1981): 87-92, these authors ask three questions. What is planning? What sustains it? How stable is it? A number of new books testify to the growing vitality

of planning now that it has been more closely identified with the political process and administrative implementation. Examples are *Politics and Planning: A National Study of American Planners* (Chapel Hill: University of North Carolina Press, 1979) by Michael Lee Vasu; Robert W. Burchell and George Sternlieb, *Planning Theory in the 1980's: A Search for Future Directions* (New Brunswick, N.J.: Rutgers University Press, 1978); Herbert H. Smith, *The Citizen's Guide to Planning,* rev. ed. (Chicago: The Planners Press [American Planning Association], 1979); and Jiri Pill, *Planning and Politics: The Metro Toronto Transpor-*

tation Plan Review (Cambridge: Massachusetts Institute of Technology Press, 1979).

Indicative planning, with its emphasis on increasing efficiency and innovating better products and techniques, was strongly advocated by Andrew Shonfield in *Modern Capitalism: The Changing Balance of Public and Private Power* (New York: Oxford University Press, 1965). Michael D. Reagan wrote "Toward Improving National Policy Planning," *Public Administration Review* 23 (March 1963), followed by *Political Economy and the General Welfare* (Chicago: Scott, Foresman, 1965). The idea of incremental (gradual)

planning, on a pragmatic basis, was stressed in Charles Lindblom's "The Science of Muddling Through," *Public Administration Review* 19 (Spring 1959) and *The Policy-Making Process* (Englewood Cliffs, N.J.: Prentice-Hall, 1968). See also Norman Beckman's symposium "Policy Analysis in Government: Alternatives to 'Muddling Through,'" *Public Administration Review* 37 (May–June 1977). On scientific planning, see Harlow Person, "Planned Execution, the Issue of Scientific Management," *Advanced Management* 10 (December 1945).

CHAPTER 11

In Chapter 9, entitled "Organizations and Administration of the Future: A Multifaceted Crystal Ball," Dwight Waldo, in his book *The Enterprise of Public Administration* (Novato, Calif.: Chandler & Sharp, 1980), deals with competing theories of organization and suggests that they may be markedly modified by "futurism." Some of the same ground is covered by Herbert Kaufman in *Limits of Organizational Change* (Tuscaloosa: University of Alabama Press, 1971) and "The Direction of Organizational Evolution," *Public Administration Review* 33 (July–August 1973).

On the practical, operating aspects of organization, the following will be found useful: Harvey Sherman, *It All Depends: A Pragmatic Approach to Organizations* (Tuscaloosa: University of Alabama Press, 1966); James D. Thompson, *Organizations in Action* (New York: McGraw-Hill, 1967); Chris Argyris, "Some Limits to Rational Man Organization Theory," *Public Administration Review* 33 (May–June 1973); Peter Drucker, "Managerial Organization" in *Management: Tasks, Responsibilities, Practices* (New York: Harper & Row, 1973), pp. 517-602; Warren G. Bennis, *Organization Development: Its Nature, Origins, and Prospects* (Reading, Mass.: Addison-

Wesley, 1969); and Daniel Katz and Robert L. Kahn, *The Social Psychology of Organizations* (New York: Wiley, 1966).

William G. Scott and Terence R. Mitchell have written *Organization Theory: A Behavioral Analysis for Management*, 3d ed. (Homewood, Ill.: Irwin, 1976). See also Rensis Likert, *The Human Organization: Its Management and Value* (New York: McGraw-Hill, 1967). "Organization Theory and Political Science" was contributed by Dennis J. Palumbo, in *The Handbook of Political Science*, edited by Fred I. Greenstein and Nelson W. Polsby (Reading, Mass.: Addison-Wesley, 1975), vol. 2. There are also some trenchant observations in Harlan Cleveland, *The Future Executive: A Guide to Tomorrow's Managers* (New York: Harper & Row, 1972). Herbert Emmerich, who once headed the public administration program of the United Nations, gave some lectures published as *Essays on Federal Reorganization* (Tuscaloosa: University of Alabama Press, 1948); and John D. Millett deals with organization and reorganization in *Management in the Public Service* (New York: McGraw-Hill, 1954), chs. 7 & 8.

CHAPTER 12

In Chapter 5, dealing with supervision, John D. Millett, *Management in the Public Service* (New York: McGraw-Hill, 1954), says there are six main aspects, pp. 98-122. See also John M. Pfiffner and Frank P. Sherwood, *Administrative Organization* (Englewood Cliffs, N.J.: Prentice-Hall, 1960), ch. 16. Rensis Likert deals with supervision in *Patterns of Management*

(New York: McGraw-Hill, 1961), ch. 4. Directing and disciplining is considered in William H. Newman, *The Process of Management: Concepts, Behavior, and Practice* (Englewood Cliffs, N.J.: Prentice-Hall, 1961), ch. 24. See also Harold L. Wilensky, *Organizational Intelligence, Knowledge, and Policy in Government and Industry* (New York: Basic Books,

1967). Also Herbert Kaufman, *Administrative Feedback: Monitoring Subordinates' Behavior* (Washington: Brookings Institution, 1973). William Dowling and Leonard Sayles, *How Managers Motivate,* 2nd ed. (New York: McGraw-Hill, 1978) remains the best text in the field.

On managing by objectives, consult Saul W. Gellerman, *Management by Motivation* (New York: American Management Associations, 1968). Also see Jerome M. Rosow, *The Worker and the Job: Coping With Change* (Englewood Cliffs, N.J.: Prentice-Hall, 1974); and Alfred J. Marrow, David G. Bowers, and Stanley E. Seashore, *Management by Participation* (New York: Harper & Row, 1967). The philosophy of administering by objectives is admirably set forth in

Ordway Tead, *The Art of Administration* (New York: McGraw-Hill, 1951), chs. 3 and 11.

Decision making in management is developed in Herbert A. Simon, *Administrative Behavior: A Study in Decision-Making Processes in Administrative Organizations,* 2d ed. (New York: Free Press, 1957); in William J. Gore, *Administrative Decision Making: A Heuristic Model* (New York: Wiley, 1964); and William J. Gore and J. W. Dyson, eds., *The Making of Decisions: A Reader in Administrative Behavior* (New York: Free Press, 1964). See also William G. Scott and Terence R. Mitchell, *Administrative Behavior: A Study of Decision-Making Processes in Administrative Organization,* 2d ed. (New York: Free Press, 1957).

CHAPTER 13

The tendency toward autarchic insularity is dealt with by an experienced Washington official, Rufus E. Miles, Jr., in "The Origin and Meaning of Miles' Law," *Public Administration Review* 38 (September–October, 1978): 399–403. The theme of conflict is consistently developed by Bertram Gross in *The Managing of Organizations,* 2 vols. (New York: Free Press, 1964) and *The Legislative Struggle: A Study in Social Combat* (New York: McGraw-Hill, 1953). How to cope with conflict is the theme of Rensis Likert and Jane Gibson Likert, *New Ways of Managing Conflict* (New York: McGraw-Hill, 1976); and Stuart Chase, *Roads to Agreement: Successful Methods in the Science of Human Relations* (New York: Harper & Row, 1951). See also Daniel Katz, *Bureaucratic Encounters* (Ann Arbor: University of Michigan Press, 1975). Daniel Katz and Robert L. Kahn also wrote *The Social Psychology of Organizations* (New York: Wiley, 1966).

Good books on motivation and morale are Rensis Likert, *Motivation: The Core of Management* (New York: American Management Associations, 1953); Abraham Maslow, *Motivation and Personality* (New York: Harper & Row, 1954); Morris S. Viteles, *Motivation and Morale in Industry* (New York: Norton,

1953); William F. Dowling and Leonard Sayles, *How Managers Motivate* (New York: McGraw-Hill, 1978); Frederick Herzberg et al., *The Motivation to Work* (New York: Wiley, 1959); and Lyman W. Porter and Edward E. Lawler III, *Managerial Attitudes and Performance* (Homewood, Ill.: Irwin, 1968). On "self-starters" see David McClelland, *The Achievement Motive* (New York: Appleton-Century-Crofts, 1953).

On the question of public interest, a beginning point might be Herbert J. Storing, "The Crucial Link: Public Administration, Responsibility and the Public Interest," *Public Administration Review* 24 (March 1964): 34–36. For strong objection to the concept see Glendon Schubert, *The Public Interest: A Critique of a Political Concept* (New York: Free Press, 1960) and his article "'The Public Interest' in Decision-Making," *American Political Science Review* 51 (June 1957): 346–348. For a more sympathetic view see Carl J. Friedrich, *Nomos V: The Public Interest* (New York: Atherton Press, 1962); and Marshall E. Dimock, *The New American Political Economy* (New York: Harper & Row, 1962), ch. 4, "The Public Interest."

CHAPTER 14

On the problem of internal coordination a good starting point is International City Management Association, *Effective Supervisory Practices: Better Results*

Through Teamwork (Washington: ICMA, 1978), ch. 3, "Basic Management Skills." Peter Drucker also has a discussion of the span of managerial relationships in his *Management: Tasks, Responsibilities, Practices* (New York: Harper & Row, 1973) commencing on p. 412. He discusses the matter further in *The Practice of Management* (New York: Harper & Row, 1954). See also John D. Millett, *Management in the Public Service* (New York: McGraw-Hill, 1954), ch. 7, "Organization as a Technical Problem." Other good references are Alfred D. Chandler, Jr., *Strategy and Structure* (Cambridge: Massachusetts Institute of Technology Press, 1962); Harold Koontz and Cyril O'Donnell, *Principles of Management* (New York: McGraw-Hill, 1972); and Douglas McGregor, *The Professional Manager* (New York: McGraw-Hill, 1967). Two other good references are Robert Albanese, *Management: Toward Accountability for Performance* (Homewood, Ill.: Irwin, 1975); and Dale D. McConkey, *No-Nonsense Delegation* (New York: American Management Associations, 1974). Bruce T. Barkley writes "The Program Management Officer in the Public Service: His Role in Policy Formulation and Administration," *Public Administration Review* 27 (March 1967): 25–30.

A real coordination, with emphasis on headquarters-field relationships, is dealt with by James M. Fesler, "Field Organization," in *Elements of Public Administration*, ed. F. Morstein Marx (Englewood Cliffs, N.J.: Prentice-Hall, 1946). See also George M. Goodrich, "Integration and Decentralization in the Federal Field Service," *Public Administration Review* 9 (August 1949): 272–277; Earl Latham, *The Federal Field Service* (Chicago: Public Administration Service, 1947); and John D. Millett, "Field Organization and Staff Supervision," in *New Horizons in Public Administration* (Tuscaloosa: University of Alabama Press, 1945).

The coordination of line and staff activities is considered by Ernest Dale and L. Urwick in *Staff in Organization* (New York: McGraw-Hill, 1960); by David S. Brown in "The Staff Man Looks in the Mirror," *Public Administration Review* 23 (June 1963); and by Melville Dalton in "Staff and Line Relationships: A Study in Conflicts," in *Human Relations in Administration*, ed. Robert Dubin, 4th ed. (Englewood Cliffs, N.J.: Prentice-Hall, 1974).

CHAPTER 15

Most of the fear of bureaucracy out of control, says Herbert Kaufman, is rhetoric devoid of substance: see his article "Fear of Bureaucracy: A Raging Pandemic," *Public Administration Review* 41 (January–February, 1981): 1–10. Peter Drucker distinguishes between "control" and "controls," the former being part of a needed strategy, in *Management: Tasks, Responsibilities, Practices* (New York: Harper & Row, 1973), ch. 39, "Control, Controls, and Management." Similarly, see William Guth, *Organizational Strategy: Analysis, Commitment, Implementation* (Homewood, Ill.: Irwin, 1974); Stafford Beer, *Decision and Control* (New York: Wiley, 1966); Marvin Bower, *The Will to Manage* (New York: McGraw-Hill, 1966); or the earlier classic by Paul E. Holden et al., *Top-Management Organization and Control* (New York: McGraw-Hill, 1951). A shorter treatment of the subject is that of Philip M. Marcus and Cora Cafagna, "Control in Modern Organizations," *Public Administration Review* 25 (June 1965): 121–127. The perennial issue of efficiency is dealt with by Marshall E. Dimock in "The

Criteria and Objectives of Public Administration," in *The Frontiers of Public Administration*, by John M. Gaus, Leonard D. White and Marshall E. Dimock (Chicago: University of Chicago Press, 1936), ch. 7; and by Herbert A. Simon in *Administrative Behavior*, 2d ed. (New York: Macmillan, 1957), pp. 180–186.

A useful guide is *Developing the Municipal Organization* (Washington: International City Management Association, 1974), chs. 2, 12–15. See also Douglas M. Fox, *Managing the Public's Interest: A Results-Oriented Approach* (New York: Holt, Rinehart, & Winston, 1979). References to state government include Coleman B. Ransone, Jr., "The American Governor in the 1970s," *Public Administration Review* 30 (January, 1970): 1–44; Robert Connery and Gerald Benjamin, eds., *Governing New York State: The Rockefeller Years* (New York: Academy of Political Science, 1974); and "Gubernatorial Executive Orders as Devices for Administrative Direction and Control," *Iowa Law Review* 50 (Fall 1964): 78–98.

CHAPTER 16

A good introduction to the scope and utility of program evaluation is found in Orville F. Poland, ed.,

"Symposium: Program Evaluation," *Public Administration Review* 34 (July–August, 1974). This might be followed by thoughtful analyses of the *raison d'être* of social science analysis in Alice M. Rivlin, *Systematic Thinking for Social Analysis* (Washington: Brookings Institution, 1971); Carol Weiss, *Evaluation Research: Methods of Assessing Program Effectiveness* (Englewood Cliffs, N.J.: Prentice-Hall, 1972); and Carol Weiss, ed., *Using Social Science Research in Policymaking* (Lexington, Mass.: Heath, 1977). Another lucid statement is found in Edward A. Suchman, *Evaluative Research: Principles and Practices in Public Service and Social Action Programs* (New York: Russell Sage Foundation, 1967) and "Action for What? A Critique of Evaluative Research," in *The Organization, Management and Tactics of Social Research,* ed. Richard O'Toole (Cambridge, Mass.: Schenkman, 1971). A more recent analysis is Barry Bozeman, *Public Administration and Policy Analysis* (New York: St. Martin's Press, 1979). For state and local government, see Harry P. Hatry et al., *Practical Program Evaluation for State and Local Government Officials* (Washington: Urban Institute, 1976). On the critical side, consult James E. Prather and Frank K. Gibson, "The Failure of Social Programs," *Public Ad-*

ministration Review 37 (September–October 1977): 556–564; and V. F. Ridgway, "Dysfunctional Consequences of Performance Measurements," *Administrative Science Quarterly* 1 (September, 1956): 240–247.

The subject of productivity in management and government also has a large literature. A good introduction is Chester A. Newland, ed., "Symposium: Productivity in Government," *Public Administration Review* 32 (November–December 1972). Good references to local government are John P. Ross and Jesse Burkhead, *Productivity in the Local Government Sector* (Lexington, Mass.: Lexington Books, 1974), and Patrick Manion, *Improving Municipal Productivity: Work Measurement for Better Management* (Washington: U.S. Government Printing Office, 1975). On state government consult Edgar G. Crane, Barry Lentz, and Jay Shafritz, *State Government Productivity: The Environment for Improvement* (New York: Praeger, 1976); or National Center for Productivity and Quality of Work Life, *The Status of Productivity Measurement in State Government: An Initial Examination* (Washington: U.S. Government Printing Office, 1975).

CHAPTER 17

A good introduction to information systems is found in Harold L. Wilensky, *Organizational Intelligence, Knowledge, and Policy in Government and Industry* (New York: Basic Books, 1967); in Dennis J. Palumbo, *Program Development and Administration* (Washington: International City Management Association, 1965); or in Herbert A. Simon, *The Shape of Automation for Men and Management* (New York: Harper & Row, 1965). Gilbert Burck and the editors of *Fortune* brought out *The Computer Age and Its Potential for Management* (New York: Harper & Row, 1965); as did John Diebold, the management consultant, *Beyond Automation: Managerial Problems of an Exploding Technology* (New York: McGraw-Hill, 1964).

On the utilization of information systems in state and local government, see Kenneth L. Kraemer and John Leslie King, *Computers and Local Government,* Volume 1: *A Manager's Guide* (New York: Praeger, 1977). See also Geoffrey Y. Cornog, "Change, Management, and Electronic Data Processing in State and Local Government," in Geoffrey Cornog et al., *EDP Systems in Public Management* (Chicago: Rand McNally, 1968). Alternatively, see Harold Hovey, "Some Perspectives on Data Processing in State Government," in *Computer Systems and Public Administrators,* ed. Richard A. Bassler and Norman L. Enger (Alexandria, Va.: College Readings, 1976).

CHAPTER 18

Two well-known texts on public personnel administration are those of O. Glenn Stahl, *Public Personnel Administration,* 7th ed. (New York: Harper & Row, 1976) and Felix A. Nigro and Lloyd G. Nigro, *The New Public Personnel Administration,* 2d ed. (Itasca,

Ill.: Peacock, 1981). In the July/August 1981 issue of *Public Administration Review* there is an excellent review of four new books in the personnel management field, one of which is Nigros' book. The review is entitled "Taming Techniques for Public Purposes," and the book titles do suggest, indeed, that there may be some new thinking going on in the field. One, by N. Joseph Cayer, is called *Managing Human Resources* (New York: St. Martin's Press, 1975); another, by Donald E. Klinger, has an intriguing subtitle: *Public Personnel Management: Contexts and Strategies* (Englewood Cliffs, N.J.: Prentice-Hall, 1980); a third, by Robert D. Lee, Jr., *Public Personnel Systems* (Baltimore: University Park Press, 1976).

Frederick C. Mosher, *Democracy and the Public Service* (New York: Oxford University Press, 1968) puts the field in a larger setting. John W. Macy, Jr., who used to head the U.S. Civil Service Commission, wrote *Public Service: The Human Side of Government* (New York: Harper & Row, 1971). Winston W. Crouch, ed., *Local Government Personnel Administration* (Washington: International City Management Association, 1976), is one of the best treatments of municipal government. Other good books include Robert T. Golembiewski and Michael Cohen, *People*

in Government (Itasca, Ill.: Peacock, 1970); Wallace S. Sayre, ed., *The Federal Government Service: Its Character, Prestige, and Problems* (New York: Columbia University, The American Assembly, 1954); National Manpower Commission, *Government Manpower for Tomorrow's Cities* (New York: McGraw-Hill, 1962); and Rensis Likert, *The Human Organization* (New York: McGraw-Hill, 1967).

On civil service systems and methods, see Paul Van Riper, *History of the United States Civil Service Commission* (New York: Harper & Row, 1958); Jay M. Shafritz, *Public Personnel Management: The Heritage of Civil Service Reform* (New York: Praeger, 1975); and David T. Stanley, *Professional Personnel for the City of New York* (Washington: Brookings Institution, 1963). Two Hoover Commission reports are also good: *Personnel Management* (1949) and *Personnel and Civil Service* (1955), both published by the U.S. Government Printing Office, Washington.

CHAPTER 19

A convenient collection of articles from *Public Administration Review,* which has had a distinguished editorship, is found in Chester A. Newland's symposium, in book form, *Professional Public Executives* (Washington: American Society for Public Administration, 1980). This paper-bound book might even be worth considering for one's personal library. There is also a constructive agenda provided in a group effort in which John W. Gardner, of Common Cause fame, took part: *Agenda for the Eighties* and especially the task-force report, *The Electoral and Democratic Process in the Eighties,* both by the President's Commission for a National Agenda for the Eighties (Washington: U.S. Government Printing Office, 1980). In the latter monograph, ch. 4, "The Presidency and the Executive Branch," is particularly relevant. There is a good discussion, for example, of the Civil Service Reform Act of 1978.

The United States Office of Personnel Management publishes an attractive quarterly magazine called *Management: A Magazine for Government Managers.* Volume 2 (Spring 1981), for example, has a lead article "Linking Pay to Performance," while Volume 2 (Summer 1981) has one entitled "Appraising Performance."

A down-to-earth analysis of executive opportuni-

ties is found in John J. Corson and R. Shale Paul, *Men Near the Top: Filling Key Posts in the Federal Service* (Baltimore: Johns Hopkins University Press, 1966). Anyone undecided about a career would do well to read Frederick C. Mosher and Richard J. Stillman II, eds., "The Professions in Government," *Public Administration Review* 37 (November–December 1977): 631–685, and 38 (March–April 1978): 105–150. There is also a good profile of the government executive in Harlan Cleveland, *The Future Executive* (New York: Harper & Row, 1972).

The International Personnel Management Association has produced some good books on training and executive development: Kenneth T. Byers, ed., *Employee Training and Development in the Public Service* (Chicago: IPMA, 1968); and Felix M. Lopez, Jr., *Evaluating Employee Performance* (Chicago: IPMA, 1968).

The best discussion of coordination of policy and execution by political heads and their opposite numbers, career heads, is found in an article by Lord Boyle of Handsworth, "Ministers and the Administrative Process," *Public Administration,* published by the Royal Institute of Public Administration, London, 58 (Spring 1980): 1–12.

CHAPTER 20

On the background of union attitudes and objectives, either Gus Tyler, *The Political Imperative: The Corporate Character of Unions* (New York: Macmillan, 1968) or Jack Steiber, *Public Employee Unionism: Structure, Growth, Policy* (Washington: Brookings Institution, 1973) are rewarding. On a comparison of public and business methods there is none better than the Committee for Economic Development study, *Improving Management of the Public Work Force: The Challenge to State and Local Government* (New York: CED, November, 1978). For the federal government, see Thomas R. Colosi and Steven B. Rynecki, *Federal Legislation for Public Collective Bargaining* (Chicago: International Personnel Management Association [IPMA], 1975). For state government, see Advisory Commission on Intergovernmental Relations, *Labor-Management Policies for State and Local Governments* (Washington: U.S. Government Printing Office, September 1969); alternatively, Hugh D. Jascourt, *Public Sector Labor Relations: Recent Trends and Development* (Lexington, Ky.: Council of State Governments, 1975). Along the same line is Arvid Anderson and Hugh D. Jascourt, eds., *Trends in Public Sector Labor Relations* (Chicago: IPMA, 1975).

The Labor-Management Division of the U.S. Department of Labor has three good volumes: *Summary of Public Sector Labor Relations Policies* (1976), *Fact Finding and Arbitration in the Public Sector* (1974), and *Understanding Grievance Arbitration in the Public Sector* (1974)—all U.S. Government Printing Office, Washington. There are also two bibliographies: *Public Employment Bibliography,* by Robert V. Pezdek (Ithaca, N.Y.: Cornell University, School of Industrial and Labor Relations, 1973) and *Public Employee Relations Library* (Chicago: IPMA, series commencing 1968).

On the issues involved in the Hatch Act or the Equal Employment Opportunity Commission, see personnel management texts such as O. Glenn Stahl, *Public Personnel Administration* (New York: Harper & Row, 1976); or Felix A. Nigro and Lloyd G. Nigro, *The New Public Personnel Administration* (Itasca, Ill.: Peacock, 1976). The U.S. Merit Systems Protection Board has recently published two outstanding monographs in this field: *Breaking Trust: Prohibited Personnel Practices in the Federal Service* and *The Other Side of the Coin: Removals for Incompetence in the Federal Service* (Washington, D.C.: U.S. MSPB, February 1982).

CHAPTER 21

Useful compendia of statistics for American governmental finance include the Tax Foundation's biennial *Facts and Figures on Government Finance* (New York: odd-numbered years), and the Advisory Commission on Intergovernmental Relations (ACIR), *Significant Features of Fiscal Federation* (Washington: U.S. Government Printing Office, 1980). The ACIR conducts annual opinion surveys to see what Americans think about government finance: *Changing Public Attitudes on Government and Taxes* (Washington: U.S. Government Printing Office).

The federal government's budget policies are summarized in the *Annual Report of the President's Council of Economic Advisers and the U.S. Budget in Brief.* Indispensable for the serious student is *Special Analyses: Budget of the U.S. Government.* President Ronald Reagan's plans to cut back federal spending are contained in two 1981 publications, *A Program for Economic Recovery* and *Fiscal Year 1982 Budget Revision.* All of these are published by the U.S. Government Printing Office in Washington. A notable recent book is Allen Schick, *Congress and Money* (Washington: Urban Institute, 1980).

James A. Maxwell and J. Richard Aronson, *Financing State and Local Governments,* 3d ed. (Washington: Brookings Institution, 1977) is the best introduction to subnational public finance. James Howell and Charles Stamm, *Urban Fiscal Stress* (Lexington, Mass.: Lexington Books, 1974): and Roger E. Alacaly and David Mermelstein, ed., *The Fiscal Crisis in American Cities* (New York: Vintage Books, 1976), are excellent treatments of local government financial problems. Howard Jarvis, the antitax crusader, tells his story in the amusing, though overly lengthy, *I'm Mad as Hell* (New York: Times Quadrangle Books, 1979). Aaron Wildavsky presents a scholar's version of the same message in *How to Limit Government Spending* (Berkeley, Calif.: University of California Press, 1980).

CHAPTER 22

Albert C. Hyde and Jay M. Shafritz have edited a collection of some of the best articles in their *Government Budgeting* (Oak Park, Ill.: Moore Publishing, 1978). The collection includes several articles by two of the contemporary leaders in the field, Aaron Wildavsky and Allen Schick. Wildavsky's *Budgeting* (Boston: Little, Brown, 1975) is an excellent survey of the state of research knowledge on the topic.

Wildavsky's *The Politics of the Budgetary Process,* 3d ed. (Boston: Little, Brown, 1980) is a major work, which changed the study of the subject. It focuses on the federal budget. Allen Schick's *Congress and Money* (Washington: Urban Institute, 1980) looks at the changes brought about by the 1974 Budget Act. George Hale's superb survey, "Budgetary Politics in the States" (1978), remains, most lamentably, unpublished as this book goes to press. The best introduction to local government budgeting is Lennox L. Moak and Albert M. Hillhouse, *Concepts and Practices in Local Government Finance* (Chicago: Municipal Finance Officers' Association, 1975).

On the performance budget, see Allen Schick, *Budget Innovation in the States* (Washington: Brookings Institution 1971), and the articles on the topic in the Hyde and Shafritz reader. The Schick volume also treats the Planning-Programming Budgeting System in the states, while Hyde and Shafritz have a good collection of articles on the topic. The best introduction to the PPBS remains Charles L. Schultze, *The Politics and Economics of Government Spending* (Washington: Brookings Institution, 1969). On Zero-Base Budgeting, see the ZBB section in Hyde and Shafrtiz, as well as Peter A. Pyhrr, *Zero Base Budgeting* (New York: Wiley, 1973); and Douglas M. Fox, *Managing the Public's Interest* (New York; Holt, Rinehart & Winston, 1979), ch. 7. Thomas H. Hammond and Jack H. Knott deliver a strong attack on ZBB in *A Zero Based Look at Zero-Base Budgeting* (New Brunswick, N.J.: Transaction Books, 1980).

General textbooks on budgeting include Jesse Burkhead, *Government Budgeting* (New York: Wiley, 1956); Robert D. Lee, Jr., and Ronald W. Johnson, *Public Budgeting Systems,* 2d ed. (Baltimore: University Park Press, 1977); and Thomas D. Lynch, *Public Budgeting in America* (Englewood Cliffs, N.J.: Prentice-Hall, 1979).

CHAPTER 23

There is not much writing on the topic of the government audit that is not highly specialized and technical. On the federal audit, see Erasmus H. Kloman, ed., *Cases in Accountability: The Work of the GAO* (Boulder, Colo.: Westview Press, 1979); Frederick C. Mosher, *The GAO* (Boulder, Col.: Westview Press, 1979); and Joseph Pois, *Watchdog on the Potomac* (Washington: University Press of America, 1979). Mosher's book is the more historical and descriptive, Pois's the more analytical treatment of the actual power of the federal external auditor.

Richard E. Brown, ed., *The Effectiveness of Legislative Program Review* (New Brunswick, N.J.: Transaction Books, 1979), contains useful material on the state audit.

Peter F. Rousmaniere's *Local Government Auditing* (New York: Council on Municipal Performance, 1979) is the best introduction to the topic.

CHAPTER 24

Several major sources for this chapter have been cited in the notes, especially the 1980 report of the President's National Agenda Commission, the Luther Gulick *Perspectives* and the Dwight Waldo *Enterprise*. Another useful reference is David Nachmian and David Rosenbloom, *Bureaucratic Government U.S.A.* (New York: St. Martin's Press, 1980).

On the relation of political science and public administration, consult R. F. Ridley, *The Study of Government: Political Science and Public Administration* (London: Allen & Unwin, 1975). On theory and practice, see Emmette S. Redford, *Ideal and Practice in Public Administration* (Tuscaloosa: University of Alabama Press, 1958); also, Louis C. Gawthrop, ed., *The Administrative Process and Democratic Theory* (Boston: Houghton Mifflin, 1970).

John Gardner, whose influence on the *National Agenda* study is obvious, wrote *Toward a Pluralistic But Coherent Society* (New York: Aspen Institute for Humanistic Studies, 1980). See also James L. Sundquist, "The Crisis of Competence in Government," in *Setting National Priorities for the 1980's*, ed. Joseph Pechman (Washington: Brookings Institution, 1980). Along the same line is Anthony King, "The American Polity in the Late 1970s: Building Coalitions in the Sand," in *The New American Political System*, ed. Anthony King (Washington: American Enterprise Institute, 1978), pp. 371–395.

On the political party system a good source is Fred I. Greenstein, *The American Party System and the American People* (Englewood Cliffs, N.J.: Prentice-Hall, 1970); also Sidney Verba and Norman H. Nie, *Participation in America: Political Democracy and Social Equality* (New York: Harper & Row, 1972). On the changing role of administrators, see Hugh Heclo, *A Government of Strangers* (Washington: Brookings Institution, 1977); also William G. Scott and David K. Hart, *Organizational America* (Boston: Houghton Mifflin, 1979) and John Macy, Jr., "Executive Preparation for Continuing Change," *Public Administration Review* 29 (September–October 1969).

INDEX